W9-CFZ-182

THE ENVIRONMENT OF MARKETING BEHAVIOR

The Wiley Marketing Series

WILLIAM LAZER, Advisory Editor
Michigan State University

MARTIN ZOBER, *Marketing Management*

ROBERT J. HOLLOWAY AND ROBERT S. HANCOCK, *The Environment of Marketing Behavior—Selections From The Literature*

ROBERT MANNING
STROZIER LIBRARY

FLORIDA·STATE·UNIVERSITY
VIRES ARTES MORES
1857

Tallahassee

Gift of

Dr. Bruce Gunn

THE ENVIRONMENT OF MARKETING BEHAVIOR

Selections from the Literature

Robert J. Holloway

Professor of Marketing
University of Minnesota

Robert S. Hancock

Professor of Marketing
University of Minnesota

LIBRARY
FLORIDA STATE UNIVERSITY
TALLAHASSEE, FLORIDA

APR 25 1977

John Wiley & Sons, Inc., New York · London · Sydney

Soc
HF
5415
H742

Copyright © 1964 by John Wiley & Sons, Inc.

All Rights Reserved. This book or any part thereof must not be reproduced in any form without the written permission of the publisher.

Library of Congress Catalog Card Number: 64-25889

PRINTED IN THE UNITED STATES OF AMERICA

LIBRARY
FLORIDA STATE UNIVERSITY
TALLAHASSEE, FLORIDA

APR 25 1977

Preface

The selections from the literature included in this book represent what we consider to be some of the most basic and enlightening contributions to marketing thought. The criteria for selecting articles to be included in the book were as follows: (1) That the article contribute to the basic framework and knowledge of marketing, (2) that the article be more or less timeless insofar as the concepts expressed, and/or (3) that the article be one around which discussion or controversy could evolve in the classroom setting. The wisdom of these criteria seems verified by the use of most of these selections by beginning marketing students at the University of Minnesota. With the selections cast in the framework outlined in our Introductory Comment, beginning marketing can be a stimulating and intellectually challenging subject.

In reproducing these articles, it was nec-essary to take some liberties with them. All articles were not reprinted in their entirety, some footnotes and other reference materials were deleted, and minor editorial adjust-ments were necessary to fit them more ap-propriately to the size and style limitations of this book. For these liberties and the per-mission to reprint the articles, we are in-debted to the authors and publishers. In addition, special appreciation is expressed to Donald V. Harper, Associate Professor of Marketing and Transportation, Carl W. Rudelius, Lecturer in Marketing, Richard N. Cardozo and Donald J. Hempel, Instruc-tors in Marketing, all of the University of Minnesota, for their many helpful sugges-tions, which resulted in improvements of the selections. Meenakshisunder Venkate-san, a graduate student in marketing, was most helpful with the preparation of the manuscript. For his help, we are indebted.

University of Minnesota
July 1964

R. J. HOLLOWAY
R. S. HANCOCK

Contents

Introductory Comment

Marketing is a social and economic phenomenon which comes into being when a society removes itself from a subsistence level of existence. The precise character and dimensions of marketing differ from one society to another, and this is explained, at least in part, by the degree of specialization practiced. If the possessions and abilities of all people were the same, there would be no exchange, and hence, no need for a marketing structure and its attendant activities. Fortunately this is not the case, and most societies are characterized by people possessing different abilities and different goods—thus exchange ensues, and a marketing structure of some dimension develops. Similarly, *marketing activities* anchored in the marketing structure are carried on. Whatever the nature of marketing in a society, it will be influenced by the environment in which it is carried on. The environment of marketing also represents a number of forces which generate change in a marketing structure, and furthermore, these forces influence the character of marketing activities. If these forces and the environment of marketing explain its existence, character, and dimensions, it is probably most desirable to begin a study of marketing within such a framework.

As the title of this book suggests, major emphasis is given to the environment of marketing and the way in which the environment influences the behavior of marketing. Just what is the environment of marketing? What are the forces that generate change in marketing? In answer to these questions a rough schema, or model, of an introductory course in marketing might be like that shown on page 2.

The model depicts the environment of marketing as being social, economic, legal and ethical, technological and physical. The social aspects of marketing take on importance, because markets involve people who are conditioned and influenced by several forces and their interrelationships. Their behavior in the market place is most properly analyzed in terms of demographic factors, psychological influences, and the impact of their traditions and culture.

The economic aspects of marketing are of twofold importance. First, the economic condition of consumers contributes to their behavior and makes it possible for other influences acting on them to be realized. When the economic status of consumers is combined with the social aspects of society, the impact of their behavior in the market place becomes a reality of major significance to marketers. Second, firms operating in the market and firms moving goods into the market do so in an atmosphere of competition with price functioning as the core to exchange transactions. In this way the economic dimension is broadened, and the economic environment of the firm becomes a market force worthy of consideration.

All social and economic activities are carried on in a legal and an ethical framework. This segment of our model is concerned with the probabilities and permissive aspects of market behavior. The legal environment influences the character of pricing, competitive activities, market control, and promotional strategies. The ethical behavior (or lack of it) in the market place is a more nebulous subject. From one society to another, this aspect may be expected to vary by virtue of traditions, the mores of society, and the values of a society.

1

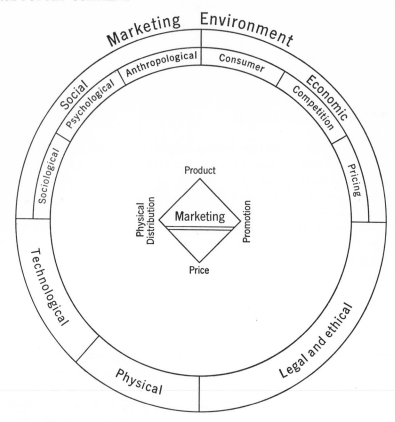

Technology is another force influencing market place behavior. Technology puts pressures on a marketing system to which it must adjust, and similarly, technology has much to do with the products distributed and their eventual acceptance.

The physical environment of marketing includes the institutional structure. Intermediaries of all types are included in this concept, and it is recognized that the structure of the intermediaries influences the physical movement of goods to their possession by a consumer.

When marketing is cast in this framework, the marketing activities of the firm should *ideally* correspond to its environment. As a result Part III, "Directing the Marketing Effort," is anchored in a research context followed by the major marketing activities which can be designed to adjust to and meet an ever changing environment.

The Focus of Marketing

A. The Role of Marketing in Society
B. Marketing in Free and Planned Economies

Part I introduces the character and nature of the subject matter of marketing. It focuses attention on marketing problems, basic concepts, the origin of trade, and on an understanding of markets.

Most marketing, as now understood, and the play of forces influencing market behavior are within a free enterprise framework. In the last reading of Part I, marketing in a free enterprise system is contrasted with marketing in a planned system.

A. The Role of Marketing in Society

1. Some Problems in Market Distribution

ARCH W. SHAW

THE ACTIVITIES OF BUSINESS

When a workman in a factory directs the cut of a planer in a malleable steel casting, he applies motion to matter with the purpose and result of changing its form.

When a retail clerk passes a package of factory-cooked food over the counter to a customer, he applies motion to matter with the purpose and result of changing its place.

When a typist at her desk makes out an invoice covering a shipment, she influences the motion of that material or merchandise, not directly to change its form or place, but indirectly to facilitate changes of one or both kinds.

Isolate any phase of business, strike into it anywhere, and invariably the essential element will be found to be the application of motion to matter. This may be stated, if you will, as the simplest ultimate concept to which all the activities of manufacturing, selling, finance and management can be reduced.

Starting with this simple concept, it is at once evident that we have an obvious and easy basis for the classification of business activities —a simplifying, unifying principle from which to proceed rather than some mere arrangement by kind or characteristic of the materials, men, operations and processes in the various departments of a business enterprise.

The nature of the motion does not of itself supply the key to this basic classification. For

⁜ SOURCE: Reprinted by permission from *Changing Perspectives in Marketing* edited by Hugh G. Wales (University of Illinois Press, 1951), pp. 32–52.

while the action may be characteristic of one part of a business and not duplicated elsewhere, like the pouring of molten metal in a foundry or the making up of a payroll, it may, in contrast, be common to all the departments into which the organization is divided, such as the requisition of a dozen pencils or a box of paper clips. It is not until we single out the common fundamental element and inquire, "What is the purpose of this motion?" that we find the key.

I do not wish to exaggerate the importance of this simple and apparently obvious concept; but for me it has opened a way to locate the activities of business and disclose their relations to one another and to their common object, and so has proved a device of daily use. For the final function of the classification, as it is the practical problem of all business, is to identify those motions which are purposeless, so that they may be eliminated, and to discover those motions, old or new, which are of sound purpose, so that they may be expedited.

When, upon studying an individual motion or operation in itself and in relation to the other associated activities, no satisfactory answer can be found to the question, "What is its purpose?", you have strong grounds for assuming that it is a non-essential and useless motion. It may have the sanction of house tradition or trade custom, but its superfluous character persists and the wisdom of eliminating it becomes plain. Conversely, a new motion proposed for adoption, though never before tried in the trade, may still have value. Purpose again is the decisive test. From the social standpoint, any motion which has no valid purpose or result is economically useless and wrong. The effect of employing such a motion in business, like the effect of omitting a useful motion, is to limit profits that otherwise might rise.

So the purpose of the analysis, from the manager's point of view, is not alone to position the activities of business and develop their relationship, but also to order his thinking so that he can more readily see what activities he should discontinue and what others he should encourage, perfect, or add.

This does not always mean a reduction in the total number of motions. In our roundabout system of production, with its minute subdivision of labor, it is possible to make a greater number and variety of motions and distribute them over a longer period of time, yet increase the eventual output or decrease the cost through the group effectiveness of all the motions.

In the three operations already mentioned—those of the factory workman, the retail clerk, and the office typist—each application of motion was for an economically valid purpose and each instance was typical of one of the three great groups of business activities:

1. The activities of production, which change the form of materials.

2. The activities of distribution, which change the place and ownership of the commodities thus produced.

3. The facilitating activities, which aid and supplement the operations of production and distribution.

Whatever the nature or kind of any business activity, its final effect is one of these three.

METHODS OF DISTRIBUTION

In the early stages of our industrial history, sales were made in bulk. At all stages in distribution, the purchasers saw the actual goods before the sale was made.

Later sale by sample appeared. The purchaser bought goods represented to be identical with the sample he was shown. The introduction of this method of sale was necessitated by the widening of the market and was made possible by improvement in commercial ethics and increasing standardization of product. The purchaser had to have confidence not only in the producer's honest intention to furnish goods identical with the sample, but also in his ability to produce identical goods. Hence, increasing uniformity in product through machine methods of applying standard materials in its manufacture was a factor in the increase of sale by sample.

Sale by description is the most modern development in distribution. Here an even higher ethical standard is required than for sale by sample. Moreover, sale by description requires a higher level of general intelligence than sale in bulk or sale by sample. Sale by description in its modern development is, in a sense, a by-product of the printing press.

All three methods of sale are in use in modern commercial life. The consumer still makes a large part of his purchases under a system of sale in bulk. He sees the goods before he buys them. The middleman, buying in larger quantities, generally purchases from sample. But sale by description becomes each year more important in every stage of the distribution system.

The root idea in sale by description is the communication of ideas about the goods to the prospective purchaser by spoken, written or printed symbols and facsimiles. This method takes the place of the sight of the goods themselves or a sample of them. It is obvious that this requires that the purchaser shall have sufficient intelligence to grasp ideas either through spoken, written or printed symbols.

The ideas to be conveyed to the prospective purchaser in sale by description are such as will awaken an effective demand for the commodity in question. The awakening of demand is the essential element in selling. It must be remembered, however, that the distributor has the further task of making it possible to gratify that demand by making the goods physically available to the buyer.

With sale in bulk, this problem merges with the selling, since the goods are physically present when the sale is made; while in sale by description the physical distribution of the goods is a problem distinct from the awakening of demand. And it is a problem that requires equal attention, for it is obviously useless to awaken the demand unless the goods to satisfy it are available.

As demand creation is the initial step in distribution, it is necessary to consider the agencies for this purpose available to the merchant-producer. There are three general agencies to be considered: (1) middleman, (2) the producer's own salesman, and (3) advertising, direct and general. The business man faces the problem of what agency or combination of agencies is the most efficient for the creation of demand and the physical supply of his particular commodity.

The number of possible combinations of methods and agencies renders the problem of the producer-merchant an intricate one. It will be seen that he has a difficult task in analyzing the market with reference to his goods, and in working out that combination of methods and agencies which will give him the most efficient system of applying motion to achieve distribution.

The middleman is a by-product of a complex industrial organization. The chart of Fig. 1 shows in rough outline the evolution of the middleman from the early period when producer dealt directly with consumer, to the appearance of the orthodox type of distribution (late in the Eighteenth Century and in the first quarter of the Nineteenth Century) when a complicated series of middlemen existed.

In the more primitive barter economy, the producer deals directly with the consumer, and middlemen take no part in the transaction. In the medieval period, as the handicrafts become specialized occupations under a town-market regime, the producer is a retailer and sells directly to the consumers. As the market widens, a division of labor becomes necessary, and the merchant appears as an organizer of the market.

Steadily the market widens until business confronts both national and world-wide markets. The merchant is no longer a single intermediary between the producer and the consumer. The merchant who takes the goods from the producer disposes of them to retail merchants who in turn distribute them to consumers. After a long period, we find the producers gradually strengthening their financial position, and freeing themselves from the control of a single merchant. They become merchant-producers. They assume the burden of production, and dispose of the product to various wholesalers, who in turn sell to retailers and they to the consumers. As a world market appears, the producer disposes of a part of his product to the export merchant.

In the early days of the factory system, shown in the chart of Fig. 2, we find that the producers have lost their character as merchants and are devoting themselves to the problems of production. The selling agent appears as a link in the chain of distribution to relieve the producer from the task of selling his product. He distributes it among wholesalers, who in turn distribute it to retailers, and the retailers to the consuming public. This may be termed the orthodox pattern in distribution, a pattern almost universal thus far in the Nineteenth Century.

Conversely, as the long period of development from a system of barter economy to the early decades of the factory system showed a continuous tendency toward increase in the number of middlemen intervening between the producer and the consumer, so recent years have shown a growing tendency to decrease the number of successive steps in distribution. Fig. 2 is an attempt to show diagrammatically the

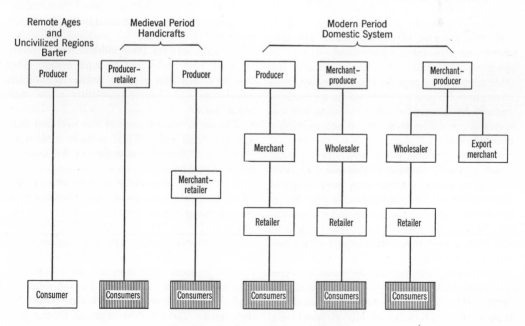

FIG. 1.   Evolution of the middleman.

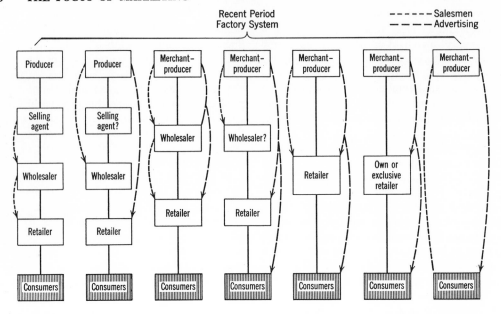

FIG. 2.   An apparent tendency to reduce the number of successive middlemen.

development of this apparent tendency to decrease the number of middlemen.

The most extreme step in the process is the complete elimination of middlemen, and the sale direct from the merchant-producer to the consumer, either by advertising alone or by salesmen supplemented by advertising.

It should be emphasized that the analogy between direct salesmen and advertising is very close. Each agency is largely used to enable the producer to take over one function of the middleman, that is, the selling function. And in each case the root idea is the same. The producer seeks to communicate most directly to the prospective purchaser, through one or the other agency, or a combination of the two, such ideas about his goods as will create a conscious demand for them. The direct salesman and advertising are different modes of accomplishing the same end.

Advertising, then, may properly be regarded either as a substitute for middlemen and salesmen, or as auxiliary to them in the exercise of the selling function. Owing to the rise of sale by description and the increasing differentiation of commodities, it tends to displace in whole or in part these other agencies in many lines of distribution.

Advertising may be said to build up three general classes of demand: (1) expressed conscious demand, (2) unexpressed conscious demand, and (3) subconscious demand. Ex-

pressed conscious demand means present sales; unexpressed conscious demand means future sales; subconscious demand means a fertilizing of the field so that future selling efforts will be more fruitful. Unexpressed conscious demand and subconscious demand are difficult to measure but must always be taken into account in any consideration of the efficiency of advertising as a selling agency.

What has gone before has been by way of analysis. The general problem of distribution, the present-day differentiation of products, the price policies open to the producer, the methods of sale, and the three chief selling agencies have all been subjected to brief review. This has been essential because neither economists nor business men have previously made such an analysis.

The social significance of the problem calls for emphasis also. While a more systematic handling of distribution means to the business man greater business success, a better organization of distribution with maximum economy of motion means to society the prevention of an enormous annual waste.

CONSIDERATIONS OF THE MARKET

The business man faces a body of possible purchasers, widely distributed geographically, and showing extremes of purchasing power and felt needs. The effective demand of the individual consumer depends not alone upon his purchasing power but also upon his needs, conscious or latent, resulting from his education, character, habits, and economic and social environment. The market, therefore, splits up into economic and social strata, as well as into geographic sections.

The producer cannot disregard the geographic distribution of the consuming public. He may be able to sell profitably by salesmen where the population is dense, while that method of sale would be unprofitable where population is sparse. If a sound system of distribution is to be established, the business man must treat each distinct geographic section as a separate problem. The whole market breaks up into differing regions.

Equally important is a realization of what may be termed the market contour. The market, for the purposes of the distributor, is not a level plain. It is composed of differing economic and social strata. Too seldom does the business man appreciate the market contour in reference to his product.

Nor does the merchant-producer always realize how intricate is his problem as to the agency or combination of agencies that will be most efficient in reaching his market.

The business man often adopts one method of reaching his market and becomes an advocate of it, entirely disregarding other methods.

While the method adopted may be more efficient than any other single method, it is apparent that a method which is relatively efficient in reaching one area may be inefficient in reaching another. So a system of distribution which has proved effective in reaching one economic stratum may be relatively inefficient when employed to reach a different economic stratum in society. Each distinct area and economic stratum may have to be treated as a separate problem.

A sound selling policy will require as its basis a careful analysis of the market by areas and strata, and a detailed study of the proper agency or combination of agencies to reach each area and stratum, taking into account always the economic generalizations expressed in the law of diminishing returns. It must also take into account not only the direct results obtained from the use of one or another agency over a short period, but also the less measurable results represented by the unexpressed conscious demand and subconscious demand which may facilitate future selling campaigns.

The crux of the distribution problem is the proper exercise of the selling function. The business man must convey to possible purchasers through one agency or another such ideas about the product as will create a maximum demand for it. This is the fundamental aim whatever the agency employed.

Editor's Note: The reader may be interested to know that Shaw's original material was published in the *Quarterly Journal of Economics* (1912) and in a book by Arch W. Shaw. *Some Problems in Market Distribution* (Harvard University Press, 1915).

2. *Notions About the Origins of Trading*

GEORGE W. ROBBINS

The origins of trade have been the concern of economists and anthropologists in the past in order to trace or to relate the present functions of trade to their primeval beginnings and to discover the basic character of this economic usage. While this preoccupation with origins is disappearing from the scientific literature, it is not uncommon to find its implications and assumptions in the more popular literature of business, and particularly on the subject of salesmanship.

References are often made to premises concerning the origin of trading as a means of explaining or analyzing the ethical position of modern selling, imputing to present practices in the market place the circumstances and virtues of an assumed primeval genesis. It is, for example, not uncommon to hear trading spoken of as universal and natural. On the other hand, anthropological evidence reveals primitive cultures with a complete lack of competitive trading and with insignificant exchange practices.

In the face of these opposing positions, it is desirable to examine the various notions concerning the origins of trading and to appraise them in the light of their usefulness in the analysis of trading in our own society. It is possible to do this without a true chronological history of trading, or without attempting to formulate an organic-evolutionary concept of trading which takes the form of extracting from succeeding cultures certain common characteristics, with the conclusion that these have been

passed down the lingering trail of institutional patterns.

Indeed, it should be evident that the accurate establishment of the origins of any human activity must await sufficient evidence from archaeological diggings.[1] The dearth of this evidence precludes a chronology that starts at the beginning. It is more profitable to avoid an historical recital in favor of an attempt to penetrate the internal logic of trading.

Our concern here is with the efficacy of employing, as either inarticulate or expressed premises, notions about the origins of trading in the evaluation of present-day trading practices from a functional or an ethical viewpoint. Is an understanding of the origins of trade an essential matter in the study of the ethics of selling and buying? Will it help to answer the problems of honesty and efficiency in selling? Does it throw light on the problems of the contests and conflicts of trading today in the economic institution?

It should be clearly understood that this inquiry differs from, and is not in conflict with, the study of trade history as it can be established through adequate records.[2] It relates to those

---

[1] See Melville J. Herskovits, *The Economic Life of Primitive Peoples* (New York: Alfred A. Knopf, 1940), Pt. I, for detailed comment on methodology in economics and anthropology.

[2] As for example: Clive Day, *A History of Commerce* (New York: Longmans, Green, 1938); George Burton Hotchkiss, *Milestones of Marketing* (New York: Macmillan, 1938); N. S. B. Gras, *An Introduction to Economic History* (New York: Harper, 1922).

✸ SOURCE: Reprinted by permission from the *Journal of Marketing* (National Quarterly Publication of the American Marketing Association), Vol. 11, No. 3, January 1947, pp. 228–236.

histories only insofar as their authors employ reference to origins; and it is, of course, possible to treat a matter historically without assuming an organic evolution based on obscure beginnings.

It is well to keep in mind that we are concerned with trading—buying and selling—as a matter of social behavior rather than as a technical process in marketing. It is essential to assume that trading is not a fortuitous or whimsical phenomenon, but rather an observable datum governed by laws of behavior that are subject to discovery. Moreover, it is no part of assumption here that trading is good or bad, strong or weak, or favorable to any given environment. These matters must emerge only as conclusions based on adequate observation of group activity in a definable situation.

THE MEANING OF TRADING

The term "trading" may mean many things to say that a trade is an act of effecting an exchange, barter, transfer of title, persuasion, or even deception. It is not an oversimplification to say that a trade is an act of effecting an exchange of goods or services between a seller and a buyer; indeed, such a statement involves complexities of subtle premises. What lies both before and after the trade is of interest to this inquiry. The mere fact of communication between two individuals is a relatively superficial datum

It may be helpful to clarify the thing we are discussing by examining definitions. Confusion will be avoided if it is remembered that a trade is a two-sided shield—it is both a purchase and a sale. While it is a popular misconception that the initiative in trading is largely with the seller, it is irrelevant to our purposes which side we take for reference. For the sake of brevity, only the selling side will be defined; and even the uninitiated may fill in a parallel definition of buying.

There are at least three types of definitions of *sale* which serve to illustrate the usual approaches to selling:

(1) The legal: "Sale is an agreement by which one of the two contracting parties, called the 'seller,' gives a thing and passes title to it, in exchange for a certain price in current money, to the other party, who is called the 'buyer' or 'purchaser,' who on his part, agrees to pay such a price." [3]

(2) The vocational: A sale is the exchange of goods or services resulting from the exercise of the art of salesmanship.

(3) The professional: A sale is an exchange of goods or services resulting from rivalry in the productive effort of creating demand and of rendering service in the satisfaction thereof.

The legal definition leads to a concept of trading that is narrow and restricted mainly to the technical fact of title transfer in a society characterized by a highly refined property concept. It fails to provide for the student of the economic or sociological aspects of trading adequate attention to the circumstances precedent or subsequent to that transfer. [4]

The vocational approach to selling, on the other hand, emphasizes the importance of the arts of persuasion rather than their functional position. By contrast, what may be called the professional approach calls attention to the fundamental circumstance of human wants and of the existence of rivalry in the performance of the services that create and satisfy those wants. [5] It is not concerned with the contractual character of the sale; for contract is a usage of convenience, and the vast majority of sales are completed without the parties being aware that a legal contract is involved. Likewise, it does not deny that there is an important body of arts practiced by both sellers and buyers, which are effective in lubricating the process; but these arts are chiefly vocational techniques (however difficult to master). The professional approach places emphasis on the fundamental creative functions of selling in a highly competitive society.

---

[3] Walter A. Shumaker and George Foster Longsdorf, *The Cyclopedic Law Dictionary* (3rd ed.; Chicago: Callahan, 1940), p. 992.

[4] This is not to say that the law has little influence on selling, but rather to emphasize that a legal definition is necessarily a cautious one and is more likely to represent a careful attempt to classify a concept rather than to penetrate it. It should be recognized, of course, that the law does place the intention of the parties to a contract in an important position as distinct from the transfer to title. See Nathan Isaacs, "Sales," *Encyclopaedia of the Social Sciences* (New York: Macmillan, 1931), VIII, pp. 511–516.

[5] By calling this approach "professional," it is not necessarily implied that selling is a profession. However the social responsibility of the seller today certainly suggests a professional attitude, and it is clear that the acceptance of business as a profession will only follow, not precede, the adoption of such an attitude on the part of sellers. Cf. Louis Dembritz Brandeis, *Business—a Profession* (Boston: Small, Maynard, 1914), pp. 1–12.

While varying in approach, these three familiar concepts of selling have in common the functional position of selling in a society whose economic institution is characterized by a high degree of competitive effort—in short, a society like our own. In juxtaposition to these definitions, another, more fundamental, approach may be more suggestive of the real character of trading. A trade must always be a human relationship involving the behavior patterns of at least two persons.[6]

Hence, it is basically a *communication* and should be viewed as a part of the sociological field of communication.[7] It is subject to all the status barriers which define and separate individuals and groups. Again, any trade must be *cooperative* in the sense that two or more persons are acting together to achieve a new relationship which manifestly could not be achieved by each acting alone. Furthermore, every trade is an *organization* because it is a system, formal or otherwise, of consciously coordinated activities of at least two persons.[8] And lastly, the term is confined to situations where the ends are economic in order to exclude the multitude of other human relations which, without this modification, would fall unwanted into the area of our present concern.

Thus, we may define trading as a cooperative organization in communication to achieve economic ends. This definition carries no connotations with respect to the characteristics which may surround trading as the result of differing practices, usages, instruments, and mores to be found in the economic institution either at different times or in different locations. Like all other organizations in communication, trading belongs to a social institutional pattern, and becomes a part of the usages of that pattern. Specifically, it is part and parcel of the system of regulating economic contest and conflict, and is itself subject to contests and conflicts with usages of the other social institutions, marital, familial, educational, recreational, religious, scientific, and governmental.[9]

From the historical viewpoint, any inquiry into the nature of trading, to be significant, must be one that takes cognizance of the particular institutional fabric of which it is a part. To say that trading in our society today has its roots in the behavior of our primeval ancestors, or to say that this notion is confirmed by the habits of our "contemporary ancestors," [10] the non-literate primitives now living, is to stretch the latitudes of scientific inquiry to the point of incredulity.

Yet it is true that many practitioners of selling base an important part of their philosophy on premises concerning the origins of trading that comprise the substance of these ideas. It is precisely this basic mistake of many writers on salesmanship that led them to attitudes which provoked the well-known, pointed, and inescapable criticism of salesmanship by Clarence Darrow.[11]

THE MAJOR HYPOTHESES

No one disputes the antiquity of trading; but the exact point and conditions of its origins provide the subject of consideration by many writers whose attempts may be classified in seven main hypotheses. Not a few students of anthropology and economics alike have supported one or more of these assumptions without even the benefit of tacit recognition of the implications.

(1) *Trading Is Instinctive*

It is perhaps most widely held that "to trade, or 'swap' is an inborn trait in the human being." [12] A variation of this view was expressed by Sombart, who believed that some have an inherent capacity to become traders (undertakers) while others do not. "Either you are born a bourgeois or you are not. It must be in the blood, it is a natural inclination." [13]

---

[6] This is the case even where impersonal or even mechanical implements are employed, (e.g., corporations, agents, or vending machines).

[7] Communication is "the process of exchanging commonly understood ideas, facts, or usages by means of language, visual presentation, imitation, suggestion." Constantine Panunzio, *Major Social Institutions* (New York: Macmillan, 1939), p. 529.

[8] This concept has been used effectively by Chester I. Barnard in his interesting analysis of business organization. See, "Comments on the Job of the Executive," *Harvard Business Review*, XVIII, Spring 1940, pp. 295–308. See also his *The Functions of the Executive* (Cambridge: Harvard University Press, 1938).

[9] Constantine Panunzio, *op. cit.*, p. 7.

[10] Melville J. Herskovits, *op. cit.*, p. 35.

[11] "Salesmanship," *The American Mercury*, V, August 1925, pp. 385–392.

[12] Charles H. Fernald, *Salesmanship* (New York: Prentice-Hall, 1937), pp. 44 ff.

[13] Werner Sombart, *The Quintessence of Capitalism* (London: T. Fisher Unwin, 1915), p. 205.

This palpable view is undoubtedly a sufficient explanation to many salesmen; it is certainly a comfortable refuge from the penetrating criticism of some of the ancient and modern practices of the market place. If it is "natural" to sell, then the criticism of traders is comment out of hand. But the evidence of scientific anthropology gives little support to this notion.

Not a few evidences exist to show that primitive peoples have existed for long periods without competitive trading.[14] The industrial civilization of the Incas is a striking case in point.[15] Polish peasants for centuries did not know the meaning of buying and selling between members of the same community. Their knowledge of trading came entirely from contacts with outsiders; and their resistance to selling has survived, since "even today, peasants dislike to trade with neighbors.[16]

While it is a rare culture that does not produce some exchanges of commodities on occasion, it is rather common to find that among primitives trading, insofar as it possessed any formal existence, arises mainly to facilitate exchange between members of different groups rather than between individual members of the same group.[17] In a culture where the institutions support a strict control of production and allocation of wealth, trading between individuals in the society becomes unnecessary, as in the case of the Incas, or vastly restricted, as in the case of Soviet Russia in the early years at least, where other stimuli than private profit were dominant.[18]

One would expect few psychologists to rank so complex a phenomenon as trading with fundamental instincts of self-preservation and sex as a basic drive. Unlike these fundamental urges, trading is not universal, intensive, or repetitive. And while it is true that trading appeared early in many different places and independently under different circumstances, these facts serve no more to demonstrate instinctiveness of trading than does the simultaneous scattered growth of the family institution prove that marriage is instinctive. Not only is this hypothesis too simple and superficial, but adherence to it may even retard the ability of present-day sales management to cope with its functional responsibilities.

(2) Trading Grew Out of Warfare

This "hostility" hypothesis has trading growing out of war between clans or tribes. It pictures primitive man as essentially warlike because of the pressure of population on the means of subsistence. It assumes that warfare has economic roots, and that it is inevitable when man searches for the satisfaction of elemental wants. The reasoning follows that whereas man could satisfy his wants by warring on his neighbor, he soon learned that trading was an alternative possibility that had merit from the standpoint of group survival.[19]

This hypothesis has many faults, not the least of which is that it leads us into the difficult path of analyzing the origins of war, a path that is as rugged and unmarked as any other that goes in the direction of primeval origins. It is sufficient here to record that the hostility notion runs afoul of evidence of trading where war is unknown, as well as testimony pointing to the conclusion that both war and trading appear to develop from the same circumstances, and independently of each other. War was unknown among some primitives who carried on a rudimentary form of trade, notably the Eskimo and the Semang of the Malay Peninsula.[20]

The Arapesh tribe of New Guinea, naturally easy-going and yet pitted against physical barrenness that might be expected to produce

---

[14] Melville J. Herskovits, op. cit., pp. 17–19.

[15] Elizabeth Ellis Hoyt, Primitive Trade, its Psychology and Economics (London: Kegan Paul, Trench, Trubner, 1926), p. 141.

[16] W. I. Thomas and F. Znaniecki, The Polish Peasant in Europe and America, 1927, as quoted by E. L. Thorndike, Human Nature and the Social Order (New York: Macmillan, 1940), p. 633.

[17] Melville J. Herskovits, op. cit., pp. 133 ff.

[18] William Henry Chamberlin, "The Planned Economy," Red Economics (Boston: Houghton Mifflin, 1932), pp. 9 ff. See also M. Ilin, New Russia's Primer (Boston: Houghton Mifflin, 1931), II, and XIII.

[19] It is interesting that the opposite view is widely held also; namely, that trading inevitably leads to warfare. Elizabeth Ellis Hoyt cites evidence to support both views, op. cit., VII.

The fact that war and trade often appeared together as effect and cause may have been attributable to the fact that the traders (foreigners) were usually more advanced culturally than those on whom they called and thus had a higher capacity to injure [cf. Max Radin, Manners and Morals in Business (New York: Bobbs-Merrill, 1939), pp. 89 ff]. But they also should have had a higher capacity to serve, which may well have prevented conflicts!

[20] Margaret Mead, "Primitive Society," Planned Society (New York: Prentice-Hall, 1937), p. 16.

strong rivalry for survival, finds great adventure in producing for others and actually regards it a sin to eat one's own kill. Motivation is achieved without competitive rivalry or war by a custom of having an official "insulter" for each man to taunt him publicly for his failure to produce feasts. So dreadful is this torture in the face of his peaceful nature, that a man looks forward to his reward—release from his "insulter" and retirement when his son reaches puberty. Thus, at least one primitive culture has institutionalized its lack of aggressiveness and self-interest, both of which would seem to be of some importance in the origin of either competitive trading or war.[21]

Nor is it easy to relate war and trading in the face of the fact that in many primitive peoples the rewards for war are personal and psychological rather than economic, and take the form of prestige supported by the evidence of another feather in the cap or another enemy's scalp on the belt. And the persistence of war, not only among primitives but in our own society, is difficult to explain if it is to be argued that trading supplanted war because of its demonstrated superior contributions to group survival; for wars have almost always provided a serious interference with economic life. Indeed, it seems well to avoid any attempt to relate trade to war as a fruitless inquiry in which observable data are altogether too lacking to support reasonable conclusions.[22]

(3) Trading Originated in Predation

The "predatory" hypothesis is closely allied with the hostility notion. Because there are a few primitive tribes, such as the Bushman and the Apache, whose economies were regularly dependent upon the capture of wealth from other tribes,[23] and because there are a few evidences that modern business "is a complex and well-integrated series of frauds,"[24] some observers may conclude that trading began with the extraction of tribute and has never succeeded in getting away from the original predatory pattern.

The difficulty here lies in the abundance of evidence, historical and anthropological, that trading flourished between peoples who were entirely friendly and to whom the idea of tribute never seemed to occur. Moreover, predatory activities are not confined to the economic institution, but pervade the other social institutions as well. Indeed, political leaders, whether they be the heads of primitive tribes or of literate nations, have been among the most notorious tribute-extracting racketeers of history, and their predacity on merchants has all too often throttled trade.[25]

(4) Trade Grew Out of Friendly Gift-Giving

This "friendship" hypothesis is an explanation in diametrically the opposite vein. Professor Hoyt cites many examples of friendly gift-giving in primitive society and suggest that this practice may have led to learning the utility of exchange.[26] In primitive societies where the ownership of things was strongly identified with personal or group spiritual entity, the giving of gifts to neighboring tribal chiefs must indeed have stemmed from a genuine gregarious feeling and friendly goodwill.[27] The cynical view that a wise chieftain would buy off the predatory nature and power of his neighbor with gifts is not sufficient to explain the facts of anthropological research.

It is perhaps sufficient here to note that both war-making and gift-giving were means of communication, either or both of which may have been helpful in the discovery of trading. Professor Hoyt's emphasis on gift-giving as an origin of trading is supported by logic; for the atmosphere of gift-giving is a congenial one in which man may learn to perceive the utility of exchange.

---

[21] Ibid., p. 23.

[22] A more fruitful approach to the question of war and trade will be found in Lionel Robbins, The Economic Causes of War (London: J. Cape, 1940).

[23] Margaret Mead, op. cit., pp. 17 ff.

[24] J. B. Matthews and R. E. Shallcross, Partners in Plunder (Washington, New Jersey: Consumers' Research, 1935), p. 400. See also Clarence Darrow, op. cit.

[25] N. S. B. Gras, Business and Capitalism (New York: F. S. Crofts, 1939), pp. 307 ff. See also Miriam Beard, A History of the Business Man (New York: Macmillan, 1938), passim.

[26] Op. cit., p. 104 and Part IV.

[27] To say that gift-giving is entirely a matter of goodwill or altruism, however, is to overstate the matter; for no matter how freely a gift is given, its presentation in primitive societies appears nearly always to create an obligation which, if neglected by the recipient, leads to loss of prestige or social disapprobation, which is a strong factor in shaping action. Cf. Herskovits, op. cit., p. 134.

(5) Trading Originated with the "Silent Trade"

Silent trade is well-known to anthropologists as an early means of economic communication, and it appears in many isolated places among primitives. In this crude form, trade is initiated when one group leaves its wares on a promontory and retires from sight to permit another group to come out of hiding to inspect the goods and deposit its offering in return.[28]

Silent trade seems to have prevailed (1) where contact was between peoples of widely different cultures, (2) where languages were different, and (3) where fear or distrust was even more highly felt than were the economic motives of the intercourse. While the silent trade is an important fact in early communication, it throws little light on the real origins of trading. Its existence proves, however, that trading did occur between peoples who were motivated by neither the desire to make friends nor the will to annihilate.

It should also be recognized that neither party to the silent trade would have acted had he failed to develop an evaluation of the exchanged wares entirely apart from his own spirit or soul. Some degree of objectivity was implicit. Moreover, it is not plausible that this form of trading was an expression of instinct; it was discovered, developed, and learned as a crude but effective usage in the framework of the existing social institutions.

(6) Trading Arose from Surpluses

Some students have suggested that trading originated because of the pressure of surplus goods resulting from the early division of labor in the primitive family or tribe.[29] Presumably the relative scarcity of goods was apparent in the periodic surpluses made available either through the efforts of nature or man. The plethora of cattle against the dearth of fodder may have suggested a gain from the exchange of cattle for fodder that was plentiful in a neighboring area.

This explanation fails on a number of grounds. There is practically no evidence that surpluses were accumulated by primitive families or clans excepting for anticipated emergencies.[30] Indeed, it is probable that excesses of things to eat or wear or use were regarded as "free goods" with respect to which transferable control did not even suggest itself until after trading as an instrument of communication developed. Moreover, much of the early trade in all parts of the world was in rare and exotic items "for which the demand was largely an expression of arbitrary value."[31] The primitive trading in ornaments and trinkets which gave their owners social prestige can hardly be said to stem from surpluses.

Too, a rational and administrative division of labor in primitive tribes, assumed in this hypothesis, cannot conceivably have preceded the need for it; and this need certainly compels outside markets as a *sine qua non*. The superficial explanation posed by the surplus hypothesis is to be found in the contemporary and popular notion that foreign trade exists because of surpluses resulting from the division of labor when in fact it is quite the other way around.

(7) Trading Grew Out of the Development of the Property Concept

Tracing the origin of trading to the growth of the concept of property is a preoccupation of those who see in the exaggerated manifestations of trading in our society an overemphasis on private ownership. It is not appropriate to our purposes here to enter the controversy over the inequalities of property ownership or over the ways by which the function of property may be molded in the interests of social progress and public welfare.

It is merely essential to point out that in the manner in which the function of property is conceived as an end in terms of private advantage, special privilege, and exploitation will have a profound bearing on the practices in the market place. That many of these practices are subject to question today is not gainsaid; but to attack trading as a major evil growing out of the property concept is to engage in ardent speculation.

If by property we refer to the claim which gives transferable control over things,[32] then the property concept is best explained by the relative scarcity of these things in terms of the con-

---

[28] N. S. B. Gras, "Barter," *The Encyclopaedia of the Social Sciences* (New York: Macmillan 1933), II, pp. 468 ff. Elizabeth Ellis Hoyt, *op. cit.*, pp. 133 ff. Max Radin, *op. cit.*, pp. 81 ff.

[29] Edward D. Page, *Trade-Morals*, 2nd. rev. ed. (New Haven: Yale University Press, 1918), p. 58. See also Charles H. Fernald, *op. cit.*, pp. 44 ff.

[30] Max Radin, *op cit.*, pp. 85 ff.

[31] *Ibid.*

[32] Frederic B. Garver and Alvin H. Hansen, *Principles of Economics*, rev. ed. (Boston: Ginn, 1937), pp. 29 ff.

test for individual and group survival.[33] While it is true that the extensive and complex exchange in our society presupposes a well-developed concept of property, it is far from true that crude trading could never have existed without even a simple property concept. Indeed, the very definition of property as anything with exchange value implies clearly that it is the need and practice of trading which called the property concept into use and aided materially in shaping its character. To say that property value existed before the fact of exchange is to indulge in a hopeless confusion of ideas and terms.

Trading and property concepts are both man-made and have developed in close relationship. They have certain characteristics in common: (1) both are dependent on the recognition of scarcity values; (2) both presuppose a divorcement of possessions from the individual's spiritual identity—an objective valuation of things; (3) both emerge from the same set of factors and must be explained in terms of a larger institutional concept.

Hence, to say that trading originated in the property concept and is a usage of property is to misinterpret the origins of both while leaving the essential character of each shrouded in confusion. In short, it is another example of the futility of tracing origins without the supporting evidences of observable data.

A RATIONAL EXPLANATION OF TRADING

The one thing in common which all of these hypotheses of the origins of trading have is a high degree of speculation unsupported by the accumulation of empirical data. It should be clear that any logic based upon premises like these is not acceptable to the social scientist. Indeed, social science has long since abandoned the methodology suggested by such speculations as those we have been examining.

If an explanation of trading is needed, it is to be found in the nature of man and of his adaptation to his environment through the institutions he builds. The universal, abiding, and repetitive characteristics of man to learn, to explore, to satisfy his curiosity, and to live with groups of other men have led him into an ever-expanding circle of experiences from which he has developed his learning and his patterns of

associated living.[34] These attributes undoubtedly stem from the character of man's genes as distinguished from those of other animals. The explanation of trading lies neither in man's instincts nor his intelligence alone, but must be seen in terms of the patterns of the accumulated deposits of his activities in associated living.[35]

The essential prerequisite to trading, original or otherwise, is the development of the ability to valuate things in terms of other things rather than in terms of spiritual or mystical beliefs— to objectify and emancipate one's belongings from his spiritual self and soul.[36] But this ability is by no means a guarantee that trading will be carried on in a society unless the folkways and mores are receptive to the changes which it imposes in the patterns of living.

Trading may be said to have been a slow discovery, made at a relatively early stage by peoples the world over, that followed the intellectual advance of valuation and which, in turn, vastly stimulated that advance, that grew out of the practices of associated living and, in turn, greatly affected these practices.

As contrasted with the other means of acquiring things, trading is by all odds the most complex. It is unique in that it alone is a two-way transaction.[37] The fact that trading has grown to such prominence and complexity as one of the dominant means of acquiring things is attributable, in part at least, to its relative survival value and to the character of the prevailing institutional patterns of which it is a part.

CONCLUSION

The answers to our original questions may now be seen in better perspective. Although it would be the height of pedantic scepticism to

---

[33] Constantine Panunzio, *op. cit.*, p. 216.

[34] A highly imaginative, yet penetrating essay on this fundamental character of man as opposed to other animals is to be found in Clarence Day, *This Simian World* (New York: A. A. Knopf, 1936).
[35] Constantine Panunzio, *op. cit.*, pp. 143 ff.
[36] Elizabeth Ellis Hoyt, *op. cit.*, Pt. IV. That this emancipation is universally or wholly accomplished today (or, indeed, should be) is not suggested. Contemporaries have "priceless" trinkets and sometimes order them interred with their remains. Businessmen have been known to defy the logic of the case by insisting on the use of their own photographs as trademarks.
[37] The other means are strictly one-way: appropriation from nature, seizure from others, cultivation and making with the hands, gifts and inheritance, and gambling. H. K. Nixon, *Principles of Selling* (New York: McGraw-Hill, 1942), pp. 41 ff.

deny validity to a hypothesis because of the absence of all conceivable verification, nevertheless, the main assumptions examined all fall in the same category of speculation without adequate empirical verification, and they involve an outmoded methodology in the social sciences.

Even by the most tolerant sense of proportion and broad feeling for the evidence, any conceivable proof of the kinship of modern competitive trading to the earliest forms of barter and exchange would fail to offer a basis for a discussion of either ethics or efficiency of trading unless it be considered in a particular institutional framework. Consequently, it is not to be argued that the ethics of selling in our own society can be related to that of the societies in which origin may have occurred.

As a basis for the evaluation of the ethics of selling and buying in our own society, the concept that trading is a cooperative organization in communication for the purpose of achieving economic ends is one that properly expresses the internal logic of trading. For it implies in trading a concept in the economic institution whose usages entail a continuing contest and conflict with other concepts and usages prevailing in all of the social institutions. This view of trading permits one to proceed with an examination of the ethics of trading in our own society without the hindrance of a cloak of prejudgment drawn about it by speculation with respect to the ultimate origins of trading usages.

3. Some Concepts of Markets and Marketing Strategy

ROLAND S. VAILE

THE BASIC DEFINITION OF MARKETING

"Marketing covers all business activities necessary to effect transfers in the ownership of goods and to provide for their physical distribution." [1] "Marketing includes all the activities involved in the creation of place, time, and possession utilities." [2] "Marketing, in the full sense of the word, must involve change in ownership; physical movements merely facilitate this change or make possible the use of the commodity by the new owner. All the rights, privileges, and responsibilities, either of use or of further sale, attach to ownership and are passed on with change in ownership." [3]

These three definitions, taken from many, pretty well represent the concept of marketing although perhaps sale of services merits more specific inclusion. Change in ownership is all important. Physical movement is facilitating. Place, time, and possession utilities are involved, but their development requires marketing only when change of ownership is also involved.

There are many other instances in which the creation of place utility does not involve marketing. For example, place utility and only place utility is created in bringing crude

[1] T. N. Beckman and others, *Principles of Marketing* (New York: Ronald Press, 1957), p. 4.
[2] P. D. Converse and others, *Elements of Marketing* (New York: Prentice-Hall, 1952), p. 1.
[3] Roland S. Vaile and others, *Market Organization* (New York: Ronald Press, 1930), p. 43.

‡‡ SOURCE: Reprinted by permission from *Changing Structure and Strategy in Marketing* edited by Robert V. Mitchell (Bureau of Economic and Business Research, University of Illinois, 1958), pp. 17–29.

oil from the bottom of a deep well to a surface tank, and yet that process is not usually included in marketing. Actually the sinking of an oil well and pumping oil from it have much in common with the laying of a pipeline and pumping oil through it. Both result in place utility, but one pair is classed with marketing and the other with production. The same point might be made with coal mining, potato digging, and many other activities which result only in place utility, but which are commonly thought of as part of production rather than marketing.

CONCEPT OF A MARKET

The term "market" may be used to designate:

(1) The place where a sale is made.

(2) The area in which a particular supply usually is sold, or the area from which a particular supply generally is procured.

(3) The particular institutions or channels that carry on the marketing processes.

(4) The complex set of forces that result in a certain price being paid for a particular bill of goods or service.

Legal controversy exists concerning the locus of a market in the geographic sense. Is the market for cement, for example, at the point where it is made, or where it is used? The primary focus of the forces of demand is at the latter point, surely, although some of the basing-point discussions seem to contend otherwise. One basic question involved is whether different proportions of common costs may properly be covered by identical sales in markets with differing demands. Retail pricing certainly results in differing contributions to common costs from the sale of different items. To what extent and under what conditions would similar leeway be appropriate between different geographic markets? In other words, is there anything necessarily nefarious in "freight absorption" per se? No completely satisfying answer has been given to this question.

A conspicuous change during the past generation is seen in the growth of individual firms through integration, both horizontal and vertical. Firms that have expanded horizontally have tended also to integrate vertically. According to data summarized in *Fortune*, six merchandising firms each had sales of over $1 billion in 1956. Each of these is engaged predominantly in retailing, but each also has undertaken many activities usually considered as wholesaling, as well as some manufacturing. Our concepts and definitions in this field are made archaic by these developments, and our statistics do not permit precise chronological comparison. Moreover, the question still is moot as to the conditions under which a firm should be permitted to own or control its principal customers so that a large portion of its "sales" are merely paper transactions.

The growth of our great suburban shopping centers and of supermarket self-service retailing is made possible, of course, by the high-income, automobile age. Rather than a move toward economy in the use of total social resources, it appears to be grossly inefficient, as is, in fact, practically every do-it-yourself program. These movements are reversions away from the principle of specialization. They can be tolerated only because specialized technology already has resulted in high productivity and considerable unused personal time and energy, together with widely dispersed ownership of idle capacity in quasi-industrial goods like washing machines and automobiles. (The importance of the automobile in our abundant economy is highlighted by the fact that six of the ten national firms with largest 1956 sales are engaged in automobile manufacture and petroleum production while three others have the automobile business as a principal customer.)

Of course there are some sociological considerations connected with do-it-yourself programs, and perhaps the sociological gains outweigh any economic inefficiency. Measurement of the net effect on our culture involves value judgment that is beyond the scope of this paper. Suffice it to say that the opportunity cost of many do-it-yourself programs is pretty low while some economic use is made of otherwise unemployed labor and equipment. The alterna-

tive use of that potential capacity may be a rather low-grade consumption activity. In any case the public seems to have accepted the trend philosophically and with considerable enthusiasm.

Melvin Copeland suggested a generation ago that consumer goods are purchased as convenience, shopping, or specialty goods, and that stores tend to concentrate on one of these lines.[4] This tendency has led to a mixing of the conventional lines of groceries, drugs, and household gadgets into a fairly complete stock of convenience goods in modern supermarkets. That this development has been going on for some time is shown by the following quotation from Chester Haring:

Of course, lines are being added to the stocks of nearly all retail merchants, but the greatest change is taking place in the drug, grocery, cigar, and five-and-ten-cent stores. While each of these groups is doing its largest business in its natural field, each is encroaching upon the fields of others, and also into entirely new fields. In short, these four classes of stores seem to be making up a new class which we may call "convenience stores."[5]

In the nearly thirty years since that statement was written, change in the concept of the most appropriate market institutions has continued. The supermarkets and the suburban shopping centers are dominant in the fashion of the moment. Completely automatic service in supermarkets is in the pilot stage and may become the fashion for tomorrow. Evidently the ultimate physical and institutional pattern for market distribution still is to be conceived and evolved. As one result our retail statistics are badly muddled, and for most useful analysis they should be reported in much greater detail.

Changes in the commodity mix are not confined to retailing. In many cases manufacturers are taking on new lines. This may be done to give more price lines as in the case of the Edsel. It may be done to improve the seasonal distribution of demand or because the firm has funds to invest and decides to spread its risks. Whatever the reasons, it appears that the concept of the market for an individual firm is broadening and specialization by manufacturers on a limited line of commodities is being reduced.

Of course many manufacturers have long undertaken to reach different segments of their

[4] *Principles of Merchandising* (New York: A. W. Shaw, 1924).
[5] *The Manufacturer and His Outlets* (New York: Harper, 1929), p. 176.

market with differentiated products. For example, canners, flour millers, some tire manufacturers, and others have sold their products both under their own brands and under wholesaler or retailer brands. Sometimes the product offered under several brands has been essentially identical, but through this multiple-brand strategy additional segments of the total market have been reached. This practice constitutes a form of semisecret, intra-firm competition, often with only minor physical differences among the products.

As individual firms have grown in size and have added to their lines of products, many of them have undertaken more direct and obvious intra-firm competition. This strategy is conspicuous, of course, in the automobile field. General Motors, for example, not only offers different named cars in different price lines, but there is considerable overlap of prices among the different makes. Strenuous rivalry exists among the retail agents that sell the several makes—as strenuous, perhaps, among the separate units of GM as between them and the members of the Ford or Chrysler families. Competition among the products of a single company is well illustrated, also, in Procter and Gamble where the sales division is organized on a competitive product basis. Recently, intra-firm product competition has become keen with cigarette manufacturers, especially following the wide introduction of the filter and mentholated brands. This practice of differentiating the products of a single seller makes it possible to satisfy the tastes and whims of segregated markets. One result is an increase in total company sales, as illustrated by the huge volume of such organizations as General Motors or Procter and Gamble. Sometimes, but not always, it permits some price discrimination.

Money makes markets. This aspect of markets deserves and receives close attention. The flow of income is of great importance to market potentials. Changes in the flow of income are reflected closely by changes in retail purchases. Forecasts of future changes in income directly affect the volume of industrial expenditures. Increases in income generally are accompanied by changes in the percentage of savings and investment. Conversely, neither increases nor decreases in income flow result immediately in equal changes in consumption expenditure. Increases and decreases in credit have much the same immediate effects as do changes in income flow. Thus when income falls, an increase in consumer credit may temporarily offset the

effect of the fall. These points are elementary, of course, and call for no amplification here.

It may be pointed out, however, that both government and private agencies have made available an increasing amount of data on income, past, present, and future. These data include the well-known estimates of GNP, national income, disposable personal income, average individual and family income, and so on. Of considerable use to some branches of marketing is the MacFadden estimate of discretionary purchasing power. All these data are available in both current and constant-value dollars. Studies in consumer economics are available to indicate many of the relations between changes in income and the accompanying changes in its use. These correlations are of great value in the planning of business decisions affecting marketing.

Perhaps it almost goes without saying, however, that relationships between income and expenditures change over the years. This is illustrated, for example, by the well-known fact that until recently the percentage of consumer income spent on food has decreased as income increased, while the reverse sems to have occurred in the past decade. Perhaps this is merely a statistical illusion due to changes in the form in which food is bought, but at least it points a finger of caution against stubborn adherence to past or present relations.

CONCEPT OF COMPETITION

Discussions among economists have been fruitful in developing, modifying, and clarifying concepts that are useful in the description and understanding of marketing as well as in the making of marketing decisions. (I am impressed by the extent to which recent management research has been devoted to how management decisions are made rather than to the decisions themselves.) A sharp dichotomy between competition and monopoly was neither realistic nor very useful in practical affairs. The newer concepts of monopolistic competition, oligopoly, workable competition, and administered prices are much more pertinent to actual business situations. The idea of cross-elasticity of demand has gained in acceptance and application to the analysis of specific market situations. So also has the idea of the kinked demand curve.

Understanding of these concepts seems to have an increasing influence on pricing policies of individual firms. However, the relation of costs to pricing policy and the influence of full costs, marginal costs, allocation of common costs, break-even analysis, and similar matters on specific prices still is somewhat moot.

In 1927 Wesley Mitchell wrote as follows: "The prices ruling at any moment for the infinite variety of commodities, services, and rights which are being bought and sold constitute a system in the full meaning of that term. That is, the prices paid for goods of all sorts are so related to each other as to make a regular and connected whole. Our knowledge of these relations is curiously inexact. . ."[6] Our knowledge of these relations is still inexact, but the economists' clarification and market research have at least helped toward an understanding of how some of them come about.

The concept or strategy suggested by Edwin G. Nourse in *Price Making in a Democracy*[7] is still hotly argued. Who should get how much of the advantage from technological improvements in production—stockholders of large firms, owners of small businesses, wage earners through wage increases, or consumers through lowered prices? Nourse argues for a large share to the consumer directly, Walter Reuther favors higher wages, some neo-Keynesians want high dividends to attract capital for an ever expanding economy. The consensus has not jelled yet. Relative prices unquestionably are of major importance in marketing strategy, but no one knows just how or to what extent they should be used.

One of the changes in the applied use of a concept as a marketing strategy is seen in the case of the single price. The basic policy of one price to all was introduced by many merchants in the nineteenth century. It gained considerable acceptance, enough so that it was considered the general policy. Trade-in allowances, package deals, trading stamps, and other devices have eroded some of the rigidity so that a recent article carried the title "One Price— Fact or Fiction?" and the implication that fiction was more nearly the case. Marshall Field is using trade-in allowances even with pots and pans!

The distinction between price competition, product-quality competition, and non-price competition still is somewhat foggy. Marketing strategies include attempts to increase sales (and profits) through lowering price, through change in product, or through mere sales effort

with no change in either price or product. Perhaps the latter is the true non-price competition. Probably in most real-life situations two or more of the three strategies are in use at the same time, but it is useful for the marketing analyst to consider their effects separately.

SALES PROMOTION

For the purposes of this paper I have divided marketing strategies into three classes, namely:

(1) Direct price competition (just discussed briefly).

(2) Product development and change (merely mentioned).

(3) Sales promotion (now to be discussed).

Attempts to sell an existing product at an established price involve many sophisticated strategies. Included are such obvious things as personal selling, advertising, and merchandise fairs. Specific tactics may change with time. In 1923, for example, Daniel Starch defined advertising as "selling in print."[8] Since the advent of radio and TV, new methods of advertising have been adopted and the definition has been broadened.

As I wrote in 1927, however, "It must be clearly recognized that 'advertising' is but a convenient name for certain forms of persuasion applied to buying and selling. At many points the economic arguments would apply with equal force to the arousing of desire . . . whether the technique used was 'advertising' or 'personal selling.' In such cases the choice between the two would be merely one of relative costs. With this in mind it seems unnecessary to define advertising; each reader may include in this category whatever technical activities suit his fancy."[9]

Probably it is likewise unnecessary to define sales promotion. It may be pointed out, however, that in addition to various forms of publicity, the extension of credit, as in installment selling, may be used as a sales-promoting stratagem. When consumer credit is expanded, consumer purchasing is stimulated as with any other form of sales promotion. Moreover, it follows that there is an increase in inflationary pressure.

In 1928 Paul Nystrom wrote that "there seems to be little to indicate that any important

[6] *Business Cycles* (New York: National Bureau of Economic Research, 1927).

[7] Washington: The Brookings Institution, 1944.

[8] *Principles of Advertising* (New York: A. W. Shaw, 1923), p. 5.

[9] Vaile, *Economics of Advertising* (New York: Ronald Press, 1927), p. 3.

trend of fashion has ever been changed by any form of sales promotion." [10] Probably this statement still holds so far as the *direction* of any trend is concerned. On the other hand, the *rate* of acceptance or decline of a fashion may be affected by sales promotion. Because of these phenomena, sales-promoting effort usually is correlated directly with industrial fluctuations, with increased effort when sales are easy to make, and with decreased effort when selling is difficult. This holds true, certainly, both for advertising and for extension of installment credit. Thus instability of economic activity is furthered by sales promotion. The over-all data suggest little change in this situation over the years. The burden placed on the monetary system and other possible devices for the control of industrial fluctuations is increased by sales promotion. The question may well be raised whether, as a general concept or stratagem, sales promotion should or could be used as an aid toward industrial stability. Some individual firms appear to have successfully used it in this manner.

"In December 1923 there were no less than ten manufacturers of milk chocolate who unqualifiedly advertised their products as 'the best.' Such a condition is possible because there is no definite standard of 'best.' " [11] Today an equal number of cigarette brands are advertised as having "the best taste." Apparently the use of claims that can neither be proven nor disproven is a continuing stratagem. This is one way that advertisers continue to play up what Borden has called the "hidden qualities" of goods.

Another stratagem that seems, if anything, to have grown in use is reference to scientific evidence. This is an age in which science is popular —as Anthony Standen tells us, Science is a Sacred Cow! Unfortunately, not all of the evidence used by advertisers is actually pertinent to the consumer's problem, but if it helps persuade him to buy, it has accomplished its purpose. Thus sales promotion continues to be opportunistic and to prey upon the gullible.

So long as these practices are continued it is doubtful that consumers are helped by advertising to make wiser or more rational choices in their general purchasing. In fact, I see little in today's advertising strategy, at least at the consumer level, to modify my 1927 statement that "if education were the principal claim of

advertising as it is now practiced, it would be an enormously wasteful enterprise." [12] Of course, as George French said years ago, "The major function of advertising is to persuade," [13] and this it seems to do pretty effectively with categorical and emotionally slanted claims.

In 1926 Clare Griffen wrote, "The third phase of the [automobile] industry will be one in which . . . annual sales will go largely to replace cars that have been eliminated from use. A majority of the industries of the United States have been in this . . . stage for a long time. . . ." [14] In 1927 I made a companion point in connection with the sales promotion of the California Fruit Growers Exchange. [15] In this case a wide expansion of supply was possible. In fact, while sales promotion had successfully expanded demand, supply had increased at about the same rate, leading to the conclusion that individuals who had owned orange orchards in 1905 had just about maintained a status quo so far as the purchasing power of the net income from these orchards was concerned. More recent data indicate that this result has been continued for another thirty years. In other words, in the long run, at least in this case, the rate of return on invested capital has not been increased by sales promotion.

Perhaps in each of these cases the professor was overly conservative or even pessimistic. Certainly the automobile industry has not yet, thirty-one years later, reached a mere replacement basis; and when control of supply is more practical, some brand advertising continues to be accompanied by high rates of return on invested capital even after more than thirty years of continuous promotion. While the two illustrations suggest the inevitable long-range result of specific sales promotion, aggressive businessmen refuse to accept the inevitable, thank goodness!

This discussion is both too broad and too episodic for successful summary or statement of specific conclusions. In closing, therefore, let me merely say that marketing is a living, growing organism. As it grows, its behavior sometimes is erratic and whimsical. Our understanding of its problems has increased materially, as has our ability to direct its further development. As with much of evolution, however, constructive and lasting change often is slow in coming.

---

[10] *Economics of Fashion* (New York: Ronald Press, 1928), p. 36.
[11] Vaile, *op. cit.*, p. 49.

[12] *Ibid.*, p. 59.
[13] *Advertising* (New York: Ronald Press, 1924).
[14] "The Evolution of the Automobile Market," *Harvard Business Review*, July, 1926, pp. 407–408.
[15] Vaile, *op. cit.*, Chap. 7.

B. Marketing in Free and Planned Economies

4. *Soviet Economic Growth*

FRANCIS M. BODDY

CAPITALISM AND SOVIET COMMUNISM

If we take the view that in the economic race between the Soviet Union and the United States the basic resource factors (except for the deficiency in Soviet agriculture) are about equal, the outcome may be determined largely by the relative efficiency with which the two economies can be managed. Here, of course, direct comparisons are difficult because of the striking organizational differences between the two systems: one is a mixed-market economy, the other is, basically, a centrally planned state socialism. Nevertheless, both the US and the USSR come up with answers to essentially the same questions. Each of them has to make decisions concerning:

1. Who shall use the available natural resources? For what purposes? How intensively? At what locations?

2. How much of current resources shall be directed to the production of investment goods —and of what kinds?

3. How shall the remaining available capital goods and labor supply be used? What goods and services shall be produced for current consumption?

4. How shall the output for current consumption be distributed to the consumers?

5. How shall resources and output be allocated between private or personal consumption and public or group consumption?

‡‡ SOURCE: Reprinted by permission from *Soviet Union: Paradox and Change* edited by Robert T. Holt and John E. Turner (New York: Holt, Rinehart and Winston, Inc., 1962), pp. 62–89.

The distinctive characteristics of capitalism and Soviet Communism can be illustrated by the location of the decision-making power in the economy and by the forces that determine how these decisions are made.

Features of Capitalism

1. Ownership and control of natural resources, capital goods, and personal labor lies with individuals or firms owned by individuals. These are the private property rights of a capitalistic society. Such rights may be temporarily (or permanently, except for labor) assigned to other persons by mutual agreement. This is the *right of contract.*

2. The organization and fundamental direction of the economic processes of production, exchange, and consumption are accomplished by the market system. This is, first of all, a system for the collection and dissemination of *information* as to current supplies and demands and market prices; and it is, secondly, a system of processes and institutions by which the exchanges of the goods and services are arranged for and accomplished. Under capitalism the market system is not directly planned nor are the prices fixed by the government or by any organized groups, but arise spontaneously and react freely to the economic actions of all the individual persons or firms in the economy.

3. The income of each individual and firm is determined basically by the market valuation of the contribution of that individual's (or firm's) labor, or of his other owned resources, to the economic output of the system.

4. Hence the economic incentives that lie behind economic decisions are (a) income for the owners of resources, (b) profits for the business firms, and (c) individual desires and satisfactions for the consumers.

In modern western capitalism generally, and in the United States, government has become an important economic sector. For defense, and for a variety of other governmental activities, the governments purchase large quantities of materials and products and hire large numbers of employees through the markets. In addition, governments of capitalist countries plan their policies of taxation and expenditure, as well as their monetary policies, in such a way as to promote full employment of resources and stability in overall economic conditions. In carrying out these activities, however, the governments have generally acted through the markets and have not used direct controls or "fixed" the market results.

In spite of the governmental effects, and in some cases controls, on the free market, however, a basic characteristic of western capitalism is the dominant role played by the free market in directing the whole economic process.

Features of Soviet Communism

1. All natural resources and all capital goods are owned collectively, that is, by the state; and the direction of their use, as well as the use of the labor of all individuals, lies with the state.

2. The organization and direction of the economic processes of resource use, production, and distribution is directly controlled by the state, although each consumer is permitted to choose, to a large degree, how he shall spend his income for the goods or services available to the consumer.

3. The incomes of individuals come solely from payments for personal contributions to the production of goods and services, and the rates of payment are determined by the state. No individuals are permitted to own or to receive the income from natural resources or capital goods (except for the "private plots" permitted to the farmers), or to hire other individuals for productive or income-earning activities.

4. The market processes and institutions are firmly and centrally controlled by the state, and the forces of supply and demand do not control market prices or economic decisions. Rather, prices and economic decisions conform to the central directive—the economic plan of the state. In the actual operation of Soviet Communism, this complete economic control and direction by the state is somewhat tempered by the economic and political necessities of permitting some degree of individualism, particularly in the agricultural sector, and permitting some freedom of choice to consumers. Some small areas of private property exist (for example, the small "private plots" allotted to the collective farmers and private ownership of some livestock). Moreover, in recent years the collective farms have been freed from the system of compulsory delivery of their produce to state agencies at state-set prices, and they may sell their output directly in consumer markets if they wish. But these are minor exceptions. The basic pattern is centralized state control over all significant economic decisions.

From this brief sketch of the two economic systems, the primary differences are apparent. First, the contrast of individual versus state ownership and control over resources; second, the contrast of a free-market system versus central planning as a means of organizing the economic life of the society.

In a mixed-market economy there is no overall economic plan that directs each individual or firm in its economic activities. Decisions on who shall make how much of what for whose consumption are decentralized. The quality and quantity of production in a given firm or industry are determined over time by the interaction of the forces of supply and demand. The future plans for a firm are made by the management as it estimates future demand for its products in relationship to anticipated costs. The resources needed for production are bought at a price determined by the market; the products produced are sold at a price determined by the market.

In the Soviet Union, on the other hand, the plans for each operating unit (the *enterprise*) are handed down from above. The resources needed for production are sent to the enterprise at a fixed-price according to the plan—management does not (in theory, at least) have to procure them. Finished products are distributed through the marketing outlets according to the plan at a price set by the plan. The plan for a firm is a segment of the plan for an industry (before 1957) or for an area (after 1957) that, in turn, is a part of the master plan for the entire economy.

To the uninitiated observer of these two different economic systems, the planned economy, in which all important decisions are centrally made by relatively few men, may seem to be the model of rational and efficient order; and a free economy may appear as a disordered array in which hundreds of thousands of entrepreneurs are making independent decisions, with only disorder and inefficiency as the inevitable results. But reality may be quite the reverse. The market mechanism in a free economy is an integrating force of great power, providing the entrepreneur with the information necessary to make rational decisions concerning the most efficient use of resources in his firm.

When in a free-market system the economy is running along at something like full employment; when general economic conditions are relatively stable, so that decision-makers have reason to be confident of their future plans; and when free competition is the dominant characteristic of the market relationships; then the economy has, in its market system, an operating process that leads to an efficient allocation of resources that, in turn, produces a maximum of desired products and services.

In fact, of course, and in spite of the effort of governments to maintain the desirable conditions, the system works far from perfectly. Unemployment obviously signals failure to achieve as much output as can and should be produced. Monopoly is neither fully prevented nor perfectly regulated when it does arise. And the rapid changes in technology and in consumer and governmental demands keep the system continually off balance. Nevertheless, free-market system achieves a very high degree of economic efficiency and preserves the highest levels of individual human freedoms.

Part of the job of the designers of a planned and centrally controlled economy is to develop incentives and mechanisms that will achieve the efficient allocation of economic resources to achieve *their* economic objectives. What they need, therefore, is a plan or set of plans that will do for their economy what the market largely does for western economies. The complexity of the problem of detailed allocation of all economic resources by a central plan may be illustrated by a vastly oversimplified example, using a very simple "economy," and posing the problem arising out of a single planned change for the coming plan period.

AN ILLUSTRATION OF THE PLANNERS' PROBLEM

One way to illustrate the difficulty of allocating resources in a planned system is to set up an input-output table for a simple economy (Table 1). This simple hypothetical economy consists in its entirety of five sectors (metal, machinery, fuel, agricultural products, and labor). The table shows the number of units of the products (outputs) of each sector required by each of the other sectors.

Across the top of the resulting table are listed sectors that consume the products of each producing sector. For example, the figures in the machinery column (reading down) show the units of output of each of the producing sectors that are consumed during the year by the machinery sector in the creation of its output. In order to make 200 units of machinery, it takes 65 units of metal, 25 units of machinery, 5 units of fuel, 10 units of agricultural produce, and 200 units of labor. The same sectors as producing sectors are listed down the side (except that the output, labor, is used as a title instead of the title of the consuming units, households). One can read across a row and find in each column the disposition of the output of that sector. The disposition of the total output of 50 units of fuel is shown by the figures in each column in the row labeled "Fuel."

An input-output table can be constructed on the basis of past records of actual operations of the economy or from knowledge of the tech-

TABLE 1. A Simple Model of an Economy

Producing Sectors	Consuming or Using Sectors					Total Output
	Metal	Machinery	Fuel	Agric.	Households	
Metal	10	65	10	5	10	100
Machinery	40	25	35	75	25	200
Fuel	15	5	5	5	20	50
Agriculture	15	10	50	50	525	650
Labor	100	200	100	550	50	1000

nical and engineering requiremnts of the available techniques for producing each product.

We can show the basic problem of a planner who is concerned with setting future production targets in each sector by looking at this table. (The establishment of such goals is, of course, one of the things the Soviet economic plan does.) Suppose that the planners decide to increase next year the amount of machinery to be made available to the household sector by 20 units. Since the total machinery output is 200 units, this is an increase of 10 percent in the total output of machines. This increase in production will require a 10-percent increase of all of the products needed to make machines: 6.5 units of metal, 0.5 unit of fuel, 1 unit of agricultural produce, and 20 units of labor, *plus* 2.5 additional units of machinery (it takes machines to make machines). Thus the other units of inputs into the machine sector will have to be increased by an additional 1.25 percent. But this is only the beginning of the computations. The additional units of metal that are required to make the additional units of machines will require increased inputs into the metal sector of the economy. Thus we can see that a change in just one column in the table requires a change in many other columns. If our planners were trying to set new goals for each of the products used by each of the other sectors, there would be hundreds of computations to make in this simple five-sector economy.

While even this simple illustration seems complex enough, the problem of Soviet planners is unimaginably more complex. Our five-sector input-output table must be replaced by one containing thousands of sectors. (A thousand-sector table would have one million entries, although many would consist of zeros.) The computational problem would be impossible if it were not for the development of high-speed electronic computers. Even these, however, could not effectively handle an input-output model that would recognize the need to break down the calculations to particular enterprises within the product classes and economic sectors. In many respects, however, the computational problem is the easy one. It is even more difficult to get the information needed to construct such a table, particularly in a rapidly changing economy where technological developments and increased labor productivity are constantly modifying the input-output relationships. Estimates have to be used, and errors in estimating even a few of the required input-output relationships will generate errors through the system. Inaccuracies of this sort will result in nonfulfillment of an output plan, or in a waste of resources or both.

As the planner runs through the computations of the input-output requirements necessary to fulfill a specified final output list, he may well find bottlenecks in the form of shortages of plant capacity, of raw materials or fuels, or of labor. This would call for a recasting of the plan to allocate more resources to break these bottlenecks by increasing investment in the critical areas, which will mean that lower output goals must be planned in the final-goods sectors. Sometimes, indeed, it may not be feasible to provide the inputs called for by a plan, and the goals may have to be adjusted to bring them within the limits imposed by resources and technology.

After the major outlines of the problem of economic decision-making in a planned economy have been laid out, there still remains the question of what administrative structure is to be established to carry out the plan that has been decided upon.

IS THERE A SUBSTITUTE FOR THE MARKET?

The Soviet Union is certainly not going to adopt, in the foreseeable future, all the features of a market system. Economic priorities will still be set by the political leaders in Moscow. But if the maturing economy is to achieve the level of efficiency necessary to maintain growth rates in the seven to nine percent range, the regime may have to borrow some of the techniques of the market system to provide rapid, accurate information on the relative scarcity of the factors of production. In other words, some type of pricing system will have to be developed in which prices reflect relative scarcity and real costs of production.

The Communist rulers have already taken a few timid steps in this direction. The freeing of the collective farms from the compulsory delivery of produce is one example. The farm manager has the option of selling produce in a market, and thus prices in the market to some degree affect his planting and investment decisions—to the extent that he is permitted to exercise any discretion. The manipulation of market prices by the planners may thus to some degree replace "the plan" as the main directive over the farmers.

In many ways, a more interesting, adaptation has been in the consumer-goods sector of the economy. In the past, the typical manner in which the USSR planned the distribution of consumer goods was to estimtae net disposable income in each republic and to provide the amount of consumer goods and/or to set the prices in such a way as to absorb this income. There was only the crudest concern for product mix and none at all for individual differences in tastes and styles. This method proved effective in an austere economy, in which consumer goods were so short in supply that the consumers had little alternative to accepting what was available. As incomes rose and as larger quantities of goods became available, however, consumers could afford to be more discriminating. A woman with enough clothes to meet her basic needs might save her money and wait until the dress style she wanted became available. A man could afford to be more particular about the quality and style of a suit. The result was that although most types of consumer goods remained scarce, some embarrassing surpluses began to appear. Indeed, certain products scarcely moved off the shelves.

In order to correct this situation, the system was modified. Now retail trade officials in the several republics are beginning to *order* the consumer goods they want from the producers or wholesalers, rather than merely distributing the goods sent to them on the basis of the economic plan. At this point, however, the retail-trade officials begin to encounter some of the fundamentals of a freshman course in the economics of the market. Since demand depends on price, the suit that will barely sell for 100 rubles may sell very well at 50. The retail-trade officials, to make the new approach an improvement, must have some device for measuring consumer demand and determining its elasticity for a wide range of products. The best and most efficient way (perhaps the only adequate way) of obtaining measures of these factors is through a market in which the consumer can use his "ruble ballot," and in which the prices are permitted to respond to supply and demand.

By 1961 surpluses in certain capital goods were also beginning to appear. The obvious solution to this problem would also be to allow factory management and *sovnarkhoz* officials to bid for their own capital goods. Here again certain elements of a market would have to be introduced to facilitate the making of a rational choice. But a decision on which capital goods should be purchased involves a consideration that is rarely present in a consumer-goods transaction; there is a range of alternative choices that would involve a different mix of capital and manpower, according to the production process in which the capital goods are to be used. The manager will want to choose the most efficient mix, but what criteria does he have to guide him?

A simple case will illustrate the problem. Suppose the *sovnarkhoz* in a region having an iron and steel complex decides to open a new iron mine and must provide for transporting the ore to the furnaces. The alternatives might be an electrified railway, a steam railway, or a road to accommodate heavy-duty trucks. Let us assume that the initial cost for the electric railway is 12,500,000 rubles; for the steam railway, 5,000,000 rubles; and for the truck highway (including the trucks), 2,000,000 rubles. The annual operating costs (including depreciation) of the electric railway are 250,-000 rubles; of the steam railway, 750,000 rubles; and of the truck highway, 1,000,000 rubles. Which alternative is the most rational and efficient? One can answer this question if he knows the marginal costs of capital in the economy. In a market economy, interest rates provide a good measure of such costs.

Not only is there nothing really comparable in the Soviet economy, but Soviet rulers have steadfastly refused to accept the idea of interest rates, regarding them as a feature of the exploitative capitalistic system. One of the fundamental themes of classical Marxist doctrine, to which lip service is still being paid, is the labor theory of value. The official ideology, in other words, denies that there can be anything like a cost of capital. If capital "costs nothing" in investment decisions, capital costs tend in fact to become enormous. This is one of the reasons for the "gigantomania" that is so characteristic of many Soviet productive enterprises. If the economy is to reach optimal efficiency, capital costs will have to be calculated as a part of investment decisions. If they are to be calculated, they must be measured. If they are to be measured, there is no really good substitute for introducing the concept of interest rates, which, in turn, must be sensitive to supplies of and demands for capital if they are to be reliable guides in decision-making.

In short, we are arguing that if the Soviet economy, rapidly increasing in complexity, is to achieve the efficiency necessary for continuing rapid economic growth, certain characteristics of the market will have to be introduced to provide reliable guides for rational economic decisions. The market, however, is not an "automatic" decision-making system. Knowing how to use the information derived from market operations requires the professional skills of the economist or of the western type businessman more than it does the talents of the successful bureaucrat or politician. For the intricate economic machine to operate efficiently, economic decision-making will probably have to become the job of economic managers rather than of politicians. The price the political elite may have to pay for economic efficiency is the diminution of some of their control over the economy.

Khrushchev has shown a strong pragmatic bent. To him the critical question is, "Will it work?" This has led him to steer the whole Soviet system, and particularly its economic system, in directions far from those indicated by Marx and Lenin.

The strength of the income incentive in persuading men to work effectively seems to have so impressed him that he told the Twenty-second Party Congress in 1961 that the present "socialist" rule (Article 12 of the Soviet Constitution)—"Work in the USSR is a duty and a matter of honor for every able-bodied citizen in accordance with the principle: 'He who does not work, neither shall he eat'"—would continue as a supreme principle under Communism as well.

Given this strong practical approach, the current Soviet regime may well permit or even encourage moves in the direction of a decentralized and partly market-controlled economy that will be heretical to the ideological Communists.

THE OUTCOME OF THE ECONOMIC RACE

The programs that the Soviet regime may have to adopt in order to win such a race, however, may in time have great impact upon the structure of Communist control over the society. We have suggested that the problems of maintaining and measuring economic efficiency in a mature economy may ultimately call for the adoption of a decentralized and, to a significant degree, market-controlled economic organization. The discussion of "synthetic" or "shadow" prices in the context of mathematical-economic analysis of economic problems by Soviet economists themselves; the use of prices rather than the plan to control and direct agricultural production; the struggle to find some "true measure" of economic costs of production; and the continued emphasis on the further decentralization of economic decision-making in the Party Program for the Twenty-second Party Congress—all these give some indication that modifications in the economic machinery may be in process. The state will undoubtedly retain ownership of the basic resources and monopoly over all economic enterprises; what is suggested here is that the *means* of control may move toward a modified market system.

If this development occurs to any significant extent, it will lead to a further strengthening of the use of economic incentives for the workers and a consequent further rise in the influence of the consumer in the system. It will also tend to attach greater importance to successful decentralized "managers" rather than to the central "planners" as key personnel in the economic system. Shifts in the locus of decision-making away from the center in the economic sphere may even be accompanied by changes in the pattern of control in other areas of Soviet life. Whether in fact such developments take place depends upon the way in which the Party moves to maintain its power. Khrushchev may discover, however, that the type of people upon whom he must depend in the economic race have a different political and psychological outlook from those of the ordinary Communist functionary. If this is true, and if such personnel begin to gain a bigger voice in decision-making, the structure of the dictatorship itself may undergo some modification over time.

The Environment and Forces of Marketing

A. Sociological and Anthropological Aspects
B. Psychology of Consumer Behavior
C. Economic Aspects of Consumer Behavior
D. The Legal Framework
E. Ethical Considerations
F. Competition and Economic Environment
G. Technological Developments and Marketing
H. The Institutional Framework of Marketing
I. Marketing's Dynamic Characteristics

M arketing functions within a complex, dynamic, and demanding environment. Deeply ingrained cultural patterns of behavior mesh with contemporary forces such as technological change. Consumption patterns are influenced by economic capabilities and by social and psychological motivations to satisfy wants and to achieve ever-changing aspirations.

It is the task of marketing to link producer and consumer within our environment. To this end, marketing institutions continually adjust to the environmental needs as they carry on their functions.

The readings in Part II have been selected because they develop the perspective of the marketing environment. An appreciation and understanding of this environment helps one immeasurably to perceive marketing in its proper focus.

A. Sociological and Anthropological Aspects

5. Business Implications of Population Growth

PHILIP M. HAUSER

WORLD INCREASES

In considering the world population outlook, it is well to bear certain perspectives in mind. To begin with, the total surface of the earth contains some 200 million square miles. Only a fourth of this surface is land. Only a tenth of the land surface is arable, and another tenth is potentially arable. These observations add up to the fact that this planet is finite and that the population that the earth can support is therefore also finite; both the available space and the ability of the earth to produce food, fibers, and other requisites for human life are restricted.

In 1950, the population of the world was estimated at about 2.5 billion. This population was distributed rather unevenly over the surface of the globe; half of the population was in Asia, a fourth in Europe, and the remaining fourth distributed over the rest of the earth. About two-thirds of the world population was concentrated in about a tenth of the land surface, in four great regions—South Asia, Southeast Asia and the offshore islands, Europe, and Northeastern United States.

The 1950 world population of 2.5 billion was reached by quite uneven rates of growth. During most of the two hundred thousand to a million years that Homo sapiens has been on the earth, his numbers could not have increased at more than 1 per cent per century. In fact, a population of the present magnitude could have been produced from an initial pop-

⠟ SOURCE: Reprinted by permission from *Business Horizons*, Vol. 3, No. 2, Summer 1960, pp. 87–96.

ulation of two dozen persons, increasing at the rate of 0.02 per cent per year over a period of one hundred thousand years. The rate of world population growth has increased explosively during the modern era, that is, the three centuries beginning in 1650. During this period, the rate increased from about 0.4 per cent per year between 1650 and 1750 to approximately 1 per cent per year between 1930 and 1940. While a 1 per cent return on capital seems niggardly, a 1 per cent annual population increase produces fantastic results in relatively short periods of time. This can be quickly documented by indicating the population that would be produced by one hundred persons reproducing at a rate of 1 per cent per year, not for the entire period that man has been on earth, but merely for the 5,000 years of recorded history. Under such conditions, there would be on the face of the earth today 2.7 billion persons for each square foot of land surface—a number that happens to be the United Nations estimate of *world* population for 1957!

At the rate of population increase in 1700, world population would have doubled every 178 years. By 1800, continued acceleration of the rate of increase reduced the period of doubling to 154 years; by 1930, to 75 years; by 1950, to 58 years. At the present rate of world population increase, 1.7 per cent per year, a doubling of the population will occur in about 40 years. World population actually doubled in the 70 years between 1887 and 1957. Thus, it took between two hundred thousand and a million years to produce a population of about 1.3 billion people and only 70 additional years to double this figure. Considerations of this type have led the demographer to use the emotionally loaded phrase "population explosion" to indicate the changes in rates of population growth during the modern era.

These changes in population growth rates are the concomitants of man's culture-building activities. The great spurt in growth rates is primarily the result of decreased death rates. These in turn were partly unanticipated by-products and partly direct results of increased agricultural and industrial productivity, improved environmental sanitation and personal hygiene, and modern medicine. The world population explosion is still under way. The United Nations outlook for world population growth is summarized in Table 1.

Breakdown by Major Areas

This global picture of population growth varies considerably, of course, by continent and nation.

Asia. With more than half the world's population in 1950, Asia will, according to United Nations projections, increase at a rate above the world average both in the third and fourth quarters of this century. Between 1950 and 1975, Asia will have an annual percentage increase of 2.4; and between 1975 and 2000, an average annual percentage increase of 3.0. Asia's population by the end of the century is projected to be about 3.9 billion. Thus, during the second half of this century, Asia is destined

TABLE 1. Estimated Population and Population Increases, 1900-2000

Year	World	Africa	North America	Latin America	Asia	Europe (incl. USSR)	Oceania
Population in millions							
1900	1,550	120	81	63	857	423	6
1925	1,907	147	126	99	1,020	505	10
1950	2,497	199	168	163	1,380	574	13
1975	3,828	303	240	303	2,210	751	21
2000	6,267	517	312	592	3,870	947	29
Average Annual Percentage Increase *							
1900-1925	0.9	0.9	2.2	2.3	0.8	0.8	2.3
1925-1950	1.2	1.4	1.3	2.6	1.4	0.6	1.4
1950-1975	2.1	2.1	1.7	3.4	2.4	1.2	2.4
1975-2000	2.6	2.8	1.2	3.8	3.0	1.0	1.6

* Arithmetic mean of percentage increase for 25-year periods as projected by United Nations; "medium" assumptions.

SOURCE: *The Future Growth of World Population* (New York: United Nations, 1958), p. 23.

During the third quarter of this century, according to the "medium" assumptions of the United Nations, world population will increase at the rate of 2.1 per cent per year, and will reach a total of over 3.8 billion by 1975. During the fourth quarter of this century, the average annual percentage increase in world population will reach 2.6 per cent, a rate that would produce a total world population of 6.3 billion by the year 2000. According to these projections, then, the population of the world will increase by 1.3 billion in the third quarter of this century and by an additional 2.5 billion —a number equal to the total world population in 1950—during the fourth quarter of this century.

to increase by some 2.5 billion persons or by as many people as were on the entire globe in 1950.

Africa. With a population of 199 million in 1950, Africa is projected to have a 2.1 per cent average annual increase during the third quarter of the century, and a 2.8 per cent average annual increase during the fourth quarter of the century. Thus, Africa will have a population of 517 million by the year 2000, a 2½-fold increase amounting to over 300 million persons.

Latin America. With a population of 163 million in 1950, Latin America south of the Rio Grande will have an average annual percentage increase of 3.4 per cent during the third quarter, and of 3.8 per cent during the fourth quarter of this century. By the year 2000, Latin America, according to this projection, will have a population of 592 million or an increase of 429 million persons in the last half of this century.

North America. In 1950, America north of the Rio Grande had a population of 168 million. With the projected increase of 1.7 per cent per year during the third quarter of the century, and 1.2 per cent during the fourth quarter of the century, North America will have a total population of 312 million in the year 2000, an increase of 429 million during the second half of this century.

Europe. Finally, Europe, with a population of 574 million in 1950, will, according to the United Nations projections, experience the lowest of the population increases of the continents: a 1.2 per cent per year increase in the third quarter and a 1.0 per cent per year increase during the fourth quarter of this century. Under these assumptions, Europe will have a population of 947 million by the year 2000, an increase of some 373 million persons during the second half of the century.

In summary, then, the population of the world by the end of the century—6.3 billion—will be about 2½ times the 1950 total. Of the world increase of 3.8 billion persons, about two-thirds, or 2.5 billion, will occur in Asia. Latin America will experience the next largest increase, well over 400 million persons, followed by Europe with an increase of about 370 million persons, and Africa with an increase of over 300 million. North America during the same period will increase by 144 million. Finally, to complete the picture, Oceania, with a total population of 13 million in 1950, will more than double during the second half of the century to reach a total of 29 million persons.

U.S. INCREASES

The United States provides one of the world's most dramatic examples of explosive population increase. The growth of the United States reflects, of course, not only a great natural increase as mortality declines more rapidly than fertility, but also the effects of immigration.

The projections show that the maintenance of the postwar birth rate for the United States would by 1980 produce a population of about 260 million; and by the year 2000 a population of 377 to 388 million, the variation being due to differing assumptions about the death rate. On the likely assumption that the post-

TABLE 2. **Population of the United States, 1950 and Projections to 2000**

(In thousands of persons)

Year	Medium Projection	Low Projection	High Projection
1950	151,683	–	–
1960	180,126	179,420	181,154
1970	213,810	202,541	219,474
1980	259,981	230,834	272,557
1990	313,538	252,361	320,761
2000*	332,239	262,516	377,486
	342,673	272,178	388,444

* Two estimates are shown for each projection for the year 2000, based on different assumptions with respect to the death rate.

SOURCES: For 1950: Bureau of the Census, U.S. Dep't of Commerce, 1950 *Census of Population* (Washington: U.S. Gov't Printing Office, 1951) For 1960–80: Bureau of the Census, "Illustrative Projections of the United States, By Age and Sex 1960 to 1980," *Current Population Reports* (1958), p. 16. For 1990–2000: Division of the Actuary, Social Security Administration, U.S. Dep't of Health, Education, and Welfare, *Illustrative United States Population Projections* (Washington: U.S. Gov't Printing Office, 1957), pp. 23–24. The Census and Social Security Administration projections as presented are not strictly comparable but are sufficiently so for purposes of this article.

war birth rate of the United States will not be maintained throughout the rest of this century, the Social Security Administration projects a population of from 332 to 343 million persons by the year 2000.

Thus, the maintenance of the present birth rate would by 1980, in a period of little more than one human generation, increase the population of the United States by about 110 million persons over that of 1950. This *increase alone* would constitute the fifth largest nation in the world today, exceeded in size only by China, India, the USSR, and the United States itself.

Drawing further on the census projections, should the birth rate decline to the wartime level, the population of the United States by 1980 would be about 231 million; and should the birth rate increase by 10 per cent, the population could be some 273 million. The population of the United States, then, in the single human generation following 1950, could increase at the lower limit by about 80 million, the equivalent of a nation the size of Pakistan;

and at the upper limit by about 125 million, the equivalent of the entire population of Pakistan and the United Kingdom combined.

In brief, the population of the United States during the second half of the century could increase by from about 171 to over 237 million persons, to reach a total of from 332 to 388 million, with the latter figure being the less likely.

WORLD IMPLICATIONS

The implications to the business community of the rapidly increasing world population may be broken down into direct implications and indirect implications. The direct consequences of the world population outlook may be gauged in terms of the world market; the indirect consequences in terms of their long-run and short-run political and economic impact on the world in general.

The World Market

Markets are people with purchasing power. The explosive increase of world population obviously means that in at least one sense the market is expanding. But, unfortunately, the world market will not increase as rapidly as world population. For the outlook for a corresponding increase in world purchasing power is dim indeed.

In 1950, North America, with 9 per cent of the world's population, enjoyed 44 per cent of the world's income. Europe (excluding the USSR), with 17 per cent of the world's population, enjoyed an additional 27 per cent of the world's income. Thus, North America and Europe combined, with about a fourth of the world's population, had over 70 per cent of the world's total income. In contrast, Asia in 1950, with 53 per cent of the world's population, had less than 11 per cent of the world's income. Per capita income (in United States dollars) was $1,100 for North America in 1950, but only $50 for Asia. The market as measured by Continental income was $237 billion for North America; whereas Asia (excluding the USSR), despite her much greater population, was at a level of $58 billion. Continental income for Europe (excluding the USSR), with less than a third of Asia's population, was $149 billion, or over 2½ times that of Asia.

During the remainder of the century there will be, in general, an inverse relationship between the per capita income of nations and their rates of population growth. The popula-

tion of the relatively underdeveloped areas of the world will increase at a more rapid rate than that of the economically advanced continents. During the last quarter of the century, for example, while North America is increasing at an average of 1.2 per cent per year, and Europe at 1.0 per cent, Asia will be increasing at 3.0 per cent, Africa at 2.8 per cent, and Latin America at 3.8 per cent.

Advanced vs. Underdeveloped Nations

If the world is divided into two economic categories—the advanced countries and the underdeveloped countries—the population outlook of each category is quite different.[1] Among the advanced countries are included North America, temperate-zone South America, Japan, Europe, the Soviet Union, Australia, and New Zealand. In 1950, these nations had a population estimated at 863 million. By 2000, the population of these nations will reach nearly 1.5 billion. Their annual percentage increase in population will average 1.2 per cent between 1950 and 1975, and 1.0 per cent between 1975 and 2000.

The underdeveloped countries include the African countries, Central America, tropical South America, Asia (excluding Japan and the Soviet Union), and the Pacific Islands (excluding Australia and New Zealand). The population of this area in 1950 was estimated at 1.6 billion. The growth of these underdeveloped countries may proceed at a rate of 2.0 per cent per year between 1950 and 1975, and 2.4 per cent per year between 1975 and 2000. The population of these nations by 2000 may be some 4.8 billion.

That is, between 1950 and 2000, the population of the economically advanced countries is likely to increase by about 600 million, whereas that of the underdeveloped countries will increase by over five times that figure, 3.2 billion. Needless to say, the market in the economically underdeveloped countries will not increase by a factor of five. The evidence indicates that, if anything, the gap between the have and have-not nations is increasing rather than decreasing.

Of special interest to United States business is the prospect of the rapidly expanding population in Latin America. The proximity of Latin America to the United States, and the special

---

[1] Population Reference Bureau, "World Population Review," *Population Bulletin*, XV, March 1959, pp. 19–20.

historical relations between the northern and southern parts of the Western hemisphere, may make the Latin American market an increasingly attractive one to United States business; Latin American development needs may make it an even more important area for United States investment. It should be noted that, although the population of North America outnumbered that of Latin America by 5 million persons in 1950, and that despite the post-war baby boom in North America, Latin America is likely to outnumber North America by 280 million people by the end of the century! During the fourth quarter of this century, Latin America will be increasing at a rate producing a doubling every eighteen years.

It would be meaningless to attempt to quantify the national income of the underdeveloped areas by the year 2000. From a market standpoint, the underprivileged areas in Asia and Africa will remain relatively impoverished. On the other hand, the market of the advanced countries of the world, together with the possibility of increasing business relations with Latin America, provides tremendous opportunities for investment and foreign-trade expansion during the remainder of the century.

Long-Run Implications

The long-run implications of explosive world population increase can be more easily grasped if they are related to the population-carrying capacity of the globe. Although such a calculation is necessarily conjectural, it is instructive to observe that such estimates vary from 5 billion to 50 billion. The latter number is the highest ever published by a responsible scholar and it is based on rather extreme assumptions. Harrison Brown, who made this estimate, indicates that a population of 50 billion persons could be sustained indefinitely on the earth under two difficult assumptions.[2] The first is that the control of solar energy or nuclear energy will be achieved so that the cost of energy will be very low. Under such a condition, we would not need to be concerned with the conservation of resources, because everything needed to support this population would be obtained from the air, the seas, and rock. The second assumption is that mankind will not only forgo meat, as the Hindu has already done, but also vegetables, and will subsist in large part on algae, a yeastlike substance raised on the ocean or developed in factories.

With present rates of growth, even this maximum figure would not be very far off; in fact, it would be reached in less than 200 years. Just how impossible it is for the present world rate of population growth to continue much longer is indicated by the fact that, at present rates, there would be one person for every square foot of land surface on the globe within less than 800 years.

Calculations of this type are admittedly academic. They are designed merely to indicate the implications of population increase, implications that obviously cannot come to pass. The mere consideration of these data, however, is one of the reasons these extreme numbers will not be reached. For mankind, by recognizing the implications of his present rates of reproduction, is bound to modify them. The calculations make it clear that present rates of increase cannot be sustained for long, if for no other reason than the limitations of space on the globe. Of course, if one assumes that we can colonize outer space, then such a limitation does not exist.

Short-Run Implications

Perhaps of more immediate concern to the world are the short-run implications of population increase. Rapid population growth is an important factor in the bipolar world political situation. It affects the bitter struggle between the free nations and the Communist nations for ascendancy and constitutes a major threat to peace.

There is a great imbalance between the distribution of the world's population and the world's utilized resources; this imbalance is manifest in international differences in standards of living. At the extreme, these differences, as was indicated by the per capita incomes cited above, may be in a ratio of as much as 20 to 1.

The great gulf between the have and have-not nations is a major source of international friction and a great barrier to world peace. The various types of technical assistance programs, those of the United Nations and the specialized agencies, the Point Four Program, the Colombo Plan, and the programs of the great foundations, together with the strenuous efforts of the less-developed countries themselves, are designed to raise world-wide standards of living, partly in the interest of international peace. Clearly, in order to increase

---

[2] Harrison Brown, *The Challenge of Man's Future* (New York: Viking Press, 1954), pp. 146, 220–21.

the standards of living, aggregate production must increase more rapidly than population. In most of the have-not nations, the more slowly that the population grows, the more that increases in production are likely to be reflected in higher output per capita and higher standards of living. Because the initial effect of induced economic development programs is to decrease the death rate and increase the rate of population growth, rapidly growing populations threaten to nullify efforts to raise standards of living.

This threat is particularly great at the present time in the context of the struggle between the free and the Communist countries. The Communist countries continuously exploit the mass poverty of the less-developed areas of the world, especially the highly strategic area of South and Southeast Asia. The Communists not only attribute the misery of the have-not nations to the "imperialist policies" of the capitalist nations, but also promise quicker methods for achieving higher levels of living. If the less-developed nations in Asia are unable to achieve higher living standards by increasing product per capita, either by controlling population growth, or by achieving great increases in productivity, or by some combination of both, they are likely to be easier prey to Communist propaganda. Should this happen, a real threat would be posed not only to world peace but also to the way of life in the free countries.

At the present time, about a third of the world's people live in the free countries and about a third in the Communist countries. The remaining third live primarily in the uncommitted countries, mainly in South and Southeast Asia. In view of the resources and the population that the uncommitted nations command, it is reasonably clear that the balance of world power in the long run may be determined by the success of the free or Communist bloc in capturing the allegiance of the uncommitted nations.

In the short run, then, what is of major concern to business about the world population outlook is its threat to world peace and the way in which population growth could affect the outcome of the gigantic struggle between the two opposing power blocs.

Concentration of Population

One further effect of the great population increases in prospect for the United States must be noted. Explosive national population growth in the United States has been accompanied by an increasing concentration of population in a relatively small number of metropolitan areas. At the beginning of the century, about a third of the population in the United States lived in areas that would qualify as Standard Metropolitan Areas as defined by the federal government in 1950. By 1950, this percentage had increased to 57 per cent. By 1980, perhaps 68 per cent of the population will be in metropolitan areas and, by the year 2000, perhaps as much as 78 per cent.

The increased size of these clumpings of people and economic activities has many direct business implications that cannot be elaborated upon here. But there is a tremendously important consequence that must be at least mentioned. This is the way in which the increased size in concentration of the population affects the role of government at the federal, state, and local levels. Increase in metropolitanism as a way of life, involving an increasing complexity in and interdependence of social and economic organization, necessitates an ever-increasing multiplication of governmental functions and interventionism. The great expansion in governmental functions that has characterized the political organization of the United States from the beginning of our national history is undoubtedly attributable to the increase in urban and metropolitan living. There can be little doubt that the combination of greatly increased population, creating pressures on national resources, and the increasing "metropolitanization" of a population, making our social and economic organization more complex and interdependent, will result in a further elaboration of governmental functions and increased government intervention in all aspects of American life, including business activities.

The business community has been inclined, with good reason, to view population changes as possessing essentially long-run implications. It has been recognized for some time that population changes have important implications for economic activity in general and specific businesses in particular. But it has been believed that population changes were of a long-run character, setting up irresistible but imperceptible influences, glacier-like in character. With the great fluctuations in the birth rate over the past several decades, however, and with the tremendous decreases in the death rate throughout the world, population changes are increasingly having significant implications for business even in the short run.

6. *Social Classes and Spending Behavior*

PIERRE MARTINEAU

All societies place emphasis on some one structure which gives form to the total society and integrates all the other structures such as the family, the clique, voluntary association, caste, age, and sex groupings into a social unity. Social stratification means any system of ranked statuses by which all the members of a society are placed in some kind of a super-ordinate and subordinate hierarchy. While money and occupation are important in the ranking process, there are many more factors, and these two alone do not establish social position. The concept of social class was designed to include this process of ranking people in superior and inferior social position by any and all factors.

CLASS SYSTEM

It has been argued that there cannot be a class system existent in America when most individuals do not have the slightest idea of its formal structure. Yet in actuality every individual senses that he is more at home with and more acceptable to certain groups than to others. In a study of department stores and shopping behavior, it was found that the Lower-Status woman is completely aware that, if she goes into High-Status department stores, the clerks and the other customers in the store will punish her in various subtle ways.

"The clerks treat you like a crumb," one woman expressed it. After trying vainly to be waited on, another woman bitterly complained

‡‡ SOURCE: Reprinted by permission from the *Journal of Marketing* (National Quarterly Publication of the American Marketing Association), Vol. 23, No. 2, October 1958, pp. 121–130.

that she was loftily told, "We thought you were a clerk."

The woman who is socially mobile gives considerable thought to the external symbols of status, and she frequently tests her status by shopping in department stores which she thinks are commensurate with her changing position. She knows that, if she does not dress correctly, if she does not behave in a certain manner to the clerks, if she is awkward about the proper cues, then the other customers and the clerks will make it very clear that she does not belong.

In another study, very different attitudes in the purchase of furniture and appliances involving this matter of status were found. Middle-Class people had no hesitancy in buying refrigerators and other appliances in discount houses and bargain stores because they felt that they could not "go wrong" with the nationally advertised names. But taste in furniture is much more elusive and subtle because the brand names are not known; and, therefore, one's taste is on trial. Rather than commit a glaring error in taste which would exhibit an ignorance of the correct status symbols, the same individual who buys appliances in a discount house generally retreats to a status store for buying furniture. She needs the support of the store's taste.

In a very real sense, everyone of us in his consumption patterns and style of life shows an awareness that there is some kind of a superiority-inferiority system operating, and that we must observe the symbolic patterns of our own class.

Lloyd Warner and Paul Lunt have described a six-class system: the Upper-Upper, or old families; Lower-Upper, or the newly arrived; Upper-Middle, mostly the professionals and successful businessmen; Lower-Middle, or the white collar salaried class; Upper-Lower, or the wage earner, skilled worker group; and Lower-Lower, or the unskilled labor group.[1] For practical purposes, in order to determine the individual's class position, Warner and his associates worked out a rating index, not based on amount of income but rather on type of income, type of occupation, house type, and place of residence.

Athough the Warner thesis has been widely used in sociology, it has not generally been employed in marketing. As a matter of fact, some critics in the social sciences have held that, since Warner's thesis rested essentially on studies of smaller cities in the 10,000-25,000 class, this same system might not exist in the more complex metropolitan centers, or might not be unravelled by the same techniques. Furthermore, many marketers did not see the application of this dimension to the individual's economic behavior, since the studies of Warner and his associates had mostly been concerned with the differences in the broad patterns of living, the moral codes, etc.

SOCIAL CLASS IN CHICAGO

Under Warner's guidance, the *Chicago Tribune* has undertaken several extensive studies exploring social class in a metropolitan city, and its manifestations specifically in family buying patterns. The problem was to determine if such a social-class system did exist in metropolitan Chicago, if the dimensions and the relationships were at all similar to the smaller cities which were studied before the far-reaching social changes of the past fifteen years. The studies were undertaken to see if there were any class significances in the individual family's spending-saving patterns, retail store loyalties, and his expressions of taste in typical areas such as automobiles, apparel, furniture, and house types.

It seems that many an economist overlooks the possibility of any psychological differences

between individuals resulting from different class membership. It is assumed that a rich man is simply a poor man with more money and that, given the same income, the poor man would behave exactly like the rich man. The *Chicago Tribune* studies crystallize a wealth of evidence from other sources that this is just not so, and that the Lower-Status person is profoundly different in his mode of thinking and his way of handling the world from the Middle-Class individual. Where he buys and what he buys will differ not only by economics but in symbolic value.

It should be understood, of course, that there are no hard and fast lines between the classes. Implicit in the notion of social class in America is the possibility of movement from one class to another. The "office boy-to-president" saga is a cherished part of the American dream. Bobo Rockefeller illustrates the female counterpart: from coal miner's daughter to socialite. As a corollary of the explorations in class, the study also tried to be definitive about the phenomenon of social mobility—the movement from one class to another.

There are numerous studies of vertical mobility from the level of sociological analysis, mostly by comparing the individual's occupational status to that of his father. There are also studies at the level of psychological analysis. This study attempted to combine the two levels, to observe the individual's progress and also to understand something of the dynamics of the mobile person as compared to the stable individual. The attempt was to look both backward and forward: tracing such factors as occupation, place of residence, and religion back to parents and grandparents, and then where the family expected to be in the next five or ten years, what were the educational plans for each son, each daughter, a discussion of future goals.

Because this article is confined primarily to social class, this section may be concluded by saying that the studies show a very clear relationship between spend-saving aspirations and the factors of mobility-stability.

FRAMEWORK OF STUDY

Following are Warner's hypotheses and assumptions for the study:

I. *Assumptions about symbols and values and about saving of money and accumulation of objects.*

---

[1] W. Lloyd Warner and Paul Lunt, *The Social Life of a Modern Community* (New Haven: Yale University Press, 1950). Also, W. Lloyd Warner, Marchia Meeker, and Kenneth Eells, *Social Class in America* (Chicago: Science Research Associates, 1949).

Our society is acquisitive and pecuniary. On the one hand, the values and beliefs of Americans are pulled toward the pole of the accumulation of money by increasing the amount of money income and reducing its outgo. On the other hand, American values emphasize the accumulation of objects and products of technology for display and consumption. The self-regard and self-esteem of a person and his family, as well as the public esteem and respect of a valued social world around the accumulator, are increased or not by such symbols of accumulation and consumption.

The two sets of values, the accumulation of product symbols and the accumulation (saving) of money, may be, and usually are, in opposition.

General working hypotheses stemming from these assumptions were: (1) People are distributed along a range according to the two-value components, running from proportionately high savings, through mixed categories, to proportionately high accumulation of objects. (2) These value variations conform to social and personality factors present in all Americans.

II. *Assumptions about product symbols, savers, and accumulations.*

American society is also characterized by social change, particularly technological change that moves in the direction of greater and greater production of more kinds and more numerous objects for consumption and accumulation.

Hypothesis. New varieties of objects will be most readily accepted by the accumulators, and most often opposed by the savers.

III. *Assumptions about the social values of accumulators and savers.*

American society is characterized by basic cultural differences, one of them being social status. Social class levels are occupied by people, some of whom are upward mobile by intent and fact. Others are non-mobile, by intent and fact. The values which dictate judgments about actions, such as the kinds of objects which are consumed and accumulated, will vary by class level and the presence or absence of vertical mobility.

IV. *Assumptions about the personal values of accumulators and savers.*

The personality components are distributed through the class levels and through the mobility types. By relating the social and personality components, it is possible to state a series of hypotheses about accumulators and savers as they are related to the object world around them, particularly to objects which are new and old to the culture, those which are imposing or not and those which are predominantly for display or for consumption.

At the direct, practical level, all of these theoretical questions can be summarized by one basic question: *What kinds of things are people likely to buy and not buy if they are in given class positions and if they are or are not socially mobile?* In other words, what is the effect on purchasing behavior of being in a particular social class, and being mobile or non-mobile?

If this is the crucial question, theoretically grounded, then a whole series of hypotheses can be laid out concerning values about money and values about buying various kinds of objects for consumption and for display. Some of these are:

1. *There will be a relationship between values held by a particular subject and the extent to which particular products exemplify those values.*

2. *There is a differential hierarchy of things for which it is worth spending money.*

3. *Veblen's theory that conspicuous expenditure is largely applied to the Upper Class is erroneous. It runs all the way through our social system.*

From these statements certain other hypotheses follow:

4. *At different class levels, symbols of mobility will differ.*

There is a differential hierarchy of things on which it is worth spending money. Class and mobility will be two of the dimensions that will differentiate—also personality and cultural background.

5. *The place in the home where these symbols will be displayed will shift at different class levels.*

The underlying assumption here is that there is a hierarchy of importance in the rooms of the house. This hierarchy varies with social class, mobility, age, ethnicity. The studies also revealed clear-cut patterns of taste for lamps, furnishings, house types, etc.

6. *The non-mobile people tend to rationalize purchases in terms of cost or economy.*

In other words, non-mobile people tend to be oriented more toward the pole of the accumulation of money. Purchases, then, are rationalized in terms of the savings involved.

The basic thesis of all the hypotheses on mobility is this: Whereas the stable individual would emphasize saving and security, the behavior of the mobile individual is characterized by spending for various symbols of upward movement. All of the evidence turned up indicates that this difference in values does exist, and furthermore that notable differences in personality dynamics are involved. For instance, the analysis of how families would make investments shows that stable people overwhelmingly prefer insurance, the symbol of security. By contrast, the mobile people at all levels prefer stocks, which are risk-taking. In Warner's words, the mobile individual acts as if he were free, white, and twenty-one, completely able to handle the world, and perfectly willing to gamble on himself as a sure bet to succeed.

CLASS PLACEMENT

Returning to the factor of social class, in this study class placement was based on a multi-state probability area sample of metropolitan Chicago, involving 3,880 households. It was found that the matter of placement could not be done by the relatively simple scoring sufficient for the smaller cities. To secure house typings, it was necessary to provide the field investigators with photographs covering a wide range of dwelling types, all the way from exclusive apartments to rooms over stores. Because of the very complexity of metropolitan life, occupations provided the biggest problem. To solve this operational problem, it was necessary to construct an exhaustive list of occupational types involving degree of responsibility and training required by each. The data finally used to calculate the Index of Status Characteristics (ISC) were:

(weighted by 5)
    Occupation (from 1 to 7 broad categories)
(weighted by 4)
        Sources of Income (from 1 to 7 types)
(weighted by 3)
            Housing Type (from 1 to 7 types)

The sum of the individual's weighted scores was used to predict his social class level as follows:[2]

ISC Scores	Predicted Social Class Placement
12-21	Upper Class
22-37	Upper-Middle Class
38-51	Lower-Middle Class
52-66	Upper-Lower Class
67-84	Lower-Lower Class

The study very clearly shows that there is a social-class system operative in a metropolitan area which can be delineated. Furthermore, class membership is an important determinant of the individual's economic behavior, even more so than in the smaller city. The one department store in the smaller city may satisfy almost everyone, whereas in the metropolitan city the stores become sharply differentiated.

This is the social-class structure of Metropolitan Chicago, typifying the transformation of the formerly agrarian Midwestern cities from Pittsburgh to Kansas City into a series of big milltowns:

Upper and Upper-Middle	8.1%
Lower-Middle	28.4%
Upper-Lower	44.0%
Lower-Lower	19.5%

While the Old Families and the Newly Arrived are still recognizable as types, they constitute less than 1 per cent of the population. A similar study in Kansas City turned up so few that they could not be counted at all. On the other hand, we see the emergence of a seventh class, the Upper-Lower "Stars" or Light-Blue Collar Workers. They are the spokesmen of the Upper-Lower Class groups— high income individuals, who have the income for more ostentatious living than the average factory worker but who lack the personal skills or desire for high status by social mobility.

There is certainly a rough correlation between income and social class. But social class is a much richer dimension of meaning. There are so many facets of behavior which are explicable only on a basis of social class dynamics. For instance, this analysis of the purchase of household appliances in Chicago over a four-

---

[2] Dr. Bevode McCall helped to solve the ISC scoring problem for Metropolitan Chicago.

year period shows a very different picture by income and by class:

Nine Appliance Types—Four-Year Period

By Income

Over $7,000	36.2%
4,000-6,999	46.0%
Under 4,000	17.8%

By Social Class

Upper and Upper-Middle	16.6%
Lower-Middle	29.2%
Upper-Lower	45.7%
Lower-Lower	8.5%

Income analysis shows that the lowest income group represents an understandably smaller market, but nevertheless a market. Social-class analysis highlights a fundamental difference in attitudes toward the home between the two lower classes. The Upper-Lower Class man sees his home as his castle, his anchor to the world, and he loads it down with hardware—solid heavy appliances—as his symbols of security. The Lower-Lower Class individual is far less interested in his castle, and is more likely to spend his income for flashy clothes or an automobile. He is less property-minded, and he has less feeling about buying and maintaining a home.

Several *Tribune* studies have explored the way of life and the buying behavior in many new suburbs and communities. All of them quickly become stratified along social-class and mobility dimensions, and, therefore, differ tremendously among themselves. *Fortune* has reported on Park Forest, Illinois, a Middle-Class suburb of 30,000 and only ten years old. It is characterized by high degrees of both upward and geographical mobility. The people are overwhelmingly those who had moved from other parts of the United States, who had few local roots, and who consequently wanted to integrate themselves in friendship groups. But this was not typical of the new Lower-Status suburbs where the women did relatively little fraternizing. It was not typical of the new Upper-Middle Class mobile suburbs where the people were preoccupied with status symbols, not in submerging themselves in the group.

One new community had crystallized as being for Higher-Status Negroes. This was a resettlement project with relatively high rents for Negroes. Eighty-five per cent of them had come from the South where social class was compressed. But, as soon as they came to Chicago, the class system opened up and they were anxious to establish a social distance between themselves and other Negroes. Almost all of them said they enjoyed the "peace and quiet" of their neighborhood, which was their way of insisting that they were not like the "noisy" Lower-Class Negroes. They deliberately avoided the stores patronized by other Negroes.

CHOICE OF STORE

All of these studies reveal the close relation between choice of store, patterns of spending, and class membership. In the probability sample delineating social class, such questions were asked in the total metropolitan area as:

"If you were shopping for a good dress, at which store would you be most likely to find what you wanted?"
"For an everyday dress?"
"For living room furniture?"
"At which store do you buy most of your groceries?"

To assume that all persons would wish to shop at the glamorous High-Status stores is utterly wrong. People are very realistic in the way they match their values and expectations with the status of the store. The woman shopper has a considerable range of ideas about department stores; but these generally become organized on a scale ranking from very High-Social Status to the Lowest-Status and prestige. The social status of the department store becomes the primary basis for its definition by the shopper. This is also true of men's and women's apparel stores, and furniture stores, on the basis of customer profiles. The shopper is not going to take a chance feeling out of place by going to a store where she might not fit.

No matter what economics are involved, she asks herself who are the other customers in the store, what sort of treatment can she expect at the hands of the clerks, will the merchandise be the best of everything, or lower priced and hence lower quality? Stores are described as being for the rich, for the average ordinary people, or for those who have to stretch their pennies.

The most important function of retail advertising today, when prices and quality have become so standard, is to permit the shopper to make social-class identification. This she can do from the tone and physical character of the advertising. Of course, there is also the factor of psychological identification. Two people in the same social class may want different stores. One may prefer a conservative store, one may want the most advanced styling. But neither will go to stores where they do not "fit," in a social-class sense.

In contrast to the independent food retailer, who obviously adapts to the status of the neighborhood, the chain grocers generally invade many income areas with their stores. Nevertheless, customer profiles show that each chain acquires a status definition. The two largest grocery chains in the Chicago area are A. & P. and Jewel; yet they draw very different customer bodies. A. & P. is strong with the mass market, whereas Jewel has its strength among the Middle Class.

While the national brand can and often does cut across classes, one can think of many product types and services which do have social class labels. The Upper-Middle Class person rarely travels by motor coach because none of his associates do so, even though there is certainly nothing wrong with this mode of transportation. On the other hand, even with low air-coach fares, one does not see many factory workers or day laborers on vacation around airports. Such sales successes as vodka and tonic water, and men's deodorants and foreign sports cars, were accomplished without benefit of much buying from this part of the market.

COMMUNICATION SKILLS

There is also a relation between class and communication abilities which has significance for marketing. The kind of super-sophisticated and clever advertising which appears in the *New Yorker* and *Esquire* is almost meaningless to Lower-Status people. They cannot comprehend the subtle humor; they are baffled by the bizarre art. They have a different symbol system, a very different approach to humor. In no sense does this imply that they lack intelligence or wit. Rather their communication skills have just been pressed into a different mold.

Here again, style of advertising helps the individual to make class identification. Most of the really big local television success stories in

Chicago have been achieved by personalities who radiate to the mass that this is where they belong. These self-made businessmen who do the announcing for their own shows communicate wonderfully well with the mass audience. While many listeners switch off their lengthy and personal commercials, these same mannerisms tell the Lower-Status individual that here is someone just like himself, who understands him.

Social Research, Inc., has frequently discussed the class problem in marketing by dividing the population into Upper-Middle or quality market; the middle majority which combines both the Lower-Middle and Upper-Lower; and then the Lower-Lower. The distinction should be drawn between the Middle Classes and the Lower-Status groups. In several dozen of these store profiles, there is scarcely an instance where a store has appeal to the Lower-Middle and Upper-Lower classes with anything like the same strength.

It would be better to make the break between the Middle Class, representing one-third of the population and the Lower-Status or Working-Class or Wage-Earner group, representing two-thirds of metropolitan Chicago. This permits some psychological distinctions to be drawn between the Middle-Class individual and the individual who is not a part of the Middle-Class system of values. Even though this is the dominant American value system, even though Middle-Class Americans have been taught by their parents that it is the only value system, this Lower-Status individual does not necessarily subscribe to it.

WHO SAVES, WHO SPENDS?

Another important set of behavioral distinctions related to social class position was revealed in the "save-spend aspiration" study. The question was asked: "Suppose your income was doubled for the next ten years, what would you do with the increased income?" This is a fantasy question taken out of the realm of any pressing economic situation to reflect aspirations about money. The coding broke down the answers to this question into five general categories: (1) the mode of saving, (2) the purpose of saving, (3) spending which would consolidate past gains, meet present defensive needs, prepare for future self-advancement, (4) spending which is "self-indulgent-centered," (5) spending which is "house-centered."

Here are some of our findings:[3] The higher the individual's class position, the more likely is he to express some saving aspirations. Conversely, the lower his class position, the more likely is he to mention spending only. Moreover the higher the status, the more likely is the individual to specify *how* he will save his money, which is indicative of the more elaborate financial learning required of higher status.

Proceeding from the more general categories (such as saving versus spending only) to more specific categories (such as non-investment versus investment saving and the even more specific stock versus real estate investment, etc.) an increasingly sharper class differentiation is found. It is primarily *non-investment* saving which appeals to the Lower-Status person. Investment saving, on the other hand, appeals above all to the Upper-Status person.

Investors almost always specify how they will invest. And here in mode of investment are examples of the most sharply class-differentiated preferences. Intangible forms of investment like stock and insurance are very clearly distinguished as Upper-Status investments. Nearly four times as many Upper-Middles select insurance as would be expected by chance, whereas only one-fifth of the Lower-Lowers select it as would be expected by chance. By contrast, Lower-Status people have far greater preference for tangible investments, specifically ownership of real estate, a farm, or a business.

To sum up, Middle-Class people usually have a place in their aspirations for some form of saving. This saving is most often in the form of investment, where there is a risk, long-term involvement, and the possibility of higher return. Saving, investment saving, and intangible investment saving—successively each of these become for them increasingly symbols of their higher status.

The aspirations of the Lower-Status person are just as often for spending as they are for saving. This saving is usually a non-investment saving where there is almost no risk, funds can be quickly converted to spendable cash, and returns are small. When the Lower-Status person does invest his savings, he will be specific about the mode of investment, and is very likely to prefer something tangible and concrete— something he can point at and readily display.

Turning from mode of saving to purpose of saving, very significant class relationships are likewise evident. Consider the verbalization of saving purpose. Lower-Status people typically explain why one should save—why the very act of saving is important. On the other hand, Middle-Class people do not, as if saving is an end-in-itself, the merits of which are obvious and need not be justified.

Spending is the other side of the coin. Analysis of what people say they will spend for shows similar class-related desires. All classes mention concrete, material artifacts such as a new car, some new appliance. But the Lower-Status people stop here. Their accumulations are artifact-centered, whereas Middle-Class spending-mentions are experience-centered. This is spending where one is left typically with only a memory. It would include hobbies, recreation, self-education and travel. The wish to travel, and particularly foreign travel, is almost totally a Middle-Class aspiration.

Even in their fantasies, people are governed by class membership. In his day-dreaming and wishful thinking, the Lower-Status individual will aspire in different patterns from the Middle-Class individual.

PSYCHOLOGICAL DIFFERENCES

This spending-saving analysis has very obvious psychological implications to differentiate between the classes. Saving itself generally suggests foresightedness, the ability to perceive long-term needs and goals. Non-investment saving has the characteristics of little risk-taking and of ready conversion, at no loss, into immediate expenditures—the money can be drawn out of the account whenever the bank is open. Investment spending, on the other hand, has the characteristics of risk-taking (a gamble for greater returns) and of delayed conversion, with possible loss, to expenditures on immediate needs.

Here are some psychological contrasts between two different social groups:

Middle-Class

1. Pointed to the future
2. His viewpoint embraces a long expanse of time
3. More urban identification
4. Stresses rationality
5. Has a well-structured sense of the universe
6. Horizons vastly extended or not limited
7. Greater sense of choice-making
8. Self-confident, willing to take risks
9. Immaterial and abstract in his thinking
10. Sees himself tied to national happenings

[3] The saving-spending aspiration analysis was carried out by Roger Coup, graduate student at the University of Chicago.

Lower-Status

1. Pointed to the present and past
2. Lives and thinks in a short expanse of time
3. More rural in identification
4. Non-rational essentially
5. Vague and unclear structuring of the world
6. Horizons sharply defined and limited
7. Limited sense of choice-making
8. Very much concerned with security and insecurity
9. Concrete and perceptive in his thinking
10. World revolves around his family and body

CONCLUSIONS

The essential purpose of this article was to develop three basic premises which are highly significant for marketing:

I. *There is a social-class system operative in metropolitan markets, which can be isolated and described.*

II. *It is important to realize that there are far-reaching psychological differences between the various classes.*

They do not handle the world in the same fashion. They tend not to think in the same way. As one tries to communicate with the Lower-Status group, it is imperative to sense that their goals and mental processes differ from the Middle-Class group.

III. *Consumption patterns operate as prestige symbols to define class membership, which is a more significant determinant of economic behavior than mere income.*

Each major department store, furniture store, and chain-grocery store has a different "pulling power" on different status groups. The usual customers of a store gradually direct the store's merchandising policies into a pattern which works. The interaction between store policy and consumer acceptance results in the elimination of certain customer groups and the attraction of others, with a resulting equilibration around a reasonably stable core of specific customer groups who think of the store as appropriate for them.

Income has always been the marketer's handiest index to family consumption standards. But it is a far from accurate index. For instance, the bulk of the population in a metropolitan market today will fall in the middle-income ranges. This will comprise not only the traditional white collar worker, but the unionized craftsman and the semi-skilled worker with their tremendous income gains of the past decade. Income-wise, they may be in the same category. But their buying behavior, their tastes, their spending-saving aspirations can be poles apart. Social-class position and mobility-stability dimensions will reflect in much greater depth each individual's style of life.

7. The Concept of Reference Group Influence

FRANCIS S. BOURNE

Sub culture

On the common sense level the concept says in effect that man's behavior is influenced in different ways and in varying degrees by other people. Comparing one's own success with that of others is a frequent source of satisfaction or disappointment. Similarly, before making a decision one often considers what such and such a person or such and such a group (whose opinion one has *some* reason to follow) would do in these circumstances, or what they would think of one for making a certain decision rather than another. Put in these ways, of course, reference group influence represents an unanalyzed truism which has long been recognized. The problem to which social scientists have been addressing themselves intensively only for the last two decades, however, concerns the refinement of this common sense notion to the end that it might be applied meaningfully to concrete situations.

The real problems are to determine which kinds of groups are likely to be referred to by which kinds of individuals under which kinds of circumstances in the process of making which decisions, and to measure the extent of this reference group influence. Towards this end empirical researches have been conducted in recent years which have at least made a start in the process of refining the reference group concept.

Reference group theory as it has developed has become broad enough to cover a wide range of social phenomena, both with respect to the relation of the individual to the group and with respect to the type of influence exerted upon the individual by the group in question.

Kinds of Reference Groups

Reference groups against which an individual evaluates his own status and behavior may be of several kinds.

They may be *membership* groups to which a person actually belongs. There can be small face-to-face groups in which actual association is the rule, such as families or organizations, whether business, social, religious, or political. On the other hand, there can be groups in which actual membership is held but in which personal association is absent. (For example, membership in a political party, none of whose meetings are personally attended.)

Reference groups may be *categories* to which a person automatically belongs by virtue of age, sex, education, marital status and so on. This sort of reference group relationship involves the concept of role. For example, before taking a certain action an individual might consider whether this action would be regarded as appropriate in his role as a man or husband or educated person or older person or a combination of all of these roles. What is involved here is an individual's perception of what society, in general or that part of it with which he has any contact, expects people of his age, or sex, or education or marital status to do under given circumstances.

They may be *anticipatory* rather than actual membership groups. Thus a person who aspires

❋ SOURCE: Reprinted by permission from *Group Influence in Marketing and Public Relations* edited by Francis S. Bourne (Ann Arbor, Michigan: Foundation for Research on Human Behavior), 1956, pp. 1, 2, 7–11.

to membership in a group to which he does *not* belong may be more likely to refer to it or compare himself with its standards when making a decision than he is to refer to the standards of the group in which he actually belongs but would like to leave. This involves the concept of upward mobility. When such upward mobility is sought in the social or business world it is ordinarily accompanied by a sensitivity to the attitudes of those in the groups to which one aspires, whether it involves the attitudes of country club members in the eyes of the aspiring non-member or the attitudes of management in the eyes of the ambitious wage earner or junior executive.

There are also negative, *dissociative* reference groups. These constitute the opposite side of the coin from the anticipatory membership groups. Thus an individual sometimes avoids a certain action because it is associated with a group (to which the individual may or may not in fact belong) from which he would like to dissociate himself.

Influence on Individual Behavior

Reference groups influence behavior in two major ways. First, they influence *aspiration levels* and thus play a part in producing satisfaction or frustration. If the other members of one's reference group (for example, the neighbors) are wealthier, more famous, better gardeners, etc., one may be dissatisfied with one's own achievements and may strive to do as well as the others.

Second, reference groups influence *kinds* of behavior. They establish approved patterns of using one's wealth, of wearing one's fame, of designing one's garden. They set tabus too, and may have the power to apply actual sanctions (for example, exclusion from the group). They thus produce *conformity* as well as *contentment* (or discontentment).

These two kinds of influence have, however, a good deal in common. Both imply certain perceptions on the part of the individual, who attributes characteristics to the reference group which it may or may not actually have. Both involve psychological rewards and punishment.

DIFFERENT KINDS OF DECISIONS AND REFERENCE GROUP INFLUENCE

Marketing and Reference Group Relevance

As has already been suggested, the reference group constitutes just one of the many influ-

ences in buying decisions, and this influence varies from product to product. How then does one determine whether reference group influence is likely to be a factor in buying behavior in connection with a given product or brand? Research has been conducted on the various factors that influence buying behavior with reference to several products, and out of this have emerged some general ideas about how reference group influences may enter into purchasing.

Buying may be a completely individualistic kind of activity or it may be very much socially conditioned. Consumers are often influenced by what others buy, especially those persons with whom they compare themselves, or use as reference groups.

The conspicuousness of a product is perhaps the most general attribute bearing on its susceptibility to reference group influence. There are two aspects to conspicuousness in this particular context that help to determine reference group influence. First the article must be conspicuous in the most obvious sense that it can be seen and identified by others. Secondly it must be conspicuous in the sense of standing out and being noticed. In other words, no matter how visible a product is, if virtually everyone owns it, it is not conspicuous in the second sense of the word. This leads to a further distinction: reference groups may influence either (a) the purchase of a product, or (b) the choice of a particular brand or type, or (c) both.

The possible susceptibility of various product and brand buying to reference group influence is suggested in Figure 1. According to this classification a particular item might be susceptible to reference group influence in its purchase in three different ways, corresponding to three of the four cells in the above figure. Reference group influence may operate with respect to product alone (Brand + Product −) as in the upper left cell, or it may operate both with respect to brand and product (Brand + Product +) as in the upper right cell, or it may operate with respect to product but not brand (Brand − Product +) as in the lower right cell.

Only the "minus-minus" items of the kind illustrated (Brand − Product −) in the lower left cell are not likely to involve any significant reference group influence in their purchase *at the present time.*

What are some of the characteristics that place an item in a given category, and what sig-

Reference Group Influence Relatively:

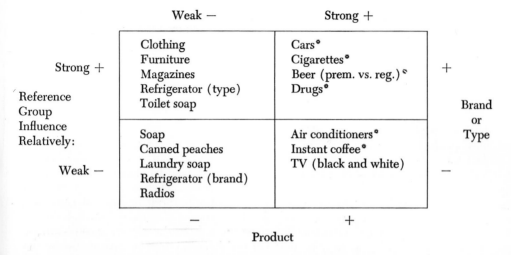

FIG. 1.   Products and brands of consumer goods may be classified by the extent to which reference groups influence their purchase. *Source*: Bureau of Applied Social Research, Columbia University (Glock, unpublished).

* The classification of all starred products is based on actual experimental evidence. Other products in this table are classified speculatively on the basis of generalizations derived from the sum of research in this area and confirmed by the judgment of seminar participants.

nificance do such placements have for marketing and advertising policy?

"Product-plus, brand-plus" items. Autos constitute an article where both the product and the brand are socially conspicuous. Whether or not a person buys a car, and also what particular brand he buys, is likely to be influenced by what others do. This also holds true for cigarettes, for drugs (decisions made by M.D.'s as to what to prescribe) and for beer with respect to type (premium vs. regular) as opposed to brand. Cigarettes and drugs, however, qualify as "plus-plus" items in a manner different from cars.

For example, while the car belongs to a class of products where brand differentiation is based at least substantially on real differences in attributes, the cigarette belongs to a class of product in which it is difficult to differentiate one brand from another by attributes: hence attributes are ascribed largely through reference group appeal built up by advertising. Popular images of the kinds of people who smoke various brands have been created at great cost, and in some cases additional images are being created to broaden a particular brand's market. In the case of drugs, it was found that the reference group influencing *whether* the product was used was different from that influencing the particular *brand* selected. Reference group influence was found to be prominent in determining whether or not beer was purchased at all, and also in determining whether regular or premium beer was selected. It did not appear to influence strongly choice of a particular brand.

"Product Plus, Brand Minus" Items. Instant coffee is one of the best examples of this class of items. Whether it is served in a household depends in considerable part on whether the housewife, in view of her own reference groups and the image she has of their attitudes towards this product, considers it appropriate to serve it. The brand itself in this instance is not conspicuous or socially important and is a matter largely for individual choice. In the case of air conditioners, it was found that little prestige attached to the particular brand used, and reference group influence related largely to the idea of purchasing the product itself. Analysis in one city revealed that the purchase of this often "visible from the outside" product was concentrated in small neighborhood areas. Clusters of conditioners were frequently located in certain rows and blocks. In many cases clusters did not even cross streets. Immediate neighbors

apparently served as a powerfully influential group in the purchase of these appliances. In this general class may also be found the b'ack and white TV set, with its antenna often visible on the outside of the house. As the saturation point in black and white TV set ownership rapidly approaches, however, the influence of reference groups may soon become minor, and the product can then be put in the "brand minus, product minus" quadrant, along with refrigerators. Color TV may remain in the "brand plus, product minus" quadrant, with type (color) rather than brand per se the element which is strongly related to reference groups.

"Product Minus, Brand Plus" Items. This group is made up essentially of products that all people or at least a very high proportion of people use, although differing as to type or brand.

Perhaps the leading example in this field is clothing. There could hardly be a more socially visible product than this, but the fact that everyone in our society wears clothing takes the *product* out of the area of reference group influence. The *type* of clothing purchased is, however, very heavily influenced by reference groups, with each subculture in the population (teenagers, zootsuiters, Ivy League collegians, western collegians, workers, bankers, advertising men, etc.) setting its own standards and often prescribing within fairly narrow limits what those who feel related to these groups can wear. Similarly, though not quite as dramatically, articles like furniture, magazines, refrigerators and toilet soap are seen in almost all homes, causing their purchase in general to fall outside of the orbit of reference group influence. The visibility of these items, however, coupled with the wide variety of styles and types among them make the selection of particular kinds highly susceptible to reference group influence.

"Product Minus, Brand Minus", Items. Purchasing behavior in this class of items is governed largely by product attributes rather than by the nature of the presumed users. In this group neither the products nor the brands tend to be socially conspicuous. This is not to say that personal influence cannot operate with respect to purchasing the kind of items included in this group. As with all products, some people tend to exert personal influence and others tend to be influenced by individual persons. Reference groups as such, however, exert relatively little influence on buying behavior in this class

of items. Examples of items in this category are salt, canned peaches, laundry soap and radios. It is apparent that placement in this category is not *necessarily* inherent in the product itself and hence is not a static placement. Items can move in and out of this category.

While it is true that items which are essential socially inconspicuous, like salt and laundry soap, are natural candidates for this category, it is not entirely out of the realm of possibility that through considerable large scale advertising and other promotional efforts images of the kind of people who use certain brands of salt or laundry soap could be built up so as to bring reference group influence into play on such items, much as has been the case with cigarettes. The task here would be more difficult, however, since the cigarette is already socially visible. On the other hand, items such as radios and refrigerators which are conspicuously visible and whose purchase was once subject to considerable reference group influence have now slipped into this category through near saturation in ownership.

Implications of Strong and Weak Reference Group Influence for Advertising and Marketing

It should be stressed again that this scheme of analysis is introduced to show how reference group influence might enter into purchasing behavior in certain cases. It cannot be regarded as generally applicable to marketing problems on all levels. There is still a need to know more precisely where many different products or brands fit into this scheme. Attempts to fit products and brands into the classification above suggest research that needs to be done to obtain more relevant information about each product.

Assuming, however, that a product or brand has been correctly placed with respect to the part played by reference groups in influencing its purchase, how can this help in marketing the product in question?

Where neither product nor brand appear to be associated strongly with reference group influence, advertising should emphasize the product's attributes, intrinsic qualities, price, and advantages over competing products.

Where reference group influence is operative, the advertiser should stress the kinds of people who buy the product, reinforcing and broadening where possible the existing stereotypes of users. This involves learning what the stereotypes are and what specific reference groups enter into the picture, so that appeals can be "tailored" to each major group reached by the different media employed.

Although it is important to see that the "right" kind of people use a product, a crucial problem is to make sure that the popular image of the product's users is as broad as possible without alienating any important part of the product's present or potential market in the process. Creating or reinforcing a stereotype of consumers which is too small and exclusive for a mass-produced item may exclude a significant portion of the potential market. On the other hand, some attempts to appeal to new groups through advertising in mass media have resulted in the loss of existing groups of purchasers whose previous (favorable) image of the prod-uct-user was adversely affected. One possible means for increasing the base of the market for a product by enlarging the image of its users is to use separate advertising media through which a new group can be reached without re-ducing the product's appeal to the original group of users. Another method might be to appeal to a new group through cooperative ad-vertising by a number of companies producing the product, possibly through a trade associa-tion. This would minimize the risk to an indi-vidual producer who, trying to reach a new group of users through his own advertising (women as opposed to men or wealthy as op-posed to average people, for example), might antagonize people who had a strong need to identify with the *original* image of the product's kind of user.

8. America's Tastemakers

THE TARGET IS THE CONSUMER

At the center of our perplexities as market researchers has been the realization that no matter how sophisticated our methods of analysis, no matter how ingenious our mathematical models, the events we are trying to predict are human events. It is consumer behavior that determines sales trends, industry performance, national indices—and not vice versa.

Management, of course, has always operated on this fact. By improving products, by developing new ones, by advertising and promotion and corporate reputation building, by training an effective sales staff, by virtually all its activities in short, management aims to influence consumer behavior. Past sales trends, etc., are studied only as guides to accomplishing this.

From whatever angle we approach the problem, therefore, we come back to the same base: the consumer and his needs, desires, aspirations, likes and dislikes, tastes, and pocketbook. In brief, to a very complex matter of human behavior.

In recognition of this reality, market research has bent its efforts increasingly on studying King Consumer. Here again, there has been a genuine growth in knowledge, sophistication, technique. But here too our growing skills and insight seem to reveal ever more serious problems that limit our ability to predict.

✜ SOURCE: Reprinted by permission from *Taste-maker Research Report No. 1* (Princeton, New Jersey: Opinion Research Corporation, April 1959).

WHY TRADITIONAL CONSUMER IDENTIFICATION LIMITS PREDICTIVE POWER

Researchers have noted three major flaws in the standard background analyses used in consumer research. One of them has to do with the built-in assumptions that are entailed. The second flaw has to do with the way we use categories—we work with aggregates of *characteristics* of people, not with aggregates of whole individuals. Third, our categories may appear to stay the same in size, while the people in them change radically. Or the categories may change, without revealing which persons are doing the changing.

WHERE IS OUR SOCIETY HEADING?

Our concern here is not philosophy or the long sweep of history, but the way people manage their lives.

Where are we as a people moving? Toward what new dimensions of experience, of aspirations, of taste and custom and habit? How can we best ascertain this?

In the free society of America there is no single man at the helm. We are a vast collection of societies: big governments and little governments, religious bodies and educational institutions, corporations and partnerships, clubs and lodges and sewing circles.

WHO ARE THE LEADERS?

Within every society there is a leadership elite. For our purposes, which are those of prediction, the critical question is one of identification.

The time-honored means—identifying leaders by title—does not serve us well. Titles designate leadership *roles;* they do not tell us how individuals behave in those roles.

Bearing these difficulties in mind, the nature of the task may be set forth in successive steps as follows:

1. If we are to predict changing consumption patterns in our society, we must get wind of upcoming social change—changes arising in the whole society, in its values, its way of life, its activity patterns.

2. If we are to predict social change, we must be able to identify those individuals most responsible for it—the leadership elite for change.

3. If we are to identify the leadership elite, we must search for the golden cord that binds the dynamic individual and his society together.

THE DIMENSIONS OF KINSHIP MOBILITY

The "break with the past" has long been a feature of the American psychology. We have termed this complex phenomenon "Kinship Mobility." Included within it are these increasing trends in American life:

1. The disappearance of what anthropologists call "the extended family"—a tightly-knit group of people of all generations related by blood, often living under the same roof, usually in the same community.

2. The dominance of what is called "the nuclear family"—man, wife, and dependent children—as the basic social unit.

3. The geographical spreading of blood relatives from the local neighborhood to towns and cities across the map—a process affecting even parents and their grown children to an increasing degree.

4. The continued growth of occupational shifting between generations. Both sons and daughters are increasingly likely to be following an occupation different from that of their parents.

5. The continuing rapid increase in educational difference between Americans and their parents and grandparents.

In all of the standard demographic categories, in short—ranging from place of residence, ethnic background and social ties to income, education and family size—the American is increasingly shaking loose from blood ties and moving out into the world on his own.

A NEW SET OF SPECTACLES: MOBILITY

In searching for a common denominator, to characterize our society, have we not overlooked *the fact of movement and change itself?*

If we are to gain predictive power over our changing environment, we clearly are in bad need of a new way of viewing it, a new set of spectacles. As a summary way of stating it, we will call this hypothetical common denominator in modern society "Mobility."

Since what we are attempting to develop is a scientific theory of marketing (and ultimately of social change in other spheres), we must set forth as precisely as we can what is meant by the term mobility.

As used in this research, *the term mobility refers to movement of the individual or group in relation to his human and physical environment.*

THE TASTEMASTER THEORY

The central thread of our modern society is mobility. The leadership elite is that group of people who possess this quality in greater degree than do other people.

Having identified significant aspects of mobility that characterize our mobile society, we can now proceed to identify the people who possess them in greater degree than do others. We will call them The High Mobiles. The means of identifying them may be described, in highly condensed form, as follows:

Prime Characteristics of The High Mobiles Compared With Other Americans

1. They travel more and change residence more often.

2. They show more movement through the occupational structure.

3. They are more likely to change their economic status.

4. They associate with a wider variety of people, of different types.

5. They move through more educational levels and institutions.

6. They move through more intellectual influences.

7. They are more selective and variable in their politics.

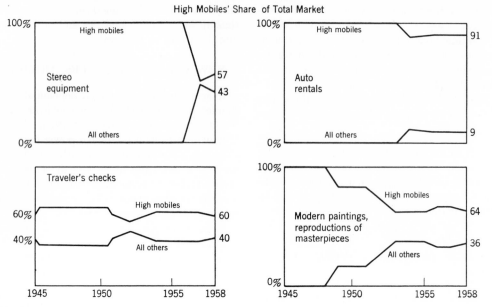

FIG. 1. Research on the tastemaker theory shows that high mobile households strongly dominate present "fledgling" markets.

8. In these various dimensions, they have moved a greater distance from their family of birth.

The High Mobiles are not to be identified by any one or two main characteristics. It is the *pattern* of their mobility that serves to distinguish them.

Our search for a predictive approach to changing U.S. markets then leads us to these three steps:

1. Identify the High Mobiles.
2. Determine the changing pattern of their values.
3. Relate the High Mobile value patterns to the ways in which they are expressed in styles, tastes, and ultimately product preference.

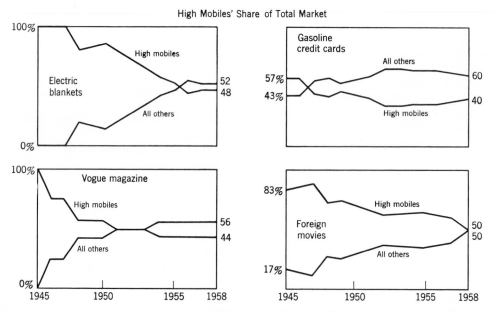

FIG. 2. As the market broadens, high mobile households naturally account for a dwindling share of the total market.

9. Anthropology's Contributions to Marketing

CHARLES WINICK

The relative slowness of anthropologists and marketers in finding common ground is surprising.[1] Anthropologists have served as colonial administrators, in foreign-aid programs, and in other situations requiring a special sensitivity to foreign cultures. They have also developed sales-training procedures which involve the analysis of the rate of speech of salesmen with potential customers, through devices which measure the rate of interaction between people talking.[2] Another specialized industrial situation in which anthropologists have worked involves the application of their knowledge of the field of anthropometry or measurement of the body, in the design of products like chairs and knobs.[3]

Other anthropologists have worked in applied fields such as: reactions to disaster, the operation of internment and relocation centers, mental health, medical care, labor-management relations,[4] the culture of a factory,[5] community organization, social work,[6] military government, the cultural change associated with economic development,[7] contact between cultures, the nature of small-town life, behavior in extreme situations, the study of culture at a distance,[8] the reconstruction of the themes of a culture, relations among minority groups, the social structure of a hospital,[9] American national character,[10] and television.[11]

Although anthropologists have published their findings on America in very accessible formats,[12] there has been little discussion of how their findings could be applied to marketing problems.[13] One advertising publication has

[1] John Gillin, "The Application of Anthropological Knowledge to Modern Mass Society," *Human Organization*, Vol. 15, Winter 1957, pp. 24–30.

[2] Eliot D. Chapple, "The Interaction Chronograph," *Personnel*, Vol. 25, January 1949, pp. 295–307.

[3] Earnest A. Hooton, *A Survey In Seating* (Cambridge: Harvard Department of Anthropology, 1945).

[4] Charles R. Walker, *The Man on the Assembly Line* (Cambridge: Harvard University Press, 1952).

[5] Eliot Jaques, *The Changing Culture of A Factory* (New York: Dryden Press, 1953).

[6] Franklin K. Patterson, Irving Lukoff, and Charles Winick, "Is Society the Patient," *Journal of Educational Sociology*, Vol. 30, October 1956, pp. 106–112.

[7] Almost every issue of *Economic Development and Cultural Change* carries relevant articles.

[8] Margaret Mead and Rhoda Metraux, *The Study of Culture At A Distance* (University of Chicago Press, 1952).

[9] Charles Winick, "The Hospital As A Social System," *New York State Nurse*, Vol. 26, January 1954, pp. 9–13.

[10] David M. Potter, *People of Plenty* (University of Chicago Press, 1954).

[11] Charles Winick, *Taste and the Censor In Television* (New York: Fund For the Republic, 1959).

[12] Margaret Lantis, editor, "The U.S.A. As Anthropologists See It," *American Anthropologist*, Vol. 57, December 1955, pp. 1,113–1,380.

[13] Richard C. Sheldon, "How The Anthropologist Can Help The Marketing Practitioner" in W. David Robbins, editor, *Successful Marketing at Home And Abroad* (Chicago: American Marketing Association, 1958), pp. 209–304.

published an article on the possibility of using anthropology in advertising.[14] The journal of applied anthropology, formerly called *Applied Anthropology* and now called *Human Organization*, almost never carries any material on marketing; and the national journal, *American Anthropologist*, also ignores the subject.

ANTHROPOLOGY, SOCIOLOGY, AND PSYCHOLOGY

Anthropology is usually defined as the study of man. Such a definition is so all-inclusive that the field is generally divided into four subfields: archeology, cultured anthropology, linguistics, and physical anthropology. Archeology is concerned with the historical reconstruction of cultures which no longer exist. Cultural anthropology examines all the behaviors of man which have been learned, including social, linguistic, technical, and familiar behaviors; often it is defined as the study of man and his works. Linguistics is the comparative study of the structure, interrelationships, and development of languages. Physical anthropology is concerned with human biology and the development of the human organism, with special interest in race differences.

When anthropology is employed in marketing, it is usually cultural anthropology which is relevant. Cultural anthropology began with the study of primitive cultures, and its comparative analyses documented the different ways in which cultures have solved their problems of living.

Cultural anthropology has much in common with psychology and sociology. All three are concerned with the examination of man in his cultural setting. They differ in the emphases which they place on different elements of the relationship between a person and his environment. It can be said that all human behavior essentially is a function of the interrelations of personality, the social system, and culture.

Oversimplifying, psychology is concerned with personality, sociology addresses itself to the social system, and anthropology explores the culture. The interdisciplinary field of social psychology may draw on all three of these fields, and there are integrated social psychology texts which do so.[15]

A sharper focus on the differences among these three social sciences may be obtained by speculating on how each of the three might look at a family.

The psychologist would be interested in the personal adjustment and emotional health of each member of the family. He would want to examine their attitudes, mutual perceptions, and motivational systems. Their happiness or lack of it would interest him.

The sociologist would be concerned primarily with the dimensions of role and status within the family and with the number of different kinds of families. He would examine how the social structure created various kinds of internal arrangements which made it possible for the family to exist. He would be interested in the norms of behavior and the stresses and strains shown by the deviations from the norm and resulting from role conflict. He would study class membership as well as the rates of various kinds of behavior, such as the birth rate.

The cultural anthropologist would examine the technological level which the culture had reached and the interrelations of technology with culture. He would scrutinize the procedures for inheritance of property and how kinship was reckoned and described, and how the spouses got to know each other. He would study the family's food and housing. He would be interested in the language level and dialects and in who talked to whom. He would be concerned with how the age of different members of the family affected their behavior, and with trends in illnesses. He would study how the culture "rubbed off" on the family unit. The anthropologist thus does not have information which it would be impossible for the sociologist or psychologist to obtain, but he has a special sensitivity to certain facets of social life.

The sociologist and psychologist bring a powerful and varied arsenal of concepts and approaches to the study of social life. In what ways is the anthropologist able to contribute insights and experience toward the science of "marketology," and to what extent may they not be immediately accessible, for example, to the sociologist?[16] The anthropologist is especially

---

[14] Alan S. Marcus, "How Agencies Can Use Anthropology in Advertising," *Advertising Agency*, Vol. 49, September 14, 1956, pp. 87–91.

[15] Steuart Henderson Britt, *Social Psychology of Modern Life* revised edition (New York: Rinehart, 1949). S. Stanfeld Sargent and Robert C. Williamson, *Social Psychology* (New York: Ronald Press, 1958).

[16] Robert Bartels, "Sociologist and Marketologists," *Journal of Marketing*, Vol. 24, October 1959, pp. 37–40; Christen T. Jonassen, "Contributions of Sociology to Marketing," *Journal of Marketing*, Vol. 24, October 1959, pp. 29–35.

trained to have empathy with groups other than his own and to "tune in" on their patterns of culture. Inasmuch as his training has exposed him to a wide variety of cultures, he can take a global view of a situation and see it in the context of a larger background. His training makes him sensitive to cross-cultural differences which may be of crucial importance in many different situations, because his entire training is geared toward awareness of such differences.

Anthropology has less of the factionalism which characterizes psychology and sociology. This is not to suggest that all is serene in anthropology or that it has never been troubled by theoretical or methodological issues. However, even though anthropologists may disagree on something like the exact value of the contribution of a particular anthropologist, they would generally agree on what the cultural anthropologist looks for, and there are standardized check lists on how to view a culture.[17] In contrast, a psychologist's allegiance to the Gestalt, behaviorist, psychoanalytic, learning-theory, or perception schools is likely to influence what he does with a given problem. A sociologist's commitment to the structure-function, historical, ecological, "middle range," environmental-determinism, or demographic schools would largely determine the emphases of his approach to a problem. Since such divergent schools are less likely to exist in cultural anthropology, it is probable than anthropological guidance on a given marketing problem would be relatively consistent.

WHAT THE ANTHROPOLOGIST KNOWS

The anthropologist is specifically trained to study national character, or the differences which distinguish our national group from another. He should be able to provide measures for distinguishing the subtle differences among a Swede, a Dane, and a Norwegian; or between a Frenchman and an Englishman; or a Brazilian and an Argentinian; or between a typical resident of Montreal and one of Toronto. The anthropologist is also a specialist in the study of subcultures. He would be able, in a city like New York, to differentiate the patterns of living of such disparate but rapidly homogenizing groups as Puerto Ricans, Negroes, Italo-Americans, Jews, Polish-Americans, and Irish-Americans.

Because almost any large community consists of a variety of subcultures, this awareness of subcultural trends can be especially useful. A more subtle area of special interest to anthropologists is the silent language of gesture, posture, food and drink preferences, and other nonverbal cues to behavior.[18]

Related to this is the anthropologist's professional interest in languages and symbols. He might, for example, be especially concerned about why a particular shape has special significance as a symbol in a society, or how the structure of a language or a regional speech pattern was related to how people think.[19]

Another area of concern to the anthropologist, because of its symbolic meanings has to do with "rites de passage" or the central points in a person's life at which he may ritually be helped to go from one status to another, for example, birth, puberty, or marriage.[20]

Taboos represent a continuing area of interest to the anthropologist.[21] Every culture has taboos or prohibitions about various things, such as the use of a given color, or of a given phrase or symbol. The anthropologist is aware of the larger values of a culture, which represent the substratum of custom which is taken for granted and the violation of which represents a taboo.

The anthropologist's method is primarily the exposure of his highly developed sensitivity to the area in which he is working, via observation and extended interviews with informants. Projective tests have also been widely used in anthropological studies. The anthropologist can bring a wealth of insight to marketing situations.

USE OF ANTHROPOLOGY IN MARKETING

There are at least three kinds of situations in which the knowledge of the anthropologist has been employed in marketing: specific knowledge; awareness of themes of a culture; sensitivity to taboos.

---

[17] Royal Anthropological Institute, Notes and Queries on Anthropology (London: The Institute, 1956).

[18] Edward T. Hall, The Silent Language (New York: Doubleday, 1959).

[19] Benjamin Lee Whorf, Collected Papers on Metalinguistics (Washington: Department of State Foreign Service Institute, 1952).

[20] Jan Wit, Rites De Passage (Amsterdam: De Windroos, 1959).

[21] Franz Steiner, Taboo (London: Cohen and West, 1957).

Specific Knowledge

Here are a few cases in which the specific knowedge of an anthropologist was applied to marketing situations.

A manufacturer of central heating equipment was planning to introduce central heating to an area which previously had used other heating. Since people generally grow up to accept a certain approach to heating which they take for granted, introduction of the new central heating posed marketing problems in coping with deeply imbedded consumer resistance to what would be a major innovation. An anthropologist was able to draw on his knowledge of the folklore and symbolism of heat and fire in order to suggest methods of presenting the new system, so as to make it as consonant as possible with the connotations of heat, even though the nature of the heating method had changed radically. There was considerable consumer resistance to the central heating, but it decreased substantially after the first year.

In addition to a marketing problem, the introduction of central heating also posed problems of public policy which the manufacturer had to overcome before he could obtain approval for the introduction of the heating equipment. The area was one which suffered from a declining birth rate, and officials were concerned about the extent to which central heating might cause the birth rate to decline further, because of their belief that heated bedrooms would cause a decline in sexual activity and ultimately in births.

The anthropologist was able to point to some cultures in which the birth rate had declined and some in which it had not done so after the introduction of central heating. The anthropologist's data made it possible for the manufacturer of the central-heating equipment to discuss its probable effects realistically with the appropriate officials.

Another field in which the anthropologist has specific knowledge that other social scientists are not likely to have is that of clothing and fashion. The only empirical study of the fashion cycle in woman's clothing which has successfully been used for predictive purposes by clothing manufacturers was conducted by anthropologists.[22] In marketing situations, the anthropologist has often been able to combine his

special knowledge of the needs of the body for clothing of various kinds at different ages, his sensitivity to what technology makes possible and his awareness of fashion.

For example, an anthropologist was consulted by a leading manufacturer of overalls for young children, a product which had remained unchanged for decades. He examined the product in the light of the special needs of children who wear overalls, the growing use of washing machines to launder the overalls, their relative frequency of laundering, and contemporary technology. He suggested that the overall straps have a series of sets of metal grippers instead of buttons, thus making it possible to use different sets of grippers as the child grew instead of tying or knotting the straps. Noting that the straps often fall off the shoulders when children played, he suggested that the shirts which children wore under the overalls have either a loop for the straps to pass through or a synthetic fastener which faced matching material on the strap, so that the shoulder of the shirt could be pressed against the strap and remain attached to it until shoulder strap and shirt were pulled apart.

He also recommended that the seams of the overalls, previously single stitched, be double stitched like those of men's shirts, which have to withstand frequent launderings. The double-stitched overalls would be less likely to come apart as a result of frequent launderings in a washing machine. These recommendations were adopted, and within a few years substantially changed and expanded the nature of the overall market for young children. The children's parents were more pleased with the overalls because they lasted longer and looked better on the children, and they were far more functional than before.

The special knowledge of the anthropologist has been called into play where there are special subcultural groups to which the marketer wishes to address himself. One beer manufacturer wished to extend his market share among Negroes in a large eastern city in the United States. He was advised about reaching this group by an anthropologist who was familiar with the special subculture of Negroes, and who pointed to the profound effects of Negroes' caste membership on their purchasing behavior. The ambiguity of their role has led many Negroes to be especially aware of articles that have status connotations and of whether a brand symbolizes racial progress. Examination of the manufacturer's marketing program by

---

[22] Jane Richardson and Alfred L. Kroeber, *Three Centuries of Women's Dress Fashions* (Berkeley: University of California Press, 1940).

the anthropologist led to several recommendations for change. The manufacturer began to help in the support of several major social events related to the arts in Negro communities, and to stress that the beer was a national brand with quality-control procedures. He changed the content of his advertising in the direction of enhancing its status and quality connotations. These changes were all directed toward improving the status connotations of the beer to Negroes.

Guidance on related problems with respect to the Puerto Rican and Jewish markets has also been used constructively. Since 35 to 40 per cent of the population of the United States consists of minority subcultures, the anthropologist's contributions may be considerable.

Another situation had to do with the selection of specific symbols for various purposes. A major manufacturer of women's products was uncertain about whether to continue using the Fleur de Lis emblem on his package. Anthropological analysis of the symbol suggested that its association with French kings and other cultural connotations of maleness made it more masculine than feminine. The anthropologist's recommendations were confirmed by subsequent field testing.

In a related case, a manufacturer of women's cosmetics conducted an anthropological study of the comparative symbolism in our culture of women's eyes and mouth, which suggested that the eye tends to be experienced as a relatively protecting organ while the mouth tends to be experienced as more nurturing. This knowledge of the differences between the special meanings of eye and mouth could constructively be used in marketing the products, and especially in advertising. The advertising explicitly and implicitly mentioned the role of the eye in protection of the woman. It stressed the role of the mouth as the organ which both symbolically and literally gives love. This replaced the manufacturers' previous advertising, in which both eye and mouth were treated in the same way, as organs which could be made beautiful.

Awareness of Themes

The anthropologist has functioned in situations in which he can use his special understanding of themes of a culture, oftentimes taken for granted.

A major chain of candy shops was suffering a decline in sales. A marketing-research study had established that the brand was usually bought as a gift, either for others or as a gift for the purchaser. The chain was unable to develop any ways of using this finding that were not hackneyed. Anthropological guidance on the symbolism of gift-giving enabled the chain to develop merchandising, packaging, and advertising formats for the gift theme. Anthropological study of the connotations of the major holidays suggested themes for window displays, and advertising of the candy in conjunction with the holidays. The chain's marketing strategy was revised on the basis of the anthropological interpretation and clarification of the marketing-research study. Anthropologists are the only social scientists who have systematically studied gift-giving and gift-receiving.[23]

Another example of anthropological interpretation of a marketing-research study was provided by a shirt manufacturer. The study had established that women buy more than half of men's shirts in a particular price range. The anthropologist was able to interpret this finding in the light of several anthropological studies of the relations between husbands and wives in America. The manufacturer had been thinking of placing advertising for his men's shirts in selected women's magazines. The anthropologist was able to point to a number of studies of husband-wife relations which suggested growing resentment by men over the extent to which women had been borrowing and buying men's clothing, and which suggested that the proposed advertising campaign might not be propitious.

Another anthropologist's special sensitivity to the "rites de passage" helped a shoe manufacturer whose sales were declining because of aggressive foreign and domestic competition. The anthropologist was able to point to the extent to which shoes represent major symbols of our going from one stage of life to another, and to assist the manufacturer in developing methods for using the relationship between shoes and "rites de passage."[24]

A landmark along the road of an infant becoming a child usually is found between the ages of 4 and 6 when he can tie his own shoe laces. The manufacturer developed some pamphlets and other instructional material for

[23] Marcel Mauss, The Gift (London: Cohen and West, 1954).

[24] Charles Winick, "Status, Shoes, and the Life Cycle," Boot and Shoe Recorder, Vol. 156, October 15, 1959, pp. 100–202.

parents on how to help children to learn to tie their shoe laces. Distribution by local retailers contributed toward making parents favorably aware of the brand's line for children in this age group.

The teenager signalizes her entrance into a new social world by her first high heels. Window displays and advertising which explicitly stressed the new social activities of the teenager wearing her high heels, and naming specific shoe models after teenage social events ("The Prom") contributed toward associating the manufacturer's name with the excitement of the new world symbolized by the high heels.

Older people see the wearing of special "old people's shoes" as the ultimate reminder that they are becoming old. The manufacturer was able to redesign his line for older people so that it retained its special health features but still looked as stylish as any adult shoe, and had no visible stigma of "old people's shoes."

Sensitivity to Taboos

Marketers may unwittingly violate a taboo, whether cultural, religious, or political, especially in selling overseas. Blue, for example, is the color for mourning in Iran and is not likely to be favorably received on a commercial product. Green is the nationalist color of Egypt and Syria and is frowned on for use in packages. Showing pairs of anything on the Gold Coast of Africa is disapproved. White is the color of mourning in Japan and, therefore, not likely to be popular on a product. Brown and gray are disapproved colors in Nicaragua. Purple is generally disapproved in most Latin American markets because of its association with death. Feet are regarded as despicable in Thailand, where any object and package showing feet is likely to be unfavorably received.

The anthropologist can cast light on taboos and on their opposite: favored colors and symbols. The reason for the people in a country or an area liking or not liking a particular color or symbol may be a function of political, nationalist, religious, cultural, or other reasons.

SOME APPLICATIONS IN CANADA

Canada represents a special opportunity for the application of anthropology in marketing situations. Twenty-nine per cent of the country's entire population is in French-speaking Quebec, and over half of this number know no English. Canada thus offers a changing kind of

bilingual and culture contact situation with major cross-cultural differences for anthropological analysis.

Both the farm community and the industrial community of Quebec have been studied by anthropologists.[25] The re-evaluation of the nature of Quebec family and community life sparked by Dean Phillipe Garigue of the University of Montreal and a team at Laval University has led to renewed interest in Quebec on the part of anthropologists. Their studies have produced considerable information on styles of life in Quebec which should be translatable into marketing data on pricing policies, colors, package size, flavor and taste of various food items, tetxure of fabrics, automobile symbolism, product scents, and related subjects.

Specific Knowledge

Perhaps the most frequent occasion for the anthropologist to demonstrate specific knowledge in Canada has to do with language. One laundry-soap company had point-of-sale material on its soap describing it as extra strong and the best one to use on especially dirty parts of wash ("les parts de sale"). After sales of the soap had declined, an anthropologist who was called in by the company pointed out that the phrase is comparable to the American slang phrase "private parts." This kind of mistake might have been avoided if anthropological guidance had been available before sales declined.

Some products do not sell well in Quebec because the English name may be almost unpronounceable to a French speaker, or the name of the product may be meaningless even when translated idiomatically. Even the English spoken in Montreal differs somewhat from the English spoken in Toronto, creating potential hazards for the marketers who may not know, for example that a "tap" in a "flat" in Toronto is likely to be a "faucet" in a Montreal "apartment."

Awareness of Themes

A study done by an anthropologist for a food manufacturer demonstrated the relationship between the purchases of certain food items and the gradual decline of the wood-burning stove which used to be a staple of Quebec farm

---

[25] Horace Miner, *St. Denis* (University of Chicago Press, 1939); Everett C. Hughes, *French Canada In Transition* (University of Chicago Press, 1943).

kitchens. The wood stove would almost always have a stew pot ("pot au feu") simmering all day. Various ingredients were put into the pot to provide flavor. With the introduction of gas and electric kitchen ranges, it not only became relatively expensive to keep the stew pot going but the simmering could not be sustained because the pot would tend to boil rather than simmer.

This change was accompanied by some radical adjustments in food consumption which were of great relevance to food marketing. The manufacturer was able to begin distribution of canned soups and stews which soon found a very large market and rapidly replaced the "pot au feu."

Taboos

Alertness to taboos was illustrated by an anthropologist's suggestion to a manufacturer of canned fish for changing a series of advertisements which were appearing in Quebec magazines and newspapers. The same advertisement was run repeatedly. The advertisements showed a woman in shorts playing golf with her husband. The caption read that the woman would be able to be on the golf links all day and still prepare a delicious dinner that evening if she used the product. Every element in the advertisement represented a violation of some underlying theme of French Canadian life; the wife would not be likely to be playing golf with her husband, she would not wear shorts, and she would not be serving the particular kind of fish as a main course. In this case, the anthropologist was consulted *after* the series had been running for awhile.

THE MARKETER AS AN ANTHROPOLOGIST

A good case could be made for the thesis that marketing researchers do more anthropological research on modern cultures than do anthropologists. Marketing researchers are studying national character, subcultures, themes, and ways of life. The kind of information which marketing-research studies seek on how peope live and what products they use represent first-rate material for the cultural anthropologist.

The questionnaire, panel, audit, sales analysis, and other methods of modern marketing differ in degree but not in kind from the trained observations of the anthropologist, but there is no reason why the two methods cannot complement each other. Greater communication between these two fields can and should lead to mutual enrichment of both.

B. Psychology of Consumer Behavior

10. Psychological Dimensions of Consumer Decision

WALTER A. WOODS

Motivational research has grown at such a great pace because consumer attitudes and behavior are so important in solving marketing and advertising problems. But motivational research as commonly practiced has often been undisciplined and even capricious. Psychological and sociological theories are often ignored. Old dimensions, often inadequate, are not replaced with new dimensions to provide a systematic way of looking at the consumer.

One reason is a common tendency to miss the differences between motivational and psychological research. Today the two terms are often used incorrectly as interchangeable.

As a result of these errors in definition, other psychological points are often understressed. Theories of consumer behavior have tended to ignore important determinants such as habit, cognition, and learning.[1]

CONSUMER DIMENSIONS VERSUS PRODUCT DIMENSIONS

Consider two distinct processes which work to determine that a particular product will be bought or consumed: (1) The process of motivation—someone is hungry and needs food. (2) The process of discrimination—the hunger

is satisfied by selecting particular foods, or particular brands of foods.

This is oversimplification, of course. To be sure, the factors underlying eating (food consumption) are motivational. Theoretically, people eat for several reasons: they are hungry, they are bored, it is time to eat, or they require an outlet for some psychological force.

But what a person (or group) eats at a particular time is usually outside the realm of this kind of motivation. Cereal may be eaten at breakfast because (1) cereal is always eaten for breakfast (habit); (2) the cereal box was in view as breakfast was considered (impulse); (3) cereal is "healthy" (motivation); or (4) everyone else was having cereal (social pressure).

As to why cereal was available in the household, there are other possibilities: (1) cereal is always purchased (habit); (2) there was no cereal but mother wanted a change (cognition plus motivation); (3) cereals are inexpensive (cognition); or (4) the young son shopped with her, and he liked the package (impulse).

As to brand selected, there are also several possibilities: (1) the same brand is "automatically" purchased (habit); (2) brand X is considered best (cognition); or (3) brands of "big" manufacturers are preferred (motivation).

Contrast this with the purchase of a car, where there is a basic need for transportation (motivation), and a secondary need for ownership. When we inquire as to make of car, the question, "What car for what purpose?", is raised. New reasons come into play: cost and economy (cognition), appearance (impulsivity), prestige (motivation).

---

[1] An attempt to remedy this is represented in James A. Bayton, "Motivation, Cognition, Learning—Basic Factors in Consumer Behavior." *Journal of Marketing*, Vol. 22, January 1958, pp. 282–289.

‡ SOURCE: Reprinted by permission from the *Journal of Marketing* (National Quarterly Publication of the American Marketing Association), Vol. 24, No. 3, January 1960, pp. 15–19.

Cereals and cars are different. Habitual and rational forces are more at work with cereals, irrational forces with cars. Consumers identify with and get more involved emotionally with automobiles than with cereals. All consumer behavior is motivated, but actual choices made to satisfy motives may depend on other psychological variables. Motivation, per se, is most often a secondary factor in consumer choice, although it underlies all consumer behavior. Two sets of factors determine the choices which are made: personality of the purchaser, and character of the product. There are thus two sets of variables:

1. Consumer variables, the differences among consumers in their habits, cognitive structure, and motives which cause them to behave differently in purchase situations.

2. Differences among products in "demand character" which cause consumers to become more ego-involved with some products than with others.

CONSUMER VARIABLES

Consumers pass through an organizing and integrating process during which patterns of behavior are established with respect to purchasing and product use. The newly married woman brings certain attitudes to her new home, but she has no set ways of running her new home. Because of the major recurring problems of personal, family, and social growth, she solves her minor problems by establishing routines (a motive common to everyone).[2] Frequently these routines are established without awareness or deliberate intent.

Among the behaviors frequently relegated to routine are menu planning and preparation, and shopping. Once housewives have routinized these activities, they become relatively "closed" to new product introductions and to brand promotion.

But no consumer solves all problems at the same time. For example, the problem of cake baking may persist long after the problem of coffee preparation is solved. Also, problems are not solved once and for all. The problem of storing perishables may be solved by a new refrigerator; but the problem may recur if, for

instance, the family grows in size and more space is needed.

Thus, particular buying habits persist because they have solved some household problems, and they continue until changes in circumstances or outlook present new problems. No published studies are known which discuss the extent to which such behavior (habit-determined behavior) exists, but for some product areas about 60 per cent of the market may be habit dominated.

On the other hand, consumer behavior may remain unstable. Brands and products may be freely changed on the basis of rational factors (cognitive behavior) such as price or convenience. One study suggests that cognitive behavior exists in about 20 per cent of the market.[3]

The cognitive-habit dimension does not explain all purchasing behavior. Purchasing decisions may be made on the basis of other forces. Two such types of behavior may be identified: behavior in response to *affective* appeal and behavior in response to *symbolic* appeal.[4] Although these behavior types are often loosely grouped together as "irrational," they do differ.

Response to affective appeals is probably best described as "impulsive" behavior. As used here, it refers to reactions to product qualities which are primarily physical. Included would be such qualities as color, design, flavor, odor. For example, a shopper impulsively purchases candy because of its inherent physical appeal; or a shopper impulsively selects an automobile because of the inherent appeal of its color and design.

Response to symbolic appeals might best be termed "emotional" behavior. As used here, it refers to behavior which is generated by thinking about the meaning of a product purchase rather than the function of the purchase. Thus, the perceived prestige of owning a Cadillac may be more important in bringing about its purchase than is the function which the Cadillac would serve. This is irrational behavior.

This discussion of consumer variables has suggested that particular people tend consist-

[2] As exemplified by the principle, referred to in psychological literature as "The Principle of Least Effort"; see G. K. Zipf, *Human Behavior and the Principle of Least Effort* (Boston: Addison-Wesley, 1949).

[3] Ben Gedalecia, "The Communicators: An All-Media Study"; a report made at the 3rd Annual Advertising Research Foundation Conference, November 14, 1957.

[4] The term "cathectic," as used by T. Parsons, E. A. Shils, and others in *Toward a General Theory of Action* (Cambridge: Harvard University Press, 1951), pp. 8–12, appears to include both "affective" and "symbolic" as used here.

ently to behave in particular ways. Although it is unlikely that a given consumer always reacts in one way rather than another, people do react predominantly in one way rather than in other ways. The market for consumer products probably is composed of:

1. *A habit-determined group* of brand loyal consumers, who tend to be satisfied with the last purchased product or brand.

2. *A cognitive group* of consumers, sensitive to rational claims and only conditionally brand loyal.

3. *A price-cognitive group* of consumers, who principally decide on the basis of price or economy comparisons.

4. *An impulse group* of consumers, who buy on the basis of physical appeal and are relatively insensitive to brand name.

5. *A group of "emotional" reactors*, who tend to be responsive to what products symbolize and who are heavily swayed by "images."

6. *A group of new consumers*, not yet stabilized with respect to the psychological dimensions of consumer behavior.

This discussion of consumer variables has been concerned with behavior and *not* with attitudes. Behavior and attitudes are not the same. A favorable attitude toward a TV message is not the same thing as in-store purchasing of the product advertised.

PRODUCT VARIABLES

Superimposed across the entire gamut of consumer cognition and motivation is the character of the product itself. Some products have the capacity to get consumers ego-involved to a high degree. That is, consumers identify with the product. Other products have this capacity to a lesser degree. Still other products depend on their sensory appeal, and others on the function they perform.

Thus, the demands of products on the consumer fall into three classes:

A. Demands of ego-involvement in the external symbols which the product conveys. ("All executives ride in big cars like mine.")

B. Hedonic demand. ("It's so beautiful, I can't resist it.")

C. Functional demands. ("Here it is Tuesday again; we may as well have tuna casserole for dinner.")

Although product variables have been studied to a much lesser degree than consumer variables and less is known about them, it is possible to describe rather unambiguous variables of this sort. Group A above can be broken down into four sub-classes of products where ego-involvement is at issue: (1) prestige products; (2) maturity products; (3) status (or membership) products; (4) anxiety products. These four, along with B and C, provide six psychological product classes.

1. Prestige Products. Prestige products are those which themselves become symbols. The product not only *represents* some image or personality attribute, but *becomes* that attribute. For example, ownership of a Cadillac is not only a symbol of success, but is evidence of success. Products which fall into this class include automobiles, homes, clothing, furniture, art objects, newspapers, and magazines.

The function which these products serve is to extend or identify the ego of the consumer in a direction consistent with his self-image, in such a way as to give him individuality.

2. Maturity Products. Maturity products are those which because of social customs are typically withheld from younger people. The initial use of such products symbolizes a state of maturity on the part of the consumer. Intrinsic product merit is not a factor, at least in the beginning stages of use. Products in this category include cigarettes, cosmetics, coffee, beer, and liquor.

3. Status Products. Status products serve the function of imputing class membership to their users. The intrinsic merit of products in this class is an important factor in continued usage. However, consumers tend to select "big-name" brands because they believe such brands impute "success," "substance," "quality," or similar attributes. "Bigness," in turn, is often imputed from familiarity or frequency of exposure of the consumer to the brand. Packaged foods and gasoline are often in this category. While prestige products connote leadership, status products connote membership.

4. Anxiety Products. Anxiety products are those products which are used to alleviate some presumed personal or social *threat*. Products in this category include soaps, dentifrices, "health" foods, perfumes, and razors. This group of products involves ego-defense, whereas the three preceding categories are concerned with ego-enhancement.

5. Hedonic Products (or Product Features). Hedonic products are those which are highly dependent on their sensory character for their appeal. Moreover, their appeal is immediate and highly situational. This category includes snack items, many types of clothing, pre-sweetened cereals. Visual (style) features of any product fall within this area; automobile design and color are examples.

6. Functional Products. Functional products are those products to which little cultural or social meaning has, as yet, been imputed. Included in this category are the staple food items, fruits, vegetables, and also most building products.

The differences between these product classes have important implications for competitive marketing. Where ego-involvement can be developed, a high degree of interest can be won on the basis of product image. This, in turn, means a high susceptibility to "other-brand" image and a less habit-bound audience. For such products, marketing success hinges heavily on motivational selling.

On the other hand, where involvement is low, loyalty to one's brand must be achieved differently. Product image becomes unimportant, while product identity and familiarity become very important. Once loyalty is established, threat from "other-brand" penetration is considerably less than with "ego-involving" products. Moreover, "other-brand" success will be much more costly for the "other" manufacturer to achieve, since the other brand must get through on the basis of cognitive appeals to a habit-bound, closed-out audience. For this reason, "lead time" becomes a highly important requirement for success of a product whose appeal is primarily functional or hedonic.

INTERRELATIONS OF VARIABLES

It might seem that the above listed person variables and product variables are two views of the same panorama. But this is not the case.

The psychological character which a product has is a true character which has been imputed to it by society as a whole through long periods of time, and is independent of the psychological character (or personality) of particular individuals. For example, no matter whether the consumer be "habit determined," "cognitive," or "impulsive," he will still acknowledge that Cadillacs do convey prestige connotations of some sort, and that cosmetics do represent a means of conveying "maturity."

Yet, while product variables and person variables represent two sets of variables, it is also true that interrelations do exist. The very nature of impulsivity as a personality characteristic leads to greater susceptibility to products with hedonic appeal. Similarly, social needs will lead to association with products with status connotations.

Although interrelations may exist between these two sets of variables, treatment as a duality is necessary in the development of marketing programs. A true differentiation is required in order to distinguish between market (or consumer) segmentation and product description. A study of consumer variables leads to a description of the market in terms of consumer segments and needs. A study of product variables leads to a definition of product concept and product attributes. Both are required in the development of a product philosophy.

11. A Psychological Approach
to Consumer Behavior Analysis

WARREN J. BILKEY

During recent years there has been considerable interest in obtaining a scientifically verifiable theory of consumer behavior. One of the most recent attempts at such a formulation is the vector hypothesis which is an application of Lewinian vector psychology to consumer analysis. The purpose of this article is to summarize briefly the main features of the vector hypothesis, to describe the techniques thus far advanced for measuring the psychic tensions involved, and finally to present some of the author's findings in his exploratory attempt to apply one of these measuring techniques in a small consumer study.

SUMMARY OF THE VECTOR HYPOTHESIS

Since the theoretical aspects of the vector hypothesis have been described in an earlier issue of the JOURNAL its basic features merely will be summarized by means of the following four postulates.[1]

1. *Consumption is but one aspect of a person's total pattern of activities.*[2]

For this reason an analysis of his purchasing behavior should take account of his entire situation, (e.g., of the limitation of his time and of his unwillingness to devote thought and energy to buying, as well as of the limitation of his funds). Interview findings indicate that people do seek to achieve a *satisfactory* allocation of their funds among the various alternatives available to them, but whether this involves a deliberate attempt at maximization has not yet been determined.

2. *A person's actual (as distinguished from his planned) disbursement pattern is the end resultant of many separate disbursement acts.*[3]

Typically there is no single all-inclusive decision point for a consumer's disbursement pattern. Rather, he buys or fails to buy whenever a disbursement opportunity presents itself. The reason for this is that all purchases do not occur at the same time nor at the same frequency so as to permit an effective weighing of alternatives when making a particular disbursement act. That is, for some categories (e.g., food), purchases occur at a regular rate, but for other categories (e.g., furniture and automobiles) purchases occur very infrequently and cannot be accurately anticipated. For this reason a separate choice is required for each purchasing act. Thus, particular purchasing acts occur throughout the course of the consumer's income period, and the choices made are affected by circumstances existing or believed to be existing at the moments in question. The sum total of the disbursements made then constitute the person's disbursement pattern.

[1] See W. J. Bilkey, "The Vector Hypothesis of Consumer Behavior," *The Journal of Marketing*, Oct., 1951.

[2] This postulate is derived from Gestalt psychology, and is confirmed by interview findings.

‡‡ SOURCE: Reprinted by permission from the *Journal of Marketing* (National Quarterly Publication of the American Marketing Association), Vol. 18, No. 1, July 1953, pp. 18–25.

[3] This postulate is based upon empirical observation, and the analysis of family expenditure records.

3. *A person's disbursement acts are the net outcome of his psychic tensions regarding each item or activity involved, together with habits, carryovers of past commitments and external impositions such as taxes.*[4]

According to Lewinian vector psychology, the underlying basis for an actively made consumer choice is an internal psychic conflict between the person's attrition toward (positive valences) certain attributes of the item or service in question, and his repulsion against (negative valences) other attributes regarding that good or service, including its cost. If his positive valences for it are greater than his negative valences against it the purchase will be made, and vice versa (see Fig. 1). Thus, an active psychic conflict is regarded as being a person's way of achieving a desirable over-all disbursement pattern. This, however, places him in a dilemma, for an active psychic conflict involves psychic effort which is undesirable to him. For this reason there is a tendency for a person to attempt wherever possible to avoid such conflict by impulse-buying or by reducing many of his purchasing decisions to routines or habit patterns—however, such attempts to avoid psychic conflict can be followed only within limits, or his income utilization would eventually become intolerably inefficient.[5]

4. *If a homogeneous group of consumers all have an identical likelihood of making a par-*

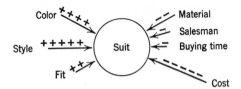

FIG. 1. Hypothetical psychic tension relationship for a person buying a suit. Each arrow represents a force direction or vector regarding the suit (hence the term vector hypothesis), and the strength of these vectors is represented by the valences (plus and minus signs) shown on them. Assumptions are that he likes the suit's color, style and fit, and that he dislikes the salesman, the material, buying time involved, and the cost. This relationship aggregates to 11 + 's and 9 — 's or to a net difference of 2 + 's; hence the suit would tend to be purchased.

ticular purchase, a frequency distribution of their psychic tensions regarding the purchase in question will tend to form a normal probability curve.[6]

This postulate is the theoretical basis for applying the vector hypothesis to the analysis of a large number of families—as was done in this study.

The above four postulates are the pillars upon which the vector hypothesis rests. Taken together, they point to the conclusion that a person's (or group's) disbursement behavior for any given item can be analyzed in terms of his (or their) psychic tensions regarding it—when due consideration is given to impulse behavior, habits, past commitments and impositions.[7] Before turning to the author's study

[4] This postulate is based upon Lewinian Vector psychology. See Kurt Lewin, "Group Decision and Social Change" in T. M. Newcomb, E. L. Hartley and others, *Readings in Social Psychology* (N. Y.: Henry Holt, 1947).

[5] Two methods used by housewives to side-step psychic tensions for food purchasing are: (1) to buy in constant physical terms, i.e., to follow certain menu routines and then simply to maintain the inventory of the pantry shelf (thus, as food prices change, their total food expenditures change), or (2) to buy in constant monetary terms, i.e., to allocate and spend a certain amount of money per time period for food (thus, as food prices change the quantity or quality of their food purchases vary). By following habit patterns, by obeying impulses, or by employing arbitrary guides, active decision making can be avoided, but the achievement of such simplification is generally done at the expense of efficient buying. (Both habit and impulse behavior may be conditioned.) See W. J. Bilkey, "The Basic Relationships in Consumer Expenditure Behavior," *Harvard Studies in Marketing*, No. 4-H, bulletin (Cambridge, Mass., 1951).

[6] This postulate is adapted from Abba P. Lerner, *The Economics of Control* (N. Y.: Macmillan, 1946), pp. 29–32. The main evidence supporting it is that in each of two independent studies when the psychic tensions for a group of consumers were averaged, the data behaved in a regular and consistent manner as if the postulate were true. This occurred with Professor Lewin's data as well as with the author's. Essentially the same principle also is involved implicitly in the consumer buying anticipation studies of the University of Michigan Survey Research Center.

[7] During the course of the study which will be described shortly, the interviewees experienced no changes in external impositions, and the individual variations in impulse buying, habits and past commitments tended to cancel out. For this reason, an averaging of the data for the 63 families studied resulted in their expenditure behavior apparently being almost exclusively a function of variations in their psychic tensions for the items in question.

which was an exploratory attempt at such an analysis, we will now discuss briefly the techniques available for measuring these psychic tensions.

MEASURING TECHNIQUES

Thus far two techniques have been devised for approximating the magnitude of consumers' psychic tensions: (1) the self-rating method which involves having the persons rate their own tensions on a "0-100 centigrade thermometer scale," and (2) the inferential method which involves asking consumers particular questions and then having the analyst rate their psychic tensions on the basis of the answers received. The self-rating method will be described in detail later in this article. The inferential method may be illustrated by a study performed by the psychologist, Prof. Kurt Lewin.[8] In it he asked a sample of consumers the following three questions (it should be noted that food prices were rising at the time): (a) "Which foods are you already cutting because of the increase in the price of food?" (b) "If prices continue to rise, which foods might you cut?", and (c) "Even if food prices continue to rise which foods are you particularly anxious not to cut?" He then assigned arbitrary weights to the replies as follows: a weight of one to foods mentioned in answer to only one of these three questions, a weight of two to foods mentioned in answer to both questions (a) and (b), a weight of three to foods mentioned in answer to both questions (b) and (c), and a weight of four to foods mentioned in answer to both questions (a) and (c). He then classified the respondents according to their income, and averaged the scores obtained. His results are shown in Table 1. Considering that frozen foods were becoming popular around the time his study was made, Lewin's results are quite in accord with what one might expect on strictly *a priori* grounds. Unfortunately, he made no attempt to compare these psychic tensions with the respondents' actual purchases.

In that study Professor Lewin was concerned merely with the general level of the consumers' psychic tensions i.e., their conflict rating for various foods. In terms of Fig. 2, he was concerned only with the question of whether their positive valences and negative valences were both high or both low, not with the values of each.

[8] Kurt Lewin, "Forces Behind Food Habits and Methods of Change," *National Research Council Bulletin*, No. 108, 1943.

TABLE 1. Conflict Ratings of High, Middle and Low Economic Groups for Specified Food Items —as Presented by Kurt Lewin

Food	High Group	Middle Group	Low Group
Vegetables	.89	1.44	.57
Milk	.70	.89	.33
Meat	.65	1.28	.95
Butter	.30	.94	.67
Fruits	.43	.94	.62
Potatoes	—	.33	.76

The higher the numerical value, the greater the average psychic tension regarding the food. Values less than 1.00 mean that some interviewees never mentioned the food in reply to any of Lewin's three questions.

SOURCE: Kurt Lewin, "Group Decision and Social Change," T. M. Newcomb & E. L. Hartley, eds., *Readings in Social Psychology*, 1947, p. 332, by permission of Henry Holt and Co., Inc., publishers.

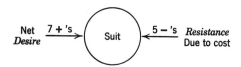

FIG. 2.   Simplified *Desire–Resistance* relationship as used for this project; the tension relationships are taken from Fig. 1. The desires (+ valences) indicate the net total of all liked attributes minus all disliked attributes except those relating to cost. The resistances (− valences) indicate only the resistance due to cost. This relationship yields a net excess of 2 + 's (the same as for Fig. 1). Note the general similarity of *Desire* to the marginal utility of a good, and of *Resistance* to the marginal utility of money.

As we compare the self-rating and the inferential measuring techniques it appears that both have strong and weak points. First let us consider the inferential method. Its advantages are: (1) interviewees don't have to evaluate their psychic tensions, they need only answer specific questions, and (2) it can be administered reasonably easily. Its shortcomings are: (1) there is no adequate objective criterion available to the analyst to determine what values to assign to the answers obtained,[9] and (2) interviewees

[9] For an appraisal of the various methods for determining scoring weights see L. W. Ferguson, *Personality Measurement* (N. Y.: McGraw-Hill, 1952), pp. 128–132.

often dislike repeating statements which they feel can be logically inferred from their earlier answers. The latter difficulty seems to be of considerable practical importance.

The advantages of the self-rating method described below are: (1) it can be easily administered, and (2) answers are taken at face value without having to assign arbitrary values to them. Its shortcomings are: (1) the interviewee has no objective criterion upon which to base his answers and (2) there is no *a priori* evidence to indicate the degree to which the answers are interpersonally comparable.

Fortunately, these two measuring techniques are not mutually exclusive. Both methods may be employed in a single study, and there is a possibility that the results obtained will be complementary. Another possibility is to develop a hybrid of these two techniques.

DESCRIPTIONS OF STUDY

The research now to be described was intended as a pilot study to discover whether any significant relationship seemed to exist between the interviewees' purchases of particular items and their measured psychic tensions regarding those items. A secondary objective, to ascertain whether these measured psychic tensions seemed to be influenced by variables which are economically meaningful, will be reported upon in a subsequent paper.

Because of the exploratory nature of this study, the author wished to work only with persons who would actively cooperate in it, hence a random sampling technique of selection was not used. Instead, mimeographed leaflets explaining the nature of the study were distributed. Persons interested in helping with it then submitted their names, and from these names 63 interviewees were selected as randomly as possible.[10]

The purchasing head of each family was interviewed once every month during the course of the study (each interview being made as near

to the middle of the month as circumstances permitted), and the family's expenditures for the month in question then were recorded during the following month's visit. Thus, the psychic tension data for each month were obtained prior to the completion of that month's expenditures. That is why psychic tensions (*net valences*) are shown as the independent variable in Figure 4.[11]

To minimize the possibility that the families might deliberately adjust their purchases to harmonize with their interview statements, the following precautions were taken: (1) most of the questions called for numerical responses, the full significance of which was not explained to the interviewees, (2) the interviewees never were shown their preceding month's answers, and (3) a large number of questions were asked so as to make memorization of their numerical responses difficult—each interview lasted about one and one-half hours and covered all of the family's major disbursement categories.

To be theoretically precise, the interviews for this study should have been made in terms of the vector relationship as illustrated in Fig. 1; however, during this pilot study phase of the analysis a more easily workable concept was wanted. For this practical reason, the model shown in Fig. 1 was reduced to the simpler desire-resistance relationship in Fig. 2. This was accomplished by letting *desire* constitute the arithmetic total of the person's valences regarding all of the attributes shown in Fig. 1 except cost. *Resistance* then involved only the person's unwillingness to incur the money cost of the item in question. The interviewees were asked to rate their *desires* and *resistances* for each of their disbursement categories on a modified Allport-Vernon value scale (see Fig. 3). The numerical answers which they gave then were treated as if they were the person's psychic tensions for the categories or items in question.

INTERVIEW FINDINGS

Consumer Durables. Several of the interviewees indicated that they were giving some consideration to the purchase of a consumer

---

[10] Of the 63 interviewees, 45 were interviewed once a month for 12 months, 8 for 6–11 months, and 10 for 1–5 months. In terms of occupation: 46 were on the faculty or staff of this University, 14 were small businessmen or laborers and 3 were married university students. In terms of location: 12 were from New London, Connecticut, and the remainder were from the Storrs-Willimantic area. No significant differences in tension-purchasing relationships were found between any of these groups.

[11] *Net valences* are merely the net difference between the person's positive valences for a given item (or category) and his negative valences regarding it. (e.g., in Fig. 1 the person has 11 positive valences for the suit and 9 negative valences against its purchase, or 2 positive *net valences* regarding its purchase.)

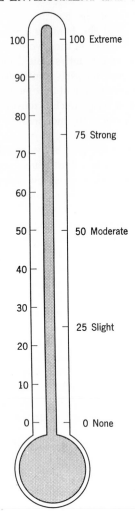

FIG. 3.   Self-rating scale.

100 Extreme

75 Strong

50 Moderate

25 Slight

0 None

which was not purchased—a car. Note the general tendency over time for the *desire* (+ valences) answers to decrease relative to the *resistance* (− valences) answers. In every case where the interviewee failed to purchase the item in question, the responses obtained all followed this general pattern.

Food. Since food is bought continuously, it was analyzed in terms of whether or not changes in its rate of purchase might occur. This involved asking the following four questions, each to be answered in terms of the scale shown in Fig. 3:

Desire questions:
1. "How strong is your desire to increase your food items consumed (in quality or quantity) by 10% from last month's amount?"
2. "How strong is your desire to avoid cutting your food items consumed (in quality or quantity) by 10% from last month's amount?"

Resistance questions:
3. "How strong is your desire to reduce your food expenditures by 10% from last month's amount?"
4. "How strong is your desire to avoid increasing your food expenditures by 10% from last month's amount?"

To obtain the psychic tension ratings for food, answers to the two *desire* questions were averaged and answers to the two *resistance* questions were averaged; the difference between these two magnitudes then being referred to as *net valences.*

Fig. 4 shows the relationship between the *net valences* for food averaged for all families by months with the corresponding averages of their food expenditures for the same months. Note that the April relationship in Fig. 4 seems to be out of place. That apparently was due to a general tendency on the part of many of these families to have reduced their food inventories during that month. A considerable number of the interviewees stated that their food expenditures were unusually low then because they had cleaned out their frozen food lockers in April. Most of them commented that they had eaten unusually well then. The conclusion drawn from the data shown in Fig. 4 is that there was a rather close quantitative relationship between the interviewees' psychic tensions for food and their corresponding food expenditures when allowance is made for inventory variation.

Food Components. The analysis presented thus far has indicated the existence of a relationship (presumably causal) between net va-

durable good such as a car, washing machine, sewing machine, rug, etc. During each interview they then were asked to rate their psychic tensions (in the sense as illustrated in Fig. 2) for the item in question. Using the self-rating scale shown in Fig. 3, they were asked: (1) "How strong is your desire for the (good)?" and (2) "How strong is your desire to avoid the expense which the (good) would entail?" Table 2 illustrates the responses obtained for an item which finally was purchased—a rug. Note the general tendency after June for the *desire* (+ valences) answers to increase relative to the *resistance* (− valences) answers. In every case which finally culminated in a purchase, the responses obtained behaved in this general manner. Table 3 illustrates the responses obtained for an item

TABLE 2. Valence Relationships which Culminated in a Purchase—a Rug. Data as Obtained from Interviewee No. 4; Comments Made by Her During the Interviews Are Given Below

The Vector	Feb.	Mar.	Apr.	May	June	July	Aug.	Sept.	Oct.
Desire for rug (+ valences)	75	—	50	25	25	—	75	90	fin
Resistance to expenditure for rug (− valences)	0	—	25	0	100	—	50	50	fin
Net valences	75+	—	25+	25+	75−	—	25+	40+	fin

Feb.—Had an even stronger desire for a new stove (100+'s and 0—'s). The interviewer failed to ask resistance against expenditures for a stove plus a rug.
Mar.—Brought a new electric range. Missed March interview because of sickness in the family.
Apr.—No comment.
May—Interviewee commented: "Now that I have a new stove I'm so satisfied that I have no desire for a new rug. Also there's the fact that I got new shoes and a dress." (She had been clothes shopping a few days before the May interview).
June—Prior to the interview she had priced rugs and found that the kind she wanted would cost around $300; her earlier estimates had been that such a rug might cost around $150. She stated, "I simply won't pay that."
July—Missed interview because family was vacationing.
Aug.—Interviewee commented: "Now I have a desire for a rug."
Sept.—No comment.
Oct.—Interviewee had purchased a rug shortly before the October interview. She commented: "Now I want a new refrigerator." (75+'s and 50—'s).

TABLE 3. Valence Relationships which did not Culminate in a Purchase—a Car. Data as Obtained from Interviewee No. 69; Comments Made by Him During the Interviews Are Given Below

The Vector	July	Aug.	Sept.	Oct.	Nov.	Dec.	Jan.
Desire for car (+ valences)	50	50	50	50	50 to 75	50	50
Resistance to expenditure for car (− valences)	50	50	50	75	25 to 50	75	75
Net valences	0	0	0	25−	25+	25−	25−

July—No comment.
Aug.—No comment.
Sept.—Interviewee commented that he might buy a car within a month or he might not do so for two years, and that he was watching ads conscientiously. His present car had been repaired a few months earlier and he expected no further trouble for a couple of years.
Oct.—Interviewee commented: "A new car looks more hopeless than ever." He had committed $500 to his wife for the purchase of furniture, and there was a possibility that she also might need an operation.
Nov.—Interviewee commented that he was now thinking more about a car; that he had been inconvenienced a few days earlier by a break-down with his present car.
Dec.—The interviewee stated that his wife had been taken to a hospital shortly before the interview, and had had an expensive operation.
Jan.—No comment; no purchase.

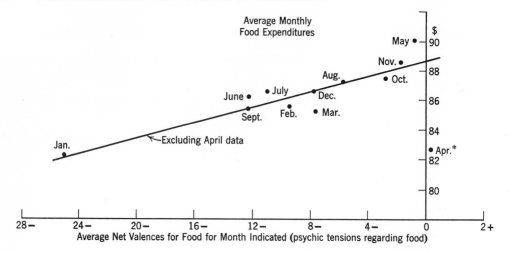

FIG. 4. Relationship between monthly averages of net valences for food and average net food expenditures for the same months. *April data seems to be out of place because of inventory de-accumulation; many of the families stated that they closed out their lockers and finished eating their canned goods in April, so that their food consumption then was greater than their expenditures indicate. Excluding April data: $Y = 88.87 + 0.27X$, and $r = + 0.910$. Including April data: $Y = 87.51 + 0.17X$, and $r = + 0.550$.

lences and purchases for both consumer durables and for food. The question then arose whether such a relationship might also hold for the components within a category (e.g. for particular food items). To test this, the interviewees were requested during the course of the study to maintain purchasing records for meat and eggs. Only a portion of the interviewees complied with this request, however the results from those who did keep records indicate that a valence-expenditure relationship does exist for these items as well as for food as a whole, although it was less close. When cast in the form shown in Fig. 4, the following relationships were obtained between the interviewees' psychic tensions and their corresponding monthly expenditures: for meat $r = + 0.761$ and the regression line was $Y = 15.27 + 0.13X$, for eggs $r = + 0.635$ and the regression line was $Y = 4.73 + 0.05X$.

CONCLUSIONS FROM STUDY

As indicated earlier, the research project described above was intended as a pilot study to ascertain: (1) whether a significant relationship appears to exist between people's psychic tensions regarding particular items and their purchases of those items, and (2) whether these postulated psychic tensions in turn are influenced by considerations which are economically meaningful.[12] It should be recalled that only 63 families were studied, that they were not randomly selected, that the families in question were aware that they were being studied and that techniques for measuring psychic tensions are barely in process of development. Under these circumstances we can conclude only that the results obtained suggest an affirmative answer to the above two questions, and that further research seems definitely to be warranted. On the basis of his experience with this and with other studies, the author is convinced that the vector hypothesis provides a useful theoretical framework for consumer analysis, even with the measuring techniques currently available.

_____

[12] To be reported in a later paper.

12. *The Autonomy of the Consumer*

NELSON N. FOOTE

Depression and war, fascism and communism, have taught us that freedom and equality must have an economic content if they are to be real to the mass of the people. This content Americans are getting in the growth of the "middle market." Some 1953 issues of *Fortune* provide numerous texts to illumine this assertion. In the August 1953 issue, carrying Mr. Whyte's critique of the loss of individuality among the interchangeable Park Foresters, appears the first of a series on the changing American market. Therein is presented the economic background for this intriguing cultural phenomenon: a nationwide multiplication of middle-income families, a correlative shrinking of upper and lower income groups, a substantial rise in real income every year, and, as a result, a mounting ratio of discretionary income. As the *Fortune* editors note, the American today has more things to be independent *about* than ever before.

Conventionally, consumer sovereignty is conceived as an all-or-none matter. Among economists it refers to the right of the consumer to buy or not to buy. In this sense, it might be said that his sovereignty is what the psychological warriors of business are bent on reducing. Consumer autonomy, however, is not an all-or-none possession. For by autonomy I mean the consumer's self-determined use of his sovereignty, his utilization of the opportunity to create his own style of spending.

In general, the autonomy of the consumer has probably been increasing. It is less important for consumer research to document the current trend, however, than to ascertain the conditions under which autonomy develops optimally. For I submit that *the researcher and his employer have more to gain from cultivating the autonomy of the consumer than from discouraging or frustrating it.*

Let us suppose a fully autonomous researcher, deeply interested in consumer behavior, supplied with unlimited resources, and ready to choose the problems of most interest to himself.[1] What would they be?

It would make a great deal of difference who the researcher is. I speak here as a family sociologist. Most of the research on consumer behavior has been done by psychologists and economists, but it is not mere professional bias that leads me to urge that the sociologist and the cultural anthropologist have much to offer. It is the sociologists who have given greatest attention to the effects of stratification upon the behavior exhibited as styles of life within our society. And it is the anthropologists who have given most attention to styles of life in comparing whole societies, not merely in the fine arts as done by the art historian but across the whole breadth of culture.

The psychologist and the economist alike tend to start from individuals and proceed to aggregates of individuals, with insufficient attention to the processes by which these aggre-

✖ SOURCE: Reprinted by permission from *Consumer Behavior: The Dynamics of Consumer Reaction*, edited by Lincoln H. Clark (New York University Press, 1955), pp. 15–24.

[1] This article is based on a paper given at the second annual conference of The Committee for Research on Consumer Attitudes and Behavior, September 17, 1953.

gates become formed into really social phenomena like classes and communities, institutions, and associations. I cannot claim that the sociologists have done much better. For instance, I have not yet seen a satisfactory way of treating families statistically as constellations rather than as mere combinations of individuals, though fortunately I do know of several persons who are working on this. Census definitions take into account about eighteen different types of living units; they include dependency and relationship characteristics but omit the social-psychological aspects, which are of greatest interest from the standpoint of consumption. What seems badly needed is research on group factors in consumer behavior that will deal with phenomena falling between, let us say, brand preferences at one end of the scale and the national consumption function, as theoretical economists call it, at the other. The home economists should have stepped in here long ago, but they have been so dominated by ideas of productive efficiency that they have contributed little in this area. Their current reorientation toward the family may, however, cause them to come up with something before long.

IDENTIFICATION WITH CONSUMER URGED

Assuming that this hypothetical researcher is a sociologist or group psychologist, I would paradoxically urge that he identify with the object of his study, the consumer himself. This is normally not done; usually the researcher takes his employer's attitude and tries to anticipate and outwit the consumer.

But we now have before us a consumer less predictable than before. Even if we still wanted to outwit him, we would have to enter into his thinking, his doubts, changes, growth, and fickleness. But the job is much more that of helping the consumer, by creating a stability or predictability congenial to him. Why hunt in a dark room for the famous black cat that isn't there? If we are to study regularities in behavior, I think we will be able to find far more by helping create them, rather than simply by searching for them.

To create them will mean that the researcher will *participate with the consumer in the orderly development of consistent patterns of choice*. His role would not be that of a bird dog engaged in sniffing out unsaturated markets; it would be the much more professional—and even artistic—role of experimentation in the creative

development of markets. Instead of simply boosting sales, he could simultaneously help make distribution more efficient and thus continue to justify his services.

With autonomy as our theme and identification with the consumer as our starting point, the variations upon our theme will be specific research hypotheses, arbitrarily set at ten. Because economics seems so basic, we shall start from the income end and work over to psychology. But, throughout, the emphasis will be upon the social conditions for development of style in consumption.

Increase in the "Middle Market"

1. As real income continues to rise, the "middle market" will continue to grow, almost regardless of national fiscal policy.

Whatever may have been true in the past, the Protestant ethic of striving and straining, of scrimping and saving, is no longer necessary to the continuous advance of real income. From here on out that advance will come principally through technical improvement, the conditions for which have already been built into our institutional structure in the endless frontier of engineering colleges and industrial research centers. The effect of these is cumulative. For the mass of people, the significance of this fact has still not been fully grasped. They still do not realize that we can all get ahead without exertion and self-denial. I could go further in undermining puritan mores by pointing out that large amounts of idle reflection are an important aid in creativity, and creativity is the basic capital of industry of the future.

As real income goes up, the motivation to enhance personal income and accumulate property will level off. This curvilinear feature of the motivation to increase one's income can already be observed among individual deviants, but it will be found more frequently among whole groups, as in shortening of hours, the multiplication of vacation and holiday clauses.

Progressive taxation, union wage bargaining, and the relative increase of salaried positions have probably received more than their share of credit, for the equalization of family income in the last decades. Given the increased security, which makes saving against catastrophe pointless, the craving for expansion of income is likely to approach some kind of ceiling for most people. This ceiling will no doubt continue to drift upward due to distribution of the benefits of enhanced productivity, but the pursuit of wealth for its own sake has already lost its former status as the be-all and end-all of human existence for masses of Americans. Leisure seems already preferable to work for all but the fortunate few whose professions are their hobbies.

Almost as important as the number of people drawing middle incomes is the increasing stability of these incomes. For the person on salary or annual wage is the one who can truly budget, who has the best chance of creating an orderly style of spending his income. The relative equality of incomes in this middle range likewise reduces the pressure to compete in primarily quantitative terms with others. Conspicuous consumption is on the decline, while the development of qualitatively distinctive taste is on the upgrade.

All this presents for the researcher a need to analyze styles of spending among people of more or less equal income. Problems of calculating the effect of changes of income upon aggregate patterns of spending will remain for the economist, and there is an inviting opportunity here for some genuinely experimental research in economics—something in which the dismal science has hitherto been peculiarly lacking. But the most novel and exciting research, even in the field of income distribution, will be in the study of that nonutilitarian calculus by which the values of leisure limit and condition the individual pursuit of income until a point of indifference is reached.

Increase in Leisure Time

2. As this point, at which leisure becomes preferable to further work, recedes, considerations of time expenditure will further condition money expenditure in consumer behavior.

The puritanical injunction that "time is money" will no doubt continue in force in factories and offices where people are paid for their time. Off the job, however, it is being reversed to read "money is time," in the sense that the worker, as his income goes up, becomes able to bid against his employer for his own time. The more money he makes per hour—a function of productivity as much as of distribution—the more time he can take off. And what he does after hours may or may not be exhibited in cash expenditures.

For the consumption researchers who must serve a commercial employer, purchasing behavior is what counts. But even this can best be understood against the background of non-purchasing behavior. Once the consumer gets beyond the point at which he is governed mainly by anxiety to survive, the consumption of time may become the basic common denominator of consumer behavior.

Currently there is a booming market in do-it-yourself items. This market could not have been predicted by extrapolations from other expenditures, but a theory of the place of crafts in any complete regime of play would afford a basis for fairly precise and detailed anticipation of where and when it will develop further. In doing it for himself, the consumer does not simply calculate the cost of a paper hanger against his own rate of pay but the interest and value of the play and creativity involved. One of the great, underrecognized values of home ownership is the play it gives to the pursuit of home crafts. Thus the growth of suburbs is not simply to be accounted for in terms of the tax structure of cities not to be halted except by economic catastrophe.

We know that the so-called laws of expenditure on food, clothing, housing, medical care, and the like, keep breaking down in the face of new conditions. Engels' law on the proportion of income spent on food, for example, apparently depended upon a set of cultural conditions. As long as they obtained, the law was "verified" in many repeated studies. But now it appears that many of our "middle-incomers" have increased the proportion they spend on food. This suggests that the social rituals of cooking and eating are being elaborated into an art of boundless proportions; not only is cooking becoming more and more efficient, it is becoming an end in itself. It consumes increasing time, attention, and ingenuity; attracts a more and more critical and appreciative audience; requires improved techniques for achieving aesthetic ends.

There is still need for further study of family budgets; also some of the archaic categories need to be refined, to take account of matters like reciprocal gift giving, philanthropy, and the value of self-produced items. We must take into account large quantities of consumption not directly purchased—free public services, receipt of charity, non-profit institutional services, bequests of goods, being a dependent, unpaid services to others. Then there are tax exemptions and illegal gains and chance winnings. Some qualitative analysis of borrowing and saving is also called for, to distinguish the effort and cost devoted to stabilization of expenditure. Just as there is food and "food," there is saving and "saving."

Here again we may see at work not a traditional motive of thrift or an unwise use of credit, but a steady effort by consumers to work out a self-conscious and orderly pattern of spending— a genuine standard of living, albeit of developing one—over and above their interest in stabilizing income. But, beyond these improvements in analysis of money budgets, the big call, theoretically at least, is for time-budget studies. The time spent with children by a mother, as against the time spent with organizations to which she belongs, may more truly index her values than the amount of money she spends on either.

Increased Effect of the Stage of the Family Cycle

3. As this enlarging market of middle-income consumers becomes more stable and homogeneous, it will become progressively more differentiated in terms of stages of the family cycle.

The high and rising rate of physical and social mobility among the American population is tending to break down traditional communities of custom and taste. To count upon any new and regularizing differentiations to appear in this squirming mass might seem futile. Evidence is accumulating, however, that patterns already visible are going to become more pronounced.

As Mr. Whyte has noted, most families found in suburbs like Park Forest live there only during a certain period in their careers. The very rate of mobility helps to account for the internal homogeneity, the external distinctiveness, of such suburbs. Birds of a feather can more readily flock together than before. What are the feathers that guide their flocking? Within the middle-income group, the most visible appears to be the stage of the family cycle. This correlates with the development of personal careers, but it is family, not occupation, that stands out in determining one's residence and style of consumption. As we look around, we find suburbs, neighborhoods, even single apartment buildings, that consist homogeneously of young-married couples, young parents, middle-aged people, bachelor girls and boys, empty-nesters, and the retired. It is easier to move than to rebuild, and thus people in metropolitan areas (and who is not?) tend to segregate themselves voluntarily among their peers. Among peers the old way of selecting friends on the basis of propinquity can once more operate without one demeaning one's autonomy.

Not the census categories, which classify families as combinations of individuals, but the family-stage categories seem the more appropriate for consumption research. Take, for example, the varieties of dependency. Internal Revenue definitions are almost beside the point if what we are interested in is the development of style of spending. Where is the authority and the leadership in the family? Children, especially adolescents, are often the missionaries of change. The psychological structure of a family in which the wife works or has another source of income than her husband is quite different from the traditional patriarchy in which wife and children are not only dependents but subordinates.

Increased Need for Criteria of Judgment

4. As freedom of choice in expenditure increases in the tangible form of discretionary income and time, the need for explicit criteria of judgment will become more consciously felt among consumers.

Any sudden or even rapid accession of wealth is likely to lead for a time to behavior like that of Molière's famous bourgeois gentleman. This is a nation of nouveaux riches, one might say, and it is to be expected that its buying will appear whimsical, uninformed, suggestible, unbalanced, and full of admitted mistakes. It is not to be expected that this awkward phase will last indefinitely, however, for criticism and the correction of error are incessant. I would not say we are swamped with wealth, but I would say the rate of stimulation to spend has run ahead of our rate of assimilation.

Better judgment is needed, and the more the consumer develops it, the more likely is he to be autonomous. And the more autonomous he is given a chance to become, the better judgment he is likely to develop. He needs to become able to state what he likes and what he does not and why. This implies practice in criticism. If sellers are as tender to criticism as Bernard De Voto alleges, they are not likely to take kindly to the proposition that they have an interest in developing the judgment of the consumer. I hope De Voto is wrong, though I half fear he may be right. Sellers may pine only for ways to control consumer decision making.

New Wants Develop

5. As income and leisure increase, not only are old wants more fully satisfied but new wants are created.

In market research, it is an undeserved compliment to the consumer to assume that he always and infallibly knows what he wants, that he can articulate his wants accurately in answer to questions, and that what he says will match what he later does. At the same time, it is an undeserved disparagement of his judgment and an intrusion of his autonomy to assume the role of trying to mold his wants to suit the seller. Concretely, the middle ground between these alternatives is best illustrated in the collaboration between seller and buyer that has developed markets of adepts for high-fidelity recordings, power woodworking tools, garden seeds, backyard barbecue equipment, and books.

Wants are not given. Once learned or acquired, they may remain quite stable, but many wants are not stable and none are permanent. They are generally in a constant process of elaboration, definition, integration, realization, fluctuation. One's wants are very much influenced by the other persons with whom he identifies himself. Rhetoric directed at producing an identification is often as effective in creating a new want as direct stimulation of existing wants or associations with previous values.

It would be valuable to explore the whole conception of wants in terms of psychological theory. But, at least, we should raise a question about the very title of the Committee for Research on Consumer Attitudes and Behavior, under whose auspices these papers are presented. If by the phrase "attitudes and behavior" it is implied that attitudes are entities resident in the consumer that may be discovered and utilized to explain his behavior, I would say the conception involved is highly debatable. I think the exploration of motivation, using the concept of identification, is going to be far more fruitful than employment of the concept of attitude. In particular, when we talk of the creation of wants as a social process in which one party creates wants in another or both participate in developing their wants, we must get around to the psychology of rhetoric, which is inevitably a psychology of identification, not of pre-existent attitudes or static preferences.

In conceiving of the growth of a market, it makes a great deal of difference whether that market is conceived as a mass of more or less unrelated individuals or as a structured and organized network of interpersonal and intergroup relationships. Even when markets are treated in terms of income levels, social strata, regions and age groupings, it may still be true that people in these categories are nonetheless conceived pretty much as individual agents rather than as members of identifiable group formations. I think all practical strategies are based on some assumption about the nature of society, and certain familiar conceptions of society are quite unrealistic and frequently ambiguous. On the one hand, they posit an isolated, thinking individual, who is to be influenced by rational appeals to his self-interest. On the other hand, his autonomous capacity for critical acceptance or rejection of group values and fashions is discouraged by the notorious tactics of band-wagon appeals, glittering generalities, the "plain-folks" device, and the testimonials originally indicted by the Institute for Propaganda Analysis.

Need for a Style of Life

6. As wants develop for a wider array of goods and services, the need for their unification through a satisfying and coherent style of living, based on aesthetic rather than economic criteria, becomes increasingly manifest.

One of my former students who became a union organizer wrote me recently the following reflections on what is happening among the people she serves.

That is why unionism has its appeal to me. It has the seeds for the developing of the workers' control of those factors that affect his life, give him a voice in determining those decisions. But unionism, in its quest for more and more, doesn't necessarily bring a sense of well-being to many workers caught up in the never-ending acquisition of gadgets, of latest models, of newest fashions, of passive recreation. How to rechannel the values people have so that they don't spend at routine work their valuable hours of life supporting cars and television sets but engage in pursuits that do develop their own potentialities; so that they don't sit back, having their entertainment spooned out to them, but have a hand in creating their own? Boredom is a problem to think about with the trend toward more leisure hours, earlier retirement, longer life.

It is a striking turn of events when a union organizer becomes as concerned about boredom off the job as on it. The two are very much related, but there is no opportunity here to deal with boredom on the job or even to do more than touch upon its relationship to boredom during leisure. The important point is: the mule can be as harassed and driven by a bewildering array of carrots as by the stick. In fact, there are already prophets to deplore the fractured multiplicity of life under constant bombardment of consumers' goods, prophets who recommend a return to rigorous simplicity. But who could without malice urge another depression or another escape from freedom? Save to these reactionaries, the problem is not that of simplification but of organization.

The organization of a style of life is not a simple product of rational deduction. It requires countless decisions contingent one on the other. As a process, it is more like the practice of art than of algebra. The artist is not governed by scarcity of paints but by self-imposed criteria. To be sure, if we think of expenditure, there is a definite vocabulary, grammar, and syntax. Rules are necessary to give some form to the composition, but the rules only set limits, they do not determine content. One can criticize an insufficient diet from the standpoint of the biochemistry of nutrition, but neither biochemistry nor guilt feelings provide a sufficient basis for planning artistic menus. Neither can mere recipes for tasty dishes form the basis for a satisfying style of eating. We are now hearing that obesity is the nation's number one health problem. Obesity, thus, rather well serves to symbolize the importance of developing a discriminating style of consumption.

As with diet, most patterns of consumption are family-wide customs rather than individual habits. The development of style in consumption, however, ought to start as near to the individual as it can without being unrealistic. Food habits are a case in point. Whether habit or custom, some researchers conceive their problem as that of overcoming resistance to change.

But food habits are neither more recalcitrant nor more pliable than most other consumer behavior. Everyone knows the fight that children can put up against being forced to eat something they do not like. They do not become less resistant as adults. It is just that no one pushes them any more (unless it be their own consciences). On the other hand, children and adults will put almost anything in their mouths, especially if encouraged by others whose example they esteem and trust. The development of any style of consumption involves as much the organization of groups of people in concerted patterns of action as it does the more intellectual subordination of purchasing decisions to autonomous styles of living.

Development of an Individual Style

7. As the autonomy of consumers develops, it is going to produce a renewed concept of style as belonging to specific persons and groups.

Style as popularly conceived is a mass phenomenon almost synonymous with fashion—transitory, shallow, anonymous. There is a large element of chance and uncertainty in its manifestations, which gives rise to a speculative fever for windfall profits through "playing the market right" or getting an edge on rivals in quick exploitation of nascent fads. All this gives to contemporary style a synthetic, ephemeral, and irresponsible character, which is continually deplored by critics.

To critics of aristocratic pretensions, there is a ready retort. The growth of the mass market has made it possible to put finer and finer things into the hands of more and more people. Given time and the continued working of the beneficent forces of advertising and mass production, the masses will graduate from low-brow to at least middle-brow levels of taste. The standard example is the sale of records of classical music.

This standard retort is satisfactory as far as it goes, but it fails to answer a more fundamental criticism. The critics and defenders of popular culture tend to focus upon the vocabulary of consumption, to criticize the qualities of the objects and events purchased, and to berate buyer or seller or someone else for their low standards or praise him for high ones. But the far more important issue is whether the standard that the seller or buyer follows is genuinely his own. If it is his own, it should and would be more continuous, more cumulative, more authentic; in other words, it would be a style and not a fashion. It would not necessarily be more individualized, though this too would be more likely. Some persons create styles uniquely expressive of themselves, but these styles tend rather soon to get adopted by others. If style is conceived as pertaining to persons rather than products, its development runs no conflict with mass production and entails no return to custom work. It may mean that the producer who aspires to make and market fine things can increasingly afford to do so.

The consumer is able nowadays to select from a wider range of sources than ever before. That is the glory of the modern market: it gives us the whole world to choose from. But let there be choice, rather than mere collective whim. Let a pattern of choice be created self-consciously among the items we buy. That is what I mean when I say that regularities in buying behavior are more likely to be created than to be discovered through research. Research can provide the basis for evaluating experiments in the development of style, for the development of judgment, autonomy, and creativity. I think we need to develop measures of these three abilities more than we need further refinements in the measurement of preference.

The consumer needs help, however, in the development of his style, and not help of a patronizing sort any more than condemnation. He needs the help of the humanities as much as that of the social sciences.

The humanities in our colleges and universities, however, are unfortunately about the last remaining refuge of the obsolete class-mass division of culture. It may be that the humanities departments are beyond hope of redemption. Home economics colleges offer only slightly more basis for optimism, owing to their rural connections. Perhaps quite new educational institutions will have to be created to aid the contemporary consumer, and perhaps the merchandiser himself—if he can honor the autonomy of the consumer—will be able to help in creating them. I doubt if any of our present commercial institutions, ostensibly devoted to raising the standards of consumership, as yet qualify, though some of the better consumer magazines, and especially certain of the new critics of consumption who appear in their columns, are beginning to show the way.

Professionalizing Marketing Skills

8. *As the autonomy of consumers develops, the occupations of advertising, marketing, merchandising, and selling will become more professionalized.*

In order to complete a circuit, communication requires a two-way flow of information. The role of market research, like that of these other intermediary occupations, may be seen as that of completing the flow of communication between producer and consumer.

Both the consumer and the producer may be viewed as engaged in creative activity. One is making a specific product. The other is fashioning a whole style of life. If they are to collaborate, they need to communicate. Failure to do so frustrates the aims of both. In the days of village enterprise and custom work, they could communicate face to face. With mass production and mass markets, we have the reign of commodities as rather eloquently and provocatively described by Karl Marx.

However, we cannot go back to handicrafts and county fairs while retaining the benefits of modern technology. And after all, the do-it-yourself phenomenon is primarily a form of recreation, with no prospect of putting General Foods or General Electric or General Mills out of business. Rather, the power of the consumer to express his wants in his own way will increasingly become a means of restoring communication between himself and the producer. This implies that all who play a part in the function of distribution must see themselves not merely as merchants but as channels of communication, of criticism and appreciation, of teaching and demonstration.

Such a prophecy may seem to contradict certain evident trends toward reducing the numbers and cost of sales personnel. I do not think it does. Merchandising can move toward self-service further than it has, but that will only increase the need for communication, not obviate or diminish it.

Something quite positive can be said, as a matter of fact, for the steady divorce of selling (*and of sales research*) from specific products. The strategic intermediary position of the distributive trades has not been sufficiently utilized, because the interests of the producer in simple expansion of sales have tended to dominate both the intermediaries and ultimately the consumer, despite the verbal emphasis on service and consumer sovereignty. As the consumer's autonomy increases, however, there is a benevolent circle or spiral, through which the intermediaries can increase their autonomy also. As this happens, producers can shift their attention from the marketing of specific products to the cultivation of the consumer's style. To use David Riesman's phrase, they tend to become "taste counselors." Their customers, as in the professions, meanwhile begin to take on the characteristics of a clientele. Instead of the commercial vocabulary, which implies gloating over maneuvering consumers into "impulse buys" and "tie-in sales," a professional vocabulary of objectivity and impartiality, a professional ethics of merited trust, are likely to be the newer sources of pride, as they are among architects.

As with persons, so with institutions. When the department store can achieve a sufficient degree of independence from manufacturers, it has the opportunity to take the part of the consumer and to market goods on their merits. I think it is more likely that stores will develop along this line than that the average consumer will sit down and study Consumers Union reports. We have something like taste counseling already in specialty shops, such as certain men's clothing stores, sporting goods departments, and travel agencies. I have found myself willing to pay the price that includes the competent professional advice of salesmen in these establishments, because I trusted them to guide the development of my taste, rather than to pursue the short-run benefits of loading me with things I was not sure I wanted. I doubt if I am unique in responding favorably to this kind of treatment.

Who are the taste counselors who exhibit this professional competence, independence, and integrity? The kind of person who best resembles what I have in mind is the unhampered writer for the less commercial magazines or the freelance independent. Names like these come to mind: Russell Lynes, Jane Nickerson, Duncan Hines, Edward Tatnall Canby, John Crosby. At the local level, everyone can name his own trusted face-to-face mentors, employed by this store or that newspaper, or simply an amateur. It is worth mentioning that, as the professionalization of salesmanship occurs, it will become evident that the judgment of these taste counselors will be of the greatest value to industrial designers in all fields.

Manufacturers have discovered, one could almost say stumbled into the realization, that in the long run good design is as much in their interest as in that of the consumer. Before long they may find that close liaison between their design departments and the taste counselors is in their interest also and that the professional integrity and independence of these professions is as worthy of being cherished as is academic freedom in the universities. Selling in the old sense of mere expansion of sales may have had its place in a certain phase of the development of the national economy. With the approach of some kind of regularly evolving equilibrium between the values of work and play, the relation of intermediary persons and institutions to the array of producers and the array of style groups must almost inevitably be transformed. Observations of its manifold emergence in other fields make me almost smugly secure in predicting the professionalization of salesmanship.

Commercial institutions and the advertising media will principally employ these taste counselors, but it will still take a university to train them. As yet, I do not know a single school that is fully capable of doing so. Probably we will have to staff such a school by hiring the best of the self-taught ones. In the university environment, they can compare and systematize, as they cannot now, under conditions of still greater protection of their autonomy. Out of such really interdisciplinary thought and research, we may then get our general science of consumption, our general theories of work and play, our positive criteria for the criticism of popular taste, our experiments in the development of judgment.

Development of Consumer Leadership in Style

9. *As the development of style in spending becomes more self-conscious and critical, leadership in the creation and propagation of style will develop among consumers themselves, making them less dependent on counselors.*

At present the phenomena of indigenous leadership in style are visible in popular culture only in patches and in connection with particular products. The vogues in dresses, haircuts, and mammary glands seem to be set as much by movie and television queens as by the designers. I do not know whether the vogue in loud, tieless sport shirts for men is traceable to Harry Truman or Dwight Eisenhower, to Bing Crosby or Arthur Godfrey, but in general there is not even yet what could be called the development of style in clothing among men, despite the fact that their taste is less fickle than that of women. Genuine growth of style through identification of large numbers with important personalities is visible in the fine arts, as in the influence of Hemingway in writing or Le Corbusier in architecture. But about the only place where fine art has really permeated mass taste to a substantial degree is in the field of furniture and tableware. American interiors have been vastly improved as a result, and today one can no longer speak of a single modern style in these fields, but recognizes considerable differentiation as he takes in the shows and the literature. These differing modern styles are coming to be identified with particular designers who develop followings. This differentiation of style is likely to become far more common as consumers take an interest in the quality of their own purchasing decisions and become equipped with resources and training for interrelating these decisions according to chosen master-themes.

This image of man constructively engaged in formulating himself is in sharp contrast to the well-known caricature of the consumer as a container of definitely satiable wants, whose only aim in life is to reach the zero point of tension. To involve man in the creation of a major style is to demand of him a commitment of which he is not often thought capable. Yet, the original development of Gothic style called for real sacrifice, and today there are communities whose inhabitants tax themselves equally hard to realize the values they have for the schooling of their children.

Public buildings in the United States used to be little short of monstrous, and they still exhibit a false dependence upon classical and medieval styles. I hope to see in my time the appearance of styles of consumption as authentically expressive of our time as Gothic and Corinthian were of theirs, styles that spread across all the categories of consumption—food, clothing, housing, transportation, association, hygiene, education, recreation, government, and family life.

We do not have to sit and pray for the return of the golden days. Social science is something they did not have in classical times, and no people anywhere ever had the quantity of resources available to us. What we do not have and need desperately to recapture is the creativity at the grass roots, and the identification with creativity at the level of genius and leadership, which some other times have had. I think that research can do something with the problem of engendering creativity in consumption as it has with creativity in production. We cannot all be poets and prophets, but there is vast need for explorers and inventors, for teachers and critics, in every community. If we can ascertain the conditions for reproducing such creativity, we may be able in this generation to gain a community better than that the Lynds pictured in their compelling indictment of the commercial civilization of Middletown.

Development of Consumers Organizations

10. As the autonomy of consumers increases, a variety of consumer organizations will arise through which consumers may exert their power in markets.

These remarks may appear subversive to the average seller who fears that such a step will bring the American way of life tumbling down around his ears. But what is wrong about organizing the consumer? And is it really against the interests of commerce for the consumer to organize? Management felt it was against its interests for employees to organize, yet it now admits that the wide distribution of purchasing power has much to do with the continuation of prosperity.

I have no idea what forms consumer organization will take. There are numerous rudimentary forms of consumer organization that may furnish some clues, but I am quite skeptical of the hopes and claims of their partisans. Too many of them are already declining because of their adherence to outdated concepts of merely helping the consumer to save his money or of protecting him from the alleged confidence men who operate the nation's business.

Perhaps the policy era of consumer behavior will be ushered in by the unions' extending their function. More likely, however, are analogous organizations that will represent different kinds of consumers. Thus, we might get bodies like the Arts Council of Great Britain to criticize and encourage the standards achieved in the entertainment field. We already have the PTA, such as it is, as a medium for expression and advancement of consumer wants in education. Our rod and gun clubs do a very good job of promoting the interests of their members before state legislatures, as do the automobile clubs.

The unions offer a second analogy. For the autonomous researcher, the organization of consumers offers no cause for alarm. Arbitrators and the rule of reason came into their own in industrial relations when the power of management was equalized by the power of unions. Similarly, the influence of the professional intermediary between producer and consumer will reach its height when the autonomy of organized consumers countervails the power of the now increasingly less competitive, more and more organized producers.

What I do not doubt is that the American genius for organization will operate in the field of consumption as in all other fields of contemporary activity, and that it will construct channels through which the will of consumers will more directly and efficaciously be brought to bear upon the making of distribution policy. As that happens, our hypothetical autonomous researcher who begs to cultivate the autonomy of the consumer will have to beg no longer. At that point, the producer and seller will be begging the researcher for predictions of what turn consumer policy will take next. And consumer behavior will no longer be merely the aggregate of collective decisions by individuals, more or less cajoled in loose herds, but policy in the self-conscious, affirmative sense that demands execution by responsible agents.

C. Economic Aspects of Consumer Behavior

13. Our Changing Consumer Market

ROBERT FERBER

Had anyone predicted ten years ago that the mainstay of postwar prosperity was to be consumer spending, he would have been ridiculed. Traditionally, business investment in plant and equipment and in inventories had been the spark plug, as well as the foretoken, of business conditions; it helped determine consumer income, which then led to a more or less predetermined level of consumer expenditures.

The experience of the last decade has shown, to almost everybody's surprise, that the process can also work the other way around. In 1948-49, and then again in 1953-54, it was consumer spending that remained high and paved the way for further prosperity, while activity faltered in other sectors of the economy.

These developments have been among the most spectacular and widely publicized characteristics of consumer spending in the postwar years. Yet, they reflect in large measure more basic changes that have been taking place over many years, and particularly during the past two decades. These include changes in the characteristics as well as the number of consumers, changes in consumer income and assets, and changes in consumer wants and preferences—all of which add up to a strikingly different present-day market structure for consumer goods, and which presage additional changes yet to come.

The slowing down of the postwar boom and the concomitant availability of a major new set of data on consumer expenditures make this a convenient time to take stock of these changes and to evaluate their effects in relation to pos-

‡‡ SOURCE: Reprinted by permission from *Business Horizons*, Vol. 1, No. 2, Spring 1958, pp. 49–66.

sible future trends in business conditions. These new data were obtained in the course of a nationwide survey of consumer income and expenditures completed in 1957 under the sponsorship of *Life* magazine. They represent the most extensive private study of this market ever undertaken to date, and rival in scope the mammoth 1950 consumer expenditures study of the U.S. Bureau of Labor Statistics.[1] Comparable in many respects with these earlier government studies, the *Life* data enable us to bring up to date the broad developments that have been taking place in the consumer market and to examine the current state of affairs.

MONEY, MONEY, MONEY

Consumer income after taxes has more than quadrupled during the past two decades, from 1936 to 1956 (Fig. 1). In 1957, disposable income after taxes appears to have hit a new peak of almost $300 billion, or an average of well over $5,000 for each of the 50 million families in the country. (Some of this $300 billion is not earned by families, but by trusts, individuals in institutions, and so forth.)

---

[1] Some pertinent statistics are: The *Life* sample contained 17,173 households selected by an area probability design from the population at large. Of this number 15,003 supplied some of the information requested, and 10,243 supplied all information. Data were collected from each household in four "waves" of interviews conducted between October, 1955, and the end of 1956. All together 110,314 interviews were carried out during the course of the study, each interview averaging about two hours.

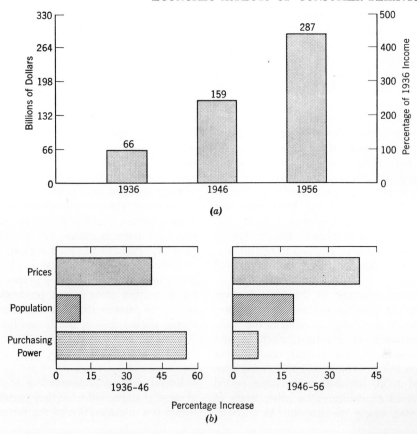

FIG. 1.   (a) Much of the rise in incomes after taxes   (b) is attributable to higher prices and a larger population. Nevertheless, purchasing power has risen substantially too. *Source:* Computed from U. S. Department of Commerce: *Survey of Current Business* and various supplements; U. S. Bureau of the Census, *Census of the United States* and various supplements.

Almost half of this increase has been brought about by rising prices—about 40 per cent during the first of these decades, and about 60 per cent in the postwar decade. Another portion of this increase can be attributed to our growing population, particularly during the postwar decade when the number of people in the country rose almost 20 per cent—almost twice the rate of the preceding decade. However, even after allowance is made for these increases in prices and population, the fact remains that consumers' purchasing power has undergone a rather hefty increase; in 1956, the real income of the average consumer was 71 per cent more after taxes than it was in 1936. Most of this increase came during the war years; the increase in purchasing power since 1946 has been less than 10 per cent.

The rise in consumer spending that has taken place during the past two decades has paralleled the rise in incomes. More important, it has varied markedly with different types of goods and services. Homes, cars, and household durables are among goods that have experienced the main increases, partly because of their unavailability during the war and partly because of rapid technological advances in their design and operation. Among the services, education and foreign travel have registered the largest gains, reflecting the newly found discretionary spending of millions of families and the growing popularity of overseas vacations. Consumer spending has risen much less than average for rental housing and for purchased local and intercity transportation, which have suffered because of the shift to home and car ownership; for clothing, which has lost for the time being much of its former glamor; and for domestic service, which has declined as a result of the widespread labor shortage, enabling workers in this field to make more money elsewhere.

Of course, much of this rise in expenditures

—approximately 60 per cent of it—is due to increases in price and population. However, much the same pattern of consumer spending emerges when allowance is made for the effects of price and population changes. This is supported by a comparison of household expenditures in 1936 with the corresponding *Life* magazine data for 1956 (Fig. 2).

Such a comparison shows that gadgetry, particularly in the form of durable goods, and pleasure have been occupying an increasingly important position in the American family budget. The average urban household in 1956 went in relatively more for home furnishings and equipment (including appliances), recreation, and automobiles, and related expenses (much of which in turn can be charged to recreation), and less for clothing, rent, and household operation.

In fact, symptomatic of the great postwar prosperity has been the decline in the proportion of the family budget devoted to the traditional necessities of life—food, clothing, and shelter. American families roughly doubled their outlays on food, clothing, and shelter between 1936 and 1956, but during the same period their over-all expenditures on other items of family living nearly quadrupled. As a result,

the importance of food, clothing, and shelter in the family budget fell from nearly two-thirds of the total in 1935-36 to just a little over half in 1956—and this is without allowance for the sharp increase in purchases of such luxury items as fancy foods and air conditioning.

When we get down to individual products, differences between family outlays then and now become much more pronounced. For some products, such as fresh fruit, potatoes, railroad travel, and domestic service, expenditures have risen hardly at all in dollar terms, and have actually declined, once price increases are taken into account. However, purchases of such items as new homes, washing machines, and margarine have risen in some cases almost fourfold (Fig. 3). Perhaps the most striking indication of the changes that have taken place in consumer markets is the growing proportion of the family budget going to new products that had no counterparts in 1936—air conditioning, television, clothes dryers, and frozen foods.

THE STORY BEHIND THE STORY

Essential to an understanding of the nature of these changes and what they portend for the future is a consideration of the factors respon-

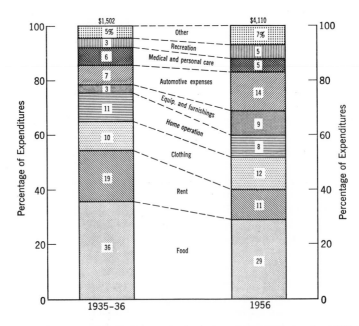

FIG. 2. The effect of prosperity on the consumer budget. *Source:* Percentages for 1935–1936 are derived from National Resources Committee, *Consumer Expenditures in the United States, Estimated for 1935–1936,* and supplementary reports by the Department of Labor, Bureau of Labor Statistics. Percentages for 1956 are derived from *Life Study of Consumer Expenditures,* copyright 1957 by *Time,* Inc.

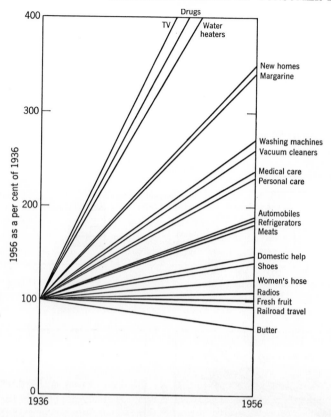

FIG. 3.   Trends in purchases of selected goods and services. *Source:* Percentages for 1936 are computed from U. S. Department of Commerce, *National Income, 1954 Edition: A Supplement to the Survey of Current Business.* Percentages for 1956 are computed from U. S. Department of Commerce, *Survey of Current Business,* July 1957.

sible for the changes. In general, among such factors there seem to be four principal ones (Fig. 4):

    1. income
    2. population
    3. assets
    4. credit

Income. The tremendous rise in the level of consumer incomes alone would have been sufficient to bring about pronounced changes in consumer spending. This rise has been reinforced by the decline in the concentration of incomes. There has been in particular an increase in the proportion of middle-income families brought about by the needs of a full-employment economy. Higher wages, especially for unskilled labor, serve to increase the earnings of those already employed and, at the same time, induce more family members to enter the labor force.

These developments have produced a more equal distribution of incomes. Thus, in 1935-36

the 10 per cent of families with the highest incomes accounted for 36 per cent of total family income in that year, whereas in 1956, according to the *Life* data, the same highest 10 per cent of families accounted for only 24 per cent of total incomes. More families were above what would be defined as a subsistence income in 1956 too—about 44 per cent in 1956 as against 24 per cent in 1935-36 (taking $4,500 and $1,750 as the corresponding respective subsistence levels). The result has been not only higher levels of spending but the creation of mass markets for goods previously in the luxury category.

Population. That more people need more goods is axiomatic. However, when characteristics of the population that are closely related to spending patterns change markedly, shifts in consumer markets are an almost inevitable consequence. The changes in the present instance are indeed pronounced. During the past two decades, our population has become more edu-

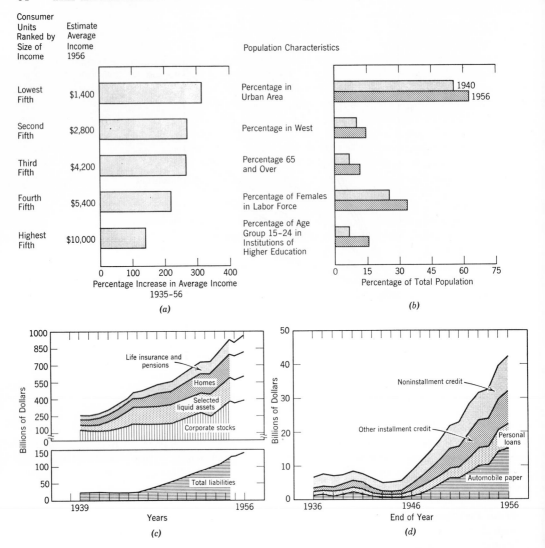

FIG. 4.   Contributing to the changing consumer market have been: (a) rising family incomes, particularly at the lower income levels, (b) a changing population structure, (c) a tremendous increase in financial assets, while liabilities rose much more slowly, and (d) a concomitant expansion of consumer credit, particularly for auto purchases. *Source*: Computed from various issues of U. S. Department of Commerce, *Survey of Current Business* and supplements; U. S. Department of Labor, Bureau of Labor Statistics, *Monthly Labor Review*; and Board of Governors of the Federal Reserve System, *Federal Reserve Bulletin*.

cated; more white collar and professional in class; more suburban; older, yet, paradoxically, with more children and larger families.

These changes, interacting with the growth and redistribution of incomes, have led to a growing sophistication in tastes and preferences (or at least so people like to believe), as well as to substantial expansion in markets for various products. The current boom in hi-fi sets, in foreign foods, in sports cars, in white shirts

(as against colored shirts), and in wines and brandies is largely a manifestation of these changes. When a family moves into a different income or population group, its spending patterns invariably tend to conform to those of the new group, albeit with some lag.

The growth of suburban living has led especially to pronounced shifts in consumer purchases; producing, among other things, a booming market for home improvement and do-it-yourself materials, a not unrelated surging market for bandages and medical supplies, and a fertile new field for novelists in search of material.

Assets. When a person has money in the bank, he is more likely to spend liberally out of current income than when his pocket is holding his last dollar. If, in addition, his holdings have risen well above customary levels because of a scarcity of goods and pressure to accumulate government bonds, he is likely to spend very well indeed once the emergency lets up; and this is what appears to have happened in the postwar years.

The high proportion of aggregate consumption expenditures to personal disposable income during this period—nearly 94 per cent—would hardly have been reached had most consumers not had a cushion to fall back on in case of sudden reversals. This cushion not only has been a comfortable one but, what may not be widely realized, has been increasing throughout the postwar period. Thus, savings (time) deposits of individuals rose from $232 per capita at the end of 1936 to $771 per capita in 1946 and then further still to $1,077 per capita at the end of 1956. At the same time, there is some evidence that liquid asset holdings (savings and checking accounts and U.S. government bonds) have become more concentrated during the past decade. Ten per cent of American households were reported to have $5,000 or more of liquid assets in early 1956 as against 6 per cent in 1946. At the same time, the proportion of households without any assets rose slightly, to one-fourth of the total.

Credit. To a large extent, the expansion of consumer credit can be alleged to be an outgrowth of these other changes. After all, really poor people are not able to borrow! The most frequent users of credit in recent years have been households in the middle-income brackets, earning between $4,000 and $7,000 per year. Many of these households have liquid assets as well but prefer to borrow anyway, treating repayment of the loan as a form of disciplined saving. The cost of this borrowing seems to be of little consequence to the consumer as long as his income is sufficient to cover the payments.

On the whole, there is little doubt that credit expansion has served as a major stimulus to consumer spending, bringing about many purchases which would not otherwise have been made—especially of cars, homes, and other durable goods. In effect, this credit expansion can be interpreted as a reflection of the growing importance of capital goods in family living, spurred in part by the sharp decline in the availability of competent household help at reasonable prices. As in business operations, outright purchase of consumer capital goods is often too costly. The consumer therefore follows the alternative of purchasing these goods on credit, thereby obtaining for himself the services and pleasures provided by these capital goods well before the time he can actually afford to own them. Whether one likes it or not, paying in the future for present enjoyment is becoming an increasingly popular way of life.

Other Factors. Diverse price movements could to some extent be labeled a fifth factor accounting for the present structure of our consumer market. It is not so considered here because during a period of rapidly rising incomes such as have characterized the last two decades, price considerations become of secondary importance in most purchase decisions. There have been notable exceptions, however, when the price of a product went completely out of line with that of competing products. This invariably has had disastrous results—as in the case of butter.

Many other factors have also contributed in one way or another to the present state of our consumer market. Most notable of these is perhaps technology, which has spurred demand for new or improved products, often at the expense of other, more prosaic products. Advertising, changing styles, and mass communications (especially the homogenizing influence of mass media) have also contributed in one way or another. Competitive pressures for mass production and standardization are also not to be ignored. Indeed, some maintain that these are the principal factors impelling consumers to "be alike and live alike."

A TELESCOPIC VIEW

The present consumer market can be eulogized in terms of a tremendous variety of adjectives. It is bigger, better, broader than at any time in our history. There are more different goods and services for sale, more of most items available, more people and more money bidding for the goods—and, of course, more advertising exhorting us to buy still more goods.

Huge as this present market may be, all indications are that it will be dwarfed by consumer markets of the future. Estimates of the size of these markets can be obtained by extrapolating past aggregate growth trends, a favorite parlor exercise of business analysts. Such an approach may yield a rough idea of the general size of these markets, but it tells us little about their characteristics—how expenditures will be distributed among different types of consumers, how expenditure patterns will be adjusted to different economic circumstances, how competition will affect expenditure patterns, and many other questions. These questions can only be answered by studying current expenditure patterns of a cross section of the population and using this as a springboard for insights into the future. Such data, if current enough, can also throw considerable light on the structure of the present consumer market and thereby serve as a basis for gauging short-run market potentials, guiding the use of promotional efforts, constructing more effective sales territories, and determining investment plans.

In a rapidly moving economy such as ours, expenditure patterns can change substantially within a few years, and it is therefore of particular importance to have data recent enough to yield an up-to-date cross section of the consumer market. It is in this sense that consumer expenditure studies, such as the recent *Life* survey, come in so handy. Changes in early postwar consumer expenditure patterns have already been pinpointed by the 1950 Consumer Expenditures Study of the U.S. Bureau of Labor Statistics and the University of Pennsylvania, and this new study indicates the extent to which further changes have taken place.

Diminishing Influence of Income. One of the striking characteristics of the present consumer market brought out by this study is its apparent homogeneity. This is true, on the whole, even with regard to income; for within a few percentage points, high-income households distribute their expenditures in much the same way as do low-income households. (See Table 2.) The only exception of any consequence is the tendency for the higher-income households to spend less on food and more on automobiles, homes, furnishings, and appliances.

The principal effect of income on the household budget seems to lie in determining how large a proportion goes for food; the allocation of the budget among other types of expenditures is determined by the homogenizing influence of mass tastes and preferences, modified by specific social and demographic factors affecting particular households.

Of course, this is a very general tendency, and numerous exceptions will be found when data for individual households are examined. In addition, we have to consider that although households in different economic and social circumstances may allocate their expenditures among different categories in the same manner, this does not mean that the same products are bought. Not only may altogether different products be bought, for example, steak and lobster as against hamburger and smelt, but the quality of product may differ substantially. The high-income family may purchase a Cadillac or an Imperial while the low-income family goes in for a Ford or a Studebaker. It may well be these quality differentials that constitute the main difference between household expenditures at different levels of income; for preliminary examination of the distribution of household budgets among individual products shows, on the whole, surprisingly small differences.

Further evidence of the declining role of income is provided by the large number of expenditures that seem to be relatively insensitive, or *inelastic*, to income changes. As incomes move up, manufacturers and distributors of goods possessing high income elasticities are in a favored position, since a given rise in income produces proportionately more outlays on these goods than on others. This approach has also provided a basis for sales forecasting and gauging market potentials, by estimating the income elasticity of demand for a good from consumer expenditure surveys and then applying it to alternative projections of future income levels and distributions.

In 1956, however, only a few of the 65 groups of goods and services used in the *Life* study exhibited elastic demand:

TABLE 1. Categories with Elastic Demand

Between Low (0-$2,000) and Middle ($4-5,000) Income Levels	Between Middle and High ($7,000 up) Income Levels
Miscellaneous home improvements	Wines, brandies, liquors
Small appliances	Miscellaneous home improvements
Furniture	Floor coverings
Automobiles	Photographic equipment
Photographic equipment	Sport goods
Games and toys	
Sport goods	

If finer classifications were used and individual products treated separately, this list would become many times longer. It is nevertheless apparent from the above and from what has been said before (Fig. 3) that the importance of income, although still great, is diminishing and will continue to do so as incomes rise further.

This is not to say that income effects can be ignored. Clearly, without income there could be no purchases, and even at present levels of income, substantial variations in purchases exist among different income levels. This is particularly true when quality considerations are taken into account. Then, too, income effects interact at times with other characteristics, so that the direction of change in consumer expenditures shifts as the level of income is varied. Thus, expenditures for infants' clothing are higher among low- and middle-income families whose heads have more education, but the reverse is true among high-income families.

Concentration of Markets. The present-day consumer market is highly concentrated. This has been brought about on the one hand by the steady migration of the population to urban centers, particularly to metropolitan areas and their environs, and, on the other hand, to the not unrelated fact that incomes are highest in these areas. Nearly six out of every ten American households resided in metropolitan areas in 1956. These families earned on the average over $5,000 apiece in that year (in the suburbs of the large cities nearly $6,000), while household incomes in other parts of the country were averaging not much over $4,000.

This huge metropolitan market of nearly 30 million households accounted for two-thirds of the total purchases of goods and services by American households in 1956. More than three-fourths of household expenditures for beer, liquor, housing, and floor coverings took place in this area. As one would expect, there are substantial variations in the market shares of various goods and services between the central cities and the suburbs of metropolitan areas. Central city households accounted for disproportionately large shares (in relation to their number) of expenditures on liquor, women's and girls' clothing and footwear accessories and clothing care, housing, spectator fees, and writing equipment; while expenditures in the suburbs were disproportionately high for nearly all housing items, appliances, and house furnishings; as well as for liquor (those exurbanites

again!), automotive items, sporting goods, and pet foods—all reflecting the emphasis in the suburbs on comfortable living.

The consumer market is also highly concentrated in various other ways. Thus, households with children spent considerably more than other households, particularly on most food items (not to mention baby food!), clothes, decorating material, and writing equipment.

Concentration by income is also pronounced: The one-third of households with the highest incomes accounted for nearly half of the total household expenditures for goods and services. However, this percentage was actually greater when incomes were lower and more unequally distributed. Geographic concentration is a much more recent development.

Despite this concentration, the fact remains that the consumer market has become so large that even the smaller segments comprise substantial markets in themselves. A commodity that appealed to only 1 per cent of this market would still have a sales potential of half a million units, representing a population exceeding that of all but four of our cities. It is largely for this reason that markets for such specialty goods as custom-made furniture, motor scooters, and such canned "delicacies" as maggots and rattlesnakes have been able to do so well alongside the development of the homogenizing mass market.

Emergence of Other Forces. Occupation, education, family size, and other social forces have always influenced consumer expenditures to some extent. Now, however, with income gradually losing its traditional role as the principal, almost sole, determinant of the types of goods and services a household will buy, these social and demographic factors are assuming positions of new importance. Differences in expenditure patterns already appear to lie about as much between households of different social characteristics, different age levels, different educational attainments and sources of livelihood, and different geographical locations, as between households of different income levels.

Many of these differences become especially pronounced when comparisons are made of expenditure patterns of households possessing different social and demographic characteristics but at the same levels of income. Thus, whether a household is earning less than $3,000 a year or over $10,000 a year, we find that the one headed by a college graduate spends relatively less on food, clothing, and medical and personal care, but spends more on the home and on automotive expenses. (See Table 2.) Again irrespective of income, families headed by younger people spend proportionately less than older families on food and medical and personal care but spend more on clothing and automotive supplies.

Region and marketing location seem to exert special influences of their own on the allocation of household expenditures. Households in the Northeast devote more of their expenditures to food than households in the South or West. At the same time, as the size of the community increases, more of the household budget goes to food, shelter, education, and recreation expenses and less to automobile expenses. (See Table 2.)

Indicative of the growing importance of other factors is the diversity of changes in household expenditures between households at the same levels of income but with differing social and demographic characteristics. In fact, for some expenditure catagories, the relative variation in purchases is larger for one or more of these characteristics than it is for income; this is true of several food products, beer and ale, tobacco, some clothing items, laundry soaps, radio and TV, medical supplies, writing equipment, and building materials. Yet these are not the only relevant characteristics that influence consumer expenditures, and indeed for some of the products listed in the table, none of these may be the most *relevant* characteristic. Again, much more frequent and substantial variations can be expected when individual product purchases are considered.

THE CONSUMER IN THE BRIGHT NEW WORLD

There is little doubt that the consumer market of the future will, with occasional setbacks,

TABLE 2. Where the Money Goes

(Percentage of all expenditures in each category, by selected household characteristics)*

Expenditure Category	Income Only	
	Under $3,000	$10,000 and Over
Food and tobacco	35	24
Clothing	11	14
Home operation	18	18
Home furnishings and appliances	7	10
Medical and personal care	6	6
Automotive	12	15
Recreation and other	11	13
Average size of household	2.9	3.8

Expenditure Category	Income and Education			
	Under $3,000		$10,000 and Over	
	Not Through Grade School	College or Beyond	Not Through Grade School	College or Beyond
Food and tobacco	37	31	27	22
Clothing	12	9	20	13
Home operation	16	24	18	20
Home furnishings and appliances	7	7	8	11
Medical and personal care	6	5	13	5
Automotive	11	13	7	14
Recreation and other	11	11	7	15
Average size of household	2.9	2.5	4.2	3.8

Columns under each household characteristic total 100 per cent.
SOURCE: *Life Study of Consumer Expenditures,* copyright by *Time,* Inc.

	Income and Occupation			
Expenditure Category	Under $3,000		$10,000 and Over	
	Nonfarm Labor	Professional	Nonfarm Labor	Professional
Food and tobacco	36	30	27	24
Clothing	10	10	16	15
Home operation	17	28	23	13
Home furnishings and appliances	7	6	9	9
Medical and personal care	7	7	3	3
Automotive	13	10	11	13
Recreation and other	10	9	11	23
Average size of household	3.6	2.9	4.4	3.8

	Income and Age of Household Head					
Expenditure Category	Under $3,000			$10,000 and Over		
	Under 30	40-49	65 and Over	Under 30	40-49	65 and Over
Food and tobacco	32	35	34	22	23	29
Clothing	11	12	10	12	15	8
Home operation	19	16	19	22	18	17
Home furnishings and appliances	9	8	8	12	10	7
Medical and personal care	4	5	7	3	5	11
Automotive	15	13	10	17	14	8
Recreation and other	10	11	12	12	15	20
Average size of household	3.3	3.9	2.0	3.1	4.1	2.8

	Income and Life Cycle					
Expenditure Category	Under $3,000			$10,000 and Over		
	No Children; Head under 40	Children under 10	No Children; Married Head 40 and Over	No Children; Head under 40	Children under 10	No Children; Married Head 40 and Over
Food and tobacco	32	35	37	22	24	24
Clothing	9	10	9	12	14	13
Home operation	22	18	17	16	20	18
Home furnishings and appliances	8	8	8	9	10	10
Medical and personal care	5	6	6	3	5	8
Automotive	12	14	12	19	13	15
Recreation and other	12	9	11	19	14	12
Average size of household	1.8	4.8	2.2	2.3	4.9	2.6

TABLE **2.** (cont.)

Expenditure Category	Income and Region (Met. Areas Only)					
	Under $3,000			$10,000 and Over		
	Northeast	South	West	Northeast	South	West
Food and tobacco	38	31	32	29	24	24
Clothing	13	12	9	15	11	16
Home operation	20	20	22	16	22	18
Home furnishings and appliances	6	9	7	8	8	9
Medical and personal care	6	6	6	4	7	6
Automotive	7	9	13	15	15	12
Recreation and other	10	13	11	13	13	15
Average size of household	2.5	2.9	2.1	3.9	3.9	3.8

Expenditure Category	Income and Marketing Location					
	Under $3,000			$10,000 and Over		
	Met. Area, 500,000 or More Central City	Suburbs	Towns under 2,500	Met. Area, 500,000 or More Central City	Suburbs	Towns under 2,500
Food and tobacco	39	34	33	27	24	25
Clothing	10	9	10	12	11	14
Home operation	25	22	15	18	22	16
Home furnishings and appliances	5	7	8	9	13	9
Medical and personal care	5	7	6	3	5	5
Automotive	7	9	17	13	13	22
Recreation and other	9	12	11	18	12	9
Average size of household	2.4	2.6	3.4	3.8	4.0	3.9

be still bigger and more grandiose than anything yet seen. Rising incomes and standards of living will take care of that. The implications of these trends are many, but perhaps the principal ones are the following:

1. *Consumers are becoming increasingly able to act differently from each other, yet in practice they seem to act more like one another.*

This paradoxical behavior of the consumer may well be such as to give market analysts and psychologists alike a completely new set of frustrations. For as incomes rise and consumers obtain more leeway in allocating expenditures, the former emphasis on subsistence gradually fades into the background. Already, probably not much more than half of the average household income goes for subsistence expenditures, and this proportion will undoubtedly decline further. Thus, consumers will have at their command an ever increasing latitude in allocating expenditures, so that consumer budgets might be expected to differ increasingly from each other.

But what has been happening? Despite the growing potential for increasing heterogeneity between consumer budgets, the trend seems to be in the other direction. Consumer budgets on the whole are very similar to one another, even when comparisons are made by income levels; the main differences appear to lie in the qualities of the goods and services that are bought rather than in what is bought. Whether it is due to mass communications, to a pervading desire for conspicuous consumption, to pressures from manufacturers, or to some other forces, consumers appear to be becoming more homogeneous in an era when they are being endowed increasingly with the capacity to behave differently.

To be sure, individual exceptions are numerous, as is only to be expected in an economy containing 50 million households. Hardly ever are we likely to reach a stage when the behavior of all individual consumers conforms to the average. In the present situation, dispersion about the average is yet to be determined, but indications are that the same tendency toward uniformity will be found to exist.

2. *New concepts of market analysis are needed.*

The growing impact on consumer expenditures of a host of factors other than income means that the past practice of predicting sales by deriving a simple relationship between income and expenditures will yield increasingly inferior results as time goes on. Accurate forecasts will entail the use of methods that take into account the effects on expenditures of a number of different factors simultaneously. This is not the place to go into such methodological issues, but it might be mentioned that some "multivariate" techniques already exist for handling such problems and other techniques are in developmental stages.

3. *The role of the consumer as a purely passive agent in business fluctuations is a relic of the past.*

With incomes well above subsistence levels and with enormous reserves of unneeded spending power in the form of durable assets and unused credit, consumers are much more free to spend as they please. Concomitantly, consumer expenditures are less likely than before to vary with moderate fluctuations in income. A substantial portion of the national income is brought about by sales at the consumer level. If incomes in other sectors of the economy dip but consumers keep on spending, the net effect can be a considerable boost to these other sectors and renewed prosperity. Postwar experience, particularly in 1949 and 1954, has demonstrated conclusively how effectively consumer spending can support the economy and mitigate the effects of recessions.

To be sure, consumer spending can work the other way, and precipitate a recession when one might not otherwise have occurred. Then, again, consumer spending may at times assume a passive role while more traditional forces, such as business investment or government spending, call the turn. The point is that the consumer has become, with these other forces, a potential catalyst in business fluctuations. His influence cannot be ignored. Whether he will choose to take the initiative at a particular time may well be the $64 billion question of the future!

14. Economic Psychology

GEORGE KATONA

In 1923, the year of the great inflation in Germany, when the price of a loaf of bread rose to 214,000 million marks and one could make a living by buying cigarettes in a retail store in the morning and selling them in the evening, I was a young psychologist engaged in experiments on visual perception at à university. Like many of my colleagues, I had to leave my work and get a job in a bank, where we were paid daily at noon so that we could spend the money right away. I also began to read economics to try to find out what was going on.

I read that inflation is the result of an increase in the money supply—of more purchasing power competing for the available goods. Observing that hardly anybody had ready cash, and finding out from statistical tables that the German note circulation was exceedingly small when expressed in real purchasing power, I wondered. Then I discovered in the literature a second vicious character, called "velocity of circulation," which joined forces with the major culprit, the "quantity of money." But naming the phenomenon did not seem to explain it. I pondered whether the explanation should not have been looked for in the psychological factors that induced the German people to get rid of their money as fast as they received it, rather than in the high rate of turnover itself.

During the mild inflation in the U. S. that followed the outbreak of the Korean War in 1950, I was again impressed by the disagreement between actual events and what I had

‡‡ SOURCE: Reprinted by permission. Copyright © 1954, by *Scientific American, Inc.* All rights reserved. Vol. 191, No. 4, October 1954, pp. 31–35.

read in economic textbooks. Prices rose rapidly before there was any appreciable increase in Government spending or money supply. But when, in the spring of 1951, rearmament expenditures really got under way, prices stopped rising. U. S. families ceased their rush buying and began to hold on to their money.

It seemed that here again, as in Germany in 1923, the answer must lie in psychology; the people's economic behavior appeared to be governed more by their expectation of what was going to happen than by the situation of the moment. And so in 1950–1951 at the Survey Research Center of the University of Michigan we undertook to examine the developments with a new approach, that of economic psychology. There were available then, as there had not been in 1923, conceptual tools and measuring sticks, such as sample interviewing, for investigating changes in mass behavior.

Let us consider first the theoretical background of economic psychology. In traditional economics the term "economic behavior" has been used in three different ways. In one sense it has purported to explain the behavior of businessmen and consumers in terms of a norm: how rational men should seek a maximization of profits or of utility, on the assumption that they have full knowledge of and control over all means of achieving the postulated economic end. In a second sense economic behavior has been used to mean the behavior of prices, of incomes and of the economy of a nation. Economists with this outlook have been concerned with the relationships that exist between changes in supply, prices, incomes, consumption, saving and investment.

These two approaches have been of great value. But they disregard the fact that it is human beings who supply the goods, make prices, strive for incomes, spend, save and invest money. They leave out of the equation human needs and desires, hopes and fears, opinions, prejudices and misinformation.

Traditional economics has, to be sure, done some exploration of economic behavior in the third sense of the term—the behavior of businessmen and consumers as people. It has made case studies of business behavior, statistical studies of business cycles and theoretical studies of mass behavior. But the information obtained was of a general nature. It was known, for instance, how national income changed from one year to the next, but it was not known how many families had an increase and how many a decrease in income, what kinds of families these were or how they reacted to their income development. Nor were there any data on changes in attitudes and expectations, the frequency of such changes or their causes and effects.

In recent years the development of the sample interview survey has made it possible to investigate these matters. Economic psychology maintains that businessmen and consumers are not marionettes pushed around by the law of supply and demand; they have some discretion and latitude, within limits. We shall illustrate both the latitude of the actors on the economic scene and its limits with reference to consumer behavior. We select the consumer because the influence of his psychology on employment and business conditions has not been generally recognized.

In our studies of consumer behavior we distinguish five sets of variables. First there are the *enabling conditions* that set the limits to the consumer's discretion: his income, assets and access to credit. Second, his economic behavior is influenced by *precipitating circumstances*: an increase or decrease in purchasing power, a change in family status, the birth of a child, a move to a new house or locality, the wearing out or breakdown of possessions, and so on. Third, there is the important factor of *habit*: the set patterns of behavior that operate, for instance, in such matters as the purchase of groceries. Fourth, we have to take into account *contractual obligations*: for example, rent, repayment of debt, life insurance premiums, taxes, dues and the like. Previous actions, such as the purchase of an automobile on installments, make both for contractual obligations

(repayment of debt) and for consequent actions (purchase of gasoline). Finally, we must deal with the consumer's *psychological state*. Whether a rise in income, a transfer to a new locality, the breakdown of an old refrigerator or any other event will result in important changes in spending depends on the prevailing motives and attitude. If the attitude is conducive to spending, one kind of decision will be made; if it is not, another decision.

How does all this affect the economy as a whole? Can the actions of individuals, influenced by these variables, produce a general economic trend? Sometimes it has been assumed that the attitudes of different people, their optimism and pessimism, for instance, should cancel out. Our studies, however, show that trends do appear. As a result of group identification and mass communication, similar changes in attitudes often occur among very many people at about the same time. This proposition serves as the starting point for quantitative studies of the origin of changes in attitudes and their influence on economic fluctuations.

The power of consumers to influence economic fluctuations will not be the same in different economies. In a subsistence economy, in which the entire income of most consumers is devoted to the acquisition of minimum necessities, the consumer and his attitudes may perhaps be disregarded. But today in the U. S. we find substantial discretionary income in the possession of broad groups of people, and also widespread ownership of liquid assets and easy access to credit. Moreover, the things that people consider necessities now include numerous durable goods (automobiles, television sets) the purchase of which can be postponed or advanced. Therefore economic psychology is particularly important in this country at this time.

The sample interview survey offers a bridge between individual attitudes and aggregate behavior, as measured by national statistics on income, spending, saving and so on. Individuals are interviewed, and for each individual respondent who falls in the sample three kinds of measures are obtained: (1) demographic data, such as occupation, education, age, marital status and the like; (2) economic data, such as income, expenditures, assets and debts; (3) psychological data, such as motives, expectations and intentions. From representative samples it is possible to determine the frequency of each type of measure at successive time points; for instance, we may find that one year

25 per cent and the next year 30 per cent of U. S. families had annual incomes over $5,000; or that one year 20 per cent expected their incomes to go up and the next year 30 per cent. We can also measure functional relations between different variables. We may find, for instance, that of those who say they feel better off, 50 per cent buy durable goods in a given year, while of those who say they feel worse off, only 25 per cent buy such goods. By repeating such measurements under different circumstances the sample interview survey may serve to test hypotheses.

What insights were obtained from such surveys in 1950–1951? They disclosed dramatic shifts in attitudes which were connected with the shifting fortunes of the Korean War. When military reversals came in the summer of 1950 and again a few months later after the intervention of the Chinese Communists, many people feared that World War III was imminent. Fear of war evoked not-too-distant memories of shortages of goods and of rapid and substantial price increases. The buying sprees of consumers in 1950 occurred in two waves, coinciding with the two periods of adverse military news.

Early in 1951 the situation changed completely. When the military front in Korea was stabilized, the expectation of World War III gave way to the notion that we were living in a period of cold war. Acute fear gave way to uneasy anxiety. The expectation of shortages disappeared; people learned that the U. S. economy could supply both butter and guns (for a cold war). By the summer of 1951 many experts spoke of a buying lull and attributed it to saturation due to previous extensive purchases. But it appeared to us who studied people's opinions and feelings that this was not an adequate description of the developments. "Lull," says Webster, means "temporary cessation," but there was nothing temporary in people's attitudes. We found that in many cases money was not lacking, and on the whole needs and desires for new and better things were expressed as frequently as before. But "this is not a good time to buy" was a frequent comment. The business outlook did not appear favorable; people complained of high taxes and high prices. Many decided to postpone the purchase of automobiles, television sets and furniture. The prevailing attitudes resulted in a low rate of spending and a correspondingly high rate of saving during 1951 and most of 1952. It is not money in the possession of consumers that moves goods off the shelves; it is people who decide to spend their money. In order to predict the trend of consumers' spending, it is necessary to obtain data both on the resources of consumers and on the motives that tend to encourage or discourage the spending of money.

What generalizations can we draw from the recent research in economic psychology?

The economic theory of Lord Keynes, which has dominated the thinking of economists in recent decades, put great stress on the effects of changes in income on spending and saving. We have found that in a period of good business, those who suffer declines in income reduce their rate of saving so as to maintain their accustomed standard of living, as the Keynes theory predicts, provided they expect the decline to be temporary and have liquid assets. On the other hand, with an increase in income, spending often rises faster than the income if the economic trend is upward. That is to say, an increase in income often leads people to reduce saving, contrary to the Keynes theory. If an economist were asked which of three groups borrows most—people with rising income, stable income or declining income—he would probably answer: those with declining income. Actually in the years 1947–1950 the answer was: people with rising income. People with declining income were next and those with stable income borrowed least. People's readiness to step up their level of living in response to their feeling that their situation has improved contributes to the dynamic nature of American society. Similar investigations carried out in Great Britain at the same time yielded different results, more in accord with traditional assumptions about saving and spending.

Another traditional assumption is that if people expect prices to go up, and have money, they will hasten to buy; if they expect prices to go down, they will postpone buying. But our surveys showed that this is not always true. Often the expectation of price increases does not stimulate buying. One typical attitude was expressed by the wife of a mechanic in an interview at a time of rising prices. "In a few months," she said, "we'll have to pay still more for meat and milk; we'll have less to spend on other things." Her family had been planning to buy a new car, but they postponed this purchase. Furthermore, the rise in prices that has already taken place may be resented and evoke buyers' resistance. For example, there is this typical comment of a teacher in 1951: "I just don't pay these prices, they are too high. Prices will go up still more. Nobody will be able to buy anything." As we have seen, expectations of war, shortages and very large price increases may result in different behavior.

The effect of price reductions varies. If people believe them to be the beginning of a downward trend, buying may freeze up. If they feel that they are being offered a bargain which will last only a short time, they hurry to buy.

The condition most conducive to spending appears to be price stability. If prices have been stable and people have become accustomed to consider them "right" and expect them to remain stable, they are likely to buy. Thus it appears that the common business policy of maintaining stable prices with occasional sales or discounts is based on a correct understanding of consumer psychology.

Finally, consumers' spending is influenced by the general economic outlook as well as by their personal circumstances and the immediate price picture. Even though a family head does not expect a cut in his own income, if he fears a general recession he may say no to the family demand that he trade in the old television set for a new one with a 21-inch screen. It appears that many people feel vaguely that their own income is an insensitive indicator; that sooner or later economic trends prevailing in the country will affect them personally. Group influences, experiences shared with neighbors and friends, also shape people's attitudes. Most United States families have an abundance of unsatisfied needs. (The rich are no exception.) Under what conditions are needs most likely to be transformed into effective demand? When people are confident about the future of the economy. They are most likely to postpone such satisfactions when they feel uneasy about the future course of the economy.

The notion of "saturation" of the market is based on old-fashioned psychological assumptions which in turn rest on the analogy of biological drives: for example, if an animal is hungry, it is motivated to search for food; after it has eaten, the motive disappears or becomes weak. The saturation concept has resulted in dire predictions about the future of the U. S. economy. Some people point to the large proportion of U. S. families that already possesses major goods, such as refrigerators (over 80 per cent) or automobiles (about 70 per cent), and they argue that in the future sales will be limited largely to replacement needs.

But social motives are different from biological ones. Levels of aspiration—in sports, for school grades, for position, for income and for goods—most commonly rise with achievement. A beginner in golf, for instance, may strive hard to achieve a score of 100; when he has achieved his goal, he invariably raises his sights. We give up aspirations when we have failed, not when we have succeeded.

In the economic field, a family that has saved enough to buy a home usually sets out on a new objective, such as college education for the children; fulfillment of one aim leads to striving for another. Indeed, in a recent survey it was found that this applied to goods already owned; families with a refrigerator in good operating condition often were preparing to buy a larger one, or one with shelves on the door and a better freezing compartment.

We translate our needs into demand when we are optimistic, confident and secure. We are "saturated," on the other hand, when we are pessimistic, insecure and especially when our past endeavors have been unsuccessful.

America is prosperous. Prosperity means that many more people than ever before own houses, automobiles, refrigerators, TV sets and the like. Is prosperity its own gravedigger; must a few years of high rates of purchasing inevitably be followed by saturation and slump? The answer is no: it is not automatic or inevitable that prosperity be followed by depression or that cyclical movements occur. This, of course, does not mean that we already know how to avoid depressions. But an understanding of what motivates people, and of how motives change, should contribute to this goal.

The few generalizations derived from recent surveys of consumer attitudes and expenditures represent a promising beginning. As yet we know far too little about the origin of mass attitudes, their spread among people and the effects of different attitudes on action. But what we do know is that economic psychology may usefully supplement the theoretical and statistical approach of traditional economics. It contributes to the understanding and prediction of economic fluctuations, and thereby promises to provide policy makers with better tools which they may use to combat the recurrence of periodic depressions and inflations. It should also contribute toward the attainment of the ultimate goal of the behavioral sciences—the development of a theory of social action.

15. *The Significance of Fashion*

PAUL H. NYSTROM

The general interest in fashion has increased enormously during recent years. This interest, formerly believed to have been the result of rising incomes and standards of living, is apparently unaffected by business adversity. It continued as strong after 1929 as before. It will undoubtedly continue to grow in years to come.

THE IMPORTANCE OF FASHION IN MODERN BUSINESS

Fashion, once the pursuit of the wealthy and aristocratic few, is now followed by the masses. In the past fashion was considered solely as a quality of goods at the highest price. It is now a necessary factor of goods at every price. It is as essential to the merchandise in a 5 and 10 cent store as to the wares of the most exclusive specialty shop. Excellence of material and the highest quality of workmanship mean little in present-day demand unless also clearly marked with current fashion.

Fashion is one of the greatest forces in present-day life. It determines both the character and the direction of consumption. Fashion makes men shave every day, grow moustaches, cut their hair in certain ways, wear certain colors in hats, clothing and shoes, certain shapes in collars, four-in-hand neckties, trousers creased, and low shoes all the year round. For women it changes the tint of the face powder, the odor of the perfume, the wave of the hair,

‡‡ SOURCE: Reprinted by permission from *Fashion Merchandising* by Paul H. Nystrom (New York: The Ronald Press Company, 1932), pp. 31–39.

the position of the waist line, the length of the skirt, the color of the clothes, and the height of the heels. Fashion sometimes makes people wear more clothes and sometimes less. Fashion is a more important factor than wear and tear in displacing furniture, kitchen utensils, radio instruments, and automobiles. Fashion causes all of these changes and, at the same time, makes people like it. To be out of fashion is, indeed, to be out of the world.

Business succeeds when it goes with fashion but fails when it goes against the tide. Millions of dollars are wasted yearly by manufacturers and retailers who try to stem the trends of fashion by offering goods that are not in fashion and have not the slightest chance of becoming the fashion. Even during the depths of business depressions, goods that are in fashion are in demand. The only goods that sell during such periods, as we have recently seen, are the goods that are decidedly in fashion. When the purchasing power declines, the desire to secure the utmost of good fashion follows prices downward. Goods that are not in fashion cannot be sold in either good or bad times. Indeed, such goods cannot be given away.

Fashion is the result of powerful forces in human nature. Foolish and shallow-minded people have laughed at fashion but the wiser ones have tried to find explanations and to understand. The influence of fashion over all of us is such as to make certain designs in goods of common use seem beautiful at one time and hideous at others. It is hard to believe now that the hoop skirt, the bustle, and the leg-of-mutton sleeve were once considered very charming and highly appropriate. No doubt the present fashions will in time seem just as ridiculous and even as hideous as these past styles seem to us now.

The subject of fashion is therefore of utmost importance, not only from the standpoint of the consumer who follows it, not only from the standpoint of designers and business organizations that cater to it, but also from the standpoint of the student of human nature.

DEFINITIONS

The first step to clear thinking about any subject is clear definition of the terms used. There is an unusually special need for such definition when dealing with the subject of fashion, for fashion, style, and design are terms that are constantly confused by most people. There is a world of difference in meaning among these three terms, but even the dictionaries have not, so far, made adequate distinctions. Our first step in the understanding of fashion and how it works will be taken by distinguishing between it and style.

A Style is a Characteristic or Distinctive, Artistic Expression or Presentation. A style is a fact of art. Thus we have styles of architecture, of sculpture, of painting, of literature, of drama, or of music. Similarly we have characteristic or distinctive conceptions, that is, styles, in the applied arts such as· in textiles, in dress, in interior decoration, and in advertising. There are styles in millinery and in automobiles, in dancing and in playing golf. There are styles in conversation, in gesturing, in pronunciation, and in penmanship.

A Fashion, on the Other Hand, is a Style Accepted and Used by People. A fashion is always based on some particular style. But not every style is a fashion. A fashion is a fact of social psychology. A style is a creation of an artist or a designer. A fashion is a result of social emulation and esthetic imitation. A style may be new or old. It may be beautiful or ugly. It may be good or bad. A style is still a style even if it never receives the slightest acceptance or even approval. A style does not become a fashion until it gains some popular use, and it remains a fashion only so long as it is so accepted.

A Design is a Particular or Individual Interpretation or Version of a Style. A style may be expressed in a great many designs, all different, yet all related because they are in the same style.

It is clearly possible, then, for a style to be-

come a fashion repeatedly. Thus every important historic style such as the Greek, the Roman, the Renaissance, the Louis XV, or the Empire, has at one time or another been a fashion. There are in every field of both pure and applied art countless possible styles. There are large textbooks and enormous encyclopaedias describing the styles in such limited fields as interior decoration, furniture, architecture, and dress. Every library and museum is a repository of the records of styles.

Obviously, you and I as consumers, and the business people who supply us, must of necessity be interested in fashions rather than in styles. As consumers we confine most of our purchases to goods that approximate current fashions. Not to do so would brand us as being queer, and social interrelationships are today so interlaced that not only our friendships but our very jobs depend upon our being and looking normal and not queer. Yet we preserve our individuality because that invaluable quality of good taste helps us at every stage to bridge what is in fashion with what is individually beautiful and becoming.

Let us try to define two or three other terms in common use related to the subject of fashion. One of these is mode and another is vogue. These words, *mode and vogue, are synonyms of fashion.* Both imply a wave-like social acceptance of some manner of action, some design or style. *A fad is a miniature fashion* usually running for a shorter time and usually applying to some unimportant matter or detail in style of apparel, home furnishings, or other articles of use in which the quality of art is present and important.

From henceforth let us think of styles as products of art and of fashions as social acceptances of styles. This distinction will help us tremendously in understanding what fashion really is and how it works. We shall be able to see at once that current fashions are styles that for the time being have obtained public acceptance. We shall also see that there are at any given time but a few fashions. Finally, we will be able to agree that these fashions are constantly changing.

CHARACTER OF FASHION MOVEMENTS

In this constant change of fashions, however, there is a definite orderliness of rise, of culmination and decline, a wave-like movement so regular, in fact, that it may be readily traced and even predicted with a fair degree of accuracy. There are already a few successful business concerns, those who have learned to distinguish between style as such and fashion, who are concentrating all of their efforts on fashions, who are able to forecast the coming fashions in their lines of business with marked success and with great profit to themselves as well as satisfaction to their customers.

DIFFICULTY OF CHANGING OR INFLUENCING THE DIRECTION OF FASHIONS

It was formerly believed, and the view is still common, that any style, if launched with enough prestige and promoted intensively by advertising and display, could be made a successful fashion. There is no business fallacy which has wasted so much energy and money as this one. We now know that while styles may be created by the thousands, the final acceptance which determines the fashion rests with the consumer who has in recent years shown remarkably strong tendencies to follow certain fashion trends rather than others and to resist all prestige sales promotion, no matter how forcefully applied, to trends in other directions. If there were any kings or dictators of fashion in the past, there are certainly not any that are making a success of it today, except those who are able to forecast what consumers are going to want and then give it to them.

Success in design or style creation today requires a great deal more than merely artistic ability and the prestige of great names. Style creation, to stand any chance of fashion acceptance, must not only offer beautiful designs but must also mold its designs to a proper expression of the spirit of the times. A keen and sensitive appreciation of this spirit is a necessary foundation for fashion merchandising. The style that is most likely to become a fashion is one that expresses what the people most desire, that touches the sympathies and moves the imaginations of the public. To do this the style must be timely or modern as well as artistic.

There is undoubtedly a great deal of current dissatisfaction with the artistic qualities of goods now on our markets. Much of this dissatisfaction is largely due to a lack of clear comprehension on the part of designers and dealers of the importance and power of current trends in consumer taste. In other words, a great many artists as well as those who make and sell their creations are failing to meet the requirements of current fashion. They still apparently have the faith that a fashion can be made out of any style.

WIDESPREAD MODERN INTEREST IN FASHION

There is a fundamental reason for the widespread consumer interest in fashion. It may be explained by reference to the part it plays in your and in my life. We are all members of society. We all participate in greater or less degrees in the material and artistic advantages provided by this age. We not only participate but we must also cooperate or at least go along with the major movements of our time. Our surroundings, our equipment, and our furnishings in some measure represent our contacts with the artistic conceptions and the tempo of our age. Since fashion is essentially the current, artistic expression of this spirit, we accept it just as we accept the automobile, the airplane, and the radio for their utilities. Fashion is the social, esthetic representation of present life. Fashion is the expression of mass taste, just as law and its administration is the expression of the mass desire for order.

FASHION AND INDIVIDUALITY

This does not mean that people must or do slavishly accept specific current designs and styles, either in apparel, home furnishings, or in domestic architecture, without exception or without modification. Even a deep interest in fashion does not, of course, exclude the expression of individuality or the opportunity for the development of individual taste. Indeed, the very essence of the philosophy underlying modern fashion movements is the scope that it gives to individuality. There is nothing so tiresome to modern taste as the unimaginative, literal, mass use of certain styles under any or all circumstances by enormous numbers of people.

There is, indeed, both the need and the opportunity for the development of individuality within the more or less generalized but constantly changing molds set by fashion. In every item of merchandise affected by style there are elements that must of necessity conform to current standards of good taste, and that means fashion. But there are likewise the individual artistic adaptations which, while they do not carry the user beyond the parallels of fashion, produce the ever-changing interest that is individuality.

BUSINESS EXECUTIVES WHO NEED TO KNOW HOW TO WORK WITH FASHION

It is for these reasons that a correct understanding of fashion and how to work with it is obviously of importance to every business owner, executive, and employee who has any constructive activity to carry on in the production or marketing of fashion goods. The artist or designer who combines beauty and individuality with current fashions in the creation of styles also needs the facts concerning fashions and their trends. In this group may be mentioned the factory manager who executes the designs in such detail as to convey the precise feeling of the fashions; the salesman of the firm who must be able to discuss the fashionableness as well as other qualities of their merchandise in intelligent terms; the retail store buyer who wants to be assured that the stock purchased and carried in his store shall be what his customers will want; and, finally, the salespeople of the store, who should have at least a rudimentary acquaintance with the nature of fashion and the way it works.

Every one who sells fashion goods needs to be able to describe the fashion features of his or her goods accurately. Every salesperson should be properly equipped with the current vocabulary of style and fashion terms. Every salesperson needs sufficient knowledge of present fashions to be able to make his or her statements about the goods to customers with confidence and authority. It would also be helpful if salespeople had sufficient knowledge of the technique of observing fashion changes so as to make satisfactory observations and reports to their employers and store heads on precisely what styles their customers seem most interested in and thereby help to carry on the store's necessary fashion analysis.

The advertising manager, his assistants, the copywriters and those who make the illustrations for use in advertising, as well as the display men who prepare window and interior store displays, need continuously authoritative information on present fashions and their trends. Nothing could be more harmful either to a manufacturing or to a retail organization than advertising or display which presents inaccurate information on current fashions. Errors made by advertising writers in such a simple matter as the names of specific styles are laughable to a sophisticated outside world and pathetic to business. In a recent advertisement of a well-known department store a chair was described as "Queen Anne," but the illustration accompanying clearly showed "Chippendale" characteristics. A lady called at a metropolitan store and asked for a Queen Anne mirror. The salesman replied, "Queen Anne is a leg, not a mirror!"

Statements purporting to be true as to current fashions when not in accord with actual facts are, of course, as dishonest as misstatements in the descriptions of other qualities of the goods. Most progressive, reputable business concerns have long held to the principle that a fabric made of a mixture of wool and cotton may not be described as "all wool," but must be described as a mixture and preferably in exact percentages of each kind of fibre. Similarly, all reputable businesses now insist that advertising statements should accurately state whether colors are fast or not, and, if possible, what degree of fastness may be expected. Any departures from this principle of truth in statement as applied to such points as materials, construction, or fastness of dye would not now be countenanced for a moment, but many concerns otherwise proud of their integrity frequently permit statements that articles of style are leading fashions when they are not, and in some cases have not the slightest chance of ever becoming fashions.

Accuracy of statement as applied to fashions is as necessary to modern business as accuracy in other respects and will come when it is recognized that there is not only no excuse for misstatement but great harm in such dishonesty. Fashion is, as we shall see, objective. There need be no guesswork as to what is in fashion. Consumers who are fooled by retailers' or manufacturers' statements are as likely to resent this as any dishonesty in statement about materials of construction.

D. The Legal Framework

16. How Much Control Can Business Endure?

EARL W. KINTNER

Explosive things are capable of producing great good and great evil. Thus, TNT can be used to erect a dam or destroy a city. So it is with concepts; and of all concepts, none is more explosive than that of power.

In fact, all man-made holocausts that humanity has endured have been caused by disputes over the allocation of power. Whenever two human beings associate, one question inevitably arises: Who shall exercise the power of decision? The omnipresence of this struggle is felt in the family, the work group, the tribe, the municipality, the nation, and the world.

The question is basic. Think for a moment of how many forms the elemental query takes: democracy or totalitarianism, centralism or localism, the individual or the state, parent or child, teacher or pupil, union or management. All human relationships and all the adjustments that they imply involve, at bottom, the problem of the proper allocation of power.

No man can stand above the agonizing struggle to answer the basic question that every society—using that word in its most fundamental sense—must resolve. Probably the vast majority of human relationships have been organized on a totalitarian basis. In this connection, note that we call our government and way of life the "American Experiment." Our permissive, plural, decentralized way of life was a very new thing only a minute ago in the history of mankind.

⁑ SOURCE: Reprinted by permission from the *Journal of Marketing* (National Quarterly Publication of the American Marketing Association), Vol. 25, No. 5, July 1961, pp. 1–6.

IS POWER AN ALIEN CONCEPT?

Examinations of the naked concept of power have been infrequent in the American experience. Somehow we have always preferred to use other terms. However, it may be refreshing to dissect the anatomy of power without benefit of euphemism.

The American system in all its aspects—political, economic, and social—places individualism at the highest point on its scale of values. We have never wavered from the theory that the power of decision should be dispersed as widely as possible . . . that each citizen is capable of, and entitled to, determine his own fate. Our faith in individualism has cost us dearly at times, but we have reaped inestimable benefits from it.

Of course, there are limitations on the individual exercise of power. Rampant individualism means anarchy, not freedom.

Dr. Johnson once said, "Power is always gradually stealing away from the many to the few, because the few are more vigilant and consistent." This pithy description illuminates a great deal of human history. The transition from unrestrained individualism to unrestrained tyranny is very swift. One need only say "Athens" or "Rome" to prove the point. The American people, dedicated as they have been to the principle of individualism, have nevertheless found it necessary to evolve a series of restraints on individualism through trial and error. The first element in the equation that is the American government describes these restraints.

Any government necessarily must impose some restraints. Lord Melbourne opined that "the whole duty of government is to prevent crime and to preserve contracts." This is a very skeletal idea of the role of government, but it does encompass restraint, however minimal that restraint may be. At first we were content with an absolute minimum of restraint. But as the industrial revolution gained impetus and as our society became more complex, the need for more sophisticated restraints became painfully evident. In the dawn of our industrial development, some few used their individual freedom without regard to the many.

Tolstoy described 19th Century Czarist Russia in terms that describe any nation in the midst of industrial revolution: "If the arrangement of society is bad and a small number of people have power over the majority and oppress it, every victory over nature will inevitably serve only to increase that power and that oppression. That is what is actually happening."

Restraints upon rampant individualism were necessary in America, and restraints were imposed. But the *nature* of the restraint devised has a peculiarly American cast.

THE EVILS OF CENTRALIZED POWER

Americans posit the centralization of power as an absolute evil, regardless of whether that power be political or economic. Just as we reject the unchecked exercise of the power of decision by the state, so also do we reject the concentration of power in a few private hands. The centralization of a nation's economy may well lead to the centralization of its polity. A brief reference to the status of guilds in early mercantile economies is enough to establish the point.

By guarantees against the undue concentration of political power, by the system of checks and balances embodied in the Constitution, by the adoption of the Bill of Rights, and by the subsequent extension of suffrage, Americans by the late 19th Century had demonstrated an effective solution to the problem of determining the proper allocation of political power. When our political system was organized, devices to insure the dispersal of power were woven into the basic framework of government.

Viewed in one light, the separation of powers is nothing more than a means of insuring that autocracy will not gain a foothold through the exercise of total governmental power by a single entity. Viewed in the same light, federalism is no more than a device to insure the decentralization of power. The dispersal of power is not a total answer to autocracy; but insofar as formal organization of government can prevent autocracy, the American adaptation of these two basic devices provides a firm barrier to centralization.

But as the frontier closed, and as the potentialities of the corporate form of business organization in reaping the fruits of the industrial revolution were realized, it became obvious that a pattern of private autocracies was enveloping the American economy.

Americans are activists. They are not disposed to apathy in the face of a threat to their vision of the good society. It became clear that some means had to be devised to shake off the spread of private economic autocracy.

Consider the intellectual picture at the moment of decision. By that time a large number of Continental theorists had grappled with the problem. Saint Simon and the other academic socialists had long since published their answer to concentration of economic power in private hands. Karl Marx had completed his labors at the British Museum. The authors of the Paris Commune had furnished a brief augury of things to come. This chorus of Continental voices sang one song: The answer to the undue concentration of economic power in a few private hands was the concentration of economic power in the state.

But in America a people wedded to the dispersion of power would not easily accept statism as a reply to monopolization. The instrument devised to snip the tentacles of monopoly was the antitrust laws. Instead of transferring economic power from one monolith to another, a method was invented to promote dispersal of power among private entrepreneurs. The major premise of antitrust is an unshakable belief in the efficacy of a competitive, free enterprise economy. The ideal to be realized is unlimited opportunity for entry into the market place, unlimited opportunity for self-development, and the resolution of economic issues by the unchecked exercise of free market forces.

In draining power from monopolists, only a minimum of power was transferred to the state. The sole reason for that transfer was to provide a governmental device for the dispersion of monopolistic power and the prohibition of harmful economic aggrandizement.

A LESSON FROM ANTITRUST LAW

One example taken from the body of antitrust decisions illustrates the depth of the American commitment to the decentralized private exercise of economic power. In 1951, the U. S. Supreme Court decided the case of *Kiefer-Stewart Company* v. *Joseph E. Seagram & Sons*, 340 U. S. 211. An Indiana wholesale liquor dealer sued the Seagram and Calvert Corporations for treble damages under Section 1 of the Sherman Antitrust Act. The complaint charged that the respondent had conspired to sell liquor only to those Indiana dealers who would resell at prices fixed by Seagram and Calvert, and that this agreement deprived the petitioner of a continuing supply of liquor.

So far this seems like a standard antitrust action; price fixing has long been held to be illegal *per se*. However, when this case went to trial, the evidence showed that the distiller had fixed *maximum* prices above which the wholesalers could not resell. The U. S. Court of Appeals for the Seventh Circuit held that there was no violation of the Sherman Act, because an agreement to fix maximum resale prices was not anti-competitive in effect. Rather, such prices promoted competition and aided the consumer.

To the surprise of many, the Supreme Court reversed. It held that agreements fixing maximum resale prices "crippled the freedom of traders" in the same manner as agreements to fix minimum resale prices. It is the restraint upon the ability of traders to sell in accordance with their own judgment that the Sherman Act reaches.

Thus, we see that price fixing, even when done with a laudable motive, that of securing lower prices to the consumer, is illegal *per se*. At first the result seems anomalous; but if we refer again to the notion of a pluralistic decentralized society, all becomes clear. It is the exercise of power by a dominant concern to the detriment of the establishment of market conditions by the aggregate of individual decisions that is condemned. Far from being anomalous, this decision shows that the American people, speaking through its judiciary, are willing to commit themselves to freedom even where centralism would seem to provide highly desirable short-term goals.

To be sure, antitrust was not the only American answer to economic concentration. The fruits of Populism were many. Another American device forged in that time of crisis was the economic regulatory agency. Although the regulatory agency inevitably presupposes a transfer of some economic power to the state, the employment of this device represents a minimal transfer. The industries chosen by supervision were, without exception, industries peculiarly affected with a public interest and industries not adapted to the checks and balances imposed by unlimited competition. They were industries in which concentration of power was inevitable; and it was inevitable that a democratic nation would require a diaspora of private power.

But there was never a complete transfer of power. The regulatory agencies have never warred against private enterprise. They have merely insured that private enterprise affected with a public interest performed its responsibilities in a reasonable manner, and every agency was swathed in an elaborate net of guarantees against the unbridled exercise of power.

The American answer to the problem of monopoly has been a good one. There has been no attempt to convert unlimited private power into unlimited governmental control. Instead, the single thrust of our political effort has been to guarantee individual freedom by limited governmental regulation. There has been no departure in theory from the ideal of a plural, decentralized, permissive society dedicated to individualism.

THE CONTRADICTORY PRESSURES

Unfortunately there have been departures, and pressures for still more departures, from these ideals in practice.

Acceptance of the idea that free enterprise bestows unparalleled benefits upon our nation does not negate the conclusion that the consequences of economic freedom have been and can be painful to many individuals and groups within the nation.

These painful consequences have led many to attempt a reshaping of the meaning of free enterprise in the mold of self-interest. To these people economic freedom may mean freedom to receive governmental subsidies to maintain uneconomic or dying industries. Or it may mean freedom to seek legislation to restrain competition and promote the stability and security of an industry or segments of an industry.

Contradictory pressures to present at least a facade of devotion to national economic ideals and at the same time to protect economic positions that could not withstand unrestrained competitive pressures have produced some public statements that are glaringly contradictory.

One of the most distressing habits of speech common to some businessmen is the tendency to say something like this: "Yes, of course I believe in free competition . . . but what *my* business (or *my* market, or *my* industry) really needs is less competition and more stability." These businessmen place their reliance upon legislation, not competition, to secure the prosperity of their enterprises.

No intensive search is necessary to uncover examples of this distressing tendency. Bills that would extend resale price maintenance, provide territorial security to dealers in various commodities, erect barriers to market entry, and establish or expand exemptions from the antitrust laws are introduced in great numbers in every session of the Congress. Proposals of this character are naked departures from the concept of economic freedom embodied in the nation's antitrust and trade regulation laws. For implicit in these laws is a recognition that the freedom to start a business, to win markets through fair competition, and to make business decisions independently cannot be enjoyed absent the risk of displacement by stronger fair competitive efforts.

Even as we extol the benefits of economic freedom, we must recognize that no free society can guarantee every individual complete insulation from painful consequences.

THE NEW CHALLENGE

The preservation of the ideal of a free-enterprise economy from the threat engendered by the rise of the trust was a signal accomplishment. The governmental devices designed to preserve economic individualism have, on the whole, been very successful.

However, new challenges threaten this ideal and new responses are continually needed. The pace of change defies description. The velocity and intensity of economic evolution approaches a state of constant revolution. New ways of accomplishing economic tasks proliferate. In space technology, for instance, we are seeing the onset of what may be a significant trend in economic organization. The rise of the government-sponsored, non-profit corporation and the university-sponsored, non-profit corporation and the development of ever more sophisticated relationships between prime contractors and subcontractors may have unforeseen consequences in the allocation of industrial power.

There is nothing sinister in these new developments. They are simply one indication of the constant need to assess the impact of organizational innovation on our traditional ideals.

Another massive challenge facing the American pattern of economic organization is the Gargantuan need of awakening populations faced with the task of expanding a narrow industrial base to meet the ever-rising expectations of ever-increasing populations. Another factor now shaping the future is the prolonged and unremitting struggle now taking place between statism and individualism.

Many thoughtful citizens are actively debating the question of whether an economy dedicated to individualism and the profit motive can adequately satisfy great public needs for education, research, resources development, foreign aid, and defense.

A clear look at the shape and pace of change does not reveal either that our ideal must be abandoned or that the instruments that we have devised to effectuate that ideal have become obsolete.

The best way to answer challenge is to set imaginative and daring men free, not to impose more shackles on human activity. Mankind is best served in a society where the power of decision is dispersed—where an educated and responsible citizenry is capable of wise and effective solutions to national problems by the aggregate of wise and effective individual decisions.

Economic individualism, then, must be defended. The antitrust and trade-regulation laws will continue to be the most effective weapons in the conduct of that defense. So long as we insure that entry to the market place and opportunity to compete in the market place are not foreclosed by coercion or unlawful combination or stifling monopoly, then the creative and talented individual—our ultimate, last, and only hope—will have the opportunity to exercise his talents.

So long as the free play of competition guarantees that the obsolescence means failure, we need not fear change. Compliance with the antitrust laws by responsible businessmen and vigorous enforcement of the antitrust laws by responsible government agencies, therefore, become primary duties of those immediately charged with the defense of the national belief in free enterprise.

THE QUESTION OF GOALS

"It is all very well to talk of preserving the reward of the daring free enterpriser," you may say, "but the nation may yet flounder if the wants satisfied by an abundantly productive free-enterprise economy are idle wants. A nation can flounder very quickly if the imaginative enterprisers devote themselves to producing kewpie dolls and electric highball stirrers when space vehicles and cyclotrons are what the nation needs."

It may be granted that dedication to free enterprise is bootless if free enterprise is doomed to end on a dungheap full of tail fins and discarded comic books. However, the necessity for some sort of hierarchy of national goals does not dictate an abandonment of freedom in favor of centralism. Rather, that need calls for an increased emphasis on enlightened individualism. Sacrifice is not incompatible with individualism, nor is excellence. *The good society cannot be achieved by the imposition of goals on a subdued populace.* The good society is composed of good individuals. As citizens, we can ultimately insure excellence only if we as citizens demand excellence.

The business community has very special responsibilities in the pursuit of excellence. The business community is skilled in the gathering of intelligence and the formulation of programs on the basis of that intelligence. It is supremely skilled in the art of persuasion.

Accordingly, if the business community wishes to insure the preservation of all the concepts embodied in the phrase "free enterprise," it must engage in a concerted effort to raise the national standards, to explain the perils that face this nation, to identify the tasks that must be accomplished, and to reinforce the will to accomplish them.

The business community has a special responsibility for education in a free society. It has the responsibility for improving the qualitative as well as the quantitative aspects of American education. Truth makes men free. The spread of truth insures that freedom will endure. Only by awakening a universal thirst for truth and by providing a means to slake that thirst can we even approximate the good society.

Democracy is a most hopeful way of life; but, unlike statists, the advocates of democracy can promise no Utopia. The dreams of free men are bounded by the limitations of the human condition. But the condition of intelligent, free men and women is not an ignoble one. A promise that problems will be faced and solutions will be sought, that tragedy will be endured and that perseverance will not fail, is far more noble than any promise that cares will cease.

RESPONSIBILITIES OF BUSINESS

Our deepest responsibility is to insure that the promise of the open society and the promise of free enterprise are realized. Business must meet the bewildering variety of demands now being made on our economy without surrendering freedom.

Inevitably this means that business must pledge renewed devotion to the principles embodies in our antitrust laws. Free enterprise cannot survive contamination either by monopoly or by statism. The best way to avoid both of these perils is to attain maximum compliance with the antitrust laws.

No one need be afraid that advocacy of vigorous enforcement of the antitrust laws is tinged with wide-eyed radicalism. Indeed, these laws are conservative in the truest sense of that much-abused term. They represent an undertaking by government designed to prevent still wider undertakings by government; for, if competition is abused and monopolistic practices become widespread, unfettered control over the economy will inevitably pass to the state.

The struggle for the preservation of free enterprise imposes great burdens upon the government also. Governmental agencies charged with enforcement of the antitrust laws and the proscription of unfair trade practices must exploit every resource available to them to insure that competition is free and fair. The malefactor must be restrained with swiftness and certainty, in order to deter others who may be tempted. And every businessman willing to accept the responsibilities that freedom brings must be educated in the letter and the spirit of the ground rules of competition, so that no one may transgress through ignorance.

But governmental proscription or regulation of economic activity must be limited, in the main, to the promulgation and to the enforcement of the "ground rules" under which fair and vigorous competition may take place, and to the penalization of those who wax strong through unfair methods. The government in its regulatory role fails if the monopolist or the predator imperils the freedom of the market place; it also fails if an iota of the freedom of individuals is sacrificed unnecessarily in the effort to contain the monopolistic or to fence in the predator.

Woodrow Wilson wrote, "Human nature is much the same in government as in the dry-goods trade. Power and strict accountability for its use are the essential constituents of good government." The prescription can be completed by stating its obverse: Human nature is much the same in business as in government. Exercise of power by the individual and strict accountability for its use are the essential constituents of free enterprise.

17. Trade Regulation and Small Business

Government regulation of monopolistic and unfair trade practices directly affects and benefits small business. The broad body of Federal legislation designed to foster free private enterprise includes the Sherman, Clayton, and Federal Trade Commission Acts.

Among the significant amendments to these laws are:

1. *The Miller-Tydings Resale Price Maintenance Amendment to the Sherman Act,*
2. *The Robinson-Patman Price Discrimination Amendment to the Clayton Act,*
3. *The Celler Antimerger Amendment to the Clayton Act,*
4. *The Wheeler-Lea Amendment to the Federal Trade Commission Act, and*
5. *The McGuire Resale Price Maintenance Amendment to the Federal Trade Commission Act.*

There is, in addition, a substantial body of comparable State laws.

The purpose of the antitrust and related laws is to encourage competition by prohibiting or restricting certain types of business activities. Although relative freedom in the operation of an enterprise exists, certain controls have been established and must, to preserve free competition, be adhered to under Federal and State trade regulation laws. The Federal laws apply to interstate commerce, and the State laws apply to intrastate commerce. In its broad aspects, legislation of this type is designed to aid smaller enterprises.

:: SOURCE: Reprinted from "Trade Regulation and Small Business," *Small Marketers Aids,* (Washington, D. C.: Small Business Administration, June 1961), No. 67.

FEDERAL LAWS

The *Sherman Antitrust Act* is essentially an anti-monopoly law. It was enacted in the era when trusts and combinations exercised power considered dangerous to the public welfare. The fundamental purpose of the Act is to prevent restraints to free competition which tend to limit production, raise prices, or otherwise control the market. It also seeks to secure equality of opportunity for businessmen and to protect purchasers of goods and services.

The *Clayton Act,* on the other hand, is designed to reach devices or practices that are discriminating and, under certain circumstances, might lead to the formation of trusts. It is intended to supplement the purpose and effect of the Sherman Act.

The Clayton Act prohibits price discriminations, knowingly inducing or receiving a discrimination in price, exclusive dealing arrangements and tying contracts, mergers, interlocking directorates and intercorporate stockholding, having the requisite adverse effect on competition. Additionally, it prohibits discriminations in the payments for and the furnishing of services and facilities and illegal brokerage payments. (Note: While the Clayton Act prohibits activities of this type, they do not necessarily constitute violations of the Sherman Act.)

The *Federal Trade Commission Act* which created the Federal Trade Commission as an enforcement agency, prohibits unfair methods of competition and unfair and deceptive acts and practices which occur in commerce. The FTC Act was passed in 1914, the year the Sherman Act was supplemented by the Clayton Act, and it broadened regulation of business and trade practices.

RESALE PRICE MAINTENANCE

Although a number of laws complementary to the Sherman Act have been enacted since 1890, the Sherman Act itself was not directly amended until 1937. During that year the *Miller-Tydings Amendment,* dealing with resale price maintenance, was passed.

Resale price maintenance is a system of distribution under which the owner of a trademark or brand name or, in some cases, any seller of a trademarked or otherwise identified product, establishes the resale price at which such may be sold. This is accomplished by entering into a contract with at least one distributor and notifying all other distributors in the State who are then obligated to maintain the price named in the contract.

Agreements fixing resale prices of commodities are invalid under the Sherman and Federal Trade Commission Acts because they constitute restraints of trade or unfair methods of competition. A movement toward legalization of resale price contracts in intrastate commerce was begun by the States and resulted in the Miller-Tydings Amendment to the Sherman Act.

This law, in effect, exempts from the Federal antitrust statutes resale price maintenance agreements which are valid under State law. It has been supplemented by the *McGuire Amendment* of 1952 to the Federal Trade Commission Act. This amendment makes it clear that the exemption from the Federal antitrust laws is extended to valid agreements entered into under State laws which make resale prices binding on distributors who do not themselves sign contracts.

Horizontal (group) agreements in which manufacturers, wholesalers, or other resellers fix resale prices, violate the provisions of the Sherman Act and the Federal Trade Commission Act. Vertical (individual) agreements, on the other hand, between a manufacturer and his wholesalers or between a wholesaler and his retailers have been legalized in interstate commerce when permissible in the State in which the resale is to be made or into which the commodity is to be transported for resale.

EXCLUSIVE DEALS, PRICE, AND OTHER DISCRIMINATIONS

Two features of the Clayton Act of direct interest to small businessmen relate to prohibitions against exclusive dealing arrangements and price discriminations. The former declares unlawful leases and sales on condition that the lessee or purchaser will not use or deal in the commodities of a competitor of the lessor or seller, where the effect might be to substantially lessen competition. The latter prohibits price discrimination where the effect is to lessen competition.

The provisions on price discriminations were amended in 1936 by the *Robinson-Patman Act.* The purpose of this Amendment was to strengthen and remedy certain defects in the price discrimination provisions of the law. Generally, with certain exceptions, it prohibited any direct or indirect discrimination in price between different purchasers of commodities of like grade and quality where the effect might be to substantially lessen competition.

While price discriminations are prohibited, certain differentials are permissible. The law authorizes differentials which make only due allowance for differences in the cost of manufacture, sale, or delivery resulting from differing methods or quantities in which commodities are sold or delivered to purchasers.

Thus, prices may be varied in accordance with differences in cost which must be justified by the seller. In addition, price differentials are permitted as the result of changes in the value of the product or in market conditions, and where commodities are not of like grade and quality.

Two other important aspects of the Clayton Act as amended by the Robinson-Patman Act relate to refusals to sell and liability of persons receiving prohibited price discriminations. The law expressly provided that sellers shall not be prevented from selecting their own customers in bona fide transactions and not in restraint of trade. Thus, while price discriminations are prohibited, the right of individual traders to discriminate in the choice of customers was reaffirmed. Finally, not only are price discriminations by sellers prohibited, but buyers who knowingly induce or receive illegal price discriminations are guilty of violation.

Of interest, also, are those provisions of the Clayton Act relating to prohibitions against the granting of discriminatory allowances or payments to favored customers for services or facilities furnished by them, or the discriminatory furnishings of services or facilities to favored customers, by the seller in connection with the distribution of his product.

ANTICOMPETITIVE MERGERS

The Clayton Act originally prohibited intercorporate stock acquisitions where the effect may be to substantially lessen competition, or restrain competition in any section or community, between the two corporations involved. This, however, did not impede corporations from acquiring the assets of other corporations. Since the acquisition of stock of a corporation is significant chiefly because it permits control of the assets of the acquired corporation, failure to prohibit direct purchase of the assets impaired the effectiveness of the Clayton Act.

This situation was corrected by the 1950 Celler Amendment. That amendment prohibited the acquisition of the whole or any part of the assets of another corporation when the effect of the acquisition may be substantially to lessen competition or to tend to create a monopoly.

The amendment also modified the Clayton Act in two other ways: (1) it did not make the lessening of competition between the acquiring and the acquired firms a test of violation, and (2) it related to commerce in any section of the country rather than in *any section or community*.

Therefore, the stock or asset merger of two small companies, which would, of course, eliminate competition between them, would be prohibited only if other competitors in that line of commerce were not so numerous or relatively large that the merger would produce a significant change in the intensity of competition in any section of the country.

In any event, this provision does not apply, as the courts have held, to the sale of stock or assets to a competitor by a company in a failing or bankrupt condition.

UNFAIR BUSINESS PRACTICES

Government regulation of improper business practices was expanded by the Federal Trade Commission Act, which prohibited "unfair methods of competition in commerce." Determination of what was an unfair method of competition was left to the Federal Trade Commission and the courts.

The powers of the Commission were extended under the *Wheeler-Lea Act* of 1938 which also declared unlawful "unfair or deceptive acts or practices in commerce" whether or not in competition. In addition, the amendment expressly provides that the dissemination of any false advertising by United States mails, or in commerce by any means, for the purpose of inducing, or which is likely to induce the purchase of food, drugs, devices, or cosmetics constitutes an unfair or deceptive practice.

The duties of the Commission include legal activities in the enforcement of the prohibitions against unfair methods of competition and unfair or deceptive acts or practices. Some typical methods and practices that have been condemned in cease and desist orders of the Commission involve making false and disparaging statements regarding competitors' products and businesses; selling rebuilt second-hand and old articles as new; passing off goods as products of competitors through simulation of trade names or labels; bribing employees of customers to obtain patronage; buying up supplies for the purpose of hampering competitors and stifling or eliminating competition. These illustrations are only a few of the many prohibited unfair trade practices.

Another important phase of the Federal Trade Commission's activities relates to the prevention of unfair competitive practices through rules of fair competition. The trade practice conference procedure provides for the formulation of rules for the protection of industry and the purchasing public against unfair competitive practices and monopolistic restraints. Under this procedure effective means are made available for groups to participate voluntarily with the Commission in providing for the elimination of trade abuses in particular industries. Any interested person or group in an industry, large or small, may apply to the Commission for conference proceedings to establish rules of fair practices or the Commission may institute a trade practice conference on its own motion.

Additionally, the Commission administers a Guide program under which it has approved and issued Guides interpretive of Commission law relating to certain advertising practices and discriminatory payments for and the furnishing of services and facilities by sellers.

Finally, it offers a service whereby small businessmen, either personally or through correspondence, may inquire as to the requirements of Commission law and the application thereof to their particular problems.

ENFORCEMENT OF LAWS

With a few exceptions, enforcement and administration of the Federal antitrust and related laws are centered in the Federal Trade Commission and the Department of Justice. Complaints by small businessmen of suspected antitrust violations by competitors are welcomed by these agencies and usually form the basis for a large part of the antitrust investigation program.

In addition, under the Sherman and Clayton Acts a small businessman injured by an antitrust violation may himself bring suit in the Federal courts and recover three times the damage sustained.

THE STATE LAWS

There is, in addition to the Federal laws, a substantial body of comparable State laws usually administered and enforced by the State attorney general. These State trade regulation laws fall within four main groups:

1. General antitrust statutes,
2. Resale price maintenance laws—popularly known as fair trade acts.
3. Price discrimination laws, and
4. Statutes prohibiting sales below cost—sometimes referred to as unfair practices acts.

Almost all States have enacted general antitrust laws. The provisions of such statutes, usually directed at the prevention and elimination of monopolies by prohibiting agreements in restraint of trade, vary in scope and detail from State to State. There is a considerable degree of connection between the Federal Sherman and Clayton Acts and comparable State legislation.

Closely related to the Miller-Tydings and McGuire Acts are the fair trade laws which have been enacted in 46 States. All, with the exception of Alaska, Missouri, Texas, Vermont, and the District of Columbia, have statutes expressly legalizing resale price maintenance agreements, although in a number of states such statutes have been invalidated by the courts.

The purpose of these laws is to allow the manufacturer of a product bearing a distinctive mark or name to control its resale price. The fair trade laws, with variations in some States, usually specify:

1. that manufacturers and distributors of trade-marked or branded goods may make contracts with purchasers establishing resale prices;
2. that such agreements, however, are not permissible between groups of producers or between groups of wholesalers or between groups of retailers;
3. that such contracts may be disregarded in sales of damaged goods, clearance sales; sales to the State and their political subdivisions, and sales by court orders; and
4. that dealers who do not sign resale price contracts must, nevertheless, maintain prices specified in such agreements between manufacturers and other dealers.

Comparable to the Robinson-Patman Act are the anti-price discrimination statutes that have been enacted in approximately half the States. The general objective of such laws is to prevent differences in prices between purchasers of commodities of like grade and quality when the effect may be to injure competition. Anti-price discrimination statutes, with variations in some States, authorize price differentials in certain cases. They include those which can be justified because of differences in grade or quality, or in manufacturing, selling, or delivery costs.

The last group of laws, in force in approximately three-fifths of the States, concerns prohibitions against sales below cost. While there is no Federal statute expressly covering this subject, selling below cost has in some instances been held a violation of the Federal antitrust laws.

A fairly typical provision of the State laws makes it unlawful for a vendor to sell any article at less than his cost for the purpose of injuring competitors. Unfair practices acts usually exempt certain types of transactions, including sales of seasonal or perishable goods, clearance sales, and sales to meet the legal prices of a competitor.

SOME ILLEGAL PRACTICES UNDER FEDERAL LAWS

Against what types of practices can the Federal antitrust law enforcement agencies be expected to take action? The following listing is by no means complete. However, it does highlight some of the more important practices that violate the trade regulation laws.

1. *Price fixing:* A pricing agreement among competitors is illegal both under the Sherman Act and the Federal Trade Commission Act.

In a 1940 decision the Supreme Court said that "Under the Sherman Act a combination formed for the purpose and with the effect of raising, depressing, fixing, pegging, or stabilizing the price of a commodity in interstate or foreign commerce is illegal per se."

2. *Exclusive deals:* The Clayton Act declares it illegal for a seller to make sales conditional upon a buyer's promise not to make purchases from the seller's competitors, if this type of sale may result in substantial lessening of competition. The law also prohibits a seller from making a buyer promise that he will purchase all his requirements of similar commodities from the seller when it has the same effect on competition.

3. *False and deceptive advertising:* A wide range of court decisions have underlined the fact that a seller violates the Federal Trade Commission Act if he misrepresents his product in a material respect or fails to disclose pertinent information, where such practice has the tendency or capacity to mislead and deceive purchasers or prospective purchasers, or injure competition.

4. *Price discrimination:* The Clayton Act as amended by the Robinson-Patman Act prohibits price discrimination which may result in a substantial lessening of or injury to competition. This means not only injury to competitors of a seller, but also injury to purchasers who are damaged because their competitors receive unjustifiably low prices or unjustifiably large discounts.

5. *Payment of brokerage to buyers:* The Robinson-Patman Act forbids a seller to pay brokerage to a buyer. This is true regardless of whether payments are made directly, or through third parties who eventually hand the money over to the purchaser.

18. A Marketing Appraisal of the Robinson-Patman Act

W. DAVID ROBBINS

The Robinson-Patman Act of 1936 is one of the most complicated and controversial of antitrust laws. Twenty-three years of enforcement have produced crystal-clear confusion regarding some of its provisions, although some sections are now reasonably understandable.

There are few legal authorities in the competitive pricing field, and even they cannot assure their clients of correct advice in all Robinson-Patman matters. Several of the most important recent U. S. Supreme Court cases have been closely divided decisions.

Although the wording of the original Act has not been altered, in effect there have been three different Robinson-Patman Acts! This has come about through changing interpretations of the courts and of the Federal Trade Commission. The early years of Robinson-Patman reflected limited enforcement. The middle and late 1940's were marked by strict to radical enforcement; the "high-water marks" were the Moss,[1] Corn Products,[2] and Morton Salt[3] cases which rendered practically all price differentials illegal. The 1950's have shown both the courts and the Commission to be more temperate and reasonable in their interpretations of the Act.

It is little wonder that marketing authorities have largely "left it to the lawyers." Yet the Robinson-Patman Act is a *marketing* statute and the most basic pricing law with which the marketing executive must deal.

The Robinson-Patman Act does not prohibit all price discrimination. By its terms it reaches only those price discriminations:

. . . where the effect of such discrimination may be substantially to lessen competition or tend to create a monopoly in any line of commerce, or to injure, destroy, or prevent competition with any person who either grants or knowingly receives the benefit of such discrimination, or with customers of either of them. . . .[4]

PRICE DISCRIMINATION AND JUSTIFICATION: SECTION 2(a)

The basic provision of the Robinson-Patman Act is Section 2(a). Under the language of Section 2(a) quoted above, the charging of different prices to different customers is unlawful only when it has the proscribed adverse effect on competition, that is, where there is a substantial (1) lessening of competition; (2) a tendency to create a monopoly; or (3) an injury, destruction, or prevention of competition. Section 2(a) also confines the statute to discriminations between purchasers of commodities of "like grade and quality."

Two provisos of Section 2(a) then go on to state exceptions to the foregoing general prohibition as follows:

1. Provided, That nothing herein contained shall prevent differentials which make only due

---

[1] Samuel H. Moss, Inc. v. F.T.C., 148 F.2d, 378 (1945).

[2] Corn Products Refining Co. v. F.T.C., 324 U.S. 746 (1945).

[3] F.T.C. v. Morton Salt Co., 334 U.S. 37 (1948).

⁂ SOURCE: Reprinted by permission from the *Journal of Marketing* (National Quarterly Publication of the American Marketing Association), Vol. 24, No. 1, July, 1959, pp. 15–21.

[4] Robinson-Patman Act, 49 Stat. 1526 (1936).

allowance for differences in the cost of manufacture, sale, or delivery resulting from the differing methods or quantities in which such commodities are to such purchasers sold or delivered. . . .
2. Provided further, That nothing herein contained shall prevent price changes from time to time . . . in response to changing conditions affecting the market. . . .

Recent developments concerning Section 2(a) relate primarily to competitive effects of price differences and to cost justification. Functional or trade discounts,[5] geographic pricing,[6] and the establishment of quantity limits[7] are not considered in this article, as there have not been recent developments of particular significance in these areas.

Competitive Effects of Price Differences

During the 1940's, anything more than a minute price difference was automatically considered illegal under the Robinson-Patman Act, and a factual inquiry into the actual or probable adverse competitive effects of the difference was not permitted. Recently the Commission and the courts have shown an inclination to make an analysis of the economic facts involved rather than to decide cases on the basis of arbitrary rules of law.

One of the most important developments of recent years in the interpretation of the Robinson-Patman Act has been the burden of proving injury to competition, a seemingly procedural technicality. The Commission has held that under Section 2(a) the counsel supporting the complaint has the burden of proof to establish the necessary competitive injury.[8] Quotations

---

[5] Doubleday and Co., F.T.C. Docket 5897 (1955) helped to clarify the status of functional or trade discounts. (Integrated distributors could lawfully be reimbursed so long as the size of discount was reasonably related to the expenses assumed by the buyer.)

[6] National Lead Co., 49 F.T.C. 791 (1953) to some extent settled the controversial "mill net" theory. (Delivered price quotations themselves must differ to constitute a price discrimination.)

[7] F.T.C., et. al. v. B.F. Goodrich Co., et al., 242 F. 2d 31 (CA D.C. 1957) where one of the few quantity limit rules issued by the Commission was held invalid. (Findings based on fewness of purchasers over $600,000 did not support a quantity limit of one 20,000-pound carload.)

[8] General Motors Corp. and A C Spark Plug Co., Dkt. 5620; The Electric Auto-Lite Co., Dkt. 5624.

from FTC cases illustrate this "new" philosophy toward competitive effects of price differences:

Differences in price without competitive injury are not illegal.[9]
The fact that a competitor has been injured in a local price-cutting case may tend to show that competition with the grantor has been affected but it does not follow in every case that because a competitor has been injured, competition has been affected.[10]
Any . . . price differential remain[s] lawful under the Robinson-Patman Act unless endangering adverse effects on competition. . . .[11]

In 1958 the Tenth Circuit Court upheld the trial court's instructions to the jury which placed upon the plaintiff the burden of proof in establishing price discrimination:

The Clayton Act, as amended, does not have the effect of making any and every differential in price in various areas illegal price discrimination within the intent and meaning of the Act. The Act concerns itself with price discrimination which is reasonably calculated to lessen competition, or tends to create a monopoly, or to injure, destroy, or prevent competition. . . .[12]

In another 1958 case, the court held that the plaintiff's claim was insufficient because it failed to show that the alleged discrimination had any unlawful effect on competition:

The amended complaint does not charge that Texaco committed an unlawful price discrimination since ultimate facts are not alleged showing that Texaco's price differences resulted in an anti-competitive effect proscribed by the Robinson-Patman Act.[13]

The courts are also more willing to accept a "rule of reason" in judging the economic effects that price differentials may have on competition. In 1951 the U. S. Court of Appeals (7th Circuit) held: "Price differences are not invalid unless potentially impairing the vitality of competition itself . . . it could not be said the effect . . . was substantially to injure competition."[14]

---

[9] General Foods Co., F.T.C. Docket 5675 (1954).

[10] Purex Corp., Ltd., F.T.C. Docket 6008 (1954).

[11] Doubleday and Co., F.T.C. Docket 5897 (1955).

[12] Elgin Corp. v. Atlas Building Products Co., 251 F. 2d 7 (10th Cir. 1958), cert. denied June 13, 1958, 26 L.W. 3368.

[13] Victor N. Alexander v. The Texas Co. (D.C. W.D. La. Aug. 22, 1958).

[14] Minneapolis-Honeywell Regulator Co. v. F.T.C., 191 F.2d 786 (7th Cir. 1951) cert. dismissed, 344 U.S. 206 (1952).

The statutory phrase "substantially to lessen competition" should be the key to enforcement of the Act. Price differences which do not impair competition need not be outlawed. It must be remembered that price discriminations are often the first step in general price reductions in an industry, thereby lowering the price to consumers through *all* competitors.

Cost Justification

Under the "due-allowance-for-cost" proviso, price discriminations are permitted which properly reflect differences in "costs." Although "cost of manufacture" is specifically mentioned in Section 2(a), proof of savings in the cost of serving different customers (marketing costs) has been the only cost defense which has been successful. If the merchandise is *not* of "like grade and quality," significant production-cost differences can occur; however, if the products are not of "like grade and quality," the Act does not apply and there can be no violation regardless of the extent of the discrimination.

The cost-justification proviso is the "sleeper section." It has only recently been aroused after an almost twenty-year sleep and is not yet fully awake. In only five formal cases have the cost justifications been entirely successful.[15] In three more cases cost studies were accepted in part as justifying some portion of the price differential.[16]

This is a pathetic record to be sure; however recently the Commission and the courts have been attempting to make some sense out of the "cost-justification" defense. Businessmen must accept much of the blame for the fact that a cost defense has not succeeded in more cases. All too often a businessman attempts to reconstruct distribution-costing information *after* he has been charged with price discrimination—a very late date indeed!

The real benefits of attempting to comply with the "cost-justification" proviso are in the improvement of marketing efficiency for the individual firm, while also preserving for the public the benefits of efficient marketing methods. Actually, a major justification of instituting cost-distribution accounting is not just to create a defense to a price-discrimination charge, but rather to improve a firm's marketing program and its profits.

Unless a seller has knowledge of his most profitable customers, territories, and lines of merchandise, he cannot most effectively direct and concentrate his marketing efforts. Although distribution-cost accounting is hardly an exact science, it is sufficiently accurate for sound marketing decisions.

If a distribution-cost accounting system is established in good faith and in accordance with acceptable accounting doctrines, it should satisfy the requirements of the Robinson-Patman Act. Speculation and guesswork are not satisfactory, nor should they be. It is usually too late and often very expensive to attempt to reconstruct the necessary cost information after a discrimination charge has been filed.

GOOD FAITH MEETING OF COMPETITION: SECTION 2(b)

When the Robinson-Patman Act was passed, Congress recognized that competitive price situations would arise wherein it would be necessary to safeguard the right to compete. Section 2(b) provides that a seller may show as justification to a charge of prohibited price discrimination that the lower price "was made in good faith to meet an equally low price of a competitor."

The Supreme Court's decision of 1958 in the *Standard Oil* case is by far the most important decision in this regard since the Act was passed.[17] Indeed, it is the first recorded case in which the seller has succeeded in justifying a challenged discrimination by recourse to Section 2(b)'s "meeting competition" defense.

The Commission had contended since 1936 that the "good faith meeting of competition" was only a "qualified" defense and would afford the seller no protection if potential injury to competition was shown. The U. S. Supreme Court rejected this construction and ruled that the "meeting-competition" proviso afforded a complete defense, incidental "injury" notwithstanding.[18] Section 2(b) has now become a substantive rule of law rather than a mere procedural rule of evidence.

[15] Bird and Son, Inc., 25 F.T.C. 548 (1937); B. F. Goodrich Co., F.T.C. Docket 5677 (1954); Sylvania Electric Products, Inc., F.T.C. Docket 5728 (1954); Reid v. Harper and Bros., 235 F. 2nd 420, 422 (1956), cert. denied, 77 S. Ct. 326 (1956); Hamburg Bros., Inc., F.T.C. Docket 6721 (1957).
[16] Bissell Carpet Sweeper Co., F.T.C. Docket 4636 (1945); Minneapolis-Honeywell Regulator Co., 44 F.T.C. 351 (1948); U.S. Rubber Co., 46 F.T.C. 988 (1950).

[17] F.T.C. v. Standard Oil Co., 355 U.S. 396 (1958).
[18] Standard Oil Co. v. F.T.C., 340 U.S. 231 (1951).

The Commission had also insisted that a seller is precluded from competing in a local market unless he was willing to make across-the-board reductions in each place of doing business. But the Supreme Court rejected this theory, saying:

There is, on the other hand, plain language and established practice which permits a seller, through section 2(b) to retain a customer by realistically meeting in good faith the price offered to that customer, *without necessarily charging the seller's price to its other customers.*[19] (Italics added.)

Unless there is legislative change, the "meeting-competition" defense will certainly become a more significant justification in pricing cases in the future. Prior to the *Standard Oil* case, however, certain limits to the "meeting-competition" defense had been spelled out by the courts. Both in 1956 and 1957 the U. S. Court of Appeals (7th Circuit) said that the competitive price must be responsive to an actual competitor or specific lower prices.[20]

Note that the *Standard Oil* decision is not concerned with entire markets—only individual customers. Also the *Standard Oil* case dealt with preventing the loss of present customers and not with gaining new customers. The competitive price must be defensive rather than aggressive.[21] Further, the competitive price may not be set pursuant to a pricing system.[22] And it was earlier held that "equally low prices" meant prices for similar quantities.[23]

Although Section 2(b) does not expressly limit its application to competitors' "lawful" prices, the Supreme Court's opinion in the *Standard Oil* case adverted to competitors' "lawful" prices.[24] The "lawful" offer of a competitor was not mentioned in the 1958 *Standard Oil* case other than in the dissent (5–4 decision). The Commission failed to determine that the competitive price cuts which Standard Oil was meeting were illegal. The "lawful" price problem was clearly expressed in the dissenting

opinion in the 1953 *Standard Oil* case when it was emphasized that there were insurmountable obstacles confronting a seller who would try to determine the legality of a competitor's price.

In 1956 the U. S. Court of Appeals (5th Circuit) dealt directly with this problem and held:

To establish this [2(b)] defense, a seller does not have the burden of proving that the competing price was lawful. Section 2(b) should not to be construed as if it were written "was made in good faith to meet a *lawful* equally low price."[25]

Another interesting and undecided problem concerning application of Section 2(b) is the "like-grade-and-quality" phrase of Section 2(a). In three different cases[26] the Commission has rejected the "meeting-competition" defense when a seller of merchandise who normally sold at a premium because of "superior public acceptance," unrelated to actual quality, reduced his prices to match competitors' lower prices.

The meaning of the phrase, "like grade and quality," is perhaps as confused today as when the Act was passed. Most of the sparse interpretations have considered only the purely physical characteristics of products and have not taken into consideration differences or unlikeness in consumer preferences.

BROKERAGE CLAUSE: SECTION 2(c)

Section 2(c) forbids the payment or acceptance of any form of commission as brokerage to or by any person who does not in fact perform the services of a broker. There were many cases in the 1930's and 1940's concerning the brokerage clause, but relatively few in the 1950's. Several seafood canners and their sales agents or brokers have recently been cited by the FTC for alleged violations of Section 2(c)[27] and consent orders have been approved by the FTC on a number of earlier complaints under this section.[28]

[19] Same reference.
[20] E. Edelmann and Co. v. F.T.C., 239 F. 2d 152 (7th Cir. 1956), cert. denied, 355 U.S. 941 (1958); C.E. Niehoff and Co. v. F.T.C., 241 F. 2d 37 (7th Cir. 1957), cert. denied, 355 U.S. 941 (1958).
[21] Standard Oil Co. v. F.T.C., 340 U.S. 231, 249 (1951) (dictum).
[22] F.T.C. v. National Lead Co., 353 U.S. 419 (1957).
[23] F.T.C. v. Standard Brands, Inc., 189 F. 2d 510 (2d Cir. 1951).
[24] Standard Oil Co. v. F.T.C., 340 U.S. 231 (1951).

[25] Standard Oil Co. v. Brown, d.b.a. Bob Brown's Standard Service, 238 F. 2d 54 (1956).
[26] Anheuser Busch, Inc., F.T.C. Docket 6331 (1957); Standard Brands, Inc., 46 F.T.C. 1495 (1950), aff'd on other grounds, 189 F. 2d 510 (2d Cir. 1951); Minneapolis-Honeywell Regulator Co., 44 F.T.C., 351, 371, 396 (1948), rev'd on other grounds, 233 F. 2d 649 (7th Cir. 1956).
[27] F.T.C. Dockets 7200, 7204, 7208, 7209, 7210.
[28] F.T.C. Dockets 6977, 6978, 6979, 6980, 6981, 7021.

This section has proved to be a highly restrictive provision which limits the type of middleman who can qualify to wholly "independent" brokers. The major beneficiary has been the food broker. Section 2(c) has also been construed by the Commission and the courts to exclude any of the justifications permitted under Section 2(a).[29] The Brokerage Clause has not been reviewed by the Supreme Court although certiorari was denied several times in the 1940's.

"PROPORTIONALLY EQUAL" PROMOTION PROVISIONS: SECTIONS 2(d) AND (e)

Sections 2(d) and (e) forbid a seller to enter into co-operative promotional arrangements of any type except on "proportionally equal" terms with all competing customers. No injury to competition is required to establish violation of these sections.[30] The Commission insists that the seller notify all qualified customers, including retailers who purchase through wholesalers,[31] of his willingness to pay for such services as well as their entitlement to participation.[32]

The most obvious defense to a charge of discrimination in the furnishing of "services and facilities" is found within the language of Section 2(e), namely, that in fact the facilities furnished were accorded to all purchasers on proportionally equal terms. However, under the proviso to Section 2(b), two other defenses are also available: by a showing that the facilities were furnished in good faith to meet the facilities furnished by a competitor,[33] or that the discrimination could be cost justified.[34] In a 1958 case involving a Section 2(e) charge, the U. S. Court of Appeals (D.C. Circuit) set aside a FTC finding on the ground the manufacturer was not given the opportunity to present evidence of cost justification.[35]

Perhaps some progress has been made in the interpretation of Sections 2(d) and (e) with "broader antitrust objectives." Nevertheless, a manufacturer has a much better chance of defending an outright price discrimination charge than a "proportionally equal" promotion charge.

BUYERS' LIABILITY: SECTION 2(f)

Section 2(f) is addressed directly to buyers rather than to sellers, and declares it "unlawful for any person engaged in commerce, in the course of such commerce, knowingly to induce or receive a discrimination in price which is prohibited by this section." When the Robinson-Patman Act was passed, it was generally expected that this section would receive vigorous prosecution. Until 1953, however, it was sparingly invoked; and since the Supreme Court's *Automatic Canteen*[36] decision the Commission has seldom challenged bargaining by buyers.

In *Automatic Canteen* the Supreme Court had occasion to review for the first time—and the only time to date—the meaning and effect of Section 2(f). The Commission's interpretation of this Section was drastically altered when the Court held that:

> . . . the Commission is, on this record, insisting that once knowledge of a price differential is shown, the burden of introducing evidence shifts to the buyer . . . we think the fact that the buyer does not have the required information, and for good reason should not be required to obtain it, has controlling importance. . . . We therefore conclude that a buyer is not liable under 2(f) if the lower prices he induces are either within one of the seller's defenses such as the cost justification or not known by him not to be within one of those defenses.[37]

Following the *Automatic Canteen* case many authorities stated that Section 2(f) would be little used by the Commission, and this has certainly been true to date. However, the Court in that case pointed out, "We are here asked to settle a controversy involving simply the burden of coming forward with evidence under 2(f) of the Act."[38]

[29] Biddle Purchasing Co. v. F.T.C., 96 F. 2d 687 (1938); Oliver Brothers, Inc. v. F.T.C., 102 F. 2d 763 (1939); Great Atlantic and Pacific Tea Co. v. F.T.C. 106 F. 2d 667 (1939); Southgate Brokerage Co., Inc. v. F.T.C., 150 F. 2d 607 (1945).

[30] Great Atlantic and Pacific Tea Co. v. F.T.C., 106 F. 2d 667 (3rd Cir. 1939); Corn Products Refining Co. v. F.T.C., 144 F. 2d 211 (7th Cir. 1944); Elizabeth Arden, Inc. v. F.T.C., 156 F. 2d 132 (2nd Cir. 1946).

[31] Elizabeth Arden, Inc. v. F.T.C., 156 F. 2d 132 (2nd Cir. 1946).

[32] Kay Windsor Frocks, F.T.C. Docket 5735 (1954).

[33] Elizabeth Arden, Inc., 39 F.T.C. 288 (1944).

[34] Simplicity Pattern Co., Inc. v. F.T.C. (D.C. Cir. 1958).

[35] *Ibid.*

[36] Automatic Canteen Co. v. F.T.C., 346 U.S. 61 (1953).

[37] *Ibid.*

[38] *Ibid.*

Only future decisions can determine how the courts and the Commission will ultimately construe the *Automatic Canteen* decision. To date the Commission has been noticeably silent; but a more stringent enforcement of Section 2(f) can be expected from the Commission sometime in the future.

PARTICIPATION IN DISCRIMINATION AND CO-OPERATIVE ASSOCIATIONS: SECTIONS 3 AND 4

There have been no recent developments concerning these sections of the Act. Section 3, which is enforced in the courts and not by the FTC, declares it unlawful for any person knowingly to be a party to or assist in discrimination between competing purchasers. It further prohibits "selling at unreasonably low prices for the purpose of destroying competition or eliminating a competitor." Section 4 declares that nothing in the Act shall prevent a cooperative association from returning to its members net earnings or surplus resulting from its trading operations.

IMPLICATIONS

The most significant development concerning the Robinson-Patman Act is that in the 1950's an Act different from the original one is being enforced. Business conditions as well as the personnel charged with the interpretation and enforcement of the Act have also changed. Some of the new members of the FTC have as yet to prove their appreciation of the value of competition. As yet, it is difficult to predict the philosophy of the reconstituted Commission.

The three major recent developments under Robinson-Patman have been:

1. To the plaintiff has shifted the burden of proving injury to competition in a price discrimination case.

2. The defense of "meeting competition in good faith" has been vitalized and is today a complete defense to a price discrimination charge.

3. The cost-justification defense has proved to be of more benefit, and is expected to have more substance in the future.

19. *The Nature and Background of the Fair Trade Problem*

Nature of Fair Trade; the Fair Trade Issue

Fair trade is a system of price control by which the owner of an article identified by brand name or trade-mark sets a minimum price below which the article may not subsequently be resold. Control is exercised normally by the producer (occasionally a dealer) who owns the brand name. The one who is controlled is normally a retailer. In practice, therefore, fair trade is a method of vertical price control whereby the manufacturer (or wholesaler) sets minimum prices for the sale at retail of his products. It is a form of resale price maintenance.

Forty-five states have enacted laws legalizing fair trade practices. Under these laws, a manufacturer and his retailers can enter into contracts whereby the former establishes minimum resale prices which the latter are obligated to observe. In addition, the manufacturer may establish his prices by notification and announcement. All state laws provide that if a manufacturer negotiates a contract with one retailer in the state and announces the terms of this contract including his minimum prices to other retailers, he may enforce these prices on the latter even though they have refused to agree to his contracts. This is the so-called non-signer provision.

State fair trade laws apply directly only to intrastate trade. Under the Miller-Tydings Act, however, state law is extended to interstate sales

‡‡ SOURCE: Reprinted from report of the Select Committee on Small Business, U. S. Congress, House, Select Committee on Small Business, House Report No. 1292, 82nd Congress, 2nd Session, 1952, pp. 3–15.

taking place within each state. This statute, which was enacted in 1937, exempts from the Sherman and Federal Trade Commission Acts contracts to maintain prices in interstate sales in states which have laws authorizing such contracts.

On May 21, 1951, the Supreme Court in *Schwegmann Bros.* v. *Calvert Distillers Corp.* ruled that the immunity granted by Congress in the Miller-Tydings Act does not extend to the maintenance of prices against retailers who are not parties to specific contracts. This decision thus rendered the non-signer provisions of state laws null and void as applied to interstate commerce. The issue now confronting Congress is whether the Federal Trade Commission and Sherman Acts should be further amended so as to legitimatize the provisions of state fair trade laws which make price maintenance enforceable against retailers who have not voluntarily agreed with manufacturers to observe the minimum prices set by the latter. Bills to accomplish this have been introduced in the 82nd Congress (H. R. 4592, H. R. 4662, H. R. 5767, and H. R. 6184.) (H. R. 5767 is included as Exhibit B.) In the meantime, a bill has also been introduced to repeal the Miller-Tydings Act altogether (H. R. 4365).

Development and Present Scope of Fair Trade

Modern price maintenance is an outgrowth of two basic developments in merchandising techniques that appeared at the close of the last century. One was the growing use of brand and trade names to identify products. The other was the expansion in advertising to secure consumer acceptance of these identified commodities. There soon appeared a realization on the part of certain retailers that a definite personal advantage could be gained by cutting prices on these nationally known brands. The situation was aggravated by the local price cutting practices of the huge trusts of that era. In self-defense, manufacturers and non-price-cutting retailers began to enter into agreements relative to the maintenance of resale prices.

The Sherman Act of 1890 and the Federal Trade Commission Act of 1914 erected formidable legal barriers to price maintenance. There upon a vigorous movement arose to obtain legislation that would exempt price maintenance contracts from the antitrust laws. From 1914 to 1933 numerous bills to accomplish this were introduced into Congress. None, however, were enacted until 1937 when the Miller-Tydings Act was passed as a rider to the District of Columbia Appropriations Act.

In the meantime, an equally determined drive had been launched to secure favorable legislation in the states. In 1916 New Jersey enacted a statute permitting price maintenance "by notice." California in 1931 enacted a statute without the non-signer provision and in 1933 added the non-signer clause. Other states fell into line very rapidly until by 1941 all but three states and the District of Columbia had adopted fair trade statutes.

The near blanketing of the country with fair trade law does not mean the blanketing of all commerce with fair trade practice. As a matter of fact, the percentage of all retail trade that is subject to fair trade is still relatively small. Although estimates vary widely—all the way from four percent to twenty percent—the most reliable studies point to about ten percent. Price maintenance is not found to any extent in staple commodities, unbranded goods or goods whose prices fluctuate rapidly. The following lines are those usually listed as being the ones in which fair trade is most significant: drugs and pharmaceutical products, cosmetics, books, alcoholic beverages, cameras and photographic supplies, certain hardware products, electrical appliances, packaged foods, jewelry, automobile accessories and sporting goods.

Although resale price maintenance started as a movement among manufacturers as a device to protect their brand names, it is today primarily a retailer movement. The most ardent supporters of fair trade are the conventional type of retailers, particularly the retail druggists.

THE CASE FOR FAIR TRADE

Fair Trade Protects the Public From the Evils of Unrestrained Price Cutting

The case for fair trade is based on the alleged evils of unrestrained price cutting at the retail level. Price cutting is viewed by the supporters of fair trade not as a legitimate expression of healthy competition, but as competition "running wild." Its purpose is not to sell the low-priced commodity but is either to ruin the market for competitors or to lure customers into the store whereupon other brands are substituted for the one whose price serves as the "bait." Recently emphasis has been placed not on "predatory price cutting" but on "price juggling." In the words of the Director of the Bureau of Education on Fair Trade:

Nobody likes to be treated as a sucker. And nobody likes a businessman who juggles his figures, his books or his prices. In loss-leader selling, the familiar prices of a few well-known brands go down to bankruptcy levels to fool the customers—and a host of unfamiliar prices go up. This is the juggling act, the essence of the unfair competition that Fair Trade prevents.

Fair Trade Protects the Producer of Branded Merchandise

The price cutter, it is said, in effect, preys on the goodwill of the producer of branded and trade-marked merchandise. The latter has developed the product and has spent large sums in obtaining consumer acceptance. If one store starts cutting prices, other dealers find that price comparisons are to their disadvantage. They stop featuring the article and may take it off their shelves altogether. The price cutter likewise discourages his own sales because he has cut his margin of profit to the vanishing point. Eventually the product disappears from the market altogether.

The price cutter is thus a parasite living off the good name of the manufacturer. He deprives the latter of his property and converts it to his own advantage. Price cutting is as unfair as physical misrepresentation.

Price Cutting Threatens the Existence of the Independent Merchant

The effects of price cutting on retailers are even worse. "Prolonged selling at cut prices results in freezing out small dealer competition," we are told. The price cutter either deprives other dealers of their legitimate margin of profit or forces them to discontinue stocking the article altogether or both. While one store is cutting on toothpaste, another is cutting on soap until all products are sold at a loss. No store derives any permanent advantage because what one can do, others can do until all are selling at a loss.

Advocates of fair trade claim that "The very existence of our small business economy is at stake." Fair trade is necessary to stop the predatory tactics of mass distributors who use price cutting as a weapon to force the independents out of business. "Fair trade is designed to give the small businessman a chance to compete fairly and on equal terms with large distributors, and thereby to preserve for small enterprises the field in which they can function most efficiently—that of distribution," the Bureau of Education on Fair Trade says.

Fair Trade Protects the Consumer from the Deception and Loss of Unrestrained Price Cutting

The advocates of fair trade vigorously contend that price maintenance is beneficial even to the consumer. Price cutting means a lack of standardization and its elimination is merely an additional step to protect the consumer. A standard price, it is argued, like a distinguishing brand name gives the consumer a yardstick of value. The standard price and the standard brand together enable the customer to determine for himself whether he is getting the proper quality at the right price. The consumer always shares in the financial losses created by unrestrained price cutting. Loss-leader selling is a form of advertising and its cost must be charged against the consumer. The public cannot get something for nothing.

Fair Trade is Consistent with Competitive Principles

The supporters of fair trade believe that price maintenance is entirely consistent with competitive principles. Their views are based primarily on the fact that control under price maintenance operates on a vertical basis rather than horizontal. They recognize that direct price competition between retailers is eliminated but believe this to be unimportant in view of the fact that competition prevails between manufacturers. Horizontal, i.e., "monopolistic," control is not possible because the state laws as well as the Miller-Tydings Act require that to be on the fair trade list, an article must be in free and open competition with similar articles produced by others. This is cited as a guarantee of free competition.

Much also is made of the fact that fair trade is entirely permissive. It permits a manufacturer to put his trade-marked article on fair trade but it does not compel him to do so. Fair-traded products and nonfair-traded products always compete with one another. No group of rival producers or dealers can force a manufacturer to establish minimum prices if he does not wish to do so.

Fair Trade Imposes a Strong Curb on Monopoly

Advocates of fair trade also contend that price maintenance is a powerful deterrent to monopoly because (1) it stops local price cutting and (2) it equalizes competitive strength. In respect to the first, a statement of former Justice Brandeis is frequently quoted. "Americans should be under no illusions as to the value or effect of price-cutting," Brandeis said. "It has been the most potent weapon of monopoly —a means of killing the small rival to which the great trusts have resorted most frequently. It is so simple, so effective." By preventing this price cutting fair trade helps to check the growth of monopoly.

Fair trade is necessary to equalize the competitive strength of the independent retailer with that of the mass distributor. The latter can establish branches, sell through agents, develop his own private brands and in other ways control prices. The small retailer can be placed on a par with these giants only through fair trade.

Fair Trade Prices Are Fair Prices

Fair trade is not designed to force consumers to pay higher prices nor has it in practice had that effect, according to its supporters. As evidence such studies as the following are cited:

1. Professor H. J. Ostlund of the University of Minnesota and C. R. Vickland conducted a survey under the sponsorship of the Research Bureau of the National Association of Retail Druggists which showed that in the drug stores of 42 fair trade states, prices of leading fair trade items showed little change between the time they were placed under contract and 1939. Fifty leading trade-marked items were included in the survey and the weighted average price of these articles declined about one percent.

2. A study made by the National Association of Chain Drug Stores indicates that since 1939 prices of fair trade articles have resisted

THE LEGAL FRAMEWORK   119

inflation better than prices of other goods. According to this study, the prices of 7,334 controlled drug products increased only 3.1 percent from 1939 to 1947, whereas food prices went up 93 percent and the over-all cost of living rose 59 percent.

3. The Bureau of Education on Fair Trade states that a recent study made by an "independent research agency" shows that "Consumers cannot expect to pay less without Fair Trade than they are now paying under Fair Trade."

Nor is it true, as the opponents of fair trade allege, that maintained prices tend to be unduly rigid and inflexible. Manufacturers are as capable as retailers of adjusting their prices to changing market conditions. If a price is too high, declining sales will force a reduction. Neither the manufacturer nor the retailer can pursue a policy for long that is contrary to the consumers' interests. In any event, flexibility does not require uncoordinated actions by individual retailers. It can be procured by simultaneous action with the initiative taken by the manufacturer.

Fair Trade Does Not Lead to Excessive Mark-Ups

To obtain higher mark-ups, we are assured, is not even one of the primary objectives of fair trade. This viewpoint has been expressed by the National Association of Retail Druggists in the following words:

The typical merchant is not worried about *average* mark-ups. . . . What concerns him most is to retain his volume, so that the accepted percentage of mark-up will produce enough gross margin to pay his operating cost. When competitors are permitted to use wanted brands as loss-leaders, they can, without reducing their own average margins, draw his customers away from him and thereby so impair his volume as to make it impossible for him to remain competitive.
The typical merchant wants Fair Trade, not in order to enable him to exact a greater profit, but in order that margins may be equalized in the different departments of his business.

Fair Trade Promotes Efficiency in Retailing and Reduces Costs of Distribution

Advocates of fair trade vigorously deny the charge that price maintenance leads to the preservation of inefficient stores and generally tends to increase the cost of distribution. Typical of the evidence they offer in support of this

view is a study made by Eli Lilly & Co. and cited by the Bureau of Education on Fair Trade. This study compared the operating efficiency of 1,122 drug stores—1,051 in the fair trade states and 71 in the non-fair trade areas. Using operating costs as a yardstick of efficiency, it revealed that drug stores in fair trade states have lower operating costs—26.17 percent of sales—compared with 27.57 percent in the non-fair trade area. This indicates that "retailers are actually more efficient when operating under Fair Trade."

Fixed prices, it is claimed, do not lessen the drive to increase efficiency and to reduce costs. These savings are passed along to consumers in the form of lower prices set by manufacturers. Margins are so small that even to remain in existence, retail stores must conduct an unrelenting search for economies of operation. Competition among retailers, among manufacturers, and between private brands and controlled brands tends to maintain a high degree of efficiency.

The Non-Signer Clauses Must Be Restored in Order to Make Fair Trade Effective and Applicable to All Retailers

The basic reason for the "non-signer" provision is freely admitted to be the very practical fact that without it, systematic price maintenance simply is not effective. There will always be some retailers who in the absence of compulsion will not observe the established prices. Experience under the California law of 1931 shows the futility of relying on voluntary price maintenance. Furthermore, although the number of confirmed price cutters is very small, the presence of even a single price cutter in a market has a demoralizing effect on the entire price structure. If one retailer starts to cut prices, others must follow. The only way to avoid the flood is to stop the first trickle.

The Non-Signer Provisions Are "Fair" and "Democratic"

This being true, there is no valid reason for objecting to the non-signer clauses. If it is good public policy to allow a manufacturer to stipulate the minimum resale price of his product at all, it does not cease to be good merely because a few retailers want to sell at a lower price. In fact, once the principle of fair trade is accepted, the extension of the practice to those who refuse to cooperate is a logical and practical necessity. To hold that fair trade contracts are good when voluntarily signed but that they cannot be protected against non-contract nullification, "is to say that the body may live but the heart must die."

The non-signer clause is "fair," "democratic" and "the American way of doing things." It is merely the principle of majority rule applied to commercial practices. A retailer, it is claimed, is not forced to handle articles subject to price maintenance. But, if he does and retains their distinguishing trade-marks, then fair trade prices must apply to him, "just as the traffic laws apply to everyone driving a car."

The States Should Be Allowed to Determine for Themselves Their Own Fair Trade Policy

When the Miller-Tydings Act was under consideration in 1937, the claim was repeatedly made that it was merely an enabling act designed to support existing state fair trade statutes. Today with 45 states having fair trade laws the argument is made even more strongly. Advocates of fair trade call attention to the fact that nearly the entire country is now blanketed by state fair trade laws. They also remind us of the fact that with the exception of the few non-fair trade areas, even interstate trade is covered by all provisions except the non-signer clause. We are told, therefore, that what was good in 1937 is even better today. Additional federal legislation is now needed merely to make it possible for the states to continue along the course already charted. The states should have the "right to be wrong" if they so desire.

The advocates of states rights believe that the authority granted by Congress to the states is not too broad nor that there is any danger that it may lead to widespread misuse by state legislatures. We are assured that the restrictions in the Miller-Tydings Act are adequate to prevent abuse and to protect non-fair trade states and the national interest.

THE OBJECTIONS TO FAIR TRADE

The Suppression of Predatory Price Cutting Is Not the Real Objective of Fair Trade

Most critics of the fair trade movement are inclined to agree that under certain conditions price cutting is undesirable. It is generally recognized, for instance, that extreme loss-leader or "bait" selling and discriminatory price cutting are contrary to the public interest. It is contended, however, that it is folly to stop all price cutting merely to eliminate the few undesirable forms. The opponents of price mainte-nance also claim that what the advocates of fair trade really are working for is not the suppression of predatory or discriminatory price cutting, but rather the elimination of all price competition at the retail level. The offering of merchandise at lower prices by super-markets, chain stores, and other mass distributors usually is not price cutting at all. Yet fair traders would put a stop to this legitimate commercial practice as well as to true price cutting. If they were really interested in shooting at the target they publicly have set up, they would be content with simple loss-leader laws.

Few Manufacturers or Retailers Are Seriously Injured by Predatory Price Cutting

Although price cutting of the loss-leader type may be undesirable, the opponents of fair trade believe it is not common. Only a few large stores in metropolitan centers have adopted it as a general business policy. Most chain organizations require each store to use minimum mark-ups. What looks like loss-leader selling is in most instances merely low-cost distribution. As for price cutting of the discriminatory type, it is claimed that the Robinson-Patman Act provides a much better remedy than the fair trade laws.

The opponents discount the effects of so-called price cutting on the producer of branded merchandise. They believe that the record indicates that thoroughly entrenched brands backed by vigorous sales efforts frequently profit from retail price competition. They refer to the Federal Trade Commission's statement that it had found no instance in which an article of real merit had been driven off the market by price cutting alone. It is highly significant, we are told, that manufacturers today have little interest in price maintenance. The opponents also feel that the goodwill argument is greatly overemphasized and that there is no reason in law or economics why the owner of a branded article should retain the right to control the resale. Goodwill is attached to the producer not the product and he receives full compensation in his sales price.

In respect to the effect on retailers, opponents of fair trade point out that certain retailers will always suffer from price competition. By the same token, other stores gain. Super-markets, chain stores, limited-service stores, stores in low rental areas and others find a definite advantage in free pricing. Even the old-line, full-service retailer encounters difficulties in fair trade. His advertising and service costs tend to rise. Competition with private brands becomes more intense. He may be forced to reduce his prices on uncontrolled items. Statistics do not bear out the assertion that in the absence of discrimination the welfare of the independent retailer is endangered by price cutting.

Fair Trade Is Essentially Monopolistic in Character

Opponents of fair trade object to price maintenance because they believe it to be a significant departure from our policy of free competition. They point to the fact that price competition among retailers is virtually suspended. They also believe that fair trade indirectly creates conditions favorable to monopoly. Typical of this view is the statement of the Federal Trade Commission in its 1945 Report on Resale Price Maintenance. In this report the Commission asserts that "the essence of resale price maintenance is control of price competition," and concludes:

Both the results of the Commission's present special study of the operation of legalized resale price maintenance and information developed over a period of many years in connection with complaints strongly confirm these earlier conclusions and point to the further conclusion that in the absence of effective Government supervision in the public interest, resale price maintenance, legalized to correct abuses of extreme price competition, is subject to use as a means of effecting enhancement of prices by secret agreements and restraint of competition by coercive action on the part of interested cooperating trade groups of manufacturers, wholesalers, and retailers in such ways and to such an extent as to make it economically unsound and undesirable in a competitive economy.

The Temporary National Economic Committee and the Antitrust Division of the Department of Justice have come to substantially the same conclusion.

The so-called guarantees in the law, that articles whose prices are maintaned must be in "free and open competition" and that there can be no collusion between manufacturers or dealers, are considered to be meaningless as legal tests and utterly incapable of effective enforcement.

Fair Trade Laws Are Not a Remedy for Discriminatory Pricing

Opponents of price maintenance strongly object to the claim of fair traders that the standardization of prices is an effective remedy for price discrimination. They deny even that the policy of fair trade is in harmony with the public condemnation of price discrimination as expressed in the Robinson-Patman Act. They point out that fair trade is designed to produce uniformity of prices regardless of costs whereas the true test of discrimination is the relationship of prices to costs. In many instances compulsory uniformity of prices is directly violative of the basic principle of the Robinson-Patman Act. The economist testifying on behalf of R. H. Macy Co. in 1937 referred to what he called the "strange inconsistency" in the views of those who advocated both price maintenance and anti-price discrimination laws. In the Robinson-Patman Act, he said, "you aim to conserve production economies for the consumer" whereas in the Miller-Tydings Act "it is proposed to prevent those and other economies from being passed on to the consumer." Furthermore, discrimination would still persist even if all retail prices were placed under control. It is felt that if the Robinson-Patman Act were properly enforced, the evil of discriminatory price cutting would disappear.

Fair Trade Means Higher Prices for Consumers

As to the effects of fair trade on prices, the following are typical of the conclusions drawn by the critics:

1. *Report to the Temporary National Economic Committee*—"Such figures as are available show almost universally that price-maintained items sell for higher prices than non-maintained goods; that prices of contractual articles rose after the law was passed; that prices average higher in cities where maintenance is legal than in comparable cities where it is not legal."

2. *The Federal Trade Commission*—The most common effect of resale price maintenance is that "chain stores, department stores, and certain independent stores that were selling below the minimums set by resale price maintenance contracts in resale price maintenance territory were obliged to increase prices."

3. *E. T. Grether*—"All the evidence available and *a priori* theorizing point indubitably to the conclusion that the patrons of lower price, limited service firms are forced to pay higher prices for the goods under contract than previously."

4. *Fortune Magazine*—In non-fair trade states, "prices are consistently lower than where

the same articles are 'fair' traded. How big a bill the American public is paying to give the retailer this protection no one has ever figured out. But to argue that there is no bill at all is simply disingenuous."

Fair Trade Leads to an Undesirable Price Uniformity and Rigidity

Fair trade is frequently condemned because of its alleged tendency to introduce an undesirable uniformity and rigidity into the retail price structure. The purpose of price maintenance is to establish a common floor to prices. Although officially only minimum prices are established, fair trade prices tend in practice to become actual prices. Thus, all stores sell at uniform prices regardless of costs and other operating conditions.

This uniformity of prices is felt to be highly undesirable. It prevents stores from adjusting their prices to peculiar needs of their own markets and robs low income families of the opportunity to profit by patronizing limited service and other low price stores.

Nor do controlled prices, so it is argued, respond readily to changing economic conditions. According to Malcolm McNair:

As abundantly demonstrated during the depression, there are numerous manufacturers who will resort to many expedients before they will change prices; they will even in some instances reduce production and lay off labor first.

The Real Purpose of Fair Trade Is to Obtain Higher Retail Margins

The opponents of fair trade fail to see any reason why old-line retailers should be so insistent on fair trade if it did not enhance the margin of profit. In fact, Grether believes that to retailers the effect on gross margins is "the prime test" of the success of fair trade. It is pointed out that, in the efforts to sell fair trade to other retailers, proponents of fair trade have always stressed the advantage derived from more profitable markups. According to Grether, the 1933 California Act was followed by a very substantial increase in retail margins.

In the same connection opponents of fair trade point to what they consider to be a very significant development in fair trade philosophy. This is the grudging support given to the fair trade movement by certain large chain organi-

zations. The reason for this, so it is claimed, is that fixed margins give a definite competitive advantage to mass distributors in the fact that with free prices on their own private brands, they can undersell the fixed prices on national brands. *Fortune Magazine* believes that fair trade "has greatly strengthened the chains."

Fair Trade Tends to Discourage Efficiency in Retailing and to Increase Costs of Distribution

The critics of fair trade believe that price maintenance discourages the introduction of measures to increase efficiency in retailing, and generally adds to the cost of retailing. As evidence they cite the following:

1. The primary appeal of many new retailing devices such as super-markets, limited service stores, low-rental shopping centers, etc., is price. By making it impossible for these stores to quote lower prices, fair trade deprives them of their chief attraction and retards their development.

2. Fair trade tends to preserve those stores which will not or cannot improve their methods of operation. The drive for efficiency loses its vigor. Merchants become apathetic toward new selling methods. Existing distributive processes are frozen into a fixed pattern.

3. Under fair trade the whole distributive structure is based not on efficiency but on the shaky foundation of fixed prices. The Report to the Temporary National Economic Committee declares that price maintenance "protects the inefficient, the unprogressive, and those who have abandoned the hazardous struggle for profits in a preference for security, while it penalizes the ambitious and resourceful merchants. It thus safeguards the living of one group, but reduces the opportunities for the more progressive. . . ."

4. Price maintenance is itself a costly and uneconomic method of pricing. As competition in prices diminishes, competitive advertising and the offering of purely competitive services tend to increase.

5. Guaranteed margins, according to E. T. Grether, are "powerful magnets to new enterprises." The result is over-crowding, diluted volume of sales, slow turnover and high costs. Fair trade, it is said, is partly responsible for the recent rapid growth of drug counters in department stores, super-markets, "dime" stores, and the like.

The Non-Signer Provisions Are Coercive, Oppressive, Unfair, and Undemocratic

Many persons who see no objection to purely voluntary price maintenance are bitterly opposed to the non-signer clauses in state laws and hence to the proposal to lend Congressional support to these clauses. They believed that to force retailers to conform to contracts which they have not signed and the terms of which they have not voluntarily accepted is contrary to the whole idea of contract as it has developed in American commercial law.

The analogy to traffic laws and other regulations which everyone must obey is felt to be utterly unsound. The fair trade laws are not in most instances, criminal statutes nor does the Miller-Tydings Act, specifically authorize such statutes. Enforcement procedure under fair trade is civil in character and merely establishes certain rights of action by one person against another. There is no reason for public policy to demand universal compliance with what are essentially the terms of a private contract. It is *not* the American way of doing things, but definitely un-American. Frequently it leads to nothing short of a monopolistic conspiracy against a retailer who is guilty of no crime against society. It is offensive to American standards of due process of law and the right to fair trial.

What makes this situation worse are the methods employed by fair trading retailers to force non-signers into line. In most states "fair-trade committees" have been formed to check on price cutters, report violations to manufacturers and, if need be, to institute legal action. The record of the activities of these private enforcement groups compiled by the Federal Trade Commission is offered as proof of their coercive tactics.

The "permissive" character of fair trade is described as illusory. A small retailer does not have an option in handling fair trade items. In some lines, in fact, all competing products are subject to control. Nor does he have either the market or the resources to develop his own private brands.

True Regard for States Rights Demands the Rejection of the Proposed Non-Signer Amendment

To the opponents of fair trade, the states rights argument presents a false issue. They believe that the proponents of fair trade are not sincere in making a plea for states rights and that the issue would never have been raised if the proponents of fair trade had not found it easier to obtain favors from state legislatures than from Congress.

Furthermore, it is contended that a true regard for the prerogatives of the states would lead to a rejection of the Miller-Tydings type of statute and particularly of the proposed non-signer amendment. The Miller-Tydings Act authorizes states in which the product is resold to determine policy. But, it is asked, how about the state in which the product originates? If this state believes price maintenance to be inimical to public welfare, should it not have as much right to determine policy as the state in which the product is resold? It is doubted that the Miller-Tydings Act contains positive guarantees that a state will be free from price maintenance merely because it refrains from enacting a fair trade statute. The force of that Act is operating in only one direction. In fairness to states which do not want price maintenance applied to non-signers, Congress should not enact the proposed amendment.

It is further argued that Congress cannot constitutionally and should not morally renounce any part of its control over interstate commerce. For over 60 years it has been a well-established principle that the regulation of monopolistic practices is a prerogative and a duty of the Congress. To turn back to the states an important area such as resale price maintenance is reversing this long-term trend and runs counter to our whole experience in regulating monopoly.

One of the strongest objections to giving additional authority to the states is based on the fear that the states will exceed the specific authority granted. In the debate on the Miller-Tydings Act the charge was made time and again that its enactment would be giving a "blank check" to the states. The very situation which has produced the demand for further legislation is cited as evidence that these fears were well founded. The Miller-Tydings Act authorizes price maintenance only by specific contract between manufacturer and dealer. Yet every state which has enacted fair trade legislation has attempted to extend price maintenance to all dealers whether or not they are parties to contractual arrangements. To legalize these actions now will be merely to extend an invitation to commit even more objectionable excesses in the future.

20. The Protection of the Consumer and Competition, Some Fundamental Issues

WILLIAM F. BROWN

The debate between those who believe that only government can solve certain of our problems and those who denounce the intervention of federal authority in business affairs seems to be a never-ending one, and it is fortunate that this is so. As our economic environment changes and as our knowledge of business economics becomes more complete and precise a balance between business and government that may be satisfactory at one point in time may become patently inadequate at another. But the issue is always an important one and any changes in the balance, in either direction, deserve to be sharply challenged—to be reviewed carefully in terms of their possible influence upon our progress toward the goals of our society. Among the most important of these goals, it seems to me, is the advancement of the welfare of the individual—all individuals, not merely a select few. And we have interpreted this welfare not only in terms of material progress, i.e., increasing amounts of desired goods and services, but also in terms of individual freedom—freedom of speech, freedom and religion, freedom to choose occupations, freedom to choose among goods or services, freedom to take risks or to minimize them, to name but a few. We have not reached perfection in moving toward these objectives; we have been guilty of contradictions and we have been compelled by the very nature of the problem to accept compromises. For purposes of compari-

‡‡ SOURCE: Reprinted by permission from *Effective Marketing Coordination*, edited by George L. Baker, Jr., Proceedings of the 44th National Conference of the American Marketing Association, June 1961, pp. 426–438.

son, too, I might add that other nations or societies may have goals that differ from our own with the welfare of only a limited class of individuals and others may place much greater emphasis upon material progress rather than upon individual freedom.

REGULATION FOR MORE RAPID PROGRESS TOWARD OUR GOALS

In our own case the present balance between government and private enterprise has been the result of a process of development within our democratic system. It is still going on. Fairly early in this process we rather firmly committed ourselves to a competitive capitalistic economy because we believed that it preserves a reasonable maximum of individual freedom while at the same time assuring an expending flow of desired goods and services to the greatest possible number of individuals. But many questions arise in the implementation of this economic philosophy, as in any other, including the development of technical capabilities, the rate of formation of capital, the control of unemployment, the distribution of rewards, and so on. Over the years, we have modified our approach in a number of ways; it is by no means the sort of complete laissez-faire attitude that was once envisaged as typical of the competitive capitalistic system.

These modifications have come in a number of different forms. From the very first we have recognized that certain activities should be a monopoly of the federal government—for example, those related to foreign affairs, the

Army, the Navy, the Post Office, and so on. Second, in order to foster the development of better methods and improved products we have provided, by means of our patent system, for the granting of an absolute monopoly to individuals who can contribute such inventions, though we have done this only with rather strict reservations, particularly with respect to the time during which such monopoly shall be valid. Third, we have taken the position that there are peculiar circumstances in some industries which make the unrestrained action of competition unsatisfactory, and we have designated these industries as public utilities, and, while conferring upon them certain monopolistic or semi-monopolistic advantages, we have protected the public interest by setting up regulatory agencies in order to control the services and prices offered by firms in these industries. Fourth, we also have recognized that for some trades or professions the protection to the consumer requires that certain standards of competition and ethics be maintained and thus we have established boards or commissions in such fields as law, medicine, barbering, undertaking, laundry and dry cleaning, to ensure that these minimums be met by practitioners. Fifth, we have modified the freedom of action of entrepreneurs in all businesses in a great variety of ways, in some instances more or less positively by the enactment of such measures as tariffs and farm price support programs and in other cases by the enactment of legislation which influences pricing, promotional activities, labor practices, and financial arrangements of various kinds in our economic society.

In theory, at least, it seems clear that we have justified these modifications of a free competitive enterprise system on the grounds that with them we can advance more rapidly and more surely toward our material goals than we would without them. The question we must continuously raise is: To what extent does any particular form of regulation actually make progress toward our goal of maximizing production and distribution of desired goods and services for the maximum number of people?

With this question in mind I propose to examine briefly the major kinds of regulatory activities (thus excluding the first four types of modifications of competition mentioned above) which more or less directly have influenced marketing in the past three quarters of a century. Frankly, my judgments will not be concerned as much with the success and freedom

of business decision-making of the particular entrepreneur as with the welfare of the populace served by him. The justification for his existence as an entrepreneur, it seems to me, resides in the values which he can contribute to the total welfare. Fortunately, it is the fundamental strength of a competitive economy that most of the actions of the individual entrepreneur designed to further his own well-being are likely to result in the improved welfare of the general populace. Of course, the areas of activity in which the nation relies upon competition rather than upon some kind of centralized control mechanism in order to attain its goals must indeed be characterized by competition. This assurance is essential. Also, the effective satisfaction of the material wants of the greatest possible number of people within a framework of freedom of choice requires that the individual buyer have available to him reasonably satisfactory sources of information about products and services. And this is also a necessary requirement for the proper functioning of the competitive system as a whole. The business firm which has a new or improved product or which can produce at lower cost must be able to inform potential buyers of the merits of its position. In general, the modifications which we have introduced into our system are those which have appeared necessary—at least to some observers—because conditions in particular areas of activity have indicated a divergence between the basic similarity of interest between some entrepreneurs and the public.

THE EXTENT REGULATION HAS PROGRESSED TOWARD OUR GOALS

The forms of the kinds of regulations with which we are now concerned and which have been most important in their influence on marketing activities fall into two categories: first, those regulations which are designed to protect the consumer from misinformation or from his lack of information and second, those which are intended to ensure the competitive character of our system. The first type has become important because in the past century the number and variety of products which the typical consumer may select from has increased so enormously and many of them are of such technical character that the ordinary buyer cannot be expected to possess enough information or scientific training to make buying decisions on a basis reflecting complete knowledge of the characteristics of the product, the characteristics of competitive products, and knowledge of market conditions generally.

By the turn of the century the position of the consumer had changed so much and hence questionable practices in some fields had developed so extensively that in 1906 Congress enacted the first Food and Drug Act. Thereafter the basic enactment was amended some thirteen times and then completely re-written in 1938. In general the law prohibited the adulteration and misbranding of products in these categories. Until the passage of these measures, the consumer could not be sure that such products as milk or other foods or drugs were not diluted or even falsely described on the label. Today the buyer has reasonable assurance that the foods or drugs he purchases are what they claim to be, that they are pure and safe to use under prescribed conditions, and that they have been produced under acceptably sanitary conditions. That the buyer must possess these assurances if our goals are to be attained seems to be beyond question. No other method than governmental interference seems to have been able to provide this guarantee. Apparently the fringe of unethical producers could not otherwise be prevented from taking advantage both of the consumer and their more honest competitors.

But the 1938 Food, Drug, and Cosmetic Act went considerably further than simply to protect the consumer from the carelessness or downright dishonesty of some producers. It may be said that it attempts to protect the consumer from his own ignorance by providing that the Administrator may establish official standards of identity for specific products within the purview of the Act. The issue is placed squarely in focus by the decision of the United States Supreme Court in the *Quaker Oats* case first upholding the 1938 measure. The Administrator had established a standard of identity for enriched farina which required the addition of a minimum quantity of each of a selected list of vitamins. No farina which did not contain at least the minimums could be labelled enriched or could even state the addition of any vitamins to the product. In upholding the Administrator the Court adopted the argument that consumers in general did not possess enough information about various vitamins to be able to distinguish between one product which had an adequate quantity of a proper

variety of vitamins and another product which might have an unnecessarily large amount of an inexpensive vitamin and little or no addition of an important but costly vitamin. Hence even truthful statements were not permitted if the state of consumer knowledge was such that the consumer might be falsely impressed by them. In order to achieve the level of consumer want satisfaction which I have postulated as a goal of our society it seems imperative that there be some standards of identity for many kinds of products and some method of obtaining reasonable adherence to these standards, and again delegation to a central authority for the determination and enforcement of standards has seemed to be the only practical alternative. It does carry risks, as some later administrative actions indicate, but fortunately the courts in most instances can be relied upon to provide a balancing point of view.

Because consumers obtain much of their knowledge about products and services not only from the label, but also from the advertising and personal selling that may be done by the producer or his representatives or dealers, there is an equal need in these areas of marketing activity for assurance that the buyer can rely upon them. And again, without governmental interference this assurance is not obtainable. The leaders of the advertising profession themselves recognized this need and in 1911 the Associated Advertising Clubs of the World vigorously supported the enactment of a standard regulatory measure at the state level, the so-called Printer's Ink Model Statute. Then in 1914 Congress passed the Federal Trade Commission Act, a measure intended to reinforce antitrust activities of the government by preventing unfair competition. Although the Act had not been viewed as a measure designed to protect consumers directly, the Commission, supported by the courts, quite logically took the position that false advertising was an unfair competitive method and early began to proceed against instances of such advertising (in general, I might add, with more success than it achieved in undertaking the expected kinds of antitrust actions).

As Judge Baker of the Seventh United States Circuit Court of Appeals pointed out in the *Sears, Roebuck & Company* case, the first to come up under the law, the Act was intended to initiate a new era in business morality and it did so. Many kinds of practices which had been accepted as commonplace began to disappear, except perhaps at the "fringe." True, there were difficulties in procedures under the law and unnecessary delays often ensued; hence, in 1938 the Wheeler-Lea Act, amending the original measure, was enacted. In addition to streamlining some of the procedures required of the F.T.C., the law broadened its mandate to specifically include the protection of the consumer and to cover false advertising. For the first time, too, false advertising was defined, and in sweeping terms, as follows in Section 15:

The term "false advertisement" means an advertisement, other than labeling, which is misleading in a material respect; and in determining whether any advertisement is misleading, there shall be taken into account (among other things) not only representations made or suggested by statement, word, design, device, sound, or any combination thereof, but also the extent to which the advertisement fails to reveal facts material in the light of such representations or material with respect to consequences which may result from the use of the commodity to which the advertisement relates under the conditions prescribed in said advertisement, or under such conditions as are customary or usual . . . .

In view of the rather sweeping terms in which false advertising is described in the act, one can only wonder at times that the Federal Trade Commission has not proceeded against certain kinds of advertising that still appear with too great frequency.

To repeat, the consumer must have information upon which he can rely, that is, which he believes, if he is to obtain maximum satisfaction from his buying and if the competitive system is to function most effectively. A very high proportion of all advertising is truthful and performs its vital functions reasonably well. But there exists a fringe of untruthful, highly exaggerated or misleading advertising which unfortunately is sometimes quite prominent. As a result, this relatively small fraction of advertising has a much greater influence on public believability of advertising than its absolute volume or importance justifies and thus advertising's greatest asset, its believability, is impaired.

The second major aspect of marketing regulation, the protection of competition, raises much more complicated and controversial problems. The reasons for these difficulties are varied: First, it is not easy to define competition in a realistic manner in the practical market place. Second, the protection of competition inevitably leads to the necessity of distinguishing between desirable and undesirable methods of competing. Judgement values then become increasingly significant. And here we must start out by recognizing a fact whose importance in this connection it is almost impossible to overemphasize, namely, competition necessarily involves injury to competitors. Each time an individual firm makes a sale that might have gone to a competitor, he thereby injures the competitor, that is, he makes the competitors' business less profitable or more difficult. The question is not "Has there been an injury to a competitor?" but rather, "How has the injury been inflicted?" If the sale has been made "fairly," then the natural working of competition has been effective. If made "unfairly," then the method should be circumscribed. Obviously, the critical problem here is that of defining the terms "fair" and "unfair." If we believe in a competitive society we must, it seems to me, keep as a guiding factor in our definition of what is fair and unfair in competition at least the criterion that anything which basically impairs or eliminates competition is unfair.

It was in order to give effect to this concept that Congress enacted the early antitrust laws, the Sherman, Clayton, and Federal Trade Commission Acts, hoping then to prevent practices which the great trusts of the post Civil War period had employed to obtain their monopolistic positions. The use of discriminatory price cutting in order to ruin smaller competitors, tying the sale or lease of many other items to a monopolized product, buying out or merging with the remaining competitors in an industry, agreeing to set artificially high prices or to divide markets, arranging interlocking directorates to ensure coordinated and non-competitive action, were among the most prominent of these practices. It seems to me that there can be no argument about the desirability of preventing such practices when they are clearly employed to eliminate all competition and give the user a monopolistic position in the market.

However, the problem of regulation is confused by the fact that these basic methods also may be employed in many situations simply to enable an individual firm to compete more effectively in the market. The dilemma becomes one of establishing an operational set of rules which, when applied, will distinguish between the desirable and undesirable use of the methods. "Desirable," of course, is equated to "maintaining the beneficial effects of competition." Unfortunately the phrases that appear in the Antitrust Acts include words which, necessarily, do not set absolute standards. "*Substantially* lessen competition" and "*tend* to create a monopoly" require interpretation. In recent years there seems to be developing a "take no chances" attitude. A few examples may suffice to indicate the significance of this point.

The ability to merge firms has been a very useful device in the past permitting a speed-up in the processes of both horizontal and vertical integration with consequent benefits to consumer in terms of greater efficiency, lower costs, and so forth. In some instances the merger of smaller firms (for example, those in the automobile industry) may lead to more effective competition between the merged firms and the giants of the industry. On the other hand, any merger between two firms which sell or might sell similar products to some of the same buyers clearly results in the elimination of competition between them insofar as these buyers are concerned. Only the facts in each situation can indicate how substantial this specific lessening of competition can be, and even these facts in many cases cannot provide a basis for accurately forecasting the ultimate effect on the vigor of competition in the industry.

In attempting to obtain solutions in specific merger situations many different questions may be raised, among them the following: What share of the market will the company possess if the merger is consummated? (And this query requires a definition of the market—in terms of product, function, and geographic limits—generally a knotty problem in itself.) What degree of concentration now exists in the relevant market and how will the merger change this pattern? How easily can new firms enter the market and achieve substantial positions in it? How flexible has pricing been in the industry? What economies of scale may result from the merger? Is the merger likely to encourage or impel a wave of additional consolidations in the same market? Unfortunately, in attempting to obtain answers to these questions, and particularly in putting them together to create a sound solution I think that we must confess that we really know very little with precision. In two recent actions, the Bethlehem Steel–Youngstown Sheet and Tube and the Brown Shoe Co.–Kinsey Shoe Company merger cases, the respective United States District Courts have concluded that the concentrations were such that, in the light of all the circumstances, they presented a "reasonable probability that (they) may substantially lessen competition or tend to create a monopoly . . ." And the courts brushed aside arguments that the mergers would enable the firms to compete more effectively and operate more efficiently. In the Brown Shoe Co. case, particularly, the vertical integration of a shoe manufacturer and a chain of retail stores was prohibited even though substantial efficiencies were claimed for the combination. The courts have seemed to indicate that they simply would not take the risk of potential damage to the character of competition in order to permit possible increases in efficiency.

The threat posed by vertical integration of the sort projected by the Brown-Kinsey merger is one which clearly implies injury to competing non-integrated shoe manufacturers, particularly if this merger were to be followed by others which eventually led to the formation of a number of huge manufacturer-retailer enterprises which might then account for a half, two-thirds, or even more of the industry's entire volume at all levels. In such a case the non-integrated manufacturer would be foreclosed from a great part of the market. Even so, would competition be less and would the consumer suffer? The chain grocery retailing institution developed rapidly in the 1920's, integrating the retailing and wholesaling functions and by "tying up" approximately 40 per cent of the retail market for groceries unquestionably caused the subsequent elimination of many of the conventional wholesale grocery firms. But competition in grocery retailing and manufacturing seems not to have been reduced and if anything, to have increased. And certainly there have been significant reductions in the overall costs of marketing food products. Presumably, then, it would have been unfortunate had the chain grocery development been dependent upon an illegal merger pattern. Of course, the possible advantages of integration in the grocery situation seemed to have been greater than those which may exist in the shoe industry at present.

In the situations described above regulatory action is designed to protect competition and in doing so almost inevitably also protects some types of competitors. Protection of groups of competitors is, nominally at least, only a by-product of most of the provisions of the antitrust laws, but important exceptions to this general principle appear in sections 2(c), (d), and (e) of the Robinson-Patman act. These provisions, dealing with brokerage payments, advertising and similar allowances, and the furnishing of services to buyers, protect individual competitors or groups of competitors without regard to the possible effect on the state of competition generally. Nor can possible benefits in the form of cost savings be employed to justify variations from the concepts enunciated in these sections. In this type of legislation we have gone far in attempting to equalize the conditions of competition in order to protect less efficient competitors. In doing so we have introduced rigidities in pricing and other business practices which reduce the opportunities of well managed firms to improve operations with subsequent long-run benefits to consumers. In such situations, unfortunately, the interests of the few not only have been permitted to restrict the freedom of action of others, but also may be said to have interfered with our progress toward our more general goal, the improvement of the general welfare.

E. Ethical Considerations

21. Marketing and Moral Values in an Acquisitive Society

EUGENE J. KELLEY

The issues discussed in this paper center on whether or not marketing teachers should be concerned with moral values and ethical questions in the teaching of marketing. Marketing professors as individuals might not separate material and spiritual factors. As professionals, they usually have not linked ethics with marketing in their teaching, research, and writing.

Some marketing teachers maintain marketing should not be concerned with ethical questions, perhaps because ethical discussions involve value and moral judgments which might conflict with the advancement of science in marketing. Other teachers have grown sensitive to criticisms that we are preparing students for a field described as "huckstering," using "hidden persuaders," contributing to a "pitchman's prosperity," producing "artificial obsolescence," and comprised of "wastemakers." This group believes students should be able to evaluate criticisms of marketing at both factual and ethical levels and that it may no longer be adequate to justify marketing solely in terms of economic accomplishments.

Critics and opinion leaders are increasingly critical of marketing policies—charging deliberate programs of planned obsolescence, consumer manipulation, and proliferation of products without functional differences. Marketing teachers should not ignore or react defensively to such criticisms. To do so would only broaden the schism between intellectuals and the business community.

Marketing teachers can communicate ideas

on the positive values of a free marketing system based on a hierarchy of values including customer service, individual and societal development, freedom of choice, in addition to profit maximization. There are numerous illustrations of the concern of marketers with the principles of business responsibility, public service, veracity, social welfare, and consumer sovereignty. These are as much parts of the ethical dimensions of marketing as are the aspects the critics are prone to comment on such as deceptive promotion and the stimulation of meaningless and wasteful consumption. The basis of the necessary dialogue lies in a discussion of the ethical dimension of marketing thought and practice.

DEFINITIONS[1]

Ethics. Ethics is one division of philosophy. In the sense that the term is used in this paper, ethics refers to the philosophy of moral values or moral norms, i.e., normative ethics. In this case, ethics does not belong to empirical science, but to philosophy. Ethics is the study and philosophy of human conduct with emphasis on the determination of right and wrong. It is concerned with good and evil, with what is right and what is wrong. "The purpose of philosophical, or normative, ethics is to state norms for human action or judgments about moral values." [2]

⚉ SOURCE: Reprinted by permission from *Marketing: A Maturing Discipline*, Proceedings of the Winter Conference of the American Marketing Association, December 1960, pp. 195–203.

[1] I am indebted to Dr. J. Whitney Bunting of New York University for a helpful discussion of definitions.

[2] Morton White, *The Age of Analysis* (New York: The New American Library, 1955), p. 217.

Moral. Moral refers to the degree of conformity to right conduct, to being actuated by a sense of the good, true, and right. Thus, ethics refers to the rules of human behavior deemed right and proper by society at a point in time; moral is a descriptive adjective denoting a standard of ethical behavior.

Acquisitive Society. The term acquisitive society is used to describe one view of our consumeristic society underlying many ethical discussions. In many respects our society is more materialistic than others. In the United States greater emphasis seems to be placed on acquiring material things in the belief that this is one way to achieve the age old dream of the good life. Our national faith in this belief is reflected in our economic, social, and marketing system and accounts, in no small measure, for the American standard of living.

Ethical concepts and moral standards always exist and moral decisions are endless for all in any society. It is not suggested that problems of marketing ethics are more numerous or difficult than in medicine, law, teaching, or any other field. Marketing is by nature a more visible and conspicuous activity than most fields and, therefore, more likely to be noted and criticized. Professionals in any field have an obligation to respond objectively to criticisms, even to anticipate criticisms of the ethical norm.

ETHICS ARE ABOVE CULTURE

The conflict between ethical concepts and marketing practice exists because philosophers are concerned with an ideal in which ethical values are superimposed on the culture according to the highest moral standards. But the norms of ethical behavior in business are taken from the prevailing culture of the time and may be far from the philosophic ideal. Unfortunately, all too often the ethics practiced in a field are the worst of the culture, not the best. Examples can be found in international law, religion, politics and other fields besides marketing.[3]

By definition, ethics is a subject not related primarily to business practice, but to the promise and potential of a higher moral climate. Thus, at one level of ethical study it is possible to identify issues with ethical dimensions and to develop an appreciation of the relation between existing business practice and ethical standards.

SOME MARKETING QUESTIONS

Some marketing issues with ethical dimensions are illustrated by the following questions. The questions may indicate the discussion and research possibilities of the ethical dimension. Each question can be discussed on two levels: factual and ethical. The ethical level would be one which would consider standards for approval and disapproval.

1. What are the ethics of persuasion and promotional strategy? What are the ethical responsibilities of the motivation researcher and the manager who uses his findings? How far should researchers go in probing into the subconscious of the individual to try to influence or manipulate purchase behavior?[4]

2. Is it ethical to persuade someone to do something which might not be in his long term interest—to spend money on liquor instead of education, or to spend money, more than he can afford, on a deluxe refrigerator while the present one has utility?

3. Planned product obsolescence is a major issue. Is it ethical to "make" a product obsolete before it is completely worn out? Are marketers wastemakers? Is wasteful product obsolescence necessary to product development programs?

4. To what extent are marketers, as practical businessmen, concerned with anything but the efficient movement of volume at a profit?

5. The new marketing concept has required wide-reaching changes in organization, philosophy, promotion, and product organization. All this has involved people, and many people have been, or think they have been, adversely affected. To what extent do we or can we set up safeguards to minimize this impact on people in undertaking reorganization which we know is inevitable and essential to survival? Where does "cruelty" begin (or end) and where does "toughness" take over in dealing with human beings, with frustrated ambitions, regroupings which inevitably "put someone under some-

---

[3] Kenneth S. Carlston, *The Province and Role of Marketing Theory* (Urbana, Illinois: unpublished manuscript, 1960).

[4] Some of the newer techniques of advertising raise interesting ethical questions. Consider, for instance, the discussion possibilities of the recent FTC ruling restricting Colgate in the "invisible" shield case. This is an example of many situations where to illustrate something on TV the advertising technician must fake it. Where whipped cream tinted grey is used to imitate shaving cream on a model's face, is there deception or isn't there?

one else?" How can we safeguard the freedom of thought and inquiry that are so essential in all creative jobs?

6. Many people have said that integration and coordination were the outstanding developments and gains from the marketing concept. Does this imply an intensification of the "organization man?"—the elimination or subduing of individualism and of creating "aloneness," without which there is no individual progress?

7. One of the significant changes taking place today is in the field of distribution channels. Many manufacturers are setting up their own branches, bypassing the distributor; many others sell through distributors to the small, unprofitable accounts, but sell direct where the volume makes this profitable (and would make it profitable for the distributor as well). To what extent do we have any moral responsibility to keep the independent merchant in business? Is the disappearance of tens of thousands of small merchants of any concern to the efficient marketing executive? Is this entirely a matter for political reformers, welfare economists and others?

8. Do we, as marketing people, have any responsibility in developing standards for measuring contributions, other than cold efficiency? Is it, or should it be, any of our concern that the theory of "the survival of the fittest" should be seriously questioned by sociologists and some economists? Should we concern ourselves with this question in appraising the "value added" by distribution?

9. What are the ethical implications of the indications that profits are taking on a subsidiary role in many business problems? Economic stability, public relations, fear of government intervention are strong influences on executive decisions and have modified the traditional view of profit maximization. The term "corporate conscience" has been used to describe this change.

10. Are the existing legal structure, individual personal standards, and the general level of ethical expectations of the times sufficient guides to ethical marketing conduct in a changing world?

11. One more question: should such questions be introduced from time to time in the framework of marketing courses?[5]

Many of these complex questions have, in one form or another, been considered by thoughtful men for centuries. Most individuals, whether consciously or not, have arrived at positions. Some of the questions suggested have political as well as moral and economic overtones. None of them are posed to deny that the prime responsibility of business is to perform an economic function. Underlying such questions is the view that, in the long run, it is not likely that a business, or the enterprise system as we know it, can survive if the narrow view of ethical questions is taken.

The ethical and social demands being placed on business administrators are part of the environment influencing many market decisions. To ignore social and ethical considerations is to ignore the will of the market. The importance of the market in setting ethical standards is one reason why marketing men must lead the way in developing the social responsibilities of business enterprise.

CRITICISMS OF PRESENT STANDARDS

Some critics believe that business ethics have declined in recent years and that some forms of corruption in the United States today are deeper and more widespread than 10 or 20 years ago. This is the view communicated in one form or another in books such as *The Operators, The Organization Man, The Hidden Persuaders, The Status Seekers, The Wastemakers, The Affluent Society, The Lonely Crowd, The Exurbanites*, and *Life in the Crystal Palace*. Some of these books can be regarded as non-scholarly works with serious errors and distortions. However, the cumulative criticism of present standards of business responsibility cannot be ignored, even though many of the writers are straining hard to make a journalistic point. Time does not permit a detailed analysis of these books. One common denominator can be pointed out. All these authors are highly critical of "Madison Avenue" and of many marketing practices. All portray "a society uprooted by great changes, losing its certainty about moral values, and trying to substitute social approval for morality . . . ."[6]

Students who have heard only one side of the debate will find two recently published books provide some of the answers to criticisms being

[5] Dr. Hector Lazo of the Graduate School of Business Administration of New York University has discussed such questions in his courses and has contributed to the above list of questions.

[6] Speech by Robert L. Fegley, General Electric Company, before Williams College Undergraduates, Williamstown, Mass., January 31, 1960.

directed to this field. These are *The Spenders* by Steuart Henderson Britt and *The Strategy of Desire* by Ernest Dichter.

Some scholars believe that western society is facing an inevitable mental, moral, and sociocultural revolution and that we are not in one of the ordinary crises which happen every decade, but in one of the greater transitions in human history.[7] Business and marketing leaders must be perceptive enough to appreciate the nature of the extraordinary character of the contemporary crisis of our culture and society. As Sorokin put it, "he is a poor doctor who treats dangerous pneumonia as a slight cold."[8]

ETHICS AND THE DEVELOPMENT OF MARKETING AS A DISCIPLINE

The level of ethical behavior in a field seems to be related to the stage of development of a discipline. In the context of marketing as a maturing discipline it might be helpful to recall Whitehead's suggestion for applying Hegel's ideas to educational theory. The Hegelian analysis of progress, Thesis, Antithesis, and Synthesis, in relation to intellectual progress, was compared by Whitehead to the stage of romance, the stage of precision, and the stage of generalization.[9]

In an historical sense, marketing has completed the laissez faire period, where each businessman and economic unit operated with a minimum of restraint. We may now be in an era where ethics and legality are generally equated and operating under a kind of minimum ethic in which some rules have been established and others are understood. Much marketing activity seems to exist in this rather elastic, legally dominated ethical framework.

A third stage was suggested by Cabot when he identified a stage of Christian ethics, "a sample of which is the effort to satisfy real, deep, and permanent desires, and not merely obvious desires in others as well as ourselves."[10] This might be called an ideal or maximum ethic. These ethical levels, laissez faire, legally determined, and maximum seem to parallel White-

head's stages of intellectual progress of romance, precision, and generalization.

Many marketers tend to confine themselves to the second stage of the cycle, the stage of precision, and to view ethical problems in essentially legalistic terms. This seems to minimize the ferment which underlies the precision stage of marketing and the potential educational meaning of the intellectual stage of generalization.

As Whitehead points out, the stage of precision is barren without a previous stage of romance; he says, "unless there are facts which have already been vaguely apprehended in their broad generality, the previous analysis is an analysis of nothing."[11] The final stage of generalization, Hegel's Synthesis, "is a return to romanticism with added advantage of classified ideas and relevant technique. It is the fruition which has been the goal of the precise training. It is the final success."[12]

This may be a critical transitional period for marketing. The marketing pioneers have done their work well; we now seem to be at a point of revising approaches to the study of marketing. Is it possible we may be on the verge of moving from the stage of precision to generalization, from an essentially descriptive, institutionalized, functional approach to the study of the process of marketing from an administrative and social viewpoint, and from a minimum ethic towards a maximum ethic?

If marketing is in such a transition period, teachers charged with preparing students for the future are confronted with a major challenge. In the kind of changing world associated with transition periods, a premium is placed on men who can operate effectively in a climate of change and who can innovate and lead in the implementation of innovation. Such innovative capacity is not likely to be found among marketing men who do not understand the nature of the ethical, social, political, economic, and other environmental forces influencing their innovations.

Conclusion

Marketing and moral values are related if the appropriate time span is taken and student and business attention shifted to the creation of long run rather than short run personal and professional values. This task is probably best

[7] Pitirim A. Sorokin, *The Crisis of Our Age* (New York: E. P. Dutton, 1957), p. 315.

[8] *Ibid*, p. 315.

[9] Alfred N. Whitehead, *The Aims of Education* (New York: The New American Library, 1949), p. 29.

[10] Richard C. Cabot, *Adventures on the Borderlands of Ethics* (New York: Harper, 1926), p. 89.

[11] Whitehead, *op. cit.*, p. 30.

[12] Whitehead, *op. cit.*, p. 31.

performed in the university. The university must do it because it has obligated itself to society to anticipate the future.

A colleague, Peter Drucker, has said the business schools are the major organ for the anticipation of tomorrow. It is, therefore, not enough that they teach yesterday's mistakes to today's students to prepare them to be tomorrow's managers. They must teach today what will be needed tomorrow. Indeed, the function and mission of a professional school is to make the tomorrow.

The opportunity to consider ethical and moral issues reaffirms my belief that the study of marketing can be truly liberal, if not humanistic, as well as professional. Pragmatically, to avoid rising public standards of ethical expectations would be as unwise marketing as to ignore rising educational, income, or population levels.

The answer to the question whether or not marketing teachers should teach or even be concerned with the ethical and broader social implications of marketing practices probably depends on one's view of the professor's role. If the professor's role is seen merely as the dissemination of existing knowledge, without appraisal, then perhaps it is not necessary to consider the ethical dimensions of marketing. If the professor's function in society is to appraise, increase, and disseminate knowledge, it seems mandatory to consider carefully the types of questions raised in the beginning of this paper at both descriptive and normative levels. Does the first view enable marketing professors to fulfill their full potential of service to students and society? Is it calculated to provide students able to evaluate the ideas, human values, and social ponderables raised in this session and this conference? If not, it may be time for teachers of marketing to raise some questions which will make our job even more complex and our responsibilities more personal.

22. Is Advertising Morally Defensible?

ARNOLD TOYNBEE

"It is argued that marketing—including the kinds of new products introduced, the design of those products, and advertising—reflects public wants and tastes rather than shapes them." I have been asked whether I believe this to be true. I do not believe that. If advertising were just an echo of desires that were already in the housewife's mind, it would be a superfluous expense of time, ingenuity and money. It would be nothing more than a carbon copy of a housewife's own shopping list. I believe that advertising does have an effect. I believe it stimulates consumption, as is suggested in the second point put to me:

"It is argued that personal consumption, stimulated by advertising, is essential for growth and full employment in an economy of abundance." If this were demonstrated to be true, it would also demonstrate, to my mind that an economy of abundance is a spiritually unhealthy way of life, and that the sooner we reform it the better. This may sound paradoxical to modern Western ears. But if it is a paradox, it is one that has always been preached by all the great religions. In an article published in *Printers' Ink* on October 20, 1961, Mr. James Webb Young dismisses the example set by St. Francis of Assisi. "Americans today," Mr. James Webb Young writes, "see little merit in these medieval hairshirt ideas." St. Francis got his ideas from a premedieval teacher, Jesus. These ideas cannot be dismissed without rejecting Christianity and all the other great religions, too.

‡ SOURCE: Reprinted by permission from *Yale Daily News*, Special Issue 1963, p. 2.

WILLIAM BERENBACH

Mr. Toynbee's real hate is not advertising. It's the economy of abundance or, as we have all come to know it, capitalism. This is perfectly all right if only he would make clear the real target he is shooting at. There are many things about capitalism that need correcting, and Mr. Toynbee would be doing the world a great service if he could persuade us to make these corrections. But he's never going to do that if he throws up smoke screens with tirades against a tool that happens to be used by big business in its efforts to sell more goods.

Advertising, like so many techniques available to man, is neither moral nor immoral. Is eloquence immoral because it persuades? Is music immoral because it awakens emotions? Is the gift of writing immoral because it can arouse people to action? No. Yet eloquence, music and writing have been used for evil purpose.

Only recently we were asked to prepare an advertisement by the National Committee for a Sane Nuclear Policy. We conceived an ad featuring Dr. Spock. Its purpose was to discourage nuclear testing. If Mr. Toynbee will agree that this is a good purpose, then he must also agree that in this case at least, advertising was not an instrument of "moral mis-education." He would also be happy to learn that here was an advertisement so persuasive that it prompted one of the chairmen of SANE to telegraph his congratulations for "by all odds the most powerful single statement I have seen over the imprint of SANE."

For the past two years we have run advertis-

The moral that I draw is that a way of life based on personal consumption, stimulated by advertising, needs changing—and there are dozens of possible alternatives to it. For instance, we could still have full employment in the economically advanced countries if we gave up advertising and restricted our personal consumption to, say, the limits that present-day American monks and nuns voluntarily set for themselves, and if we then diverted our production to supply the elementary needs of the poverty-stricken three-quarters of the human race. Working for this obviously worthwhile purpose would bring us much greater personal satisfaction than working, under the stimulus of advertising, in order to consume goods that we do not need and do not genuinely want.

But suppose the whole human race eventually became affluent; what then? Well, I cannot think of any circumstances in which advertising would not be an evil. There are at least three bad things intrinsic to it:

Advertising deliberately stimulates our desires, whereas experience, embodied in the teaching of the religions, tells us that we cannot be good or happy unless we limit our desires and keep them in check.

Advertising makes statements, not in order to tell the truth, but in order to sell goods. Even when its statements are not false, truth is not their object. This is intellectually demoralizing.

Advertising is an instrument of moral, as well as intellectual, mis-education. Insofar as it succeeds in influencing people's minds, it conditions them not to think for themselves and not to choose for themselves. It is intentionally hypnotic in effect. It makes people suggestible and docile. In fact, it prepares them for submitting to a totalitarian regime.

Therefore, let us reform a way of life that cannot be lived without advertising.

ing for Volkswagen cars with the purpose of persuading Americans that simplicity, craftsmanship and low price were available to them in an automobile. These were ads that conveyed facts simply and honestly to the customer. They seemed to sell the country on filling their automotive needs modestly and with good taste. Would Mr. Toynbee call this effort evil merely because advertising was involved? The Volkswagen was built to give the buyer the greatest value in automotive transportation. Isn't advertising performing a valuable function by making that fact clear to the buyer?

No, advertising is not moral or immoral. Only people are. I can cite many instances in commercial advertising that would prove Mr. Toynbee's point of view. I can cite just as many that would disprove it.

If Mr. Toynbee believes a materialistic society is a bad one (and I am not saying he is wrong in that belief), then he owes it to mankind to speak to the point. He owes it to mankind to speak out against such a society and not merely against one of the tools that is available to any society. He may even find that nothing will "sell" his point as effectively as advertising.

F. Competition and Economic Environment

23. *Bigness and the Economic Analysis of Competition*

R. S. MERIAM

Most businessmen never use the tools of economic analysis in making day-to-day decisions or in shaping policy for the future. Yet economic theory is important to them. The course of business obviously is affected by government action, as for example in proceedings under the Sherman Antitrust law and under the laws administered by the Federal Trade Commission; and government policy in such matters makes considerable use of theoretical analysis. The theory of "monopolistic competition," specifically, helps explain much of the government drive against "bigness."

The purpose of this article is to discuss problems of economic analysis which are common to many public issues, such as basing point pricing and freight absorption; uniformity and parallelism among the pricing and marketing practices of competitors; injury to competitors and damage to competition; prices, price restraints, and profits in a period of inflation; and many others. The thought is that these issues exemplify problems which are significant for all who are concerned with public responsibilities of business beyond the mere need of conforming to existing requirements of the law; and that corporate management might profit from a clearer knowledge of how theoretical economists, in and out of government, interpret the facts of business situations involved therein.

In particular, the article treats and attempts to make understandable for businessmen two different economic analyses of competition: (1)

‡‡ SOURCE: Reprinted by permission from *Harvard Business Review*, Vol. 28, No. 2, March 1950, pp. 109–126.

the theory of so-called "monopolistic competition" and (2) the concept of "workable competition." Monopolistic competition is the older analysis. Of academic origin, it has brought academic economists both clarity and confusion; fortunately, in academic circles clarity is now gaining and confusion is losing. Workable competition, also of academic origin, is an outgrowth, an improvement, a corrective supplement. It is in closer touch with the realities of practical business. It has not yet entered the thinking in government circles to any significant extent, while some confused versions of monopolistic competition are very prevalent there. Of course, despite the fact that monopolistic competition analysis helps explain some of the intellectual content of government attacks on big business, no one would claim that academic thinking provides the ignition or the explosive power or, still less, that it explains the will to attack.

Only problems of *economic* analysis are dealt with here. A search for other common elements among such issues as basing points and price restraints in a period of inflation would doubtless reveal similarities of a political, legal, and sociological nature, as well as applications of business administration in a narrow sense; but such other elements are not considered. Moreover, there are more economic problems common to many of the public issues mentioned than this article attempts to cover. For example, the question of how much is known about the relative efficiency of small, medium, and large business units as producers and distributors of wealth and of how to go about finding out more than is now known is obviously a significant question of economic analysis; the article does little more than refer to it.

No attempt is made to draw forth any "rules" or "guides" for business conduct. Because the article deals with the common elements of a wide variety of complex practical problems, it has the general quality which is inherent in any attempt to avoid getting lost in the details of concrete cases and to look at them from a detached point of view. Although some readers may be disappointed by the lack of immediate applications and the absence of specific findings, others may realize value in the very fact that such a general approach often helps in the end to achieve understanding.

MONOPOLISTIC COMPETITION THEORY

In this section the endeavor is to state the essentials of the monopolistic competition theory, to discuss some of its implications for businessmen, and to point out certain difficulties and weaknesses inherent in it. Monopolistic competition, it should be noted, is a term devised by economists to describe conditions where most business operations represent neither pure monopoly nor pure competition but rather something between those two extremes. Such conditions are recognized as typical of modern business.

We will repeatedly call attention to conclusions of monopolistic competition theorizing which are critical of business. Such references may give the impression that the theorizing has been used exclusively by hostile critics and has been developed by them for that purpose. If monopolistic competition theorizing is made to appear as nothing but ingenious rationalization by men who seek the breakup of big business or its subjection to governmental control, we should correct this erroneous impression. The theory consists, with a few exceptions, of logical syllogisms where the conclusions must be accepted if the premises are. (The exceptions usually arise when the reasoning rests upon some unstated premises which, when stated, make the conclusion more special than general.) It provides tools of intellectual analysis to be used by any competent craftsman regardless of his personal sympathies or political convictions.

Essentials. There follow the essentials of the theory stated in as simple terms as possible without too great a loss in precision:

1. A basic premise of monopolistic competition theory is that the businessman tries to make his decisions so as to get as much profit as possible. This basic premise holds for each of the three periods which economic theorists use in their analysis: immediate or "market," intermediate or "short-run," and "long-run."

2. In his endeavor to make as much profit as possible a businessman must weigh three considerations. He must try to buy cheap, sell dear, and do a considerable volume of business. Because the first two objectives may conflict with the third, he must strike a balance among them. As he tries to increase his volume, the margin between price and cost is likely to shrink; his point of maximum profit is where the volume times the margin is the greatest. Because in real life a businessman would recognize that many factors besides these three affect his profit, this view of business motivation can be defined as "narrow."

This narrow point of view is usually assumed by a theorist no matter which of the three time periods is involved. The principal difference between the three time periods lies in the nature of the costs to be considered when the volume of output is being adjusted. In the long run there is an opportunity to adjust all factors, including the quantities of physical capital investment in plant and equipment. In the short run some factors are more or less variable, such as purchases of raw material, while others, such as plant and equipment, are fixed or sunk costs. Under market or immediate conditions, the only relevant costs are those connected with the preservation or storage of the finished product or those involved in transporting the product from one market to another; the position of an agricultural commodity in the period after the harvest serves as an example of a "market" time period.

Attention may be called to another difference between the three periods: the longer the time period, the more likely it is that the customers will restrict their purchases of a dear commodity or increase their purchases of a cheap one.

3. The monopolistic competition theory points out that, when a market is crowded with buyers and sellers, few of the individuals in the market have any big opportunities to buy cheap or to sell dear. Under strictly competitive conditions, they say, no competitor has any significant influence on price. This condition is a brief statement of the economist's definition of "pure competition." Under conditions of pure

competition, then, there are so many buyers and sellers that not one of them can have a price policy; they can only decide whether or not to buy or sell at the price they find in the market.

In the case of "pure monopoly," on the other hand, with 100% of the supply of the commodity controlled by a single individual, the monopolist can adjust his purchasing price, his selling price, and his volume to one another; he can get the greatest return by finding the volume where his aggregate receipts from his customers provide the greatest profit margin over the aggregate costs for the same volume.

4. There are many markets which do not meet either the conditions of pure competition or those of pure monopoly. They range from those with only a few more sellers than one to those which just fall short of having many sellers. The theorists of monopolistic competition give particular attention to markets where the sellers are few. Such a market is called an "oligopoly." The analysis of such markets is, of course, particularly relevant to the problem of "bigness." In such markets the sellers have less opportunity to buy cheap, sell dear, and do business in volume than would a real monopolist, but they have more such opportunities than would the very many buyers and sellers in a perfectly competitive market. In general, the fewer the sellers, the greater the opportunities for the individual seller. These conditions—i.e., markets with not many sellers—are an in-between land where profit opportunities are neither so good nor so clear as in the case of a real monopoly but are far more numerous than in a "strictly competitive" situation where an individual has no control at all over price.

5. In "oligopoly" each of the few sellers knows that the other sellers will react to any move he makes. In particular, if he cuts his price, that fact will not escape the attention of his few competitors. He must therefore anticipate that a price cut on his part will not succeed in drawing to him many of his competitors' customers. If the seller believes that a price cut will not succeed in bringing more business to the entire industry, he will decide against a price cut, for he knows it will surely be copied at once.

6. Where each of the few sellers knows that a price cut will surely be copied, a condition may arise which we will call "as if collusion." The several sellers may not in fact confer with one another about their price changes, but no express agreement or illicit communication is necessary to bring about the economic result. Prices stay put, are lowered, or are advanced with exactly the same effects on the pubic as though the Sherman Antitrust law had been violated by conspiracy in restraint of trade. It is not inconceivable that a few sellers, by "as if collusion," could attain the same economic result as perfect monopoly. Each might do a regular share of the selling dear, buying cheap, and seeking business in volume without any agreement to divide territories or to accept quotas.

Under conditions of "as if collusion," price uniformity exists in a very close approximation to identical prices. Such price uniformity may be contrasted with "approximate competitive uniformity of price," such as exists in open competitive markets. There prices are approximately uniform at any time, but price changes are relatively frequent. These peculiarities of price uniformity under conditions of "as if collusion" need to be noted, for they have great economic significance and might well have considerable legal significance.

The term "as if collusion" seems appropriate even though it has no recognized place in the literature of economic theory as have "pure competition" and "pure monopoly." It has about the same meaning as the term "conscious parallelism of action," which has recently come into some prominence. We may note in passing that it is far safer to infer price uniformity from an assumed condition of "as if collusion" than it is to infer a condition of "as if collusion" from the existence of uniform prices. For example, even if many candy bars sell at 5 cents, it may be doubted that the market can be accurately described as a condition of "as if collusion"; the probable explanation is simply that 5 cents is a convenient price for the buying public.

7. Another possible result of a situation where sellers are few is that no one dares tamper with an existing price. This price may well have been set so high that it affords a considerable margin over cost. More and more sellers may enter the field, but each seller as he enters may realize that it is to his advantage to maintain the going price. As this process goes on, more and more of the capacity to produce the commodity is left idle, because every competitor cannot dispose of his entire output at the going price. The eventual outcome is that the old price remains where it was, but none of the competitors make abnormal profits; the

profits of each are gobbled up by the carrying charges of their excess capacity.

This case rests upon the special assumption that the going price is rigid over a long period of time during which the capacity of the industry is increased. A case of "excess capacity" where the going price is not rigid presents an entirely different problem.

8. Price differences may also be the outcome of a situation where sellers are few, though the foregoing discussion may make such a statement appear paradoxical. Price differences may take the particular form of "price discrimination," where the seller in two markets persistently gets a wider margin between price and cost in one than in the other. A persistent difference between price and cost (all kinds of cost included) indicates that competitive leveling of margins is not taking place.

The explanation is found in the relative attractiveness of avoiding price competition in the two markets. In a market where sellers are very few or where substitution of other commodities is highly unlikely, the seller gets a big margin as compared with his margin in a market where competition or substitutes are more to be feared. "Dumping" in foreign markets is perhaps the best known example of the sort of price discrimination which the theorists of monopolistic competition have in mind. Adherence to basing point systems, where some mills realize better margins from sales nearby than from sales at more distant points by "freight absorption" or "phantom freight," is often said to be another example.

Here again the special meaning, in economic theory, of "price discrimination" must be noted. It is not identical with the apparent legal meaning of "price discrimination" among different customers condemned in the Robinson-Patman Act, for the different customers there are customers in competition with one another in the same market; and it should not be confused with the price differences which constantly appear and disappear in open competitive markets. The sort of price discrimination discussed here results, so the monopolistic competition theorists assert, in a maldistribution of products between the two markets. They do not share in proportion to their respective demands as they would if the competitive leveling of margins had made the prices the same.

9. The fear of immediate retaliation may make price competition unattractive where sellers are few. Because price competition is unattractive, the few sellers compete in other ways. They produce slightly different commodities or put the same commodity in different containers; they brand their products and spend large sums on advertising. All this expense, say the theorists, is for the purpose of building up an immunity against the immediate impact of competition; if patents can be obtained for new developments, they help further to build up an immunity from competitive pressure. We may note in passing that it is from the monopolistic competition analysis that critics of business have acquired the glorification of price competition as the ideal condition.

10. The analysis by the theorists of monopolistic competition leads to the conclusion that the division of manpower and capital equipment among the various industries of the country is unbalanced. The "maldistribution" argument runs along the following lines: The condition where sellers are relatively few is found in many branches of modern industry, but there is a wide variation between the several branches of industry. In industries where the sellers are very few, there is a relatively strong tendency for them to be in a position to keep up price, keep down output, and keep employment opportunities limited. Where sellers are more numerous, there is less likelihood of a combination of high price, limited output, and limited opportunity for employment of men and machines. Because of the varied degrees of concentration within the different branches of industry and trade, the analysis would claim that some fields are undeveloped. In more technical jargon, the result is a maldistribution of the nation's productive resources among the several branches of industry. This "maldistribution" argument, we repeat, is distinct from the "excess capacity" point developed under 7.

11. Monopolistic competition ideas lead to the general conclusion that prices where sellers are few tend to be "too high." According to the analysis, the public is harmed by high prices whether the high prices go into the pockets of the competitors as profits or whether they are absorbed by the expenses of nonprice competition and the costs of idle capacity. The theorists are therefore not pacified by low profits on investment; such profits do not mean the absence of harm to the public if the public pays for waste. Wastes of this sort are burdens on the public which arise from the competitive elements in conditions of monopolistic compe-

tition; they would not appear under conditions either of pure competition or of pure monopoly. With this exception, the burdens on the public under conditions of monopolistic competition are of the same sorts as the burdens under conditions of monopoly.

Difficulties and Misconceptions. Before proceeding further with an examination of the validity and significance of the various ideas of monopolistic competition, we should like to examine some of the difficulties which readers may have encountered thus far. Though some of those difficulties arise from our efforts to distill a few essential theorems from a voluminous literature, there are other difficulties more fundamental in character.

One such difficulty is with the vocabulary. The theorist of monopolistic competition uses some of the same words the businessman has always used and still uses, but he uses them with particular meanings. The businessman uses the term "competition" in an ordinary sense

which is an acceptable description of the world in which he operates. When he hears the economic theorist use the word, he thinks he knows what the economist is saying. How can he fail to be amazed when he comes to realize that the economist uses the term "pure" or "perfect" competition to describe a hypothetical situation which has never existed, does not now exist, and has no prospect of existing?

His difficulty is compounded when he then learns that some economists consider this hypothetical situation as a standard for appraising the results of the existing business system and tries to understand how it can be so applied. This particular point needs the further consideration it will be given later in this article.

Another vocabulary difficulty is the use of newly invented terms such as "oligopoly" (to denote a market with few sellers), "duopoly" (two sellers), "monopsony" (one buyer), and so on. The economists have developed a vocabulary for their own professional use, not for purposes of wide understanding.[1]

---

[1] "Oligopoly" is a term which is suffering from the distortions which a technical word undergoes when it passes into wider use. Apparently it has a peculiar fascination, for it rarely fails to provoke hilarity. An example is provided by the record of the *Hearings before the Subcommittee on Study of Monopoly Power* of the House Committee of the Judiciary (81st Congress, 1st Session, pp. 366–367), with Mr. Herbert A. Bergson, Assistant Attorney General, in charge of the Antitrust Division, Department of Justice, testifying:

Mr. Keating. Is there a numerical limit to an oligopoly?
Mr. Bergson. No; it is the circumstances that exist.
Mr. Keating. Could it be 10?
Mr. Bergson. I doubt very much that it could be 10. It would be rather difficult for them to operate that way. I think it is usually a Big Two or Three or Four. I would not want to say that is the limit, but it would be more apt to happen in an industry of that type.
Mr. Michener. One of the newspapermen suggested that we have inserted in the record somewhere your definition in plain simple language of "oligopoly."
Mr. Bergson. You know that qualification of "plain, simple language" almost tongue-ties me, Mr. Michener.
Mr. Michener. The words are significant. [Laughter.]
The Chairman. Somebody said that the economists—and I presume if you tried to define in plain,

simple language "oligopoly" you would be an economist—someone said that the economists are those who make common sense more difficult. [Laughter.]
Mr. Michener. We would like to have your view.
Mr. Bergson. My view of an oligopoly is an industry in which two or more companies—probably three or four, maybe five—control, can control, production, and can control prices following principles of live-and-let-live so far as each other is concerned; where the attitude of one company is, "I am not going to lower my prices and increase my production because my competitor has the power to lower his prices and increase his production to such an extent that I will have to lower my prices more and increase my production to a greater degree. So I will just leave it where it is safe in the knowledge that my competitors have the same feeling about me, and they will do the same thing."
Now, I do not know whether that is plain or simple.
Mr. Michener. Then, so the ordinary layman can best understand your using the term, it is quite similar to the symbols used by the shorthand writer, and in order that one might understand the whole meaning of the word, as envisioned by you, if there were parentheses following each word, with your statement, then the reader would know what it was all about.
Mr. Bergson. Mr. Michener, I do not even know what that was about. [Laughter.]
Mr. Michener. It just shows how difficult it is for the economist to talk in the language of the average person.

Another difficulty is with the type of thinking used by economists in theoretical analysis. Economic theory is abstract. In endeavoring to see some things clearly, it proceeds by artificial simplification. Many significant realities are excluded, and the reader is sometimes left in the dark whether the theorist is leaving out something merely because he finds it convenient, or because he thinks it of little importance, or because he knows nothing about it.

Another difficulty with the theory of monopolistic competition arises from its systematic character. The various theorems constitute a body of doctrines which are all tied together. Though the individual theorems can be studied separately, there is danger in doing so because attention may be diverted from such assumptions, common to all the theorems, as that the businessman seeks to maximize profits; because the conclusion of one theorem becomes the premise of another; and because the assumptions are deliberately shifted to bring out such contrasts as that between "pure" competition and "pure" monopoly.

If businessmen readers are skeptical about the merits of such theorizing, with its peculiar vocabulary and with its refined assumptions, they should know that some economists, both in the present and in the past, have rejected economic theory as incomprehensible, unscientific, or useless. In any event, the sort of thinking done by the theorists of monopolistic competition is radically different from the sort of thinking done by the business executive in running his company's affairs.

Some businessmen feel that economic theory is or should be a kind of basic science, one which would have the same relation to actual business that, say, chemistry has to chemical engineering. If businessmen readers think that the economic theorists are trying to construct a basic science of business, they are harboring a misconception. Economic theory has been developed partly because economists have been attracted by this sort of intellectual activity and partly because they believe that it may be used in clarifying the economic aspects of questions of public policy. If it has provided any intellectual tools useful to the business administrator, it has not done so purposely. Economic theorizing is a form of intellectual activity about as far different from the comprehensive and realistic thinking which precedes and accompanies executive action as is the study of analytical geometry.

A final difficulty which may have persisted, although we have tried to prevent it, arises from the fact that many of the conclusions of monopolistic competition theorizing are critical of business, particularly of the big few. In much of the best theoretical writing these conclusions are clearly nothing more than the results of good reasoning from the assumptions and are not used for passing judgment on practical affairs. Other writers have not been so careful. We have not undertaken to distinguish the contribution of one author from that of another or to point out where some writers have lost sight of some of the careful work of the leading writers on monopolistic competition.

Mr. Bergson. Well, what I mean is, as simply as possible, a situation where the normal forces that ordinarily set production figures and prices, the competitive forces do not operate.

Mr. Michener. That is right.

Mr. Bergson. Where you have a situation of that kind, and you are most likely to have it in a monopoly industry or an oligopoly industry, then you have monopoly power, whether it is in the hands of the one or in the hands of the four or the three or the two.

In such an instance we think that the Sherman Act is violated and that we can proceed under the Sherman Act. And we are proceeding in some cases under the act.

Mr. Michener. I think I understand.

The Chairman. In other words, usually where there are oligopolies there is what has been called conscious parallelism—

Mr. Bergson. That is right.

The Chairman (continuing). And price leadership and price maintenance.

Mr. Bergson. That is right.

Mr. Michener. Would you call the automobile industry an oligopoly?

Mr. Bergson. I would not like to call any specific industry an oligopoly until I file a case against it. [Laughter.]

The economist would say that the original and standard definition of oligopoly as "a market with few sellers" met any desire for "plain, simple language." We would venture the prediction that if there is ever to be a legal definition of oligopoly as a violation of the Sherman Act, it will be neither plain nor simple. This prediction is based on observation of the difficulties the Department of Justice is having explaining that "bigness" is not a violation of the Sherman Act but "unexercised monopoly power" which accompanies bigness is a violation. All this confusion is amusing, of course, but it is not entirely amusing to the businessman who is trying to live "well within the law."

In fact, we have ignored many significant differences among various writers on monopolistic competition, and the fact that we have grouped them all together does great injustice to many professional economists. It also may alarm and confuse readers of this *Review*. It may alarm them because it leaves them with the impression that most professional economists are a closely knit group hostile to business, particularly to big business. It may confuse them because they find it difficult to see how the theorists can be careful craftsmen and careless critics. The truth is that some individuals are the one and some the other, and still other individuals are mixtures of the two. The author regrets that an article which emphasizes the realities of business and the many differences between cases of business experience is open to the charge that it has ignored the realities of professional economics and the many differences among the writers on monopolistic competition.

The theory of monopolistic competition, we repeat, provides tools of intellectual analysis to be used by any competent craftsman regardless of his personal sympathies or political convictions. They are used well, and they are misused. Even when they are used well, however, the conclusions of monopolistic competition theorizing need not be accepted. We are free to criticize the assumptions which are used for premises as being so few that the conclusions are of little significance or as being so far from the truth that the conclusions are either useless or misleading. Nor does it follow that the end results of such theorizing are not important to businessmen, especially to those concerned with the "bigness" problem.

Practical Importance. The ideas of monopolistic competition are of considerable current practical importance, and such importance is likely to increase. They range beyond the older notions of monopoly, restraint of trade, and unfair competition, but mingle with them to so great an extent that the novel combination is confusing and possibly alarming.

Monopolistic ideas are of some importance in regard to the existing antitrust laws and their current interpretation. A number of such instances have already been mentioned. A further specific example may be seen in the sense in which the word "monopoly" is used in the language of a recent decision of the United States Supreme Court in an antitrust case. In *United States* v. *Griffith et al*, Mr. Justice Douglas, speaking for the Court, said "Anyone who owns and operates the single theater in a town, or who acquires the exclusive right to exhibit a film, has a monopoly in the popular sense."

If it is true that the word "monopoly" has been extended in popular usage to cover such instances—which, incidentally, is hard to imagine—it would appear that popular usage has left the competition part out of monopolistic competition, has retained the monopolistic part, and now applies the word "monopoly" to very small markets indeed. In any event, Mr. Justice Douglas goes on to say "But he usually does not violate § 2 of the Sherman Act unless he has acquired or maintained his strategic position, or sought to expand his monopoly, or expanded it by means of those restraints of trade which are cognizable under § 1."

If these statements mean that all monopolies in the popular sense are not included in the monopolies condemned under the Sherman Act, then it no longer seems safe to make the accepted observation that the act also covers strong strategic positions that are not monopolies in the popular sense. If the theory of monopolistic competition has played any role in bringing such statements into the Court's decision, it has lost some of its clarity and precision while doing so.

Another trace of monopolistic competition thinking may be seen in the proceedings of Congressional investigating committees where interest is shown in industries in which a few companies—usually three or four—control some significant percentage of the national output of some commodity. The House Judiciary Committee, of which Representative Celler is chairman, provides a current illustration. An earlier one is contained in the monograph, *The Structure of Industry*, prepared for the Temporary National Economic Committee by Willard L. Thorp and Walter F. Crowder, then of the Department of Commerce. Still earlier is a study under the same title, prepared for the National Resources Committee by Dr. Gardiner C. Means in 1939. These earlier studies, it should be noted, may be stronger indications of Administration interest than of Congressional concern.

THE CONCEPT OF WORKABLE COMPETITION

The concept of workable competition was introduced by Professor J. M. Clark in an article entitled "Toward a Concept of Workable Competition," first printed in the *American*

Economic Review in June 1940. Professor Clark wrote:

. . . the conception of "perfect competition" has itself for the first time received really specific definition and elaboration. With this has come the realization that "perfect competition" does not and cannot exist and has presumably never existed, for reasons quite apart from any inescapable tendency toward collusion, such as Adam Smith noted in his familiar remark on the gettings-together of members of a trade. What we have left is an unreal or ideal standard which may serve as a starting point of analysis and a norm with which to compare actual competitive conditions. It has also served as a standard by which to judge them.

I am not quarreling with proper use of this standard as an ideal. However, it has seemed at times to lead to undesirable results, in that it does not afford reliable guidance to the factors which are favorable to the closest available working approximation to that ideal, under actual conditions.[2]

The "toward" in the title Professor Clark chose for his contribution is significant because it reveals that he considered the concept of workable competition as one under development rather than one which was fully completed. The concept is still under development.

Relation to Standard of Perfect Competition. Readers will have noted that Professor Clark's concept expressly refers to "perfect" (or "pure") competition as a standard by which to judge actual competitive conditions. Perhaps it will be of some help if we try to explain, at this point, how such a contrary-to-fact hypothesis can be transformed into such a standard.

Under conditions of pure or perfect competition, the competition would function to bring about certain results. One specific result would be its apportionment, in a definite manner, of the available supplies of any commodity among the various consumers. Some would get much, some little, and some none at all. This function of price is sometimes called "price rationing" nowadays—in the sense that the free play of prices determines who is able and willing to buy—in contrast to the division of supplies on a first-come, first-served basis or on some basis imposed by governmental authority.

Another specific result is the apportionment

of each consumer's expenditures among various commodities. Still another is the apportionment of the available human and material productive resources among the various commodities or branches of production, as, for example, the division of the available mechanics skilled in the operation of turret lathes among the many various factories in which such machines are installed.

By such divisions or apportionments, the nation's output and consumption are affected in both character and amount. Under conditions of perfect competition, small changes in any of the elements included in the complex balance which may be assumed will be followed by appropriate and numerous changes elsewhere.

These many imaginary results of the hypothetical pure or perfect competition are what makes it a standard. When and if the economist looks at the specific results and finds them good, he is prepared to accept perfect competition as a standard. Instead of trying to enumerate all the separate results which are good in themselves or which often are good only because they are good in relation to one another, the easy way to sum up all the accepted standard results is to say: "Let's accept pure competition as a standard."

Such a standard may be applied to actual competitive conditions. If advertising expenditures, for example, contribute to increased sales of a commodity or to a "better" distribution of the commodity among the consumers, and if, further, there are smaller disadvantages in other directions or none at all, the advertising expenditures are good according to the standard or standards of pure competition.

As we interpret the standard, it must be not the departure from the *conditions* of pure competition but the departure from the *results* of perfect competition that is significant. If the significant thing were the departure from the conditions of pure competition, a pure monopoly would be unqualifiedly condemned, regardless of the monopolist's behavior. If the results count, a pure monopoly which keeps prices lower than they otherwise would have been, and which produces so much more than would otherwise have been produced that its profit rate would be no greater than the profit rate obtained in competitive fields, will not be condemned under the standard of pure competition. Any characteristic of an actual market, such as the number of competitors, the differentiation of the competing products, or the por-

---

[2] Volume XXX, No. 2, Part 1, pp. 241–256. It is reprinted in *Readings in the Social Control of Industry*, pp. 452–475, Volume 1 of the Blakiston Series of Republished Articles on Economics (Philadelphia: Blakiston Company, 1942).

tion of the market supplied by the big few, is used only as a help in classifying problems to be discussed. Such market characteristics assist in stating the questions to be examined, but they are nothing more than starting points. They lead to significant conclusions, not by logical necessity, by elaborate chains of reasoning, but by greater realism, by further consideration of pertinent factors of experience. At the end of the discussion only the results of actual conditions of competition are appraised, and only results count in the final score.

Upon the basis of this interpretation, we would call attention to some errors into which some users of the pure competition standard have fallen: Starting from the proposition that no competitor can have a price policy under conditions of pure competition, a business which admits it has a price policy will be condemned regardless of what the policy is. A more common and more serious error is the glorification of price competition as superior to all other types of competition. Starting from the belief that price competition is characteristic of pure competition, price competition is hailed as the essential and easily ascertained characteristic of healthy competition.

This enthusiasm has gone so far that it has left businessmen with the impression—which the economists themselves never intended to convey—that the economists think the world would be "perfect" if price wars were continuous, severe, and universal. In general, when parts of monopolistic competition analysis are applied to such marketing problems as pricing, sales promotion, advertising, and selection of distribution channels, the results are often unhappy. The intellectual roots of this unhappiness are, in our view, the failure to distinguish between the *results* of pure competition, on the one hand, and the *conditions, structure, and adaptive mechanisms* of pure competition, on the other hand; and the failure to use only the standard of results.

Other Standards. We would call the reader's attention to the fact that Professor Clark referred to pure or perfect competition as *a* standard, not as *the* standard. Under conditions of pure competition, economists might wish to look at questions of progressive taxation or the direction of public expenditures in order to consider possible improvements in the state of the nation. In other words, they might apply ethical or political standards to an existing situation and recommend changes from it when both the existing and the proposed situation

would meet all tests of pure competition. This example provides only one of several possible illustrations of the simultaneous use of other standards along with that of perfect competition.

Another example would be the use of standards of economic progress or development, in contrast to the standard of pure competition which is essentially a product of economic statics or the analysis of economic equilibrium and the effect of small departures therefrom. We call particular attention to a standard of economic progress, because, as will be shown later, the doctrines of workable competition do apply directly to problems of economic progress. A standard of economic progress is not so sharply defined as a standard of pure competition, and some economist may be prepared to demonstrate that his standard of economic progress is derived from that of pure competition. No investigation of such a position is needed for our present purposes, which do not include any more discussion of the "systematic" aspects of economic theorizing than we have already included.

The doctrines of workable competition have not yet acquired a systematic character and may never acquire it. That is why we have included some points made by writers who have not to our knowledge accepted or used the term. For example, we have drawn heavily upon Professor Joseph A. Schumpeter's book, *Capitalism, Socialism, and Democracy,*[3] though we do not recall that he uses the term workable competition and do not find it in the index.

We may not speak, at least for the present, of the doctrines of workable competition as those of a school of thought. The various writers who have contributed to our collection of doctrines and stimulated our own thinking differ among themselves in important matters of emphasis and arrangement. What the various writers most clearly have in common is the use of the *two* standards of pure competition and of economic progress. When they apply these two standards to the complex problems of actual competitive conditions, they cannot be expected to arrive at the same judgments.

A word of warning is needed to prevent readers from gaining a wrong impression. It is true that workable competition doctrines reject many of the conclusions which others have drawn from applying to actual business conditions some results of the monopolistic competition

---

[3] 2nd ed. (New York: Harper, 1947).

analysis. They do not reject the analysis as such. Among the conclusions which they reject are many which are highly adverse to bigness or to business generally. That fact does not mean that writers on workable competition are not themselves critical of business, that they have chosen the role of the apologist for business, or that they find nothing objectionable in the behavior of business. We hope the truth of this statement will be apparent in our own summary of the doctrines, though we emphasize primarily their conflict with the apparent or suggested conclusions of monopolistic competition theorizing.

The doctrines of workable competition have been grouped under three headings: (1) price competition and small number of competitors, (2) realistic dynamics, and (3) the business cycle. Because the doctrines of workable competition are not separate propositions but reinforce and strengthen one another, this three-fold classification is adopted for convenience only. We have included only the highly significant doctrines, and we have not attempted to elaborate their implications.

Price Competition and Small Number of Competitors

The doctrines of workable competition contain less enthusiastic praise for price competition and less unqualified alarm at a small number of competing units than the theory of monopolistic competition has suggested.

Under some conditions price competition may be as beneficent as the monopolistic competition theorists believe it to be, but under other conditions it may be destructive. When all the conditions assumed, consciously or not, by the theorists of monopolistic competition are present, price competition does help the process of adjusting supply to demand and does help to allocate the productive resources of the country among their various fields of employment in a desirable fashion. Under these conditions anyone who is dissatisfied with the present employment of his labor or capital is free to move elsewhere where the opportunities are better.

In the real world, however, both labor and capital are often closely tied to their present employments and cannot easily shift to others. This condition is particularly likely to exist when, because of a business depression, opportunities in all fields appear to be distinctly limited. The point is that where labor and capital are not free to move out of a particular employ-

ment, price competition is likely to lead to low prices and low wages without leaving any real gain to anyone. The purchasing power of the laborers and that of the capitalists are both reduced, and both reduce their demand for the products of other industries. What the consumers save through lower prices they do not always spend on other commodities, either because they anticipate that other prices will come down too and hence they hold off buying or because they fear that their own incomes will be lower in the future and hence they keep money idle to provide for the rainy day they anticipate.

The possibilities of ruinous price competition can be seen in the history of the bituminous coal industry and of the clothing trades. There is an important difference between price competition as a means of passing on the benefits of more economical production to the public over the long run and price competition which, under the particular conditions of the industry or the particular state of general business, either results in a depressed industry or intensifies a business depression if one has already set in.

The doctrines of workable competition raise doubt whether there is any necessary significance in the mere fact of a small number of competitors in any given industry or trade. It is possible that, where the number of competitors is very few, each may follow the leader with the result of low output and high prices. But this is not the only possible result. Even where competitors are few, each may independently pursue his own advantage and may explore the possibilities of low prices and abundant output and employment. The significant thing to look for is the independence and competitiveness of the rivals, not the number of competitors.

Over the long pull the possibilities of making significant profits by a policy of restricted output and high prices are often much exaggerated in the statements of monopolistic competition theory. Monopolistic competition theorists have assumed extreme cases to make their points clear and have left the impression that they are typical. In a more realistic view, a wide gap between price and cost would ordinarily be obtainable only at so great a loss of volume that profits would be seriously impaired. Because of the indirect competition from other industries for the consumer's dollar, higher prices are likely to result in the public's being willing to take only a greatly reduced volume of output, and the possibilities of reducing costs through exploring the economies of large-scale manufacture are often effective hindrances to a restrictive policy.

This same point can be restated in terms of markets. In the market there are few competitors, by assumption, but what is the market? If there are two motion-picture theaters in a town, is the market divided between two competitors? The market that is really significant probably has much competition—theaters in near-by towns, the pleasures of listening to the radio and of automobiling (which may be combined), local sports events, boxed chocolates, and so forth. Thus in many markets the small number of competitors are actually affected by influences from other markets; if these competitors have business foresight, they look further around and further into the future.

Definitions of "markets," "trades," or "industries" which we use for statistical convenience must not be interpreted to mean that everything of significance to the economist or businessman is contained within such limited definition. In *United States* v. *Griffith,* Mr. Justice Douglas spoke of the owner of the single theater in a town as a monopolist in the popular sense. If this narrow definition is to be accepted, the significant question has to be changed: How is this monopolist's behavior affected by the fact that his market is surrounded by the markets of many other competing monopolists?

The absence of unlimited price competition or of a large number of competitors may harm the actual competitive results in the market; it may have little or no effect; or, indeed, it may actively improve the results by increasing output and employment. Unlimited price competition may be immediately destructive; and in many markets only a look at the most immediate situation would find few competitors and significant opportunities for monopolistic restrictiveness in any limitation of price competition. In these doctrines of workable competition there is no sharp break between the market or immediate situation, the short-run period, and the long-run period, because the factors the economist and the businessman should consider cut across such periods. It may be convenient to retain the distinctions, for they have limited usefulness and significance; but the limits must not be overlooked.

Realistic Dynamics. We next turn to the workable competition doctrines where the emphasis is upon the longer range aspects of a progressive economy. Workable competition provides a doctrine of realistic dynamics; it is not a doctrine based upon an assumed almost unchanging equilibrium of demand and supply. In realistic dynamics the changes are greater in number and size than in equilibrium economics. These changes include population growth, the discovery of natural resources, developments in technology, advances in the arts of management, and many others.

1. In the doctrines of workable competition stress is laid on the constructive role of the businessman in expanding demand and improving product. Demand, particularly in markets with a limited number of sellers, is not something which exists independently of the businessman's own efforts, as is often assumed to be the case in the monopolistic competition analysis. Advertising and selling effort is something more than an effort to avoid price competition, and the businessman's introduction of improved products consists of something more than insignificant changes to confuse the public and escape the full impact of competition; such business moves are also a major source of economic progress. Thus the doctrines of workable competition recognize persistent efforts of business to improve the services that it gives to the consuming public. There is no denial that advertising can be wasteful or that product differences can be trivial, but such waste is not found to merit conspicuous weight in the overall appraisal of actual competitive results.

2. In the concept of workable competition stress is laid on the constructive role of the businessman in investing in equipment and new processes. The businessman often makes these investments of time and money ahead of the current demand of the consumers. Thus, in the development and application of technological progress, the businessman plays a leading role.

Likewise patents are a desirable means of stimulating technological progress, not merely a device to hold back the impact of competition. If there could be no patents under conditions of pure competition, so much the worse for pure competition. A genuine understanding of the patent problem could not rest upon the monopoly character which can be given to patents by some definitions. The full impact of competition would destroy any effective incentive to make technological discoveries or to make large pioneering investments in their practical application and would reduce the income from which come the means to continue on the road to technological and commercial development.

3. In the light of realistic dynamics idle capacity takes on other meanings than those revealed by the monopolistic competition analysis. Technological improvements render some

capacity obsolete, and it is scrapped. If the pressure of technological change is not so great, the old capacity may be retained in order to meet large pressure for supplies. Such capacity will be used despite its high cost when that action is justified by the market conditions. The existence of a certain amount of idle capacity is therefore no evidence of any monopolistic restriction of production or monopolistic rigidity of prices.

Moreover, in a dynamic world a certain amount of spare capacity is a necessary condition for competitive rivalry. For example, if two competitors each have 15% spare capacity, their salesmen may compete for additional business even though neither of the competitors thinks that there is enough business to be found to permit both of them to operate at full capacity. If both companies were ever operating at 100% of their capacity, sales effort to secure greater volume would not make sense. Some additional capacity is therefore a condition for two or more competitive rivals, each soliciting the orders of the same customers. The dynamics of shifting customers from one competitor to another brings with it certain costs of sustaining such rivalry, and one of these costs is that of a certain amount of unused capacity. In ordinary business language this is the distinction between spare capacity and overcapacity.

4. In the doctrines of workable competition, there is no denial that, under some circumstances, large business units may put more competitive pressure on smaller units than is desirable. But every injury to some competitor is not an injury to competition as a functional process to bring about the varied economic results which were outlined above when the use of perfect competition as a standard was under discussion. Competition in a dynamic economy is bound to put pressure on any inefficient competitors, large or small. This pressure is not desirable for itself but as a means of bringing about needed economic readjustments.

5. The discussions of workable competition would seem to indicate marked skepticism toward the frequent assertion that a few big businesses tend to drive out a great multitude of efficient small competitors. There is no denial that it is most important that the nation not be confronted with the political problems which would appear if the small businessman were to be eliminated. The relative roles of small, medium, and large business present many difficult economic problems, but the threat of extinction to small business is not one of them.

SIGNIFICANT QUESTIONS

The outline of workable competition doctrines which we have just given will have provided many illustrations of a point developed earlier in discussing perfect competition as a standard: Workable competition looks to results, not to the number of companies in a market or to the presence or absence of price competition or sales promotion. It is interested in business performance.

From the discussions of workable competition, an effort is being made to derive more satisfactory tests of business performance. The goal toward which this effort is directed is that of tests which are widely approved, which put questions which can be answered on a factual basis, and which do not depend largely upon the insight, the sympathy, or the politics of the tester. Even if such a goal is not reached, progress in that direction is most welcome.

It is fortunate that Dean Edward S. Mason has been able to announce that he and some associates from Harvard and Massachusetts Institute of Technology are proceeding further with the development of tests of business performance. The direct purposes of the study are to provide economists and government officials with more understanding of what sort of business performance is in the public interest. The author of this article, who owes so much to Dean Mason's published[4] and unpublished discussions of workable competition, is confident that the study will be of value to businessmen as well.

For the benefit of businessmen readers, we will list some tests which we have found useful. To call them tests of business performance might appear to claim too much for them, but at least they may be called usable and significant questions. The merits of these questions are found not so much in the direct factual answers to them as in other questions which arise when these questions are pursued.

There are, first of all, two kinds of very general questions which are significant: (1) Is the industry progressive? Does it make technological improvements, improve products, and take an active part in expanding output and employment? (2) Do the companies in the industry act competitively? Does each of them make its own decisions and pursue a policy on prices

---

[4] See especially "The Current Status of the Monopoly Problem in the United States," 62 *Harvard Law Review* 1265 (June 1949).

and output which is the product of its own thinking rather than an attempt to follow the example of its competitors?

More specifically, the doctrines of workable competition raise the following questions:

1. Are the prices in the industry made on a follow-the-leader basis, in which one firm announces all the price changes which the others adopt; or is there evidence that the general uniformity in prices comes about through competition, in which price changes are initiated in no regular pattern and some price changes are followed generally, whereas others are not followed?

2. A second specific question bears on market quotas or market positions. Does the industry show a relatively unchanging division of the market among the various competitors; or do these market positions change up and down, with the individual companies exploring the possibility of increasing or decreasing their positions in a particular part of the industry, either geographically or by product, and competing against one another in various localities and on various product lines as determined by their own views on the present and future profit possibilities?

3. A third specific question concerns cost reduction. Do the various competitors in an industry act similarly on questions of investing in a process or using some manufacturing technique, of following some method of distribution or effective way of attracting the custom of the public; or does each pursue his own independent judgment on such questions?

4. A fourth specific question concerns the relatively inefficient and high-cost units in an industry. Does the industry function to hold an umbrella over the inefficient, perhaps pursuing a policy directed toward increasing the solidarity of the trade by catering to the inefficient; or do the various companies in the industry let the inefficient go to the wall through their separate and individual efforts to expand their own business? To pose the question in another way: Does stabilization mean the preservation of inefficient competition; or does it not?

5. A fifth specific question looks the other way from that suggested in the previous question. Are inefficient competitors who are only inefficient because they are starting in business or are the victims of some purely temporary circumstances driven out; or is the industry so organized that companies which are likely to be efficient over the long pull can enter the industry and remain in it?

6. A sixth specific question concerns the expansionist activities of the company or industry in question. Does the industry merely adapt itself to the favorable conditions the country as a whole affords it; or does it take an active part in technological progress, product improvement, and expansion of markets, output, and capacity?

7. The final question is on price quotations and pricing formulas. Do these make it so easy to detect any departure from "proper prices" that the larger companies do not want to engage in any form of price cutting and smaller firms fear retaliation if they make any price cuts; or do they facilitate price comparisons by buyers and thus broaden the market in which any one seller can operate? If we cannot devise any system of price quotations that will make price comparison easy for the buyers and that will not also make it easy for the sellers, the question should be posed in terms of the actual price behavior of the industry: Do the big companies avoid any or all price reductions and do the smaller firms really fear retaliation if they cut prices; or do they not?

These questions are, we believe, usable and significant for the businessman in appraising his own situation in the competitive world. It is no part of our discussion of the economic analysis of competition to consider whether satisfactory answers to these questions would provide immunity from prosecution under the various antitrust laws, from political attack, or from the censure of some segments of public opinion. The list includes only questions derived from the economic analysis of competition; there are many others from such fields as law and public relations. Nor is it by any means an exhaustive list of economic questions, because further study of workable competition will reveal more and better questions as it proceeds.

Continuation of such study will also eliminate some of the difficulties with the monopolistic competition analysis. With defects thus removed or repaired through the help of the concept of workable competition, the usefulness of the theory of monopolistic competition, one of the major contributions to economics in the first half of this century, will become more and more clear. Professional discussions and criticisms are in the process of making the analysis of competition both more realistic and more accurate. The discussions which are permitted and encouraged by the liberties of a free society and especially by "academic freedom" are bearing fruit.

24. Competition as Seen by the Businessman and by the Economist

JOEL DEAN

RESEARCH METHODS

The two people who ought to know most about competition are the economist, whose profession it is to study it, and the businessman, whose profession it is to practice it. The purpose of this little disquisition is to contrast the views of these two experts.

Economists, of course, differ greatly among themselves, and their views on this subject range over a broad continuum. Any attempt to lump together the opinions of such a notoriously discordant group of people must, therefore, be at best a bold simplification, and more probably a foolhardy caricature. Business executives also cover a wide spectrum of attitudes toward competition and differ strikingly in their penchant for looking at the economic mechanism as a whole. Hence, any attempt to speak about the views of "the businessman" necessarily abstracts from the great variation among individual executives, and runs the risk of merely reflecting the prejudices of the generalizer.

Instead of attempting to mitigate these hazards, I have accentuated them. No effort has been made to survey systematically a wide range of businessmen's opinions on the subject, and no effort has been made to present a central tendency of the views of the typical executive. Dr. Kinsey has established that statistics can make anything dull. So I have steered

‡‡ SOURCE: Reprinted by permission from *The Role and Nature of Competition in Our Marketing Economy* edited by Harvey W. Huegy (Bureau of Economic and Business Research, University of Illinois, 1954, pp. 8–15.)

clear of statistics and confined my inquiries to businessmen whose views intrigued me.

I have maintained the same high standards of statistical thoroughness and Olympian objectivity in summarizing my dinner table findings with respect to economists. Observing that the inner soul of the academician is seldom bared in the learned journals, I have religiously abstained from any examination of the literature on the subject and instead have gone out into the byways and the unbeaten paths of casual conversation and taking my cocktail in hand, have coaxed cozy confidences from my cloistered colleagues.

Economists, doubtless as a consequence of the rigor of the scientific method and the broad factual foundation for their science, vary in their views on competition over a vast range. One can move along this continuum from the managerial economist with intimate participation in the highest policy decisions of huge corporations (like myself) along a trajectory of marginal futility down through the geologic strata of sophistication to the neoclassical, welfare economist who still takes the model of atomistic competition seriously.

A simple, scientific, and completely satisfactory solution for the annoying individuality of economists has been found. It consists of classifying them into two groups: (a) sophisticated industrial economists and (b) foolish cloistered economists. Following the pattern of our scientific treatment of the businessman, we shall ignore altogether the views of the sophisticated economists and confine ourselves to the foolish ones.

What Competition Is

By these research methods we obtained impressions about the economist's and the businessman's view of the characteristics of a competitive situation.

Hallmarks of Competition Listed by Businessman

Generally speaking, competition, to the businessman, is whatever he has to do to get business away from his rivals and whatever they do to take sales away from him. To be more specific let us look at nine hallmarks of an intensely competitive situation, as seen through the eyes of our businessman:

1. *Price uniformity.* Close similarity of quoted prices of rivals, usually accompanied by undercover price shading.
2. *Price differentiation.* A structure of price discounts characterized by wide spreads between the lowest and the highest net price, e.g., the discount structure that is usual for suppliers of fairly standardized products to the automobile industry.
3. *Selling activities.* Substantial promotional outlays, i.e., much advertising, point-of-sale merchandising, and direct personal salesmanship.
4. *Product differentiation.* Preoccupation with the modernity, quality, and style of the company's products as compared with rivals' products and with "good service."
5. *Product research.* Large outlays on product research that is focused on creation of new products and continuous improvement in the firm's existing products.
6. *Selective distribution.* A strong dealer organization, i.e., rivalry through and for sponsored, franchised (and often exclusive) distributors.
7. *Market share.* Acute consciousness of the activities and position of competitors, and preoccupation with the company's market share and with the market occupancy of individual rivals.
8. *Market raiding.* Uninhibited efforts to detach big customers from rivals, often by price shading, or special concessions, business patronage, and "services." Sporadic penetration of the market by distant rivals, who frequently dump, so that their net-back is much lower than from sales in their own backyard territory. The converse is customer-freezing,

i.e., the use of sewing-up devices such as requirements contracts, reciprocity, and lavish gifts, which make good customers hard to alienate.

9. *Customer sharing.* Widespread acceptance of the strike-born doctrine that for each important material or component the buyer needs the protection of having at least two suppliers.

Economist's View — Appraisal

Influenced by fashionable doctrines of "imperfect competition" and "monopolistic competition" many neoclassical economists have taken the view that only atomistic competition is the real thing; that any form of rivalry that departs from the paragon of perfect competition falls from grace, i.e., is monopoly. Classifying all departures from the purity of atomistic rivalry as monopolistic is a simplifying analytical device of proven pedagogical value. The inference drawn by many students and, unfortunately, by some of their teachers is that all aspects of rivalry among sellers which deviate from "perfect" competition are "monopolistic," and therefore, are not competition at all.

The result of this doctrinaire dissection of the geometry of competition is the unconscious conviction on the part of many young economists that monopoly, rather than competition, is now the dominant characteristic of American capitalism. The impression that competition has been "declining" is a frequent, though not necessary, corollary.

A weird consequence is that the same behavior traits which the businessman sees as hallmarks of competition are viewed by many economists as indicia of monopoly.

Price Uniformity. To many economists close similarity of prices quoted or bid by rivals is an almost classic indication of a monopoloid situation. Some economists view "price matching" as conclusive proof of culpable collusion. Undercover price concessions have been regarded not only as buttressing the evidence of collusion but also as pernicious in themselves because they are a particularly insidious kind of price discrimination.

The businessman sees uniformity of official prices as evidence that rivals' products are such close substitutes that competition is driven underground, where dark and terrible subterranean struggles produce differences in quality, service, and terms which work out to differences in real prices.

The businessman sees no practical competitive alternative to similarity of quoted prices where products are standardized and competitors are few. Each seller knows that official price cuts will be promptly met. Overt price reduction is, therefore, a futile device for extending a firm's market share. And since open price reductions are not easily reversible undercover concessions provide the necessary mechanism for flexible adjustment to rapid changes in economic and competitive environment.

Price Differentiation. Charging different prices to different people makes the economist suspect price discrimination, roughly defined as price differences that are not "justified" by cost differences. Price discrimination is an indication of monopoly power, since it is unthinkable under atomistic competition. Price discrimination may also be employed to acquire, perpetuate, or abuse market power. Accordingly, most economists have been "agin" it. But few have recognized that under modern technology it is very difficult to define price discrimination, and almost impossible to measure, detect, or avoid it. (See *Managerial Economics,* pp. 504-10.)

The businessman sees his structure of price discounts as an instrument of competitive strategy in fighting for position in different sectors of the market. Aware of the furious consequences of failing to meet rivals' net prices as they differ among market sectors and aware of the impossibility of finding the full cost of serving different sectors he sees the sort of cost-price disparity (price discrimination) that distresses the economist as an everyday unavoidable and not particularly culpable practice. He is amazed that price differentiation that is so directly geared to market conquest and defense should be viewed as a symptom of monopoly and is even more puzzled that it should be viewed as culpable or as avoidable.

Selling Activities. By our economist, all sales effort has characteristically been viewed with serious misgivings. His ire has been concentrated on the purest forms of selling cost, such as advertising, but it has slopped over into every aspect of promotional effort. Economists, particularly of the more dedicated neoclassical persuasion, have seen in selling efforts a device for enhancing the monopoly power of the firm by differentiating the product in the minds of the prospective buyers. According to this view, the resulting "consumer franchise" is an island of monopoly power largely created by selling efforts.

To the businessman, selling activities seem the essence of competition. Pained by the unfamiliarity and indifference of consumers to the virtues of his product and service, he sees sales effort as dissolving the rigidities of ignorance and inertia that block access to substitutes. Thus it converts the incipient rivalry of substitutes into effective competition.

Product Differentiation. Physical differences among sellers' products have come under opprobrium similar to psychological differentiation. These economists consider that commercially successful product competition which develops a distinctive product that people want creates a monopoly power. This power is limited, to be sure, by the adequacy of substitutes, but nevertheless product innovation and adaptation to consumers' desires bears the opprobrium of monopoly. Thus these economists see in each new product and each improvement of an existing product an effort to escape from the competitive struggle into a stronghold of monopoly. In contrast, the businessman, in industries where product innovation and improvement is a dominant aspect of rivalry, would look upon it as the very core of competition. (Witness the workings of real-world rivalry in the automobile industry.)

Product Research. Many neoclassical economists have looked on the outlays of large corporations for technological research with apprehension. The results of research are patented; patents constitute legalized monopolies, and patents build barriers to entry. Hence research expands and perpetuates a firm's monopoly power in the view of some economists.

The businessman sees whatever monopoly power he succeeds in building up by technological research as being transient. It is eternally threatened by the competitive inroads of rivals. His experience indicates that perpetuation of his power to compete can be achieved only by research which creates new products and which keeps existing products abreast of the technological innovations of his rivals. He properly sees his existing products and methods threatened, to an extent never experienced before, by inborn substitutes that may provide dramatically cheaper solutions for his customers' problems. He sees patents as poor protection in today's dynamic, fluid technology.

Selective Distribution. Flowing the product to consumers through an organization of sponsored, franchised (and sometimes exclusive) dealers has been viewed by some economists not only as evidence of monopoly power but also as an unwarranted extension and consolidation of the market power of product differentiation. The businessman, in contrast, sees an effective dealer organization as a major weapon of competition. In some industries a dealer organization appears essential to make the manufacturer's competition operational at the point where competition counts, namely, in the decisions of the ultimate consumer.

Economists have not only feared the distributive power conferred by a strong dealer organization, they have also looked upon exclusive dealerships as a grant of locational monopoly and as a monopolistic denial of access to rival sellers. To the businessman, exclusive dealerships are a means of assuring single-minded and dedicated effort to compete with dealers of rival manufacturers.

Market Share. Preoccupation with the company's market share has ominous monopolistic overtones to the neoclassical economist. For a firm to have market occupancy big enough to make its market share perceptible is in itself a significant departure from the standard of perfect competition. Making market-share goals pivotal for pricing and promotional policy is, to these economists, a sure sign of a monopoloid situation. Similarly, when the very awareness of rivals as individuals is a sinful slip from atomistic competition, overt study of rivals' reactions to the firm's market thrusts is to these economists clear litmus of "monopoly power." To the businessman who watches his market share apprehensively and at considerable cost and who frequently sacrifices immediate profits for long-run strengthening of his sinews for market-share rivalry, it is incredible that his concern about his "competitive position" should be damned as monopolistic.

Even more culpable in the eyes of the economist is industry-wide cohesion in the face of threatened encroachment by rival industries (for example, the movie industry's battle with television and radio for consumer attention and for the amusement dollar). The businessman, more painfully impressed with the realities of substitute competition, sees industry solidarity as improving his competitive effectiveness in this wider arena and hence as intensifying rather than diminishing competition.

Market Raiding. Muscling in on stable and satisfied (established) customers is to the businessman proof of voracious competition. To the neoclassical economists, however, the very existence of long-lived, uninterrupted commercial relationships with individual large customers is an indication of monopoly power, since it is unthinkable under perfect competition. And the subterranean efforts to dislodge the favored supplier smack of discriminatory tactics.

Similarly, raiding by suppliers who are geographically (or in other ways) distant strikes the businessman as indicating that the arena of competition has been widened and hence intensified. Also, the hit-and-run tactics of the raider disturb the price peace and may force a substantial realignment of market occupancy. To the neoclassical economist, in contrast, raiding demonstrates the existence of a private preserve to raid, and raiding tactics produce disparity in the net revenue between backyard and distant sales which have discriminatory results, presumably possible only with the substantial degree of monopoly power.

Customer freezing is in a sense the converse of market raiding. To the businessman it indicates the length to which he must go to keep his established customer relationships intact and protect them against the heartless and ceaseless competitive efforts of his rivals. To some economists these sewing-up devices look like the creation of noncompetitive nooks which impose barriers to the access of rivals.

Customer Sharing. Customer sharing is to many economists proof that rivalry is imperfect. Predetermined sharing of the business even of an individual customer is a departure from the essentially anonymous and happenstance division of patronage that is assumed under perfect competition.

To the businessman, who is forced by the growing acceptance of the dual-supplier doctrine to share his established customers with rival suppliers, customer sharing shows the essential equivalence of their products and services and often sales volume, thereby intensifying competition.

Sad Conclusion

No plaudits had been expected by our businessman for his little foray into economics. But it is downright discouraging to find that his nine telltales of a tough competitive setup are to our economist sure symptoms of monopoly. Recognizing that competition is clearly just the opposite of what it seems, our business friend sadly climbs back through the looking glass.

G. Technological Developments and Marketing

25. *Effects of Technology on Marketing*

A. E. REYNOLDS

A great many of the items used and talked about in everyday life are the results of recent technical research. We speak commonly these days of nuclear powered submarines, wear clothing made of synthetic fibers, spend countless hours watching a television set perform, and hardly become excited when watching the winter Olympics on television relayed to this country "via satellite."

The technological research which has brought the world these and many other new things is also the major cause of the great rise in total national productivity, an increase of over 50 percent in the short span of two Olympiads.

If this record of past achievement is not sufficient evidence of the rapid rate of technological growth brought about by research, then we need only listen to the forecast of things to come. We are told by numerous authorities that industrial research alone will more than double by 1975, and that government-sponsored research may exceed total industrial research. It is certain that such tremendous increases in research effort will result in even greater increases in productivity and product selection than have been seen in the past decade.

Such progress will have profound effects on everyone. The purpose of this article is to consider some of the effects on *marketing*.

Marketing, defined in its broadest scope, is the business of moving products from the producer to the ultimate consumer. Marketing is affected by technological change in the following ways:

‡ SOURCE: Not Previously Published.

1. By changes in goods and production methods.
2. By changes in the ultimate consumer.
3. By changes in marketing itself.

Let us consider each of these areas in some detail.

CHANGES IN GOODS AND PRODUCTION METHODS

Changes in the products and the methods used in producing them are the most obvious result of technological research and development.

Today's products are on the average far more complex than those of a generation ago. The 1964 automobiles are many times more complicated than the Model-A Ford of the 1930's. Television sets are more complex than the early radio receivers. Even a simple, everyday item, such as a loaf of bread, is far more complex than the neighborhood baker used to make—incorporating homogenation, vitamin and mineral supplements, slicing, dating, and specialty packaging.

This greater degree of complexity has forced marketing to give much more consideration to the *multiple* features of the products to be sold. In the case of the automobile, for instance, marketing has had to learn that it is no longer selling simple transportation when it is selling an automobile. It is now also selling seat belts, automatic transmissions, self-adjusting brakes, synthetic finishes, more horsepower, fashion interiors, lubrication-free bearings, and many other new technical developments. These multiple features result in multiple benefits to the consumer—comfort, safety, convenience, reliability, style, snobbery, service, name, reputation, quality, durability, price, terms, trade-in value, and so on. Marketing must constantly study this multitude of features and benefits of its products, and incorporate them in the proper proportion and perspective into a marketing program which will be effective against competitors selling similarly complex automobiles. In every industry the increasing complexity of new products requires marketing to acquire a deeper understanding of the technical aspects of the products it is trying to sell.

Technical developments have given birth to whole new kinds of competition, forcing marketing to battle against entirely new competitors. In the construction trade, for instance, wood stood for centuries as the basic material for siding homes and buildings. It was unchallenged. The only competition was among a few *kinds* of wood. Now this traditional material is competing with synthetic plastics, ceramics, metals, and various combinations of these. Marketing programs for both the newer and the older materials have to be constantly updated and modified to cope with increasing competition.

Greater production and design technology has brought about more rapid development *and* obsolescence of products. The classical product life cycle shown in Fig. 1 is constantly being compressed from both ends. Evidence of the change in growth rate is shown in Figs. 2 and 3. The acrylic fibers, as Fig. 2 notes, had a growth rate of 45 percent per year, three times that of the rayons 20 years earlier. Fig. 3 shows similar increases in the growth rate of home appliances. The ability of industry, through combined efforts of research, production, and marketing to promote faster growth of new products, tends also to shorten the period of maturity of established products and hasten their decline. This shortening of product life cycles requires more careful planning of marketing programs and long-range schedules. It also emphasizes the need to plan introduction of *new* products *and* the withdrawal of obsolete products. This withdrawal decision is another marketing function which is becoming more prevalent because of greater technological capability.

CHANGES IN THE ULTIMATE CONSUMER

Since the Second World War the attitudes, appetites, and habits of the average American family have changed tremendously. A few examples point this out.

1. The much dreaded childhood disease of polio myolitis is no longer a constant threat in the minds of American mothers. This disease has been brought under control through technological research. We have even seen a transition from the injection technique to the now prevalent oral vaccine—another example of shortening product life cycles.

2. With coin-operated washers and driers

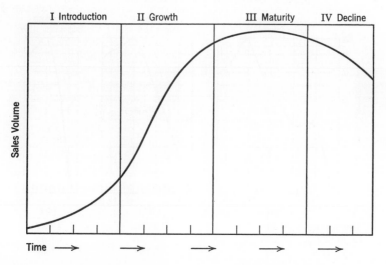

FIG. 1.   The classical product life cycle curve. *Source*: Robert D. Young, *Product Growth Cycles — A Key to Growth Planning* (Menlo Park, California: Stanford Research Institute).

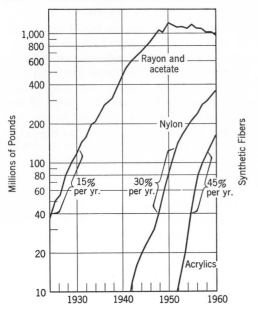

FIG. 2.   Growth cycles are shortening. *Source:* Robert D. Young, *Product Growth Cycles.*

in every community, a family does not need to buy its own machines.

3. The American family now consumes three times the amount of frozen foods it did just ten years ago.

4. Credit and discretionary income have risen 60 percent in the past eight years.

5. Leisure time and the *importance* of leisure time activities have soared in the average American family.

Another way of describing this change is to say that we have passed from the traditional state of mankind, in which shortages of commodities prevailed, into a period where commodities are in surplus. Faced with such a variety of commodities to choose from, and having a broad credit base with which to purchase these commodities, the consumer is placing greater and greater importance in his decision making on another factor—*time.* The consumer realizes that time cannot be purchased, only conserved, and that only by conserving his time can he fully enjoy leisure activities. Purchasing is being influenced more and more by the time factor—the time it takes to make a purchase, the time required to use the product, the time saved by engaging an outside service or by using a different product. This change in attitude of the consumer, brought about by technological growth, is affecting the design of products and services. It is also affecting the marketing of these same products and services.

CHANGES IN MARKETING

The slogan "the customer is always right" has been in use much longer than it has been practiced. For centuries the *real* practicing philos-

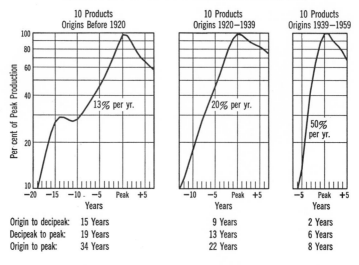

FIG. 3.   Growth cycles are shortening. Note: Three-year moving averages plotted. War years 1942–1945 omitted. *Source:* Robert D. Young, *Product Growth Cycles.*

ophy of marketing was *caveat emptor* or, "let the buyer beware." Henry Ford expressed it some 40 years ago with his now famous statement, "Customers for my automobile can have any color they want, so long as it's black." As long as goods and services were in short supply, this attitude did not inhibit business. But as commodities became more and more plentiful and competition increased, marketing men were forced to realize that customers had peculiar tastes in their likes and dislikes which did not necessarily correlate with the tastes of research and production. Marketing learned that it paid to adapt products and marketing approaches to the things customers liked. Nowadays marketing is concerning itself more and more with the job of finding out what the customer really wants and then, by feeding back this information, taking advantage of technology to create the products to suit the customer.

In this "Age of Research" marketing men have ceased being peddlers to become scientific businessmen. To accomplish this, largely a phenomenon of the years since the mid-1930's, marketing men have had to hurdle two important changes in the concept of their profession: first, that scientific methods could be applied to marketing problems, and second, that the customer was always right.

The pioneer in the application of scientific methods to marketing problems was the chemical industry. Emerging as an important part of the economy, the industry began to realize that it was marked by high investment costs which yielded high volume at low production costs. The question of "How much can we sell?" was a crucial one in weighing investment in new plant facilities for a new chemical product developed by research. Through scientific means, the highly trained scientific personnel of the industry sought to find the answer to this all important question. By studying its customers and interviewing potential new ones, and by using some basic statistics, these men began the successful application of scientific marketing research. Soon nearly all industries in the country followed suit. Inspired by the lead of the chemical industry, they have adopted market research as an important part of their total market function.

Having made this start, modern marketing is rapidly becoming a technology in itself. It is making use of many other disciplines to develop information and to design marketing programs. Schools and universities are offering growing numbers of courses in marketing subjects. More and more associations and publications are being created to serve the needs of this specialized part of business life. Even a Marketing Science Institute has been founded. Scientific marketing is growing rapidly now, yet it seems certain that the accelerating rate of growth of technology will cause an even greater pressure to be exerted on the spread of scientific marketing if the total products of technology are to be moved from producer to consumer.

In summary the technological growth we are experiencing today provides business with an ever increasing array of products and services. These products are being turned out at an increasing pace, resulting in ever greater competition for the consuming public's purchasing power. This results in the marketing effort becoming a more and more important part of a successful business operation. Marketing is beginning to learn to apply technology in solving its problems, in moving the goods which this same technology has produced. Marketing is also learning that it can have an effect on technological progress which will lead to more marketable products, better business operation, and happier customers.

26. *Marketing Myopia*

THEODORE LEVITT

Every major industry was once a growth industry. But some that are now riding a wave of growth enthusiasm are very much in the shadow of decline. Others which are thought of as seasoned growth industries have actually stopped growing. In every case the reason growth is threatened, slowed, or stopped is *not* because the market is saturated. It is because there has been a failure of management.

FATEFUL PURPOSES

The failure is at the top. The executives responsible for it, in the last analysis, are those who deal with broad aims and policies. Thus:

¶ The railroads did not stop growing because the need for passenger and freight transportation declined. That grew. The railroads are in trouble today not because the need was filled by others (cars, trucks, airplanes, even telephones), but because it was *not* filled by the railroads themselves. They let others take customers away from them because they assumed themselves to be in the railroad business rather than in the transportation business. The reason they defined their industry wrong was because they were railroad-oriented instead of transportation-oriented; they were product-oriented instead of customer-oriented.

¶ Hollywood barely escaped being totally ravished by television. Actually, all the established film companies went through drastic reorganizations. Some simply disappeared. All of them got into trouble not because of TV's

‡‡ SOURCE: Reprinted by permission from *Modern Marketing Strategy*, edited by Edward C. Bursk and John F. Chapman (Harvard University Press, 1964, by the President and Fellows of Harvard College): pp. 24–48.

inroads but because of their own myopia. As with the railroads, Hollywood defined its business incorrectly. It thought it was in the movie business when it was actually in the entertainment business. "Movies" implied a specific, limited product. This produced a fatuous contentment which from the beginning led producers to view TV as a threat. Hollywood scorned and rejected TV when it should have welcomed it as an opportunity—an opportunity to expand the entertainment business.

Today TV is a bigger business than the old narrowly defined movie business ever was. Had Hollywood been customer-oriented (providing entertainment), rather than product-oriented (making movies), would it have gone through the fiscal purgatory that it did? I doubt it. What ultimately saved Hollywood and accounted for its recent resurgence was the wave of new young writers, producers, and directors whose previous successes in television had decimated the old movie companies and toppled the big movie moguls.

There are other less obvious examples of industries that have been and are now endangering their futures by improperly defining their purposes. I shall discuss some in detail later and analyze the kind of policies that lead to trouble. Right now it may help to show what a thoroughly customer-oriented management *can* do to keep a growth industry growing, even after the obvious opportunities have been exhausted; and here there are two examples that have been around for a long time. They are nylon and glass—specifically, E. I. duPont de Nemours & Company and Corning Glass Works:

¶ Both companies have great technical competence. Their product orientation is unquestioned. But this alone does not explain their success. After all, who was more pridefully product-oriented and product-conscious than the erstwhile New England textile companies that have been so thoroughly massacred? The DuPonts and the Cornings have succeeded not primarily because of their product or research orientation but because they have been thoroughly customer-oriented also. It is constant watchfulness for opportunities to apply their technical know-how to the creation of customer-satisfying uses which accounts for their prodigious output of successful new products. Without a very sophisticated eye on the customer, most of their new products might have been wrong, their sales methods useless.

Aluminum has also continued to be a growth industry, thanks to the efforts of two wartime-created companies which deliberately set about creating new customer-satisfying uses. Without Kaiser Aluminum & Chemical Corporation and Reynolds Metals Company, the total demand for aluminum today would be vastly less than it is.

Error of Analysis

Some may argue that it is foolish to set the railroads off against aluminum or the movies off against glass. Are not aluminum and glass naturally so versatile that the industries are bound to have more growth opportunities than the railroads and movies? This view commits precisely the error I have been talking about. It defines an industry, or a product, or a cluster of knowhow so narrowly as to guarantee its premature senescence. When we mention "railroads," we should make sure we mean "transportation." As transporters, the railroads still have a good chance for very considerable growth. They are not limited to the railroad business as such (though in my opinion rail transportation is potentially a much stronger transportation medium than is generally believed).

What the railroads lack is not opportunity, but some of the same managerial imaginativeness and audacity that made them great. Even an amateur like Jacques Barzun can see what is lacking when he says:

I grieve to see the most advanced physical and social organization of the last century go down in shabby disgrace for lack of the same comprehensive imagination that built it up. [What is lacking is] the will of the companies

to survive and to satisfy the public by inventiveness and skill.[1]

SHADOW OF OBSOLESCENCE

It is impossible to mention a single major industry that did not at one time qualify for the magic appellation of "growth industry." In each case its assumed strength lay in the apparently unchallenged superiority of its product. There appeared to be no effective substitute for it. It was itself a runaway substitute for the product it so triumphantly replaced. Yet one after another of these celebrated industries has come under a shadow. Let us look briefly at a few more of them, this time taking examples that have so far received a little less attention:

¶ *Dry cleaning*—This was once a growth industry with lavish prospects. In an age of wool garments, imagine being finally able to get them safely and easily clean. The boom was on.

Yet here we are 30 years after the boom started and the industry is in trouble. Where has the competition come from? From a better way of cleaning? No. It has come from synthetic fibers and chemical additives that have cut the need for dry cleaning. But this is only the beginning. Lurking in the wings and ready to make chemical dry cleaning totally obsolescent is that powerful magician, ultrasonics.

¶ *Electric utilities*—This is another one of those supposedly "no-substitute" products that has been enthroned on a pedestal of invincible growth. When the incandescent lamp came along, kerosene lights were finished. Later the water wheel and the steam engine were cut to ribbons by the flexibility, reliability, simplicity, and just plain easy availability of electric motors. The prosperity of electric utilities continues to wax extravagant as the home is converted into a museum of electric gadgetry. How can anybody miss by investing in utilities, with no competition, nothing but growth ahead?

But a second look is not quite so comforting. A score of nonutility companies are well advanced toward developing a powerful chemical fuel cell which could sit in some hidden closet of every home silently ticking off electric power. The electric lines that vulgarize so many neighborhoods will be eliminated. So will the endless demolition of streets and service interruptions during storms. Also on the horizon is solar energy, again pioneered by nonutility companies.

Who says that the utilities have no competition? They may be natural monopolies now, but tomorrow they may be natural deaths. To avoid

---

[1] Jacques Barzun, "Trains and the Mind of Man," *Holiday*, February 1960, p. 21.

this prospect, they too will have to develop fuel cells, solar energy, and other power sources. To survive, they themselves will have to plot the obsolescence of what now produces their livelihood.

¶ *Grocery stores*—Many people find it hard to realize that there ever was a thriving establishment known as the "corner grocery store." The supermarket has taken over with a powerful effectiveness. Yet the big food chains of the 1930's narrowly escaped being completely wiped out by the aggressive expansion of independent supermarkets. The first genuine supermarket was opened in 1930, in Jamaica, Long Island. By 1933 supermarkets were thriving in California, Ohio, Pennsylvania, and elsewhere. Yet the established chains pompously ignored them. When they chose to notice them, it was with such derisive descriptions as "cheapy," "horse-and-buggy," "cracker-barrel storekeeping," and "unethical opportunists."

The executive of one big chain announced at the time that he found it "hard to believe that people will drive for miles to shop for foods and sacrifice the personal service chains have perfected and to which Mrs. Consumer is accustomed." [2] As late as 1936, the National Wholesale Grocers convention and the New Jersey Retail Grocers Association said there was nothing to fear. They said that the supers' narrow appeal to the price buyer limited the size of their market. They had to draw from miles around. When imitators came, there would be wholesale liquidations as volume fell. The current high sales of the supers was said to be partly due to their novelty. Basically people wanted convenient neighborhood grocers. If the neighborhood stores "cooperate with their suppliers, pay attention to their costs, and improve their service," they would be able to weather the competition until it blew over. [3]

It never blew over. The chains discovered that survival required going into the supermarket business. This meant the wholesale destruction of their huge investments in corner store sites and in established distribution and merchandising methods. The companies with "the courage of their convictions" resolutely stuck to the corner store philosophy. They kept their pride but lost their shirts.

Self-Deceiving Cycle

But memories are short. For example, it is hard for people who today confidently hail the

twin messiahs of electronics and chemicals to see how things could possibly go wrong with these galloping industries. They probably also cannot see how a reasonably sensible businessman could have been as myopic as the famous Boston millionaire who 50 years ago unintentionally sentenced his heirs to poverty by stipulating that his entire estate be forever invested exclusively in electric streetcar securities. His posthumous declaration, "There will always be a big demand for efficient urban transportation," is no consolation to his heirs who sustain life by pumping gasoline at automobile filling stations.

Yet, in a casual survey I recently took among a group of intelligent business executives, nearly half agreed that it would be hard to hurt their heirs by tying their estates forever to the electronics industry. When I then confronted them with the Boston streetcar example, they chorused unanimously, "That's different!" But is it? Is not the basic situation identical?

In truth, *there is no such thing* as a growth industry, I believe. There are only companies organized and operated to create and capitalize on growth opportunities. Industries that assume themselves to be riding some automatic growth escalator invariably descend into stagnation. The history of every dead and dying "growth" industry shows a self-deceiving cycle of bountiful expansion and undetected decay. There are four conditions which usually guarantee this cycle:

1. The belief that growth is assured by an expanding and more affluent population.
2. The belief that there is no competitive substitute for the industry's major product.
3. Too much faith in mass production and in the advantages of rapidly declining unit costs as output rises.
4. Preoccupation with a product that lends itself to carefully controlled scientific experimentation, improvement, and manufacturing cost reduction.

I should like now to begin examining each of these conditions in some detail. To build my case as boldly as possible, I shall illustrate the points with reference to three industries—petroleum, automobiles, and electronics—particularly petroleum, because it spans more years and more vicissitudes. Not only do these three have excellent reputations with the general public and also enjoy the confidence of sophisticated investors, but their managements have become known for progressive thinking in areas like

---

[2] For more details see M. M. Zimmerman, *The Super Market: A Revolution in Distribution* (New York: McGraw-Hill, 1955), p. 48.
[3] *Ibid.*, pp. 45–47.

financial control, product research, and management training. If obsolescence can cripple even these industries, it can happen anywhere.

POPULATION MYTH

The belief that profits are assured by an expanding and more affluent population is dear to the heart of every industry. It takes the edge off the apprehensions everybody understandably feels about the future. If consumers are multiplying and also buying more of your product or service, you can face the future with considerably more comfort than if the market is shrinking. An expanding market keeps the manufacturer from having to think very hard or imaginatively. If thinking is an intellectual response to a problem, then the absence of a problem leads to the absence of thinking. If your product has an automatically expanding market, then you will not give much thought to how to expand it.

One of the most interesting examples of this is provided by the petroleum industry. Probably our oldest growth industry, it has an enviable record. While there are some current apprehensions about its growth rate, the industry itself tends to be optimistic. But I believe it can be demonstrated that it is undergoing a fundamental yet typical change. It is not only ceasing to be a growth industry, but may actually be a declining one, relative to other business. Although there is widespread unawareness of it, I believe that within 25 years the oil industry may find itself in much the same position of retrospective glory that the railroads are now in. Despite its pioneering work in developing and applying the present-value method of investment evaluation, in employee relations, and in working with backward countries, the petroleum business is a distressing example of how complacency and wrongheadedness can stubbornly convert opportunity into near disaster.

One of the characteristics of this and other industries that have believed very strongly in the beneficial consequences of an expanding population, while at the same time being industries with a generic product for which there has appeared to be no competitive substitute, is that the individual companies have sought to outdo their competitors by improving on what they are already doing. This makes sense, of course, if one assumes that sales are tied to the country's population strings, because the customer can compare products only on a feature-by-feature basis. I believe it is significant, for example,

that not since John D. Rockefeller sent free kerosene lamps to China has the oil industry done anything really outstanding to create a demand for its product. Not even in product improvement has it showered itself with eminence. The greatest single improvement, namely, the development of tetraethyl lead, came from outside the industry, specifically from General Motors and DuPont. The big contributions made by the industry itself are confined to the technology of oil exploration, production, and refining.

Asking for Trouble

In other words, the industry's efforts have focused on improving the *efficiency* of getting and making its product, not really on improving the generic product or its marketing. Moreover, its chief product has continuously been defined in the narrowest possible terms, namely, gasoline, not energy, fuel, or transportation. This attitude has helped assure that:

1. Major improvements in gasoline quality tend not to originate in the oil industry. Also, the development of superior alternative fuels comes from outside the oil industry, as will be shown later.

2. Major innovations in automobile fuel marketing are originated by small new oil companies that are not primarily preoccupied with production or refining. These are the companies that have been responsible for the rapidly expanding multipump gasoline stations, with their successful emphasis on large and clean layouts, rapid and efficient driveway service, and quality gasoline at low prices.

Thus, the oil industry is asking for trouble from outsiders. Sooner or later, in this land of hungry inventors and entrepreneurs, a threat is sure to come. The possibilities of this will become more apparent when we turn to the next dangerous belief of many managements. For the sake of continuity, because this second belief is tied closely to the first, I shall continue with the same example.

Idea of Indispensability

The petroleum industry is pretty much persuaded that there is no competitive substitute for its major product, gasoline—or if there is, that it will continue to be a derivative of crude oil, such as diesel fuel or kerosene jet fuel.

There is a lot of automatic wishful thinking in this assumption. The trouble is that most refining companies own huge amounts of crude oil reserves. These have value only if there is a market for products into which oil can be converted—hence the tenacious belief in the continuing competitive superiority of automobile fuels made from crude oil.

This idea persists despite all historic evidence against it. The evidence not only shows that oil has never been a superior product for any purpose for very long, but it also shows that the oil industry has never really been a growth industry. It has been a succession of different businesses that have gone through the usual historic cycles of growth, maturity, and decay. Its over-all survival is owed to a series of miraculous escapes from total obsolescence, of last-minute and unexpected reprieves from total disaster reminiscent of the Perils of Pauline.

Perils of Petroleum

I shall sketch in only the main episodes:

¶ First, crude oil was largely a patent medicine. But even before that fad ran out, demand was greatly expanded by the use of oil in kerosene lamps. The prospect of lighting the world's lamps gave rise to an extravagant promise of growth. The prospects were similar to those the industry now holds for gasoline in other parts of the world. It can hardly wait for the underdeveloped nations to get a car in every garage.

In the days of the kerosene lamp, the oil companies competed with each other and against gaslight by trying to improve the illuminating characteristics of kerosene. Then suddenly the impossible happened. Edison invented a light which was totally nondependent on crude oil. Had it not been for the growing use of kerosene in space heaters, the incandescent lamp would have completely finished oil as a growth industry at that time. Oil would have been good for little else than axle grease.

¶ Then disaster and reprieve struck again. Two great innovations occurred, neither originating in the oil industry. The successful development of coal-burning domestic central-heating systems made the space heater obsolescent. While the industry reeled, along came its most magnificent boost yet—the internal combustion engine, also invented by outsiders. Then when the prodigious expansion for gasoline finally began to level off in the 1920's, along came the miraculous escape of a central oil heater. Once again, the escape was provided by an outsider's invention and development. And when that market weakened, wartime demand for aviation fuel came to the rescue. After the war the expansion of civilian aviation, the

dieselization of railroads, and the explosive demand for cars and trucks kept the industry's growth in high gear.

¶ Meanwhile centralized oil heating—whose boom potential had only recently been proclaimed—ran into severe competition from natural gas. While the oil companies themselves owned the gas that now competed with their oil, the industry did not originate the natural gas revolution, nor has it to this day greatly profited from its gas ownership. The gas revolution was made by newly formed transmission companies that marketed the product with an aggressive ardor. They started a magnificent new industry, first against the advice and then against the resistance of the oil companies.

By all the logic of the situation, the oil companies themselves should have made the gas revolution. They not only owned the gas; they also were the only people experienced in handling, scrubbing, and using it, the only people experienced in pipeline technology and transmission, and they understood heating problems. But, partly because they knew that natural gas would compete with their own sale of heating oil, the oil companies pooh-poohed the potentials of gas.

The revolution was finally started by oil pipeline executives who, unable to persuade their own companies to go into gas, quit and organized the spectacularly successful gas transmission companies. Even after their success became painfully evident to the oil companies, the latter did not go into gas transmission. The multibillion dollar business which should have been theirs went to others. As in the past, the industry was blinded by its narrow preoccupation with a specific product and the value of its reserves. It paid little or no attention to its customers' basic needs and preferences.

¶ The postwar years have not witnessed any change. Immediately after World War II the oil industry was greatly encouraged about its future by the rapid expansion of demand for its traditional line of products. In 1950 most companies projected annual rates of domestic expansion of around 6% through at least 1975. Though the ratio of crude oil reserves to demand in the Free World was about 20 to 1, with 10 to 1 being usually considered a reasonable working ratio in the United States, booming demand sent oil men searching for more without sufficient regard to what the future really promised. In 1952 they "hit" in the Middle East; the ratio skyrocketed to 42 to 1. If gross additions to reserves continue at the average rate of the past five years (37 billion barrels annually), then by 1970 the reserve ratio will be up to 45 to 1. This abundance of oil has weakened crude and product prices all over the world.

Uncertain Future

Management cannot find much consolation today in the rapidly expanding petrochemical industry, another oil-using idea that did not originate in the leading firms. The total United States production of petrochemicals is equivalent to about 2% (by volume) of the demand for all petroleum products. Although the petrochemical industry is now expected to grow by about 10% per year, this will not offset other drains on the growth of crude oil consumption. Furthermore, while petrochemical products are many and growing, it is well to remember that there are nonpetroleum sources of the basic raw material, such as coal. Besides, a lot of plastics can be produced with relatively little oil. A 50,000-barrel-per-day oil refinery is now considered the absolute minimum size for efficiency. But a 5,000-barrel-per-day chemical plant is a giant operation.

Oil has never been a continuously strong growth industry. It has grown by fits and starts, always miraculously saved by innovations and developments not of its own making. The reason it has not grown in a smooth progression is that each time it thought it had a superior product safe from the possibility of competitive substitutes, the product turned out to be inferior and notoriously subject to obsolescence. Until now, gasoline (for motor fuel, anyhow) has escaped this fate. But, as we shall see later, it too may be on its last legs.

The point of all this is that there is no guarantee against product obsolescence. If a company's own research does not make it obsolete, another's will. Unless an industry is especially lucky, as oil has been until now, it can easily go down in a sea of red figures—just as the railroads have, as the buggy whip manufacturers have, as the corner grocery chains have, as most of the big movie companies have, and indeed as many other industries have.

The best way for a firm to be lucky is to make its own luck. That requires knowing what makes a business successful. One of the greatest enemies of this knowledge is mass production.

PRODUCTION PRESSURES

Mass-production industries are impelled by a great drive to produce all they can. The prospect of steeply declining unit costs as output rises is more than most companies can usually resist. The profit possibilities look spectacular. All effort focuses on production. The result is that marketing gets neglected.

John Kenneth Galbraith contends that just the opposite occurs.[4] Output is so prodigious that all effort concentrates on trying to get rid of it. He says this accounts for singing commercials, desecration of the countryside with advertising signs, and other wasteful and vulgar practices. Galbraith has a finger on something real, but he misses the strategic point. Mass production does indeed generate great pressure to "move" the product. But what usually gets emphasized is selling, not marketing. Marketing, being a more sophisticated and complex process, gets ignored.

The difference between marketing and selling is more than semantic. Selling focuses on the needs of the seller, marketing on the needs of the buyer. Selling is preoccupied with the seller's need to convert his product into cash; marketing with the idea of satisfying the needs of the customer by means of the product and the whole cluster of things associated with creating, delivering, and finally consuming it.

In some industries the enticements of full mass production have been so powerful that for many years top management in effect has told the sales departments, "You get rid of it; we'll worry about profits." By contrast, a truly marketing-minded firm tries to create value-satisfying goods and services that consumers will want to buy. What it offers for sale includes not only the generic product or service, but also how it is made available to the customer, in what form, when, under what conditions, and at what terms of trade. Most important, what it offers for sale is determined not by the seller but by the buyer. The seller takes his cues from the buyer in such a way that the product becomes a consequence of the marketing effort, not vice versa.

Lag in Detroit

This may sound like an elementary rule of business, but that does not keep it from being violated wholesale. It is certainly more violated than honored. Take the automobile industry:

Here mass production is most famous, most honored, and has the greatest impact on the entire society. The industry has hitched its fortune to the relentless requirements of the annual model change, a policy that makes customer orientation an especially urgent necessity.

---

[4] *The Affluent Society* (Boston: Houghton Mifflin, 1958), pp. 152–160.

Consequently the auto companies annually spend millions of dollars on consumer research. But the fact that the new compact cars are selling so well in their first year indicates that Detroit's vast researches have for a long time failed to reveal what the customer really wanted. Detroit was not persuaded that he wanted anything different from what he had been getting until it lost millions of customers to other small car manufacturers.

How could this unbelievable lag behind consumer wants have been perpetuated so long? Why did not research reveal consumer preferences before consumers' buying decisions themselves revealed the facts? Is that not what consumer research is for—to find out before the fact what is going to happen? The answer is that Detroit never really researched the customer's wants. It only researched his preferences between the kinds of things which it had already decided to offer him. For Detroit is mainly product-oriented, not customer-oriented. To the extent that the customer is recognized as having needs that the manufacturer should try to satisfy, Detroit usually acts as if the job can be done entirely by product changes. Occasionally attention gets paid to financing, too, but that is done more in order to sell than to enable the customer to buy.

As for taking care of other customer needs, there is not enough being done to write about. The areas of the greatest unsatisfied needs are ignored, or at best get stepchild attention. These are at the point of sale and on the matter of automotive repair and maintenance. Detroit views these problem areas as being of secondary importance. That is underscored by the fact that the retailing and servicing ends of this industry are neither owned and operated nor controlled by the manufacturers. Once the car is produced, things are pretty much in the dealer's inadequate hands. Illustrative of Detroit's arm's-length attitude is the fact that, while servicing holds enormous sales-stimulating, profit-building opportunities, only 57 of Chevrolet's 7,000 dealers provide night maintenance service.

Motorists repeatedly express their dissatisfaction with servicing and their apprehensions about buying cars under the present selling setup. The anxieties and problems they encounter during the auto buying and maintenance processes are probably more intense and widespread today than 30 years ago. Yet the automobile companies do not *seem* to listen to or take their cues from the anguished consumer.

If they do listen, it must be through the filter of their own preoccupation with production. The marketing effort is still viewed as a necessary consequence of the product, not vice versa, as it should be. That is the legacy of mass production, with its parochial view that profit resides essentially in low-cost full production.

What Ford Put First

The profit lure of mass production obviously has a place in the plans and strategy of business management, but it must always *follow* hard thinking about the customer. This is one of the most important lessons that we can learn from the contradictory behavior of Henry Ford. In a sense Ford was both the most brilliant and the most senseless marketer in American history. He was senseless because he refused to give the customer anything but a black car. He was brilliant because he fashioned a production system designed to fit market needs. We habitually celebrate him for the wrong reason, his production genius. His real genius was marketing. We think he was able to cut his selling price and therefore sell millions of $500 cars because his invention of the assembly line had reduced the costs. Actually he invented the assembly line because he had concluded that at $500 he could sell millions of cars. Mass production was the *result* not the cause of his low prices.

Ford repeatedly emphasized this point, but a nation of production-oriented business managers refuses to hear the great lesson he taught. Here is his operating philosophy as he expressed it succinctly:

Our policy is to reduce the price, extend the operations, and improve the article. You will notice that the reduction of price comes first. We have never considered any costs as fixed. Therefore we first reduce the price to the point where we believe more sales will result. Then we go ahead and try to make the prices. We do not bother about the costs. The new price forces the costs down. The more usual way is to take the costs and then determine the price, and although that method may be scientific in the narrow sense; it is not scientific in the broad sense, because what earthly use is it to know the cost if it tells you that you cannot manufacture at a price at which the article can be sold? But more to the point is the fact that, although one may calculate what a cost is, and of course all of our costs are carefully calculated, no one knows what a cost ought to be. One of the ways of discovering . . . is to name a price so low as to force everybody in the place to the highest point of efficiency. The low price makes everybody dig for profits. We make more discoveries concerning manufacturing and selling under this forced method than by any method of leisurely investigation." [5]

Product Provincialism

The tantalizing profit possibilities of low unit production costs may be the most seriously self-deceiving attitude that can afflict a company, particularly a "growth" company where an apparently assured expansion of demand already tends to undermine a proper concern for the importance of marketing and the customer.

The usual result of this narrow preoccupation with so-called concrete matters is that instead of growing, the industry declines. It usually means that the product fails to adapt to the constantly changing patterns of consumer needs and tastes, to new and modified marketing institutions and practices, or to product developments in competing or complementary industries. The industry has its eyes so firmly on its own specific product that it does not see how it is being made obsolete.

The classical example of this is the buggy whip industry. No amount of product improvement could stave off its death sentence. But had the industry defined itself as being in the transportation business rather than the buggy whip business, it might have survived. It would have done what survival always entails, that is, changing. Even if it had only defined its business as providing a stimulant or catalyst to an energy source, it might have survived by becoming a manufacturer of, say, fanbelts or air cleaners.

What may some day be a still more classical example is, again, the oil industry. Having let others steal marvelous opportunities from it (e.g., natural gas, as already mentioned, missile fuels, and jet engine lubricants), one would expect it to have taken steps never to let that happen again. But this is not the case. We are now getting extraordinary new developments in fuel systems specifically designed to power automobiles. Not only are these developments concentrated in firms outside the petroleum industry, but petroleum is almost systematically ignoring them, securely content in its wedded bliss to oil. It is the story of the kerosene lamp versus the incandescent lamp all over again.

Oil is trying to improve hydrocarbon fuels rather than to develop *any* fuels best suited to the needs of their users, whether or not made in different ways and with different raw materials from oil.

Here are some of the things which nonpetroleum companies are working on:

¶ Over a dozen such firms now have advanced working models of energy systems which, when perfected, will replace the internal combustion engine and eliminate the demand for gasoline. The superior merit of each of these systems is their elimination of frequent, time-consuming, and irritating refueling stops. Most of these systems are fuel cells designed to create electrical energy directly from chemicals without combustion. Most of them use chemicals that are not derived from oil, generally hydrogen and oxygen.

¶ Several other companies have advanced models of electric storage batteries designed to power automobiles. One of these is an aircraft producer that is working jointly with several electric utility companies. The latter hope to use off-peak generating capacity to supply overnight plug-in battery regeneration. Another company, also using the battery approach, is a medium-size electronics firm with extensive small-battery experience that it developed in connection with its work on hearing aids. It is collaborating with an automobile manufacturer. Recent improvements arising from the need for high-powered miniature power storage plants in rockets have put us within reach of a relatively small battery capable of withstanding great overloads or surges of power. Germanium diode applications and batteries using sintered-plate and nickel-cadmium techniques promise to make a revolution in our energy sources.

¶ Solar energy conversion systems are also getting increasing attention. One usually cautious Detroit auto executive recently ventured that solar-powered cars might be common by 1980.

As for the oil companies, they are more or less "watching developments," as one research director put it to me. A few are doing a bit of research on fuel cells, but almost always confined to developing cells powered by hydrocarbon chemicals. None of them are enthusiastically researching fuel cells, batteries, or solar power plants. None of them are spending a fraction as much on research in these profoundly important areas as they are on the usual run-of-the-mill things like reducing combustion chamber deposit in gasoline engines. One major integrated petroleum company recently

---

[5] Henry Ford, *My Life and Work* (New York: Doubleday, Page, 1923), pp. 146–147.

took a tentative look at the fuel cell and concluded that although "the companies actively working on it indicate a belief in ultimate success . . . the timing and magnitude of its impact are too remote to warrant recognition in our forecasts."

One might, of course, ask: Why should the oil companies do anything different? Would not chemical fuel cells, batteries, or solar energy kill the present product lines? The answer is that they would indeed, and that is precisely the reason for the oil firms having to develop these power units before their competitors, so they will not be companies without an industry.

Management might be more likely to do what is needed for its own preservation, if it thought of itself as being in the energy business. But even that would not be enough if it persists in imprisoning itself in the narrow grip of its tight product orientation. It has to think of itself as taking care of customer needs, not finding, refining, or even selling oil. Once it genuinely thinks of its business as taking care of people's transportation needs, nothing can stop it from creating its own extravagantly profitable growth.

Creative Destruction

Since words are cheap and deeds are dear it may be appropriate to indicate what this kind of thinking involves and leads to. Let us start at the beginning—the customer. It can be shown that motorists strongly dislike the bother, delay, and experience of buying gasoline. People actually do not buy gasoline. They cannot see it, taste it, feel it, appreciate it, or really test it. What they buy is the right to continue driving their cars. The gas station is like a tax collector to whom people are compelled to pay a periodic toll as the price of using their cars. This makes the gas station a basically unpopular institution. It can ever be made popular or pleasant, only less unpopular, less unpleasant.

To reduce its unpopularity completely means eliminating it. Nobody likes a tax collector, not even a pleasantly cheerful one. Nobody likes to interrupt a trip to buy a phantom product, not even from a handsome Adonis or a seductive Venus. Hence, companies that are working on exotic fuel substitutes which will eliminate the need for frequent refueling are heading directly into the outstretched arms of the irritated motorist. They are riding a wave of inevitability, not because they are creating something which is technologically superior or more sophisti-

cated, but because they are satisfying a powerful customer need. They are also eliminating noxious odors and air pollution.

Once the petroleum companies recognize the customer-satisfying logic of what another power system can do, they will see that they have no more choice about working on an efficient, long-lasting fuel (or some way of delivering present fuels without bothering the motorist) than the big food chains had a choice about going into the supermarket business, or the vacuum tube companies had a choice about making semiconductors. For their own good the oil firms will have to destroy their own highly profitable assets. No amount of wishful thinking can save them from the necessity of engaging in this form of "creative destruction."

I phrase the need as strongly as this because I think management must make quite an effort to break itself loose from conventional ways. It is all too easy in this day and age for a company or industry to let its sense of purpose become dominated by the economies of full production and to develop a dangerously lopsided product orientation. In short, if management lets itself drift, it invariably drifts in the direction of thinking of itself as producing goods and services, not customer satisfactions. While it probably will not descend to the depths of telling its salesmen, "You get rid of it; we'll worry about profits," it can, without knowing it, be practicing precisely that formula for withering decay. The historic fate of one growth industry after another has been its suicidal product provincialism.

DANGERS OF R & D

Another big danger to a firm's continued growth arises when top management is wholly transfixed by the profit possibilities of technical research and development. To illustrate I shall turn first to a new industry—electronics—and then return once more to the oil companies. By comparing a fresh example with a familiar one, I hope to emphasize the prevalence and insidiousness of a hazardous way of thinking.

Marketing Shortchanged

In the case of electronics, the greatest danger which faces the glamorous new companies in this field is not that they do not pay enough attention to research and development, but that the pay *too much* attention to it. And the fact that the fastest growing electronics firms owe their eminence to their heavy emphasis on technical research is completely beside the point. They have vaulted to affluence on a sudden crest of unusually strong general receptiveness to new technical ideas. Also, their success has been shaped in the virtually guaranteed market of military subsidies and by military orders that in many cases actually preceded the existence of facilities to make the products. Their expansion has, in other words, been almost totally devoid of marketing effort.

Thus, they are growing up under conditions that come dangerously close to creating the illusion that a superior product will sell itself. Having created a successful company by making a superior product, it is not surprising that management continues to be oriented toward the product rather than the people who consume it. It develops the philosophy that continued growth is a matter of continued product innovation and improvement.

A number of other factors tend to strengthen and sustain this belief:

1. Because electronic products are highly complex and sophisticated, managements become topheavy with engineers and scientists. This creates a selective bias in favor of research and production at the expense of marketing. The organization tends to view itself as making things rather than' satisfying customer needs. Marketing gets treated as a residual activity, "something else" that must be done once the vital job of product creation and production is completed.

2. To this bias in favor of product research, development, and production is added the bias in favor of dealing with controllable variables. Engineers and scientists are at home in the world of concrete things like machines, test tubes, production lines, and even balance sheets. The abstractions to which they feel kindly are those which are testable or manipulatable in the laboratory, or, if not testable, then functional, such as Euclid's axioms. In short, the managements of the new glamour-growth companies tend to favor those business activities which lend themselves to careful study, experimentation, and control—the hard, practical, realities of the lab, the shop, the books.

What gets shortchanged are the realities of the *market*. Consumers are unpredictable, varied, fickle, stupid, shortsighted, stubborn, and generally bothersome. This is not what the engineer-managers say, but deep down in their consciousness it is what they believe. And this accounts for their concentrating on what they know and what they can control, namely, product research, engineering, and production. The emphasis on production becomes particularly attractive when the product can be made at declining unit costs. There is no more inviting way of making money than by running the plant full blast.

Today the top-heavy science-engineering-production orientation of so many electronics companies works reasonably well because they are pushing into new frontiers in which the armed services have pioneered virtually assured markets. The companies are in the felicitous position of having to fill, not find markets; of not having to discover what the customer needs and wants, but of having the customer voluntarily come forward with specific new product demands. If a team of consultants had been assigned specifically to design a business situation calculated to prevent the emergence and development of a customer-oriented marketing viewpoint, it could not have produced anything better than the conditions just described.

Stepchild Treatment

The oil industry is a stunning example of how science, technology, and mass production can divert an entire group of companies from their main task. To the extent the consumer is studied at all (which is not much), the focus is forever on getting information which is designed to help the oil companies improve what they are now doing. They try to discover more convincing advertising themes, more effective sales promotional drives, what the market shares of the various companies are, what people like or dislike about service station dealers and oil companies, and so forth. Nobody seems as interested in probing deeply into the basic human needs that the industry might be trying to satisfy as in probing into the basic properties of the raw material that the companies work with in trying to deliver customer satisfactions.

Basic questions about customers and markets seldom get asked. The latter occupy a stepchild status. They are recognized as existing, as having to be taken care of, but not worth very much real thought or dedicated attention. Nobody gets as excited about the customers in his own backyard as about the oil in the Sahara Desert.

Nothing illustrates better the neglect of marketing than its treatment in the industry press.

The centennial issue of the *American Petroleum Institute Quarterly*, published in 1959 to celebrate the discovery of oil in Titusville, Pennsylvania, contained 21 feature articles proclaiming the industry's greatness. Only one of these talked about its achievements in marketing, and that was only a pictorial record of how service station architecture has changed. The issue also contained a special section on "New Horizons," which was devoted to showing the magnificent role oil would play in America's future. Every reference was ebulliently optimistic, never implying once that oil might have some hard competition. Even the reference to atomic energy was a cheerful catalogue of how oil would help make atomic energy a success. There was not a single apprehension that the oil industry's affluence might be threatened or a suggestion that one "new horizon" might include new and better ways of serving oil's present customers.

But the most revealing example of the stepchild treatment that marketing gets was still another special series of short articles on "The Revolutionary Potential of Electronics." Under that heading this list of articles appeared in the table of contents: "In the Search for Oil," "In Production Operations," "In Refinery Processes," "In Pipeline Operations."

Significantly, every one of the industry's major functional areas is listed, *except* marketing. Why? Either it is believed that electronics holds no revolutionary potential for petroleum marketing (which is palpably wrong), or the editors forgot to discuss marketing (which is more likely, and illustrates its stepchild status).

The order in which the four functional areas are listed also betrays the alienation of the oil industry from the consumer. The industry is implicitly defined as beginning with the search for oil and ending with its distribution from the refinery. But the truth is, it seems to me, that the industry begins with the needs of the customer for its products. From the primal position its definition moves steadily backstream to areas of progressively lesser importance, until it finally comes to rest at the "search for oil."

Beginning and End

The view that an industry is a customer-satisfying process, not a goods-producing process, is vital for all businessmen to understand. An industry begins with the customer and his needs, not with a patent, a raw material, or a selling skill. Given the customer's needs, the industry develops backwards, first concerning itself with the physical *delivery* of customer satisfactions. Then it moves back further to *creating* the things by which these satisfactions are in part achieved. How these materials are created is a matter of indifference to the customer, hence the particular form of manufacturing, processing, or what-have-you cannot be considered as a vital aspect of the industry. Finally, the industry moves back still further to *finding* the raw materials necessary for making its products.

The irony of some industries oriented toward technical research and development is that the scientists who occupy the high executive positions are totally unscientific when it comes to defining their companies' over-all needs and purposes. They violate the first two rules of the scientific method—being aware of and defining their companies' problems, and then developing testable hypotheses about solving them. They are scientific only about the convenient things, such as laboratory and product experiments. The reason that the customer (and the satisfaction of his deepest needs) is not considered as being "the problem" is not because there is any certain belief that no such problem exists, but because an organizational lifetime has conditioned management to look in the opposite direction. Marketing is a stepchild.

I do not mean that selling is ignored. Far from it. But selling, again, is not marketing. As already pointed out, selling concerns itself with the tricks and techniques of getting people to exchange their cash for your product. It is not concerned with the values that the exchange is all about. And it does not, as marketing invariably does, view the entire business process as consisting of a tightly integrated effort to discover, create, arouse, and satisfy customer needs. The customer is somebody "out there" who, with proper cunning, can be separated from his loose change.

Actually, not even selling gets much attention in some technologically minded firms. Because there is a virtually guaranteed market for the abundant flow of their new products, they do not actually know what a real market is. It is as if they lived in a planned economy, moving their products routinely from factory to retail outlet. Their successful concentration on products tends to convince them of the soundness of what they have been doing, and they fail to see the gathering clouds over the market.

CONCLUSION

Visceral Feel of Greatness

Less than 75 years ago American railroads enjoyed a fierce loyalty among astute Wall Streeters. European monarchs invested in them heavily. Eternal wealth was thought to be the benediction for anybody who could scrape a few thousand dollars together to put into rail stocks. No other form of transportation could compete with the railroads in speed, flexibility, durability, economy, and growth potentials. As Jacques Barzun put it, "By the turn of the century it was an institution, an image of man, a tradition, a code of honor, a source of poetry, a nursery of boyhood desires, a sublimest of toys, and the most solemn machine—next to the funeral hearse—that marks the epochs in man's life." [6]

Even after the advent of automobiles, trucks, and airplanes, the railroad tycoons remained imperturbably self-confident. If you had told them 60 years ago that in 30 years they would be flat on their backs, broke, and pleading for government subsidies, they would have thought you totally demented. Such a future was simply not considered possible. It was not even a discussable subject, or an askable question, or a matter which any sane person would consider worth speculating about. The very thought was insane. Yet a lot of insane notions now have matter-of-fact acceptance—for example, the idea of 100-ton tubes of metal moving smoothly through the air 20,000 feet above the earth, loaded with 100 sane and solid citizens casually drinking martinis—and they have dealt cruel blows to the railroads.

What specifically must other companies do to avoid this fate? What does customer orientation involve? These questions have in part been answered by the preceding examples and analysis. It would take another article to show in detail what is required for specific industries. In any case, it should be obvious that building an effective customer-oriented company involves far more than good intentions or promotional tricks; it involves profound matters of human organization and leadership. For the present, let me merely suggest what appear to be some general requirements.

Obviously the company has to do what survival demands. It has to adapt to the requirements of the market, and it has to do it sooner rather than later. But mere survival is a so-so aspiration. Anybody can survive in some way or other, even the skid-row bum. The trick is to survive gallantly, to feel the surging impulse of commercial mastery; not just to experience the sweet smell of success, but to have the visceral feel of entrepreneurial greatness.

No organization can achieve greatness without a vigorous leader who is driven onward by his own pulsating *will to succeed*. He has to have a vision of grandeur, a vision that can produce eager followers in vast numbers. In business, the followers are the customers. To produce these customers, the entire corporation must be viewed as a customer-creating and customer-satisfying organism. Management must think of itself not as producing products but as providing customer-creating value satisfactions. It must push this idea (and everything it means and requires) into every nook and cranny of the organization. It has to do this continuously and with the kind of flair that excites and stimulates the people in it. Otherwise, the company will be merely a series of pigeonholed parts, with no consolidating sense of purpose or direction.

In short, the organization must learn to think of itself not as producing goods or services but as *buying customers*, as doing the things that will make people *want* to do business with it. And the chief executive himself has the inescapable responsibility for creating this environment, this viewpoint, this attitude, this aspiration. He himself must set the company's style, its direction, and its goals. This means he has to know precisely where he himself wants to go, and to make sure the whole organization is enthusiastically aware of where that is. This is a first requisite of leadership, for *unless he knows where he is going, any road will take him there.*

If any road is okay, the chief executive might as well pack his attaché case and go fishing. If an organization does not know or care where it is going, it does not need to advertise that fact with a ceremonial figurehead. Everybody will notice it soon enough.

---

[6] *Op cit.*, p. 20.

27. Research and the Marketing Concept

W. B. REYNOLDS

Marketing literature has for some time devoted space to the so-called total marketing concept in American business and has developed a substantial rationale for the benefits which potentially can be derived through the intelligent application of the concept. I emphasize the words "intelligent application of the concept" since a few marketing experts seem to feel that total marketing concept means turning over management of all aspects of the company's business to them. These people are delighted by articles such as that by Theodore Levitt entitled "Marketing Myopia" which appeared in the *Harvard Business Review* of July-August, 1960. That this article is filled with sweeping generalizations based upon factual distortion seems to escape them.

If the total marketing concept is an opportunity to reappraise marketing thinking, it at the same time makes demands upon marketing organizations which they must realistically face. One of the most important of these demands is the understanding of the proper relationship between the total marketing concept and the intelligent use of research and development.

A successful manufacturing corporation today rests upon three essential bases—(1) an informed, aggressive and intelligent executive management, (2) sound marketing concepts administered by superior marketing management, and (3) sound technology developed

‡‡ SOURCE: Reprinted by permission from *Marketing Innovations*, Proceedings of the 8th Biennial Marketing Institute, American Marketing Association, Minnesota Chapter, November 1961, pp. II: 14–21.

by superior scientific and technological personnel. Enlightened executive management will see to it that a proper partnership develops between marketing and technology and that neither becomes subservient to the other. Each has an important and easily defined area of basic contribution requiring a high ·degree of creativity and innovation. Creativity thrives best when free of undue pressure and domination.

Since authors like Mr. Levitt are reaching unwarranted conclusions based upon irrelevant or incorrect facts, I should like to reexamine the general area of the Marketing-Research relationship.

At the outset I want to make it clear that I agree thoroughly with Mr. Levitt's thesis that marketing has been frequently neglected and that many companies and even a few industries have declined because of what Levitt terms "marketing myopia." Levitt's basic fallacy is not that he emphasizes the marketing concept but that he suffers from acute technological myopia.

Permit me to illustrate by referring to the petroleum industry which seems to be Mr. Levitt's favorite whipping boy. Although Levitt's "Perils of Pauline" analogy is clever journalism, it completely begs the question of the greatness of today's industry. What happened during the first 50 years after Col. Drake spudded in his first well at Titusville is rather academic at this stage. Any new industry in a nineteenth-century environment was likely to experience growing pains. But the petroleum industry was never in any real danger of demise as Levitt implies because petroleum was then and still is inherently the cheapest practical source of energy and it will continue to be so in the forseeable future. And modern civilization, friend Levitt, is based upon cheap energy. The petroleum industry has developed to its present enormous strength and virility because it has used sound technology to provide a better product at lower prices. And it has never lost sight of its basic mission of finding and exploiting the cheapest sources of fossil carbonaceous deposits.

To assert that the petroleum industry is in the energy business and should, therefore, quickly jump into atomic energy, fuel cell technology or any other energy producing or converting innovation that happens along without regard for the technological "fitness" for so doing is an error as grave as marketing myopia. Take the fuel cell.

Mr. Levitt castigates the petroleum industry for its "watch and wait" attitude on fuel cell technology. To quote: "We are now getting extraordinary new developments in fuel systems specifically designed to power automobiles. . . . Over a dozen firms now have advanced working models of energy systems which, when perfected, will replace the internal combustion engine and eliminate the demand for gasoline." end quote. Specifically this weird generalization seems to be based upon the fuel cell, storage batteries, and solar energy converters. And Mr. Levitt complains that none of the oil companies are enthusiastically researching fuel cells, batteries, or solar power plants. Here his technological myopia is quite evident.

In the first place, none of these represents a serious immediate threat to gasoline as the prime fuel for automobiles. A moment's reflection should make this obvious. The only presently developed practical fuel for the fuel cell is hydrogen. Can you imagine an automobile powered with hydrogen? Hydrogen is a light gas which cannot be liquified under any practical conditions for use in automobiles. Even under very high pressures which would require enormously heavy cylinders a practical amount of hydrogen could not be carried in an automobile. And to cap it all, hydrogen is one of the most highly explosive substances known, when mixed with air. A hydrogen cylinder leak in a home garage could blow a whole neighborhood apart. In short, hydrogen will not be used to power automobiles. If it is ever used to power stationary engines or generate electrical power, it will doubtless be obtained from methane, a petroleum product.

Because of these considerations the oil companies have worked with hydrocarbons as fuel for cells. This is the only practical approach for moving power plant use and was motivated by sound technical considerations, not an obsession with their basic raw material as Levitt contends.

The use of batteries and solar cells to power automobiles is equally impractical. The last time I used a battery-powered golf cart both the battery and my patience gave out on the fourteenth fairway. The new gasoline-powered golf carts are rapidly taking over. Even assuming great technical progress in batteries and solar cells, they cannot be regarded as more than very long-range technical possibilities. The petroleum industry has quite correctly adopted a wait-and-see attitude. In the first place, the odds are strongly in favor of petroleum fuels, and in the second place the technology involved in batteries and solar cells doesn't fit. A company should move into an entirely new field of technology only when there are compelling reasons such as unusual profit opportunities or a dire and imminent threat to present lines. Finally, the timing of potential obsolescence of motor fuel by *anything* is such that the oil industry will have at least ten years warning of a serious threat. To dilute its efforts today by moving away from established technology into an entirely new technology (in this instance electronics and electrical equipment) because of a minor and long-range threat just doesn't represent sound business judgment for the petroleum industry.

The petroleum industry is basically engaged in finding, producing and upgrading fossil deposits. In this they have had preeminent success. Mr. Levitt is quite incorrect in his statement that ". . . major improvements in gasoline quality tend not to originate in the oil industry." On the contrary, *all* major improvements in gasoline quality, with the possible exception of tetra ethyl lead, have originated in the oil industry, e.g., thermal cracking, catalytic cracking, catalytic reforming, alkylation, etc., etc. The octane rating and other performance characteristics of unleaded gasolines have consistently improved from year to year. Tetra ethyl lead was discovered by Thomas Midgeley, who took it to DuPont for production because DuPont was technologically qualified to produce it. It remained in the chemical industry because that was where it belonged technologically. On the other hand, petrochemical technology does fit the petroleum industry and many petroleum companies now derive a substantial percentage of their profit from petrochemicals. Levitt feels that petroleum management cannot find much consolation today in the rapidly expanding petrochemical industry since petrochemicals represent only 2% of the volume of oil processed. But, in fact, petrochemicals represent a much higher percentage of the *value* of hydrocarbons processed. It is not unusual for a petrochemical to sell for 50 to 100 times the value of the hydrocarbon from which it was made. The oil companies have moved rapidly into petrochemicals because the technology is right.

To emphasize the marketing myopia of the oil industry Levitt points out that gasoline users strongly dislike the bother, delay and experience of buying gasoline. Hence, the industry must quickly develop an efficient, long-lasting fuel to eliminate filling-station stops. I might point out to Mr. Levitt that there is also great popular demand for a safe, economical magic carpet and a really workable Aladdin's lamp. Where does Mr. Levitt suggest we look for this magic fuel? Atomic energy? Fuel cell? Solar devices? The petroleum companies are in the business of producing and upgrading *oil*. A company must put its research dollars into technological areas with the maximum chance of success. Otherwise like Ponce de Leon, they will die withered and frustrated. In connection with the utility of that great American institution, the filling station, I might parenthetically ask Mr. Levitt if he has ever taken a motor vacation with a carload of youngsters.

I have dwelt upon Levitt's treatment of the petroleum industry for the purpose of making a single point, namely, that the total marketing concept cannot be successful unless it is administered wisely in the light of sound technological considerations. As marketing men you have not only an opportunity but a compelling responsibility to know and understand important aspects of the technology underlying your field of interest and to benefit by what that technology can bring to your company in the way of new product opportunities.

Levitt says that an industry begins with the customer and his needs, not with a patent, a raw material or a selling skill. But I submit, on the contrary, that most new industries have grown out of technological progress leading to the development of new products which fulfill basic human needs. Dr. Wallace Carothers developed nylon, not because marketing people were clamoring for a synthetic fiber, but because his fundamental research on polyamide resins re-

vealed that these resins had interesting fiber-forming characteristics. The great, modern plastics industry has grown from exploratory research on high polymers which, for the most part, was not slanted toward any particular market needs. Once these new products were developed, effort was then directed toward their place in the market and, if no need was apparent, extensive applications research and market development soon found many customers, frequently in unexpected places.

For some time after polyethylene was discovered there was little demand for it. Little by little, new uses were found and, most important, the price was brought down through intensive research until today sales of this product approach half a billion dollars annually. This achievement was brought about by a successful marriage of marketing and technology. And the flow was fundamental research, new products, applications research, new end product, marketing and sales to the customer, not the Levittized or backward process. The customer demand for most polyethylene products did not exist until it was created by creative applications research and marketing. And I might say parenthetically that most of the creative marketing in polyethylene and polypropylene has been carried out by the petroleum industry, whose development of low-cost olefins has made the whole thing possible.

Please do not interpret my strong disagreement with Mr. Levitt's version of the marketing concept as a lack of appreciation for the value of an enlightened total marketing concept. Whereas Levitt castigates technology and scientists in management and downgrades unreasonably the position of technology in the profit picture, an enlightened marketing concept will exploit to the utmost the contributions of technology.

In my discussion today I have been asked to emphasize the decision-making process in new product development. One of the most basic decisions executive management and marketing management must make relative to new products is whether or not *all* research projects should arise from consumer studies and marketing research. If this decision is affirmative, I submit that executive and marketing management suffer from technological myopia and have, per se, cut themselves away from tremendous profit possibilities. As I have pointed out, many of the most highly profitable new products have resulted from unexpected discoveries made during the course of fundamental and exploratory research. These products would never have been developed as an answer to consumer wants arising from marketing research for the twofold reason that the consumer want often was not recognized *a priori* and usually the product grew out of developing technology which would not have developed in response to a defined product need.

On the other hand, many profitable new products *have* developed as a result of clearly-defined consumer needs. Frequently, but by no means always, these consumer needs have received corporate notice as a result of marketing research. Others, such as synthetic rubber, have been so obviously needed that they became prime objectives of technology, itself.

The point to be emphasized is that new products arise in *two* ways; one, in response to clearly-defined consumer needs and, two, from fundamental and exploratory research, i.e., developing technology. The first and most important management decision relative to new products is to take full advantage of both sources of new products and to organize so that products and concepts from each source can and will be fully evaluated as to both marketing and technological appropriateness. This will avoid the pitfalls of (a) trying to sell a new product out of technology for which no basic need exists or (b) senselessly spending research money to develop a product which might satisfy a need but for which the technological chances of success are nil or very small.

Once a product has been placed on the market it must be supported continuously thereafter by aggressive research to improve quality and lower cost. This is the technological input that keeps a product on the market long after it otherwise would have become obsolete. But simultaneously, vigorous exploratory research must be carried out to develop new products and processes which will make the old ones obsolete. This is a continuing responsibility of research and development and here, at least, it seems that Mr. Levitt and I are on common ground. Except, and the exception is very important, I would emphasize that the limited research dollar be aimed toward programs that make technological sense both from the standpoint of technical feasibility and proper fit with the company's established technology and marketing capabilities.

If I have managed to make the point that technology, itself, has a major contribution to make to the product development function, the question naturally arises as to how this can be accomplished in a consumer, marketing oriented company. Assuming that executive and marketing management are aware of this gold in the technological rainbow, its exploitation becomes an easy organizational matter. Fundamental and exploratory research from which these products arise is set up as a corporate function, financed by the corporation and responsible only to executive corporate management. Here we are dealing with the creative talents of skilled scientists and, in the words of Mr. James F. Bell, "We must follow where research leads."

This is the kind of research that led to nylon, to the transistor, to polyethylene and to a host of other new products. True, these products were successful only because they fulfilled basic needs, but the scientists who developed them were not consciously slanting their efforts toward the fulfillment of those needs. They were pushing forward the frontiers of science simply to find out what was there. Since no one knows *a priori* what is there, it is a bit ridiculous to say that this aspect of the research program should be market directed or even strongly influenced by market considerations.

On the other hand, once the outline of a definable product begins to emerge from this black box of technology, an enlightened market research becomes as important as the product itself. The decision to perfect the product through further applied research should be made only in the light of basic marketing considerations. Through this stage of the development marketing plays an important supporting role. Once the product is perfected, the final decision to manufacture and sell becomes a dominant marketing function. The important factor in the decision-making process relating to these technology-nurtured products is proper liaison between research, marketing, and executive management. It is important that this liaison be at the highest research and division management level.

As already noted, the other prime source of new product concepts comes directly from studies of consumer wants and needs. Usually the product can be reasonably well visualized and its development becomes a matter of short-term, applied research. This type of product-development may be carried out by the operating department, itself, or it may be carried out by the corporate research function under conditions assuring the satisfaction of marketing needs. Decisions regarding new products arising in this way are straightforward and relatively easy to make. If the economics are right and the original marketing input was right, the product should make money.

However, not all consumer wants and needs can be met by easily defined products. For example, it doesn't require a very erudite marketing study to know that one of the most urgent human needs is a cure for cancer. This does not at all mean that the chemical and pharmaceutical industry should (on the basis of business judgment) devote their major research efforts toward chemotherapy agents for cancer. A mature scientific evaluation of the difficulty of the problem and hence the chances for success requires prudence in research expenditures in this field. In fact, the technology is so difficult, even though the potential rewards are great, that most cancer research has been carried out with government or non-profit foundation funds. The point here is that a compelling market need is not per se an adequate reason for an extensive product development program. This is the point missed by Theodore Levitt in his castigation of the petroleum industry for not developing a "permanent" motor fuel to eliminate filling station stops. Technical considerations practically eliminate this idea as something to be taken seriously. Thus another of the basic decisions regarding new product research must be that purely marketing considerations must be fully evaluated 'in the light of sound technology.

This again emphasizes the corporate tripod of sound management, sound marketing and sound technology. My marketing friends tell me there is little consumer interest in a two-legged stool. And my corporate experience tells me that there are few if any successful companies balancing on a bipod. Strong marketing doesn't offset weak technology, and strong technology cannot offset marketing myopia.

Since product decisions are based in substantial part upon market research and since in a short run research and development manpower and budgets are relatively fixed, marketing managements have an increasing responsibility to be sure that the wants and needs which they are communicating to research and development personnel are more real than imagined. These must be supplemented with a rigorous examination of factors such as competition, trends in the industry, investment requirements, advertising appropriations necessary, channels of distribution, and a host of other critical factors. For despite the wants and needs of the consumer, and they are many and varied, corporate managements are asking for a more realistic assessment of the total risk.

In its final form the identification and interpretations of consumer wants lead ultimately to a prediction problem; and the information which managements are really asking of marketing management is prediction of consumer behavior at some future point in time. Under these conditions, and if research and development effort is not to be misdirected, it would appear that the tools and techniques to be applied in predicting consumer behavior now need the same kind of scrutiny that predictive mechanisms in the physical sciences have undergone for a hundred years.

The question becomes one of maximizing the corporation's opportunity for being right, since once the decision has been made to move in any given product area with the research and development program, valuable manpower and time is committed. If this commitment is made, and if it later develops that the commitment was improperly made, then not only has the research and development time and manpower been used unwisely but valuable time has been lost which could have been devoted to more adequately thought-through projects.

Both marketing and research managements are sensitive, to greater or lesser degrees, to the action of competitors. To a reasonable extent, this is necessary. However, the most desirable situation would be one in which the consumer's wants were being interpreted on a constant and rolling basis with an applied development program closely geared to these wants and the capacity of the individual corporation. Research and development programs cannot be all things to all men and there must come a point at which management makes a series of judgments as to what will and will not be researched. These decisions are critical to the well being of the organization and demand more complete evaluative techniques.

Even assuming that the ability to predict future consumer behavior becomes more sensitive as we learn to live with the marketing concept, the responsibilities of marketing managements do not end here. The reason for this is that the purpose of predicting and interpreting is to provide intelligent outlines for research and development programs which, if successful, will find acceptance with the consumer. The consumer, however, is not the only governing factor. Research managements must at the same time evaluate their applied projects in view of a total evaluation of the future climate in which the proposed products will find themselves competing. Research and development departments have a real responsibility in technological forecasting just as marketing managements have a responsibility in demand and business forecasting. The rate at which technology is growing has accelerated to the point where decisions must be made today on the possible impact of tomorrow's technology. The rate at which our decisions can be made obsolete is truly staggering.

An enlightened total marketing concept requires three major technical programs. These are a fundamental research program engaged in a search for new knowledge, an exploratory research program which becomes more immediate than the fundamental program, and an applied product development program aimed specifically at introducing new products in time and with particular characteristics which will satisfy consumer wants as interpreted through marketing managements. With these three programs, it is possible to work not only from the consumer back toward development, but also to work from a developing technology toward the consumer.

It is important for marketing people to understand what the research and development process is. Accustomed as they are to dealing with the uncertainties of human nature, they frequently fail to understand the uncertainties of technology. A new product should not be ordered from research as one would order a toothbrush from the drug store. There are many difficult uncertainties in product development both as to timing and quality. Frequently undue pressure from marketing leads to hastily conceived products of questionable quality. It takes a great deal of time and painstaking effort to develop good products, and requests from marketing to research should be most carefully considered and documented. Otherwise there is tremendous spinning of wheels and little forward motion.

Marketing is in the van of corporate thinking and action. The responsibility is very great as are the potential rewards. An enlightened marketing management will seek neither to direct the methodology of product development nor to dominate the conception of new products. Rather will it recognize the joint responsibility of marketing and research and seek to make its corporate contribution through supporting and promoting exploratory research and constructive guidance and mature understanding of the problems of applied research.

As one of my colleagues puts it, research is not sheer adrenalin. It is a mechanism through which the corporation can satisfy consumer wants at a profit.

H. The Institutional Framework of Marketing

28. *Fundamental Differences Between Industrial and Consumer Marketing*

INTRODUCTION

The subject of this monograph concerns modern marketing with its many ramifications, apparent cross currents, and obvious parallelisms. It is manifestly impossible to lay down "hard and fast" rules which encompass all of the fringe differences between industrial and consumer marketing. So many exceptions exist in most areas that these differences, as well as similarities, can only be stated in general terms.

There is, however, a definite need for "bench marks" to which the reader may return from time to time like a surveyor to check the accuracy of his work or to serve as a "point of departure" into other parts of the geography surrounding the bench marks.

For us, these fixed points will be definitions basic to the subject.

Marketing

Marketing includes those business activities involved in the flow of goods and services from production to consumption.

Goods and services are of two types; consumer and industrial.

Consumer Goods

Goods destined for use by the individual ultimate consumer and in such form that they can be used by him without further commercial processing. . . .[1]

This is a portion of the definition prepared by the Committee on Definitions and the balance of the statement does not include consumer services such as hairdressing, window-washing, furnace-cleaning, laundry, etc., yet these are an integral part of the broad consumer marketing field.

Industrial Goods

Goods which are used in producing consumers' goods, other business or industrial goods, and services and/or in facilitating the operation of an enterprise, may include land and buildings for business purposes, equipment (installation and accessory), operating supplies, raw materials, fabricated materials.[2] Thomas A. Staudt of Indiana University boils this down to "Industrial goods are commonly defined as those goods used in the production of other goods and services." (This definition seems to omit industrial services which are playing an increasingly important part in the operation of a number of industries such as acid-treatment for oil wells and prospecting services, aerial surveys, and the like.)

⁑ SOURCE: Reprinted by permission from the *Journal of Marketing* (National Quarterly Publication of the American Marketing Association), Vol. 19, No. 2, October 1954, pp. 152–158.

[1] Prepared by the Committee on Definitions of the National Association of Marketing Teachers: Professors R. S. Alexander of Columbia University, G. R. Collins and John W. Wingate of New York University, Robert F. Elder of Mass. Institute of Technology, and Charles E. Bellatty of Boston University.

[2] *Ibid.*

Even with these definitions there must be an awareness that in many instances a specific commodity may either be an industrial good or a consumer good, depending upon the use to which it is put. Two examples will suffice to illustrate the points:

1. A manufacturing company may buy the same kind of powdered soap for use in soap dispensers in lavoratories which the housewife buys in an identical package for use in her washing machine;

2. The typewriter used for making out production orders for machine tools, wire rope, office furniture or what-have-you, may be identical with the one purchased at the local office equipment store for occasional use in the home.

DIFFERENCES OWING TO THE NATURE OF THE MARKET OR THE BUYERS

1. A part of the demand for industrial goods is a derived demand from consumer goods and services and a part from government, defense, and war purchases. The apparent influence of the derived demand for various types of industrial goods is diluted rapidly as the chain of purchases recedes from the consumer product application.

2. Rational buying motives appear to predominate in the industrial field (as against emotional motives in the consumer field) but their influence declines with the increase in product similarity.

3. Industrial buyers usually purchase raw materials and component parts on a policy formulation basis expressed in quantity, price, and specification; capital production equipment on a projected cost analysis; and supplies from habit and availability. Consumer purchasing policies and methods are less well-defined.

4. The number of industrial buyers is much smaller than the number of consumer buyers. (In 1947 there were 240,881 manufacturing plants as contrasted with the 1950 census population figure totaling 42,520,000 family units.) Some specialized industrial markets may comprise less than a dozen potential customers.

5. Industrial markets are likely to be much more concentrated geographically. For example, the 1947 Census of Manufacturers shows that the 53 metropolitan areas in the United States each having over 40,000 industrial wage earners had 59 per cent of the total industrial wage earners but only 24 per cent of the total United States population. The disparity is much more pronounced if the top ten industrial metropolitan areas are compared—37 per cent of the wage earners but only 13 per cent of the population.

6. Single unit or small volume purchases are characteristic in consumer marketing. Industrial buying covers not only single unit purchases but also a prevalence of volume purchasing of raw materials and component parts and may include volume purchasing of supplies.

7. Multiple-buying responsibility is commonplace in the industrial field in the purchase of major items of equipment and in the establishment of formulas for purchases of raw materials and component parts.

8. Successful development of "yardsticks" for industrial market determination from a sample depends on the individual product-market situation. Consumer buying can be measured more universally through sampling techniques, panels and inventory movement studies.

9. In the industrial market there is a higher degree of sensitivity to satisfactory product performance than there is in the consumer market because of the time lag through the longer trade channels usually found in the latter.

10. There is a greater fluctuation in the volume of industrial goods as a whole from the high to the low of the business cycle.

11. The need for and influence of *service* both before and after the sale is greater in industrial marketing.

12. Leasing and renting of equipment (with or without the option of purchase) is important for many industrial products because of the possibility of the production cost savings being used to liquidate the first cost. In consumer marketing instalment selling spreads the cost and brings immediate physical possession.

DIFFERENCES ARISING OUT OF THE CHARACTERISTICS OF THE PRODUCTS

1. Industrial products are usually marketed by giving the purchaser more factual and technical data than are consumer products, since the former generally are bought on a basis which requires *proof* of suitability for the particular use.

2. Prices of industrial goods are likely to fluctuate within narrower limits than consumer goods. "Loss leaders" and "clearance—markdowns" are devices of consumer marketing.

3. Industrial goods are usually bought and sold on a more complete and usually more pre-

cise description or specification basis. (Mail order catalogs for consumer goods, although quite descriptive, are usually not as detailed as the specifications for industrial goods.) An important portion of industrial selling activity may be in influencing the preparation of specifications to favor the vendors' products.

4. Bids may or may not be submitted in marketing industrial goods. Bids are less prevalent in manufacturing industries than in government, leasing, construction procurement, or wherever the comparison of offers can be reduced to a common dollar denominator. In marketing to manufacturing industries, however, quotations or contracts, evaluated in terms of projected product performance, are more often the basis of purchase.

Although there is much shopping in the consumer field, there is little formal bidding or negotiation.

5. The descriptions, specifications and acceptance tests for industrial goods are usually more precise than in the case of consumer goods. These are physical or chemical measurements, or both, rather than measurements of taste, flavor and style. (An example of the difference in preciseness might be the measurement of color—the industrial user of colors is likely to use the spectrophotometer to measure the precise shade of blue, whereas the consumer wants to "see it in daylight" to know if that shade of blue is suitable.)

6. Industrial goods are subject to greater standardization as the influence of obsolescence in industrial goods is largely in utility, while consumer goods suffer from the impact of fashion, style, and utility. The necessity of design changes for increased salability are more pronounced in the consumer field.

DIFFERENCES ARISING OUT OF ORGANIZATION OR OPERATIONAL SETUP

1. The channels of distribution for industrial goods are likely to be shorter than channels for consumer goods. There are fewer middlemen in the industrial distribution chain and a much larger percentage of industrial goods is sold direct to the buyer in industrial marketing than the percentage sold direct to the consumer in consumer marketing.

2. The media used and the types of advertising copy (used in the broad sense) prepared to carry the message vary considerably between the two types of products. The industrial marketer usually reaches his prospects through the trade and business publications and the consumer marketer through the so-called "mass publications," radio and television.

3. Reciprocity, a factor of indeterminate importance in the industrial field, appears to be less prevalent in the consumer field.

4. In industrial marketing the seller commonly goes to the buyer—the reverse is the situation in the consumer field, with the exception of door-to-door selling.

5. Production for inventory is less widespread in the industrial field than in the consumer field, partially due to the shorter "pipe lines" of distribution.

OTHER DIFFERENCES

1. Speed and dependability of delivery are important in the marketing of both types of goods. Consumer goods are more readily available to the buyer than are industrial goods (other than supplies), since consumers usually buy direct from local or nearby inventories.

2. Longer periods of salesman training are generally required for industrial marketing as compared with consumer marketing, often due to the technical nature of products sold to industrial goods manufacturers.

3. Sales promotion expense (including advertising but excluding direct selling) in relation to the selling price is likely to be much lower in industrial selling than in consumer marketing.

4. Industrial salesmen's compensation on raw materials and production equipment is likely to be in the form of salary or a combination of salary plus bonus; on smaller items and supplies it is more likely to be either salary plus a bonus or some form of drawing account plus commission to straight commission.

5. Major equipment items may be purchased only once every 10 or 20 years unless expansion or obsolescence is an overriding factor. In the case of fabricated parts, materials, and operating supplies, buying is often done on a contract basis.

6. The industrial marketer has a greater problem in keeping contact with customers to avoid possible loss of orders and yet not incur needless sales expense.

7. The number of women who exert direct influence upon industrial purchases is very small compared to the number in buying positions

throughout the trade channels for consumer goods. It is, of course, obvious that women exert a dominant influence in purchasing for the millions of family units in the country.

8. In the field of industrial marketing a large proportion of sales is in raw materials, semi-finished products and component parts, while in the consumer marketing field the largest proportion of sales is in finished products.

9. In measuring a majority of industrial markets through marketing research, it is essential that well-trained technical people do the basic interview work because of the technical problems involved and technical questions which may be asked during the interview. In the consumer field, however, interviewers with a less technical background may often be used, and in the case of much consumer marketing research housewives or others with no technical training may obtain valid answers.

10. The packaging of industrial products, often in much larger units than is required for consumer goods packaging, is both functional and serviceable, lacking the eye appeal or definite advertising or promotional slant. Containers for industrial goods are often designed for return to the manufacturer and re-use for the same purpose, whereas consumer goods are often placed in an attractive package which later serves the consumer in an entirely different way. (As an example, certain foods are packaged in glass or metal suitable for table use as glasses or with jar tops usable as coasters or ashtrays.)

SIMILARITIES BETWEEN INDUSTRIAL AND CONSUMER MARKETING

1. Industrial marketing and consumer marketing are both carried on under the following common objectives:

a. To result in a profitable operation.
b. To obtain a growing share of the market or at least to maintain the present share of the market.
c. To achieve efficiency in the expenditure of all monies involved in the operation.
d. To develop and use advertising and promotional efforts which will both find new customers and maintain current customers.
e. To market at all times the right product or products to meet customer needs or desires.
f. To be alert to the development of new products in the same or related fields which will affect the marketing operation.
g. To maintain the good name of the producer.

2. Where there is no distinguishable product difference there are marked similarities in buying motives and buying motivations.

a. Habit, the universal resistance to change in buying patterns, is equally important in both industrial and consumer marketing fields.
b. The personality of the salesman is important in both fields.

3. The use of contracts is characteristic in the marketing of both industrial and consumer goods. Industrial equipment, raw materials, component parts and even supplies may be purchased on this basis, an infrequent occurrence in the field of consumer marketing.

4. Well organized and highly skilled purchasing groups are found both among the customers of industrial marketers and the customers of consumer goods marketers.

5. In measuring the market for either industrial goods or consumer goods the manufacturer can obtain much basic data from his internal sales and production records. The marketer of industrial products, however, can place more reliance on his sales and production record information due to his much closer relationship with his customers than can the manufacturer of consumer goods in measuring his ultimate consumer market, since the trade channels are usually longer and in some cases rather devious.

CONCLUSIONS

Few rules can be formulated to portray the fundamental differences or similarities between industrial and consumer marketing.

Although both industrial marketing and consumer marketing have as a common goal the satisfaction of the wants and needs of the customer, the two are significantly different in many important respects. The differences can be attributed to a number of reasons, the most evident of which seems to be the difference in the products themselves.

Industrial goods move in a series of steps from the mine, forest, farm, air or ocean in which the raw materials originate through everything from a simple to a very complex set of manufacturing and marketing operations before reaching that final step where they are assembled into the end product, whether it be an industrial good or a consumer good.

Consumer goods as they leave the manufacturer and head into the channels of distribution, regardless of how complex the channels may be, are finished goods and usually require no further processing.

Every practitioner of marketing, whether it be industrial or consumer, should become, if he is not already, thoroughly conversant with the ramifications of those phases of marketing with which he is engaged and constantly be on the alert to visualize new relationships, new exceptions to his previously accepted theories, and new approaches to his chosen profession.

Every teacher of marketing who does not already do so should visualize our modern marketing machine as being at least as complex as an electronic computer. Each marketing teacher should teach the fundamental principles underlying the entire marketing setup, rather than the methodology by which the results are achieved. Students of marketing would thereby obtain not only a head full of rules with a magnificent array of exceptions but an ability to trace the right path or paths through the maze of this complicated distribution system which will result in his finding the right answer to the particular problem at hand. After all, teaching is lighting a lamp, not filling a bucket.

29. *Some Basic Concepts [of Wholesaling]*

DAVID A. REVZAN

The field of wholesaling represents by far the most significant segment of marketing based on any or all of several points of view: Annual gross cumulative sales volumes; the variety of types of middleman operations compared with retailing; the range of kinds of business involved; the number of levels and complexity of the transactions involved; or the complexity of the problems involved. It entails as well, cutting across the above, the critical evaluation of the position of primary and intermediate markets. Many of these points of view will be treated in detail in later chapters. The levels of business transactions involved are many, ranging from the extractive industries through basic and secondary manufacturing levels, going on to the service businesses, the various wholesale and retail middlemen, and, finally, to many governmental levels, educational institutions, and other agencies as well. These are only some of the aspects which underlie the importance and complexity of wholesaling.

But however viewed, wholesaling is a part of marketing which emphasizes matters of structural arrangement based upon degrees of specialization of both types of business and kind of transaction. Some aspects, as will be noted in a later section of this chapter, create no questions as to whether or not the transaction involved is wholesaling in nature. But other aspects, because of their relationships with retailing activities, cannot be classified so easily and certainly as wholesaling in nature. Additional differences

‡‡ SOURCE: Reprinted by permission from David A. Revzan, *Wholesaling in Marketing Organization*, (New York: John Wiley & Sons, Inc., 1961), pp. 1–22.

and difficulties, as will be noticed, arise from variations between the specifications contained in existing forms of legislation; from legal interpretations in cases; from Bureau of the Census definitions; and from other sources. These differences and difficulties can and do lead, in turn, to sharp differences in the quantitative measurement of the importance of wholesaling.

VARIOUS MEANINGS OF WHOLESALING

Orthodox Marketing Meanings

The orthodox marketing definition of wholesaling generally stresses, among other things, the nature and motivation of the buyer as the single most important criterion. Based on this criterion, wholesaling may be defined, in the orthodox sense, as that part of marketing in which goods and services move to various classes of buyers (or agents thereof) who will: (1) engage in the resale of such goods and services with profits in mind; (2) use the goods and services in order to facilitate the production of other goods to be sold with profits in mind; or (3) use the goods and services for various institutional purposes (e.g., educational, charitable, governmental).

On this basis, it follows that all remaining sales and movement of goods and services to persons who use these goods and services to satisfy their respective wants and desires represent retailing transactions. These persons can combine, of course, in any form of living-spending unit relationship without affecting the retailing nature of the transaction. Thus, if the total quantitative measure of goods and services is known in any year, the division as between the volume of wholesale and retail sales can be made by using these criteria.

Two refinements need to be introduced into the discussion of the orthodox definition at this point. First, the prices charged for a given product sold at wholesale may or may *not* be lower than prices charged at retail, although a lower price for the wholesaling transaction *usually* is the prevailing situation. But if, for example, a person operating an office buys a single typewriter, he may pay the identical price charged to a student buying the product for his own needs (a retail transaction). Second, the quantity purchased at wholesale *usually* is, but need not necessarily be, larger than the quantity purchased at a single retail sales transaction. Many important variables affect this factor of the quantity purchased at each transaction.

From the preceding discussion, several characteristics or criteria emerge which may be useful in identifying a wholesale transaction: (1) The motive of the purchaser; (2) the quantity purchased at each transaction; (3) the wider varieties of goods offered for sale compared with retail sales; (4) the wider geographical base for wholesale sales; and (5) usually, the lower prices per unit involved. In addition, it may be inferred, because of the varieties of business and other activities involved, that wholesale transactions frequently involve the sale of the same product two or more times; while, on the other hand, retail transactions involve selling the same category of product only once.

LEVELS OF WHOLESALING ACTIVITIES

The various concepts of wholesaling make it necessary to discuss the activity levels of wholesaling. These levels call attention not only to the possibilities for the varieties of customers and transactions noted briefly above but also to the variety and complexity of channel arrangements. Perhaps, the best methods in which to consider these levels is to classify them, in some detail, from producing levels to retail middlemen levels as follows:

I. *Production Levels*
  A. Extractive industries (domestic and foreign).
    1. Agriculture.

2. Mining (metals, coal, other).
    3. Fishing.
    4. Quarrying.
    5. Petroleum.
    6. Others (not elsewhere classified).
  B. Manufacturing industries (domestic and foreign).
    1. Primary, by kinds of goods.
    2. Secondary, by kinds of goods.
II. *Construction Industry* (domestic and foreign, by type)
  A. Roads, etc.
  B. Factories, commercial properties, etc.
  C. Residential.
  D. Others (not elsewhere classified).
III. *Transportation Industries* (domestic and foreign)
  A. Railroads—passenger and freight.
  B. Local railways and bus lines.
  C. Highway—passenger and freight.
  D. Water—passenger and freight.
  E. Air—passenger and freight.
  F. Pipelines.
IV. *Communications Industries* (domestic and foreign)
  A. Telephone, telegraph, and related services.
  B. Radio broadcasting.
  C. Television broadcasting.
V. *Utilities: Electric, Gas, Oil, etc.* (domestic and foreign)
VI. *Wholesale Middlemen*
  A. Merchant.
  B. Manufacturers' sales branches and sales offices.
  C. Petroleum bulk stations, etc.
  D. Agents and brokers.
  E. Assemblers of farm products.
VII. *Government Agencies*
  A. Federal.
  B. State.
  C. County.
  D. Municipal.
  E. Foreign.
VIII. *Services*
  A. Agricultural.
  B. Business and commercial.
    1. Professional.
    2. Repair.
    3. Others (not elsewhere classified).
  C. Hotels and motels.
  D. Personal.
    1. Professional.

2. Repair.
3. Entertainment.
4. Others (not elsewhere classified).
IX. *Financial Institutions*
X. *Educational Institutions*
XI. *Office and Other Commercial Buildings*
XII. *Retail Middlemen*
A. Store retailers.
B. Nonstore retailers.
  1. Mail-order houses.
  2. Direct selling (house-to-house)
    organizations.
  3. Merchandise vending machine
    operators.

Thus, as defined above, wholesale sales may
be made by wholesale middlemen to any or all
of the above groups; or from a type of whole-
sales middlemen to one or more other types of
wholesale middlemen; or between separate establishments within the same classification of
wholesale middleman.

FUNCTIONS AND PROCESSES

Although it is true to say that wholesaling
involves the same group of processes and functions applicable to the whole field of marketing,
some special adaptations and applications need
to be noted. The term "function" is used at this
point in the sense of a group of purposeful
activities which are homogeneous in the sense
of having common objectives and molding (as
well as being molded by) managerial organization units. Since these functions will be discussed in detail in the internal-management section of this book, the following classification
scheme will suffice:

I. *Functions of Exchange and Contact*
A. Merchandising: the function of mar-
  keting strategy.
B. Buying and selling: the tactics of
  marketing.
II. *Functions of Physical Distribution*
A. Transportation.
B. Storage.
III. *Facilitating* (auxiliary) *Functions*
A. Standardization and grading.
B. Financing.
C. Communication and research.
D. Risk.

Of more importance at this stage of the discussion is an analysis of the marketing *pro-*

cesses. Processes, in their marketing context,
deal with meaningful groupings of functions, as
outlined above. These processes may be useful
in describing and analyzing the flow-of-com-
modities aspect of marketing and, in addition,
to emphasize the division in specialization between wholesale and retail market levels; (i.e.,
between the primary and intermediate markets,
on the one hand, and the final markets, on the
other).

THE GENERAL STRATEGY OF WHOLESALING

To understand something of the importance
attached to wholesaling in marketing, it is necessary to emphasize, at this stage of the discussion, the general strategy of wholesaling,
wholesale markets, and the various types of
wholesale middlemen.

The Strategic Aspects of Wholesaling and Wholesale Markets

The general strategic aspects of wholesaling
in marketing, stem from the following conditions:

1. The development of diversified, large-
scale mass production in factories located at a
distance from the areas of principal use of the
output thus produced.
2. An increase in the volume and proportion
of such production made prior to, rather than
for, the specified order of users.
3. A corresponding increase in the number
of levels of intermediate-user consumption between the production of basic raw materials at
the beginning of the channel and the areas of
final use at the end of the channel.
4. The increasing need for adaptations of
products to the needs of intermediate and final
users in terms of quantities, shapes, packages,
and other elements of assortments, as well as in
pricing arrangements.
5. Continuing increases in both the quantities and varieties of goods and services in relation to the foregoing.
6. The necessity of establishing primary and
intermediate markets (organized and unorganized) in which the various stages of wholesale
exchange and the establishment of wholesale
price levels (systematic and unsystematic)
would take place.

Given these forces, then, wholesaling developed in structure as attempts were made by

producers and other business firms—mainly in the forces of the various types of wholesale and retail middlemen—to solve the problems of marketing thus created, and to bridge the growing marketing gap between the various types and levels of producers at one end, and the various types and levels of users at the other.

But the bridging of this gap should not be thought of as merely the physical forms of a pipeline or as a series of links. Rather, it should be thought of as a composite of a complex schematic framework which regulates physical flows both as to quantities and qualities in terms of spatial allocations; of locating potential users, or intermediate "users" in the form of middlemen, and convincing them to buy; of establishing the prices at which exchanges would take place in the primary and intermediate markets; and of feeding back various kinds of data to guide the management efforts of the various extractive and manufacturing producing agencies.

From the above discussion, it may be inferred that a considerable segment of wholesaling has to do with a theory of primary and intermediate markets. By primary and intermediate markets are meant the organized or unorganized institutional arrangements within which the prices and other aspects of the whole-sale marketing transactions are determined. They exist at the extractive and primary manufacturing industries levels in connection with the concentration process. And they are located at strategically located trading centers in connection with the equalization process. Depending upon channel complexities to be investigated at a later point, they may be found either in single or in multiple combinations. Specialization may exist for a single class of products, or opportunities may be present in the channel for dealing in assortments.

The Strategic Intermediate Position of Wholesale Middlemen

The various types of middlemen that conduct their businesses in these primary and intermediate wholesale markets are, accordingly, the instrumentalities through which the general strategic position of wholesaling is made effective. Figs. 1 and 2 show the *combined* importance of wholesale middlemen under the following set of assumptions: (1) The total number of buying units is 200,000 but with no assumption of equality of buying strength; (2) the *average* purchase per buying unit per unit of time accounts to $100, and consists of 25 *separate* products; and (3) the total number of

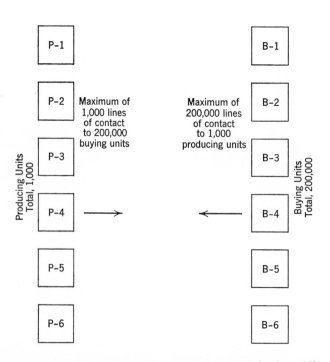

FIG. 1.   Wholesaling structure without intermediate markets and wholesale middlemen.

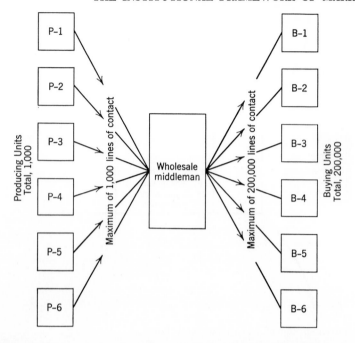

FIG. 2.   Wholesaling structure with intermediate markets and wholesale middlemen.

products handled by each buying unit is 5,000, produced by 1,000 separate producing units, with no assumption of equal producing strength.

Given these assumptions, Fig. 1 shows the generalized pattern of the necessity for the marketing system to provide 200,000 lines of contact from each of the 1,000 producing units, if *all* buying units are potential customers for all 5,000 products and if the producing units assume the marketing initiative in searching for each buyer. Similarly, these will be 200,000 lines of communication from the buying units to each producing unit for each buying transaction *if* the buyers assume the marketing initiative. Thus, given these assumptions, there could be a minimum of 200 million and a maximum of 400 million individual lines of communication for each buying operation. The multiplication by the average dollar volume of sales for each purchase, and the number of products involved, gives the total dollar volume of sales and the total physical flow.

With the introduction of wholesale middlemen of various types handling the output of all producing units and selling this output to all buying units, Fig. 2 indicates the reduction in lines of communication that would take place as compared with the 200 to 400 million noted in Fig. 1. The actual reduction would depend

on how many business establishments would be involved at the wholesale middlemen's level. In actual practice, of course, there are variable combinations found in the marketing structure depending upon the numbers and types of producing units, the numbers and types of wholesale middlemen, the numbers and assortments of products involved, and the size and variety of the buying interest.

The Funnel Concept

Given the above analysis of the marketing processes and of the strategic importance of wholesaling, wholesale markets, and wholesale middlemen, an additional important aspect of the general strategy of wholesaling can be obtained through the funnel concept.

The analogy to be developed is designed to explain the position and strategy of wholesaling as a funnel made of stretchable (expandable) materials which permit adaptation to variations in the total physical output of products to be handled. In addition, this funnel incorporates a series of regulatory valves designed to control the rate of flow into the hands of middlemen and intermediate and final classes of users. This funnel may be thought of as being made up, as well, of a series of openings through which the

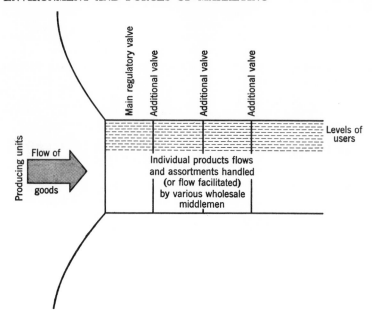

FIG. 3.   The wholesaling funnel (composite total form).

regulated flow of various assortments of products takes place. Fig. 3 presents a simplified cross-section diagram of this funnel.

The various types of wholesale middlemen have varying kinds of functional interrelationships within this funnel. In a sense, the funnel shown in Fig. 3 is a composite funnel. Actually, the funnel concept includes the notion of a set of individual funnels for each meaningful grouping of products, and with each having a systematic positioning within the channel pattern. Similarly, these series of individual product funnels have spatial adaptation.

It has been indicated that the funnel in the wholesaling structure is something more than the physical unit of simple dimension outlined in the dictionary definition. The funnel in Fig. 3 acts as a marketing medium through which moves the flow of goods from producers in a fashion designed to match as closely as possible the needs of intermediate and final users in terms of desired quantities, qualities, package, time, and geographical considerations. Furthermore, as has been indicated in the explanation of the equalization process, the prices and terms of sale at which these matchings and exchanges take place are negotiated in the funnel.

The notion of the funnel in Fig. 3 as a composite of a series of individual funnels needs some additional explanation at this point. Much of this concept of composite and component

funnels stems from the following variables as being suggestive:

1. *The type of product*—that is, whether raw material, semi-processed, or finished, and whether for example, it has single or multiple uses.

2. *The physical volume* of the commodity flow and its time divisions within a year's cycle.

3. *The monetary value* of the physical flows in (2).

4. Variations in the *types of middlemen* found in the channels of distribution for the product.

5. The *varieties and levels of users* for the product based upon the characteristics noted in (1).

6. The *number of assortment combinations* —actual and potential—in which the product appears.

7. *Geographical variations* in the commodity flows, channel patterns, and types of users.

WHOLESALING AND MARKETING ORGANIZATION THROUGH THE CHANNEL

General Meaning of Marketing Organization

Since wholesaling is but one aspect of marketing organization, some discussion is needed at this point of the general meaning of marketing organization. The concept as it is used in this introductory context is not concerned with the internal aspects of particular firms. What is being emphasized here is the way in which many different kinds of individual firms and establishments array themselves in *formal, systematic* manner within various producing, buying, selling, and facilitating agencies in making possible the systematic, continuous movements of goods and services from producing to using units, together with the necessary determinations of prices and terms of sale for their exchange. Depending upon the ideology of the political environment, the maximization of alternatives for final users may or may not result, and the operation of the organization within some framework of "efficiency" may or may not take place.

The marketing organization is formal and systematic in the sense that there has evolved over a long period of time: (*a*) specialized production units both at the extractive and at the manufacturing levels which account for the highest percentage of all goods produced; (*b*) a series of specialized wholesale middlemen who, together with integrated types, operate in various types of wholesale primary and intermediate markets; (*c*) a series of specialized retail middlemen who, together with integrated types, operate similarly in retail markets; and (*d*) many types of facilitating agencies offering services to establishments at all levels, and who act in a buying capacity as well including professional transportation, storage, financial, communication, research, and related facilitating functions.

Thus, to summarize, the marketing organization is a cross-sectional or dissectional study of the agencies and mechanisms of marketing as they array themselves in systematic fashion each to the other in moving goods and services from producing units.

Marketing Organization and Channels of Distribution

Marketing organization is made effective through channels of distribution. Since the flow of goods and services through the marketing organization is not an automatic process, what must be recognized at the beginning is that marketing organization involves a complicated network of buying and selling agencies, of varying periods of negotiation, of physical handling agencies and intermediaries, and of facilitating business units of various sizes in various locations, grouped together in varying combinations to link particular producing units with particular using units. In addition, they combine in varying patterns of complexity to account for the over-all movement of particular commodity categories and groups of categories.

The channel thus becomes the linking vehicle by means of which marketing organization takes place and becomes effective. And as the marketing aspects of a nation grow in complexity parallel to the nation's total social and economic development, so do its channel aspects develop into more intricate patterns along functional, commodity, spatial, and control components.

The Position of Wholesaling in the Marketing Organization

Viewed in this way from the dual vantage points of marketing organization and channels of distribution, the strategic position of wholesaling is once again reaffirmed. It constitutes the single most important sector of marketing organization, regardless of the measuring standard used. This sector covers a wider variety of goods and services than any other sector of marketing organization. It has more types of middlemen agency operations than does the retail sector; and their combined sales volume exceeds that of any other group in the channel.

In addition, wholesaling, by virtue of the factor discussed earlier, gives more depth, more variety, and more complexities to marketing than any other sector. Every technological development of production which affects the volume and variety of goods, must be reflected in, and become magnified through the wholesaling sector. Viewed in this framework, the funnel concept takes on a more complex perspective not apparent if only the purely physical aspects of the funnel are considered. The waves of effects flowing from the wholesaling structure move forward and backward in the marketing channels. These wavelike movements widen, in turn, the interrelationships between marketing organization and the rest of the business economy.

WHOLESALING AND INTEGRATION

The role of wholesale middlemen as independent intermediaries in the market channel is a precarious one. As is true of any intermediary, either the originating or the terminal end of the channel may attempt either to eliminate him or to reduce his importance. Thus, the producing level may attempt elimination or increased control by means of vertical integration based upon direct ownership of the intermediary; from restrictive controls by means of contracts or marketing policies; by granting exclusive dealership franchises in return for the middleman's to reduce his buying alternatives and to restrict his area of selling activity; and by indirect pressures resulting from selling and advertising efforts directed at the ultimate user.

Partially to offset these attempts by producers, and partially for reasons of pressure and control, both retail middlemen and users may indulge in reverse or backward vertical integration efforts. These efforts may be based upon direct ownership of either the wholesale middlemen agencies or of the producers, or both. Or they may represent contractual devices designed to secure both price and product identification advantages. Or, finally, they may represent a mutual pooling of retail and wholesale middlemen's financial resources and management know-how into some cooperative agency effort.

The wholesale middleman may do nothing actively in either combatting or joining these attempts at vertical integration. Or he may retaliate in kind against each by moving either backwards or forwards, or in both directions, in the channel in order to control directly or indirectly the business units involved. Or he may strengthen his competitive defenses by incorporating changes in internal organization and policies in other directions, including the pooling of similar wholesale middlemen's resources on a common or wider geographical front.

As a result, these various aspects of integration keep changing the patterns of linkages and blockages in the channel. These changing patterns result, in turn, in ever-changing patterns of channel arrangements. The complexities of these various types of integration will become more apparent in the classification of wholesale middlemen in the next chapter and in later chapters discussing channel structure.

MEASURES OF THE IMPORTANCE OF WHOLESALING

As a final part of this introduction to the wholesaling sector of marketing, some reference should be made to measures of the importance of wholesaling. Because wholesaling involves a considerable amount of multiple handling and sales of goods, any realistic measure of its importance must include measures of *gross* as well as of *net* importance. These measures of gross importance may be noted here: (1) The total value of all extractive industries' output, *plus* the total value of all domestic manufacturers' output, *plus* the value at wholesale of all imports; (2) the total dollar sales of all wholesale middlemen as reported by the Bureau of the Census; and (3) the ratio of total wholesale sales to total retail sales.

Most of the measures of the *net* importance of wholesaling stem from the program of national income statistics prepared by the Department of Commerce. Of the many possibilities, these are especially useful in the present context: (1) The ratio of full-time equivalent employees in wholesale trade compared with the total number in all industries; (2) the ratio of corporate sales for wholesale trade establishments to the sales of all industries; and (3) the proportion of the national income accounted for by wholesale trade as compared with all industries.

30. The Personality of the Retail Store

PIERRE MARTINEAU

¶ One of the leading retail grocery chains in Chicago has been exceptionally successful in the newer communities and particularly in the suburbs. In one neighborhood after another, stores of this chain far outsell competing stores offering the same services, the same merchandise, the same prices, the same parking capacity, the same amount of advertising. Why such an overwhelming preference?

¶ One midwestern dealer has become a leading seller of foreign sports cars without advertising either special "deals" or the engineering superiority of his cars. How does he manage to do it?

¶ One Chicago quality department store has tremendous customer draw for the middle-class Negro, far more than all the other department stores put together. Some actual research on the underlying causes of this consumer behavior stresses the absence of any classical price considerations or functional factors. Again, why the preference?

What is it that draws the shopper to one store or agency rather than another? Clearly there is a force operative in the determination of a store's customer body besides the obvious functional factors of location, price ranges, and merchandise offerings. I shall show that this force is the store personality or image—the way in which the store is defined in the shopper's mind, partly by its functional qualities and partly by an aura of psychological attributes. Whereas the retailer thinks of himself as a merchant concerned with value and quality,

‡‡ SOURCE: Reprinted by permission from *Harvard Business Review*, Vol. 36, No. 1, January-February 1958, pp. 47–55.

there is a wide range of intangibles which also play a critical role in the success or failure of his store.

POWER OF THE IMAGE

What kinds of intangibles are important? What is the effect of a retail store's personality? For answers, let us turn to the customers themselves—and, to make it specific, to the customers of the three retailers cited at the beginning of the article.

In the case of the grocery chain, for instance, one new unit developed over twice the sales of a new competing store of the same size and description. Research showed that the women of the community characterize the store as "clean and white," "the store where you see your friends," "the store with helpful personnel." This chain unit conveys a pleasant feeling of independence to the shopper. The aisles are spacious and not cluttered. In short, shopping in this store is a pleasurable experience instead of a routine duty. It is significant that not once did any of the shoppers interviewed mention lower prices, better bargains, or greater savings.

The tip-off to the automobile dealer's success is in the agency personality he has created.

This dealer is a former yacht captain, so that he developed outside the rituals and mythology of automobile retailing. Instead of belaboring "deals" and carburetors, economics and functions, he has imbued his establishment with the symbolic appeal of the foreign sports car.

All the salesmen are British—no matter what they know about car mechanics, as long as they are recognizably British. Reinforcing their accents, they wear slacks and blazers with "Sports Car Club of America" emblems.

Also, the dealer energetically promotes sports car clubs for different age groups, and he writes a column on sports cars in the classified advertising. In short, he has built and is constantly reinforcing a symbolic image congenial to a particular customer group.

In the example of the department store, the consumer group ascribe their preference to an atmosphere of acceptance for them. "I get a warm feeling of acceptance," "It makes you feel good to go shopping there," "I like it because it seems to have a warm atmosphere," and similar comments typified most of the customers' explanations. By contrast, Negroes dislike other stores in the neighborhood because of the feelings of rejection they have—even though the managements have been trying to serve them.

Retailers vs. Shoppers

Despite all of this, the typical retailer's promotions and advertising proclaim price cuts and huge savings to the shopper, as if that were the only consideration in a buying decision. Tire store advertising, liquor store advertising, furniture advertising, appliance advertising—all have the same monotonous chant. Chain drugstore advertising is typically a bargain potpourri of nondrug items such as alarm clocks, salad bowls, TV tables, flashlight batteries. A grocer builds a beautiful store in a modern shopping center and promptly plasters his windows with gaudy signs giving it a fire-sale atmosphere.

Yet research indicates that women do not believe there is any substantial difference between the pricing of various supermarkets. They are all competitive in price, customers think, and it is impossible to make any material savings by shopping at one chain instead of another. A woman's primary reason for reading a particular advertisement is "this is my store." If she glances at other advertising, it is largely to reassure herself that her favorite store *is* competitive in price. Instead of comparing prices, she evaluates the supermarket from a different set of criteria: variety of goods, orderliness of the store, services and nonservices, personnel, other shoppers, and goals of the owner or manager.

When our researchers talk to women about department stores, their comments invariably cover a wide range of elements which bear on whether they will or will not shop in a particular store. They are quite vocal about the physical plant itself, the elevator banks, the wash-rooms, the location; about the attitudes of the clerks and the other people in the store; about service facilities such as credit policies and returns; about whether the styling is extreme, conservative, smart, ageless, or in poor taste; about the displays and windows; about such intangibles as odors and colors—all these in addition to price considerations.

Personality Identification

When the shopper looks at a store's particular advertising, she unconsciously asks herself these questions: "What is the status of the store? Is it high-class or low-class or what?" "What can I expect of it in over-all atmosphere, product quality, and personal treatment?" "How interestingly does it fulfill its role?" "How does this image match my own desires and expectations?"

Of course, she is not oblivious to price; in fact, she may be proud of what she *thinks* is price-conscious in order to justify her choice of a store. But plumb her mind—go beneath any pat answers—and you will find that she is not the "economic woman" that American businessmen have so long and glibly assumed.

The Typological Approach

The shopper seeks the store whose image is most congruent with the image she has of herself. Some stores may intimidate her; others may seem beneath her. A store may be acceptable for one type of goods and not for others. A shopper may go to one department store for bargains, children's clothes, or housewares, and to another one for gifts or personal items. Thus, when the question was asked in a city-wide study about the preferred store for an everyday dress, two mass-appeal department stores were overwhelmingly chosen by the wage earners' wives. But when asked where they would buy a good dress, most of the women selected different stores. In fact, one store clearly stood out as the luxury store for the lower-income families.

Economic factors will always be important. But unless the store image is acceptable to the shopper, price announcements are meaningless. The upper-status woman cannot conceive of herself shopping in the subway store of a large department store. Regardless of bargains, she is repelled by the thought of odors, milling crowds, poorly educated clerks. Conversely, the wage earner's wife is not going to expose herself to the possibility of humiliation by shopping in the quality store, whether it be Bonwit Teller or Nieman Marcus or Lord and Taylor—even if she has the money to buy something there. In other words, regardless of ability to pay, all shoppers seek stores whose total image is acceptable and appealing to them individually.

This concept of the store image goes hand-in-glove with a growing realization that retailing generally must take a typological approach to marketing. As Virgil Martin, general manager of Carson, Pirie, Scott, has stated:

It is high time we retailers recognize that we cannot be all things to all people. When we try to do that, we end up with no particular appeal for anybody. Each of us has his own individual niche in the market place. It is up to us to determine where we fit, who comprises our customer body, and then to fulfill as completely and satisfactorily as possible the expectations of our particular group and our logical market.[1]

Illusion of Mass Appeal

As a researcher with some crude tools for describing customer groups along both sociological and psychological dimensions, I am continually confronted with amazing disparities be-

[1] From a speech, "The Dynamics of the Present," 1957 National Conference, American Marketing Association.

tween the retailer's concept of his customer draw and the actuality. For example:

¶ One Chicago retailer believes that his store does the largest volume in its product category in the market. When we discussed his marketing philosophy and future goals, I asked him about the character of his customer body. He did not hesitate to state that the entire market was his oyster—people from all income brackets, all surrounding areas, and all social groups.

But an analysis of his sales tickets reveals that nothing could be further from reality. An extremely disproportionate share of his customers is concentrated in the lowest economic third. Although his store is located in the Chicago central shopping district and should attract traffic flow from all parts of the area, his customers are coming in a statistically significant ratio from the south part of the city and the southern suburbs.

¶ In making a social class analysis of the customers of Chicago retail organizations, we asked this question: "If you were going to buy new livingroom furniture for your home, at which store would you be most likely to find what you want?" Fig. 1 summarizes the answers in profile form for two leading stores. If the customer body of each store had been truly representative of the social classes in the metropolitan area—or, more precisely, if it had corresponded with the chance expectancy of choice based on the numbers of people in these classes —the result would have shown up as the hori-

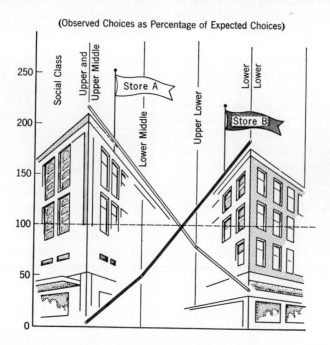

(Observed Choices as Percentage of Expected Choices)

FIG. 1. Customer profiles: store choices of people in different social classes.

zontal broken line opposite the figure 100. But in neither case did it turn out this way, as the thick lines show. Store A appealed strongly to people in the upper and middle classes, and Store B appealed strongly to shoppers from the lower social classes.

Yet the advertising director of Store A, a leading department store with a broad range of price lines and a basement store, was astonished to learn that not every person read his stores' advertising. And the executive vice president of Store B, one of a chain of retail furniture stores, was on record as saying: "We sell everybody. We have stores throughout the area, we advertise in all the mass media, we have furniture in all price ranges."

Not by any stretch of the imagination do these stores have universal appeal. Each organization is successful, yet each is attracting out of the market a distinctive customer group.

Stores of Distinction

The foregoing examples are not unusual ones. A lengthy list of customer profiles in many categories and along several dimensions makes it perfectly clear there is no such thing as a store image with equal appeal for all income groups, all social classes, all ages, all types. The store that is successful in the new communities and suburbs has competitive difficulties in the mill districts and the lower economic areas, and vice versa. The competitive pricing structure may be the same, but the elements of the store image which are so attractive to one group of shoppers are not attractive to another group.

It has to be this way. Different classes and different types of shoppers have different psychological outlooks on the world and different ways of life. Each segment of the market looks for a different emphasis. In general, the lower-status shopper looks at goods in a functional sense; she wants the store image to reflect her values of concreteness, practicality, and economy. She is concerned with quality of the merchandise and dependability of the store. The upper-status shopper, by contrast, is interested in whether the symbolic meaning of the store reflects her status and her style of life.

Take, for instance, the Marshall Field store in Chicago. It is much admired by perceptive competitors because all of the organization's activities are consistent and reinforce its strong symbolic character. The advertising, windows, merchandising events, restaurants, architecture, store policies, and attitudes of the sales personnel—all say the same thing symbolically. A shopper may feel she cannot afford to buy there, she may feel more comfortable in the atmosphere of another store. but she knows precisely what to expect. Marshall Field epitomizes elegance and sophistication. It creates a mood that helps to transform the shopping trip into an exotic adventure. It is described by shoppers as a "little world in itself" where the shopper can browse and enjoy her fantasies.

But just as the Marshall Field store represents so much to one kind of shopper, so does Sears, Roebuck & Co. have tremendous appeal to another kind. It is considered the friendliest and most comfortable department store in Chicago, with outstanding strength in all kinds of appliances, household staples, paint, tires, and children's wear. The type of woman considered typical of Sears' customers is pictured as hardworking, careful, practical, and home-minded. Sears has created a public image of itself as a family store, both in the type of merchandise it carries and in such intangible meanings as warmth, comfort, friendliness, honesty, dependability, and even unselfishness. Whereas the wife is more apt to go shopping alone at Marshall Field, it is not uncommon for the Sears shopping trip to be a safari for the entire family.

Sears, Roebuck and Marshall Field are the two largest department stores in Chicago, yet their store images are entirely different. The very merchandising strategies and personality aspects which are so successful for Sears are not uppermost for the Marshall Field audience, and vice versa. The upper-status woman expects a respect and a restrain from the salesclerk that would be interpreted by the wage earner's wife as formal and forbidding. On the other hand, the family atmosphere and the great emphasis on savings which attract the Sears customer are distasteful to the Marshall Field shopper.

The Dull Personality

What happens to the retail store that lacks a sharp character, that does not stand for something special to any class of shoppers? It ends up as an alternative store in the customer's mind. The shopper does not head for such a store as the primary place to find what she wants. Without certain oustanding departments and lines of merchandise, without a clear-cut attraction for some group, it is like a dull person.

When we asked Chicago women to characterize a department store on a range of qualities, the one attribute most applied to the alternative store was, "You don't hear much about it." It may spend many millions annually for advertising and promotion events, yet many, many shoppers will characterize it this way. Here is an interesting story of what happened to a store that lost its personality and then regained it:

A leading southern department store originally possessed a distinctive image emphasizing the traditionalist values of its city. The lighting and the fixtures were old-fashioned, and the total store atmosphere was congruent with the city-wide interest in antiques, old families, old homes, old restaurants, and historical monuments.

Then the women's apparel merchandiser modernized his department. He introduced new fixtures and lighting, more high-fashion styling, and a promotional flavor similar to any aggressive chain store in this field. The fortunes of the store declined in definite progression—first women's apparel, then children's, then men's, and finally all the hard-line departments.

A management consultant determined that the store had dissipated the strongest component in its image, the key to which lay in the women's apparel department. It had become indistinguishable from any other store. On his advice, the store set about restoring its traditionalist, distinctively period personality. The old-fashioned lights and fixtures and the ultra-conservative styling were brought back. As management reformulated the symbolic meaning which had given the store distinction and character, its fortunes changed sharply for the better in the same progression as they had declined—first women's apparel and ultimately the hard lines.

PERSONALITY FACTORS

What makes up a store's image in the minds of customers? There are many elements—architecture, color schemes, advertising, salespeople, and others. Let us look at the most important ones.

Layout and Architecture

The layout and architecture of the store itself invariably come in for comment. Women in modest-income suburbs are likely to describe changes in department stores over the years in terms of the modernization of the physical plant

itself: "Modernization in the better stores is the big item nowadays." "They are all modernized inside now and are much better than they were ten years ago—in appearance and comfort for the customer."

Sometimes when elevators and escalators are set too deep in the store, women experience a panicky feeling of being lost. A shopper in such a store complained, "One day I thought I never would find my way out." Some shoppers are overwhelmed by counters and displays which are built too high. "They build up the display way over eye level so that things are staring at you and it bears down on you," they may comment; or, "On entering that store, the whole place gives you the feeling of crushing you."

Especially when comparing the advantages and disadvantages of the department store with those of the specialty shop, a very sizable proportion of women express feelings of confusion, of being overwhelmed by the crowds and size of the department store. Very possibly, the same reaction may be created by huge supermarkets.

The fixtures of a store add in a subtle but potent way to the general décor and atmosphere management wants to create—or subtract from it. They affect the success of promotions and can be used to transmit any elegant, exotic, or unusual emphasis in store policy. Thus:

¶ J. L. Hudson's new Eastland Center in Detroit, while located in a higher-income area than the same firm's fabulously successful Northland Center, is designed to be more colorful and lively while still reflecting highest quality. The entire décor of the first floor presents a subdued effect of dark woods, cherry showcases in center islands, but with a greater use of color on wall panels and in various metal displays running from floor to ceiling. Hardware finish is bronze, of the richest type of finish available. Besides the effect of various woods and colors to create personality, the type of fixture is significant. A quality store such as this uses a large number of showcases and center islands which lend a rich feeling to the store, as compared to a table-top presentation.

¶ T. A. Chapman's new Capitol Court in Milwaukee uses bronze profusely throughout, including bronze displays, plus many species of wood, to express a modern but high-fashion character.

¶ Julius Garfinkel's which is an outstanding carriage trade department store in Washington, made two fixture changes in its new lower-level store in Fairfax County, Virginia, in deference to the modern age. While the design is similar to the fixtures in the downtown Washington store that express conservatism and fashion, the new store uses a light ash wood plus more open selling to create greater accessibility of merchandise.

¶ Harvey's in Nashville, created a lively Victorian personality by buying an old carousel and placing the animals throughout the store and on the marquee. The store restaurant is in the form of a carousel, and the cashier's booth resembles a ticket seller's booth.

Symbols and Colors

In a psychological study which was conducted for us on gasoline brands and companies,[2] by far the most distinctions and meanings were created by the emblems and the color schemes used on the retail stations, rather than by any product differences or verbalized claims of the companies. Sometimes these meanings were positive, sometimes negative. But whereas the differences between individual companies and brands were mostly blurred in the motorist's mind, rich meanings were conveyed to him by the symbols and colors.

A similar study, conducted by a New York industrial designer,[3] took the symbols of midwestern gasoline companies to eastern motorists who presumably were not familiar with them. Their evaluations of the companies were based therefore entirely on the shape and color of the symbols. Wherever this study examined the same symbols as our study did, the respondents' evaluations were in almost complete agreement. For example, the company using an oval-shaped symbol and a red, white, and blue color scheme was accorded by far the most positive evaluations. The company using a triangle was rated lowest on every scale. A dark color scheme used by another company cast an aura of dirtiness over its stations. Still another design and color created a company image that was "old-fashioned" and "inadequate" in motorists' minds.

What applies to gasoline stations applies with equal force to many other types of retailers. In the customer's mind color schemes and designs have an intrinsic meaning. They tell him something about the company as surely as the architecture, fixtures, and other visual factors. The association may not be logical, but it is real.

Advertising

The retailer's advertising is an especially important factor in expressing the character of the store. But while the retailer thinks mostly of the factual *content* of his advertising—item, price, timeliness, quality of merchandise—the shopper is impressed by the physical appearance, general tone, and style of the advertising as well as by the words. Just as we instinctively make judgments about another person from his clothing and his mannerisms, so does the shopper believe she can abstract symbolic cues from the advertisement. To illustrate: This year, in a study of retail grocery advertising, we took characteristic advertisements of several Chicago chains to different parts of the country where the shoppers were totally unfamiliar with the stores. When the judgments of women who knew nothing whatever about the stores were compared with the opinions of Chicago women familiar with the stores, they were in remarkably close agreement.

Retail advertising has become a language unto itself. It accurately conveys to the shopper whether the store is exotic and high-style, a dependable family store, or a promotion store hammering at bargains and pennies saved. She decides which atmosphere is most appealing and where she fits. Certain elements of the advertising lend themselves by logical extension to the store itself and to the goals of the owner. High-style art and restraint of tone and typography convey that the store is expensive and formal. The advertisements which are overly black and filled with typographical tricks indicate that the store is disorderly, with cluttered aisles and a strictly volume-turnover philosophy.

Obviously, there is no one advertising style which is best for all stores because each is trying—or should be trying—to convey different meanings about itself. The promotion store and the predominantly mass-appeal store would be mistaken to run the beautiful advertising of the exclusive shop and the quality department store; for a grocery in one neighborhood it might be mandatory to promote trading stamps, but for a grocery in another section of town, very unwise; and so on. In other words, the

---

[2] William E. Henry, *Gasoline, Gasoline Companies and Their Symbols* (Chicago: *The Tribune*, 1957).
[3] *A Study of Consumer Response to Oil Company Gas Station Signs* (New York: Lippincott and Margulies, 1957).

symbolic meaning of the advertising has to be consistent with the character of the store itself.

Sales Personnel

Perhaps the biggest single factor in the store image is the character of the sales personnel, in spite of the fact that so much discussion of retailing in recent years has virtually disposed of the salesclerk. The success of the supermarket and the extension of self-service into other fields has led some to assume that personnel will someday disappear from the retailing scene. We talk about robot retailing and the necessity for preselling; we say the store clerk performs only a wrap-up function in the typical store; we detail how the automobile salesman is now only a sharp-pencil operator instead of an aggressive outside salesman.

Moreover, many department-store executives to whom I have talked appear resigned to a steady downgrading in the quality of their sales help. They feel they cannot compete in the labor market with other industries and are therefore forced to take whatever is available.

Yet the fact remains that shoppers almost invariably evaluate the personnel in discussion of specific stores. Even in the grocery chains that have no salesclerks, women will talk about the checkers and the stock boys, whether they are friendly or indifferent, cooperative or brusque. As the shopper tries to imagine how her family would like some new dish or some unfamiliar brand, she naturally is anxious for support and information from some source. She is unhappy when the stock boys are so engrossed in their tasks of refilling shelves that she feels her questions would interrupt them and be resented.

In the case of department stores, clerks are mentioned more often than any other image-creating factor. Here are typical comments: "A salesperson's personality makes the store." "If the clerks are courteous and friendly and act as if they enjoy their work and their merchandise, I enjoy shopping." "The employees make you feel at home or uncomfortable in a store by their attitude when they wait on you. Sometimes if you decide not to buy, they can make you feel like you'll never go back." "I was just browsing in the millinery department of the store when a snippy saleswoman asked me not to handle the merchandise. That was enough for me. I would never return there again."

In contrast to the impersonality of the down-town-store salesperson, the relationship between clerk and customer in the outlying center can be more personalized. The fact that both usually live in the same community or general area makes the clerk more perceptive to the shopper's attitudes and wants. As one shopper said; "You get to know the same salespeople in the local stores, and they know just what size and style and price you want."

I believe that the courtesy and adequacy of sales personnel is one of the decisive factors in the growth of the outlying and suburban store. In the words of another woman, "Why shop downtown when the local stores are so much friendlier?"

It is ironical that at the very time when a better educated and discriminating shopper expects more from the store and the clerk, management is dragging its feet in upgrading salespeople. The stores are more beautiful and interesting; they have escalators, air conditioning, and improved fixtures; they have buyers ranging far and wide to offer the broadest merchandising selection. But what about the salespeople.

TRENDS IN BEHAVIOR

Perhaps a great many retailers will consider this concept of the store image as vague and inexact. While they may find it pleasant to know that there is such a thing, they are far too much concerned with the operational problems of being good merchants to devote any mental energy to it. But I believe that somebody in top management should think about these intangibles of store reputation and public attitudes. Somebody high up should ponder whether the over-all store image is positive and appealing or negative and dull, and whether it is in tune with what shoppers want today. The image plays an increasingly vital part in the fortunes of business.

Some of the reasons for this are economic—for instance, the increase in discretionary spending power, or the rise of new types of competition. Such trends make the subjective element of choice more important at the same time that the consumer is presented with more alternative ways of spending his money. But there are other reasons why top management should give more attention to the company image—reasons that are not so obvious. Some of them apply with particular force to department stores; some are of interest primarily to other types of retailers. Let us see what they are.

Suburban Shopping

Today with the customer flow in most great cities moving outward toward the periphery and the beautiful new shopping centers, with so much of the population moving away from the heart of the city, the retail executive is concerned with placing stores in various strategic outlying locations. Just as the manufacturer is weighing the risks of product diversification, so is the retailer studying the uncertainties of geographical diversification. In the central shopping district of the past, he did not have to concern himself with store personality so much because all roads figuratively led to Rome. All shoppers found their way to the downtown area.

Now the situation is quite different. The executive has to take his store image into fairly stratified communities whose shopping expectations and style of life may be totally out of keeping with the traditional image of his store. In one instance, when a promotional bargain store was located in a community of ambitious, mobile, well-educated young families, these people took the store as almost an insult to their set of values. In another situation, a high-status and a low-status store both entered a middle-class community, and both were rejected because shoppers said, in effect, "I don't trust them."

The problem is far more difficult than merely locating a store where there are population concentrations and doing research to learn what kind of a personality to give the new store so that it will "fit in." The branch store and the suburban store partake of the personality and character of the big downtown store. Even though management may build very attractive branch stores which in themselves would be congruent with the new community, these stores cannot dissociate themselves from the core meanings of the main store image, which are deeply etched into the shopper's consciousness. If, for example, merchandising techniques and promotional approaches have made the downtown store successful with lower-income families, a branch will operate under a cloud in a smart new suburb. And, conversely, when the high-status store locates a branch in a fairly prosperous mill district, the advertising which is building an image of sophisticated modernity for the main store's customers is also visible to shoppers in the mill district, who shy away from such a store image.

The spectacular growth of the outlying shopping center has created another problem. Very often this center has included whatever stores the real estate promoter could interest, quite without regard to how their images fitted together. As a result, the stores in many centers are pulling against each other. The smart high-fashion department stores and apparel stores find themselves in centers with drugstores, grocery stores, and a miscellaneous assortment of small shops negating their image, so that the center becomes a hodgepodge to the shopper.

If the opposite is true—if most of the store images *do* reinforce each other—a "shopping-center mood" will result that will make these stores more successful than they could have been operating by themselves. But any stores that are out of character with the over-all image will have a harder time than they would otherwise. As an illustration, one grocery chain is having difficulty in a very successful center which is dominated by stores that create a mood of elegance, ornateness, formality, and sheer luxury throughout. The shopper coming to this center is dressed for the occasion and not likely to be attracted to a routine grocery store.

Earlier I stated that the question of the image was one for top management. It should now be easy to see why this is so whenever store location is the issue. It makes no sense to ask a group of executives to operate a branch in a new location until careful attention is first given to the store personality they will be working with. It can bless their efforts or plague them! Either way it is a factor of tremendous importance.

The New Customer

In a study of the new community shopper, based on four rising communities which I felt were typical of different social classes and income groups, I noticed two large-scale trends:

¶ A new set of family values is developing. There has been a shift from the philosophy of security and saving to a philosophy of spending and immediate satisfaction, to rise of the child-centered family, more self-indulgent spending, a tendency to equate standard of living with possession of material goods, and great emphasis upon community values.

¶ The influence of the store image is increasing. People place great stress upon their interaction with other people—talking and socializing with others. How do they react to the growing impersonality of metropolitan life? Cutting all her ties with friends and family to move to a new city or new suburb, shopping in stores where she cannot know the owner or the clerks or where there may be no clerks, the shopper compensates for less personal contact by personalizing the store. She behaves in considerable measure toward this inanimate object as if it were a person. It becomes a symbol to which she can form deep attachments or dislikes. A department store, like a person, is characterized as "modern, practical, casual, and exciting." A grocery chain is characterized as "young, progressive, growing, friendly." Another store is called "dull," and still another is described as if it were somebody she did not like.

The National Association of Retail Grocers has conducted seminars for its member stores whose sole theme was the importance of developing an appealing and distinctive store personality. Throughout the country there are countless instances of imaginative independents successfully competing with the chains because they have created their own character in many and diverse ways. One Chicago grocer recently opened a "kiddy theater" which adults cannot enter without crawling on hands and knees. The youngsters sit entranced on benches watching cartoons while mother enjoys her shopping.

Brand Products

Much of what applies to stores also applies to products and packages. Package designers startle our moral sense when they say that today's consumer is more interestd in the package than in what is inside; she takes the contents for granted. Styling and décor are the key to the automobile sales picture today, not engineering. Refrigerators present the "sheer look." Today even the most prosaic products are offered in a choice of many colors.

All of these are externals which have nothing to do with economics or function, yet which are demonstrably important in the sales fortunes of the brand.

Service Organizations

Company image and personality are also important to the success of service organizations. Here the primary differences between competing companies are generally not matters of price and service so much as they are stereotyped attitudes in the public mind. Whether true or not, they exercise tremendous influence upon buyer choice. For example: Airlines offer the same rates and much the same services. Yet a Chicago *Tribune* study of the airlines serving Chicago shows very wide differences in their company images. In fact, no two of the seven airlines studied have anything like the same profile.

United Airlines is accredited with a broad range of rich meanings: safe, up-to-date, good for traveling with children, efficient stewardesses, extremely dependable, excellent food, comfortable, excellent personal attention, luxurious service, and attractive interiors in the planes.

Capital Airlines has a very different image, stemming largely from its use of Viscounts: fast, quiet, smooth, good views, comfortable seats, an ultramodern, progressive line.

Interestingly enough, the same feelings were expressed by those who had flown in Viscounts and those who had only heard about them. This confirms findings of other studies that the attitudes toward a company image are not necessarily formed from experience. Rather, they may be shared ideas relayed by word of mouth.

A POINT OF VIEW

Management is accustomed to look at shopping in an atomistic way—in terms of how many items were bought in what stores and at what prices. It should and must analyze retailing in this way. But it must not forget that statistics on sales provide only a partial basis for intelligent decision making. It must not be so captivated by the logic of figures that it overlooks the nonlogical basis of shopping behavior. Whether the customer is buying airline tickets, gasoline, hardware goods, or department store merchandise, his actions defy analysis in terms of after-the-sale statistics alone. To understand "why," management must look for deeper insights on customer behavior.

I have focused much of this article on department store customers not because they are different (they are, after all, the same people who buy automobiles, life insurance, and so on), but because studies of them offer some of the most dramatic evidence to support my points. We have found that the customer generally thinks of shopping as a total experience which runs through a number of departments in a number of stores and ends when she (or he) returns home. This is particularly true when she shops downtown or in a major shopping center requiring some travel and time. She faces many extraneous problems: How does she get there? If she drives, where does she park? Which store does she go to first? Is it the store where she plans to buy, or will it be the comparison point? If she expects to be gone for long, what about the restroom and restaurant facilities?

Curiously, the lowest-income shoppers mentioned the holiday aspects of such a trip more than any other group, probably because their routine lives are closer to humdrum practicality.

The shopping situation must therefore include many things not directly associated with specific items but closely connected with various patterns of consumer behavior. As the shopper fits the stores into her planning, she manipulates store images in her mind—not images of this counter or that department but impressions or pictures of entire stores. In large part, where she goes and what she buys depends on the subjective attributes that are part of these store images—atmosphere, status, personnel, other customers. Consciously or unconsciously, they sway her expectations and direct her steps.

I. Marketing's Dynamic Characteristics

31. A Continuous Audit of Distribution Policies

HARVEY W. HUEGY

Considering the traditional optimism of the American spirit there has been an amazing reluctance to accept the idea that our American economy can operate at a high and constantly expanding level. This intellectual lag may have some interesting explanations, perhaps it could even be given political implications. At present, however, we content ourselves with the point that the early voices which called upon us to raise our sights went unheeded. It is encouraging to prophets that some of those who early held this goal before us are on this program. For example, with the publication of "America's Needs and Resources" in 1947 Dr. Dewhurst pointed to the amazing potential of the American economy, and, perhaps, finding himself by 1955 to have been overly conservative has recently revised that publication. Arno Johnson was also a pioneer in analyzing the changes which had occurred and in emphasizing their impact on markets. But we were slow to believe. Fortunately while we may now differ as to the exact level which will be attained we at least agree that the potential is there and when we fully accept the goal of an expanding economy it will be realized.

The theme of this conference indicates that if distribution is to play its full part in attaining this expanded and expanding economy which we have finally accepted as a desirable goal, and agreed upon as attainable, we must accept constant modification of distribution methods, institutions, and policies. Indeed, to play its part in an expanding economy distribution must change. Thus constant change should be both a

‡ SOURCE: Reprinted by permission from *Boston Conference on Distribution*, 1955, pp. 58–61.

result of past expansion and a basic cause of future expansion.

Under such circumstances there is no question of the inevitability of change. The major question should be how to conform to, or anticipate, change. It is my present thesis that this can be facilitated best by a continuous audit of distribution policies. The results of the continuous audit will supply the facts concerning change and indicate modifications of distribution policies consistent with the situation. There is no question that this implies some elements of discomfort—it will present problems and require thought. But solace should be found in the suggestion that most problems are difficult because of inadequate information. Thus the price of not having problems is the cost of collecting the information which allows them to solve themselves.

SOURCES OF CHANGE IN DISTRIBUTION

It is difficult to separate cause and effect in the pattern of change and adjustment caused by the expanding economy for, in the intimately interconnected modern market, there is a constant interaction from sources both without and within the market. *Institutional* changes within the market occur with the development of new types of retail operation such as suburban branch stores, discount houses, and specialized outlets for new products. Wholesalers also change their manner of operating and lines of goods, as witness rack jobbers, and voluntary and cooperative group wholesalers. *Functional performance* can also be modified. It is no longer

199

sufficient to simply identify a function as present. It is now requisite to take a three dimensional view of marketing functions: their presence, the extent of performance of the function, and the quality of the functional performance.

Growth itself is a basic and obvious cause of changes in distribution. In the last two decades we have witnessed an enlargement of the market in numbers of persons because of the unpredicted, almost unbelievable, increase in the birth rate and have felt the additional impact of a high level of income more widely distributed with millions of families moving into newer and higher brackets of family income. Further expansion of markets followed as firms expanded their facilities and enlarged their production to satisfy the demand. Movements of population and industry have been rapid and substantial. Unfortunately some of our market practices still prevent full realization of the potential from past growth itself and thus inhibit growth to the full future potential. Enlargement of retail stocks and facilities are still necessary to realize sales potential fully, and increased production facilities are needed to both satisfy existing demand and encourage additional demand. Thus to realize on potential growth there must be expansion of distribution on the basis of both actual and potential growth.

The *manner of living* of our people has also changed. Product modification, new products, even innovative products are a natural accompaniment of an expanding economy. Our producers have indeed brought to the market a parade of products not known to previous generations. Our consumers have embraced them eagerly adding new products to their list of wanted goods readily, even avidly. This is indeed a healthy attitude for an expanding market for, were it not, present access to market would be denied some new products and made much more difficult and much slower for many others. Our consumers have also shown themselves to be flexible in adapting their patterns of consumption to the higher levels of income they are currently enjoying. It seems there is practically no time lag between the possession of additional purchasing power and the addition of either new commodities or increased usage of older commodities. Probably we should give a large measure of credit for this well-nigh perfect adjustment to the American women. For they seem always to know what to do with any additional family income. In the process of adjustment we have accepted new social goals and aspirations. We have entered joyfully upon "casual but gracious" living; we have embarked wholeheartedly upon "do it yourself" ventures with considerable investment in tools, garden supplies, hobby equipment, liniment and splints. The threat of additional leisure time does not dismay our consumers; they seem supremely confident they will add leisure time spending and leisure time commodities to their manner of living with no difficulty at all.

THE DISTRIBUTION AUDIT

Such then is the flux and change of distribution under conditions requisite to an expanding economy. Sometimes it is difficult to discern its course but discernment is essential to manufacturers and to distributors; essential to survival and success of the firm and to the continuance of the industry of which the firm is a part. The conditions of the changing and expanding economy can be met only by planned and systematic observation, careful analysis, and imaginative action. This requires that the requisite information be gathered regularly and in accordance with a standing plan. Only thus can the shifting, changing, confusing picture of distribution in an expanding economy be made meaningful in terms of direction of change, importance of new developments, and appropriate adjustment to the situation.

The observational stance should be provided through a continuous audit of distribution. This observational stance should cover sales, customers, and distributors.

To audit distribution policies three broad types of information gathering and analysis are indicated.

Analysis of Sales. The analysis of sales should cover both the firm and the industry and show movement of the product by geographical divisions, trade channels, product types, and to significant customer segments. Changes in the relative importance of geographical areas, types of retail or wholesale outlets, or of different products are obvious stimulants to action. Analysis in terms of homogeneous groups of customers permits identification of significant market segments. Thus growth or decline in the relative importance of market segments can be anticipated and met and the emergence of new segments capitalized upon. When the exploitation of the generalized market has been exhausted additional market opportunity can often be realized through deeper penetration of segments. This provides both additional volume potential and strengthened market position.

Consumer Surveys. The consumer surveys appropriate to a continuous audit of distribution policies should penetrate deeper than surveys for product development, new packaging, or price policy. For the purpose of the continuous audit they should supply information as to consumer purchase behavior. Thus they should cover the decision making process, the shopping history, and the purchasing plans and intentions. These surveys should also supply information as to what various groups of consumers want from the marketing institutions and what services provided by distributors are desired. Thus they should reveal the degrees of satisfaction or dissatisfaction with the marketing facilities and services provided by the present organization of distribution and the present distribution institutions. A continuous flow of information should reveal shifts in buying behavior or in marketing facilities desired and new types of distributors and new services can then be developed.

Distributor Surveys. Through periodic survey of distributors information will accumulate as to the relative importance of various channels and outlets—for the subject firm, for the industry, and by various products. It should show shifts and changes in the relative importance of types of outlets. As a guide to distribution policies information should be gathered to show margins and costs by type of distributor. Thus services of distributors and their costs can be matched against consumer wants and desires in the market. Through distributor surveys information relative to new methods, even innovations, at various trade levels should be available.

IMPACT OF CHANGE ON DISTRIBUTION POLICIES

Where and how economic and social changes have an impact on distribution policies can only be illustrated within the compass of this discussion. Obviously such fundamental changes have an impact which is as varied and extensive as the entire economy. We shall be content to illustrate them in a few major areas of distribution policy.

Movement of population and industry obviously leads to increased demands for distribution facilities in the growth areas. If the market potential of the growth areas is not realized by sales management, this can cost the firm marketing position in the more promising markets of tomorrow. Equally significant, and not so obvious, is the change in the importance of sub-

urban markets. Not only have they increased in number of people, they have also increased in income. The impact of these changes has been felt by the downtown areas with unhappy consequences relative to land values, retail sales, and tax collections. The newly developing suburban shopping areas have meant opportunity for newly established businesses and for those already established downtown who had the courage to seek their opportunity where the people wished to trade. Department store managements slow to sense the change and reluctant to conform to it have lost market position for their firms and now adjust belatedly.

Mr. and Mrs. Consumer are also making some of their new desires felt as to the time when they want retail services available to them with consequent need for modification of store hours. The practice of family shopping, the hours of work, and the changed social patterns dictate reexamination of convential store hours.

Consumers have also accepted modification of the extent and quality of retail services which the distributive institutions make available to them. They have cooperated in the performance of many of the tasks of retailing through their acceptance of self-service. They have apparently accepted self-selection for many of the products offered on this basis. The limits to further development of self-service and self-selection have not as yet been determined.

At the same time that consumers have indicated their willingness to accept stripped down service they have been offered another opportunity to vote upon this issue through the rise of discount houses. With the elimination of certain service features and the attraction of a discount from conventional prices discounters have attracted substantial patronage in certain lines. The success of manufacturers in establishing confidence in whole classes of products has presented them with a difficult distribution problem. The public now has such confidence in the product class and in the manufacturers' reputation that they will purchase many such products, at a saving, from distributors who may not merit confidence in their own operation. The manufacturer has to decide whether he will confine his lines to the so-called "regular" dealers or permit some to flow through "irregulars." The prospect of losing position with the "regulars" has to be balanced against the volume prospect offered by the "irregulars." A dilemma from which few have yet escaped.

While consumers have thus indicated their willingness to accept limited service, or to perform many of the services of retailing themselves, they have not been entirely consistent in their attitude. For the extent to which they have availed themselves of installment credit shows no general preference for cash over credit. They forego credit service on foods but want installment credit for durables. The new revolving credit plans and the development of charge account banking plans indicate that credit can be a powerful sales inducement with soft goods and that the ingenuity of the marketing system in offering new services has not been exhausted. There is also evidence that installation and designing services are desired by the homeowner in the extended use of interior decorators, landscape gardeners, and architects. It also seems probable that the more complex products may cause consumers to seek professional, or at least skilled, service in the design and installation of air conditioners and similar complex mechanical commodities.

The consumer has also shown an amazing flexibility and adaptability in the assortment of goods he will accept from various retail outlets. The drug store may have pioneered in the scrambling of merchandise lines, but they are now the victims of their own invention as they find traditional drug lines offered in supermarkets. It almost seems as though the country general store is returning to the merchandise scene when the lines offered by 'supermarket, mail order retail stores, and junior department stores in suburban shopping centers are examined. Which leads to the suggestion that perhaps this is not scrambling of merchandise at all but really an unscrambling based on a new classification scheme. A classification which rests on the attitudes and convenience of consumers when shopping, not on the physical characteristics of the merchandise, not on the source of supply, not on the wishes of retailers, and certainly not on convention.

The shifts of lines from conventional channels to new channels has presented a problem to wholesalers and to manufacturers. The drug manufacturers have had to devise ways to reach food markets, the rack jobber arose to fill the need for a new type of wholesaling service.

In the process of mergers and consolidations which have been going on in business many firms find themselves in markets heretofore foreign to them. Thus a firm formerly confined to heavy chemicals may find itself deeply involved in the soap business, a firm once limited to original equipment for automotive manufacturers has aspirations to become a major element in the household appliance field, or a firm in the food processing business becomes a factor in pharmaceuticals. Technology as well as merger has played a part in this process of getting into the other fellow's back yard. Many times production and technical "know-how" are not equal to marketing requirements and such firms find themselves in considerable marketing difficulty. However, sometimes a newcomer can make trouble for those already established in the industry and can stake out a sizeable market share before older members of the industry recognize that they have been joined by a "stranger." Perhaps this may occur because the "stranger," unhampered by tradition, dares to be different and in the process finds a new basis for success.

In the process of successful entrance into markets new to the firm, or in the effort to retain market position, manufacturers have had to consider the nature of the service performed for them by wholesalers and the price charged by wholesalers in the form of margin. They have had to measure this cost against the performance of wholesaling function and the cost of alternative ways of performing the tasks. The measurement has necessarily been tri-dimensional. Not only the performance of the various functions, but the measurement of the extent of their performance, and the appraisal of the quality of the performance. Not simply stocking or selling, but how much stock and how much selling, and the quality of the selling or the stocking. In some instances this has led manufacturers to perform these tasks themselves. In other cases it has led to ingenious modifications of operations or a new division of labor with the manufacturer aiding in the sale or the stocking.

Margins, which may be viewed as the price paid for the performance of marketing services, are an area which has been much subject to the stultifying effect of custom. Margins which may have been proper for the performance of a task initially may no longer be necessary under the changed conditions. Not only does the distribution task change but the position of commodities changes also. A margin necessary for creative selling may be continued after the commodity has become a repeat purchase item. A product which required installation and service may be improved in design and performance to the point where it is a "plug-in" installation. But the margin remains sanctified.

Obviously margins are a sensitive area. They are the basis of profits and as such a reduction is strongly resisted. But a margin too high for the task invites entry by other systems of distribution not bound by the same tradition. Such entry is facilitated by the establishment of customary levels of retail prices which make the amount of the saving obvious.

Margin renegotiation may be the answer for established products but complete reliance on low margin systems may not be the appropriate answer for product innovation. If new products are to be presented to consumers and are speedily to find their place in the household assortment they must be supported by creative selling. That the low margin systems can also do creative selling is doubtful. There is also some question whether they can assure satisfaction in use through proper installation, service after sale, and adequate repair and maintenance.

Margin convention appears to prevent the established systems from accepting dual margin levels. Operating methods appear to prevent the low margin systems from assuming the task of creative selling. A route out of this impasse must be found which combines the low price for the services of distribution appropriate to the established products and the higher margins appropriate for the services and creative selling needed for the innovative products.

SUMMARY

These then are the conditions found in a market which accompanies an expanding economy. To cope with the rapid change inherent under such conditions there must be a plan for gathering information in an orderly and regular manner. The accounting term audit emphasizes the regularity of the informational gathering process and the planned and orderly character of the array of information. But an audit is not in itself enough. The breath of life must be brought to the problem through managerial analysis and review of the information and imaginative decisions as to courses of action. Broadly the action may be to improve performance through better execution of current policies, through changes in the emphasis given to institutions or channels used, or through modification of policies to conform with current developments.

These results can be attained only when management recognizes that distribution is not a constant, that it is dynamic. Thus, it *has* a distribution problem and the proper answer to changing problems of distribution is *essential* to maintaining an expanding economy.

32. Which Automobiles Will be Here Tomorrow?

ROBERT J. HOLLOWAY

During 1960 the 180 millionth automobile produced in the United States rolled off the assembly lines. This represents approximately $156 billion of automobiles, unadjusted wholesale value.[1] There are more passenger cars registered in the United States than there are telephones in the Bell System, extensions included.

Despite these impressive figures, Detroit has been almost frantic in its desire to provide "something for everybody."[2] More new brands were introduced during 1960 than in any year since 1922.

But will the Comet, Corvair, Falcon, Lark, and Valiant be remembered longer than the Bay State, Gray, Jewett, Rickenbacker, and the Star, all of which were introduced in 1922? Will plans for the 1961 Cardinal, F-85, Lancer, Special, and the Tempest prove successful in capturing profitable shares of the large but elusive automobile market? Accurate predictions of consumer buying behavior are not easily made. Even with engines, the "car manufacturers were taken by surprise by the suddenness of the switch in public preference."[3]

Today there are twenty-three brands fighting for a market which amounted to 7,920,000 units in 1955. By contrast, in 1920 there were sixty-one brands competing for a 2,000,000-unit market.

Still, the consumer today may be confused by the multiplicity of domestic and foreign brands. During our automotive history, there have been approximately 2,750 brands of automobiles sold in the United States.[4] At least one brand has originated in each of thirty-seven different states, although the five states of Michigan, Ohio, New York, Illinois, and Indiana have accounted for 40 per cent of the brands produced in the United States.[5]

Most of the early brands were introduced when financial requirements were relatively modest. Maxwell-Briscoe was operating in 1904 at a production rate of "not less than two per day" with a capitalization of $875,000.[6] By contrast, George Romney, Chairman and President of American Motors, said in 1958 that it would require $576 million for a new company to break into the market with 250,000 units.[7]

Although forty-four new brands of automobiles entered the market during the 1920-1960 period, there has been a steady diminution in the number of brands; during this same period, eighty-six brands were withdrawn.

[1] "Automobile Facts and Figures," Automobile Manufacturers Association, Detroit, 1959–60, p. 3.
[2] "End of the Annual Style Change?" *Business Week*, No. 1,603, May 21, 1960, pp. 30–31.
[3] *Wall Street Journal*, June 15, 1960, p. 1.

[4] "Roll Call of 2,726 Automobiles Sold in the United States During the Past 50 Years or More" (*Saturday Evening Post*, 1952).
[5] G. R. Doyle, *The World's Automobiles, 1880–1955* (London: Temple Press, 1957), p. 21.
[6] John B. Rae, *American Automobile Manufacturers* (New York: Chilton, 1959), p. 54.
[7] United States Senate, *Administered Prices* (Subcommittee on Antitrust and Monopoly, 1958), Appendix, p. 3809.

‡ SOURCE: Reprinted by permission from the *Journal of Marketing* (National Quarterly Publication of the American Marketing Association), Vol. 25, No. 3, January 1961, pp. 35–36.

Today five firms are producing nineteen brands. Some of these have survived depressions, wars, and changes in consumer buying preferences, and in that sense can be considered the "survival of the fittest." However, age of a brand is not a guarantee of continued success. A matching of the ages of today's nineteen brands with ages of selected brands withdrawn during the last forty years demonstrates the point. See Table 1. The brands selected were on the market the longest of any of the eighty-six brands withdrawn during the 1920-1960 period.

The various reasons for withdrawing a brand have included trading down (Packard), design (Franklin), timing of introductions (Cord and Edsel), price selection (Marmon), retail outlet selection (All State), and intra-firm competition (La Salle).

Successes and failures continue. A Rambler "catches on," as it goes from 21,674 units in 1950 to 401,422 in 1959. An Edsel fails to "hit," as it tries to carve out a market in a price bracket which slipped from 2 million units in 1955 (Buick, Oldsmobile, and Pontiac only included), to 790,000 units in 1958. A Buick has its "ups and downs" as it attains first place (back in 1908); holds third place in 1954, 1955, and 1956; and then slips to eighth place in 1960.

Which brands will be here tomorrow?

TABLE 1. Age Comparison Between Existing Brands of Automobiles and Selected Withdrawals 1920 to 1960

Existing Brands—Years of Age, 1960		Selected Withdrawals—Years of Ages at Time of Withdrawal	
1. Oldsmobile	64	59	Packard
2. Studebaker	58	49	Hudson
3. Cadillac	57	40	Nash
4. Buick	57	38	Auburn
5. Ford	57	37	Pierce Arrow
6. Chevrolet	49	33	Franklin
7. Dodge	46	32	Hupmobile
8. Lincoln	40	32	Reo
9. Chrysler	37	32	Peerless
10. Pontiac	35	31	Marmon
11. DeSoto	34	31	Willys Overland
12. Plymouth	33	31	Stearns Knight
13. Mercury	23	30	Locomobile
14. Rambler	11	27	Haynes
15. Imperial	4	27	Winton
16. Comet	1	25	Moon
17. Corvair	1	25	Oakland
18. Falcon	1	24	Stutz
19. Valiant	1	25	Kissel

Directing the Marketing Effort

M arketers' efforts are carried on within the environmental framework developed in Part II. Marketing effort should match the firm's resources with segments of the market. More specifically, these efforts are concerned with the development of the markets. The development of markets involves planning. Planning encompasses the price, design, promotion of the product, and the utilization of efficient channels of distribution.

The success with which marketing strategies are derived and later implemented is due in some measure to the use of marketing information. For this reason the readings in Part III begin with marketing research and then proceed to the important marketing efforts. These efforts, though described one by one, are integral parts of the total marketing program.

A. Introduction

33. *The Marketing Revolution*

ROBERT J. KEITH

The consumer, not the company, is in the middle.

In today's economy the consumer, the man or women who buys the product, is at the absolute dead center of the business universe. Companies revolve around the customer, not the other way around.

Growing acceptance of this consumer concept has had, and will have, far-reaching implications for business, achieving a virtual revolution in economic thinking. As the concept gains ever greater acceptance, marketing is emerging as the most important single function in business.

A REVOLUTION IN SCIENCE

A very apt analogy can be drawn with another revolution, one that goes back to the sixteenth century. At that time astronomers had great difficulty predicting the movements of the heavenly bodies. Their charts and computations and celestial calendars enabled them to estimate the approximate positions of the planets on any given date. But their calculations were never exact—there was always a variance.

Then a Polish scientist named Nicolaus Copernicus proposed a very simple answer to the problem. If, he proposed, we assume that the sun, and not the earth, is at the center of our system, and that the earth moves around the

❖ SOURCE: Reprinted by permission from the *Journal of Marketing* (National Quarterly Publication of the American Marketing Association), Vol. 24, No. 3, January 1960, pp. 35–38.

sun instead of the sun moving around the earth, all our calculations will prove correct.

The Pole's idea raised a storm of controversy. The earth, everyone knew, was at the center of the universe. But another scientist named Galileo put the theory to test—and it worked. The result was a complete upheaval in scientific and philosophic thought. The effects of Copernicus' revolutionary idea are still being felt today.

A REVOLUTION IN MARKETING

In much the same way American business in general—and Pillsbury in particular—is undergoing a revolution of its own today: a marketing revolution.

This revolution stems from the same idea stated in the opening sentence of this article. No longer is the company at the center of the business universe. Today the customer is at the center.

Our attention has shifted from problems of production to problems of marketing, from the product we *can* make to the product the consumer *wants* us to make, from the company itself to the market place.

The marketing revolution has only begun. It is reasonable to expect that its implications will grow in the years to come, and that lingering effects will be felt a century, or more than one century, from today.

So far the theory has only been advanced, tested, and generally proved correct. As more and more businessmen grasp the concept, and put it to work, our economy will become more truly marketing oriented.

PILLSBURY'S PATTERN: FOUR ERAS

Here is the way the marketing revolution came about at Pillsbury. The experience of this company has followed a typical pattern. There has been nothing unique, and each step in the evolution of the marketing concept has been taken in a way that is more meaningful because the steps are, in fact, typical.

Today in our company the marketing concept finds expression in the simple statement, "Nothing happens at Pillsbury until a sale is made." This statement represents basic reorientation on the part of our management. For, not too many years ago, the ordering of functions in our business placed finance first, production second, and sales last.

How did we arrive at our present point of view? Pillsbury's progress in the marketing revolution divides neatly into four separate eras —eras which parallel rather closely the classic pattern of development in the marketing revolution.

FIRST ERA—PRODUCTION ORIENTED

First came the era of manufacturing. It began with the formation of the company in 1869 and continued into the 1930's. It is significant that the *idea* for the formation of our company came from the *availability* of high-quality wheat and the *proximity* of water power—and not from the availability and proximity of growing major market areas, or the demand for better, less expensive, more convenient flour products.

Of course, these elements were potentially present. But the two major elements which fused in the mind of Charles A. Pillsbury and prompted him to invest his modest capital in a flour mill were, on the one hand, wheat, and, on the other hand, water power. His principal concern was with production, not marketing.

His thought and judgment were typical of the business thinking of his day. And such thinking was adequate and proper for the times.

Our company philosophy in this era might have been stated this way: "We are professional flour millers. Blessed with a supply of the finest North American wheat, plenty of water power, and excellent milling machinery, we produce flour of the highest quality. Our basic function is to mill high-quality flour, and of course (and almost incidentally) we must hire salesmen to sell it, just as we hire accountants to keep our books."

The young company's first new product reveals an interesting example of the thinking of this era. The product was middlings, the bran left over after milling. Millfeed, as the product came to be known, proved a valuable product because it was an excellent nutrient for cattle. But the impetus to launch the new product came not from a consideration of the nutritional needs of cattle or a marketing analysis. It came primarily from the desire to dispose of a by-product! The new product decision was production oriented, not marketing oriented.

SECOND ERA—SALES ORIENTED

In the 1930's Pillsbury moved into its second era of development as a marketing company. This was the era of sales. For the first time we began to be highly conscious of the consumer, her wants, and her prejudices, as a key factor in the business equation. We established a commercial research department to provide us with facts about the market.

We also became more aware of the importance of our dealers, the wholesale and retail grocers who provided a vital link in our chain of distribution from the mill to the home. Knowing that consumers and dealers as well were vital to the company's success, we could no longer simply mark them down as unknowns in our figuring. With this realization, we took the first step along the road to becoming a marketing company.

Pillsbury's thinking in this second era could be summed up like this: "We are a flour-milling company, manufacturing a number of products for the consumer market. We must have a first-rate sales organization which can dispose of all the products we can make at a favorable price. We must back up this sales force with consumer advertising and market intelligence. We want our salesmen and our dealers to have all the tools they need for moving the output of our plants to the consumer."

Still not a marketing philosophy, but we were getting closer.

THIRD ERA—MARKETING ORIENTED

It was at the start of the present decade that Pillsbury entered the marketing era. The amazing growth of our consumer business as the result of introducing baking mixes provided the immediate impetus. But the groundwork had been laid by key men who developed our sales concepts in the middle forties.

With the new cake mixes, products of our research program, ringing up sales on the cash register, and with the realization that research and production could produce literally hundreds of new and different products, we faced for the first time the necessity for selecting the best new products. We needed a set of criteria for selecting the kind of products we would manufacture. We needed an organization to establish and maintain these criteria, and for attaining maximum sale of the products we did select.

We needed, in fact, to build into our company a new management function which would direct and control all the other corporate functions from procurement to production to advertising to sales. This function was marketing. Our solution was to establish the present marketing department.

This department developed the criteria which we would use in determining which products to market. *And these criteria were, and are, nothing more nor less than those of the consumer herself.* We moved the mountain out to find out what Mahomet, and Mrs. Mahomet, wanted. The company's purpose was no longer to mill flour, nor to manufacture a wide variety of products, but to satisfy the needs and desires, both actual and potential, of our customers.

If we were to restate our philosophy during the past decade as simply as possible, it would read: "We make and sell products for consumers."

The business universe, we realized, did not have room at the center for Pillsbury or any other company or groups of companies. It was already occupied by the customers.

This is the concept at the core of the marketing revolution. How did we put it to work for Pillsbury?

The Brand-Manager Concept

The first move was to transform our small advertising department into a marketing department. The move involved far more than changing the name on organizational charts. It required the introduction of a new, and vitally important, organizational concept—the brand-manager concept.

The brand-manager idea is the very backbone of marketing at Pillsbury. The man who bears the title, brand manager, has total accountability for results. He directs the marketing of his product as if it were his own business. Production does its job, and finance keeps the profit figures. Otherwise, the brand manager has total responsibility for marketing his product. This responsibility encompasses pricing, commercial research, competitive activity, home service and publicity coordination, legal details, budgets, advertising plans, sales promotion, and execution of plans. The brand manager must think first, last, and always of his sales target, the consumer.

Marketing permeates the entire organization. Marketing plans and executes the sale—all the way from the inception of the product idea, through its development and distribution, to the customer purchase. Marketing begins and ends with the consumer. New product ideas are conceived after careful study of her wants and needs, her likes and dislikes. Then marketing takes the idea and marshals all the forces of the corporation to translate the idea into product and the product into sales.

In the early days of the company, consumer orientation did not seem so important. The company made flour, and flour was a staple—no one would question the availability of a market. Today we must determine whether the American housewife will buy lemon pudding cake in preference to orange angel food. The variables in the equation have multiplied, just as the number of products on the grocers' shelves have multiplied from a hundred or so into many thousands.

When we first began operating under this new marketing concept, we encountered the problems which always accompany any major reorientation. Our people were young and frankly immature in some areas of business; but they were men possessed of an idea and they fought for it. The idea was almost too powerful. The marketing concept proved its worth in sales, but it upset many of the internal balances of the corporation. Marketing-oriented decisions resulted in peaks and valleys in production, schedules, labor, and inventories. But the system worked. It worked better and better as maverick marketing men became motivated toward tonnage and profit.

FOURTH ERA—MARKETING CONTROL

Today marketing is coming into its own. Pillsbury stands on the brink of its fourth major era in the marketing revolution.

Basically, the philosophy of this fourth era can be summarized this way: "We are moving from a company which has the marketing concept to a marketing company."

Marketing today sets company operating policy short-term. It will come to influence long-range policy more and more. Where today consumer research, technical research, procurement, production, advertising, and sales swing into action under the broad canopy established by marketing, tomorrow capital and financial planning, ten-year volume and profit goals will also come under the aegis of marketing. More than any other function, marketing must be tied to top management.

Today our marketing people know more about inventories than anyone in top management. Tomorrow's marketing man must know capital financing and the implications of marketing planning on long-range profit forecasting.

Today technical research receives almost all of its guidance and direction from marketing. Tomorrow marketing will assume a more creative function in the advertising area, both in terms of ideas and media selection.

Changes in the Future

The marketing revolution has only begun. There are still those who resist its basic idea, just as there are always those who will resist change in business, government, or any other form of human institution.

As the marketing revolution gains momentum, there will be more changes. The concept of the customer at the center will remain valid; but business must adjust to the shifting tastes and likes and desires and needs which have always characterized the American consumer.

For many years the geographical center of the United States lay in a small Kansas town. Then a new state, Alaska, came along, and the center shifted to the north and west. Hawaii was admitted to the Union and the geographical mid-point took another jump to the west. In very much the same way, modern business must anticipate the restless shifting of buying attitudes, as customer preferences move north, south, east, or west from a liquid center. There is nothing static about the marketing revolution, and that is part of its fascination. The old order has changed, yielding place to the new— but the new order will have its quota of changes, too.

At Pillsbury, as our fourth era progresses, marketing will become the basic motivating force for the entire corporation. Soon it will be true that every activity of the corporation—from finance to sales to production—is aimed at satisfying the needs and desires of the consumer. When that stage of development is reached, the marketing revolution will be complete.

B. Marketing Research

34. The Place of Marketing Research in Economic Activity

D. MAYNARD PHELPS

Marketing research is concerned with getting the best possible answers to certain major questions of business; namely, what to produce or handle, when and how much to produce, where to place the product over the market, where to direct sales effort, and what price to charge. Questions such as these are never permanently answered, rather they are constantly recurring ones. Frequently—in many cases each season— decisions must be made anew. Therefore, the marketing research task is never completed. Although these questions are simple and easily understood, they are most difficult to answer with any degree of assurance that error is avoided. Undoubtedly the simplicity of the questions belies the difficulty of arriving at correct answers. Yet they must be answered with a considerable degree of effectiveness if an enterprise is to be successful, and, furthermore, if the economic system under which we live is to operate effectively. In a capitalistic economy, responsibility for decisions on these questions may be taken by consumers directly, by producers, or by market intermediaries. As a matter of fact, it is taken partially by each of these groups. But regardless of which group takes responsibility, there must be anticipation of demand, and this leads to observation of the market. First, each of the questions previously enumerated will be considered briefly by way of introduction to the general problem, and the importance of the questions will be discussed. Later, attention will be given to the direction of productive effort—the extent to which the re-

❧ SOURCE: Reprinted by permission from *Marketing Research* (Bureau of Business Research, Graduate School of Business Administration, University of Michigan, 1937) pp. 69–74.

sponsibility for answering these questions is assumed by consumers, producers, and market intermediaries. Finally, the difficulties of market observation and the results of faulty decisions will be considered in some detail.

QUESTIONS OF MARKETING POLICY

What to Produce

Deciding what to produce is obviously the initial step toward production activity. Agriculture furnishes an illustration in which the individual in charge of a production unit must make a decision at the beginning of each crop year. Yet the farmer's decision is a relatively simple one. Climate and soil conditions narrow the range of product choice appreciably. Moreover, there is in farming, as compared with manufacturing, little opportunity for choice regarding variations in such characteristics of the product as size, quality, and color. Many of the variations in the product as harvested depend not upon independent choice but upon the vagaries of nature during the production period. The manufacturer's problem is essentially more difficult because there is a greater range of possible variations in the finished product and because an independent choice must be made in regard to those variations. When we consider the great variety of products even within narrow classifications, including differences in size, shape, color, and other distinguishing characteristics, likewise the tendency to change products frequently from period to period, the difficulty involved in deciding just what to produce becomes fully apparent.

When and How Much to Produce

We now come to questions concerning the quantity which the market will take and the correct timing of productive effort. Obviously these questions are closely connected. They are not of great importance if the product is one for which the production period is relatively short, for then adjustments to demand can be made without difficulty and errors in judgment are not costly. But when, because of the duration of the production process, a manufacturer must start production many months prior to sale, these questions assume major significance. Moreover, demand for most products has pronounced cyclical and seasonal variations, and if similar fluctuations in production are to be avoided, the manufacturer must be able to produce in advance and store his product. But advance production necessitates the forecasting of demand over a still longer period than the duration of the production process, and thus the problem is further complicated. Nor are problems of cyclical and seasonal demand particularly easy to solve. Moreover, in the usual situation the extent of total demand is not immediately apparent, nor the part of total demand which a company can expect to secure in competition with others. Yet, in order to operate profitably, business executives must arrive at reasonably accurate decisions. Shortage of goods when demand appears, too heavy inventories, perhaps waste through obsolescence, may result from ineffectiveness in determining the correct time at which to produce varying quantities of product.

Where to Place Products Over the Market

A business enterprise must determine where to place its products geographically in order to meet demand as it appears. Since demand often needs to be satisfied immediately, stocks must be placed in various parts of the country. By a correct placement of stocks it is possible to avoid a shortage at one place and a surplus elsewhere at the same time. If, for example, immediate delivery is wanted for certain units of equipment in one of the southern states and supplies are lacking, heavy supplies in Chicago are of very little value. Particularly is this true in an active competitive situation. Another company with supplies in the South which the buyer can purchase for immediate delivery is likely to secure the order.

In another sense it is likewise necessary to have the product spread correctly over the market. Here we are thinking not of the physical product but of knowledge of the product. Those individuals or institutions who are potential buyers must know of the existence of the product, its qualities and distinguishing characteristics, and the utility which it will give. Although questions of expediency may temporarily dictate otherwise, in general, knowledge of the product should be disseminated over the market in accordance with potential demand. This involves the determination of what type of people or institutions will be likely to purchase the product, and of where they are located.

What Price to Charge

Most manufacturers enjoy some measure of independence in price determination. The unusual features which differentiate one product from those manufactured by competitors create for the manufacturer a semi-monopolistic situation. While too high a price will lessen demand by causing substitution, it will probably fail to stop purchases completely. A lower price will induce greater purchases. Therefore, an executive must think of varying demands in relation to a range of prices and decide what combination of sales volume and profit per unit sold will result in the highest net profit. Thus it appears that the question of what price to charge often resolves itself into three subordinate questions: (1) How distinctive is the product in question when compared with others of its class? (2) How important are the distinguishing features of the product to consumers? (3) How much extra will consumers be willing to pay for a product embodying these characteristics?

Importance of Questions Enumerated

Admittedly these questions are not the only important ones which those in charge of business activity are called upon to answer. Still it must be conceded that they are questions of "first degree." The fact of their basic importance does not depend for its demonstration merely upon logical reasoning. It is attested by the heavy expenditures of many large corporations for the designing and perfecting of new products which they hope will be acceptable from the market standpoint, and by the increase in statistical and commercial research departments which attempt to answer the *how much, when,* and *where* questions. Moreover, many business failures can be directly traced to the omission of careful and painstaking study of these questions. In any type of economic system, whether it be socialistic, communistic, or capitalistic, these questions, with the possible exception of that regarding price, must be answered.

Perhaps the comment might be made that the previous remarks assert the obvious, that no one doubts the importance of the questions discussed. But it is all too evident that business concerns frequently blunder along and do not produce the right products, in the correct quantities, at the right time, and that both stocks and sales effort are *not* placed strategically over the market. This indicates one of two things: either those in charge of production do not realize the importance of these questions and consequently neglect them, or, although realizing their importance, they have been unable to answer them effectively. It may likewise indicate the essential difficulty of the problems involved. More will be said of this later. First, it is our task to consider the broad bases upon which the individual business man arrives at conclusions regarding these questions, and the part which he actually plays in directing production.

THE DIRECTION OF PRODUCTION

Immediately, of course, certain individuals in each concern decide whether a product shall be manufactured. If their decision is in the affirmative, production schedules are arranged, and sooner or later units of product are ready for the market. But in a broader sense the selection of what shall be produced is not in the hands of producers but in those of consumers. In a regime of free enterprise, a capitalistic economy, production is guided by consumers' choices acting through the price system. Individuals receive money incomes as a result of their separate contributions to the productive process, and they are largely free to apportion their incomes among various goods and services as they desire. Whether a person uses a part of his income to buy this or that article depends upon the utility which he thinks it will give him, and upon its cost in relation to the cost and utility of other articles. In a situation where all wants cannot be satisfied, each expenditure is necessarily an alternative one. One product, or perhaps additional units of it, can be had only at the sacrifice of other products. Each individual, therefore, within the limits of his own income and the products and services which are available, determines his own demand schedule. When one product is chosen rather than another, its total demand is thereby increased and the total demand for some other product is necessarily less than it otherwise would be. Increased price is likely to follow increased demand; at any rate, the producer is encouraged to increase output, perhaps through higher prices and therefore greater profits, perhaps through decreased production costs as a result of greater volume at the same prices. Thus it appears that, through the price system, the extent of demand for various products, which is simply an agglomeration of many individual choices, determines what shall be produced, and that, in a very real sense, consumers as a group direct production.[1]

While economists largely agree on the conclusions of this analysis—that consumer choice is the final determinant of what shall be produced—we must recognize that consumers are influenced by producers in their selections of product and that, in many instances, demand does not appear prior to the time that production is started. When an entirely new product is designed and ready for manufacture, or when a well-known product is greatly changed, consumer choice has not had an opportunity to "direct" production and is therefore of little immediate aid to the business man in determining whether the new product should be placed in manufacture, or whether the old product should have been changed. Consumer choice will tell the business executive *later* whether more or less should be produced. But whether it is a good venture to go ahead in the first place is a question that must be decided independently of consumers, or at least without any definite act on their part. Unless a manufacturer has orders in advance, he must *anticipate* what consumer wants and choices will be. Thus, in many cases, production is directed, not by consumers' choices in the first instance, but by *anticipation* on the part of producers of what consumers' choices will be. The tool which the business man must then use is *observation* of the market. Thus we see that, in determining what and how much to produce, the business man follows one of two guides—either orders in advance or observation of the market.

[1] See F. M. Taylor, *Principles of Economics* (New York: The Ronald Press, 1925), chap. 45; also R. T. Bye and W. H. Hewett, *Applied Economics* (New York: Alfred A. Knopf, 1928), chap. 3.

35. *Market Measurement in a Free Society*

RALPH CASSADY, JR.

In a free society, some knowledge of consumer demand is not merely desirable but an absolute necessity if vendors are to be successful.[1] Those offering goods and services must know not only the type of merchandise desired by consumer-buyers, but also the style of item preferred, the amount consumers will take, the nature of service desired, where consumers can expect to buy the product, the particular time the item is required, and how much prospective buyers will pay for it. It is only after knowing these things that vendors can safely attempt to promote the sale of their merchandise offerings without incurring losses due to consumer resistance.

The key to intelligent competitive activity is market research which seeks information about consumer wants and behavior patterns to serve as a basis for effective marketing activity.

HOW THE MARKET IS INVESTIGATED

There are, of course, various methods of obtaining market information available to those who undertake the responsibility of providing for consumer wants. It is the main purpose of this paper to consider such procedures and to relate them to various specific marketing problems.

Before examining the several market research methods in detail, a number of preliminary points should be made about market research as compared with other types of scientific investigation.

BASIC RESEARCH METHODS

As in every other field of knowledge, only a limited number of basic research methods are available to the investigator who is interested in probing markets. This is not to say that there are not innumerable research techniques available for use in our investigatory activity, but only that various devices possess basic characteristics which permit classification into only one of a very few categories.

While hypothesis-testing[2] is used as a research device in economic (including market) analyses, its use is not as extensive as in some other areas. One reason for this, perhaps, is that the state of knowledge in the marketing field is such that research has been confined largely to exploratory investigation, and less emphasis has been placed on precise explanations for various developments.

It is in this latter phase of research activity that hypotheses are most useful. One might add

---

[1] The only exception to this is in a sellers' market when the competition for supplies of goods is much more intensive than the competition for customers, e.g., in wartime.

⚜ SOURCE: Reprinted by permission from the *California Management Review*, Vol. 2, No. 2, Winter 1960, Copyright 1960 by The Regents of the University of California.

[2] According to Webster's (*Webster's New International Dictionary*, 2nd ed., Unabridged) a hypothesis is "2. A proposition, condition, or principle which is assumed, perhaps without belief, in order to draw out its logical consequences and by this method to test its accord with facts which are known or may be determined."

that those engaged in economic investigations often appear to confuse hypotheses (tentative explanations) with theory (confirmed generalizations).

In economic investigations, heavy reliance is placed on inference for conclusions. This is due, in part at least, to the difficulty of employing experimentation in this field. For example, if in an analysis of market data a marked change appears in the statistical pattern, which upon further analysis is found to coincide with a particular development that reasonably could have had an effect on the results, an inference is apt to be drawn that it did indeed have such an effect.

But research which leads to inferential conclusions is not unique to economic analysis. It will be recalled that the cigarette-lung cancer researches have thus far been mostly statistical, with inferential conclusions being based upon the apparent relationship between heavy smoking and the incidence of this disease.

While statistical studies may result in a strong inference toward a cause and effect relationship between cigarette smoking and lung cancer, the heavy smoking and the cancer might conceivably both stem from a common cause. Hence experimentation must be employed to confirm or invalidate the hypothetical conclusion that heavy smoking is the causal factor.[3]

Market researchers must, in large part (as in some other new areas of investigation) devise their own apparatus for market-measurement purposes. The mark of a good research man in this field is his ability to design effective methods of measuring various market phenomena, such as buying habits, brand preferences, market potentials, etc. Thus, over the years, there have been contrived all kinds of ingenious devices for measuring market behavior, including pantry surveys (which serve as the basis for drawing inferences concerning consumer brand preferences), mechanical recorder attachments for radios and television sets (which reveal the listening and viewing habits of householders), retail-store brand-preference audits (which reflect consumer buying habits),

consumer diaries (which provide invaluable information concerning buyer preferences and practices), and automobile license number studies (which reveal much information about consumer patronage habits in relation to various retail institutions).[4]

Research methods in the marketing field as in other disciplines may be classified as deductive (seeking answers by the application of logic to a problem) and inductive (seeking answers by empirical study of the problem).

DEDUCTIVE ANALYSIS

Although stress in market research is laid on inductive investigation, those who are well versed in research methodology do not "look down their noses" at deductive analysis. Deduction is an extremely effective supplementary research tool. Indeed, inductive research would lose much of its effectiveness without the aid of deductive analysis.

Some deductive activity is merely hypothesizing,[5] designed either to provide tentative explanations of certain phenomena or to suggest a possible behavior pattern, say, which might be subject to test later on. However, deductive investigation may extend knowledge at least in the sense of making clear the full implications of inductively-established conclusions.

Thus deductive analysis may serve at least three purposes in market investigation:

1. It may suggest hypothetical relationships whose actual existence may be later subject to test through inductive means.

2. It may provide tentative explanations of phenomena which may later be confirmed or vitiated through inductive study.

3. It may make possible the extrapolation of knowledge gained from inductive investigations by providing inferential conclusions based on fact-founded premises.

There has been considerable advancement in our thinking concerning buyer attitudes and competitive behavior at the abstract level during the past 25 years as a result of investigative effort which might reasonably be classed as market research. Thus, the work of Prof. Edward H. Chamberlin and Mrs. Joan Robinson

---

[3] A difficulty here might be the devising of experimental methods which would not endanger the health of human "guinea pigs." This does not mean, however, that investigations that endanger health are precluded. It will be recalled that Dr. Walter Reed made use of volunteers in his famous yellowjack investigations of sixty years ago which were designed to test the hypothesis that mosquitos were carriers from which infection resulted.

[4] See Ralph Cassady, Jr. and Harold M. Haas, "Analyzing the Market of Mail Order House Retail Stores," *Harvard Business Review*, Summer 1935, pp. 493–502.

[5] See footnote 2.

is based almost entirely on deductive analysis and, while still largely hypothetical, has led to the development of the area of nonperfect competition with its classification based on variation in numbers, differentiation of product, and amount of market information in possession of buyers and sellers.

The author's own studies have been in part deductive in nature also. For example, some years ago, J. M. Clark published a trail-blazing article on what he called "workable competition." [6] In this presentation Prof. Clark suggested the possibility (or perhaps better, the probability) that elasticity of demand was substantially conditioned by the passage of time.[7] This led to a great deal of reflection by this author on the time element as it affects consumer demand, and ultimately to a publication of his views.[8]

While these hypotheses are still subject to confirmation, some headway has been made by isolating the issues and thus simplifying the task for the inductive investigator and indeed in informing practical marketing executives about probable consumer behavior patterns.

To take another example, this author was a participant in a recent international round-table on fisheries and fishery products. The discussion included the nature of the demand for fish by American consumers. One part of the analysis was concerned with cross-elasticity of demand between fish and meat (i.e., the impact on the sale of one product resulting from a change in the price of another).

Ordinarily, a high degree of cross-elasticity between two competing products would mean that when the price of one goes up the amount taken of the other increases and vice versa. Fish, however, is considered by Americans to be a second-class food and hence—according to this hypothesis—cross-elasticity would appear to be much lower when a change in price favors fish than when a change in price favors meat.[9]

While this hypothesis still remains to be tested, the formulation of the hypothetical proposition is a definite step toward the solution of the problem because it isolates the question which needs to be answered and prevents wasted investigatory effort. Although no suggestion is being made at this time regarding a scheme which one might use to test this hypothesis, there is little doubt that a testing device can be devised in time.

It is this writer's opinion that even without confirmation deductive analysis may be valuable because of the fact that it provides the practitioner with a suggestion as to possible behavior patterns that might alert him to potential dangers and opportunities. The possibility for instance that the impact of a price change will be greater over time than it is at the moment the change is made may be of great significance to those engaged in actual market operations.

Similarly, practitioners stand to gain greatly from a hypothetical finding that consumer demand for various products and services may vary greatly during a day or week and that greater response can be expected to the offerings of vendors if consideration is given to the place where consumers are when they feel the need of the item most keenly.[10]

INDUCTIVE ANALYSIS

Despite the valuable contributions of deductive analysis, the large bulk of market research activity is inductive in nature. That is, findings are the result of actual market investigation. While the methods utilized in field study differ greatly in details, basically there are only three inductive approaches available to market researchers.[11] These will be discussed briefly in the following paragraphs.

OBSERVATIONAL METHOD

Under this scheme (which is, of course, relied on very heavily by astronomers) information is derived either directly or indirectly by observing and recording the phenomena under study, for example, the behavior of people who are going about their normal daily tasks—pre-

[6] J. M. Clark, "Toward a Concept of Workable Competition," *The American Economic Review*, June 1940, pp. 241–256.

[7] See p. 247 of footnote 6.

[8] See Ralph Cassady, Jr., "The Time Element and Demand Analysis," Cox and Alderson (eds.), *Theory in Marketing* (Chicago: Richard D. Irwin, 1950), pp. 193–207.

[9] Ralph Cassady, Jr., "The Marketing of Fishery Products in the United States," Turvey and Wiseman, (eds.), *The Economics of Fisheries* (Rome: Food and Agriculture Organization of the United Nations, 1958), p. 201.

[10] E.g., ice-cold "Coke" in service stations and places of work.

[11] The author is indebted to Professor D. M. Phelps for his extremely able analysis of marketing research methodology as described in *Marketing Research* (Ann Arbor: University of Michigan Press, 1937).

paring meals, keeping house, listening to the television, moving about the community, shopping, performing marketing functions, etc. As was suggested immediately above, observation may be performed directly in a first-hand manner or it may have been performed by someone else at an earlier time and only later reported by the observer as a result of second-hand investigation.

DIRECT OBSERVATION

In the use of this approach, observations are made at the time the event is taking place. For example, an observer at some carefully selected vantage point is able to tell a great deal about consumer acceptance of a particular style (e.g., the number of men out of every hundred wearing Homburg hats). The author participated in a foot-traffic study for a certain location on Market Street in San Francisco some years ago in order to determine, by actual count, the types of persons passing by the place under study and the time of passing. This information then could be utilized as a basis for deciding the most effective use of the retail location under study.

Similarly, a tabulation of automobile license numbers found in parking lots of two Midwestern retail establishments yielded vast amounts of useful market information, such as the number of patrons at different times of the day and week, the distances traveled by customers from home to the store, and (determined from the location of the home of each car owner) the estimated income bracket of the patrons.[12]

One recently reported application of the direct observational method in American business is the use of a one-way mirror (so-called) to permit a study of the reactions of children to various types of toys with which they have been invited to play, without awareness on their part that they are being observed.

Diary studies, based on detail records of consumer purchases and commonly used by market researchers to derive information about family living and purchasing habits, are basically similar to the schemes just discussed except that the diarist is often both the observer and the observed.

INDIRECT OBSERVATION

Under this scheme, observations are made after the event has taken place (although some

recording of events might have taken place earlier) and reliance is placed on existing evidence of what has occurred in the past rather than on personal observation of the event as it occurred. Essentially, this is feasible because past developments usually leave in their wake some evidence in the form of records or reports by participants or primary observers which may be utilized as a basis for determining what took place at an earlier time.[13]

The indirect observational method may be classed either as qualitative or quantitative.

QUALITATIVE INVESTIGATION

In this type of investigation the information the researcher is attempting to obtain concerning past events is essentially subjective rather than statistical in nature. Some of our historical studies are essentially taxonomic—that is, their contribution to understanding is based largely on the systematizing of the information gathered so as to make such data more comprehensible and thus applicable in planning market strategy.[14]

A qualitative study of the Los Angeles wholesale grocery trade several years ago revealed the evolutionary change from the full-service type of operation to the limited-function method of food distribution which, of course, is a reflection of changing consumer patronage habits.[15] Similarly, the writer has been working recently on a study of price warfare (including consumer behavior patterns found therein) in which he relies to some extent on records of past events. These records may in turn be in the form of second-hand observations rather than reports by direct observers at an earlier time.[16]

---

[13] It should be noted that the indirect observational method is so designated because the researcher does not observe phenomena directly but reports on the observations that someone else has made.

[14] See, for example, Ralph Cassady, Jr., "Techniques and Purposes of Price Discrimination," *The Journal of Marketing*, October 1946, pp. 135–150, which is essentially a classification of price discrimination methods employed by various types of individuals and firms in the business and professional world.

[15] See Ralph Cassady, Jr. and Wylie L. Jones, *The Changing Competitive Structure in the Wholesale Grocery Trade* (Berkeley: University of California Press, 1949).

[16] See, for example, a description of the Santa Fe–Southern Pacific rate wars of the mid-eighties found in Glenn S. Dumke, *The Boom of the Eighties in Southern California* (San Marino: Huntington Library, 1944), pp. 17–27.

---

[12] On a basis of the relationship between income and housing cost. See footnote 4.

It is sometimes possible to interview direct observers simultaneously with the unfolding of the event observed (e.g., interrogating those actively engaged in a price war). However, there is a question as to whether participants in particular economic behavior situations (such as price warfare) should be interviewed *during* such altercations or after they are concluded.

Some argue that the former is the correct approach because the events are fresh in the minds of the participants and the researcher is therefore likely to get a more accurate appraisal of conditions and motivations. However, a major objection to this approach is that participants' views may be distorted by emotional reactions and, indeed, such individuals may be reluctant to tell the whole truth when the outcome of the struggle might be affected by such a revelation.

Qualitative historical research results may have commercial as well as pure research value. For example, some business concerns have made use of analytical studies of certain types of existing legal restrictions on selling activities, with the purpose of establishing a basis for planning future market strategy. By knowing the nature of the legislative restrictions which condition a firm's activities in relation to consumer-behavior patterns, management may be able to make a more intelligent decision as to whether it should attempt to meet consumer needs through its own method of operation or to withdraw from the particular field. Indeed, the firm may actually choose to remain in the field and seek some easing of the restrictions through the legislative process.

QUANTITATIVE INVESTIGATION

The market information sought by quantitative studies is essentially statistical in nature. One interesting application of this type of investigation to market-measurement problems is an analysis which was made of the shift of retail trade of a large metropolitan area from the central shopping district to outlying areas. This investigation was conducted by recasting Census of Business data from political subdivisions to economic subregions, thus providing a basis for measuring the movement of trade from one time to another.[17]

Similarly, some years ago a study was conducted of the seasonal behavior of apple prices to serve as a basis for a top-level executive decision in a large food chain organization. This analysis, which was predicated on published auction price statistics, had the specific purpose of providing an answer to the question as to whether a large food firm might find it more profitable to acquire title to supplies of this type of product early in the season rather than to continue purchasing the goods as needed on a hand-to-mouth basis.

It should be obvious that if conclusions are to be drawn regarding general behavior patterns which are to be considered generally applicable to other similar situations, the historical data chosen for observation must be properly representative of the whole universe under study.

INTERROGATION METHOD

This approach is relied on very heavily by researchers who inquire into human behavior and motivation (e.g., psychologists). Some types of market information cannot readily be acquired except by the use of such techniques. For example, a person's income (and hence his purchasing power) may not be accurately obtainable by observation (although, of course, certain inferences might be drawn regarding this matter on a basis of one's occupation or place of residence). Thus investigators must resort to interrogation if adequate information is to be obtained.[18]

The survey method of research (as it is sometimes called) relies not on observing what people do but on gathering information which reposes in people's minds and which must be acquired by questioning individual respondents. A large part of market research, of course, is based on the use of this general method of investigation.

[17] See William K. Bowden and Ralph Cassady, Jr., "Decentralization of Retail Trade in the Metropolitan Market Area," *The Journal of Marketing*, January 1941, pp. 270–275, and Ralph Cassady, Jr. and W. K. Bowden, "Shifting Retail Trade Within the Los Angeles Metropolitan Market," *The Journal of Marketing*, April 1944, pp. 398–404.

[18] It must be admitted that there is a danger of upward bias in attempting to gain information about incomes through interrogation, due to the element of prestige which is connected with high incomes, although this would depend to some extent at least on the agency collecting the data. (Some companies no longer require job applicants to list salaries earned on former jobs, since it has been found that these are frequently overstated by a $1,000 a year or more.) The U. S. Bureau of Census can undoubtedly obtain income data in its sample studies with a certain degree of accuracy.

Information which may be obtained by survey techniques includes the number of persons in various age groups. For example, the number of youngsters between 10 and 14 years of age might serve as a basis for estimating the market for some proposed children's magazine. Information may be obtained concerning individuals' reading habits, brand preferences, patronage habits, motivational influences, and future purchasing plans by survey also.

Just as in the observational approach, great care must be taken to obtain scientifically selected samples in survey studies. This is a highly technical procedure and requires a great amount of skill if sound results are to be obtained. In addition, however, it is necessary to prepare properly constructed questionnaires and to select and train skilled field personnel.

SIMPLE INTERVIEWING

In this type of procedure the questions to be asked are predetermined and precisely stated and the interviewer is not permitted to depart from the schedule of queries previously prepared. Care must be taken to ask questions which will elicit from the respondent the desired information with the least amount of bias or distortion.

A simple question in a gasoline patronage study, asking for the brand of gasoline purchased most recently and in which station it was purchased, should yield sound and valuable market information. Likewise, questions concerning the brand of shortening the housewife has on hand should produce equally successful results. Questions concerning the television program which one watched at a specified recent time should also result in the required information. (It is interesting, incidentally, that the latter type of information might be obtained through observational methods (i.e., a recording device can be attached to the television chassis.)

The interrogation method was utilized several years ago in a study of consumer meat-purchasing habits in a Midwestern community to determine to what extent consumer buyers shift their patronage from one institution to another in accordance with lower prices offered, as a basis for a defense against a charge of violation of a "cost floor" act.[19]

DEPTH INTERVIEWING

It is well recognized by competent market researchers that motivation cannot be accur-

ately determined by ordinary questioning, either because respondents do not know why they behave as they do or because they do know but are reluctant to tell. Motivational research techniques are those which are designed to determine why who does what when. The depth interviewing technique, undoubtedly borrowed from the psychoanalyst (who in turn borrowed it from the anthropologist), is designed to overcome the limitations inherent in simple (closed-end) interrogation. In this technique, questions to be asked are only generally outlined with the expectation that the subtle aspects of the respondent's behavior will be discovered by intensive discussion. Thus, by skillful probing, reluctance of respondents is overcome and memories refreshed.

Deep-seated information concerning preferences for certain brands of a particular food item may be discovered by means of depth-interviewing techniques.[20] A survey of Palm Springs pay-television subscribers several years ago elicited interesting and extremely valuable information concerning consumer attitudes on subscription television service which may be applicable generally. Thus, depth interviewing makes possible the substitution of basically sound responses for "top-of-the-mind" answers.

EXPERIMENTAL METHOD

Experimentation which is employed so extensively in certain of the physical sciences (e.g., chemistry), also may be advantageously employed by investigators into market phenomena. Experimentation—in a broad sense at least—may under certain circumstances be clas-

---

[19] The point here was that such legislation typically permits the meeting of competitors' lower prices for comparable merchandise, but the question in this instance was whether consumers might not shift patronage in response to lower prices for an inferior product, and hence the firm selling the superior product might have to protect its position by offering its product at lower prices.

[20] The results of one such study are given in an article by William F. Brown, "The Determination of Factors Influencing Brand Choice," *The Journal of Marketing*, April 1950, pp. 699–706. For additional information on depth interviewing see the American Marketing Association's Research Committee report, "Depth Interviewing," in the same issue of *The Journal of Marketing*, pp. 721–724, and L. M. Paradise and A. B. Blankenship, "Depth Questioning," *The Journal of Marketing*, January 1951, pp. 274–288.

sified as an observational type of investigation, but is distinguished from the first-named approach by the fact that in the experimental scheme test conditions are prearranged. Thus, people are observed not as they go about their normal tasks but in an artificial situation devised for the particular purpose. This procedure may be classified as either simple or controlled.

SIMPLE EXPERIMENTATION

This term suggests that the experiment is not controlled—that is—no attempt is made to provide a bench mark of normal expectation against which results may be measured. For example, a firm might simply wish to find out whether a certain demand manipulative scheme is likely to be successful. By the use of a consumer jury technique, it is possible to determine which of a number of different sales appeals is most attractive to consumer buyers. Or a firm, in bringing out a new brand of shaving cream, may desire to test the item simply by providing a sample of the proposed product to a panel of consumers and probing their reactions to the new item.

There are innumerable other applications of simple experimentation in market research. For example, a large retail concern may wish to test the efficacy of telephone selling by store employees. Such a test can be conducted by selecting the names of a certain segment of its charge list to whom the phone calls might be made announcing certain special offerings. Purchases of all such individuals then may be recorded and, on a basis of sales results, the promotional device evaluated. An interesting application of the technique has been employed also in the entertainment field in probing audience response to a presentation by instructing panel members to express their reactions to a test performance through the use of a recording device.[21]

Simple experimentation may be used in pricing studies also. The head of an outstanding American market research organization devised a scheme some years ago which was designed to aid in the pricing of a new brand or make of product. This scheme called for a panel of consumer jurors to evaluate the new brand

against competitive offerings.[22] The new article, unpriced, was available for examination by the jurors along with the products with which this item might be expected to compete.[23] Thus each consumer juror "priced" the product in comparison with the standard composed of all competitive items in the field.

While a control in the usual sense was absent in this experiment, a standard was provided against which consumers could evaluate the new item. It is interesting, as a side-point, that the results of such an experiment might provide the vendor with an approximation of a miniature demand curve for his product.

Each of these schemes, it should be noted, is based on some sort of prearrangement of conditions but is uncontrolled. While some types of experimental investigations may not require controls for sound research results (see above), some do. The *sine qua non* of some investigations is an evaluation of the impact of a particular stimulus on market results. In such investigations, the absence of some sort of control is a serious flaw because without it, it is impossible to isolate the stimulus under study from other stimuli which may have a simultaneous effect on market results.

CONTROLLED EXPERIMENTATION

The aim of controlled experimentation is to keep all stimuli precisely the same in the experimental as well as in the control group, except the one whose effect is being studied, so that the results from the one stimulus can be distinguished from those of others. Referring to the telephone sales study mentioned above: How is one to tell that sales made to those telephoned *resulted* from such calls when some of the individuals might have visited the store and purchased the merchandise even in the absence of the specific stimulus under study?

It is not enough to know what the sales were in a pretest period, and to assume that any increase in the test-period sales resulted from the stimulus under test, because other

---

[21] For further information on this method see Ralph Cassady, Jr., "Statistical Sampling Techniques and Marketing Research," *The Journal of Marketing*, April 1945, p. 339.

[22] See Wroe Alderson, "New Applications for Market Research," *Sales Management*, February 1, 1947, p. 46.

[23] It is not clear from Alderson's brief description of the experiment (See footnote 22) whether the prices of the competing products were indicated to panel members, but the present author would be inclined to believe that best results would be obtained if such prices were available to the test group.

stimuli (such as seasonal or industrial changes) might have occurred simultaneously and these may have caused *all* sales to increase at this time. As a basis of measuring the results of a specific stimulus (telephone calls to test group), one must compare results with the purchasing behavior of a control group made up of individuals of the same type in all respects except that they have not been subjected to the specific stimulus under study (i.e., telephone solicitation).

To take another example: A company might wish to test a formula of a proposed product by providing panel members with supplies of the item under consideration along with supplies of the leading brand in the field in masked containers as a sort of "control," [24] after which panel members may be questioned concerning preferences, and observations can be made of remaining amounts of product. [25]

And still another: A firm might wish to determine to what extent (if at all) a counter display rack would enhance sales for a particular brand of product, for example, razor blades. To determine effectiveness of the rack, sales might be recorded in a store selected for the purpose during a pretest period and then be compared with sales of the store during the test period. But the use of another store (similar in all respects to the first except that no display rack is utilized) would serve as a control which would make possible the isolation of the sales resulting from the use of the display rack from those resulting from other existing stimuli. [26]

Controlled experimentation also lends itself to studies of the effectiveness of alternative prices and pricing arrangements. [27] For example, a chain store organization may wish to know the most effective price to charge for a single unit of a specific item or for a multiple offering of the same item.

The question of a multiple offering may involve subquestions regarding the effectiveness of a multiple offering *per se* (where the price charged for the group as a whole is the same as the price of the individual unit times the number of units making up the group) as compared with multiple-unit offerings where the total price of the group reflects discounts for quantity. If the regular price of the item were 10 cents, the problem might indeed be to determine what sales results might be expected from offering the item at two for 20 cents, at 9 cents per unit, at two for 18 cents, or at two for 19 cents.

In order to obtain a definitive answer to this problem, several cooperating stores must be used, including the control store (at which the regular price is charged). [28]

This method might also be used in solving other market-measurement problems. These could include packaging problems (consumer preferences for tin versus glass containers, or mesh sacks versus paper bags, etc.), and shelving of merchandise (position in relation to eye-level, location of goods in relation to a family of related items, amount of shelf frontage for each item, etc.). It might, in addition, be used to study the effect of the introduction of new products (impact on any competing items already in stock as well as on related items), and improvements in store equipment (effectiveness in serving consumers resulting from mechanized check-out stands). Undoubtedly, controlled experimentation techniques may be utilized in other studies of consumer behavior and response. [29]

Controlled experimentation in market research is not confined to sales-test studies. The

---

[24] This type of experimentation has certain limitations. For example, its use is greatly restricted if not actually precluded in some fields (such as drugs) by legislative circumscriptions. However, this type of test may have applications in certain lines which do not appear to be promising (appliances, say), although experimental conditions must be adapted to the peculiar circumstances of the product under study.

[25] It should be noted that what panel members may say about their preferences may not jibe with the consumption habits as evidenced by residual amounts of product. When such a correlation is absent, it may reveal certain very subtle preference patterns (such as liking ease of preparation but disliking the flavor) of the product under consideration.

[26] The difficulty, of course, is to find stores which are sufficiently similar to one another (in sales, location, type of patronage, etc.) to be used as a basis of comparison.

[27] William Applebaum and Richard F. Spears, "Controlled Experimentation in Marketing Research," *The Journal of Marketing*, January 1950, p. 513.

[28] The result must, of course, be measured by the percentage change in sales between the pretest and test periods. Generally speaking, if a change in the number sold is no greater in test stores than in the control store, it indicates that the change in prices was not the causal factor.

[29] Applebaum and Spears, *op. cit.*, pp. 512–515.

projective technique (which is designed to elicit uninhibited judgments from those under study) might be considered an example of controlled experimentation. In this scheme, the respondent is asked to project himself or herself into situations which are different in only one respect, and to interpret given phenomena, thereby disclosing deep-seated attitudes or motives of such individuals.

For example, if one wishes to determine secret or subconscious consumer attitudes toward instant coffee, he might (as one researcher did) [30] prepare two lists of food items precisely the same in every respect except for the inclusion of instant coffee in one and regular coffee in the other, and ask respondents to characterize the persons who purchased each group of food items. From the respondents' attitudes toward the purchaser of a certain type of item one can infer attitudes toward the item itself.

The scheme makes possible the discovery of biases which might not be readily revealed otherwise because ostensibly the respondent is not making a self-analysis but rather an evaluation of others, and, moreover, it isolates the respondent's attitude toward the item under test by controlling all conditioning stimuli except this one. A similar scheme has been used to test the inner attitudes of housewives toward trading stamps. [31]

One final point might be made re the use of controlled experimentation in market research: While the concept of control is very simple, the effective application of this scheme to market research problems is extremely difficult. The main reason for this is that controlling all factors except the one under study, while easy enough in medical research, [32] is difficult

in market research because of the existence of innumerable variables between test and control situations which may alter results in one but not in the other, hence vitiating conclusions. However, with all of its limitations, we can look for greater and greater use of controlled experimentation in market research because of the promise of more precise solutions to demand-analysis problems.

CONCLUSIONS

The author has attempted to present an overview picture of the methods which may be employed in determining the market for firm and industry offerings. While it is true that the consumer in the free-enterprise system may choose as he pleases, hence complicating the job of the vendor, there is little excuse for ignorance on the part of sellers concerning the markets they are serving at this stage of our knowledge of research methodology. Actually, methods of investigation are available which may provide vendors with needed market knowledge.

It should be noted, however, that the various methods are not alternative schemes of investigation to be chosen as one chooses the color of a jacket to be worn on a certain day. Rather, the method should be selected as an expert chooses a golf club for a specific task to be performed. Usually only one scheme will precisely produce the results one wishes to achieve, although some studies must be based on a combination of methods because of the limitations of any one method in providing all of the information required. The trouble in golf *and* research is that one must be skilled enough to be able to choose the most effective implement to use.

One final word: Information concerning markets, no matter how complete and accurate, is no substitute for intelligent executive action. That is, the results of market investigations do not automatically provide answers to the best course to take, given all the circumstances of the problem with which the firm is faced. Moreover, decisions have to be made concerning hundreds of different questions which cannot economically be studied or which are beyond the purview of the investigator. It must be kept in mind, further, that even assuming information is available, intelligent use must be made of it. The point is, however, the market research findings should be extremely helpful tools to those who are responsible for making wise managerial decisions.

---

[30] The results of such an experiment, Mason Haire, "Projective Techniques in Marketing Research," *The Journal of Marketing*, April 1950, pp. 649–656, indicate that (a) instant coffee on food lists is viewed by certain respondents as evidence of laziness on the part of the housewife (p. 653), and (b) this attitude is fairly deep-seated because respondents having such views do not purchase the product themselves (p. 655).

[31] Bertrand Klass, "The Controversies Surrounding Motivation Research," *Proceedings of the Fourth Annual Meeting—Social Science for Industry* (Menlo Park: Stanford Research Institute, April 4, 1956), pp. 46–47.

[32] Giving a serum to every other patient, applying a medicament to burns on only one side of the face, etc.

36. *Psychology in Market Research*

ERNEST DICHTER

The fact that the businessman must market his products means that he must deal with people—his customers, the users of his services. The psychologist too deals with people. Both businessman and psychologist are interested in what makes people tick, what motivates them, and how they can be molded and influenced. This article, then, is an exploration of how businessmen can work together with modern psychologists and make use of their fund of special knowledge, particularly in the marketing of consumers' goods.

CONSUMER MOTIVATIONS

American industry has been fairly successful with machinery and technical processes, and there have also been some attempts to control the more obvious human factors like safety, labor relations, aptitudes, and morale. Likewise definite beginnings have been made in the measurement of markets: We know how to determine sales potentials, we can make product tests, we can measure attitudes, and we know something about the effectiveness of advertising campaigns.

But by and large we are still using outmoded and inefficient methods to determine and understand consumer motivations. We are only scratching the surface. In making marketing decisions, we are relying on surveys based on what people say they think and feel. Yet even in the everyday aspects of modern life we have learned to distinguish between what a man

‡ SOURCE: Reprinted by permission from *Harvard Business Review*, Vol. 25, No. 4, Summer 1947, pp. 432–443.

says and what he really means deep down. We know that to deny jealousy, for example, is very frequently only an admission of the emotion. We know that often we do things because of inferiority feelings. We also know that we forget names and objects and tasks because of an unconscious desire not to remember. We know that constant denial of pleasure to a child will frustrate him and that frustration leads to aggression.

In these and many other ways we are, bit by bit, introducing modern scientific thinking into our everyday lives. It would seem to be time to take similar steps in industry and commerce, where an understanding of human nature is basic and where so much is at stake. For instance, we already know that fear and psychological depressions are more dangerous than economic setbacks; in fact, they often cause such setbacks. The interdependence of cold, sober business statistics and deeply seated human motivations is obvious even to the completely untrained. In marketing where we have no direct control over the factors with which we must contend and where we must make decisions on the basis of what is at best intangible evidence—here especially we need all the clear insight we can get.

Cooperation between the practical businessman and the psychologist is not just a nice or desirable state; rather it is an essential development if we are to progress from a medicineman stage of selling and advertising to a scientifically controllable one. Of course the businessman will not and cannot apply to the psychologist for help with all his marketing problems. There are a number of clearly visible

225

situations, however, when he can reasonably assume that normal research resources will not suffice. Questions like the following present real challenges:

Do You Really Know Why Your Customers Like or Dislike Your Product? Your customers tell you they bought a particular make of car because of its "performance," "economy," or "trade-in value." Are you sure these are the real reasons? Many surveys have shown that they are but pure rationalizations. They were mentioned in answer to the usual type of questioning because they sounded better, more logical. This becomes clear when you compare the motivating reasons for purchase given by Ford buyers, Plymouth buyers, and Chevrolet buyers; they are exactly the same for all three.

Deeper reasoning, then, must have been at work. Emotional factors such as loyalty, fear, and tradition are usually much more important than the actual quality differences which people are likely to offer as reasons. Obviously an advertising campaign which does not rely on the answers to "surface" questioning but which capitalizes on the actual motivating forces revealed by questioning that digs down into people's minds is much more likely to be effective.

Do You Know What Kind of People Your Customers Are? Although you may know the average age, income, educational level, and so on, of your customers—the factors usually sought for in market surveys—you may still not know the real factors that determine their acceptance or rejection of your product. For example, the degree of customer security or insecurity (in a psychological sense) may be the all-important variable which you have to ascertain before you can market your product intelligently. Suppose the product is a deodorant. The appeals which will influence persons who are desperately anxious to be socially acceptable may fall flat with persons who already feel satisfied with their position.

Are You Sure You Do Not Insult Your Customers? Suppose you are in the pipe tobacco business. Your advertising uses colorful language to describe the aroma of your tobaccos in order to make them sound more desirable than your competitors' products. Yet, unless you are careful, many of the words you use may arouse feminine associations of a nature unpleasant to the pipe smoker, intent as he is on convincing himself of his masculinity. A study showed "aromatic," which on the surface sounds like a perfectly good word, to be of this type. Many times manufacturers run up against other such obscure inhibitions, deep-seated prejudices, hatreds, negative associations, and unconscious forms of resistance which, when uncontrolled, may play havoc with their sales.

These are just a few examples of the kinds of problem which a businessman selling consumer products may run into and which, when attacked by customary means, i.e., either by pure guess work or by inadequate, purely statistical market research, may lead to trouble. In a broad sense, any time a businessman is in doubt about why his customers act the way they do, or, in other words, any time he must deal with a *why* question, a truly scientific approach to his problem is indicated.

Of course there are many questions that can be answered by the customary type of market research department or outside research agency —as a matter of fact, all those questions where the answers are clear in the customer's mind. The consumer knows how many bottles of beer he consumes in one week, which brand of bread he buys, where he buys his motor oil, and so on. The reader can report that he read only parts of a certain book and which parts they were. The radio listener can reliably inform the researcher that he fell asleep during this program or laughed 14 times during that program.

But the moment the investigator attempts to get the answers to such *why* questions as what actually made respondents switch from one brand of soap to another, or to find out their *true* opinions about such matters as various brands of soft drinks, then he is in trouble. What he is doing is the same thing that the physician would be doing if he asked his patient for an explanation of his ills. The patient, looking for some causal relationship, as he saw it, might explain the pain in his right side as due to overwork and strain, whereas actually it might be the beginning of an appendicitis. Of course, the patient might also chance to be right, especially if he had picked up a smattering of physiological knowledge, but the odds are against him. Curiosity, unwillingness to accept superficial explanations, good common sense— all these may help to get the right answer. Nevertheless there are very few of us who, experiencing a bad pain, do not desire to consult the expert, in this case the doctor, because of the importance of having the best possible diagnosis.

SIGNIFICANCE OF FINDINGS

While up to about ten or fifteen years ago businessmen were entitled to assume an attitude of regretful resignation, tinged with hope that their intuitions were right, at the very times when they wanted to be sure that they understood the basic function of their products and services, this is no longer true. It is not necessary now to face with perplexity, or even to dismiss as unanswerable, questions concerning the apparently mysterious forces that control the success or failure of a product, a magazine, a service, a motion picture, a radio program, or a Broadway show. For modern social psychology has undergone considerable changes over the last decade or so; it has become much more capable of producing practical findings.

Let us look now at some examples of the kind of thing the psychologist can find out for the businessman, thus adding strength to market research in its task of measuring and understanding the interrelation of human needs and their satisfactions. We shall then, in a subsequent section of the article, go on to discuss briefly the technical methods by which such findings are produced.

The Customer's Inner Needs

The psychologist can be helpful in finding out the needs and innermost wishes the consumer expects to see fulfilled by a type of product. This is what might be called the functional approach.

In a study the author recently completed for *Time* magazine, direct questioning about why people read *Time* evoked such answers as "It condenses the news for me," or "It is written in a brilliant style," or other similar quality *descriptions* of the magazine. In the functional research approach, however, we are not so much interested in finding out what people think about the magazine, or what they think they think about it, as we are in finding out what the magazine actually *does* for them. In the case of *Time*, this approach showed that one of the major functions of the magazine was to provide what the psychologists call "ego-benefits." That is, it bolstered up the readers, because it made them *feel* like busy executives whose position demanded that they be well informed but whose schedule was so crowded that they needed to get their news quickly. As one reader actually said, in response to deeper questioning: "When I read *Time*, I like myself." Such a statement is quite different from a descriptive remark about the product itself; it depicts a real psychological effect produced on the reader.

Now such a functional finding permits action on the part of the publisher. For example, if he knows that some of his readers are looking

for such ego-benefits, then he can make use of this knowledge. The more *Time* offers those readers the opportunity to experience this kind of feeling by the way the magazine is written and edited, the better they like the magazine and the more they are inclined to buy further copies at the newsstand or to renew their subscriptions. Furthermore it can be decided, and actually has been, to make a specific appeal to this feeling in *Time's* circulation promotion efforts, where a fraction of a percentage point improvement in the rate of returns will add up to a substantial dollars-and-cents savings. Presumably the appeal will be introduced subtly and in such a way as to re-enforce the description of the magazine's quality, features, and services.

It is worth noting, too, that in this way *Time* introduces an important new aspect into the whole field of education. For hundreds and possibly thousands of years our good-intentioned educators have attempted to convince us that it is not an easy job to increase our knowledge. *Time* encourages and produces the opposite conviction. While the academic archeologist tells you that it takes scores of years really to know the field, *Time* promises you a workable knowledge after only a comparatively few pages of reading.

For the Chrysler Corporation the application of modern functional research operated in the following way. The objective of the executives concerned was to use advertising to get more people to switch from other makes of cars to Chrysler cars. To do this they needed to know why about 75% of all car buyers purchase the same make of car year after year; they wanted to change that habit. Direct questioning uncovered the apparent reason: rational satisfaction with the quality of the previously owned car. The obvious advertising approach, dealing with such surface rationalization, would have been to stress the fact that the new make of car was startlingly different and better, that it was time to get rid of the old car with all its repair bills and troubles.

From the point of view of the psychological findings this was exactly the opposite of the correct approach. A psychological survey revealed that the real reasons for the high percentage of repeat purchases were based on unconscious fear of automobiles as dangerous, powerful instruments, taking the form of fear of the unfamiliarity of a new make of car, fear of disloyalty to the old car which had demonstrated its safety, emotional attachment to the old car, and similar factors. Instead of talking down the old car, the advertiser needed to compliment the prospective customer on his friendship and loyalty to the presently owned car and to promise him that the new car would permit him to feel the old familiarity within a few hours. The Chrysler executives decided to use this approach in all their advertising and to include it in their sales training courses. The result was a 100% rise in the Starch rating of Chrysler and Plymouth advertisements and a substantial increase in sales.

For the same reasons, the salesmen's usual habit of kicking the tires of old cars brought for trade-in was found to be psychologically detrimental to the transaction. Controlled tests showed that customers actually accepted lower trade-ins when the old car was complimented —"It's easy to see this car was well taken care of"—than when it was deprecated. Thus, functional research reveals the deeper-lying, real motivations for buying behavior and permits correct, effective sales methods to be substituted for others that are often dangerously wrong business-wise.

Creative Programming

The same development of functional psychology can also be helpful in presentation of such a product as a radio program. Take the research for the CBS atomic bomb program, "Operations Crossroads," as an example. The ordinary approach would have been first at the content level—contemplating such considered questions of program format and presentation as whether it should be given in fictionalized form or as a round-table discussion or as a documentary. The functional approach, however, was to consider the desired effect of the program first, with the idea that the format and content should be subordinated to this all-important goal.

A study of polls and surveys had revealed that about 75% of the public were thoroughly scared by the atomic bomb but had largely chosen to dodge the issue. They wanted to keep the secret or build bigger battleships or have the bomb outlawed, or simply felt that things should be left to take care of themselves—all more or less inadequate solutions. It became clear that if this radio program was to have any effect at all it would have to be in the direction of cutting short all these forms of escapism.

By applying functional research techniques to the study of this problem, it was found that the main program aim should be to convince the listener that he had to face the real issue, which (it seemed to those responsible) concerned the necessity of a world government. Therefore it was necessary to demonstrate to the listener in a step-by-step, almost psychoanalytical procedure, descending from surface forms of escapism to deeper psychological mechanisms, that none of the escapist solutions could possibly work. The method decided on was to stage a series of interviews in which the people questioned began by advocating the escapist solutions and then were forced gradually to admit the illogic of their positions. Once the program had thus indirectly pushed the listener into a corner, so to speak, getting him to admit to himself that all the escapist solutions were inadequate, it then could lead him to positive suggestions. Even though it might enrage him in the course of getting him there, it could leave him at the end of the broadcast with a feeling of encouragement and clarity as to what decision he would have to make.

Once this clear concept of the psychological structure of the program had been worked out in detail, research had come very much closer to defining the job of the creative writer. While all the artistic intuition and sense of drama still had full play in the actual dramatic translation of this concept, the job of arriving at the finished product had been made a lot easier than if the nonfunctional type of research had been the only one applied to this program. Thus, the functional research approach provides a way to bridge the gap between purely descriptive research and creative work.

The same technique can be applied to any other problem in programming and advertising. (It has already been applied in studies of shoes, magazines, candy, chewing gum, and movies.) The first step is to ask what psychological function the message or product should fulfill and how it can be achieved. Then, like a medical practitioner systematically examining several hypotheses suggested by his knowledge of blood, lungs, heart, and so on, the researcher translates the clinical picture into a series of directly observable indices in a questionnaire and makes a quantitative check-up of the various buying, reading, or listening mechanisms which he has reason to think may be involved. Next comes the creative job of programming or advertising indicated by the research. The final step is a clearly focused test of whether or not the average listener has actually been induced to do what it was intended he should do. In the case of the "Operations Crossroads" program, psychological audience tests indicated the success of the methods used, and this was borne out by the many requests for rebroadcasts, the unusually large number of enthusiastic letters, and so on.

Dynamic Behavior

Many research procedures concern themselves quite properly with critical judgments made by the audience, the ad reader, and so on. Often this approach has a static aspect, however. The inquiry is concerned, for instance, with whether a particular advertisement has been accepted or rejected, or how many people have read it—and many advertisers may have a pretty accurate answer to such questions. But much more important than this is a knowledge of what *happens* in the mind of the reader as he inspects the advertisement. What are his impressions? What is he thinking about? What associations does the advertisement create? What desires or blockages does it mobilize? Even when the advertiser knows the motivations determining purchase of his product, he still has to know whether he is correctly translating these appeals into copy in terms of present-day motivations and needs of buyers.

The dynamic effects produced by advertising and other selling techniques are particularly important now that people are so concerned with help in planning for the future and with guidance in finding their way again within the intricacies of peacetime economy and the transition to a free market. While a company's advertising and sales approach may be technically excellent, special emphasis should be given now to the actual help that sales representatives can give to customers. Several magazine studies showed that the readers were mainly interested in those features which helped them chart the future, which attempted to organize their thinking, and which gave them hope. It is obvious that if the same function were fulfilled by salesmen and advertising, the customer would just as eagerly reach to the product for gratification.

To avoid soliciting meaningless aesthetic judgments from ad readers, the author has developed a procedure whereby the attitude toward the product and its verbal and pictorial associations are matched with the associations and impressions created by an advertisement. Take oleomargarine for an example. Questioning revealed that one of the major prejudices against it stems from a feeling of artificiality,

low social acceptance, and general doubt about the composition and nutritive values of the product. It would seem logical, then, that a correctly conceived advertisement would serve the purpose and effect of combating these prejudices and of rendering reassuring information. Yet questioning further revealed that most women visualize margarine as a fatty white substance which is changed into an artificial yellow by mixing a powder into it, and those asked to react to margarine ads reported that the feeling of artificiality was heightened by the extreme brightness of the ad colors (and in some cases surrealist trees in the ad). There was also a general feeling that a special effort had been made to combat consumer suspicion. Because the readers thought it was done in an obvious, exaggerated fashion, a general feeling of insincerity was created, further increasing the feeling of artificiality.

Phonograph records, especially classical records, constitute another case. When you talk to people about their record collections, they connect records with such things as memorable events in their lives, demonstrate their pride of possession with a sweeping gesture indicating the size of their record collections, and make many other references to the meaning of records in the lives of their families. Today, with a much greater consciousness of being eye-witnesses to history-in-the-making, most people have a heightened desire to enjoy themselves while they can and to hold on to their fast-moving lives in tangible forms. In addition to stressing the quality of records as exemplified by the name of the conductor or singer, the technical processes used in recording, and so on, it simply is good selling psychology to make use of more personal appeals based on what records actually mean to buyers. Yet relatively few of these basic psychological appeals are translated into record advertisements.

If psychological investigation shows a consistent discrepancy between the presently existing product attitude and the effects and impressions created by an advertisement, it is obvious that the ad is not doing the job it could, even though the figures show it to be well read. Research on advertisement effectiveness is another example of the application of modern scientific thinking which can help the sales executive or market research man to gauge the success of his attempts to win and influence the consumer. This research, instead of relying on the erratic, subjective, and static likes and dislikes of ad readers, proceeds on the basis of analysis of basic human emotions, expressions, feelings, and associations, ascertained by objective, scientific, psychological means.

Multiple Motivations

Most actions are motivated by a whole field of reasons. In other words, we speak of multiple motivations, all of them interlocking and acting together to produce the final result. Some of these reasons lie within ourselves; others, again, come from the environment. For example, you make love to a girl. Your motivations in doing so may be only partly related to a basic sex urge. You may want to feel powerful, or you may be in need of affection, or you may need to convince yourself of your manliness.

Modern motivational research has to employ methods which can investigate these multiple motivations in their natural structure and mutual relationship without tearing them apart or arranging them in the artificial atomistic order of a check list. A method which the author has tried to develop, taking into consideration the "personality" approach, is the psycho-panel. A psycho-panel is a representative group of several hundred families about which not only factors such as age, income, and marital status are known (as in the case of the consumer panels which have already proved so helpful in commercial market research), but also personality factors such as whether the individual families are governed by the authority of the father or the mother, whether the members are secure or insecure, resigned or ambitious, overspending or miserly, conspicuous or modest, emotional or rational, escapists or realists, and so on. The psychological needs of the panel members are known specifically, and they can be interviewed and questioned when needed. The continuing relations build mutual confidence between interviewer and panel members and add reliability to the responses secured.

The actual methods of interviewing and testing, such as are used in connection with the panel, will be discussed later. All we want to do here is to bring out the significance for businessmen of the personality factors which can be thus uncovered. For example, suppose two families are found to resemble each other in income, family size, education—in short, they belong to the same group according to the socio-economic criteria of typical consumer research. But the members of one family may have a strong sense of security, be well balanced, optimistic, and have reached a high saturation of their needs; they may be content with the life they can lead on their income. The family next door, however, may consider the same income just a temporary one; its members may be insecure, pessimistic, and overambitious. Advertisers who plan their campaigns efficiently must regard these families as two different units, must remember that the general market is made up of both kinds of family, and must decide which they wish to solicit, and then act accordingly.

Whenever a product attitude appears to be influenced by personality factors, which is the case very frequently, use of the psycho-panel provides an opportunity for confirmation or refutation of the existence of such a relationship, since the files of each family unit in the panel include a long list of personality information gathered by an array of psychological tests, detailed depth interviews, and frequent family contacts. The psycho-panel serves as a sort of X-ray laboratory by use of which we can discover obscure and subtle relationships. For example, if a businessman has a hunch that degree of security influences the buying habits of his particular customers, he can ask questions of the secure and insecure members of the panel and thus find out whether there does exist an actual relationship between this personality factor and buying habits. This turned out to be significant with the deodorant mentioned earlier.

Rationalization vs. Real Motivations

The discovery of the existence of several levels of consciousness—the ego, superego, and unconscious—is the basis of another reason why modern psychological methods can help market research. People rationalize their actions and beliefs, try to justify them on moral and logical grounds. We are loath to admit that we sometimes act for completely irrational and possibly idiotic reasons. Almost automatically we construct a fool-proof system of explanations which is completely logical and, if possible, moral and ethical. Psychology, however, teaches us that many of our actions are guided by irrational and emotional reasoning. This is illustrated by many of the examples already cited, particularly that of the reasons for repeat purchases of cars.

Therefore, a research approach not capable of distinguishing between rationalizations and real reasons can go very far astray. The respondent in an interview is frequently unaware of his real motivations to action; they are unconscious.

This fact is extremely important. So-called "depth psychology" teaches us that unconscious reasons are usually more basic and powerful than are the conscious ones. Obviously, direct questioning runs no chance of success in uncovering unconscious motivations, so we are forced to introduce new and different methods for the investigation of *why* problems.

RESEARCH METHODS

The approach the author uses in his work is often termed "depth interviewing." But this phrase does not represent the total picture. It is completely misleading to use the terms "depth interviewing" and "motivational research" interchangeably. Depth interviewing is only *one* of the methods used in modern motivational research. Other methods are content analysis, laboratory experiments, effectiveness tests, field observations, psycho-panels, and finally statistical methods. (The psychologist, by the way, uses statistical methods to the same extent as any other researcher; the only difference is that he considers statistics a technical tool, like all the other procedures we have just mentioned, and not something which can substitute for sound psychological thinking.) Rather than trying to define these various methods separately, let us try to see how they would all work together in solving a specific problem.

We might have a problem of how believability of the curative effect of a stomach remedy can be achieved: Should it be through *logical* arguments and testimonials, or through reference to some directly observable feature of the medicine such as its color and consistency—even if *illogical?* Or we might have a question of the real motivations for buying life insurance: Are they *fear* and *solicitude* for the man's family, or are they more in the nature of *pride* in being a good family man? Or we might want to know why individuals tend to buy ice cream in specific stores: Is it *convenience,* as they say, even though they will walk by a nearer store selling the same brand, or has it something to do with the *feeling of luxury* they experience in their favorite store? We might have any of these problems, or a thousand more. But suppose our assignment is to find out the major gratifications of a certain motion picture, that is, what the effects of its showing are on the movie-goers— an admittedly difficult job since there are so many conflicting factors to be taken into account, but for that very reason requiring added insight.

Our initial task would be to analyze the problem in a psychological sense, to investigate all the possible domains in psychology and sociology which this problem touches. We would thus become somewhat oriented and could see what general fields should be covered in our research—aesthetics, personality research, leisure time occupations, family organization, mechanisms of emotion, frustrations, and so on. From this general survey of topics, a systematic procedure evolves. We know we are dealing with communication and that in a psychological sense any form of communication represents a stimulus-response situation.

Suppose, further, that the motion picture is an MGM "Red" Skelton comedy. Because it is a comedy, we would know that we were dealing with the difference in attitudes of people toward reality and toward comedy. In one such film which was investigated by the author, there were a few initial scenes that gave the members of the test audience, although they knew they were watching what was supposed to be a comedy, the idea that all the scenes they were about to see would be realistic. As the story progressed, many of the comic scenes became completely unacceptable because they were seen through the filter of reality set up by the initial scenes, yet they probably would have been satisfactory if seen as parts of a purely comedy plot. In other words, the research had to concern itself with the domains of realism and comedy and with identification.

In such a case there are really three research jobs to do: (1) investigate the stimulus, i.e., the motion picture; (2) study the responding individual or audience member; and (3) study interactions taking place between the stimulus and the respondent, such as identification, emotional response, and so on. All three are aimed at achieving a complete psychological understanding of the problem.

Psychological Understanding

Content analysis is used for the first research task. Scripts are taken apart, and we investigate possible psychological stimuli offered by the film, types of characters in the story, settings, and lessons which could possibly be taught by the drama. Here is where we might have become aware that the two contradictory frames of reference, reality and comedy, had become dangerously mixed in the film. In any event, having acquired a familiarity with the operating stimuli of the film, we could approach our second job, the movie-goer analysis, in a sound, direct way.

The movie-goer analysis is handled by the depth interview method (sometimes called "case study" method). This method cannot be explained by calling it a longer interview, an informal interview, or any similar name. It is simply a device which has been used by many clinical psychologists who have been confronted by the problem of finding out why their clients behave in a particular way. It might best be described as a procedure by which the respondent achieves an insight into his own motivations. In other words, for the respondent it is a sort of introspective method. Psychological laboratories have been using it for decades in the investigation of the complicated workings of the human mind.

In a depth interview the interviewer attempts to bring about a full and spontaneous expression of attitudes from the respondent. It is the proof of a good interview if at its end the respondent has the feeling that he himself has expressed his own reactions. After a satisfactory interview, some people remark, "I never knew that there was so much to going to the movies (or buying a pair of shoes). It just dawns upon me now why I do all these things." Such statements prove to us that we have succeeded in bringing about an understanding in the respondent which permitted him, and us, to perceive the true reasons, the basic motivations for his actions.

In our specific example, psychological interviews revealed a resentment against the comedian, who displayed an inane shirking of life's responsibilities and yet was rewarded with the girl, the job, and the money. The respondents, seeing themselves in the same kind of awkward dilemmas as "Red" Skelton, knew they would surely have to pay for their stupidity; and the fact that he "got away with it" unconsciously upset them.

The third step, investigation of the processes taking place between the stimuli and the respondents, uses another group of methods. It is necessary to study the processes of identification, catharsis, frustration, and other psychological concepts of a relatively complicated nature. Unfortunately they cannot be approached directly, but must be dissolved into their ascertainable components. Identification, for instance, has many ramifications: It must be clearly separated from admiration. There are different forms of identification—some harmful and some desirable. And different factors serve as the basis for identification. In our particular example, we would be concerned with how the men in the audience identified themselves with the film's supposed hero.

At the end of these three research tasks, we often have found sufficiently clear understanding of the problem we tackled to permit action —whether it be in the field of communications, advertising, merchandising, selling, or public relations. In many cases such a grasp of the basic psychological mechanism at work in the effect of a movie, in the acceptance or rejection of a product, and so on, will be the final step.

Quantitative Data

In many other cases, however, we would still need more precise quantitative data. In such cases, the preceding psychological research helps in the forming of meaningful hypotheses. Then indicator or clue questions can be developed to test the hypotheses. And when answers have been collected, counted, and tabulated, we can come up with accurate and significant figures.

To make this clearer, let us take another example—the problem of finding out why one brand of chewing gum was preferred over another. Without the preliminary psychological research, we might have been inclined to compare the flavors of various brands and to conclude from the expressed preferences for one specific brand that it was better liked because it had a better flavor. Having conducted such research, however, we would know that there were other reasons why this brand was preferred, such as a suggestion of fun (bubble blowing) and a feeling of aggressiveness (tougher chewing). In the questionnaires, therefore, we would try to uncover the extent of such psychological associations, and we would not just ask for flavor preferences but would introduce such clue or indicator questions as: "Which one of these various brands makes you think of fun?" and "Which one makes you think of the feeling of getting your teeth into it?"

In this way, the preceding psychological research helps in developing the kind of questions we need to ask in order to find out the quantitative facts we are after. In the case of the film which we discussed, the questions might be: "Which one of the characters was most like yourself?" "Whom did you have a feeling of trying to help?" By analyzing the answers to such questions, we can begin to measure the strength of the psychological factors involved.

Getting the answers and tabulating the results can be handled in the usual way: by sending out a great number of interviewers or questionnaires to a correctly selected sample of people. Once the returns are in, however, we are able to go far beyond the usual type of cross tabulating of age groups, education, income, and so on, because of the thorough understanding of our hypotheses and the intimate structure of the problems given us by our previous research. We gather our information from apparently widely separated fields and fit it together into a meaningful structure. All the elements of our procedure, beginning with the case studies and ending with the mass treatment of indicator questions, can be molded into a complete and integrated unit.

Thus, it is possible to deliver a scientifically correct and adequate answer to the initial problem of people's motivations in a specific field; e.g., the film failed to make the audience laugh as much as the producer hoped it would (1) because of the confusion between reality and comedy, in the case of men and women alike, and (2) because of the resentment against "Red" Skelton caused by his getting away with being a "jerk," particularly in the case of the younger men.

What is more, once we understand the mechanism of these motivations, we can also indicate the ways by which improvements can be made. As for the motion picture discussed, the film had already been released to the public and nothing could be done. The practical thing to do with motion pictures, however, would be to test them psychologically before release. It would have been comparatively simple to cut a few feet of film and remove the realistic scenes from the beginning of the "Red" Skelton comedy, thus eliminating the sense of confusion, and also to add a scene at the end in which Skelton stumbled and fell flat on his face, thus sending out the audience with a more comfortable feeling. Both minor changes would have unquestionably enhanced the picture's commercial success. Similarly, in the case of other types of product, psychological research should be conducted before outlays of possibly thousands of dollars have been wasted in ill-conceived advertising or selling effort.

In summary, then, social psychological research embraces problems which can be solved by merely counting noses, and it also includes problems which necessitate more complicated methods. Because in the last analysis all social psychology is concerned with the individual, his attitude, his motivations, and his behavior, it uses all those methods which help in better understanding of the individual. At the same time, every scientific procedure has to be capable of yielding generalized statements about groups and populations. The single individual can only be understood because of his membership in human society. Any true social psychological method has to be able to cover both these aspects in the most modern and advanced fashion science permits.

Although at first glance it may seem that this kind of psychological research would only add expenditures to already extended research and advertising budgets, the justification for it is similar to that for an X-ray needed to insure better care of a patient. Without the outlay for the X-ray, the treatment may remain ineffective and the cure unduly delayed. With the knowledge provided by real understanding of the causes of difficulties, however, a more concentrated and sharply focused attack on the problem is possible—and quite often at an ultimate dollars-and-cents savings. It is the wise man who knows the value of expert assistance.

Of course there are many problems not important enough to warrant psychological X-rays, and there are many problems where a sound, penetrating, common-sense approach will yield answers which are reliable for all practical purposes. Yet, even here a recognition of the principles discussed in this article can be helpful, if only in stimulating and directing the thinking of a company's regular research department. There still will remain, however, many problems that need and deserve expert assistance from trained psychologists, either on a consulting basis or, in the case of large companies, as a specialized part of the company's own staff.

37. Inside Marketing Research

LEO BOGART

A variety of books and publications have attempted to deal with the body of social science as source material for the marketing practitioner. The present essay arises from the feeling that there has been very little of the reverse interest. The field of marketing research has remained remarkably free of investigation for what it is—an important contemporary institution, perhaps no less worthy of scholarly attention than such old stand-by's as the parole system, the child guidance clinic, or the college sorority.[1] (This seems to reflect a general lack of interest, by today's social scientists, in the consumption aspect of society, which so fascinated Le Play and Booth. Not only marketing research, but all the institutions of marketing—like the supermarket, the wholesale warehouse, the discount store, the advertising agency—remain almost unexplored territory for the social scientist with a reportorial curiosity about the everyday life of our time.)

The interest of sociologists in the growth of marketing research has lagged far behind that of the general literate public. With the publication of such books as *The Insolent Chariots*[2] and *The Hidden Persuaders*,[3] people have become quite used to the idea that business is engaged in a continuous and expensive effort to probe their tastes and motives, and the widespread feeling that marketing researchers are engaged in sinister manipulations may not be too distinct from the public impression of social science in general.

Research of a kind that social scientists sometimes regard as their private domain is today an accepted and integral part of the American marketing system. Vast sums are expended to study the attitudes, preferences, and choices of consumers,[4] and these studies have become increasingly relied upon by business managements in their decision making.

Much of this research entails the use of the systematic social survey method. Such surveys are done (1) to determine the position of competitive brands in the market, both in terms of actual unit or dollar sales and in terms of con-

[1] Several noteworthy efforts have been made to bridge this gap: Robert Dahl, Mason Haire, and Paul F. Lazarsfeld, *Social Science Research on Business: Product and Potential* (New York: Columbia University Press, 1959) and Christen T. Jonassen, "Contributions of Sociology to Marketing," *Journal of Marketing*, Vol. 24, No. 2, October 1959, p. 29.

‡‡ SOURCE: Reprinted by permission from the *Public Opinion Quarterly*, Vol. 27, No. 4, Winter 1963, pp. 562–577.

[2] John Keats, *The Insolent Chariots* (New York: Lippincott, 1958).

[3] Vance Packard, *The Hidden Persuaders* (New York: David McKay, 1957).

[4] In the United States alone, perhaps $300 to $400 million a year is budgeted in the general area of consumer research by companies, government agencies, and various other groups. This figure is my own estimate, developed by several alternative procedures: (1) taking research as a percentage of marketing cost, (2) adding an overhead and out-of-pocket cost factor to the total research payroll, (3) adding up some guesses of the total billings of United States research organizations.

sumer awareness and acceptance; (2) to study the prevailing consumption patterns of different segments of the population in relation to particular products and brands; (3) to understand the tastes and motivations that underlie opinion and behavior in the market place; (4) to evaluate the influences on consumer action and attitudes, including the opinions and activities of the retailer and the effects of display, promotion, and advertising; (5) to determine how successfully various techniques of persuasion and communication appeal to popular tastes and thereby influence the purchase of goods and services; (6) to compare the opportunities that various media provide for communication with different segments of the public.

But the interdependence of marketing research and social science goes beyond their common use of survey techniques. Consumer and media research represent a rich source of data on the social aspects of technological change. Marketing research includes the unsystematic collection and evaluation of field intelligence; the systematic study of statistics on distribution, sales, inventory, display, and pricing; and analysis of basic economic indicators developed through a variety of means that involve sampling but not interviewing. A great deal of this information (e.g., demographic trend analysis, studies of shifts in the income pyramid, surveys of retailing distribution, cost-of-living studies) is organized in terms of concepts drawn (consciously or otherwise) from the social sciences.

The field of consumer research has in the last decade been increasingly attractive as a source of employment by social scientists. Fifteen years ago, psychologists, sociologists, and anthropologists were almost a curiosity in marketing circles. Today their presence is taken for granted. In the days when marketing research was new and relatively unaccepted, the practitioner faced a major problem of communication with his lay colleagues, management, or clients. But in a business world made up increasingly of specialists with private vocabularies, the social scientist is no longer in a unique or disadvantaged position. And the continuing growth of the research and development function in industry has made it unfashionable to question the practicality of the scientist and his works. As in the case of R and D in the physical sciences, the growth of marketing research has broadened industry's tolerance for intellectuals, for off-beat personalities, for members of minority groups.

One effect of the widespread use of marketing research has been the development of a superficial familiarity with research terms and concepts on the part of an enormous number of people in the business community. Not only does this include almost every practitioner in the advertising field from agency presidents down to mailroom boys, but it includes the top managements of every substantial corporation in the country and middle managements in marketing and sales. All these executives are periodically (and in some cases incessantly) exposed to presentations of research findings, in which such things as sampling tolerances and social-class differences are discussed as a matter of course. This, in some instances, leads to a pseudo- or semi-sophistication in the use of terminology, so that the professional researcher in his dealings with nonresearch colleagues and clients can never be too sure of how much they really know about the underlying techniques and theories.

Some elements in the marketing research system are primarily concerned with the gathering, interpretation, and analysis of data, others more with utilization. Yet, it becomes increasingly difficult to draw the line between the two, since more and more companies that sponsor research today also to some degree conduct their own. This follows from the fact that, once an organization's research requirements pass a certain point, it requires its own staff specialist to set specifications, select suppliers, and supervise or monitor the output. But as this specialist acquires greater acceptance and greater self-confidence in the substantive field or industry that employs him, he will naturally want to become directly and closely involved with the details of the work that is done for him. And so he is likely to build his own empire, albeit without conscious imperialistic pretensions.

Research is used in marketing and advertising for a variety of reasons. Above all, it permits the businessman to observe and to influence the continuing drama of his own product's struggle in the competitive market place. Research gives him the measure of the constant change within the market. That change is wrought by the actions of individual competing companies, developments in the technology of production and distribution, and shifts in public tastes, needs, and wants.

This dynamic quality is at the root of the fascination that marketing can arouse in its practitioners. Their operating decisions on behalf of the product they sell are moves in a game, a game in which there is uncertainty about the rules and even about the identity of the other players. Marketing research provides a scorecard on which the progress of the contest is observed. It is inevitable, therefore, that the researcher is himself swept up in the game as he watches the changing position of products and brands.

Academic critics of marketing research often wonder how intelligent and well-trained people can dedicate their time to examination of the market shares for soap flakes or to comparison of advertising copy appeals for headache remedies. But the drama is not in the product itself (cultural artifact or social symbol that it may be); the drama is in the network of human institutions that surround it: rival manufacturing firms, distributors, retail outlets, advertising agencies, and media. The researcher's own intense involvement with relatively trivial data may reflect his personal loyalties or his clinical interest in the individuals and groups whose careers and fortunes face fresh uncertainties each business day.

THE MARKETING RESEARCH PROFESSION AS AN EXTENDED PRIMARY GROUP

The practitioners—professional, administrative, and clerical—who make up the marketing research community maintain a high consciousness of kind. While not all of them are personally known to each other, most of them (at least at the professional level) have at least one common acquaintance. The research world is the significant reference group by whose standards they tend to estimate their own professional actions, and the criteria thus set are often more stringent than those of their own employers or clients.

Within the total membership of the American Marketing Association, there are perhaps 2,000 or 3,000 persons whose primary preoccupation is with marketing research.[5] There are, in addition, perhaps another 10,000 or 15,000 people who belong to the research community either in a professional, analytical capacity, or as interviewers, coders, clerks, typists, field workers, punchcard or IBM machine operators, and the like. Many of the latter are in only a peripheral relationship to the research world, either because they consider their jobs to be temporary

or transient or because they see them as "just a job" within some bigger industry (advertising, automobiles, toiletries, television).

Within the larger marketing research community, there are several hundred people who constitute an elite by virtue of the importance of their jobs, the importance attributed to their jobs because of the prominence of their employers, or their public visibility in scholarly productivity or organizational politics. This is not really a single body but a set of interlocking elites, each with its own area of specialization, derived either from original professional schooling or from common interest in a particular voluntary association or friendship clique within the world of research.

The growth of the field and the proliferation of specialties within it have led to a steady growth of its professional bodies. The American Marketing Association, with its broad, large membership, has not only a national program of publications and conferences but an active local program through its chapters in all major American cities. The American Association for Public Opinion Research includes those market researchers whose original training was in sociology or psychology. The Market Research Trade Association is made up of individuals primarily concerned with field work and preoccupied with such questions as the rate of compensation for interviewers, laws restricting polling, credit and financing of research organizations, etc. On a completely different level of specialization is the American Psychological Association's Division 23 (Consumer Psychology) and Division 14 (Industrial Psychology).

There are active and ably staffed research committees or councils working with such organizations as the American Association of Advertising Agencies, the Public Relations Society of America, the Bureau of Advertising of the American Newspaper Publishers Association, the Television Bureau of Advertising, the National Association of Broadcasters, and the Magazine Advertising Bureau. There are foundations like the Advertising Research Foundation and the newly created Marketing Science Foundation, each with its own roster of professional committees. In addition, New York City houses several small but influential monthly luncheon groups with a restricted membership —the Market Research Council, the Copy Research Council, the Radio-Television Research Council, and the Media Research Directors Association. And the above is by no means a complete inventory.

---

[5] These are, again, my own estimates.

When one considers that persons active in these organizations are often as likely as not involved in other peripheral professional or trade association activity involving either their original field of academic specialization or their present field of substantive interest, it is apparent that the meetings are frequent and the personal interaction is intense.

The informal network of interpersonal relationships among marketing research practitioners represents the strongest support for the maintenance of professional standards of conduct, and keeps at a minimum the deliberate bias that uninformed outsiders sometimes attribute to commercial research.

Because the research world represents a primary group of acquaintances for so many of its active members, there is within it a relatively high tolerance of incongruous viewpoints and opposing competitive interests. Marketing research partakes of the high job mobility that characterizes the whole field of marketing. This mobility in turn reflects the fact that the marketing function occupies the pivotal position in the competitive struggle for business survival, and personnel shifts often reflect the changing fortunes of businesses themselves.

It has become common for individuals to move back and forth among university research bureaus, commercial research firms, corporations, media, advertising agencies, and government bureaus.[6]

INSTITUTIONAL STRUCTURE IN MARKETING RESEARCH

In a large corporation today, survey research may be carried on in a number of different departments—public relations or employee relations departments or the controller's office, as well as through the sales or marketing departments. Thus, research focuses on different significant groups—the general public, residents of plant communities, employees, stockholders, audiences for the company's advertising, prospective or actual users of its products. In larger companies, these different studies (all employing much the same range of techniques) are handled by separate staffs within the framework of individual operating departments, often with little or no internal communication—let alone liaison or coordination.

The institutional structure of the marketing research world is integrated with the general structure of contemporary business bureaucracy. The table of organization of the research department in a corporation or advertising agency is typically set up along hierarchical lines that are the counterpart of those in other departments of the company. Such a department will usually number among its staff some people who are not professional researchers. A trusted "old company man" with a good substantive knowledge of the business may be assigned to head up research on the assumption that practicality and administrative skill are the main qualifications for the job. Or the department may be a way station for new trainees, a strategic point at which they can learn something about all aspects of the business before they move on to executive positions elsewhere in the organization.

The traditional professional colleague relationship that exists even between junior and senior staff members of an academic institution is replaced in the commercial research organization by the conventional relationships of employee and supervisor. The junior's role too often is not that of an apprentice craftsman but that of a hired hand, just as the senior's function is less that of counselor than of administrator.[7]

As in every small service operation, the dedication of the researcher to his task is often out of all proportion to remuneration or profit. He is likely to spend a disproportionate amount of time on a project that interests him either because of its intrinsic fun or intellectual stimulation, because of the prestige of doing it and the prospects of getting further assignments, or because he likes the client. Conversely, he may slough off with a minimum of effort those projects which are routine and dull or in which the client is cold or demanding.

Research organizations chronically underestimate the cost of jobs because of their anxiety

---

[6] To illustrate: Not long ago a retiring president of the American Association for Public Opinion Research, who had held a number of top-level positions in the course of his marketing research career, joined a university research staff to study for a doctorate in sociology. At about the same time, another president of the Association left his distinguished career as a professor of sociology to become a vice president of a great corporation.

[7] This transformation applies generally to the scientist in a bureaucratic setting. Cf. William M. Evan, "Role Strain and the Norm of Reciprocity in Research Organizations," *American Journal of Sociology*, Vol. 68, 1962, p. 346.

to get the business, and this anxiety often reflects an inherent interest in the problem of the client. (Incidentally, because of this chronic underbudgeting, research reports tend to be ground out at fever pitch on overtime to meet the deadline or to get them off the researcher's back once the deadline is past.)

Nonrational considerations may also govern the operating decisions of a research department in a corporation, agency, or medium, since for such institutions research expenditures represent an investment whose ultimate return is to be measured in the success of the over-all enterprise, and so is almost immune to the rules of cost accounting.

The choice of a research supplier on the part of a company in some cases reflects a competitive award to the lowest bidder—that is, the lowest bidder among the favored few who are invited to bid. A firm with the right reputation will get assignments at a premium price that presumably reflects its higher operating costs and the superior talents it employs. (This may be justified as much by the supposition that work done by a prestige firm will have greater management acceptance as by the expectation that the job will be better done.) In an established relationship between supplier and client, issues of cost and technical competence to do a particular job may be considered wholly secondary to the research firm's understanding of the client's problems and the trust and personal rapport between the two parties to the contract.

One research firm may be chosen over another because of geographical proximity or other, reasons of convenience. Another reason might be the degree of specialization on the part of the firm, the extent to which it provides a unique service with which other firms cannot compete.

ADVERTISING MEDIA RESEARCH

Every advertising medium conducts and uses research in an effort to demonstrate that it can deliver desirable audiences more efficiently than its competitors.[8] An unusual catalytic function is served by media research, which, unlike most marketing studies, is publicized and talked about. Media research projects involve large budgets and are, therefore, sought after by research firms. Moreover, because a lot of money is involved,[9] media are reluctant to entrust such studies to research firms that do not already have an established reputation. Since the medium does research to promote its own self-interest, the methodology must be acceptable to the marketing or advertising trade, and this makes it vital to attach to it a name that is already associated with high standards of professional sophistication and integrity. Thus, major media research projects tend to be concentrated in the hands of a relatively few firms rather than to be spread out, like consumer research. The firms that conduct media research are publicized all the more. Their reputation is enhanced with each major study, and thus they are more likely than ever to attract marketing research projects from major clients.

To the degree that research is a service that must be sold, its successful practice calls for talents other than the technical and scientific: personal charm, clarity of expression, administrative skill, the ability to present or dramatize research findings, and, perhaps most important, the capacity to make results meaningful to the layman by extracting conclusions that can be acted upon. A research executive who combines these talents must redefine his personal values as his primary role becomes that of entrepreneur or corporate manager. He thus emerges as a marginal man between the worlds of business and scholarship. The "sense of conflict" that academic social scientists commonly attribute to their colleagues in the commercial world really manifests itself at this point in an individual's career rather than at the initial point, where he turns his attention away from juvenile gangs or unmarried mothers and toward the subject of soft drinks or ketchup. (Remember that the use of ketchup also reflects mysteries of human behavior. Much as the student of ketchup may wonder whether his work is truly meaningful—shouldn't he really be studying gangs?—so might the student of gangs have qualms about whether he shouldn't really be studying the social consequences of nuclear warfare.) Role conflict, far more than anxiety

---

[8] Research by media covers audience characteristics and behavior, market descriptions, and studies of product distribution and consumer attitudes. Such research is conducted by individual newspapers, magazines, radio and television stations and networks, and also by the various media associations, including the Outdoor Advertising Association, the Direct Mail Advertising Association, and the like. Studies are also made by representative firms that sell space or time in local media to national advertisers.

[9] By "a lot of money" I mean in the range of $50,000 to $1 million.

about subject matter, is at the root of the business researcher's struggle over personal values.

The world of marketing and advertising is crowded with crypto-painters, crypto-poets, and crypto-politicians who face their day-to-day assignments with varying degrees of disillusionment or cynicism, and the marketing researcher who is secretly meant for higher things must take his place on the line.

RESEARCHERS AND
RESEARCH ORGANIZATIONS

Specialized service organizations, notably advertising agencies, are important in the market research world both because of the research they do themselves, through their own internal staffs, and also because their clients often rely on them heavily for planning, interpretation, and evaluation of external studies, and for the choice and supervision of outside research suppliers. On a much smaller scale, management-consulting and public relations firms become involved in marketing projects that use survey methods.

The large corporation in American life is characteristically thought of as impersonal in its spirit and collective in its management, and the researcher who is a corporation executive necessarily conforms to its style. It is a little more difficult to position the researcher in an advertising agency, because agencies themselves span a broad spectrum. The smaller, younger agencies often reflect the presence of a single strong leader. The larger firms are relatively impersonal and bureaucratic, with compartmentalized specialties and complex systems and procedures for planning and review. Executive responsibility may be diffused among a number of personalities, each one dominant in a specialized domain or on a particular group of accounts.

From the standpoint of the advertising agency, research may be a profitable service that it seeks to sell its clients—if it can do so on the premise that research represents an extra above and beyond its normal obligation to plan advertising wisely. The agency normally absorbs the costs of desk research, like economic or media analysis of data already published. It may or may not feel that its 15 per cent commission adequately covers the cost of researching the so-called "creative product"—the possible variations in the form and content of the advertising message.

Since the agency's operating costs vary from one account to another (depending on the account's size, media use, and miscellaneous requirements), policy may dictate flexibility in the face of the client's predictable demand that the agency test its output. And in all the consequent jockeying and bargaining, researchers for agency and client alike become deeply involved, since cutting costs means changes in research design. (This merely illustrates the point that the researcher's administrative responsibilities and substantive interests continually push him to assume a role that may be out of phase, or even in conflict, with his professional interest.)

Research firms for the most part are perceived as the projection of an individual personality or founder. Even as firms become larger and more successful, and as a strong second echelon emerges who carry on the day-to-day operating responsibilities, there is a tendency for clients to insist on the services and the presence of the principal, whom they identify with the unique or special qualities of the company.

Thus the public face of the research organization is apt to be quite different from that of its internal private operations. Internally, a firm with a staff of between 30 and 150 people may be run in a bureaucratic manner with the conventional diffusion and decentralization of responsibility. But from the standpoint of the clients and of the general marketing public who follow its activities through trade media, the founder is the embodiment of all its wisdom. It is he in whose name the press releases are issued reporting the completion of new projects; it is he who bylines the articles and reports; it is he who is called upon personally to present the findings of studies over which his own personal control or direction may have been minimal. All this, plus the fact that it is his name that graces the top of the stationery, is apt to prove a source of frustration to the second echelon as it gains in maturity, professional self-confidence, and intimacy with clients and their problems.

The market research field, during its period of great expansion, has witnessed a proliferation of new ventures started by former lieutenants or seconds in command. And while the mortality rate of such businesses resembles the general survival pattern for small enterprises in today's economy, the field as a whole has undergone sufficient growth to make possible a movement of unsuccessful entrepreneurs into agencies, companies, or government jobs.

The relative youth of the field means that most of the principal firms are today still headed by their original founders, and it is only lately that the inevitable toll of retirement and death has raised questions about the capacity of these firms to continue under a collective management.

One must not underemphasize the power and influence of some of these men who led the first generation of market research entrepreneurs. Attractive and outstanding personalities, they have in many cases established close relationships with the top executives of corporations and advertising agencies. Since the subjects they study for their clients cut across the gamut of business problems, often including public and employee relations as well as marketing, their advice and counsel are often sought out on all matters of major policy. And since the stock-in-trade of the independent marketing researcher is his analytical objectivity and the capacity for keeping information confidential, he may very well become a father confessor to corporate executives who are considering business acquisitions, new product introductions, shifts in agencies, or revisions of advertising investment strategy.

But this kind of personal contact between researcher and corporate official cannot be maintained indefinitely. Within the corporation and within its advertising agency there may be distrust and resentment of an outsider who has the boss's ear, and, inevitably, as new generations assume responsibility both within the corporation and within the research firm itself, there can be a sudden weakening of the old ties built on individual trust and friendship rather than on institutional necessity.

DIFFERENCES OF PERSPECTIVE: ACADEMIC AND COMMERCIAL RESEARCH

There are essentially four areas of major difference in perspective between the researcher working within the framework of one of the marketing institutions described earlier and the same researcher tackling the same problem as an independent university scholar.[10] In part these differences reflect the general distinction

---

[10] Cf., for a discussion of some of these points, Robert O. Carlson, "High Noon in the Research Marketplace," *Public Opinion Quarterly*, Vol. 25, 1961, p. 331; Leo Bogart, "How to Get More Out of Marketing Research," *Harvard Business Review*, Vol. 34, No. 1, 1956, p. 74; Leo Bogart, "The Researcher's Dilemma," *Journal of Marketing*, Vol. 26, No. 1, 1962, p. 6.

between applied and academic research; in part they reflect the specific commercial setting of the market researcher.

1. The applied researcher is preoccupied with the substantive nature of the problem rather than with the theoretical implications of the findings. He makes more or less self-conscious use of theory in order to design and analyze his studies in a meaningful way. To the degree that he retains his academic interests he may be fascinated by the theoretical implications of his findings, and he may find the means for expressing this interest through professional channels. Only rarely does he find it possible to build his research design around a problem in theory. However, the lack of opportunity to pursue theory by no means precludes an interest in methodological innovation.

Although research is ostensibly a labor of love for the academic research man, and merely an assignment for the applied researcher, the difference in reality may not be great. (After all, much academic research is done because data are available or because of a grant, an existing research program, or a senior colleague's active interest. And much commercial research arises from proposals spontaneously initiated by the researcher.)

2. A preoccupation with substantive findings makes the marketing researcher far more likely to be descriptive rather than analytical in his approach to data. This is less true today than it was fifteen or twenty-five years ago, before social scientists and social science concepts were as prominent as they are now in marketing research. In its crudest form, marketing research is really an aspect of marketing intelligence (as when its task is to report product distribution or market share). In such research—which includes a very substantial part of all that is done—the essential figures are the global descriptive ones rather than the details which differentiate groups of consumers or segments of the market, or which illuminate variations in the over-all picture.

The social scientist is preoccupied with the "what" of human experience to the extent that it helps explain the "why." But this type of understanding is not essential to the pragmatic utilization of research findings in a commercial context.

One weakness of much consumer research is that the consumption function tends to be looked at in isolation. Market researchers are preoccupied with the behavior of individuals as consumers, as though it were, in fact, possible to divorce this one role from the many others that every individual enacts. This concentration on the single role, of course, reflects the pressures of time and money budgets in research. Lip service to the importance of other roles is given in the classification section at the end of the questionnaire, in which a few convenient demographic designations are intended to encapsulate the complex reality of multiple human interests.

3. The pace and scope of commercial applied research differs from the research of the university scholar. The latter is normally under little pressure of time, although he may also have few funds at his disposal to collect and analyze data. He therefore works his limited data intensively. The commercial researcher always works under restrictions of time and very often (contrary to impressions in the university world) within tight restrictions of budget as well. While he customarily works with larger and more representative samples than those common in academic research, restrictions of time and budget may force him to limit the number of questions he asks each respondent, the cross-tabulations he orders, and the time he spends analyzing interpretations of the data.

Very often the main value of what is learned is in the merely descriptive aspect of a study. From the standpoint of the decision maker, the most useful information is that which permits him to deploy his forces efficiently for appropriate action, and this means knowing what his competitors are up to, who buys his product, what people think of it, how it is distributed, and what audiences are reached by his advertising. The marketing executive who uses a research report is concerned with the analysis only to the extent that it gives him a reason for trusting the conclusions, but it is the conclusions that for him represent the heart of the matter. These conclusions may include interpretation and judgment on the part of the reseacher not merely as to the meaning of what he has learned but as to what should be done about it.

The separation of conclusions from interpretation or analysis is only one phase of the progressive attenuation of the evidence that commonly occurs in marketing research as a counterpart of the very division of labor that makes large-scale projects possible. The man who looks over the summary and writes the conclusions may not himself have participated in the analytical travail that preceded this stage. The analyst writing his tabulation plan for the data-processing house or preparing his report works with numbers and percentages that threaten to become demographic abstractions. These numbers are a long step removed from the human beings whose opinions the interviewers originally culled and whose recorded words were coded by still another set of specialists equally remote from interviewing and analysis. (By contrast, the independent scholar is apt to be personally involved in all stages from the field work to the writing of the complete report.)

The progressive disembodiment of the data brings about a loss of interest in the individual case and a concentration on the aggregates about which generalized statements can be made. This process is, of course, hardly unique to marketing research, but it is particularly in this field that the surveys succeed each other with such frequency and volume that the individuality of each project tends to be lost. And it is peculiarly in marketing research that the statistics emerging from surveys are quoted cheek by jowl with statistics on sales and inventories, with the danger that they, too, assume the property of "real things."

The widespread reliance on research in making business decisions is the substance of a chain of faith that stretches back eventually to the individual interviewer. In perhaps no other field is so much taken for granted about the integrity of the participants: the client trusting the conclusions drawn by the research analyst or the research firm, the analyst trusting his data processors, the field-work supervisor trusting his interviewers, and all of it, of course, eventually leading back to a faith in the ability of people to record meaningful opinions or reports of behavior on matters whose interest and significance is as slight and tangential to them as, in fact, the great mass of marketing decisions are.

4. In spite of his middle-class origins and station in life, the social scientist is, by the definition of his professional role, a freely moving agent in society. He must observe the affairs of kings and beggars with equal objectivity, and he trains himself to achieve rapport with Eskimo hunters, Bowery bums, movie stars, and coal miners, among others.

Turned marketing researcher, the social scientist acts as a link between business management and the public at large. His stock in trade is his ability to get at grass-root sentiment and report it back to those who encounter grass roots only at the golf course. To the degree that he continues to go out into the field to interview, he can continue to think of himself as *déclassé*, living outside the conventional social-class structure. But as he comes to deal with the data at several removes, he loses the immediacy of contact with the human qualities, problems, and motives of ordinary men. At the same time, his institutional life in the ivory tower becomes more demanding and the accretion of administrative duties makes his functional role more and more similar to that of other nonresearch executives in the same bureaucracy. Thus, subtly, his own personal biases and habits of thought become more and more identified with a particular social-class position—that of the business elite.

The applied social researcher shares with the academic social scientist the basic problem of asserting his professional authority as an expert in the face of the typical lay conviction that every human being is in a position to comment intelligently on the activities and motivations of every other.[11] Nowhere does this conviction hold more force than in the marketing area, where the familiar "mother-in-law" survey epitomizes the tendency to generalize from private experience. All the more is this so when the researcher deals, as he so often does, with people who have devoted a lifetime of study to a specialized subject to which he is an uninformed newcomer.

RESEARCH PRACTICE AND POWER RELATIONSHIPS

The practitioner's problem is further complicated by the fact that research may become an instrument to maintain or threaten power relationships in the business world. Research may be used as a weapon in a competitive or conflict situation directly involving corporate interests. Companies conduct studies to help offset the threat of government restrictive action through the courts or through legislation. Or they may conduct surveys to produce results of the "nine out of ten prefer our brand" type, in the hope that these will convince consumers of the superior merits of their product.

A good market position for a brand, as shown by national audits of store movement or consumer preference, will be used as evidence by a grocery salesman to convince a supermarket manager to stock his merchandise. But, since distribution in itself makes for sales, quite apart from the merits of the product or the effectiveness of the promotion behind it, this argument is of the nature of a self-fulfilling prophecy.

An advertising agency may conduct research to buttress its recommendations regarding media or copy themes, or regarding product pricing or marketing strategy. Or the agency may want a study to prove to the client that its stewardship of the account has been successful, by the criteria of the market place.

Within the corporation, research may be used as a weapon by factions who hold differing viewpoints on marketing strategy. Research findings are apt to be cited when opinions conflict between sales and advertising departments, or between product managers on established products and those charged with the development of new ones. The proposition, "Let's do a survey," may arise from an executive's conviction that he can win favor with his boss by proving himself in the right, or it may even reflect the boss's own conviction that he can prove his judgment sound in the face of the conflicting opinion of unruly subordinates.

In this respect, the research function should be seen as a by-product of bureaucratization in the large corporation, with its delicate balance of specialized but interdependent departments, each headed by an individual who can make decisions only within a framework of general managerial consensus and who may therefore be less and less likely to make any real decisions at all. Like the "Big Boss" of classical Victorian entrepreneurship, research may be the final arbiter of interdepartmental rivalries, making disinterested and Olympian judgments on which subsequent failures can always be blamed.

Just because so much marketing research is descriptive rather than analytical, it tends to support conservative business decisions. To the degree that research reports eschew explanations and hypotheses, they tend to discourage consideration of contingencies or innovations (which presume a more complex and dynamic model than the conventional division of the market into brand shares). In short, the *status quo* (be it in TV programming or soap scents) always finds support in research that reports on things as they are rather than as they might be.

---

[11] Cf. Lester C. Van Atta, "Arms Control: Human Control," *American Psychologist*, Vol. 18, 1963, p. 37: "Your fortune is to be specialists in a field that interests everybody. Your misfortune is that most laymen consider themselves to be expert psychologists. We are, in fact, all practitioners of the art, if not the science, of psychology."

C. Promotion

38. The Propaganda Function in Marketing
EDMUND D. McGARRY

The most controversial aspect of marketing is advertising. Ever since advertising began to appear, moralists and critics have complained that it distorted people's natural desires, misinformed them as to the products they needed, played upon their emotions, and led to waste of resources.

Proponents of advertising, on the other hand, have argued that it is an economical method of distributing goods, that it provides entertainment, and actually adds to the value of the goods advertised. The purpose here is not to discuss these issues directly, but rather to place the advertising process in its proper perspective as a function of marketing.

Advertising as used today is primarily a type of propaganda. The essence of propaganda is that it conditions people to act in a way favorable to or desired by the propagandist. It deliberately attempts to influence, persuade, and convince people to act in a way that they would not otherwise act. Propaganda had its birth in the attempt of the church to propagate the faith. It is used by leaders who seek a following in politics, in religion, and in all affairs which require action by large bodies of people.

In business it is used primarily by sellers to obtain a market by conditioning people in the market to accept the particular products offered. The growth of new techniques of communication has greatly extended the range of propaganda penetration, has expanded the number of products advertised, and has in-

creased the total amount of propaganda disseminated; but the aim of the messages carried is essentially unchanged since the beginning of civilization.

In fact, the use of force of argument instead of physical force marked the change from savagery to civilized living. "The creation of the world," said Plato, "is the victory of persuasion over force."

The use of persuasion is part of man's apparatus to adapt his way of life to change. Without some stimulus to action, man tends to be indifferent and apathetic to change, and unwilling to exert the effort which change necessitates. He prefers to follow his preconditioned routines rather than direct his effort in some different way. There must be some extra stimulus to action; and this stimulus is afforded either by compulsion of force or the threat of force, or by persuasion in the form of the written or spoken word.

PROPAGANDA VERSUS EDUCATION

Propaganda differs from education in that education presumably is oriented toward the dissemination of "truth"—dispassionate, objective, and unbiased. Pure education takes an impartial non-partisan point of view. It is not prejudiced; it has no slant. Yet all of us know that education must persuade to get students to study; it must propagandize to get funds.

Propaganda, on the other hand, by definition is biased, partial, and one-sided. It has an axe to grind; therefore it is always controversial. But unlike education, in which there is no sponsor, the sponsor of propaganda, particularly

✂ SOURCE: Reprinted by permission from the *Journal of Marketing* (National Quarterly Publication of the American Marketing Association), Vol. 23, No. 2, October 1958, pp. 131–139.

advertising propaganda, is known. And everyone knows what the sponsor is trying to do, what his motives are, and how he would like others to act. The sponsor of commercial propaganda must identify himself and the product he advertises and he must take the responsibility for it; otherwise, his propaganda cannot be directed to his purpose.

Every advertisement is designed to predispose its readers to a favorable consideration of its sponsor and his product. It is deliberately planned to make its readers and listeners take sides—to affiliate and ally themselves under its banner and to ignore all others.

Advertising is the obtrusive display of the conflict of interests in the market place. It represents a parade of the contestants in the battle for market supremacy, each imploring the audience to follow him. By its very nature advertising must be prejudiced in order to be potent.

THE BARRAGE EFFECT OF PROPAGANDA

Commercial propaganda is a social phenomenon, and its analysis must necessarily be in a social framework. It is, in fact, a part of our culture and at the same time exercises a considerable influence on that culture. Professor David M. Potter speaks of it "as an instrument of social control comparable to the school and the church in the extent of its influence upon society." [1]

Like other types of propaganda, advertising has a barrage effect. Although it is designed primarily to induce people who have the money and the need to buy the product, its effect cannot usually be confined to these. It creates a pattern of thought in a much larger population. Its results are diffuse and pervasive rather than selective. Because of this diffusion, many who are not in a position to buy, read, or listen to the advertisement, and many others who do not see or hear the message directly, learn of it from others by word of mouth.

Moreover, the pattern of thought created by advertising is likely to last for an indefinite period. If consecutive appeals are used, the effect tends to be cumulative both because of the widening group which sees it and because of the intensification of the impression it makes. This cumulative effect continues to a point of diminishing returns which is reached either

through saturation of the market, through the counteracting influence of competing messages, or through the saturation of receptivity.

There is another sense in which there is a spill-over of advertising effectiveness. This is what might be called the cross-product influence. It is said, for instance, that when vacuum cleaners were first advertised the demand for brooms increased; the inference is that the promotion of cleanliness in the home leads to the increased sales of any product that enhances cleanliness.

Still another type of spill-over effect is seen in the case of the firm selling a family of products in which the advertising of any one will increase to some extent the sales of other products in the same group. It seems probable also that the advertising of a particular brand influences the sales of all other products in the same use-class, even if they are marketed by competitors.

It would seem logical to assume that, when two competing advertisers attempt to promote their individual brands for a particular use, the impact will be greater than if only one is advertised; and, if the market can be expanded, the advertising of each will have a complementary effect on that of the other. If this is true, then there is a cumulative effect of advertising generally in the sense that, as more advertising is published, there is developed a greater propensity to purchase advertised goods of all kinds. The increase may be at the expense of non-advertised goods, it may be at the expense of savings, or it may result in greater effort on the part of consumers to secure more income.

Advertising vs. Personal Selling

Advertising today has to take a large part of the responsibility for making sales. To a great extent salesmen, particularly at the retail level, have become anonymous persons—unknown either to the selling firm or to the buyer—who merely facilitate the sale by formally presenting the product and accepting payment. The real job of adjusting the consumer to the product is done by the mass propaganda called advertising.

In taking over the task formerly performed by the salesman, advertising must substitute symbolic language for the personal appeal of man-to-man at a point where the merchandise is itself present and the transaction takes place. The task of persuading the customer is pushed

[1] David M. Potter, *People of Plenty* (University of Chicago Press, 1954), p. 168.

back in time to a point where it can be planned and partly executed months before the product reaches the market. It is removed in space from the point of sale to the business office, where the entire selling technique is planned and developed without benefit of the presence of the buyer. The sale must thus consist of an impersonalized message to thousands of unidentified potential customers, who have no way of communicating their impressions.

Modern advertising has many tasks to perform, which do not arise when selling is done face-to-face at the point of sale:

1. It must create or point out a need by identifying the circumstances under which it arises.

2. It must link the need to the possibility of fulfilling it with a general product, so that when the need arises the respondent will think of the product that will fulfill it.

3. It must differentiate the particular brand and its sponsor from other products which might satisfy the need approximately as well.

4. It must connect the particular branded product with the place and the conditions under which it can be obtained.

5. It must show that the need is urgent and that the task of buying is easy.

6. It must give a rational basis for action, for people do not like to buy goods which they cannot justify to their own consciences.

7. It must stimulate the respondent to make a firm decision on which he will act at a later time.

In accomplishing these tasks, advertising acts under the kleiglights of publicity. Unlike personal selling, where the promotion is carried on in private between two or more people, the messages publicized in advertising are conspicuous and cannot escape observation. This is one of the reasons why advertising comes in for a great deal of criticism that is equally relevant to selling on a personal basis. The so-called abuses which are concealed and disguised in the personal sales transaction are flaunted in the face of the public when they are published on the printed page or appear on the television screen. There is little doubt that there is more misrepresentation, deceit, and fraud in person-to-person sales relationships than in advertising.

The Purpose of Advertising

Commercial propaganda or advertising had its genesis in the need of the mass producer to sell goods in large quantities, and competition of other goods forced him to resort to an anonymous market: an aggregation of people scattered geographically, and unknown and unidentified as individuals. These conditions, and the growing separation of the locus of production in time and space from the locus of consumption, necessitated some means of making an individual manufacturer's product known and thus assuring it a continuous market.

Through the use of propaganda it was possible to create markets that were more stable than their component parts; for, although individual consumers are notoriously whimsical in changing their minds, their reactions in the market as a whole tend to cancel each other out.[2]

In order to accomplish these results the advertiser must use all the tools at his disposal. He must have an intimate understanding of the product advertised and be able to sense these characteristics whether inherent or inferred, which will fulfill the hopes and expectations of the potential owner and user. He must envisage the product in its use-setting. He must comprehend and appreciate the nature of human behavior. And he must be able to use the tricks of his trade—often the same as, and always closely akin to, those used on the rostrum and in the pulpit.

If the propaganda which the advertiser writes is to be effective, it must be expressed in terms in which the consumer thinks, with the same overtones and exaggerations of the product that the well-disposed consumer will attribute to it. It must recognize that the consumer to whom it appeals is but imperfectly rational, that he hates the labor of rational thinking, and that he is sometimes more impressed by what seems to others to be superficial than by the real merits of the product.

RATIONAL VERSUS EMOTIONAL APPEALS

In a broad, general sense advertising appeals either to man's reason or to his emotion or to both. It is difficult, of course, to differentiate in any precise way between these; but generally speaking rational appeals seem more effective in deciding alternative means to ends rather than the ends themselves. Emotion, on the other hand, is usually the trigger to action, particu-

---

[2] Compare Neil H. Borden, *The Economic Effects of Advertising* (Chicago: Richard D. Irwin, 1942).

larly when the actions mean a change of attitude on the part of the person.

There are many road-blocks to actions based on rational appeals; for rational arguments tend to raise questions rather than to answer them. Emotional appeals, on the other hand, attempt to stimulate the individual to carry through impulses which he already has. Assuming that this is true, the rational appeal is likely to be more lasting and its secondary effect to be stronger, because people are more likely to repeat rationalizations than they are to communicate their emotional feelings.

Advertising is highly concentrated on marginal products, things that one can do without, things that can be purchased with free income after the more austere basic needs such as necessary food, housing, clothing, etc., are taken care of.[3] It is these marginal products that give the real satisfactions in life. Even in the case of basic products, it is the exotic, the unusual elements—the fringe benefits—that set one off from his fellow creatures and thus claim the attention of consumers.

The Most Common Motives

Some years ago Victor Schwab suggested that there were ten leading motives or desires of the average consumer to which advertising must appeal in order to be effective:[4]

1. *Money and a better job.* "There must always be some kind of short-cut to getting ahead faster."

2. *Security in old age.* "When I get along in years, I want to be able to take it easy."

3. *Popularity.* "It's fun to be asked out all the time, to be wanted by everybody."

4. *Praise from others.* "Praise from others is a nice thing to get and I like to get it when I deserve it, and I often do."

5. *More comfort.* "A lot of people who are not as industrious or as capable as I am seem to have more comforts, so why shouldn't I spread myself once in a while?"

6. *Social advancement.* "Where would a person be if he never tried to better himself and to meet and associate with better people?"

7. *Improved appearance.* "It is awfully nice to have people tell you how attractive and well-dressed you are. If I had the time and money

some people spend on themselves, I would show them."

8. *Personal prestige.* "I am going to see to it that my children can prove that they have parents they need never be ashamed of."

9. *Better health.* "I don't feel any older than I did years ago, it's just that I don't seem to have the drive and energy I used to have."

10. *Increased enjoyment.* "I work hard, I do the best I can about things so why shouldn't I get as much enjoyment as I can?"

Advertisers have found by trial and error that these types of appeals are effective. It is evident that each appeal contains a bit of rationality with a large dose of sentimentality. The fact that these appeals are effective simply indicates that "the average human mind is a montage of hasty impressions, fuzzy generalities, bromidic wall-motto sentiments, self-justifications and sentimentalities."[5] It is out of this "jumble of ideas and feelings" that the advertiser must find a background for his appeals.

More and Better Wants

"The chief thing which the common-sense individual actually wants," wrote Professor Frank H. Knight, "is not satisfactions for the wants which he has, but more and better wants. There is always really present and operative, though in the background of consciousness, the idea of, and desire for a new want to be striven for when the present objective is out of the way."[6] Advertising attempts to present goods which are new or additional in the consumers' inventory of wants, and to indicate how they can be realized. In doing this, it both creates a want and the means of satisfying it.

The fact that advertising concentrates its efforts on changing people's customary wants has given rise to the contention that it corrupts people's desires and stimulates so-called "artificial" consuming habits. But this argument is beside the point for, as Professor Knight has indicated, "there is no issue as between natural and artificial wants. All human wants are more artificial than natural, and the expression 'natural wants,' if it has any meaning, can only refer to those of beasts. By the same token, human wants are more sentimental than real."[7]

[3] F. P. Bishop, *The Ethics of Advertising* (London: Robert Hale, 1949), p. 48.

[4] Victor Schwab, "Ten Copy Appeals," *Printers' Ink*, December 17, 1943, pp. 17ff.

[5] *Ibid.*

[6] Frank H. Knight, *The Ethics of Competition* (New York: Harper, 1935), p. 22.

[7] *Ibid*, p. 103.

Most people have always lived rather drab and unimaginative lives. The so-called golden ages of history were golden only to the few. The great masses lived by drudgery, and thought in terms of only the elemental emotions such as hunger and comfort. The so-called "democratic way of life" rests simply on the idea that our present economy is oriented to change the thinking of these masses. Propaganda, if it is to be effective, must appeal to the masses in the terms of their own mental processes.

It is sometimes alleged also that, through advertising, businessmen foist on people goods they do not want. This, of course, is sheer nonsense. There are, in fact, few acts necessarily more deliberate than that of the consumer's action in response to advertising.

Picture the consumer in his living room reading a magazine advertisement. He has had to choose the particular magazine, and pay for it; he has had to select from among the hundreds of pages those he wishes to read, and he can either accept or reject the arguments presented. Assuming that he accepts them and resolves to make the purchase, he must still wait hours or even days before an opportune time arises to make the purchase. During the interval between the time he reads the advertisement and the time he undertakes the overt act of buying, he is entirely outside the influence of the message and may deliberate and search his soul to his heart's content either in private or in consultation with his friends. There is not even mass psychology to influence him. He is a free agent and there is no possibility of coercion, duress, or constraint of any kind.

But the impossibility of advertising to force consumers to buy what they do not want should not be confused with the fact that advertisers sometime overstep the bounds of propriety to make claims for their products which cannot be justified. In some product areas effective protection has been provided by law, but in general the chief defense of the consumer lies in his own discrimination of whom he will patronize or refuse to patronize.

THE LARGER SYSTEM OF BELIEFS

In discussing propaganda generally, psychologists Krech and Crutchfield state that "suggestions which are accepted as a consequence of propaganda tend to be in harmony with some larger system of beliefs or some already existing predisposition, and therefore presumably with the major needs and interests of the subject." [8]

To put this another way, at any given time the subject of propaganda has many prejudices, beliefs, and attitudes of different intensities. Some are deeply entrenched, while others are at a superficial level. The more deeply entrenched these predispositions are, the more difficult it will be to change them, and some seem to be entrenched so deeply that they cannot be changed by propaganda at all.

Since it is easier and less expensive to modify existing predispositions than to oppose them, propagandists find it expedient to fit their messages into the current pattern of thinking rather than oppose it head on. It is for this reason that most changes in attitudes and wants achieved by advertising are almost imperceptible, and can be objectively observed only over a period of time.

Both in the selection of the characteristics of the product to promote and in the framing of appeals, the advertiser must give attention to consumers' preconceived ideas of what they want. He develops his product and its appeals to fit into these ideas and to project them further. If his advertising is successful in selling his product, competitors will find it necessary to discover other new products or new characteristics of old products, likewise in line with consumers' ideas, as a basis for their counter-propaganda. Thus, competition in advertising tends to develop a constantly increasing improvement of the product to fit consumers' wants, while at the same time it raises the standards of wants in the consumers' minds.

Discounting the Message

The very mass of advertising and the great amount that comes to the attention of consumers is often open to criticism. Critics ask, for instance, "Is there no limit to the increasing din of the market place?" "Will it continue until all businesses are wasting their substance and crying their wares?" "Are there no antidotes for this infectious disease?" We suspect there are.

The editor of *Harper's Magazine*, puts it this way: "Perhaps, however, we will in the long run have reason to be grateful to the copy-

---

[8] D. K. Krech and R. S. Crutchfield, *Theory and Problems of Social Psychology* (New York: McGraw-Hill, 1948), p. 347.

writers and press agents, even the worst of them. It may turn out that thanks to advertising and public relations, the American people will become the first people in history to be impervious to propaganda. Maybe it isn't such a bad thing that the advertisers and other word-manipulators have got us to the point that we never take words quite at their face value. In all events, it is hard to imagine that the people inured to American advertising would whole-heartedly believe the kind of promises and assurances, whereby Hitler and Stalin have enslaved two great nations in our time." [9]

When two advertisers say approximately the same things about their product, the message of one tends to neutralize that of the other, and the public learns to discount what is said by both. In a free world the right to persuade and be persuaded is one of the essential freedoms. We assume that each of us has the mentality and the fortitude to choose—to accept or reject what he hears or what he reads.

Each has the right to act or to refuse to act on the basis of all the propaganda he absorbs, whether it is in the form of advertising or word-of-mouth gossip. That he often rejects propaganda is a matter of record. But we assume that, whether a person acts wisely or foolishly, he will take the responsibility for the act and that he himself will reap the benefits or the penalties of his action. For this reason he will eventually learn to listen more discriminatingly and act more wisely in the light of all the information available.

EFFECT ON MEDIA CONTENT

It is sometimes alleged that advertising, because it pays most of the cost of magazines and newspapers, dominates and controls the information in these media. It is said that, since the advertiser pays the piper, he must call the tune.

Actually this is seldom true because the medium that publishes biased or slanted news tends to lose its circulation when its bias becomes known, and in this way it ceases to be an effective means of communication. Even the most severe critics of advertising admit that this type of direct and overt influence is pretty well eliminated by the intense competition among media themselves.

The effect of advertising on news content and editorial opinion is far more indirect and subtle.

Editors themselves are human and they live in the same environment as the rest of us. They, too, are subject to the propaganda which all of us read; and it would be too much to expect that they are not influenced in a general way by what they read. As a part of the total environment it tends to set a point of view which is not unfavorable to advertising.

The Function of Media

From the advertiser's point of view, the function of the newspaper, the magazine, the broadcasting station, or any other medium of publication is to gather a crowd or furnish an audience.[10] Once the crowd has gathered, it must be entertained, amused, or at least interested enough to hold together while the advertiser's message is being delivered. The need for holding the audience arises from the fact that advertising is selective, in the sense that a specific message is likely to have an appeal only to a scattered few among the many in the crowd. As for the many others who have no need or interest in the particular product, they become bored and resentful that their attention has been disrupted.

The fact that advertising is selective in its expectations, though not in its aims, means that its impact on those to whom the message does not apply or who do not care to listen ranges from irritation to exasperation. From the listener's point of view, it is an unwarranted intrusion on their privacy, by some "jerk" who wants to sell something.

Therefore, the advertiser must use every art he can contrive to make his message palatable, even to those who do not want to listen; and at the same time he searches for a vehicle which will capture and hold his audience while he gives them "the works." In rare cases he is able to convert his message into news which is interesting and entertaining in itself; but often there is a trail of resentment left in the listener's mind, and he deliberately tries to develop some means of shutting out the message from his consciousness. The result is that a great deal of advertising never passes the threshold of the reader's or the listener's consciousness.

Although there is danger of exaggerating the importance of advertising in causing certain changes in our culture, it would be erroneous to conclude that its influence is negligible. Ad-

---

[9] Robert Amory, Jr., "Personal and Otherwise," *Harper's Magazine*, 1948, p. 6.

[10] See G. B. Hotchkiss, *Milestones of Marketing* (New York: Macmillan, 1938), p. 10.

vertising is so prevalent, so pervasive, so extensive, and so conspicuous that it would be absurd to argue that it does not affect our attitudes.

On the other hand, the fact that advertising, in order to be successful and economical, "must be in harmony with some larger system of beliefs or some already existing predisposition" indicates that its influence is tangential rather than direct, that it tends to fit in with and supplement other motivational influences rather than act as an independent force.

EFFECT ON CONSUMER STANDARDS

Advertising, both for individual products and in the aggregate, appeals to the anticipatory aspirations of the group.[11] It offers goals of attainment that would not otherwise be thought of. It sets up ideals to be sought after. Its appeals are designed to stimulate action which will result in a more comfortable, congenial and satisfying life.

Thus, in the aggregate it creates an ever-expanding series of aspirations for the future. In doing this, it shapes the standards of living for the future; and, since man lives largely in a world of anticipation, it lays the basis for much of his enjoyment.

In American business, commercial propaganda is part and parcel of the mass-production process. Our present American business could no more operate without advertising than it could without the automatic machine or the assembly line. By means of this propaganda, the millions of people coming from many nations and races and diverse backgrounds are conditioned to want sufficient amounts of a given standardized product to make it possible to produce that product at a fraction of the cost which would otherwise be necessary.

If left without such propaganda as is found in advertising, people would not choose the same products they do choose. Whether they would choose the same product at a later date is purely a matter of conjecture, but it seems unlikely. If it is assumed that without advertising they would choose something different, then no producer would be able to secure sufficient production to provide these diverse things at prices people could afford to pay. This is another way of saying that standardization of wants through advertising is in part the basis for the economies which come through mass production.

In spite of the necessity that people's wants be so standardized as to secure mass production, the enormous market and the high-level purchasing power available in America have enabled firms to proliferate these standards and to offer a wider variety of goods for sale than would be possible even under a handicraft system where goods are presumably made to fit the consumer's specifications.

Incidentally, the assumption sometimes made, that people would make wiser choices if there were no advertising, ignores the fact that preconceived notions of what they want have themselves been formed by other types of propaganda and other influences no less biased and no more rational than the propaganda used by sellers.

As people get more income, and as competition becomes stronger among sellers for a share of this income, adjustment of goods to the consumer becomes finer. More attention is given to the marginal aspects of goods. New quality standards are developed in terms of their psychological rather than their utilitarian values. For instance, people in buying shoes are often more interested in style and how they look to others than in comfort and durability, which are likely to be taken for granted.

These types of desires are often hidden and so subtle that sellers are faced with a continuously changing market, difficult to interpret and almost impossible to predict. They are thus forced to offer their products with infinite variations in characteristics and appeals. To the consumer, the opportunity to choose from this vast variety of products is itself a major element in his standard of living.

---

[11] See Wroe Alderson, *Marketing Behavior and Executive Action* (Homewood, Ill.: Richard D. Irwin, 1957), p. 276ff.

39. The Role of Advertising in Modern Society

C. H. SANDAGE

Advertising is a form of communication in which the communicator can control the character of his message and have it delivered to either a select or a mass audience at relatively low cost. This is accomplished by the permission which such media as newspapers, magazines and radio stations grant to advertisers to purchase space or time to carry uncensored[1] messages created by the advertiser or his agent. This freedom to create messages without fear of blue pencil alteration, combined with the availability of mass media to distribute or broadcast such messages, gives to purveyors of products, services, and ideas tremendous power to influence the thoughts and actions of vast numbers of people. The speed with which messages can be delivered adds to this power to influence.

The availabiliy of mass media to serve as "retailers" of sales messages manufactured by others is relatively recent. While the seeds of the advertising industry were planted some generations ago, its flowering into a dominant force in our economy and culture has been a twentieth century development. It is, therefore, appropriate to inquire into the role which advertising is now playing and might be expected to play in our economic and social order.

ECONOMIC INFLUENCES

It shall not be our purpose to examine all areas where advertising influences the character of the American economy. Instead, discussion will be limited to the influence which advertising has on (1) high level consumption, (2) allocation of resources, (3) stimulation of product variety, and (4) consumer prices.

High Level Consumption

The American economy is today organized to produce goods and services far in excess of what would be needed to give consumers the basic necessities for comfortable living. Our economy is no longer a food, shelter, and clothing one. It is no longer built upon scarcity, but rather upon plenty and luxury. If the production and distribution facilities of America were devoted only to meeting the basic needs of the citizenry, only a fraction of our capital goods and labor force would be employed full time. With technological improvements in capital goods increasing the output per worker at the same time that population increase adds more persons to the labor force, the importance of consumption becomes more and more significant.

If we are to maintain anything like full employment of labor, it is exceedingly vital that consumption be on a high level—a level far above that of basic need, and at an increasing rate from year to year. That means a wardrobe of dresses and suits instead of a mother hubbard or a pair of overalls; motels for the traveler instead of a tent or open air camp; bath tubs and stall showers instead of the brook or wash basin; a beautiful lawn and power mower instead of a weed patch and a goat; mechanical refrigerators and deep freeze boxes instead of the oaken bucket and salt brine barrel; washing

[1] Except for violations of law or codes of good practice established by media.

‡‡ SOURCE: Reprinted by permission from *Changing Perspectives in Marketing*, edited by Hugh G. Wales (University of Illinois Press, 1951), pp. 185–196.

machines and inside running water instead of a wash-board and a horse trough; innerspring mattresses instead of straw-filled ticking; fountain pens instead of goose quills; modern, well equipped school buildings and well trained teachers instead of one room country schools run by disciplinarians; good medical clinics and health restoring drugs instead of witch doctors and asafetida bags.

Before people can have products and services of either the necessity or luxury variety, they must have purchasing power. Such purchasing power may be in the form of an ability to work, money, or both. Fundamental physiological factors are enough to motivate the able-bodied person to work or to spend his money to secure the bare necessities of life. He needs no outside prodding to tell him he is hungry and needs food. Nature soon tells him that a cave, house, or bearskin coat will keep him from dying of exposure. Thus, these physiological factors are sufficient to drive people to work and to produce the things of absolute need in preserving life.

A luxury or surplus economy cannot be built upon the physical needs of society. It depends primarily on the psychological needs and wants of consumers. If capital, labor, and natural resources are to be combined to produce non-necessities such as those enumerated earlier, the consuming public must be informed of their existence, educated as to their want-satisfying qualities, and persuaded to buy them. It is here that advertising plays an important role. It becomes the stimulator of human interest. It serves as an interpreter or translator of the products and service of industry to a psychologically hungry public. Advertising transforms a bundle of steel coils, felt, hair, and ticking into a bed of kingly comfort and health-giving rest. It builds a propensity to consume.

There are those who, with good logic, might question the social values resulting from a stimulation of a high level of consumption of products and services that are not actually needed. One should not forget, however, that human satisfactions rather than physical or moral well-being constitute the base on which our economy is built. Social values, therefore, are often different from economic values even though the individual is the final arbiter in determining both. Thus, if people want tobacco, are willing to work to get it, and get satisfaction from its consumption greater than the dissatisfaction resulting from labor expended in securing it, such action is economically justified. It may not be considered socially good.

Another point of view concerning social values should also be emphasized, namely, that the alternative to high level consumption is a greatly reduced tempo in economic activity. Closing up only a fraction of the production facilities now devoted to making luxury items might well produce economic depression. It is not to be inferred that an effective use of advertising can or will guarantee economic prosperity. The economic machine is too delicate and complex to warrant singling out one of its parts as the key to prosperity. But it is essential that consumers continue to have a strong propensity to consume products and services above the level of necessities if full employment is to be approximated. The informative and persuasive forces provided by advertising are key elements in keeping consumers flocking to the market-place.

Allocation of Resources

The allocation of economic resources is, in the long run, determined primarily by the consuming public. Natural resources, capital, labor, and management are combined to produce goods and services which will be acceptable to and purchased by consumers. It is thus necessary to key production to consumer needs and wants.

In an economy which is limited largely to supplying goods to meet only the basic physiological needs of consumers, the attitudes of the latter need not be given primary consideration. Consumers could be forced to accept the kind of food, clothing, and shelter offered by producers. The alternatives would be starvation and exposure. Under such conditions, consumers might have little voice in determining how resources would be allocated.

In an economy of plenty, where production facilities are adequate to provide goods and services far in excess of those required to meet basic physiological human needs, consumer wants become highly important. Psychological rather than physiological factors become the strong motivating forces. Under these circumstances, consumers can choose not to buy as readily as they can choose to buy. It is here that information and persuasion become vital elements in inducing consumers to buy *want-satisfying* goods and services. Because consumers need not buy items designed to satisfy wants rather than needs, they can readily transfer their favor from one producer or product to another at will. The informative and persuasive powers of advertising can hasten the acceptance of new products and influence the stability or fickleness of consumers' transfer of favor from one product to another. Thus, insofar as advertising influences consumers to buy a new product or to switch from one product to another, to that extent it influences the allocation of resources.

The power of advertising to persuade consumers to accept non-necessity goods is greatest when such goods have been engineered to satisfy existing wants. It thus behooves business firms to learn the wants and interests of consumers before products are placed on the market and before advertising is applied to persuade consumers to buy. The advertising industry has exercised some leadership in seeking to learn the wants and interests of consumers. Research is now commonplace in the field of advertising to determine not only the psychological needs and wants of people, but also the extent to which specific products and services will give satisfaction. Experimental advertising and distribution programs are often undertaken to measure the extent to which consumers accept such products and services. If acceptance is substantial, production facilities are organized to shape raw materials into that form which consumers have indicated they will buy. Thus, in many respects, consumer wants, made articulate through research and stimulated to buying pitch through advertising, become the blueprints to guide the production machinery of the country.

But let it not be forgotten that consumers are not always fickle and their wants not always associated with material things for immediate consumption. To continue an economy of plenty it is vital that capital goods be maintained and perhaps increased. This necessitates saving which is the antithesis of immediate consumption. It is perhaps conceivable that if advertising were used only to persuade people to consume to the maximum of their ability to buy, savings would become nil and the economy decay.

Such a danger is remote as long as there is a substantial amount of freedom of enterprise. Advertising is an instrument that can be used by any business. It facilitates competition. The savings bank, stock and bond broker, insurance company, and United States Treasury can use the persuasive and informative force of advertising to encourage saving and postpone consumption of material goods. The experience of firms that have used advertising to encourage

saving indicates that this force has often been more potent in increasing the amount of saving than has an increase in the rate of interest. Thus, psychological values, made recognizable through advertising, have often been more potent than price increases in producing increased savings.

Stimulation of Product Variety

In a luxury or plentiful economy consumers have a great deal of freedom to choose or reject products offered them. So potent is this freedom of choice that producers strive to not only meet the needs and basic want of consumers, but also cater to their whims, fancies, and impulses. Since final consumer choice is materially influenced by advertising in a competitive economy, it behooves the producer to differentiate his product from similar products offered by other suppliers. This makes it possible to relate advertising messages to the specific product and to associate it with the qualities described and emphasized in the advertising.

One element of difference in almost any advertised product is the brand or trade name. The attachment of a name to a product permits buyers to identify it for purposes of repeating a purchase or rejecting it if it has proven unsatisfactory. The very fact that rejection is possible stimulates producers to build into their goods those qualities which will increase human satisfaction. This competitive spirit, made more potent by advertising, has stimulated product variety and improvement.

The advertising man is always seeking to find or to have built into a product or service a particular quality around which an informational and persuasive story can be built and delivered to prospective buyers. That quality may be an automatic defrosting device for a refrigerator or an easy adjustment on a lawnmower to permit a 2-inch high cut. It may be an attachment for the mower which will pick up and shred the leaves that clutter the lawn in the fall. Many other examples could be given such as a vacuum seal for packaged coffee, no-drip pitchers, automatic transmission for automobiles, golf caddy carts, king-size cigarettes, polarized sun glasses, rayon cord in automobile tires, and automatic washing machines. Were it not for brands and advertising it is doubtful whether the increase in the variety and quality of products would have been so great.

Not all product differentiation has been of a

material character. Through advertising, psychological values have been built into a particular brand which is physically different from some other brand only in name and package design. It may be debated whether this is good or bad for the economy. Persons who hold that consumers are interested primarily in the physical features of a product would criticize differentiation on the basis of name only. The opposition would point out that the values of most goods that are not absolute necessities are psychological ones.

Through advertising the psychological values of products are often developed and enhanced. The orchid is physically comparable to the iris, but the *psychological* qualities are certainly different. Physiologists will say that identical twins possess the same physical characteristics, but parents give them different names. A mother or father learns to distinguish between them and finds a real difference as a result of the intertwining of personalities. Association patterns are established on psychological grounds that make one twin distinctly different and more appealing to certain persons. Two brands of cosmetics may be made from the same formula, but one manufacturer may, through honest advertising and adroit suggestion, build into his brand name superior beauty and a sense of well-being for the user. If maximum human satisfaction is a major objective of our economy, this use of advertising perhaps helps in achieving that objective.

There are undoubtedly elements in these efforts to provide products with a difference which are not beneficial. Such efforts have encouraged an increase in gadgets, frills, and unneeded and often unwanted adornments. They have produced too frequent style or model changes in many commodities. They have perhaps tended to waste some resources and reduce total human satisfactions in a number of instances. The great number of brands of such commodities as coffee, peas, dog food, toothpaste, fountain pens, vacuum sweepers, and soaps at times tend to confuse rather than help consumers. This is one of the costs that must be associated with the competition for consumer favor. Probably most consumers would prefer to pay this cost rather than be denied a wide variety of products from which to choose. In addition, however, they would want informative advertising that might serve as a reasonably reliable guide to buying. Such advertising could help reduce the confusion that attends a multiplicity of brands in the market place.

Consumer Prices

Advertising can influence the price which consumers pay for commodities in two ways. It can affect the costs of production and distribution and thus influence the minimum price which must be obtained by sellers to break even or continue to supply such commodities. Advertising can also affect the attitude of consumers toward specific commodities in terms of the price they are willing to pay rather than deny themselves the satisfaction they think will result from purchase.

There is abundant evidence that advertising has been of material assistance in stimulating large-scale demand for many products. This has been a significant factor in the development and perpetuation of large-scale production and distribution. Mass production and distribution do not always provide monetary economies, but, in general, lower costs have resulted from large scale operations.

The contribution of advertising to lower costs resulting from large-scale operations has been most pronounced in new industries where a primary demand for the new commodity needed to be established. Examples drawn from past experiences would include industries making products such as refrigerators, radios, automobiles, cigarettes, and rayon textiles. Once primary demand has been established on a high plane and plants of individual companies have grown to an optimum size, some companies may depend primarily on forces other than advertising to maintain a favorable sales volume. But in any event, for commodities where substitutes are readily available, it seems that continued advertising expenditures by a significant segment of such an industry are necessary if sales or consumption are to increase or continue at a high level.

A conclusion that advertising has contributed to a generally lower unit cost of production and distribution signifies only that sellers could, if they wished, offer goods to consumers at a price lower than would otherwise be economically possible. Some producers have wished to do so. Lower costs, however, have not always been passed along to the consumer. If the products of the many producers within a given industry were not differentiated in some manner, competition would be primarily on a price basis and maximum consumer price would be established primarily by the costs of marginal producers. In the case of branded goods the owner of a particular name can often avoid direct price competition and persuade many consumers to buy his product because of some supposed hidden values.

Competition becomes somewhat non-price in character, and consumer favor may be sought on grounds other than price. The owner of a brand achieves a position in the market somewhat similar to one having a monopoly, although the ease with which consumers can substitute other brands is usually great.

The level to which the owner of a brand may push his control of price will depend primarily on the attitude of consumers toward his brand in comparison with readily substitutable brands of other manufacturers. Adroit and convincing advertising may persuade a substantial number of consumers that brand X is enough better than other brands to warrant payment of a premium price to obtain it. When this occurs, consumer attitude toward the product becomes more significant than cost of production and distribution in setting price.

There are many examples of advertised products that carry a consumer price higher than would be necessary because of costs. This higher price is not dictated by advertising, but rather by the policies adopted by businessmen who utilize advertising. It takes real business statesmanship to forego pricing a commodity in terms of what the traffic will bear, but there is an increasing number of such business statesmen. The role of advertising is that of serving as an aid in reducing costs and increasing human satisfactions. If at least some of the reduced costs are passed along to consumers in the form of lower prices, without at the same time reducing the monetary value which consumers have placed on such products, a surplus of consumer satisfaction is thus provided over and above that which would have been enjoyed by supra-marginal buyers at the old price.

SOCIAL INFLUENCES

The impact which advertising has exerted in the past has been largely economic in character. While the application of advertising to material things is not diminishing, its use in the promotion of ideas is increasing rapidly. Political parties, governments, churches, business institutions, and labor groups are making greater and greater use of advertising as a means of informing people and persuading them toward a particular philosophy or point of view.

In the field of public relations, business firms in particular and labor groups to some extent now buy space or time in mass media to present their own economic, social or institutional philosophies to specific publics. Advertising is being used for such purposes because it permits the buyer of space or time to control the character of the message presented. Meanings may be distorted by the writer of the advertising message, but no editor or third party censor can distort the message without the sanction of the buyer. This places a much more potent instrument in the hands of the public relations man than that provided in the form of free publicity releases.

The Voice of America may not be classified as advertising by some people, but it is essentially that. A mass medium is used. The user of time controls the character of the message. Its purpose is to inform and persuade. The term "propaganda" may be preferred by some, but in the case of Voice of America, as in many other propaganda drives, the techniques of advertising are used to sell people or educate them to a particular point of view.

Churches have also "discovered" advertising as an instrument to promote their ideologies. The item to be "sold" may be a particular creed, the dignity of man, fundamental spiritual values, or the philosophy of Jesus. Each year millions of dollars are spent by churches for radio time and space in printed media to present their own religious messages in the unedited form they want to reach the public.

The availability of mass media to those who have ideas to promote broadens the concept and influence of free speech. No longer is it necessary to own a newspaper or magazine to further a particular ideology. It takes relatively little money to buy space in a medium of communication to present a message to large numbers of people. This greatly enlarges "Hyde Park" and increases the figurative soap boxes available to those who would persuade others to a particular way of life.

The availability of mass media for these and similar purposes is increased by the work of the Advertising Council. This organization stands ready to offer professional guidance and expert techniques in promoting, through advertising, ideas which seem to be in the public interest. The Council was born during World War II to assist the government in selling bonds, recruiting men and women for war service, urging citizens to develop victory gardens, reduce loose talk about movement of ships and troops, and to maintain a high morale among the civilian army of workers. Postwar activities have included advertising campaigns to reduce accidents, promote contributions to CARE, improve public health, develop a better understanding of the meaning of democracy, increase human tolerance, improve the status of the educational profession, and help hospitals recruit more nurses.

This trend toward using advertising to sell ideas as well as products places a new and greater responsibility on the advertising man and the advertising industry. It emphasizes the need for newer concepts of ethics. Those who devote their lives to the fashioning of language of persuasion and action should be ever conscious of the need for truth and honesty. A firm faith in what is being written, and a testing of that faith by all available evidence, should be cardinal guideposts for advertising men. Their purpose in the preparation and dissemination of messages designed to get acceptance of ideas should be to help a public choose those ideas which will increase personal satisfactions. Truth is a powerful force in achieving that purpose.

40. *Objectives of Selling*

HARRY R. TOSDAL

The objectives of selling may at first thought appear to be very simple. Some individual or business firm is endeavoring to influence other people or firms to make purchases for the selfish benefit of the seller. But there is much more to the function of selling than this. The objectives ascribed to selling and to those engaged in selling are too often based upon limited experience, observation, and contact. True, the immediate objective of selling is to make sales and to develop buying action on the part of prospective or potential buyers; but most sellers are also under heavy economic pressure to deal with buyers or whose who influence buying in such a manner that future transactions will be facilitated. Most sellers are looking forward to making repeat sales, that is, to inducing future purchases by the same customers, because the bulk of business transactions takes place between buyers and sellers who have had previous buying and selling relationships. The seller must, therefore, direct his effort so that the buyers will want to repeat the experience. Where freedom of choice prevails in our competitive economy, that repetition will not occur unless the buyer is "well satisfied" to use the words of the Supreme Court. Thus, "enlightened selfishness" tends to influence the seller to establish himself as a good source of supply and to avoid methods and practices which would harm the buyer.

Any careful examination of the objectives of selling, however, must go beyond such enlightened selfishness to reach a basic understanding. It is the failure to penetrate more deeply into objectives and results that has contributed to the misunderstanding of selling. As is so often the case in studying social phenomena, it is easy to fail to see the forest for the trees.

It is helpful in the process of the study of objectives to distinguish between individual and group objectives and to separate the purpose of the individual and the private firm from the general social objectives and goals of the total selling process. That selling has as its ultimate purpose a social goal is not quickly apparent because we do not attempt to look at the over-all purposes and results. There is need, therefore, to outline the scope of these objectives and to relate the conclusions derived from limited observation and embodied in common opinion to the broader facts of the selling situations and their significance. The objectives of selling to be discussed will be grouped therefore under four major headings:

1. The objectives of selling effort carried on by individuals, directly engaged in selling activity whatever the form.
2. The objectives of selling effort on the part of the firms and corporations in relation to those doing the selling work in those firms and in relation to the owners of the selling enterprise.
3. The objectives of selling effort in relation to our economic structure and its functioning.
4. The objectives of selling effort in relation to our society as a whole.

⁑ SOURCE: Reprinted by permission from *Selling In Our Economy*, Harry R. Tosdal, (Homewood, Illinois: Richard D. Irwin, Inc., 1957), pp. 79–90.

OBJECTIVES OF INDIVIDUALS
ENGAGED IN SELLING WORK

The objective of selling activities generally is obviously to secure buying action, to cause purchase of goods and services by buyers. This leads eventually to higher consumption by many people, although higher consumption may or may not be the objective of a particular seller. Any careful examination of the objectives of selling must lead to the conclusion that the objectives of individuals who are engaged in the practice of selling may differ widely in type and emphasis. Among these objectives are the following:

1. To make a living. From the standpoint of the individual salesman whose income and success depends on his efforts to cause people to buy, it is evident that selling constitutes a gainful occupation at the practice of which he hopes to make a living. His ambition may extend to achieving advancement into executive ranks. This ambition may in turn be motivated by desire to secure the ownership of business that will give him the income desired for the benefit of himself and his family, the enjoyment of luxuries, or the acquisition of power.

It is certainly not assured under the usual plans of compensation that salesmen will make a living, much less go beyond that. Many a young man who has started out to sell aluminum utensils, magazines, or hosiery from house to house, has found out in a very short time that he could not make a living and has given up in despair. He has learned that selling is not easy and that earnings are not automatic, particularly in normal buyers' markets. A substantial proportion of those who try selling fail for want of aptitude, industry, or basic interest in and respect for their work. Some fail also because what they are trying to sell is not wanted.

Those who work in the field of advertising or display, or who perform many other supplementary and staff duties, find that ultimate success in their jobs depends on the estimated contribution that their work makes to selling. They have the same ambitions, the same desires as those who are directly in contact with the prospective buyers. But the difficulty of measuring their contribution to selling results is a handicap to some, perhaps an advantage to others.

We cannot, offhand, condemn the motivation of the individual in trying to make a living and improve his lot in life as purely selfish and antisocial. On the contrary, one's first economic responsibility is usually to himself and family; and unless he meets this responsibility, he cannot ordinarily serve society well. But serving society may be the best way of serving himself. A possible conflict between his obligation to society and private interest may exist; but in selling it need not and usually does not. The salesman who persuades a manufacturer to install a new machine to make a better product or to cut costs is contributing to a higher standard of living, in spite of the fact that the motivation of the salesman may be to increase his own standard of living and that of the manufacturer who, in installing the machine, increases profits and avoids loss. Eventually his purchase will contribute to lower costs and higher scales of living for the people. The salesman who sells an electric washing machine to the housewife is generally raising the family's level of living.

Because selling involves a form of leadership, because it requires those practicing selling to influence other people, selling has frequently furnished a training ground for other positions in business. Selling leadership is persuasive leadership, a type of leadership that is both appreciated and greatly needed in democratic societies.

2. A second objective of those who perform selling work is likewise understandable. It is the desire to secure satisfaction from the work itself. Salesmen who believe in their products and in the benefits those products will convey to buyers feel satisfaction when they make sales, entirely apart from the contribution that such sales make to their personal welfare. In fact, success as a salesman is usually predicated on a firm belief in the merits of the product sold in terms of the satisfactions to be obtained by the buyers. There is no evidence that salesmen, any more than any other group, wish to make a living without regard to the service performed in return.

3. Again, there are special satisfactions from successful sales work which attract and hold a good many workers in the selling field. That is the desire to secure the excitement and thrills from successfully influencing people to take the desired action. Obviously, to the salesman who is ethical in his conduct, such thrills and satisfactions must be the result of selling that is mutually beneficial.

The ease of selling during periods of shortages brought about by global war has for many years obscured the fact that selling in a competitive economy is a difficult task requiring intelligent, often exhausting, effort. In a competitive economy, with high standards of living, with many products both old and new, the difficulty of making particular sales at a particular time will furnish a challenge to the keenest brain, a challenge that is paralleled only in other areas of human activity where democratic liberty prevails and freedom of choice obtains. The intense satisfactions which men have often reported at the successful conclusion of a selling project need to be experienced in order to be fully appreciated.

4. Serving buyers and customers. Since most selling is done on a repeat basis, sellers get to know buyers and become friendly with them. Particularly in the sales of technical and complex products, the salesman develops friendships that cause him to serve his buyers and customers to a point substantially beyond the length required by cold and calculating type of enlightened selfishness. The salesman who furnishes selling or merchandising services to customers is adding to the satisfactions that both his firm and the customer feel as the result of the purchasing transactions. But he also derives personal pleasure and satisfactions from the relationship with customers.

5. Lastly, except in the general desire to be engaged in useful work so that the earning of a living or the accumulation of capital for personal or family improvement is accomplished in an honorable manner, one does not expect that many salesmen will engage in such work with vague altruistic ideas of serving society. The man who believes in his product and acts honorably in bringing about a sale that leads to mutual satisfaction is actually serving society, whether the goal he seeks to reach is explicitly service to society or the same goals as characterize other vocations; to make a living, to develop security, to furnish the means for cultural or other development, to attain power, or any of the other objectives that men may hope to reach, directly or indirectly, through a chosen field of effort.

The motivation of the individual may differ from that of his firm. Sometimes the differences in that motivation are not important in the performance of a useful function for society. Sometimes they are. The behavior of the salesman who engages in sharp practice or even the use of illegal means of influence may go beyond anything either permitted or encouraged by the firm itself. In other cases, the standard of the salesman may be merely a more concrete reflection of the carelessness or low standards on the part of the executives of the selling firm itself. It is unlikely that the sales organization in its contact with the public will rise above the character of the top management, but it is also possible that top management with a large and scattered field sales organization may not be able in all areas to control the behavior of those who are exercising influence at the point of contact with the public. The parallel in political leadership is quickly apparent; it need not be spelled out. One may only mention the contrast between some top political leaders and the ward bosses of certain cities. Fortunately, checks upon "bad behavior" and unworthy motivation, inherent in selling in our economy, seem to be more quickly operative than in the political field.

SELLING OBJECTIVES IN RELATION TO BUSINESS ENTERPRISES AND OWNERS AND MANAGERS

The business enterprise which is devoted to the production of goods or services, or both, sells for various reasons, some of which are obvious and some not so apparent:

1. In the opinions of a good many businessmen, selling is fully justified if one can show that selling is essential to the survival of an enterprise in competition. In our economy distinguished by large-scale production for national or even international markets, the cessation of selling effort would, except under war shortages or monopoly of necessities, mean more or less rapid failure. If one will examine the balance sheets of many firms, he will find that if the income from sales were cut off, the firm operating at its previous level would consume its capital in a very short time, even where heavy capital investment was involved. Obviously the cessation of selling effort would not cut off all sales, because some buying would take place based in part on connections and past selling, and in part upon need for the sellers' products. Generally, however, the decline in the volume of goods disposed of in the absence of selling effort would be disastrous. For that decline in most industries is likely to be much more than proportionate to the possible decline in costs, thus quickly bringing losses because of the insufficiency of income from sales to cover costs.

To the experienced businessman, it is quite evident that production does not create demand. Sales do not come automatically and purchases are not made automatically despite implications in some economics texts. Basically, survival of the firm is the condition of continuing private profit, but it is also the condition of continuing service to society. Just as in politics the most competent man with the best motives may be forced to pay attention to his survival in office if he is to be able to carry out his program, so the businessman will look to profitable sales as a condition of real and outstanding accomplishment and growth.

It is obvious that for most business enterprises sales transactions constitute the sole source of income. Sales provide the income out of which wages and salaries can be paid and the requirements met for goods, machinery, supplies, and taxes. Without sales income, firms cannot long continue to make these payments without dissipating assets, endangering chances of restoration to economic health, and suffering eventual failure.

2. Businessmen sell in order to secure return on investment. The business executives who are responsible to a board of directors and to stockholders may aim through selling to provide the income necessary for return on investment. They realize that only an adequate volume of sales, made at a profitable price, can provide the dividends, allowance for depreciation, and reserves necessary for continuously satisfactory operation. If return is not earned for a considerable period of time, the difficulty of securing further capital is increased and becomes eventually impossible.

3. Businesses and business executives sell in order to have the satisfaction of achievement. Business executives and leaders take pride in the building of enterprises and look upon the work of building a going concern as a worthwhile economic and social objective. They know that the building of large enterprises is seldom a one-man job. The planning necessary for successful sales operations, the execution of sales plans, and the overcoming of obstacles, thereby contributing vitally to bringing into full operation an enterprise that produces useful goods and services, is an accomplishment worthy of credit. In the United States more than in some other parts of the world, such men think of businesses not only, or even primarily, as a means of deriving purely personal and family benefit. They often regard these businesses as living organisms which bring benefits to workers, users, and owners as well as to the managing groups. These benefits are realized, developed, and expanded by selling.

4. Public benefit is the ultimate goal of most selling. The objective of serving the consumer public, whether the consumers be ultimate consumers or firms or institutions, constitutes a rarely expressed but implicit objective even beyond the necessity of selling in order to make a profit. Many a businessman who disclaims altruism in his business conduct actually performs a greater social service by what he does in his own business than he could possibly perform in participating in community affairs or in his gifts to educational or charitable institutions.

The obvious connection between selling and employment constitutes a working objective that is a powerful incentive to many businessmen. Selling requires production; production requires employment. Or, to reverse the statement: Employment results in production that must be disposed of for money or other goods. Disposing of goods for money requires selling effort. "Sales means jobs" because without the continual flow of buying and selling transactions, the entire basis for attaining high and rising standards of living and for maintaining those standards which have been achieved quickly disappears.

5. Both owners and executives will, of course, share the range of objectives relating to family and personal ambitions and to standing in the community, in the industry, or in the general economic structure of the nation. The interests of the individuals in management selling and ownership may, therefore, be parallel to those of the enterprise; but at times and in varying degrees they may be divergent. The evidence is that most successful executives identify their own interest with that of the firm with which they are connected. Nevertheless, when the motivation for selling is power or is unworthy, the possibilities of abuse exist and may result in injury and harm to the buying public until correctives are applied. But in this respect as in so many others, selling leadership does not differ from leadership in other fields.

ULTIMATE OBJECTIVES OF SELLING

One must constantly keep in mind that the basic objective of decent selling effort is to sell goods and services, to influence people to purchase and consume the food, clothing, shelter, the machines and materials—all the millions of items—required for an industrial civilization intended to furnish high levels of living for all the people. In other words, selling effort in all its manifold forms has as its immediate objective buying action taken by people as individuals or as part of a business or other organization. Such action represents the buying of those material goods and immaterial services that make up the economic level of our living. The amount of household production tends to grow less as living standards rise. Only in the early agrarian, pastoral, or hunting stages of economic development could family production satisfy more than a small portion of its needs. Most of the wants of an advanced industrial society such as ours must be satisfied through purchase, because the productive efforts of the family are specialized and may produce directly nothing that the family uses or desires. But only by such employment can workers be productive enough to have their work yield a high standard of living. The fact that selling effort is directed toward all people, not just toward a few privileged persons, needs special emphasis. It aims to sell automobiles not only to the wealthy but to the workman in the factory, to the farmer, or to the teacher. Selling is not the only influence, but it is the most powerful influence to take the type of resultful and productive action that will bring automobiles to the people. It has been a major influence in bringing into operation over 56 million automobiles for 178 million people. It has placed electric refrigerators in more than 90 per cent of wired homes—and one might cite many other instances, to support the fact that it is the many, not the few, who have obtained the increasingly high levels of living.

Successful selling effort obviously implies that people have been led to buy, both for consumptive and productive purposes, those goods and services needed for the continuance of high and rising levels of living. The performance of individuals and firms in persuading many people to buy thus achieves the objective of raising actual levels and standards of living if the persuasion to buy causes people to produce desired goods and services. Therefore, it does no violence to the facts to assert that the *aggregate objective of selling effort, taken as a whole, is to raise* living levels and standards of living. It is the objective of selling not only to bring about high and rising levels of living but also to raise the goals toward which people strive so that when relatively high income levels are attained by the majority of people, there will still be a gap between levels attained and levels desired. Standards are established in a dynamic economy that are a spur to the people to attain still higher levels.

The achieved levels of living in the United States are high for the population in general, higher than anywhere else in the world. They are unique in the history of the world, even though a small portion of our population still endures substandard levels. More production is needed to bring these people up to standard. Higher standards would require even greater productivity and production.

On the other hand, it is to be remarked that the attainment of these higher levels in the United States has not been accomplished by longer or more exacting labor. Rather the reverse. High levels requiring high production do not necessarily increase the amount of time and effort involved. If it were true that high levels could only be secured by longer hours and more exacting work, the question would soon arise as to whether those levels warranted the additional effort. For high levels of living, a balance is required between the work necessary to turn out large amounts of goods and services and the requirements for health and social and spiritual growth, all of which are and should be a part of broadly conceived high levels of living. The reconciling factor, which gives greater production but shorter hours and less exacting labor, is the development and application of technological and management skills and equipment to bring about greater productivity. That this has been done is clear from the record, which will be cited below. That it will continue to enable the reconciliation to be made between greater quantities of goods and services and the burdens of labor is possible but not automatic. Automation is intended eventually to reduce the human burden of producing goods and distributing goods. Nevertheless, although much has been accomplished along this line, it must be stressed that increasing social adjustment in other than economic fields to our high material standards is required before the highest levels of living can be attained.

Logicians will quickly point out that concomitant variation is not a proof of causal relationship, that high living standards in the United States may be due primarily to other causes rather than selling, or may even have occurred in spite of it. Some economists have implied that the high standards of living come first and enable us to bear the "waste" of much selling effort. But it can and will be shown that there is a definite causal connection between high levels of living and selling, which becomes clear from a realistic study of the behavior of buyers and sellers, of businessmen, executives, and the buying public.

D. Distribution Planning

41. The Other Half of Marketing

PAUL D. CONVERSE

Before dividing Marketing into halves, let's look at the overall picture. Marketing accounts for approximately one-half the value created by the production and distribution of goods to the consumer. Sales of services and investment securities and military expenditures are omitted in making this statement. This division—of one-half by marketing and one-half by production has held true for the period for which information is available, that is for the past forty years. All the reasonably complete estimates of the cost (or value added) by marketing since 1909 have been about the same, some a little more and some a little less than 50 per cent of that segment of the Gross National Product covering the production and sale of goods. Marketing expenses appear to be a little more "sticky" than production expenses. Hence in a period of rising prices, marketing accounts for somewhat less than 50 per cent and in a period of falling prices for somewhat more than 50 per cent.

Some persons have reasoned that greater use of machinery has been made in production than in marketing and hence that production costs have decreased relative to marketing costs. Even some men engaged in distribution who have spoken before this convention have been more or less apologetic about the efficiency of marketing.

The trouble with the statement that production is more efficient than marketing is that it isn't so.

We have heard much about the "miracle of production." There has been a miracle of production but there has been an equally great

miracle of marketing. During World War II the volume of manufactured goods doubled, the volume of minerals produced increased 30 per cent, and the volume of farm products marketed increased 25 per cent. This was done with 10,000,000 of our strongest young men under arms. This was really a miracle. However, these goods were distributed and there were probably relatively fewer military deferments for marketing institutions than for production institutions.

There have been technological advances in the production of goods. There have been matching advances in the distribution of goods. Let's cite a few examples. The cost of distributing foods through the wholesaler and retailers has been cut in half since the World War I period. At that time typical wholesale grocers had expense of 10 per cent and margin of 12 per cent. The typical retail grocer had expense of 17 per cent and a margin of 18.5 or 19 per cent. Thus an article sold to a wholesale grocer for $1.00 would be sold to the retailer for $1.14 and the retailer would sell it to the consumer for $1.40. Today the typical chain or supermarket buys an article from the manufacturer for $1.00, takes a 16 or 17 per cent markup and sells it to the consumer for $1.20. The cost of distribution was cut from 40 cents to 20 cents. Most foods not passing through chains or supers move through voluntary or cooperative wholesalers to an independent retailer operating on a cash-carry-self-serve basis and reach the consumer at substantially the same price as charged by the super market.

Another illustration is the rapid growth of one story warehouses and the handling of goods on pallets by fork lift trucks and other mechan-

** SOURCE: Reprinted by permission from *Boston Conference on Distribution*, 1954, pp. 22–25.

ical devices. It has been said that the past 15 years has seen a greater improvement in the mechanical handling of goods than the previous century. One story warehouses, palletization, and fork lift trucks have reduced the cost of handling goods by some 25 per cent. A larger saving has been made by requiring the retailers to originate their own orders and so eliminate the wholesaler's salesmen. This method is almost universal in the grocery trade and several hardware wholesalers operate in this way. Another illustration of reduced costs has been in the increased use of motor trucks which save crating, and handling expenses and reduce time. A warehouse distributing to retail stores over a radius of 200 miles loads the trailers one day, the tractors pick them up that evening and deliver the goods to the retail stores the next morning. L.C.L. railroad freight would often take from 2 to 10 days. The speeding up of deliveries has been so important that some middle west stockyards receive little or no livestock by rail. The truck may by-pass one, two, or three middlemen and save two to four handlings of goods in the marketing of farm products.

Improvements in accounting procedures and machines have in many instances been relatively as important as the improved procedures and machines used in handling the goods through warehouses.

We people engaged in the practice or study of marketing have been too apologetic and have lacked confidence in our own work. We should be like a merchant in Illinois in the wildcat banking days when many of the local merchants were also the bankers. One store keeper decided to open a bank and hung out a sign announcing himself as a banker. Very much to his surprise the very first day a customer made a deposit. The second day two more people made deposits and still more on the third day. His confidence in his bank went up so much that by the end of the week he put some of his own money in it. We need more confidence in our work. We should realize that the overall record of the marketing segment of our economy is just as efficient as that of any other segment of our economy. There are inefficient producers and there are inefficient distributors. If my record as a student of marketing or your record as a distributor is not good, then we should be ashamed of our work and improve it. But let us realize that the overall record of market distribution is fully as good as the overall record of the production.

THE TWO HALVES OF MARKETING

Now let's look at the two halves of marketing. Marketing has been defined as matter in motion. There are two kinds of motion in moving goods from the farm, the mine, and the factory into the hands of the ultimate consumers. Goods must be moved through the trade channel and gotten into the possession of the consumers— that is they must be bought and sold. In the study of economics you learned that a utility is something that satisfies a human want and that there are four kinds of Utility—form, place, time and possession. The creation of form utility is called production. Marketing is that part of our economy that creates possession, place, and time utility. Goods must be moved physically— they must be sorted, graded, packed, crated, loaded, unloaded, unpacked, stored, and transported.

One part of marketing deals with buying and selling, with creating desires and demands for goods, of transferring title to the goods. This part of marketing creates possession utility. The other part deals with the physical handling of goods, transporting them from farm and mine to mill and factory and from factory to processing plant to the consumers and storing when and where necessary. This part of marketing creates time and place utilities.

It appears that these two parts contribute approximately the same amount to our national economy; or if you prefer involve about the same cost. This is a rough approximation owing to the fact there can be considerable difference of opinion as to just how the time of retail workers should be divided.

I want to emphasize that the two parts of Marketing involve about the same expense, or if you prefer, contribute the same amount to the national income. Yet in the study of marketing and the operation of marketing departments and businesses a great deal more attention is paid to buying and selling than to physical handling. In fact the physical handling of goods seems to be pretty much overlooked by sales executives, advertising men, and market researchers. When a question is raised about physical distribution, how often have you heard: "let's refer that to the traffic manager," or "we'll let the warehouse manager worry about it," or "that's a problem for the package engineer." In other words problems of physical distribution are too often brushed aside as matters of little importance. I have for many years been reading business and economic magazines. Such publications over the years have devoted relatively little space to physical distribution.

The sales manager of a medium sized company that distributes its products nationally said to me recently: "One idea that I picked up at a recent meeting of our local chapter of the American Marketing Association is saving our company $3,500 a month and we have not yet made full use of it. This is the use of in-transit rates." A student of marketing in one of our large industrial cities tells me that in-transit privileges is near the top subject of interest among the marketing executives in his city. In-transit and mixed car rates often save several hundred dollars a car in freight costs. The railroads seem willing to establish in-transit rates as this device is particularly useful in meeting truck competition since few trucking lines grant the privilege.

In-transit and mixed car rates are important but there are other devices of equal or greater importance in the physical distribution of goods. I was talking the other day to a man who only a few years ago started a wholesale business. In a very few years he has built up the business until it has sales of several million dollars annually. He preferred to start and grow in rented quarters as he could expand his space as the business grew. Now that he has the business well established he is thinking of a building of his own and estimates that he can reduce his expenses 10 per cent with a modern one-story warehouse.

Everyone needing a warehouse seems to want a one-story building on the fringe of a city. It is possible that the falling off in demand for space in multi-story warehouses will decrease until the rent of such building will decline to a point where the overall cost of operation will be as low as in a one-story warehouse.

I pointed out above that the cost of distributing groceries from manufacturer to consumer had been cut in half in the past generation. This has been done by giving attention to both halves of the marketing process—buying and selling and physical distribution. The chains first and more recently the supers and wholesaler-retailer independents have very largely eliminated the selling operation between wholesale warehouse and retail store. The retail store manager or operator, as the case may be, requisitions his goods from the check lists and order blanks supplied by the wholesale warehouse. This saves time and leads to better stock keeping on the part of the retailer and saves most of the expense of salesmen on the part of the wholesaler.

Food distributors also appear to be leaders in reducing the costs of physical distribution. The chain organizations and especially the younger ones which include most of the supermarkets have been leaders in moving into one story warehouses and handling goods on pallets by fork lift trucks and other mechanical devices. Some of the wholesalers operating on the cost plus basis and sponsoring voluntary groups of retailers have very fine, modern warehouses. Receiving goods in carlot rail shipments and supplying the retail stores by trucks seems to be the preferred method at present. The retail stores are usually operated on a self-serve basis in which the consumer assembles her own order, takes the goods to the check-out counter, and transports them home. Much attention is given to handling goods in the store, the selection of shelving and display racks, the most economical method of getting goods on the shelves, the fastest kind of checkout stands. It has been said that the retail food store is today primarily engaged in physical distribution, the goods having been presold by either the manufacturer or the distributing organization. This is an overstatement, since the display of goods in the store is very, very important.

The point is that the record of the food distributors has been made by giving attention to both demand creation and physical distribution.

One may ask why the food distributors gave more attention to reducing expenses than some other trades. The answer is that food distribution is more competitive than some other industries and they had to do so to stay in business.

SOME OTHER PROBLEMS IN PHYSICAL DISTRIBUTION

Should all goods be shipped from the factory or should regional stocks be carried? If regional stocks are desirable should wholesalers be used? Should stocks be carried in public warehouses or should the company provide its own warehouses? If regional stocks are needed where should they be located? What cities? In what locations in these cities? What are the freight rates to the towns and from the towns to the territories to be served? The use of trucks may change the preferred location of warehouses. For example most goods are manufactured in the east. In going west it was customary to locate the warehouses in the eastern part of the territory. Goods would be shipped in carlots to such towns as St. Louis, Kansas City, Omaha, or Minneapolis and be distributed in l.c.l shipments to territories located for the most part west of the distributing centers. With truck distribution it may be better to locate the warehouse in the center of the territory. For example, the Iowa warehouse may have been located in Davenport. Today DesMoines may be a better location. The Nebraska warehouse may have been in Omaha. Today, perhaps an interior town as Grand Island may be better.

Are in-transit privileges and mixed-car rates available? If not can they be secured? Is more than one railroad available? Even if the rates are the same, services may be better where there is competition. What truck services are available? Is the warehouse well located as to railroads and highways with quick access for incoming and outgoing goods? How frequent, and how reliable are the carriers? What are the insurance rates? What banking facilities are available to make loans on the goods? What about the labor situation? Is police protection adequate or must you provide watchmen?

Should goods be shipped by rail, by truck, by water, or by air? If trucks are to be used should the company operate them or use contract carriers? If operated, should they be owned or leased?

What kind of containers should be used? How should the goods be packed? Can the product be shipped in bulk or is it better to pack it? If it must be packed how and in what type and size of containers? What materials should be used for containers? Should the goods be shipped on pallets?

What type of warehouses are needed? What equipment should they have? How should the warehouse be designed? Is it to be one-story or multi-story? Should it be of fireproof construction? What materials? What refrigeration is needed? How many rooms are needed? What else? What temperature? Should the warehouse be heated? Is there room for expansion if the business grows?

What material handling equipment should be used? Gasoline, or electric, or hand trucks? Overhead or subfloor belts to move the trucks or dollies? The width of the building and passageways are important. What size docks for loading and unloading, incoming and outgoing trucks? How much railroad siding is needed?

Is it economical to have goods palletized in rail cars or in trucks?

What layout or arrangement of stock? Should goods be placed in warehouse in same sequence as on order blanks or requisition sheets? What kind of labor should be used? What use can be made of part-time workers such as students? How should workers be paid—straight time, or piece work basis?

Retail stores have special problems. How much self-service or self-help can be used? How should stock be replenished? What kind of fixtures? Should reserve stock be carried? If so, where? Should fixtures be made or bought? Can the customers be educated to assemble their orders as in a super market? Should goods be delivered to customers? If so, should this be free? In self-service stores what kind of check-out equipment is best? Can customers be educated to unload the carts and put their goods on the check-out counters?

VARIATION WITH TYPE OF GOODS

I said above that there were two kinds of movement involved in the marketing of goods and that the two kinds were of approximately equal importance. This is the overall picture. With some products buying, selling and demand stimulation are relatively more important and with other products the physical handling of goods is relatively more important. In general we say that demand stimulation, advertising, selling, advice and personal adjustment to consumer needs is of first importance in the marketing of fashion and specialty goods. On the other hand we say that physical distribution is of major importance in the distribution of staples and convenience goods.

With a new product or a specialty the good must be called to the consumer's attention, its service to the customer must be explained and demonstrated. In other words the product must win consumer acceptance and this may take time and involve heavy expense. Often the product must be tried on and altered if a garment, or delivered to the home, installed, demonstrated, and guaranteed if a home appliance.

On the other hand a staple or convenience good has won consumer acceptance. Little demonstration and persuasion is needed to sell it. Some 40 years ago Parlin pointed out that a woman usually shops in three stores before buying a fashion good. On the other hand once a customer enters a grocery or drug store she in nearly all cases makes a purchase. Thus the marketing of staples and convenience goods usually involves less expense in the buying and selling operation than the marketing of specialties and fashion goods.

CLASSIFICATION OF GOODS CHANGE

A fact too frequently overlooked is that a good does not always remain in the same classification. When new it may be a specialty requiring active promotion. When it wins consumer acceptance it may be a staple. It is said that when Gillette perfected his razor, it cost less than 50 cents to make it. He proposed to sell it for $1.00. However, before placing it on the market he consulted an "expert." (We didn't have marketing researchers in those days.) This expert told him to sell the razor for $5.00—that he could not pay the promotional and selling expenses of getting it to the consumer for 50 cents. He priced the razor at $5.00 and sold it successfully. However, once safety razors were accepted the manufacturers were glad to give them away in order to sell the blades.

Many products have gone through similar changes. Many of the leading sales managers of the 1920's won their spurs selling dry breakfast cereals in the 1900's. It took a good deal of selling to persuade us to eat the various and assorted kinds of cowfeeds that we now eat and enjoy for breakfast. But eat them we did and they soon became about as staple as anything we buy. The housewife picks them up on her trip through a supermarket. We use to sell washing machines by carting them to the homes of prospects and doing the family wash to prove to the housewife that the machine would get the clothes clean, would not tear off the buttons, and that its operation was safe. Today the great majority of consumers accept the washing machine and will buy without demonstrations. Silk stockings not so many years ago were a high priced luxury good. Today nylons are staples or almost so and can be bought in many super markets.

The good may not change its classification in all places at the same time. Today air conditioning units appear to be staples in Texas while in Illinois they still need considerable promotion.

When a good changes in classification, the type of salesmanship and advertising changes. Instead of high-pressure salesmen, order-takers may do a satisfactory job. Instead of reason-why copy, reminder copy may be indicated. Thus the type of marketing expenses changes. Physical distribution becomes relatively more important and demand creation relatively less important.

Does not much of the present turmoil over discount houses and discount selling come from the failure to realize that many home appliances and other goods are no longer specialties and that they do not require as much advertising and salesmanship as they once did? It appears that most manufacturers have set up discounts to retailers and wholesale distributors determined and adapted to the promotional stage when appliances really had to be "sold" by the use of demonstrations and high pressure advertising and salesmanship. Today many of these appliances are "pre-sold" by the manufacturers, or by the retailer (as in the case of Sears Roebuck). If the manufacturer sells the product it seems no longer to be necessary for the retailer to sell it all over again. The problem becomes more and more one of physical distribution—getting the appliance delivered to the home of the consumer. It seems that many discount houses are willing and anxious to do this for considerably less than the margin allowed by the manufacturers to the wholesale and retail distributors.

Some department stores are talking of discontinuing appliances and others of getting their own brands and doing their own promoting. Many of us can remember when the department stores sold groceries. When the chains reduced the expenses of selling groceries the department stores dropped their grocery departments. The department store is organized and operates primarily to sell goods needing promotion. The department store may have to stick to the promotional type of goods or else through changed methods of operation get its expenses down where it can handle the more staple goods competitively.

42. The Logistics of Distribution

JOHN F. MAGEE

American business is awakening to a new, exciting opportunity to improve service and reduce costs—better management of the flow of goods from plant to user. Capitalizing on this opportunity means:

1. Thinking of the physical distribution process as a *system* in which, just as in a good hi-fi system, all the components and functions must be properly balanced.

2. Taking a fresh look at the responsibilities, capabilities, and organizational positions of executives in traffic, warehouse management, inventory control, and other functions which make up the over-all system.

3. Re-examining the company's physical plant and distribution procedures in the light of technical advances in such areas as transportation, data processing, and materials handling.

STUBBORN PRESSURES

The need for progress in distribution is a product of not one but several trends—trends in costs, in product-line policy, and in the market place. More often than not, the challenge posed is to the system as a whole, not just to the particular part or function where trouble is most obvious.

‡‡ SOURCE: Reprinted by permission from *Harvard Business Review*, Vol. 38, No. 4, July-August 1960, pp. 89–101.

Rising Costs

For years, businessmen and economists have looked with mixed feelings on the increase in distribution costs in our economy. Over the past half century, tremendous strides have been made in reducing the costs of production, but these feats have not been duplicated in other areas. If the over-all efficiency of companies is to continue to improve, management must turn its attention increasingly to holding distribution costs in line. Physical distribution costs in particular, estimated by some to represent the third largest component in the total cost of business operation, are a logical center for management attention.

The problems of cutting these costs pose certain new and interesting questions for business. Whereas in many production operations it has been possible in the past to substitute a machine for human labor and to cut the cost of one operation without seriously disturbing the rest of the production system, this is hardly the case in efforts to cut physical distribution costs. Indiscriminate cost reduction in any one of the individual cost elements, such as inventory maintenance, warehousing, transportation, or clerical activities, can have a disastrous effect on the efficiency of the system as a whole. To illustrate this point:

¶ Suppose we cut inventories. Certainly a reduction in inventories will save capital investment and the costs of supplying capital, and it may save some expenses in storage, taxes, and insurance. On the other hand, an indiscriminate reduction in inventory levels may seriously impair the reliability of delivery service to customers and the availability of products in the field. An inventory reduction which saves money but destroys competitive position is hardly a contribution to a more effective distribution system.

¶ We can cut transportation costs, perhaps, by changing to methods showing lower cost per ton-mile, or by shipping in larger quantities and taking advantage of volume carload or truckload rates. But if lower transportation costs are achieved at the expense of slower or less frequent movement of goods, we face the risk of: (a) cutting the flexibility and responsiveness of the distribution system to changes in customer requirements; (b) requiring greater field inventories to maintain service; (c) creating greater investment requirements and obsolescence risks.

Similarly, blanket refusal to allow cost increases in any one part can wipe out opportunities to make the system as a whole more efficient. For instance: New methods of high-speed data communications and processing may in fact increase the clerical costs of operating the distribution system. On the other hand, they may cut down delays in feeding information back to govern production operations and to control lags in getting material moving into the distribution system in response to customer demand. Thus, they may actually cut *total* distribution system costs because of their impact on improved production and inventory control.

It takes a careful analysis of the total physical distribution system to know whether net costs will be increased or decreased by efforts to cut the cost of any one component.

Proliferating Product Lines

Physical distribution systems in recent years have been put under tremendous pressure induced by changes in product-line characteristics. Until recently, for example, products like typewriters, light bulbs, appliances, and plumbing fixtures were largely utilitarian, with differences in product characteristics rather closely related to function. A typewriter manufacturer did not have to worry about matching typewriter color to office decor or type style to company "image." Light bulbs used to be white and sometimes clear, and they varied by wattage. Now, however, typewriters come in pastels and two-tones. Light bulbs are sold not only to provide light but atmosphere, with a corresponding increase in the number of products that have to be shipped, stocked, and controlled. Appliances and plumbing fixtures are available to customers not only in the classical antiseptic white, but in a wide range of color and style combinations. In short, style and individuality have become strong competitive weapons.

In an almost unending list of products in the consumer field, variations in color, packaging, and other features have imposed heavy burdens on the distribution system. In the marketing of industrial goods, variations in grade, color, and size have had a similar impact. In paper manufacture, for example, the wide variety of package sizes required for consumer products has led carton manufacturers to demand correspondingly wide ranges of kraft board roll widths from paper manufacturers, and these demands have created difficult problems of scheduling, inventory control, and distribution.

The growth and change in product-line characteristics in both consumer and industrial products have meant that manufacturing plants have had more items to make, and the distribution system has had more items to handle and stock. More items mean lower volume per item and correspondingly higher unit handling inventory and storage costs.

Alternative Courses

Increased cost, selling, and product-line pressures suggest that management should take a hard look at alternative distribution patterns, as a means of cutting logistics costs without a major sacrifice in service. Here are a few of the possibilities:

¶ The company can carry central stocks of low-selling items only. To get the right balance of transportation costs, handling costs, and service, it may be necessary to stock these items at one central point and ship them against individual customer orders as the latter arise, perhaps by expedited service or air freight.

¶ For many items in the line, a good compromise may be to carry some low- or middle-volume items in only a few large regional warehousese, as a compromise between the excessive storage costs incurred from broad-scale stocking and the transportation and service penalties incurred by attempting to meet demand from manufacturing points alone.

¶ Warehouse points can be consolidated. With improvements in transportation and in mechanical material- and data-handling methods, large opportunities exist in many businesses for cutting down on the number of field warehouse points. With increased volume through the individual warehouses, carrying a broader product line at the local points begins to make greater economic sense.

Sales-Generating Capacity

The first and most basic job of the distribution system is to get customers, to turn interest and orders into sales. As business has grown more competitive and the public has become harder to please, management has focused increasing attention on the *quality* of its logistical operations. What can be done to make products more readily available for purchase in local markets? What improvements can be made in backing up product merchandising and advertising programs with adequate deliveries and service? Obviously, questions like these are affected by cost considerations, but as marketing objectives they deserve individual attention.

In analyzing the capacity of a distribution system to produce sales, executives will do well to examine three key characteristics:

1. *Location.* It has been estimated, for example, that from 5 distribution points a company can reach 33% of the United States consumer market within a day; while from 25 warehouse locations, 80% can be reached in one day.

2. *Inventories.* Judging from my own and associates' experience, approximately 80% more inventory is needed in a typical business to fill 95% of the customers' orders out of stock than to fill only 80%.

3. *Responsiveness.* The ability of a system to transmit needs back to the supplying plant and get material needed into the field determines how quickly the business can shift with changes in customer preferences to meet demand with minimum investment and cost.

REVOLUTION IN TECHNOLOGY

The pressures on distribution methods have led to exciting new technological advances for getting goods to the user at lower cost to the company—with less labor and materials expended and less capital tied up in inventories and facilities. When these advances are introduced in proper balance, the distribution process can better meet the needs of the consumer. Major technological changes are now taking place in transportation, information handling, and material handling. Let us examine each of them in turn.

Costs vs. Transport Time

Transportation thinking has been dominated too long by preoccupation with the direct traffic bill. Too much attention has been paid to transport cost per ton-mile and not enough to the contribution transportation makes to the effectiveness of the distribution system as a whole.

Railroad rate structures are to an outsider an eye-opening illustration of what can happen when a transportation system is put under the cost-per-ton-mile pressure for too long. Rail rate structures, despite frequent attempts to introduce some rationale, have degenerated into an unbelievable hodgepodge of unrealistic and uneconomic rate compromises as the roads have succumbed to the pressure of giving each shipper the lowest cost per ton-mile, often at the expense of service. While improvements in equipment, such as the introduction of the diesel locomotive, have led to greater efficiency on the track, in some cases at least the longer trains and increased classification problems that have resulted have meant little or no net increase in over-all distribution efficiency. The gap between traffic and marketing thinking is painfully evident in many companies' distribution methods; little has been done to relate transportation methods and service to the objectives of the distribution system in support of marketing efforts.

Transportation costs are important indeed, but they are only part of the story. For example, think of the value of materials in transit:

¶ Data collected on sample shipments in various parts of the country indicate that material may spend one to two weeks in transit and that the capital value of assets tied up in the transportation system may, depending on the pressure for capital, add as much as 1% to the economic cost of the goods.

¶ Service, or reliability of the transport system, is also important. Goods must get to the user promptly and reliably, to permit him to operate systematically with low inventories.

¶ The direct and indirect costs of damage in transport are another large item in the traffic bill that at times gets overlooked in the pressure for low cost per ton-mile.

Clearly, transport time is one of the key determinants of the efficiency of the distribution system. Its impact is not vivid or dramatic, and executives do not always appreciate what a difference it makes, but in a great many companies it is a significant factor in financing. To take a simple illustration: Suppose that in a company doing an annual business of $100 million, time in transit is reduced from 14 days to 2. Time between reorders is 14 days, communication and processing time is 4 days, and field stocks average $12.5 million. In such a situation the reduction in transit time might well lead to a reduction in distribution inventory investment of $6 million, made up of: (1) a reduction of $3.3 million in transit, i.e., 12 days' sales; (2) a reduction of $2.7 million in inventories required to protect customer service resulting from a faster, more flexible distribution system response.

Speeding Up Service

Changes in transportation leading to improved opportunities in distribution have been truly revolutionary since World War II. Major superhighway systems have been built, truck speeds have increased substantially and so have trailer capacities. The growth in the use of trucking for industrial distribution is now well known. The stimulus from subsidies is only part of the story; trucks have been able to compete at characteristically higher ton-mile costs because they have offered speed, reliability, and flexibility to shippers.

Without doubt, railroads are responding to this challenge. A recent survey showed that almost all Class I railroads are offering some form of piggyback or expedited motor-carrier service. At least some railroads are showing new merchandising awareness in concentrating on customer service. Whether the industry will be able, in the face of inherent limitations, to reverse the decline in its share of manufacturers' freight business is still an open question.

Air freight represents a challenge to both rail and over-the-road haulers. Today most industry executives still tend to view air freight as a luxury, as a service available for "orchids and emergencies." However, the trend in air freight rates has been sharply downward in recent years. With new planes coming into service, even further reductions can be projected—down to 8 cents to 12 cents a ton-mile from present-day rates of approximately 22 cents. Much depends on the success of efforts to develop aircraft equipped for freight handling and for flexible operation under a wide range of conditions (for example, modest runway lengths), and to build up the ground service needed to match air-handling speeds so as to avoid the danger faced by the railroads—the collapse of service as a result of concentration on mass, low-cost, terminal-to-terminal movement.

Impact of New Methods

What is the significance of the ferment in transportation methods? For one thing, improvement in local truck service opens up opportunities to serve wide-flung markets through fewer and larger distribution points. With larger distribution centers, the chance that mechanized material handling and storage systems will pay off is enhanced, and inventory requirements are reduced through consolidation.

To suggest the size of the opportunity, one analysis with which I am familiar showed that cutting the number of field distribution points for a national product line from 50 to 25 would increase total transport costs 7% but cut inventories 20% and cut *total* physical distribution costs 8% (the latter representing roughly a 1% cut in the total cost of delivered product). This was accomplished at the cost of serving a few small markets—about 5% of the total—with second-day instead of first-day delivery.

Rapid truck or air service increases the feasibility of relying on shipments from a few central points to back up service. Here are two ways in which this can be employed:

1. The many low-volume items in the typical product line, the items on which local storage and handling costs outweigh the penalty costs of expedited shipment, can be held centrally and moved to the market where they are needed, as needed. For example, the bottom 50% of the product line, which often accounts for only 4% of sales, may require 25% or more of the warehousing costs and inventory capital charges. Turnover of the stocks of these items is often only one eighth that of the high-volume half of the line. In a *relatively* high number of cases, special shipments could be made at a cost well below that of storing the items at local distribution centers.

2. If there are substantial reserve stocks designed to protect customer service located in the field, it is possible to pare them down in the knowledge that additional supplies can be moved in promptly to meet sudden customer demands.

In a typical distribution system a large share of the inventory—as much as 90%—is carried to protect delivery service to customers in the face of fluctuating demand and system delays. This safety stock is most likely to be used at the end of the reorder cycle, when stocks hit their low point before new receipts. Fig. 1 illustrates a common situation, with safety stocks being partly depleted at intervals just before a new shipment arrives. During the period of the first

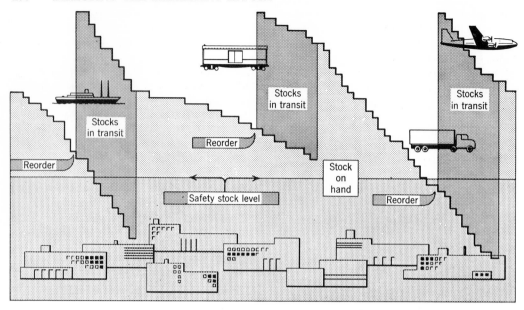

FIG. 1.   What is the characteristic inventory pattern of stocks on hand in the typical company?

reorder, demand has been heavy. In many re-order cycles, however, stocks will not be touched at all; this is the case before the second reorder in the illustration (middle of the chart) comes in. Note that inventory in transit repre-sents a fairly significant proportion of the whole.

How much of safety stocks is actually used depends on the reorder system and level of service maintained. Typically, the last 10% may be needed only once or twice a year—a turn-over rate roughly one sixth the average; and the last 30% may be needed only two to four times a year. Warehouses and inventory carry-ing charges on this portion of inventory, then, may easily run to 10%–20% of the sales they make possible.

There is an opportunity in many companies for management to cut material held in the field and back up customer service through regular-ized high-speed delivery service. This possibility will deserve increasing attention from manage-ment as the costs of high-speed transport, com-munication, and data processing drop.

Information Processing

Revolutionary data-processing methods were noisily battering at established business meth-ods some six or seven years ago, but the impact was more in noise generated than in accomplish-ment. Now that a lot of the superficial excite-ment has died away, however, a broad and solid structure of accomplishment in modern data-processing techniques is quietly being built.

For one thing, computers seem to have be-come much more broadly accepted than antici-pated. When the earliest internally programed machines were announced, computer manufac-turers' optimistic estimates were in the dozens. Today the number of machines installed or in the process of installation is in the thousands. In support of computing or processing facilities, great improvements are taking place in com-munications systems, especially systems de-signed to feed into or out of computers. In dis-tribution management, fast, reliable communi-cation is equally as important as fast, reliable processing.

The *use* being made of modern information-processing equipment in distribution is just as significant as its broad market acceptance. For instance, machines are being used to maintain local inventory balances, forecast near-term de-mand, employ forecasts and inventory balances as inputs in calculating item orders, prepare tentative purchase orders, allocate item bal-ances among stock points, and draw up pro-duction schedules and work force requirements. These are not mere compiling and accounting functions, nor is it fair to call them "decision making." In these functions, the machine systems are interpreting rules or procedures to work out the decisions implicit in them in light of the facts of the situation. In other words, the equipment is doing what we would like intelligent clerks to do: diligently following policy and weighing costs to arrive at day-to-day actions.

The forecasting function in particular deserves special attention. I refer not to the longer term economic forecasts, annual business forecasts, or even shorter term (e.g., quarterly) business predictions, but to short-term forecasts of sales, item by item, over the replenishment lead time. These forecasts are made implicitly or explicitly in every inventory control system. In most companies they are left up to the individual stock clerk or inventory controller to make as best he can, usually with little or no training or guides. Management will spend hundreds of hours of industrial engineering time simplifying or improving a job method here and there to take a few pennies out of labor cost. Yet the stock clerk making inventory control forecasts may, through his control over product distribution and assets tied up in inventories, be costing his company many pennies indeed.

Many people still argue that one cannot forecast routinely because intuition and background knowledge count too heavily. They fail to recognize that objective procedures for short-term prediction of item sales have the same merits as say, routing and tooling lists in a shop. Experience leaves little doubt that great gains can be made by substituting powerful systematic methods for casual or unrecognized ones.[1]

Changes in Material Handling

Mechanization is slowly spreading from the making of things to their handling in distribution. For instance: One company in the clothing industry has installed a new data-processing system first to handle sales orders and then inventory control and production-scheduling systems. At the same time, it has been developing a bin-and-conveyer system which will permit economical mechanization of order-filling activities. The goal toward which both of these efforts are directed is a unified system in which

the customer order not only serves as an input in automatic order handling but will also, after suitable internal mechanical processing, activate the warehouse system to select and consolidate the customer's order. This customer order data will also be processed internally for inventory management and production planning purposes.

How will such changes in warehousing and materials handling influence the planning of distribution systems? The effects will take at least three forms:

1. *Integration of systems for (a) material storage and transport and (b) information handling.* This development should create opportunities for significant "automation" of the distribution function and for reduction of manual drudgery. Ultimate full-scale mechanization of materials handling will not only require redesign of warehouse and transport facilities, but will have an impact on design of products and packages as well.

2. *Pressure to reduce the number of distribution points or warehouses.* Mechanized warehouses cost money. One way to improve the efficiency of capital utilization is of course to increase throughput.

3. *Pressure to concentrate ownership of warehousing facilities.* Mechanization takes capital. This factor will be another force behind the tendency for manufacture, distribution, and maintenance service to become integrated under one ownership roof.

GETTING STARTED

Some managers view the opportunities presented by changes in distribution technology with about the same air with which a bear views a porcupine: the possibilities look interesting, but where can you start to get your teeth in?

Improvements in distribution efficiency cost money. Higher speed, more flexible transport generally costs more per ton-mile. Mechanized warehousing systems or material-handling systems are not cheap. The cost of working out, installing, and testing new information-processing systems may make direct clerical cost savings look like a rather thin return on investment. In fact, direct payoffs from distribution changes (e.g., modified transport methods leading to a direct cut in transport costs) may often be small or nonexistent. The payoffs, often handsome ones, are likely to be indirect, coming about from "tradeoffs" such as paying a higher trans-

---

[1] See Robert G. Brown, "Less Risk in Inventory Estimates," *Harvard Business Review*, July-August 1959, p. 104.

port bill to save material investment, putting in warehouse investment to cut over-all shipping costs, and so on.

Because tradeoffs so often are involved, it is not always easy for management to get an aggressive, functionally operated group of people to think *through* the problems. It is not easy for men in production, sales, warehousing, traffic, merchandising, and accounting to grasp other functions' needs or express their own needs in terms which make the advantages of tradeoff and balance clear. Many times the distribution *system* has been run too long as a collection of more or less independent *functions*. Any changes, any tradeoffs to get the system into better, more economical balance, any modifications to take advantage in the whole system of new technical developments—these are bound to be disruptive and to some extent resisted.

The difficulties in facing up to a searching look at the distribution system are not confined to the individual functions concerned. Some of the toughest questions arise at the general management level. For example:

1. What degree of sales service is the system to provide? How far will the firm go to meet customers' service desires?

2. What standards are to be used to judge investment in facilities and inventory so that it can be weighed against any cost savings that are made possible?

3. What policy will the company take toward ownership and operation of the distribution, transport, warehousing, and information-processing facilities? Will the company operate its own facilities, lease them, contract for services, or rely on independent businesses to perform some or all of the necessary distribution system functions?

4. What is the company's policy toward employment stabilization? To what extent is the company prepared to pay higher distribution costs to absorb demand variations and to level employment?

Approach to the Issues

Grappling with all of these problems is like untangling a tangled skein of yarn. Each decision has an impact on other choices and for this reason is hard to pin down. The distribution problem is a system problem, and it must be looked at as such. If it is examined in total and if the experience and methods available for studying it are used, the issues just mentioned can be resolved in an orderly, mutually compatible way.

In my experience, three key conditions have, when present, made for a sound distribution system study and an effective implementation program:

1. Recognition by company management that improving distribution means examining the full physical distribution system.

2. Use of quantitative systems analysis or operations research methods to show clearly the nature of tradeoffs and the relation between system operation and company policies.

3. Cooperative work by men knowledgeable in sales and marketing, transportation, materials handling, materials control, and information handling.

CONCLUSION

To sum up, a number of pressures have piled up on today's distribution systems. As manufacturing efficiency has increased and product cost has come down, costs have grown. Physical distribution costs are a significant share of these.

Business in many fields is becoming increasingly competitive, with competition taking new forms, including availability of goods and reliability of delivery. Product changes are forcing new pressures on the distribution system—more items to carry, faster obsolescence, lower unit sales and inventory turnover. In particular, changes in merchandising practices, such as the introduction of style as a merchandising weapon, have significantly complicated the distribution problem. Pressures for improvement in logistics also include internal forces—for example, the need to stabilize production and insulate production levels from short-term fluctuations in sales.

In the face of these trends, a number of revolutionary changes have taken place. Substantial improvements have come about in essentially all forms of transportation methods. Tremendous strides forward have been made in information-handling methods, including schemes for assimilating and processing data dealing with product demand and with the need for replenishment. Materials-handling methods, ranging from mechanized stock keeping to extensions of the pallet concept to eliminate item-by-item handling, have been gaining acceptance. Finally, and perhaps as important as improvement in physical facilities and concepts, there has been progress in ways of looking at the logistics problem and at methods for analyzing distribution systems.

Long-Run Implications

So far, we have seen farsighted companies taking advantage of the changes I have described by redesigning their distribution systems to cut costs and increase the support given to sales programs. The next step is now beginning to be felt—the insinuation of distribution concepts into certain aspects of long-term planning and capital budgeting, especially the analysis of facility requirements, the location of distribution points, and the determination of financial requirements to support distribution.

Of course, we must avoid the trap of thinking that all management problems will be resolved in terms of efficient distribution. Nevertheless, the long-range impact of distribution-system thinking on production, on product design, and on manufacturing location may be substantial. Perhaps one of the most significant changes will be in concepts of organization, in the assignment of functions and responsibilities. Efficient physical distribution poses a challenge to business in integrating what is essentially a system approach with the functional approaches that hitherto have tended to govern business organization planning.

In the long run, at least two possible directions are open for making a wide variety of products available in local markets. On the one hand, manufacturers can move toward centralized manufacture, with the specialty or small-volume items being made in enough volume to permit reasonable manufacturing economy and then being moved rapidly, perhaps by air freight, to the local markets as needed. On the other hand, management can try to achieve diversity through superficial differences built into a few basic product lines. Low-cost mass transport methods, perhaps rail freight, can be used to move parts and components from centralized manufacturing points with heavy equipment into widespread local assembly or modification plants. At the local points, the final touches can be put on the product to meet customer demand.

One thing seems sure: the choice of distribution system each company makes will have a significant impact on product design, plant investment, and organization. Industrial logistics and trends in logistics technology will receive increasing attention from business, along with markets, capital resources, and product development, in the formulation of corporate plans for the decade ahead.

E. Product Development

43. Behavioral Science Concepts for Analyzing the Consumer

HERTA HERZOG

In earlier years, marketing, strongly influenced by economic theory, emphasized the objective factors in buying behavior although it was never unaware of the importance of "emotional" factors. It struggled with the problem but it had no systematic way of approaching the question as to the kind of psychological factors present in a given situation and as to the why and how of their importance. This was one of the main troubles with the application of the early "lists" of buying motives.

Psychological research, or what commonly goes under the name of "Motivation Research," has received new attention during the last decade when the post-war seller's market changed into a buyer's market. This economic change stimulated widespread recognition of the need to understand the consumer thoroughly. At the same time, the behavioral sciences had developed to a point where it seemed promising to attempt application of some of their concepts and methods to the specific problems of buying and consumption behavior.

The attempts so far have been quite encouraging but they represent only a beginning. Motivation researchers have been busy doing specific studies; we have not yet had enough time to think through what we are doing and what general findings emerge. We have made uneven use of the available behavioral science concepts, and for some of the marketer's problems the behavioral sciences do not yet offer concepts or methods.

‡‡ SOURCE: Reprinted by permission from *Proceedings of the Conference of Marketing Teachers from Far Western States* (Berkeley, California: September 1958), pp. 32–41.

Application of existing behavioral science material is further complicated by the fact that we are not yet dealing with a unified theoretical system. Interdisciplinary integration is far from complete and so is consensus within the various disciplines. Psychology, for instance, offers at least three major approaches to motivation.

There is the approach of the laboratory psychologists who in many instances use animals for their subjects and who have tended to focus on the physiological tensions or "body needs" as motivational forces.

There is the work of the clinical psychologists, and of dynamic psychology in particular, which has focused on the role of psychological factors. They see in the handling of the biological drives within the mores of society a key problem, and also a possibility for influencing behavior. Conflicts between basic drives or motives and social restrictions, they say, put great stresses on the individual. Since he cannot tolerate them, the motives become repressed, unconscious but not eliminated as driving forces. They continue to make themselves felt in a variety of ways.

A third approach to the study of motives is represented by the Gestalt psychologists and, particularly, the work of Kurt Lewin. This socio-psychological approach emphasizes the fact that people are reacting in an environment and that behavior must be understood as a function of the person and the environment in which he lives, with both of these being mutually dependent variables. Behavior, as these psychologists see it, is largely goal-directed and results from a person's motives as well as his perception of the environment at a given time.

In short, at this point the behavioral sciences

offer a variety of differing theories and approaches to the understanding of behavior. Thus you will find the application of behavioral science concepts to marketing varies with the theoretical orientation of the researchers, or that market researchers borrow eclectically depending on which theoretical concepts seem most applicable and fruitful in a particular case.

WHAT IS A PRODUCT?

Let me begin with the question "What is a product?"—a question of concern to every marketer. From a strictly technical manufacturing standpoint, a product consists of a number of raw materials so put together that the end result, the product, serves a useful purpose of consumption, be it in feeding, clothing, housing, transporting the consumer, etc.

You need only to think about your car, however, to realize that it represents neither the sum total of its parts for you, nor merely an instrument of transportation. This has, of course, been long recognized and one of the concerns of marketing has been to determine just which product "features" are important to the consumer. Thus market research on a food product has tried to measure the relative appeal of such features as taste, color, consistency, quality of ingredients, price etc. Studying cars, we have tried to assess the interest in engineering features such as power steering, power brakes or automatic transmission as compared with appearance, comfort, up-keep, trade-in value, etc.

These familiar classifications are not fully satisfactory. Obviously, "trade-in value" is a feature of a rather different kind than some of the others I have mentioned. To know that a consumer values "comfort" does not tell us too much. What constitutes comfort to him, we want to know: is it the upholstery, leg room, head room, trunk space, good springs, or what? Is it correct to interpret a car owner's concern with power steering as an expression of interest in engineering features or, rather, does it mean "easy parking," another comfort item to the consumer? Will the consumer tell us what he wants when we ask him to compare looks with, let's say, economy or technical quality?

In short, the traditional methods of classification are somewhere inbetween a product definition in terms of the manufacturer and a product definition in terms of the consumer. Thus they tend to fall short of telling the manufacturer how and what the consumer sees in a car

so that he can build a car that will deliver these consumer benefits.

The application of behavioral science concepts, particularly the various psychological theories, has been useful in helping us toward a better understanding of the "product."

In pointing out the subjective component in perception, they suggested that we must go the whole way in determining how the consumer sees the product, not what it is technically. The concept of the "psychological environment" includes the notion that what people "see," depends on the stimulus characteristics as well as their personality—the type of person they are, the state they are in, and their ideology. It contains a strong social and cultural component: we "see" things in the way our culture and the particular social group in which we move have induced us to see them. And we see things in context, not as isolated elements or objects but as part of the "total situation," the inner and outer environment. It is useful to add here a key concept borrowed from psycho-analytic theory, namely, that the "inner environment" may contain repressed needs and wants as well as those the individual is aware of.

These theoretical concepts have led to the notion of the *product image and the exploration of the various meanings, rational and symbolic, which the product* may have to the consumer.

For example, getting at the product image of gasoline, we asked motorists, among a number of questions, what other purchases they consider "similar" to buying gasoline, and why they are similar. We found three main types of conceptions: gasoline was likened to other types of fuel such as electricity, water, etc., by a small percentage; gasoline purchases were likened to other purchases having to do with transportation such as bus tickets, railroad fares, by another small proportion. More than half of the respondents likened gasoline to personal consumption items: things which keep the human body fed such as bread or milk, which keep it protected such as hats or shoes, which keep it pepped up, such as beer or cigarettes.

This particular study was done before the first gasoline additive broke on the market, at a time when in convential questioning the large majority of consumers stressed that gasoline is rather an uninteresting product, all main gasolines are pretty much alike, and that in buying gasoline they look for station convenience and service rather than the particular product sold at the station. The findings on the product image suggested that via the car, viewed as an extension of the body, there was a good deal more potential interest in the product itself which should be catered to in product development and subsequent product promotion.

Or take another example—airplanes and air travel. In another type of so-called projective questioning, people who like plane travel and those who do not care for it were asked to draw their idea of an airplane and tell a story about their drawings. The responses revealed marked differences in product image among the two groups, which were confirmed by other data. The fan sees himself at the controls of a wonderful instrument, while the non-fan tends to see himself as a passenger, looking at a plane mainly as a perhaps time-saving vehicle of transportation.

The famous Mason Haire study is another example of exploration of the product image. As you know, Haire made up two "shopping lists" containing a series of everyday household purchase items such as a pound and a half of hamburger, two cans of Del Monte peaches, etc. One list contained Nescafe while the other, identical with the first, substituted Maxwell House regular for the instant coffee. When he asked a matched group of housewives to describe the type of woman who would purchase each list of products, he found that a considerable proportion mentioned "lazy" housewives, "women who don't plan well," for the list containing instant coffee. Direct questioning had given no indication that this was a connotation associated with the perception of the new product.

Since the meanings associated with a product are often quite varied, it is useful to employ a variety of questioning techniques which will uncover the rational as well as the emotional connotations: direct questions, open-end type questions and projective devices, some of which I mentioned. Also, the questioning must give the respondent a variety of opportunities to say what he or she has in mind about a product. In addition to asking what she likes about the product or how she rates specific features, one might ask about the "ideal" product in a given category. Or one might invite the respondent to describe how she uses the product, or have her report her thoughts as she actually uses it. One might ascertain memories of outstanding enjoyment of the product, ask the consumer how she would feel if she had to do without the product, and why, etc.

From such types of questioning one can document that an apparently simple product such as cigarettes had a variety of "meanings"—even before the days of health concern. Some smokers, for example, saw in a cigarette something to manipulate, a means of assertion; they were particularly interested in specific features such as firm packing. For others, a cigarette was a means of comfort—deep inhaling, the strength of a cigarette, were some of the things they particularly valued. Some saw in a cigarette an outlet of nervous tension; there were no particular features that interested them more than others. Some saw in a cigarette primarily an oral sensation; taste of course was one of the features they were interested in. In each case it could be shown that the product definition was strongly linked to basic tendencies on the part of the smoker and linked also to an interest in particular product attributes.

Studies relating to product image have also taught us that the same word used loosely by the consumer, may have very different meanings. Take "taste," for example. In a study of Kippers we found that a large proportion of respondents who in direct questioning said they didn't use the product because they didn't like its taste, actually had never tasted it. In depth interviewing, it turned out that dislike of "taste" in this case was merely a way of talking about something that was unfamiliar, foreign, unacceptable, unconventional. The average American housewife had a kind of mental image of barefoot dock workers slopping around in these slimy fish in some far away port. In the case of soda crackers, liking for "taste" stands primarily for texture characteristics. In the case of toothpastes, "taste" stands for the total sensation in the mouth, not just a particular flavor. And in the case of hard liquor, "taste" is a means to describe and to anticipate effect characteristics.

Product image studies need to be repeated. Consumer conceptions about a product do not stand still: technical developments, degree of market saturation, availability, are some of the environmental factors which may restructure the consumer image. There was a time when ammoniated toothpastes had a special health connotation attractive mainly to the hypochondriac. With the subsequent advent of chlorophyll and anti-enzyme ingredients, the image of a toothpaste changed; today the anti-decay feature is a part of a modern, up-to-date toothpaste that the majority of consumers would not want to do without.

WHAT IS A BRAND?

You will have gathered from the preceding that brands, like product types, are perceived by the consumer in the form of "brand images." This is the sum total of impressions the consumer receives from many sources: from actual experience and hearsay about the brand itself as well as its packaging, its name, the company making it, the types of people the individual has seen using the brand, what was said in its advertising, as well as from the tone, format, type of advertising vehicle in which the product story was told.

All these impressions amount to a sort of brand personality which is similar for the consuming public at large, although different consumer groups may have different attitudes toward it. For instance, users generally interpret the brand image more favorably than non-users although both groups agree on its essential outline. The user may like a brand because it is "tried and true," the "first and best on the market," while the non-user may call the same brand "old-fashioned," with both agreeing that it is an old, well-established brand.

The brand image contains objective product qualities, particularly if there are observable product characteristics such as differences in strength or taste or shape or texture. These qualities themselves have rational as well as symbolic meanings which merge with the meanings created by all the other sources through which the public meets a brand.

In the gasoline study quoted before, it was found that motorists tended to think of Gulf, among other things, as a "friendly" gasoline—a notion that stemmed from associations with the name which reminded of "outdoor sports," the "Gulf of Mexico," etc. These notions were supported by the "sunny" yellow color used in its emblem, the "friendly" approach in its advertising copy (Go Gulf), and the nature of the advertising vehicle, a program called "We the People" which, although no longer on the air at the time of the study, had done its share in contributing to the brand image.

Interviews with smokers done by various motivation researchers, indicate that although they may not be able to tell brands apart in a blindfold test, they nevertheless have quite clear-cut images of various brands. Both Camels and Luckies, for example, are thought of as "strong" cigarettes as compared with Philip Morris which is associated with mildness. But there are further marked differences in the images of Camels and Luckies. This was measured, for example, by a set of questions in which people were asked to "match" each brand with a series of socio-economic and psychological characteristics, which presumably were "typical of the person likely to smoke the brand."

The concepts consumers have of a brand result from objective facts; at the same time, these concepts serve to shape sales patterns. For we find rather frequently that consumers tend to prefer the brand whose image is congenial to them. This brings me to a third point—the question "What is a consumer?"

WHAT IS A CONSUMER?

Marketing has always thought of the consumer in terms of who buys what, for what purpose, at what price, where, etc. This kind of information, derived from observable consumer behavior data, is very important in locating a product or brand in the total market picture. But certain marketing needs, specifically those of the people concerned with the creative aspects in product development and brand promotion, require more qualitative dynamic knowledge about the consumer than his age, income or family status. They require an answer to the question why consumers buy a particular product and how current non-users can be switched to a specific brand.

This statement of the problem of consumer motivation is in itself different from the way in which it used to be stated, and strongly influenced by the application of behavioral science concepts.

From trying to apply a general list of buying motives to the purchase of a particular product or brand, market research proceeded to ask the user why he bought or preferred the brand, to find out from the former user why he switched to it, and from the non-user why he never used it. This was a step ahead because it attempted to trace the purchase decision for a particular brand, and included the user and the non-user.

As you can well imagine, the non-user in particular finds it difficult to explain why he doesn't use the brand. "I just never thought of it," "I don't need it," "I like my current brand," are rather typical answers. Even more specific ones such as "I don't like the color," and "It's too expensive" do not indicate with enough certainty what appeal would be effective in inducing purchase. If one were to take the an-

swers seriously and changed the color or reduced the price, two drastic changes on the
part of the manufacturer, would the non-user
really become a consumer, one wonders? And
what impact would these changes have on the
current consumer?

In today's third stage of development we are
mindful of the concept that the consumer acts
in a total situation and we also consider that
behavior results from the interplay of his personal make-up and his perception of the environment. Thus we tend to look upon a particular brand as one possible choice the consumer
might make among other brands in the category, and even among other kinds of products.
And allowing for external situational influences
which might have a bearing on buying behavior,
motivation research proper attempts to assess
the hold the brand has on its current consumers
(some of whom might switch away from it tomorrow), as well as the appeal it might offer to
its most likely prospects (not *all* non-users). It
does so by relating the perception of the brand
to the "needs" of the consumer.

In this analysis of needs one must provide
for the fact that consumer behavior serves physiological as well as psychological needs; needs
the person is aware of and needs he may not be
conscious of although they are "projected" into
his buying behavior; needs he is willing to tell
and those he doesn't want to admit, falling back
on "rationalization." The needs are patterned
by the culture and the social class to which
he belongs, his stage of development as well as
his "personality."

Therefore, a good motivation study must be
based on a thorough knowledge of the market
in terms of such background characteristics as
socio-economic status, age, city size, region; and
it employs the total arsenal of methods that the
behavioral sciences have at their command so
far to get at conscious as well as unconscious
needs. This means personality tests and depth
interviewing, as well as direct questioning.

One of the general findings that has emerged
from this type of research is the concept of
psychological market segmentation which cuts
across and refines the traditional concept of
market segmentation based on such characteristics as age or income. Consumers tend to buy
the brand whose image most closely corre-
sponds to their own needs; the image selects
the type of consumer for whom the brand
promises particular satisfaction. This is true in
product categories where you would expect
it, such as in the cigarette field or the use of

hair tonics among men. It also holds for durable
goods such as cars, for foods down to peanut
butter, for household supplies down to dis-
infectants.

The main research task in finding out what
motivates the consumer toward product use
and brand preferences is to find the psychological dimension(s) which characterize the
user and differentiate him from the non-user.
These might have to do with the "self-image"
which the consumer acts out, as it were, in his
consumption behavior. The self-image is important, for example, in determining whether
or not a man (with enough hair on his head)
will use a hair tonic, and what type of hair
tonic he will use. The basic compulsivity of a
woman and the way she sees her role as a
housewife, have a marked bearing on the type
of household items she uses. People on comparable income levels handle the conflict between
the impulse for self-indulgence (buying) and
the demands for self-restraint (postponement
of buying) in ways which differentiate the saver
from the non-saver. In a study dealing with a
service from a "big" company, we found that
this key characteristic of the image had a positive attraction for at least two consumer groups.
Those who as personalities sought and needed
protection, bought the company's products because bigness provided assurance. At the other
end of the pole were the assertive, aggressive
people who also reacted positively because bigness provided a self-conscious gratifying identification with success.

However, there were also groups representative of many consumers who reacted negatively for a variety of reasons. In some instances
the resistance against a "big" brand was as
basic as its appeal to other consumer groups.
In other instances, the negative responses expressed merely a feeling that the company was
remote, aloof, efficient but not close enough
to the consumer.

The data not only indicated that these non-
users could be interested but the interviews
contained a number of important clues as to
just what the brand must do to hold its current
customers and come closer to these prospects.
The clues included changes in marketing strategy, media policy and selling arguments.

WHAT IS AN AD?

I will be very brief on a fourth question,
"What is an ad?" because you are probably
least interested in this area of application.

Let me make one point on layout, the physical appearance of the ad, since the application of behavioral science concepts to advertising copy follows pretty much from what I have already said about findings on consumer motivations.

Thousands of readership checks in the past have served to indicate that on the average photographs or life-like drawings are in most product fields a means of obtaining attention. Borrowing some of the concepts developed particularly by scientists working on theory of instincts, we have come to understand what accounts for the occasional very high readership obtained by ads that do not use the photographic technique.

These scientists, working with animals, have come up with the concept of "perceptual releasers." These are attributes of the stimulus which are sufficient to activate memory traces which then produce the response. For example, studying the courtship behavior of the Stickleback fish, they found that the male will pursue the dummy of a female, held into the aquarium by the experimenter, as long as it has a swollen abdomen (even though it may be only a very crude model), in preference to a life-like reproduction of a normal female. He will court the dummy particularly if it is lowered into the aquarium in the typical position of the female Stickleback in the courting situation.

The perception of an ad apparently works similarly. For example, one successful campaign featured an insurance salesman, Mr. Friendly, who was drawn in almost cartoon fashion. It was certainly not a life-like portrayal but copy research indicated that this piece of artwork served indeed to catch and release the reader's ambivalence about insurance and insurance salesmen. It was real in the sense of touching a real experience.

In conclusion, I should like to apologize that I know little or nothing about your special area of interest, the teaching of marketing. If the behavioral science approach is not part of your curriculum, I should think it worthy of your consideration—even if its application to marketing problems is not yet fully developed.

44. What Is "New" about a New Product?

CHESTER R. WASSON

Consider the case of the soup-maker who, by freezing, was able to develop commercial production of soups which previously had to be fresh-prepared—an oyster stew among them. Estimating that the market potential might be approximated by the average relationship between frozen and canned foods, he tried his soups in a single test market. The oyster stew sold out so fast that he had to withdraw it from test until he could expand production facilities even for this one market.

Or take the case of the industrial manufacturer who developed a silo-like forage storer, capable of increasing livestock production profits substantially if properly used. Yet when put into distribution through experienced dealers in heavy farm equipment, it lay dormant for more than four years. In fact, no appreciable market headway was made until it was taken out of the hands of what had seemed to be a logical channel for any kind of farm equipment.

Then, consider the business executive with soap-and-cosmetic experience who acquired rights to a promising soil improver. Trade checks indicated that consumers liked it very much, and an impartial laboratory test indicated technical properties of substance. Put into a few test garden stores with no more than nominal advertising sales seemed satisfactory. Nevertheless, jobbers would not take it on, and when direct sales to a wider group of dealers was tried, none of the outlets developed any major volume. Even though both amateurs and

‡ SOURCE: Reprinted by permission from the *Journal of Marketing* (National Quarterly Publication of the American Marketing Association), Vol. 25, No. 1, July 1960, pp. 52–56.

professionals who have tried it like it, and come back for more, and in spite of the fact that the economics of its use is reasonable and that theoretical demand seems attractive, the executive is about to write it off after four years of trying.

THE DIFFERENCE LIES IN WHAT IS NEW

All three cases are simple examples of a too prevalent failure to analyze the "what's new?" in the new product, to make sure that marketing strategy, channels of distribution, and available resources are compatible with the elements of novelty in the new product. The ease or difficulty of introduction and the characteristics of the successful marketing strategy depend basically on the nature of the "new" in the new product—the new as the customer views the bundle of services he perceives in the newborn.

Take the oyster stew—what was really new, the stew itself? In "R" months, oyster stew has been traditional in homes and restaurants from Boston and San Francisco to What Cheer, Iowa, from the Waldorf-Astoria to Harry's Diner. Assuming adequate quality in the commercial product, oyster stew was an old and welcome dinner-table friend. Was the idea of commercial preparation new? For oyster stew, yes, of course, but not for soup. Just look at the facings in the gondolas of any supermarket, or at the empty cans in the trash of any restaurant.

Of course, the idea of a frozen soup was new, but not the concept of frozen prepared foods. Food-store freezer cases had indeed established the association of fresh-quality taste with freeze-processing. But to the consumer, the only "new" aspect about frozen oyster stew was the greater availability and convenience implied in "frozen." With this particular item, the probability of great development might have been anticipated and prepared for in advance.

The silo and the soil improver, by contrast, looked deceptively similar to known items. But actually both embodied, for the consumer, radically new ideas; and both required extreme changes in user habits and user ways of looking at familiar tasks.

The forage storer looked like the familiar silo from the outside, but really embodied a new principle of preservation whose major benefits would be realized only when livestock were taken off pasture and barn-fed harvested forage the year around. Adoption of the device meant, in effect, adoption of a radically new pattern of work organization, and even of farm buildings in some cases.

No matter how great the promised benefit, such a major turnabout of habits requires a great deal of personal selling to get even the more venturesome to try it. Traditional farm-equipment channels are not prepared to carry out the prolonged and intensive type of pioneering personal sales effort and demonstration required. A reasonable degree of success began to accrue only after the manufacturer realized these facts and made the necessary changes in his selling plan.

Likewise, the soil improver resembled other growth stimulants in that it was sold in large bags and had a granular appearance. But the method of use was entirely different from, and more difficult than, the methods of surface application common to most growth stimulants in garden use. It had to be dug in, to be physically intermixed with the soil. In addition, the benefit was an unfamiliar one, and perhaps not easily believable—simple soil aeration. True, in cultivation, all gardeners practice aeration; but they think of weed killing, not aeration, when they hoe their gardens.

With such a product, success can reasonably be expected only after a strong educational campaign based on intense advertising, wide publicity, and personal contacts with consumer groups such as garden clubs and women's clubs. The resources needed were far in excess of those available in a "bootstrap" operation.

The Toni Example

Determination of the novel aspects of a new product is no simple mechanical process. What is new depends on what the prospective consumer perceives, or can be brought to perceive, in the new product.

Determining such potential aspects requires a high order of imagination, and spectacular successes such as the Toni Home Permanent are due in no small part to the introducer's skill in pinpointing the nature of the novel aspects of the product, and devising the kind of marketing strategy needed to fit the various types of "new" elements in his product.

When the Harrises first introduced Toni, they clearly perceived that their key problem was to gain credibility for the idea of a safe and satisfactory "permanent wave" done in the home. Home curling of hair was an old custom, but the home-produced curl had always been very temporary. Permanent waves had been available, and proved, for nearly thirty years, but only at the hand of a skilled hairdresser, and in a specially equipped beauty parlor. With the perfection of the cold-wave lotion, a true home permanent became possible, using a technique not very different from those already in use for temporary home curling. The principal benefit was one for which the times of the middle and late 1940's were ripe—a major saving in cost as compared with the professional job.

The problem was to gain credibility for the safety and the effectiveness of the product claiming the benefit (Toni)—a problem requiring intense selling effort. The Harris strategy consisted of: persuading the girl behind every cosmetic counter in town to use a kit herself before it went on sale; making sure that every cosmetic counter had a stock before the day of introduction; working one town at a time, putting the maximum advertising effort behind the introduction; plowing back all income into further advertising until market saturation was accomplished; and then using funds from established markets to open new ones.

If, on hindsight, this solution seems to have been the obvious, it should be noted that Toni was not the first cold-wave home permanent— merely the first successful one. The forgotten competitor, who was really first, never appreciated the intensity of consumer education that would be needed, and had so little success that his product is remembered by few.

WAYS A PRODUCT CAN BE "NEW"

In how many ways can a product be new? Of course, each case should be analyzed on its own. Nevertheless, there are at least thirteen possibilities which should be considered:

A. Six novel attributes are positive, in the sense that they ease the job of introduction:

1. New cost—or, better yet, price—if lower.
2. New convenience in use—if greater.
3. New performance—if better, more dependable and in the range of experience of the prospect—if believable.
4. New availabiliy, in place, or time, or both (including antiseasonality).
5. Conspicuous—consumption   (status symbol) possibilities.
6. Easy credibility of benefits.

B. At least four characteristics make the job more difficult, slow up market development, and usually make it costlier:

7. New methods of use (unless obviously simpler).
8. Unfamiliar patterns of use (any necessity for learning new habits in connection with performance of a task associated with the new product).
9. Unfamiliar benefit (in terms of the prospect's understanding).
10. Costliness, fancied or real, of a possible error in use.

C. Three others are ambivalent in their effect—that is, the effect on market development probably depends not only on their exact nature, but also on the cultural climate at the moment. However, extreme unfamiliarity would probably be negative in effect:

11. New appearance, or other sensed difference (style or texture, for example).
12. Different accompanying or implied services.
13. New market (including different channels of sale).

The oyster stew had four to six positive characteristics (only lower cost and conspicuous consumption omitted), and no negative ones. The silo and the soil improver had all of the negative attributes listed, and only performance among the positive. Toni had cost and performance in its favor, and marketing strategy involved an overwhelming attack on the negative aspects (fear of error and credibility of results).

The ambivalence of style should be obvious to those who have followed automobile history. The turtle-shaped DeSoto of the 1930's was one of the most spectacular design failures of history. The design was "too radical" for the motor-ists of that era. Twenty years later the very similar appearance of the Volkswagen "beetle" proved no deterrent to the initiation of a radical reorientation of the American automobile market. And while the Volkswagen brought into that market items of dependable performance, greater convenience in use, and a lower cost than had been available for some time, one element in its success was the recognition of the necessity for continuing the availability of an established implied service in the sale of the car —ready availability of parts and service. Volkswagen entered no area until it had made certain of a high-grade service network in that area.

A Fourteenth Characteristic

Omission of a possible fourteenth characteristic—new construction or composition—is purposeful. This characteristic is neutral—that is, it has no consumer meaning except to the extent that it is identified with, or can be associated with, one or more of the consumer-oriented characteristics listed above.

All that is new in any product is the package of consumer-perceivable services embodied in it. The innovator leads himself astray who analyzes the novel in his newborn in terms of physical and engineering attributes.

An Example in Television

The physical similarity of color TV to black-and-white TV probably led the electronic industry to expect, erroneously, that color-set introduction would parallel the "mushroom" market development experienced with black-and-white. Physically, the parallel was certainly there. Color adds a new dimension to the signal received, just as the picture added a new dimension to the radio signal. But black-and-white television was not, for the consumer, a simple extension of radio. To the family, and most especially to the children, it was a vastly more convenient theater—it was "movies in the parlor." In an era in which children were being granted almost everything they asked for, the pressure for ownership soon became overwhelming. And to add to that pressure, the black-and-white television set required an unmistakable and quite conspicuous symbol of possession—the distinctive aerial. Black-and-white television never had to be sold—it was bought.

Color television, however, to the consumer, *is* simply an extension of black-and-white, which he already owns, and to which he is thoroughly accustomed. The mere idea of an added color dimension has only potential interest to the adult, and probably little to the child. Programs, moreover, are fully compatible—the owner of the color TV set can talk about no program the black-and-white neighbor has not been able to see.

Color television's one positive characteristic is thus simply better performance—a degree of better performance which has not as yet acquired much value in the eyes of the consumer. Offsetting this are the factors of higher cost, questions as to perfection of color TV, and a benefit that is relatively unfamiliar, so far as the experience of most prospects is concerned.

If color television is to become dominant, it will have to gain acceptance the way most other home appliances have—by "hard" direct-to-customer personal selling, probably operating through selective retail distribution, backed up by strong advertising and shrewd publicity that will build up the latent added value of color reception into kinetic reality.

The Old Can Be New

Even the well-established can be "new" so far as the buyer is concerned. The pharmaceutical industry is well aware that when its ethical formulations can be made available for over-the-counter sales, new sales vistas can be opened by a new sales effort. Ecko discovered that an invention of the 1890's could gain quick success when reintroduced to the modern market (the case of the one-hand egg-beater). And one of the most interesting research results the author ever had was the discovery that a minor product which a client had been making for over fifty years needed only a different kind of sales effort, including a new channel of sale, to turn it into a promising new major product in the industrial-component field.

MARKET MANAGEMENT OF INNOVATION

Skilled management of the innovation phase of the enterprise is, increasingly, a prerequisite to business success. Today's fast-moving markets pay best profits to firms in the van of those with product improvements and new products. In some industries, even mere survival depends on constant, successful new-product introduction. New-product success follows only when the marketing plan is suited to the innovational characteristics of the individual product, as the customer views it, or can be brought to view it.

Really consistent success in the marketing of innovations requires an all too rare understanding that the extent and nature of the new is not measurable in terms of the physical specifications of the product nor in the logical blueprint of the service. The nature of the new is in what it does to and for the customer—to his habits, his tastes and his patterns of life.

Some aspects of the new product make familiar patterns of life easier, cheaper, more convenient, or otherwise more pleasant. These aspects aid speedy introduction and adoption. Other aspects of the innovation require new patterns of life, new habits, the understanding of new ideas or ways of looking at things, the acceptance of the difficult to believe, or the acquisition of new tastes. The latter require the maximum concentration of marketing energy, to add enough value to the strange service to counterbalance the pain of the new idea.

Finally, some characteristics can be positive, negative, or neutral, dependent on the trend of the cultural climate. The current valence of these must be carefully evaluated at the time of introduction, and the marketing plan, or even the product design, fitted to the value determined.

Skillful development of new-product marketing plans would thus seem to consist of three basic steps:

1. Careful analysis of the positive and negative aspects of the specific product.

2. Maximum exploitation of the improvements in the familiar embodied in the product, to gain added value necessary to overcome the negative aspects.

3. Application of the maximum promotional effort in countering the negative aspects and lending value to the new and unfamiliar.

F. Pricing The Offering

45. Price Policies and Theory

EDWARD R. HAWKINS

Although the theory of monopolistic competition is now almost twenty years old it remains virtually unused by marketing students, even those who are attempting to develop theory in marketing. In particular, "marketing price policies" are still treated as though they have no relation to economic theory of any sort. In the leading marketing text books there are sections describing such pricing policies as "odd prices," "customary prices," "price lining," "psychological prices," etc.[1] These are presented as descriptions of market behavior, presumably discovered by marketing specialists and unknown to economists. Even the one marketing text that explains the basic pricing formula under conditions of monopolistic competition fails to use it in the discussion of price policies.[2] Since text book writers treat the subject in this way it is not surprising that practitioners writing on pricing do not attempt to relate their policies to economic theory.[3]

It is the purpose of this article to show that these price policies are special cases of the general theory of monopolistic competition. Perhaps clarification of this point will serve to narrow the gap between the economic and marketing conceptions of pricing, and to systematize the discussions of price policies in marketing literature.

The thesis is that each of the familiar price policies represents an estimate of the nature of the demand curve facing the seller. It is not possible, on the basis of available evidence, to generalize on the validity of these estimates in various situations. The point merely is that a seller using one of these policies is implicitly assuming a particular demand curve. In the following sections various price policies are discussed in these terms, after a brief review of the general theory of pricing which is basic to all of the policies discussed.

---

[1] R. S. Vaile, E. T. Grether, and Reavis Cox, *Marketing in the American Economy* (New York: Ronald Press, 1952), ch. 22; E. A. Duddy and D. A. Revzan, *Marketing* (New York: McGraw-Hill, 2nd ed. 1953), ch. 29; P. D. Converse, H. W. Huegy, and R. V. Mitchell, *Elements of Marketing* (New York: Prentice-Hall, 5th ed. 1952) ch. 10; H. H. Maynard and T. N. Beckman, *Principles of Marketing* (New York: Ronald Press, 5th ed. 1952) ch. 35, 36; R. S. Alexander, F. M. Surface, R. E. Elder, and Wroe Alderson, *Marketing* (Boston: Ginn, 1940) ch. 16. Since these policies are fully described in marketing texts the explanation of them in this article will be brief. The attempt, rather, is to express the policies in terms of demand curves in order that the relationship to the theory of monopolistic competition may be seen.

‡‡ SOURCE: Reprinted by permission from the *Journal of Marketing* (National Quarterly Publication of the American Marketing Association), Vol. 18, No. 3, January 1954, pp. 233–240.

[2] Charles F. Phillips and Delbert J. Duncan, *Marketing, Principles and Methods* (Chicago: Richard D. Irwin, rev. ed. 1952), ch. 29, 30, 31.

[3] For example, Oswald Knauth, "Considerations in the Setting of Retail Prices," *Journal of Marketing*, Vol. 14, No. 1, July 1949, pp. 1–12; Q. Forrest Walker, "Some Principles of Department Store Pricing," *Journal of Marketing*, Vol. 14, No. 4, April 1950, pp. 529–537.

THE GENERAL THEORY OF PRICING

The theory of correct pricing under conditions of monopolistic competition, as developed by Chamberlin and Robinson is illustrated in Fig. 1. Each seller with some degree of monopoly created by product differentiation has his own negatively-inclined average revenue curve, AR. From this he derives the marginal revenue curve MR, and determines his price by the intersection of MR and MC, his marginal cost. Marginal cost can be derived from either average cost AC, or average variable cost AVC, since it would be the same in either case. In practical terms this means that for correct pricing the seller does not need to allocate over-

would result at various volumes at different prices. On each such TR curve a point can be estimated showing the sales volume that would actually be obtained at that price. If these points are connected a type of demand curve results (DD'), indicating total revenue rather than average revenue as in the usual demand curve.[4] The objective of correct pricing is to maximize the vertical distance between DD' and the TC (total cost) curve. This formulation has an advantage over the MC-MR one in that in addition to indicating the correct price and volume it also shows total cost, total revenue, and total net profit. It may also be more acceptable to business men and engineers who are accustomed to break-even charts.

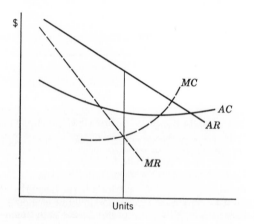

FIG. 1

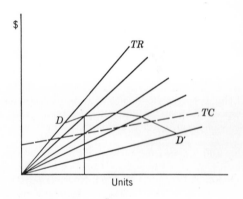

FIG. 2

head cost to individual items. For that matter, he does not even need to compute MR and MC, for the same correct price can be derived from AR and AVC by maximizing the total of the spread between them multiplied by the volume.

An alternative solution which may be more understandable to business men can be obtained from break-even charts. The customary break-even chart is deficient for pricing purposes because it is based on only one price and reveals nothing but the quantity that would have to be sold at that price in order to break even. A modification can be devised that remedies this shortcoming of the break-even chart, and even has some advantages over the MC-MR formula. Fig. 2 shows such a chart, in which a number of different total revenue (TR) curves are drawn, indicating the total revenue that

In the following discussion of marketing price policies, however, the AR curve will be used because it more clearly illustrates the points made.

MARKETING PRICE POLICIES

Odd Prices

The term "odd prices" is used in two ways in marketing literature; one refers to a price ending in an odd number while the other means a price just under a round number. If a seller sets his prices according to the first concept it

---

[4] Cf. Joel Dean, *Managerial Economics* (New York: Prentice-Hall, 1951), p. 405. Dean shows a total revenue curve without, however, indicating its relationship to break-even charts.

means that he believes his *AR* curve is like the one shown in Fig. 3.[5] In this case each price ending in an odd number will produce a greater volume of sales than the next lower even-numbered price. Many sellers appear to believe this is true, although the only large-scale test ever reported was inconclusive.[6]

The second concept of odd-pricing implies an *AR* curve like the one shown in Fig. 4, with critical points at prices such as $1, $5, and $10.[7] The presumption is that sales will be substantially greater at prices just under these critical points, whether ending in an odd or even number.

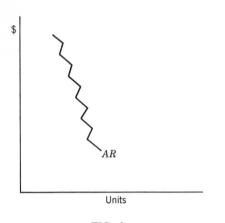

FIG. 3

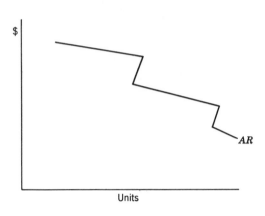

FIG. 4

[5] This curve might be regarded as discontinuous, especially since the difference between points is only one cent. But it is customary to draw demand curves as continuous even though, as Chamberlin has said, *any* demand curve could be split into segments. E. H. Chamberlin, "Comments," *Quarterly Journal of Economics*, Vol. 64, November 1934, p. 135; and A. J. Nichol, although drawing important conclusions from the supposed discontinuity of certain demand curves, states that the curves would be continuous if it were feasible to change prices by small amounts. A. J. Nichol, "The Influence of Marginal Buyers on Monopolistic Competition," *Quarterly Journal of Economics*, Vol. 64, November 1934, footnote 7, p. 126. Henry Smith believes that discontinuous demand curves might result from such heavy advertising of a certain price that the product would be unsalable at any other price. *Cf.* "Discontinuous Demand Curves and Monopolistic Competition: A Special Case," *Quarterly Journal of Economics*, Vol. 64, May 1935, pp. 542–550. This would not seem to be a very common case, however, since marketing literature reveals heavily advertised products selling at various prices.
[6] Eli Ginsberg, "Customary Prices," *American Economic Review*, Vol. 26, No. 2, 1936, p. 296. Some economists doubt the validity of positively-inclined segments of demand curves, believing either (a) that the case could happen only if consumers regard price as one of the qualities of the product, thus making it improper to show these "different" products on one demand curve, or (b) that it simply does not happen that consumers will buy more of a product at a higher price than they will at a

lower one. In regard to the first view, the important thing for purposes of the seller's pricing policy is the shape of the *AR* curve for what *he* knows is the same product. And while he may be interested in the psychology lying behind the consumer's demand curve he is not committed to the belief that it must be capable of explanation in terms of indifference curves. In regard to the second point, many marketing writers have commented on the view that a higher price will sometimes sell more than a lower one. For example, Phillips and Duncan say it may be possible to sell a greater number of a 15-cent item at 19 cents than at 15 cents (*op cit.*, p. 656). Q. Forrest Walker (*loc. cit.*), suggests that 98 cents may sell better than 89 cents. Maynard and Beckman state "It is said that more articles can be sold at 17 cents than at 14 cents." (*op. cit.*, p. 656). Converse and Huegy say "Some sellers feel that odd prices are better than even prices; others, that it makes little difference" (*op. cit.*, p. 209). A New England supermarket chain reports that their meat prices never end in the figure "1," because their price tests show they can sell more at a price ending in "3." And a U. S. Department of Commerce study reports a price of 79 cents selling more than a price of 75 cents, and a case where silk underwear sold more readily at $2 or $5 than at $1.95 or $4.95 respectively. *Cf.* F. M. Bernfield, "Time for Businessmen to Check Pricing Policies," *Domestic Commerce*, Vol. 35, March 1947, p. 20.

[7] This idea is applied even to very high prices. Thus, an automobile may be sold at $1995 rather than at $2,000.

Psychological Prices

Some of the marketing text books give the name of "psychological pricing" to policies quite similar to the one just discussed. It has been found in some pricing experiments that a change of price over a certain range has little effect until some critical point is reached. If there are a number of such critical points for a given commodity the AR curve would look like the one in Fig. 5, resembling a series of steps. This differs from the concept of odd pricing in that the curve does not necessarily have any segments positively inclined, and the critical points are

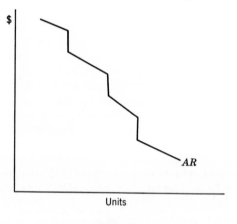

FIG. 5

not located at each round number but only at the prices psychologically important to buyers. Pricing tests at Macy's have disclosed such step-shaped AR curves.[8]

Customary Prices

Another pricing policy usually described as though it has no relationship to theory is the one using "customary prices." This is most frequently associated with the five-cent candy bar, chewing gum, soft drink, or subway fare. The chain stores have experimented, apparently successfully, with combination cut prices on such

---

[8] Oswald Knauth, "Some Reflections on Retail Prices," in *Economic Essays in Honor of Wesley Clair Mitchell* (New York: Columbia University Press, 1935), pp. 203–4. Although these tests involved *changes* in price, the important thing is that changes that reduced price below the critical points produced much greater increases in sales than changes that did not. In other words, the demand curve had very different elasticities at different points.

items, and inflation has brought about upward changes in others. In the main, however, the five-cent price on items for which it has been customary has persisted. To the extent that the policy is correct it merely means that the AR curve is like the one shown in Fig. 6, with a kink at the customary price.[9]

Pricing at the Market

Fig. 6 also illustrates the estimate of the AR curve which results in a policy of "pricing at the market." A firm that adopts this policy believes that a price above those of competitors

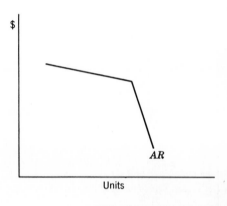

FIG. 6

would curtail sales sharply, while a lower price would not significantly increase them. This pricing policy is one of the most common, possibly because ignorance of the true shape of the AR curve suggests that the safest policy is to imitate competitors.

The policy of pricing at the market is also designed to avoid price competition and price wars. But a rule-of-thumb policy is not the correct solution to this problem, for the theory of monopolistic competition provides the basis for the proper calculation. What is required is an estimate of the AR curve after competitors have made whatever response they would make to the firm's pricing moves. In Fig. 7 this is indicated by AR_2, while AR is the customary curve based on an assumption of "all other things remaining the same." While it is very difficult for a seller to guess what competitors will do, the theory of correct oligopoly pricing along the

---

[9] Of course where the policy of customary pricing is not correct, as may be true in some of the chain-store cases mentioned, the demand curve would be quite elastic below the customary price.

AR_2 curve is quite clear, and does not necessarily call for "pricing at the market."

Prestige Pricing

It has often been pointed out in marketing literature that many customers judge quality by price. In such cases sales would be less at low prices than at high ones. This idea was the original legal basis for Fair Trade laws. While most manufacturers appear to be less impressed by this possibility than retailers are, there have been cases reported in which low prices led to reduced sales. The shape of the AR curve illustrating this situation has already been indicated in economic literature.[10] See Fig. 8.

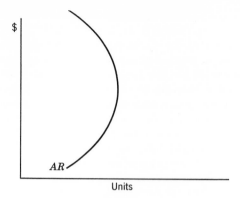

FIG. 8

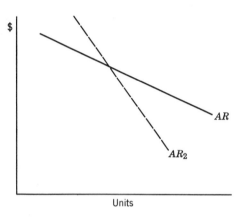

FIG. 7

Price Lining

Many retailers when questioned about their pricing policies seem to feel they have avoided the problem entirely by adopting customary price "lines." Once the lines are decided upon, prices may be held constant over long periods of time; changes in market conditions are met by adjustments in the quality of the merchandise.

---

[10] F. R. Fairchild, E. S. Furniss, and N. S. Buck, *Elementary Economics* (New York: Macmillan, 1939), 4th ed., Vol. 1, p. 166. Converse and Huegy cite an instance of aspirin being tried out at different prices, 19¢, 29¢, 39¢, and 49¢, with the highest sales resulting at 49¢ (*op. cit.*, p. 207). And they comment on this reason for positively inclined demand curves, "Thus merchandise can be priced too low as well as too high. Customers may fear that at the low price it cannot be of good quality, and will actually buy more at a somewhat higher price than they would at a lower price" (p. 206).

While this policy does not require pricing decisions, except initially and in case of special sales, it does present the seller with exactly the same choice as a variable price policy does in respect to the question of whether to equate marginal cost and marginal revenue, or to use a customary per cent of markup. This decision is made with reference to the prices paid for merchandise rather than the prices at which it will be sold. Although manufacturers and wholesalers dealing in types of merchandise which is customarily price-lined at retail usually tailor their own prices to fit the retail prices, the retailer does have some choice in regard to the quality of goods he buys. Presumably, the more he pays the more he can sell, at any given price line. That is, the lower his per cent of markup the higher his sales volume should be. Fig. 9 illustrates this situation, where P is the established price at retail, and CG shows the various quantities that could be sold at different costs of goods to the retailer. The retailer should equate his marginal cost with marginal revenue

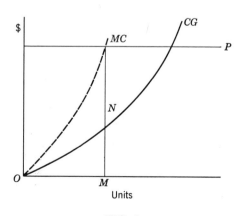

FIG. 9

(the price), paying NM for the goods and selling quantity OM. If instead he buys at a price that provides a customary or arbitrary per cent of markup it would be purely accidental if he would obtain the maximum gross margin.

Since there are few variable costs associated with the sale of most items at retail, except the cost of goods, the retailer's aim in general should be simply to maximize his gross margin dollars. If, however, other variable costs are significant they can be added to the cost of goods and a calculation made of the average variable costs, from which marginal cost can be computed. In Fig. 9 the curve CG would merely be replaced by an AVC curve.

Resale Price Maintenance

Another situation in which the retailer feels he has no pricing problem is when the manufacturer maintains resale prices by means of Fair Trade contracts. Even here, however, the retailer may find it advantageous to sell above the Fair Trade price in some cases, in states where the Fair Trade laws call for minimum rather than specified prices. In any case the retailer must decide whether to equate marginal cost and marginal revenue or to insist upon a customary per cent of markup. If he selects the latter he may refuse to handle, or to push, many low markup items which would actually be very profitable to him.

The price policy appropriate for a manufacturer using resale price maintenance is illustrated in Fig. 10. At any given retail price P, which he may set, he will have an AR curve determined by the retailers' attitudes towards the amount of markup resulting from the price at which he sells to them. At low markups some dealers will refuse to handle the item, and others will hide it under the counter. At relatively high markups dealers will push the item and will be able to sell more than consumers would otherwise take at the given retail price. The manufacturer should calculate his optimum price by computing MR from this AR curve and equating this with his MC. He should do this with the AR curve associated with each retail price and then select the combination of retail and wholesale prices that will result in maximum profit for him.[11]

Quantity Discounts

Quantity discounts are usually described in marketing texts, and explained in terms of the lower unit cost of handling large orders, or simply the desire to increase sales volume. Economic analysis of the quantity discount policy would focus on the theory of price discrimination. With reference to this theory, a quantity discount schedule, open to all buyers, is a very rough device for price discrimination, and should not be used if the laws allowed freedom of discrimination. Instead, the seller should estimate the demand curve of each buyer, and offer each the price (or prices) that would maximize the seller's revenue in respect to that buyer.[12] This might well mean lower prices for some small buyers than for some large ones, depending on the elasticity of their demand curves.

Fig. 11 illustrates a case in which the large buyer's demand curve is inelastic in the significant range, while the small buyer's curve is quite elastic. It would therefore be foolish to offer them a quantity discount schedule that would give the large buyer lower prices than the small one. The large buyer would take almost as large a quantity at high prices as at low ones, while the small buyer will not. This may not be a usual situation, but it is a possible one, and indicates that the seller should consider the elasticities of demand rather than adopt an arbitrary discount schedule.

The correct theory of price discrimination, where each buyer is to be offered a different

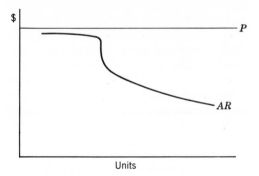

Units

FIG. 10

---

[11] For a fuller discussion see E. R. Hawkins, "Vertical Price Relationships," ch. 11 in Reavis Cox and Wroe Alderson (ed.), *Theory in Marketing* (Chicago: Richard D. Irwin, 1950).

[12] If the buyer is in a monopsonistic position he does not have a demand curve in the Marshallian sense, but it is possible to estimate how he will respond to various price offers.

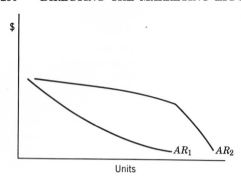

FIG. 11

price, has been outlined by Mrs. Robinson.[13] It indicates that the seller should equate the marginal revenue from each buyer with the marginal cost of the entire output.

Different costs of selling to different buyers can be taken into account by computing the AR curves as *net* average revenue curves, after deduction of the variable costs associated with the particular sales. And it would still be possible that the large buyer should be charged a higher price than the small one.

Some economists have used the term "quantity discount" to refer to a situation, unusual in marketing practice, in which each buyer is offered a quantity discount scale tailored to his own demand curve.[14] Of course a "quantity discount" of this kind would usually produce more net profit for the seller than a single price to each buyer, since it is an approach toward the maximum profit situation of perfect price discrimination, in which each buyer would be charged the highest price he would be willing to pay for each successive unit he bought. A seller may be attempting to gain some of the advantages of this type of pricing when he constructs a general quantity discount schedule with an eye to its effects on certain large buyers. In so doing, he would have to take care that the gain would not be cancelled by the adverse effect of the schedule of his net profits from other buyers.

Geographic Pricing

While some economists have long been concerned with the geographic aspects of pricing, and this interest has recently been spreading,

[13] Joan Robinson, *The Economics of Imperfect Competition* (London: Macmillan, 1933), p. 182.
[14] James M. Buchanan, "The Theory of Monopolistic Quantity Discounts," *Review of Economic Studies*, Vol. 20, No. 3, 1952-1953.

on the whole marketing specialists and economic geographers have regarded the spatial aspects of economics as their own province. Unfortunately they have developed theories which do not include the essential economic aspects of the problem. Fig. 11 may be used to illustrate some of the problems of geographic pricing. If the AR curve of each buyer is taken as a *net* average revenue curve, after deduction of transportation costs, then it is clear that the nearer buyer should not necessarily be given the lower delivered price. The elasticity of each buyer's demand curve is the important factor which should be considered. As has been indicated by Mrs. Robinson, the correct net price to each buyer would equate the seller's marginal revenue with the marginal cost of his entire output.[15]

While the Robinson-Patman Act does not permit the free price discrimination that would maximize the seller's profit, it does allow some discretion in pricing. The seller is not permitted to employ price differentials greater than his cost differentials; but he is free to give discounts less than the amount of cost saving to him. Moreover, he is allowed some discretion to employ price differentials when the buyers are not in competition with each other, or where he himself is "meeting competition." He may also, of course, discriminate by selling slightly different products, under different brand names.

CONCLUSION

The discrepancy between economic theory and actual pricing policies, as observed by marketing specialists, is more apparent than real. Most of the pricing behavior reported by marketing students is quite consistent with the general theory of monopolistic competition, and can be integrated with that theory. A considerable gain can be made on both sides if this integration is accomplished. Economists need to know more about the pricing policies actually used by businessmen. On the other hand, marketing students can understand these policies better if they appreciate the theoretical basis for them. Most of the "price policies" described by marketing specialists are merely special cases of the general theory of monopolistic competition. If so regarded, not only would clarification result, but perhaps additional insight would be gained regarding the advantages and disadvantages of each policy, and the situations to which they are appropriate.

[15] Joan Robinson, *loc. cit.*

46. *Price Decisions and Marketing Policies*

H. W. HUEGY

To reduce such a complex, even controversial, subject as modern price making to its essence, and to do so within the limits of this paper one must necessarily use some short cuts. One such short cut is to state, at the risk of being dogmatic, certain fundamental assumptions or conclusions on which the discussion is to rest.

These fundamentals are as follows:

1. Pricing can no longer be regarded as either an automatic or impersonal process.

2. Pricing must be considered as a policy question—most prices are assumed to be determined as a result of administrative judgments and differ chiefly in the degree of control and the manner of reflecting such judgments.

3. Since we still have markets through which prices continue to play their historic role of allocating resources, rewarding and penalizing performance, determining compensation of productive factors, and directing and limiting or rationing consumption, pricing can no longer be regarded as a private affair.

4. With the above constituting the matrix in which prices are made we need better information to guide those responsible for making decisions and better criteria for influencing and for judging the soundness of their decisions.

With this condensed statement of the conditions, of the consequences, and of the problem, we should proceed to some consideration of the evidence supporting these statements or of ac-

‡‡ SOURCE: Reprinted by permission from *Changing Perspectives In Marketing*, edited by Hugh G. Wales (University of Illinois Press, 1951), pp. 228–242.

tion to be taken within the framework of the existing situation.

Despite, or perhaps because of, the difficulties and complexities of administrative price making, as the pricing process has become less automatic we find many non-business groups entering more actively into the determination of prices. Government, acting on behalf of the public, early sought to prevent collusion or monopoly. From rather simple legislation we have progressed to a complex body of laws and an even more confusing series of judicial decisions; we have also entrusted certain parts of the task to various administrative bureaus. They, in turn, have erected a structure of rules and decisions and are busily engaged in adding to them.

Government, not content with preventing monopoly and collusion, has itself elected to control certain prices in the furtherance of various objectives. This was a natural step, even an inevitable consequence, with the regulated monopolies. It is not so natural or inevitable in such areas as farm prices even though there was discontent with the prices resulting from natural market forces, and dissatisfaction with the degree or quality of administration possible to farmers.

Labor, too, has entered the game of administering prices with vigor and apparent relish. Labor organization, collective bargaining, strikes are obviously attempts to administer the prices of labor services more effectively and to apply monopoly power to the bargaining process, perhaps to equalize bargaining power, perhaps to gain power.

The entry of government into the pricing

process in alliance with various numerically important special interest groups has naturally, even inevitably, injected politics into price administration.

All of which makes it clear that there are inherent dangers in the power which accompanies price administration. We have seen clearly, and for some time, that when there is monopoly or collusion in price making the rewards of the market are conferred on the basis of power, not merit. We must learn to see just as clearly that when the government enters there is a similar result and a similar risk. Political power may be as serious a threat to the common welfare as irresponsible economic power.

It does not appear that whenever there is price administration there is conspiracy, or collusion, or even monopoly as monopoly is usually defined. There is evidence that price administration can be, and is, practiced without conspiracy or collusive price agreements, and with a high level of active and aggressive competition. True this non-price competition differs from the rough and ready struggle of price competition. It is more subtle, more sophisticated, but no less vigorous or deadly.

This newer non-price competition, sometimes called quasi-monopoly, or monopolistic competition, or imperfect competition, needs further analysis and understanding. We need to know more about the practices and the results of this type of competition so we can more accurately compare its end results with the end results of the simpler and better understood direct price competition. This study and analysis must not be biased. It is certainly neither scientific nor reasonable to measure its performance against the norms and standards of pure price competition and to condemn it because it does not square with the model. Why should it be expected to when by definition it is a departure from the model?

We must find other standards against which to measure it and we must compare its accomplishments against a set of results it can be expected to attain. This would seem to call for a re-examination of the results expected from price competition and those from non-price competition and a comparison of each against standards appropriate to each and the two against standards reasonable to both.

The task of an administrator operating in markets characterized by the existence of price policies differs markedly from the task of an administrator in markets where prices are determined impersonally. Instead of being able to sell all he wishes, but at whatever price the market says is necessary to move that quantity, the price administrator has to determine a price and then accept the task of selling all he needs to sell at that price. Competition in other things than price is naturally emphasized—such things as design, quality, promotional effectiveness, dealer loyalty, brand preference, strength of consumer franchise. Price becomes a limiting factor and a determiner of the contestants rather than the decisive and exclusive competitive weapon.

Instead of allowing price to be determined by impersonal and automatic market response, the executive determining price policies has to consider the buyer's attitude toward the product and its price. He has to consider the market position of his product relative to other comparable and more directly competitive products and relative to a whole array of substitute products and services. He has to determine how his product stands marketwise—must he meet or get below others or dare he go over the price line of others? Can he go out of his class, and what is his class? Who are his competitors? What is the intensity of the indirect competition caused by alternative uses of limited purchasing power, even competition between the future in the form of savings and the present in the form of goods?

Successful price administration must recognize price policies as interrelated with all other marketing policies and must seek to bring them all into a consistent body of policy and action. One result of accepting price administration as a way of determining market prices is that responsibility has gone toward the manufacturer. By advertising prices to consumers he tends to establish the price at retail, thus he determines distributors' prices. Through fair trade contracts, or price suggestion, he even more definitely establishes retail prices. Then when he establishes his own selling price he thereby fixes the distributors' costs and margins and when distribution is through wholesale channels the chain may extend through several middlemen. The structure of prices may become highly formalized through the issuance of a schedule of list prices and of discounts for each member of the distributive channel, each discount becoming in effect a margin for that distributive level. Without such formalization of structure it may still be rather definitely stratified because of the strength of trade markup custom or habit. We thus have a whole structure of prices, and margins, resulting from his decisions. Also if he is to make sound market judgments he must work from retail back through market channels to factory price, and from there to costs. Logic thus suggests he must know channels, distributor margins and their justification, and must consciously work toward the results he wants accomplished in the market place.

Similarly the price policies of manufacturers may change the market structure or its functioning. The distributor margin allowed can encourage trade-in allowances on used items or affect the liberality of such trade practices. Special price concessions for cooperative advertising, point of sale display material, full line stocking, or other desired distributor practices can affect the type and extent of performance of functions. A level of distributor margins lower than trade custom or convention may keep some merchandise items out of certain kinds of retail stores while a level higher than conventional may make some items especially attractive to stores of a type which did not conventionally stock such items.

Sophisticated price administration must consider changes in total consumer incomes and differences in income distribution. Will the market be expanded by lower prices or restricted by higher prices and will the change be more or less than proportional to the price changes? Will gross revenue be increased or decreased? Can a larger share of an expanding market be captured by leading prices downward, or will lower prices result in the same share of market but a smaller gross?

The price administrator finds consumers with some ideas of the usefulness to them of certain goods and services and with a schedule or list of wants longer than their income will buy. With limited means they attempt to maximize their well-being by the best use of their resources. With larger total personal incomes and recent shifts in the distribution of family income the number of families with a portion of their income freed for spending at their own discretion is increased. Despite price increases the amount of discretionary spending power in the hands of the average family has continued to increase. With more purchasing power thus available for free choice of goods, or saving, the competitive sphere enlarges. The task of the marketing department is then to persuade buyers to add their product rather than other similar products competing directly; to substitute their class of product for others, thus radios compete with cars, cars with homes, and better food with better clothing. Price policies must be adjusted to competing classes of products as well as to products of the same class. Thus the price administrator must be alert to, and informed of, the value standing of his brand with consumers and of the value position of his class of product relative to a long list of alternative and substitute goods and services. He can then use prices, or design, or persuasion, or marketing skill to improve his position and to realize his goals. He must also be informed of groups excluded from the market and consider expansion of the market to such groups through price change, changes in group attitudes, or changes in their income position. Since such actions are in large measure related to the human factor, he deals with a constantly changing situation. Nor need he take the elements of any problem as given. Policy and action can be based on plans to modify attitudes which, if successful, will change the market position of the product class or of the brand. More broadly considered policies of the larger elements of an industry may be of such importance that they in themselves affect the whole environment.

In the face of such market facts price decisions cannot be the simple product of cost accounting and arithmetic—cost accounting facts are history; prices are in the future. At some time, of course, estimates of future costs must be placed alongside proposed prices. But costs are affected by volume, and volume is affected by price, so perhaps management has to assume some desired price and volume relationship and let costs become the result rather than the cause. Also there is some evidence that we should strive for price stability over relatively longer periods of time than the fiscal period and to measure profit over periods longer than the usual fiscal period rather than to attempt to keep prices flexible in their response to every fluctuation in costs.

All in all the emphasis on costs may be unfortunate. The formula of a cost increase and then an automatic price increase passes the burden to customers—not only in the form of the cost increase but in the form of a pyramided cost increase because of the percentage markup customs of distributors. This leads to price inflation through the "pass along" philosophy, which in itself interferes with the attainment of marketing objectives; in addition it encourages labor leaders to seek further wage increases which are to be "painless" to industry because they are to be passed along in prices. It also brings short term profits into the discussion when labor negotiations are in process which unfortunately for industry, is a one-way street. Further, such adjustments tend to become general throughout all industry since prices at one stage of production tend to be costs at another stage and since labor bargains tend to be industry wide.

With this far from complete sketch of the problems of making price decisions, it must be obvious that market facts bearing on the decisions, and analysis of such facts from the standpoint of price decisions, must become a more prominent part of our administrative techniques. We need to know more about the facts pertinent to pricing decisions. We need to know more about the types of analysis which will facilitate sound decisions. We need to integrate price policies closely with all our marketing policies.

Further, since such decisions have such important and far reaching effects on the well being of all of us it is clear why they can no longer be a private affair. The result of such decisions through deciding who shall use resources, where, when, and for what purpose are the most important decisions an economy can make. The deciding of rewards and penalties, the determination of compensation, the direction and limitation of consumption—such matters are basic to our economic health and common welfare. When these decisions were more largely made on the basis of automatic response to market stimuli, and when wrong decisions were of such small moment that they affected only the one individual or firm, they could safely be left to the automatic reaction of each individual or firm. But such is not the case with the price decisions of United States Steel, Du Pont, General Motors, United Automobile Makers, United Mine Workers, or the United States Government.

The bias that the great majority of price decisions should continue to be made privately rather than bureaucratically—that we should continue to operate our economy through free markets—that although price decisions have ceased to be private affairs they have not necessarily become governmental, need not be cause for apology. But though price decisions are still made by business leaders, or labor leaders, or both, such decision-makers must recognize that their decisions have become of such wide importance that they must be tested against the test of the well being of the whole economy. As they acquire such extensive powers they must accept equally extensive responsibility. Thus we need to think of some criteria for the decision making; for the individual firm, for the aggregate of all firms, for labor leaders, for special interest groups, and for the government. As suggested criteria we could well take as objectives of good and socially beneficial price making:

1. That prices should rapidly share with customers the results of technological progress.
2. That through proper price policies progress should be stimulated and encouraged.
3. That prices should assure full and continuous employment to labor.
4. That there be full and effective utilization of resources—a high level of employment and activity, resources used by those able to use them most effectively, and constant progress.

The judgment that these results can best be brought about by retaining a market economy rather than by entrusting more of these tasks to government is warranted. But it is equally certain that to carry them on properly business must be guided by better facts more effectively analyzed, and influenced and tested by better recognized and broader criteria.

47. Pricing a New Product

JOEL DEAN

New product pricing is important in two ways: it affects the amount of the product that will be sold; and it determines the amount of revenue that will be received for a given quantity of sales. If you set your price too high you will be likely to make too few sales to permit you to cover your overhead. If you set your price too low you may not be able to cover out-of-pocket costs and may face bankruptcy.

WHAT IS DIFFERENT ABOUT NEW PRODUCTS?

New products that are novel require a different pricing treatment than old products because they are distinctive; no one else sells quite the same thing. This distinctiveness is usually only temporary, however. As your product catches on, your competitors will try to take away your market by bringing out imitative substitutes. The speed with which your product loses its uniqueness will depend on a number of factors. Among these factors are the total sales potential, the investment required for rivals to manufacture and distribute the product, the strength of patent protection, and the alertness and power of competitors.

Although this process of competitive imitation is almost inevitable, the company that introduces the new product can use price as a means of slowing the speed of competitive imitation. Finding the "right" price is not easy, however. New products are hard to price correctly. This is true both because past experience is no sure guide as to how the market will

‡ SOURCE: Reprinted by permission from *The Controller*, Vol. 23, No. 4, April 1955, pp. 163–165.

react to any given price, and because competing products are usually significantly different in nature or quality.

In setting a price on a new product you will want to have three objectives in mind: (1) getting the product accepted, (2) maintaining your market in the face of growing competition, (3) producing profits. Your pricing policy cannot be said to be successful unless you can achieve all three of these objectives.

WHAT ARE YOUR CHOICES AS TO POLICY?

Broadly speaking, the strategy in pricing a new product comes down to a choice between (1) "skimming" pricing, and (2) "penetration" pricing. There are a number of intermediate positions, but the issues are made clearer when the two extremes are compared.

Skimming Pricing. For products that represent a drastic departure from accepted ways of performing a service or filling a demand, a strategy of high prices coupled with large promotional expenditures in the early stages of market development (and lower prices at later stages) has frequently proven successful. This is known as a skimming price policy.

There are four main reasons why this kind of skimming price policy is attractive for new and distinctive products: *First,* the quantity of the product that you can sell is likely to be less affected by price in the early stages than it will be when the product is full-grown and imitation has had time to take effect. This is the period when pure salesmanship can have the greatest effect on sales. *Second,* a skimming price policy takes the cream of the market at a high price before attempting to penetrate the more price-sensitive sections of the market. This means that you can get more money from those who don't care how much they pay, while building up experience to hit the big mass market with tempting prices. *Third*, this can be a way to feel out the demand. It is frequently easier to start out with a high "refusal" price and reduce it later on when the facts of product demand make themselves known than it is to set a low price initially and then boost the price to cover unforeseen costs or exploit a popular product. *Fourth*, high prices will frequently produce a greater dollar volume of sales in the early stages of market development than a policy of low initial prices. If this is the case, skimming pricing will provide you with funds for financing expansion into the big-volume sectors of your market.

A skimming-price policy is not always the answer to your problem, however. High initial prices may safeguard profits during the early stages of product introduction, but they may also prevent quick sales to the many buyers upon whom you must rely to give you a mass market. The alternative is to use low prices as an entering wedge to get into mass markets early. This is known as penetration pricing.

Penetration Pricing. This approach is likely to be desirable under the following conditions: *First*, when the quantity of product sold is highly sensitive to price, even in the early stages of introduction. *Second*, when you can achieve substantial economies in unit cost and effectiveness of manufacturing and distributing the product by operating at large volumes. *Third*, when your product is faced by threats of strong potential competition, very soon after introduction. *Fourth*, when there is no "elite" market—that is, a body of buyers who are willing to pay a much higher price in order to obtain the latest and best.

The decision to price so as to penetrate a broad market can be made at any stage in the product's life cycle, but you should be sure to examine this pricing strategy before your new product is marketed at all. This possibility certainly should be explored as soon as your product has established an elite market. Sometimes a product can be rescued from a premature death by adoption of a penetration price policy after the cream of the market has been skimmed.

The ease and speed with which competitors can bring out substitute products is probably the most important single consideration in your choice between skimming and penetration pricing at the time you introduce your new product. For products whose market potential looks big, a policy of low initial prices ("stay-out pricing") makes sense, because the big multiple-product manufacturers are attracted by mass markets. If you set your price low enough to begin with, your large competitor may not feel it worth his while to make a big production and distribution investment for slim profit margins. In any event, you should appraise the competitive situation very carefully for each new product before you decide on your pricing strategy.

WHAT SHOULD YOU LOOK AT IN SETTING A PRICE?

When you have decided on your basic pricing strategy you can turn to the task of putting a dollars-and-cents price tag on your new product. In order to do this you should look at at least five important factors: (1) potential and probable demand for your product, (2) cost of making and selling the product, (3) market targets, (4) promotional strategy, and (5) suitable channels of distribution.

DEMAND

The first step in estimating market demand is to find out whether or not the product will sell at all—assuming that the price is set within the competitive range. That is, you should find out whether or not this product fulfills a real need, and whether enough potential customers are dissatisfied with their present means of filling that need. To do this, you should make some estimate of the total potential market for the new product and all its competing substitutes and then estimate the portion of this potential that your product is likely to get.

Next, you should determine the competitive range of price. This will be easier when substitutes are relatively close or when customers are familiar with the cost and quality of substitutes and act rationally on the basis of performance.

The next step is to try to guess the probable sales volume at two or three possible prices within the price range. The best way to do this is by controlled experiments; next best is by a close estimation of buyers' alternatives in the light of market preference.

Finally, you should consider the possibility of retaliation by manufacturers of displaced substitutes. If your new product hits any one of your competitors hard enough, you may be faced with price retaliation. The limit to this price cutting is set by the out-of-pocket cost of the price-cutting competitors. Therefore, some knowledge of the out-of-pocket cost of making competing products will be helpful in estimating the probable effects of a particular price.

COSTS

Before going ahead with your new product, you should estimate its effect on your investment, your costs, and your profits. First you should estimate the added investment necessary to manufacture and distribute the new product. This investment estimate should include estimates of increased working capital that will be required at various sales volumes. Then you should estimate the added costs of manufacturing and selling the product at various possible sales volumes. The way to estimate costs is to calculate what your total costs would be with and without the new product; the difference should be assigned to the new product. Allocations of overheads that you are already incurring should not be assigned to the new product because they will be the same whether or not you go ahead with the addition to your product line.

In building up your two sets of cost and investment figures—one showing the situation *without* the new product, and the other showing the contrasting situation *with* the new product added to your line—be sure to take into account *all* pertinent items. It often happens that companies which lose money on new products have run into trouble because of unanticipated costs or investment requirements which have absorbed most of or all the profits realizable from the new idea.

New product costs may be segregated into half a dozen main categories: direct labor, materials and supplies for production, components purchased outside, special equipment (such as jigs, dies, fixtures and other tools), plant overhead, and sales expenses.

Direct Labor. Methods of estimating direct labor may be built up in one of three ways: (1) You can compare each operation on each component with accumulated historical data, from your files, on similar operations for similar components, (2) you can develop a mockup of the proposed work-place layout and actually time an operator who performs a series of manufacturing operations, simulated as accurately

as possible, (3) you can apply one of several systems of predetermined, basic-motion times which are currently available from private sources.

Make certain, however, that you include any added time used for setup work, or needed to take the item from its transportation container, perform the operations, and return the item again to its transportation container. When the total direct labor time is determined multiply it by the appropriate labor rates.

Materials and Supplies for Production. In developing reliable cost figures for materials and supplies make a methodical list of all requirements. Having listed everything in an organized fashion, you can enter the specifications and costs on a manufactured-component estimate form. Remember to include any extra costs which may be incurred as a result of requirements for particular length, widths, qualities, or degrees of finish. Allowances for scrap should also be made as accurately as possible and corrected by applying a salvage factor if the scrap can be sold or reused.

Components Purchased Outside. Place your specification for parts purchased from other concerns with more than one reliable supplier and get competitive bids for the work. But in addition to price considerations be sure to give proper weight to the reputation and qualification of each potential producer. Moreover, if you use a substantial volume of purchased parts you may want to use a "plus" factor above the cost of the components themselves to cover your expenses involved in receiving, storing, and handling the items.

Special Equipment. Take careful precautions against making a faulty analysis of your expense and investment in special jigs, dies, fixtures, and other tools which you will need to produce the new product. To avoid trouble in this area make a table showing all cases where special equipment will be needed. The actual estimating of the costs of such equipment is best done by a qualified tool shop—your own if you have one or an outside organization. Here again, competitive bidding is an excellent protection on price. Do not include costs of routine inspection, service, and repair; these are properly charged to plant overhead.

Plant Overhead. The overhead item may be estimated as a given percentage of direct labor, machine utilization, or some other factor determined by your accountants to be the most sensible basis. In this way you can allocate satisfactorily charges for administration and supervision, for occupancy, and for indirect service related to producing the new product. Overhead allocations may be set up for a department, a production center, or even, in some cases, for a particular machine. In calculating plant overhead make certain that in setting up your cost controls, your accountants have not overlooked any proper indirect special charges which will have to be incurred because of the new product.

Sales Expenses. Your estimates of sales revenue at various potential volumes can now be compared with your estimates of added costs at those volumes. The difference will be the added profits of introducing the new product. Although the costs themselves probably should not be used as a basis for setting price, you should not go into any venture that will not produce for you a rate-of-return on the added investment required that is adequate to compensate for the added risk and still be at least as high as the return you could get by investing your money elsewhere. If no price that you set will provide enough revenue to produce an adequate profit over your added costs, then you should either drop the venture, try to cut costs, or wait for a more favorable time to introduce the product.

MARKETING TARGETS

Assuming that the estimates of market demand and of cost and investment have been made and that the profit picture looks sufficiently rosy, you are now in a position to set up some basic goals and programs. A decision must first be made about market targets—that is, what market share or sales volume should be aimed at? Among other factors, you should probably consider what effect it will have upon investment requirements, whether or not your existing organization can handle the new product, how it fits in with the rest of your present product line, and so forth. These decisions should be made after a cold-blooded survey of the nature of your new product and of your company's organization and manufacturing and distributive facilities.

PROMOTION

Closely related to the question of market targets is the design of promotional strategy. As an innovator, you must not only sell your product, but frequently you must also make people recognize their need for this kind of product. Your problem here is to determine the best way of "creating a market." You must determine the nature of the market and the type of appeal that will sell the product and secure prompt acceptance by potential buyers. And you should also estimate how much it will cost you to achieve this goal.

CHANNELS OF DISTRIBUTION

Frequently, there is some latitude in your choice of channels of distribution. This choice should be consistent with your strategy for initial pricing and for promotional outlays. Penetration pricing and explosive promotion calls for distribution channels that promptly make the product broadly available. Otherwise you waste advertising or stymie mass-market pricing. Distribution policy also concerns the role you wish the dealer to play in pushing your product, the margins you must pay him to introduce this action and the amount of protection of territory and of inventory required to do so.

YOUR DECISION

These are the factors you should look at in setting a price. Estimating these factors shrewdly and objectively requires specialized training and experience. Good estimates will make your pricing more realistic and successful. But pricing cannot be established by formula. Combining these factors into a pricing policy requires judgment. In the last analysis you must pull all the estimates of the experts together and arrive at your own decision. You will want to make sure that the pricing analysis is guided by sound principles and that the activities of your specialists are all geared toward the same end—devising a sound, effective marketing and promotional program in conjunction with a price that will meet your objectives of market acceptance, competitive strength, and profits.

G. Marketing Strategy

48. Long-Range Planning in a Decentralized Company

VICTOR P. BUELL

We're in the middle of another great season of professional baseball. Major league ball offers an excellent example of the importance of long-range planning.

What the fans see is the excitement of this year's star-studded team. What good baseball management knows is that planning for this year's profit-producing team started several years ago with the scouting for young talent and the support of the team's farm clubs. It knows that if it isn't carefully selecting new talent and nurturing it through the farm clubs that the major league team will be a box office flop a few years hence—no matter how good the club's manager and coaches may be at the time.

Sometimes plans don't work out perfectly and management must find the new shortstop through a high-cost purchase or trade with another club. Occasional weak spots can be shorn up this way but no team stays in the upper division very long if it doesn't have a system for finding and developing new talent well in advance of the day it will need it.

Successful businesses are very much in the same situation. Profitable operation today is the result of two things: (1) how effectively management is managing present operations, and (2) it is the result of decisions made by management five, ten and twenty years ago.

Some business managements have failed to realize that the actions they take or don't take today will determine to a large extent what their businesses will be like five to fifteen years hence.

:: SOURCE: Reprinted by permission from *Effective Marketing Coordination*, Proceedings of the 44th National Conference of the American Marketing Association, June 1961, pp. 255–262.

This situation has been changing rapidly in recent years, however. Most managements now seem to recognize that it is not enough to manage the enterprise in a profitable fashion this year. In addition—and perhaps more importantly—they must also be laying plans for the profitable perpetuation of the enterprise. Hence, long range planning is an essential element of any business that remains profitable over a period of years—whether this planning is done formally or informally.

I start with the assumption that long range planning is necessary. But once a company accepts this tenet, how does it go about organizing for, and carrying out, the activity of long range planning?

I have been through this in a centralized company and am now going through it in a decentralized company. I can say that it is simpler to carry out long-range planning under a centralized management than a decentralized one, although many problems are common to both. The problems of tying in the planning of decentralized operations with top corporate planning, however, make the job a tougher one in the decentralized company.

My purpose is to describe the long range planning functions in my company. Archer-Daniels-Midland is a large multi-business company that only recently changed to a decentralized form of corporate organization, pledged itself to the marketing concept, and began formal long-range planning as part of its program to reverse a long term downward profit trend.

I will describe briefly our business and corporate organization, our approach to long-range planning, some of the benefits we believe we are receiving and some of the lessons we have learned. I present it in the hope that our experience may be of some help to other companies that are starting or expect to start long range planning.

BACKGROUND OF ADM

My company began making linseed oil nearly sixty years ago. It is still the leading marketer of this product, although linseed oil now accounts for only a small part of the company's volume.

Over the years, the company capitalized on its knowledge of buying, storing and processing agricultural commodities by expanding into other commodities such as soybeans, wheat, maize and alfalfa, from which it makes such products as vegetable oils, flour, animal feed ingredients, starches and proteins. These products are used in paint, bread, salad dressings, margarine, animal feeds, paper and wallboard. We store grain for the federal government and also merchandise grain for our own account.

Through technical research, ADM developed chemical processes to upgrade its linseed and soybean oils. This has led the company into the chemical field and it now produces resins, plastics and a wide line of industrial chemicals.

In addition, the company is in the foundry supply business and mines bentonite for sale to the oil well drilling and iron ore industries. It hunts sperm whales in the South Pacific for their sperm oil and for a time was in the plastic boat business, electronics business and animal feed business.

The company exports to foreign countries and owns plants in a number of countries on a joint venture basis with nationals of these countries.

Until two years ago, these far-flung operations were managed on a centralized basis with decisions made by top corporate management. Today the company's domestic operations are divided into two major groups—agricultural and chemical—headed by executive vice presidents who have complete profit responsibility. Reporting to them are ten division or operating managers who are in turn charged with profit responsibility for their operations. Our international operations are organized into an Overseas Division headed by a vice president.

Top corporate management is responsible for setting objectives and policy, corporate planning, capital investment decisions and providing services to the operating groups and divisions.

Short-range planning and control is accomplished by means of annual budgets—updated quarterly—which are prepared by the operating divisions and groups and which are subject to corporate management approval.

LONG-RANGE PLANNING

Our present management is committed to a philosophy of management by objectives, planning to meet these objectives, and measurement of performance in accordance with how well goals are achieved.

For the short range, we are progressing well through the medium of our annual budgeting procedure, although we would all agree that we still have a great deal to learn about short-range planning and budgeting, particularly in the area of forecasting.

As for long-range planning, progress is coming more slowly, although we have already received some important benefits.

Our first step in formal long-range planning was to require each operating division manager to prepare a year by year plan extending five years into the future. Our Director of Research was required to prepare five year plans for the research operations needed to support the divisions' plans.

Each division plan provided for: (1) an analysis of the division's current position; (2) its goals and plan of action by year broken down by marketing, manufacturing and management; (3) capital expenditures that would be required to support these plans; and (4) estimated profit and loss and return on investment statements for each of the five years.

As might be expected for a first attempt, these plans varied in quality and degree of sophistication. One fact was readily apparent. Our division managers—like the manager of the baseball team—had been concentrating on winning today's game. They had given less thought to how they were going to climb to the leadership of their league during the next five years. This exercise in forced planning made them aware that their jobs not only called for profitable management today but for even more profitable management in the future.

Our second step in long-range planning was to think through and put into writing our corporate objectives and policies. Perhaps this should have been our first step because our division managers could not properly think through their own goals without a clear understanding of where they fitted into the over-all corporate objectives, but the important thing is that we have now accomplished this difficult job.

The objectives and policies were hammered out over a period of a year by the Chairman, President, the President's staff consisting of the Treasurer, Secretary and the Vice Presidents for Administration, Research and Marketing, and by the Group Executive Vice Presidents. They were then reviewed by a group of fifty additional executives to make sure they were understandable and realistic. They were modified as needed and the final draft was approved by the Board of Directors and distributed to all management personnel.

Our objectives and policies have been spelled out under five categories: customers, shareholders, employees, suppliers, and the community.

The first two, dealing with customers and shareholders, examine the kind of company we want to be and how we expect to achieve our goals. For example, these state our objectives with respect to:

1. The broad types of businesses we will engage in.
2. Our growth objectives in terms of volume, profits and return on investment.

They spell out how we will achieve these broad objectives in terms of:

1. Concentration on finding and serving the needs and wants of the industries we are best qualified to serve.
2. Technical and market research.
3. Product quality.
4. Sources and use of capital.
5. Dividend policy.
6. Diversification.
7. Criteria for judging new ventures.

The above list is not all inclusive but will indicate the types of policies we have put into writing.

Our objectives and policies with respect to employees, suppliers and the community recognize that a business does not operate successfully over the long run without the good will and support of its employees, suppliers and the communities in which it lives and operates. It is in these sections that we have included our rules of ethical conduct under which we intend to achieve our over-all goals.

I might add the observation that the thinking through of a corporation's objectives and policies and getting them in writing is one of the hardest but most productive ventures a management can undertake. Not only does it clarify in the minds of management the kind of a company it wants to be, but by what operating philosophy can it be communicated to the entire organization. We found examples where people down the line had been operating unknowingly in contradiction to top management's concepts. On the other hand, management's own concepts were modified and improved as a result of discussions of the objectives and policies with middle management prior to final decision and publication.

As the result of thinking out the kinds of product lines the company would concentrate on, we have since sold three divisions and currently are selling a fourth because these businesses did not fit either the type of business we wanted to be or did not show promise of meeting our profit objectives.

In organizing for planning, we have been experimenting, trying to find the best arrangement for our company. As I have indicated each operating division and group is responsible for its own planning. If planning is done at the operating level, what functions then are to be performed at the corporate level? As we see it, there are five functions to be performed by top management with respect to long-range planning:

1. To set the broad corporate goals and to establish the policies governing operation of the business.

2. To provide the direction, stimulation and guidelines for the long-range planning that is to be performed at the operating level.

3. To provide assistance from corporate staffs.

4. To review plans of the operating divisions and groups for adequacy and completeness and to determine those plans that would have top priority call on capital funds. We have found that the total capital requirements of our divisions exceed the available supply; therefore, an important function of management is to decide which investments will result in the greatest payoff.

5. And finally, it is up to corporate management to investigate areas of growth not covered by the present operating groups. If we are to achieve our profit growth objectives, we know that we must be alert to finding new fields with greater profit potential than some of our present businesses.

The responsibility for coordinating corporate long-range planning is assigned to the corporate director of marketing. I have recently added to my staff a man whose title is Coordinator of Long-Range Planning. He is correctly called coordinator because we do not believe that responsibility for long-range planning can be assigned to one department. Corporate long-range planning, in the final analysis, is the responsibility of the president. He must actively work at it himself and he must receive assistance from all of his staff. The coordinator's job is to make sure that the long-range planning function is being performed and to see that all staff work is coordinated towards our objectives.

The Coordinator of Long-Range Planning is also secretary to a corporate strategy group, chaired by the president and consisting of the Chairman of the Board and the eight company officers that report to the president. This committee reviews plans of operating divisions and groups, gives assignments to the director of marketing and Coordinator of Long-Range Planning, and advises the president. Plans calling for major capital expenditures are submitted to the Executive Committee and Board of Directors for approval.

BENEFITS OF
LONG-RANGE PLANNING

Although we think we have a long way to go to perfect our planning procedures, we have already received a number of benefits. These are:

1. Clear cut objectives towards which everyone in the company is working.

2. Standards of profit performance by which operations and operating personnel can be judged.

3. An understanding of the types of businesses we will engage in and those we will not. This has already resulted in the sale or closing of some operations and the elimination of waste time researching and studying products or businesses our top management would not now approve even if the opportunity to enter the business presented itself.

4. A profit oriented attitude on the part of all management. We no longer are impressed by sales volume unless it results in approved rates of profit.

5. An increase in research facilities and personnel. Examination of our first five year objectives and plans made it abundantly clear that we could not achieve our goals without increased technical research.

6. A better coordination between research efforts and the abilities of our divisions to successfully produce and market products coming out of research.

7. A long-range cash flow projection which has enabled us to anticipate our long-range capital needs and arrange for capital under the most favorable borrowing conditions.

8. A more questioning attitude towards new ventures and towards expansion of present businesses. Management is asking more searching questions and saying "no" more often. Only well documented proposals with a good chance of reasonable payoff are being approved.

9. Operating managers are learning the importance of customer oriented decisions and the significance of thorough market studies. They are learning also that it is not enough to know today's market but that they must know how to determine what the market is likely to be in the years ahead.

CONCLUSION

One of the most important things we are learning is how much we have yet to learn about our businesses and the industries we serve. This realization, of course, is the beginning of wisdom and is our great hope for the future.

By and large, like other successful businesses, we have good operating managers. They know how to produce and sell and service customers. What we need is greater knowledge of our markets and to be able to anticipate the changes that will occur in these markets. This means more and better market research, a desire on the part of operating managers to use market research, and the ability to interpret findings into good long-range plans.

We are learning that long-range planning skills are not quickly or easily acquired. We know, too, that planning is hard work and time consuming. We know, also, that managers saddled with day-to-day decisions to make tend to postpone longer range planning if not required to do it and if they do not have adequate staff assistance.

In view of the progress our company has made through planning in the past two years, however, I have high hopes for the future. Planning is a skill that should improve through practice. We will make mistakes just as the New York Yankees have made them over the years, but by careful planning we expect to outhit our competitors and consistently improve our profit standing.

49. Product Differentiation and Market Segmentation as Alternative Marketing Strategies

WENDELL R. SMITH

During the decade of the 1930's, the work of Robinson and Chamberlin resulted in a revitalization of economic theory. While classical and neoclassical theory provided a useful framework for economic analysis, the theories of perfect competition and pure monopoly had become inadequate as explanations of the contemporary business scene. The theory of perfect competition assumes homogeneity among the components of both the demand and supply sides of the market, but diversity or heterogeneity had come to be the rule rather than the exception. This analysis reviews major marketing strategy alternatives that are available to planners and merchandisers of products in an environment characterized by imperfect competition.

DIVERSITY IN SUPPLY

That there is a lack of homogeneity or close similarity among the items offered to the market by individual manufacturers of various products is obvious in any variety store, department store, or shopping center. In many cases the impact of this diversity is amplified by advertising and promotional activities. Today's advertising and promotion tends to emphasize appeals to *selective* rather than *primary* buying motives and to point out the distinctive or differentiating features of the advertiser's product or service offer.

‡ SOURCE: Reprinted by permission from the *Journal of Marketing* (National Quarterly Publication of the American Marketing Association), Vol. 21, No. 1, July 1956, pp. 3–8.

The presence of differences in the sales offers made by competing suppliers produces a diversity in supply that is inconsistent with the assumptions of earlier theory. The reasons for the presence of diversity in specific markets are many and include the following:

1. Variations in the production equipment and methods or processes used by different manufacturers of products designed for the same or similar uses.

2. Specialized or superior resources enjoyed by favorably situated manufacturers.

3. Unequal progress among competitors in design, development, and improvement of products.

4. The inability of manufacturers in some industries to eliminate product variations even through the application of quality control techniques.

5. Variations in producers' estimates of the nature of market demand with reference to such matters as price sensitivity, color, material, or package size.

Because of these and other factors, both planned and uncontrollable differences exist in the products of an industry. As a result, sellers make different appeals in support of their marketing efforts.

DIVERSITY OR VARIATIONS IN CONSUMER DEMAND

Under present-day conditions of imperfect competition, marketing managers are generally responsible for selecting the over-all marketing strategy or combination of strategies best suited to a firm's requirements at any particular point in time. The strategy selected may consist of a program designed to bring about the *convergence* of individual market demands for a variety of products upon a single or limited offering to the market. This is often accomplished by the achievement of product differentiation through advertising and promotion. In this way, variations in the demands of individual consumers are minimized or brought into line by means of effective use of appealing product claims designed to make a satisfactory volume of demand *converge* upon the product or product line being promoted. This strategy was once believed to be essential as the marketing counterpart to standardization and mass production in manufacturing because of the rigidities imposed by production cost considerations.

In some cases, however, the marketer may determine that it is better to accept *divergent* demand as a market characteristic and to adjust product lines and marketing strategy accordingly. This implies ability to merchandise to a heterogeneous market by emphasizing the precision with which a firm's products can satisfy the requirements of one or more distinguishable market segments. The strategy of product differentiation here gives way to marketing programs based upon measurement and definition of market differences.

Lack of homogeneity on the demand side may be based upon different customs, desire for variety, or desire for exclusiveness or may arise from basic differences in user needs. Some divergence in demand is the result of shopping errors in the market. Not all consumers have the desire or the ability to shop in a sufficiently efficient or rational manner as to bring about selection of the most needed or most wanted goods or services.

Diversity on the demand side of the market is nothing new to sales management. It has always been accepted as a fact to be dealt with in industrial markets where production to order rather than for the market is common. Here, however, the loss of precision in the satisfying of customer requirements that would be necessitated by attempts to bring about convergence of demand is often impractical and, in some cases, impossible. However, even in industrial marketing, the strategy of product differentiation should be considered in cases where products are applicable to several industries and may have horizontal markets of substantial size.

LONG-TERM IMPLICATIONS

While contemporary economic theory deals with the nature of product differentiation and its effects upon the operation of the total economy, the alternative strategies of product differentiation and market segmentation have received less attention. Empirical analysis of contemporary marketing activity supports the hypothesis that, while product differentiation and market segmentation are closely related (perhaps even inseparable) concepts, attempts to distinguish between these approaches may be productive of clarity in theory as well as greater precision in the planning of marketing operations. Not only do strategies of differentiation and segmentation call for differing systems of action at any point in time, but the dynamics of markets and marketing underscore the importance of varying degrees of diversity *through time* and suggest that the rational selection of marketing strategies is a requirement for the achievement of maximum functional effectiveness in the economy as a whole.

If a rational selection of strategies is to be made, an integrated approach to the minimizing of total costs must take precedence over separate approaches to minimization of production costs on the one hand and marketing costs on the other. Strategy determination must be regarded as an over-all management decision which will influence and require facilitating policies affecting both production and marketing activities.

DIFFERENCES BETWEEN STRATEGIES OF DIFFERENTIATION AND SEGMENTATION

Product differentiation and market segmentation are both consistent with the framework of imperfect competition.[1] In its simplest terms, *product differentiation* is concerned with the bending of demand to the will of supply. It is an attempt to shift or to change the slope of the demand curve for the market offering of an individual supplier. This strategy may also be employed by a group of suppliers such as a farm cooperative, the members of which have

---

[1] Imperfect competition assumes lack of uniformity in the size and influence of the firms or individuals that comprise the demand or supply sides of a market.

agreed to act together. It results from the desire to establish a kind of equilibrium in the market by bringing about adjustment of market demand to supply conditions favorable to the seller.

Segmentation is based upon developments on the demand side of the market and represents a rational and more precise adjustment of product and marketing effort to consumer or user requirements. In the language of the economist, segmentation is *disaggregative* in its effects and tends to bring about recognition of several demand schedules where only one was recognized before.

Attention has been drawn to this area of analysis by the increasing number of cases in which business problems have become soluble by doing something about marketing programs and product policies that overgeneralize both markets and marketing effort. These are situations where intensive promotion designed to differentiate the company's products was not accomplishing its objective—cases where failure to recognize the reality of market segments was resulting in loss of market position.

While successful product differentiation will result in giving the marketer a horizontal share of a broad and generalized market, equally successful application of the strategy of market segmentation tends to produce depth of market position in the segments that are effectively defined and penetrated. The differentiator seeks to secure a layer of the market cake, whereas one who employs market segmentation strives to secure one or more wedge-shaped pieces.

Many examples of market segmentation can be cited; the cigarette and automobile industries are well-known illustrations. Similar developments exist in greater or lesser degree in almost all product areas. Recent introduction of a refrigerator with no storage compartment for frozen foods was in response to the distinguishable preferences of the segment of the refrigerator market made up of home freezer owners whose frozen food storage needs had already been met.

Strategies of segmentation and differentiation may be employed simultaneously, but more commonly they are applied in sequence in response to changing market conditions. In one sense, segmentation is a momentary or short-term phenomenon in that effective use of this strategy may lead to more formal recognition of the reality of market segments through redefinition of the segments as individual markets.

Redefinition may result in a swing back to differentiation.

The literature of both economics and marketing abounds in formal definitions of product differentiation. *From a strategy viewpoint,* product differentiation is securing a measure of control over the demand for a product by advertising or promoting differences between a product and the products of competing sellers. It is basically the result of sellers' desires to establish firm market positions and/or to insulate their businesses against price competition. Differentiation tends to be characterized by heavy use of advertising and promotion and to result in prices that are somewhat above the equilibrium levels associated with perfectly competitive market conditions. It may be classified as a *promotional* strategy or approach to marketing.

Market segmentation, on the other hand, consists of viewing a heterogeneous market (one characterized by divergent demand) as a number of smaller homogeneous markets in response to differing product preferences among important market segments. It is attributable to the desires of consumers or users for more precise satisfaction of their varying wants. Like differentiation, segmentation often involves substantial use of advertising and promotion. This is to inform market segments of the availability of goods or services produced for or presented as meeting their needs with precision. Under these circumstances, prices tend to be somewhat closer to perfectly competitive equilibrium. Market segmentation is essentially a *merchandising* strategy, merchandising being used here in its technical sense as representing the adjustment of market offerings to consumer or user requirements.

THE EMERGENCE OF THE SEGMENTATION STRATEGY

To a certain extent, market segmentation may be regarded as a force in the market that will not be denied. It may result from trial and error in the sense that generalized programs of product differentiation may turn out to be effective in some segments of the market and ineffective in others. Recognition of, and intelligent response to, such a situation necessarily involves a shift in emphasis. On the other hand, it may develop that products involved in marketing programs designed for particular market segments may achieve a broader acceptance than originally planned, thus revealing a basis for convergence of demand and a more generalized marketing approach. The challenge to planning arises from the importance of determining, preferably in advance, the level or degree of segmentation that can be exploited with profit.

There appear to be many reasons why formal recognition of market segmentation as a strategy is beginning to emerge. One of the most important of these is decrease in the size of the minimum efficient producing or manufacturing unit required in some product areas. American industry has also established the technical base for product diversity by gaining release from some of the rigidities imposed by earlier approaches to mass production. Hence, there is less need today for generalization of markets in response to the necessity for long production runs of identical items.

Present emphasis upon the minimizing of marketing costs through self-service and similar developments tends to impose a requirement for better adjustment of products to consumer demand. The retailing structure, in its efforts to achieve improved efficiency, is providing less and less sales push at point of sale. This increases the premium placed by retailers upon products that are presold by their producers and are readily recognized by consumers as meeting their requirements as measured by satisfactory rates of stock turnover.

It has been suggested that the present level of discretionary buying power is productive of sharper shopping comparisons, particularly for items that are above the need level. General prosperity also creates increased willingness "to pay a little more" to get "just what I wanted."

Attention to market segmentation has also been enhanced by the recent ascendancy of product competition to a position of great economic importance. An expanded array of goods and services is competing for the consumer's dollar. More specifically, advancing technology is creating competition between new and traditional materials with reference to metals, construction materials, textile products, and in many other areas. While such competition is confusing and difficult to analyze in its early stages, it tends to achieve a kind of balance as various competing materials find their markets of maximum potential as a result of recognition of differences in the requirements of market segments.

Many companies are reaching the stage in their development where attention to market segmentation may be regarded as a condition or cost of growth. Their *core* markets have already been developed on a generalized basis to the point where additional advertising and selling expenditures are yielding diminishing returns. Attention to smaller or *fringe* market segments, which may have small potentials individually but are of crucial importance in the aggregate, may be indicated.

Finally, some business firms are beginning to regard an increasing share of their total costs of operation as being fixed in character. The higher costs of maintaining market position in the channels of distribution illustrate this change. Total reliance upon a strategy of product differentiation under such circumstances is undesirable, since market share available as a result of such a promotion-oriented approach tends to be variable over time. Much may hinge, for example, upon week-to-week audience ratings of the television shows of competitors who seek to outdifferentiate each other. Exploitation of market segments, which provides for greater maximization of consumer or user satisfactions, tends to build a more secure market position and to lead to greater over-all stability. While traditionally, high fixed costs (regarded primarily from the production viewpoint) have created pressures for expanded sale of standardized items through differentiation, the possible shifting of certain marketing costs into the fixed area of the total cost structure tends to minimize this pressure.

CONCLUSION

Success in planning marketing activities requires precise utilization of both product differentiation and market segmentation as components of marketing strategy. It is fortunate that available techniques of marketing research make unplanned market exploration largely unnecessary. It is the obligation of those responsible for sales and marketing administration to keep the strategy mix in adjustment with market structure at any point in time and to produce in marketing strategy at least as much dynamism as is present in the market. The ability of business to plan in this way is dependent upon the maintenance of a flow of market information that can be provided by marketing research as well as the full utilization of available techniques of cost accounting and cost analysis.

Cost information is critical because the upper limit to which market segmentation can be carried is largely defined by production cost considerations. There is a limit to which diversity in market offerings can be carried without driving production costs beyond practical limits. Similarly, the employment of product differentiation as a strategy tends to be restricted by the achievement of levels of marketing cost that are untenable. These cost factors tend to define the limits of the zone within which the employment of marketing strategies or a strategy mix dictated by the nature of the market is permissive.

It should be emphasized that while we have here been concerned with the differences between product differentiation and market segmentation as marketing strategies, they are closely related concepts in the setting of an imperfectly competitive market. The differences have been highlighted in the interest of enhancing clarity in theory and precision in practice. The emergence of market segmentation as a strategy once again provides evidence of the consumer's pre-eminence in the contemporary American economy and the richness of the rewards that can result from the application of science to marketing problems.

50. Sales and Marketing Planning of the Edsel

HENRY G. BAKER

Market Research studies by our company on the Edsel automobile have covered a period of almost 10 years. These studies concerned owner likes and dislikes, product identification and "imagery"—the pictures in people's minds of the kind of car they would like, the reason for the Edsel, and many Market and Sales Analysis studies. As professional marketers are quite aware, we are using "imagery" in the automobile business today. We have found that cars have definite personalities of their own and that a man buys a car which he believes best exemplifies his own personality.

This made it somewhat easier for us to plan our product, as well as our Advertising and Sales Promotion, because if we could first establish a share of mind with the car-buying public, then we could more readily establish a share of market for the Edsel line.

For some years there has been a growing trend toward cars in the medium-price class. Where once the traditional makes in this field— Buick, Dodge, Mercury, and so on—were about one-fifth of industry sales, they now account for one-third of all sales. And so great has been the demand for more luxurious cars that even the so-called "low-price" makes have entered this market with models that, in price, overlap the bottom level of the medium-price class. Today, about 60 per cent of all cars sold are in this price range.

One reason for the growth of this market, of

‡ SOURCE: Reprinted by permission from *Marketing's Role in Scientific Management*, Proceedings of the 39th National Conference of the American Marketing Association, June 1957, pp. 128–144.

course, has been the tremendous rise in consumer income since World War II. Not only has disposable personal income (in 1956 dollars) increased from about $138 billion in 1939 to $287 billion in 1956, but the per cent of this income spent for automobiles has increased from around 3.5 per cent to 5.5–6.0 per cent today. And forecasts for the years ahead show that disposable income will go even higher—to just short of $400 billion in 1965.

Clearly, the economic climate favors a continued trend to medium-price cars. General Motors has threee makes—Pontiac, Oldsmobile, and Buick—in the medium-price class (which together almost equal the penetration of Chevrolet). Chrysler has two makes in the medium-price field (Dodge and Desoto). But Ford Motor Company has only Mercury, which is responsible for less than 20 per cent of the company's current business.

Let's look for a moment at the relatively common behavior of trading up one step from a low-price car to a medium-price car. Each year approximately one out of five traders of a low-price car buys up to the medium-price range. As Chevrolet traders buy up—and have three GM medium-price makes from which to choose—87 per cent stay with GM. As Plymouth traders buy up—and have two Chrysler products from which to choose—47 per cent stay with Chrysler Corporation. But as Ford traders buy up—and have but one Ford Motor Company product available to them—only 26 per cent stay with Ford Motor Company. Most go to GM's three medium-price makes. And in total volume, we can estimate quickly that Ford uptraders contribute almost as much to GM's medium-price penetration as

GM, through Chevrolet, is able to generate for itself. This has been one of the greatest philanthropies of modern business.

In search of the kind of a new make to develop, research studies also took us to the consumer's mind, where we sought to find the optimum imagery point on several scales. One, a young to old, another a masculine to feminine, and a third, workingman to well-to-do. We asked consumers which makes do you think a younger person might buy, an older person, and so on? On the basis of these interviews we planned our car to follow the personalities of those makes more centrally located between the extremes of these three scales.

A make of car is a badge that people can buy and wear, and show the world that they are the kind of people that they think they are. A make thus becomes a very real extension of the owner's *Desired* personality, and something he derives gratification from, if the personality fits.

We also researched such product images as workmanship, speed, trade-in value, and appearance, to rank them in importance. And, again, we explored social imagery by asking large numbers of consumers what car they thought of as being owned by a doctor, lawyer, dance-band leader, community leader, etc.

Our stylists have made every effort to style a car with a personality that fits a wide segment of the market, and both social and product imagery were given deep consideration.

As a result of our research, Advertising and Promotion will push Edsel as "The smart car for the young executive or professional family on its way up." It will say to the young man: "Edsel has faith in you, son." To attract families, it "Will not be exclusively masculine," but "Will seek a wholesome 'good' role." We will offer "Successful status to Ford owners who are trading up."

Edsel will attempt to exploit two rather dependable tendencies of auto buyers: To trade up, and to stick to the same family of cars.

It was determined that Edsel styling would be distinctive from any angle—front, rear, or side. General Sales and Marketing Manager, J. C. "Larry" Doyle, urged that the same fresh approach to Sales and Marketing Techniques and Programs be taken.

EDSEL STYLING

Edsel styling began in 1954, when a team of designers under Edsel's Styling Manager, Roy Brown, anticipated a go-ahead on the "E-Car"

and started making up sketches. Studying existing cars, the stylists found it difficult to distinguish makes at a distance of a city block. They even scanned cartops from the roof of a ten-story building overlooking a parking lot to see what distinguishing features might help make the Edsel stand out from the back. Edsel stylists were asked to be both distinctive and discreet, which were, in a sense, paradoxical objectives. It's easy to be distinctive *or* discreet, but not distinctive and discreet at the same time.

Since Edsel's Consumer Research could give only a general idea of the styling principles car buyers prefer, the actual features and form of the car had to be developed in a stylist's ivory tower. Stylist groups attacked various "Themes," boiled down hundreds of sketches to two dozen "Comprehensives" to show top management. Then, they boiled the "Comprehensives" down again to ten sketches, and finally started on clay or plaster mock-ups to judge three-dimensional high lights and flair. The final concept as it looked in plaster was satisfying to every designer in the company, and when you get 800 stylists under one roof to agree that they like a creation, you have unusually high agreement.

Edsel styling was "locked up" in August, 1955, except for minor alterations. By January 1956, Edsel was committed on its special tooling orders for the '58's, was ordering engines, transmissions, and other major items from other company divisions, and was arranging plant facilities to accommodate production. Last winter, orders for trim cloth, interior hardware, and other miscellany were placed. Although the first 1958 Edsel won't roll off the production line until July 15, our management is already neck-deep in the job of "Phasing In" the 1959 and 1960 models.

The new Edsel line will feature 18 models in four series—a complete line of automobiles—Ranger, Pacer, Corsair, Citation. Our price range will be about like this: The Ranger series will be priced competitively with the lowest medium-priced car you can buy, and our other three series will cover the medium-priced car segment.

Ford Motor Company has invested $250 million in the Edsel before a single car has rolled off the production lines—a major venture by any calculation, in a relatively unpredictable market. However, both the men in the company and in the division have matched the size of this risk with massive effort, in an attempt to reduce the margin of error in advance. We have studied and rehashed some 4,000 separate decisions, from the pros and cons of hubcap styling to the basic question—why build an Edsel at all?

Prototype cars have been under test since October 1, 1955, and more than 1,250,000 miles of testing have been completed. Road tests have been made including mountain, city traffic, and desert driving in Arizona—the gamut of tests conceived long before to find a car's weaknesses and get the "bugs" out. Pilot-production cars were built at Mahwah, New Jersey, during April to prove out production parts, and the results were good.

Actually, we have to figure out about two years in advance what people will want in cars. Mistakes in the auto industry are all big and must be lived with a long time.

PUBLIC RELATIONS' BUILD-UP OF THE CAR

It's not by accident that people are asking questions about the newest of new cars. Rumors of the possibility of a new Ford product circulated a number of years ago. Stories of the organization of a Special Products Division were released to the press not long thereafter.

"It's a car, not a home appliance," said the whispers that went the rounds in due course. There was plenty of speculation in the automotive columns.

Then came the announcement about the Edsel Division, and rumors in the automotive and daily press about what kind of automobile the "E-Car" would be, and what place it would take in the industry's price classes.

Releases to newspapers and radio stations, speeches by company executives, press conferences by Ford and Edsel officials served two purposes—first, to make public certain news and, second, to encourage speculation by automotive writers and commentators.

This definite pattern has emerged—step by step—one subject after another, a definite concept of the new Edsel line has been established. It has been built in a gradual crescendo of interest-arousing releases, indirect or direct, casual or formal, each more informative, and each building on those preceding. And the crescendo will grow as E-Day approaches.

Mr. C. Gayle Warnock, Edsel Public Relations Manager, keeps as a constant objective the benefits that will accrue to Edsel Division and its dealers from every news story that sees print, every telecast and broadcast that hits the air, every speech that an Edsel executive makes to a public eager to be "in the know."

MARKETING ORGANIZATION

Our General Sales and Marketing Office is headed by Mr. J. C. "Larry" Doyle. Advertising, Sales Promotion, and Sales Training are directed by Assistant General Sales Manager, R. F. G. Copeland, and Marketing is directed by Assistant General Sales Manager, N. K. Vanderzee. We have a field force of five regional and 24 district offices.

While our Market Research Department is part of our Merchandising and Product Planning Office, the Planning and Programming Department, which I administer, reports to the Assistant General Sales Manager—Marketing, and directs the field forecasting system, plans sales, reports sales, develops sales performance analysis, and engages in sales research and market analysis.

SALES AND MARKETING OBJECTIVES

Edsels will be produced in six Ford Motor Company Plants at Mahwah, New Jersey; Somerville, Massachusetts; Wayne, Michigan; Louisville, Kentucky, and San Jose and Los Angeles, California.

Our company Board Chairman, Mr. Ernest Breech, put our 1958 goal at 3.3 per cent to 3.5 per cent of the auto market. In a six-million car year, this would amount to roughly 200,000 cars. But our General Manager, Mr. Richard Krafve, pointed out that this was a very conservative estimate used for financial control. Actually, all of us in the General Sales and Marketing Office expect to do much better than this.

Since announcing that we would sell our cars through a separate dealer organization, 4,619 inquiries for dealer franchises in every part of the United States had been submitted by May 31.

To select our dealers, we made a detailed study of all United States Marketing Areas, from major cities to rural counties, carried down to such questions as the proper side of the street for an auto agency in a given town. We plan to have between 1,200 and 1,500 dealers in business when Edsel goes on the market, the bulk of them handling only Edsel (dual dealerships will be restricted to small towns). By 1960, we hope to expand the sales organization to 3,000 dealers, adding a full 25 per cent to the over-all Ford Motor Company dealer network.

While we have little chance of recovering our two-and-a-half-year backlog of development costs in 1958, we do expect to make an operating profit, and count on having the whole project in the black after the third year of production.

We have reasons to believe that the mood for consumer buying will be good at the time of our introduction. Buyers will have had three years to pay off the installment debt they used to finance their '55 automobile buying spree. More important, with consumer income and capital spending at record highs, the general economic outlook is more optimistic than it has been in months.

Where styling and zipped-up engines give auto makers their sales horsepower, it is the fundamental factors that give the market its "Torque."

SELECTION OF FOOTE, CONE AND BELDING AS ADVERTISING AGENCY

One of our first problems was advertising. The car would have to have its brand personality created almost overnight. On the face of it, the search for an agency might seem simple. Ordinarily, an account of this size would go to one of the largest agencies: it would go, furthermore, to one that did not have a competitive account. Among the top ten agencies in billings, only two were without automobile clients: Foote, Cone and Belding and Leo Burnett. Of these two, only Foote, Cone and Belding had a network of branch offices, a system nearly all of the other agencies which handle automobile accounts have found necessary to manage the regional dealer advertising.

But we did not jump at the obvious. We have, from the beginning of the division, been determined to be objective about everything, and instead of simply appointing Foote, Cone and Belding, we embarked on what became—according to Fortune Magazine—the most exhaustive examination of advertising agencies ever made by an advertiser.

General Sales and Marketing Manager Doyle, began the search in July, 1955, by polling Ford's present advertising agencies, J. Walter Thompson, Young and Rubicam, and Kenyon and Eckhardt, for their recommendations. He also asked Ford Motor Company advertising people to talk to their friends in the agencies. From the various recommendations, a list of eleven agencies was drawn up. Presentations were made by these eleven, and also by twelve other agencies which asked to be heard.

What really concerned Messrs. Doyle and Krafve was a good deal more elusive than organizational charts. They were looking for a "mature" agency. To them, this did not mean an "old" agency, but one with a healthy working climate, a good second echelon of management, widespread stock ownership, and stable clientele.

On February 7, 1956, Foote, Cone and Belding was selected as our advertising agency. Then FC and B found itself embarked on a large opportunity, but holding a big bag. In the nineteen months between getting the account and getting billings on it, the agency may go $1,000,000 in the red on its relationship with Ford Motor Company. President Cone of FC and B merely says that "we figure to invest between $700,000 and $1,200,000."

FC and B and Edsel believe that their marriage will last longer than the industry average of fourteen years. One factor in FC and B's favor, Cone thinks, is that "We know the importance of the dealer, especially on high-ticket items." Others include this agency's strong position in personnel and its chain of offices across the country.

Advertising does not build the car, but it does build the image and the desire. And while the FC and B people don't "prove" the care, they intend to prove the advertising.

ADVERTISING PLANS

Consumers will get their first taste of Edsel advertising this July. And a taste is all it will be, as we continue what we hope, and believe, is a well-planned campaign to whet the public's appetite for our new entry in the highly competitive automotive field.

Initial "pre-announcement" ads will run in magazines. In black and white spreads, they will tell about the Edsel—but only photographs of covered cars will appear. It will be late in August before pictures will be released. The magazine campaign will initiate a four-media drive—magazines, newspapers, broadcast and outdoor. This will also mark the start of a year-long "introductory" drive for the new automobile line.

We cannot release any figures on how much we plan to spend to launch the car, nor can we discuss what it will take to keep "introducing" it all through 1958. However, tentative percentage breakdowns for kick-off expenditures in various media are as follows:

Newspapers, 40 per cent—Although we plan to take full promotional advantage of our "newness" to experiment with advertising innovations, we are not breaking with the traditional emphasis on newspaper advertising that is characteristic of the auto industry.

Magazines, 20 per cent—We started our trade publication advertising on April 29 with a two-color spread in Automotive News. This is a dealer recruitment campaign and will continue in Automotive News and seven other automotive trade publications. Consumer Magazine and plans call for a "teaser" campaign starting in July, to be followed by ads illustrating the car after its unveiling late in August.

Broadcast, 20 per cent—At this moment, while Edsel has not signed to sponsor any network TV or radio shows, serious negotiations are well under way.

Outdoor, 10 per cent—Outdoor advertising will play a particularly important part during the launching, for the very simple reason that we have no car population or any "loyal owner image" established to help portray even a mental picture of the product. Outdoor advertising will be used to figuratively put the Edsel on the roads and highways of America.

Miscellaneous, 10 per cent—We know how much we have budgeted for the amount of advertising and promotion we will be doing between the time we bring out our car this fall up to January 1, 1958, and we have a tentative budget for what we think is necessary to do a top-drawer job from January 1, 1958, through the end of the model year.

We expect the task of "launching" our new car to be a two-year venture, and know that its per-car advertising costs will be competitive with other cars in our price ranges.

There is an important difference between the introduction of a new car and that of a new model of an established line by an automobile manufacturer. Ordinarily, the introductory phase of a new model automobile lasts from 60 to 90 days, when a switch into more of a holding or consolidating position is made. This will not be the case with us, for our first car, the introductory period will be the full model year.

The Edsel offers both a challenge and a unique opportunity to do a real dealer education job. For the first time in nearly 20 years, dealers will be offered something really new—a new car instead of just a new model. We at Edsel plan to take advantage of this opportunity by stressing to our dealers that they have this added increment of "newness" to sell.

There is no such thing as consumer sampling, with prototypes at about $100,000 apiece. In addition security makes it impossible, or not logical, for us to expose our product.

Also, it is not possible for us to make copy tests without exposing our hand, and it is not possible for us to do test marketing. And when we introduce, we are going to have to introduce at one time all over the country. Now, we must overcome all these handicaps and do it on a realistic budget. We are not planning on out-gate-folding, or out-shouting anybody. We intend to spend enough to properly introduce this new car, but we are not going to get tangled up in a competitive spending spree.

PROFIT-CENTERED DEALERSHIPS

Edsel's realistic new marketing concept puts every dealership department on the sales and profit team. In addition to a new kind of car, the Edsel Division introduces a new marketing concept to automobile retailing. Based upon the "costing" know-how of today's well-managed business organizations, this advanced plan for management treats every dealership department as a source of sales and, therefore, profits. Each of four basic operations of the dealership—new car sales, used car sales, service, parts and accessories—is a "profit center."

Through his management, the dealer provides the training, the leadership, and the incentives to develop every sale in every department, into a chain-reaction of further sales. Dealers have the advantage of new personnel, an impressive new product, and new opportunities to establish this profit-building concept at the start. In this sense, the dealer's office is the fifth "profit center" and the most important of all.

NEW CAR PROFIT CENTER

The first step in moving the customer along to the point of signing an order is the dealership's outside appearance. It will be transformed quickly, and at low cost, with special Edsel colors and signs. This new facade immediately identifies the dealer's place of business with Edsel's national and local advertising.

The value of "family resemblance" identification is well known in all retail lines. Once the public has identified an Edsel dealer—the man who sells a product which the public has come to know and like through publicity and advertising—he is well on his way in doing business with brand-name merchandise.

Promotion within the dealer's selling organization, as well as to the public, is provided by an Edsel Division budget aimed at getting dealers off to a flying start. Part of this program is an idea-group for salesmen's incentives and contests. Training for salesmen and sales managers is offered to help build up sales quickly. The Division is also planning an Edsel Salesmen's Club to stimulate rivalry and grant recognition to the men who produce sales.

As a basic working tool of all dealer profit centers, the Edsel Division will publish and send to dealers a marketing magazine. In this publication, "Your Edsel Marketer," dealers will find a national interchange of management ideas—field-tested answers to many common merchandising or operating needs.

USED CARS PROFIT CENTER

In the United States, the used-car business is a little known giant of retail trade. If new car sales total $15 billion in a typical year, used-car sales match them dollar for dollar. An Edsel dealer has this $15 billion market at his doorstep as an immediate source of income and profit. Edsel has made it a first order of business to give its dealers a major competitive advantage in used-car trading. Through a nationwide promotion under the general name of "Green Light," our dealers' connection with Edsel gives their used-car lots quick identity as places where prospective buyers can trade with confidence. In merchandising "Green Light" cars, a dealer will not sell used cars—he'll merchandise unused mileage or usable transportation.

The element of public confidence is universally recognized as the key to profitable used-car merchandising. There are about 35,000 independent used-car dealers in the United States, some of them large profit-producers. In practically every case, success has been based upon a firm name or slogan suggesting confidence, built up over a period of years at considerable effort and advertising expense. The Edsel "Green Light" for used cars gives our dealers this merchandising fundamental on the day they open for business.

The Edsel dealer immediately sets up a used-car operation that not only banks quick profits, but supports all future new car sales. Three out of four new cars sold today involve trades. In the 6 to 7 million-car year now considered typical, about 4.5 million are replacements for the scrappage which occurs at the low end of the car-life scale. The constant trading of still-good cars between one and eight years old is the ultimate source of the franchised dealer's retained new car profits. The successful used-car merchandiser *increases* his net profit by intelligent handling of the trades.

SERVICE PROFIT CENTER

Service makes immediate money—and our dealer's best outlook for new car prospects is through a busy shop door. On the day he hangs up his "E," the newly franchised Edsel dealer is in a revenue-producing business of servicing of all makes of cars. The Edsel dealer enjoys unusual advantages in order to profit quickly from his service shop because:

1. Good automotive service is at a premium in practically every community today—a "shortage" market ripe for cultivation.

2. Other-make dealers, overwhelmed by car population out-growing their facilities, cannot take advantage of existing conditions—while the Edsel dealer can.

3. A reputation for good service means a customer following, a prospect list for new cars, the best possible "booster" advertising for prospects. The Edsel dealer can build service reputation at a profit.

4. We at Edsel have made dealer service development our No. 1 objective of our program to aid dealers.

The Service Department of Edsel Division operates on the principle that service can make profits—which to many in the automobile business comes as a refreshing and new idea. Certain accounting theories, such as "service absorption" of entire dealership overhead, have led some dealers to conclude that their shops were not profitable. But in actual dollars, the typical well-managed service shop makes a 30 per cent gross profit.

The Edsel Division is ready with dealer-tested plans to help dealers attain immediate shop efficiency and a customer following. We believe that our "Green Light" service program of cooperating with dealers in service development is far more extensive, realistic, and closely geared to dealer needs than any ever offered by a manufacturer.

The attention the Edsel Division gives to facilities planning is also a new look at an old industry practice. By starting with the right facilities, Edsel dealers not only operate with immediate efficiency, but they make sure of retaining their service following through future expansion.

We make it possible for each of our dealers in the United States to give his mechanics thorough training. Their skill and efficiency are essential to build the dealership service reputation and thereby their ability to develop new car sales. The service manager is guided to manage men, money and machines in order to promote new business.

PARTS AND ACCESSORIES PROFIT CENTER

Although the market for Edsel parts will necessarily mature with the growth of the Edsel car population, the dealer can foresee his parts department becoming a major profit center and plan to take advantage of it. He can also earn immediate income from sales of standard or other-make parts for the shop, and especially from the sale of new car accessories. The Edsel dealer can order parts for all Ford family lines of cars direct from the nationwide system of Ford warehouses. They are located strategically to provide fast delivery to all areas via existing means of transportation. A well-charted course toward parts and accessories penetration gives the Edsel dealer still another opportunity to realize the maximum profit-dollar from his initial dealership investment.

HELPING THE DEALER TO DEAL

Under the Edsel concept of management, the dealer himself is a kind of "profit center." He makes the decisions and supplies the capital and the leadership by which each income-producing department will function. So the Edsel Division has created a special department to give the dealer every benefit of company management know-how—a consulting service that is a "first" in the automobile industry. Called Management Services, this department has an experienced management consultant in every district office, available to dealers at no cost. It also has developed modern accounting aids that clarify and simplify dealers' tasks of keeping abreast of events. And it has streamlined the work of the Edsel zone sales managers who contact dealers.

Selling cars in volume is one thing, knowing one's cost of doing business is another. Edsel Division's new, simplified financial statement is an improved management tool to help the dealer accomplish both objectives. It provides an easy-to-read summary of business results by month and year-to-date, in such a way that dealers can quickly analyze their present operating positions and plan ahead with confidence. That proven guide to efficient procedures—the daily operating control—is now so arranged that it matches the accounting line-ups on the financial statement. Dealers get a coordinated set of progress signals.

At the district level, the duties of the zone manager, dealers' principal company contact, has been given new status and importance. He will be well trained to give dealers effective assistance in a multitude of ways. Back at the district office, the zone manager's assignments will be carefully screened and organized to eliminate duplication of effort and waste of time.

Sales and profit programs will be directed by one man. His title: Management Services Manager. In this new setup, the Management Services Manager will supervise all the functions of Business Management, Sales Planning, Training and Sales Promotion of new cars, used cars, parts and service. He will be supported by Management Specialists and Analysts. In a very real sense, the responsibilities of the Management Services Manager parallel those of a Dealership General Manager. He's versed in both management and promotion—that is, in the profit twins of "more gross, less expense."

The division supplies skilled assistance to dealers because Edsel recognizes the fact that dealers' profits and Edsel's success are built precisely on the same foundation.

DEALER APPOINTMENTS

One of the most intensive market research programs in history was undertaken by Edsel to learn where to place each Edsel dealer in the nation's 60 major metropolitan areas. It consists of a series of maps and overlays, locating the major population centers, the various income groups, competitive dealers and a vast assortment of other information. We expect that this data will enable us to take advantage of the latest population shifts and trends and to have the best located dealer body in the industry. The chore now in progress is that of matching the planned dealer points with the 4,600 inquiries for the Edsel franchises.

We are not seeking to run anybody else out of business and we are not out to "shrink the economic pie" in any town, city, or state. Just the opposite. Instead of taking business away from somebody—we are out to make more business in our industry and in all the communities where we will have good businessmen for dealers.

One of the things we have done is to clarify the situation as to where we will dual. Generally, the policy will call for exclusive Edsel dealerships, with only 10–15 per cent of the dealerships in the "first wave" being dualed. The first wave of dealerships are the 1,200–1,500 dealers in the major cities and counties who must be signed by introduction day. It is expected that this wave will include about 50 per cent of the division's outlets, which will sell about 80 per cent of the volume. Progressively, over a period of several years, a "second wave" of dealerships consisting of 1,200–1,500 outlets in the smaller volume markets will be recruited.

In accepting or rejecting the various dealer applications for franchises we look for these important factors: The applicant's proposed plan, organization, and thinking about how he is going to sell and service Edsel cars. Contrary to all the things you hear and read, the factories do not want to tell a dealer how to run his business. We cannot do this because there are too many variables. We want the dealer to tell us how he is going to do it. We do have guides to help him; his reputation as a man of character; adequate finances; adequate facilities; demonstrated management ability; the ability to attract and direct good people; sales ability; proved management ability; a proper attitude toward ethical and competitive things; whether the applicant thinks in terms of being a good citizen; whether he is the type of man who will give proper consideration to his customers in sales and service.

Financial guides have been developed to determine the amount of capital needed for a certain number of car sales per year, but we are more concerned with the prospect's ideas of how much money he will require to do the job. If he has been successful before, he should know the requirements. Some men can operate with less capital than others. We are not interested in superfluous spending on bricks and mortar—but a dealer should give us adequate representation in his building, equipment and parts. A big, expensive showroom is not a requirement. We would rather see floor space devoted to pay space.

We have estimated that the mean dealer will invest between $75,000 and $125,000 in a franchise, and that he should do a mean annual volume of between $1,500,000 and $2,000,000. The automotive retail business brings a return that is generally higher than most retail businesses. Ordinarily, a dealer might invest at least $20,000 working capital, plus buildings and facilities for a 50-car franchise, but our whole philosophy in working with dealers is that each individual dealer establishes his own sales goals and his own investment requirements.

We are looking for quality dealers—men of good reputation in their communities—men of integrity. A good slogan might be—"Quality Dealers For Customer Confidence."

We want to remember "The Forgotten Man" —the customer—and start giving him the attention he deserves, because no business is any better than the customers it serves.

Edsel applicants will get the same treatment from the Ford Dealer Development Department, the agency that helps finance new dealerships, as any other Ford Motor Company division applicant.

SALES AND MARKETING JOB AHEAD IS BIG

An even richer and more brilliant tomorrow for the American economy seems just about as inevitable as anything reasonably can be. If this were not so, Ford Motor Company would scarcely have laid $250 million on the line for the new Edsel, nor would it have received 4,600 inquiries for Edsel franchises at a time when some people say there isn't any money to be made in the automobile business.

Ford Motor Company is near the completion of a 10-year capital investment program which involved $2.7 billion for new plants and equipment and plant modernization. The peak of Ford's post-war expansion is the 1956–57 period.

Most of us will agree that we have had a tremendous decade behind us, and there's every sign that another, even more tremendous decade lies ahead. The magnitude of the job to be done in changing consumer habits as well as the great opportunity for expanding sales in nearly every field of production and services suggests the need for raising our sights in the whole sales and marketing area.

Competition will be intensified by the rapid growth of advertising, sales, and marketing influence. The amount of total advertising influence directed to the United States consumers in order to change their habits and ideas of living has gone from approximately $2 billion in 1940 to the neighborhood of $10 billion in 1956. That's five times as much.

Just to keep up with our expanding productivity, which may make possible $600 billion of production by 1967, will require an expansion of $134 billion ($266 in 1956—$400 billion in 1967), or more than 50 per cent in sales of goods and services to consumers—an almost revolutionary change in living standards and concepts of the mass of our people. In other words, we must accomplish in the next ten years as much improvement in our total living standards as we accomplished in the 200 years from colonial times to 1939.

In this new environment and new pattern of life, advertising, sales and marketing will have the job of accelerating increased consumption and increased efficiency and productivity in our whole economy.

When we see our population doubling and, perhaps, redoubling in a single century, when we see the standard of living rising all over the world, when we contemplate the enormous drain on our natural resources in the coming century, when we witness man's first faltering steps in an atomic age, when we watch him seeking to penetrate outer space, when we see him trying to harness the rays of the sun, when we observe his determination to unlock, if he can, the ultimate secrets of the universe—such as the creation of matter out of energy—and when we comprehend, in short, the boundlessness and vastness of his expectations, we do know one thing: that the future is not for little men with little minds. It is not for men without vision who fear progress. It is not for timid men. The future is for men who dare to have great expectations, and who—with the guidance and encouragement of all the people for whom they strive—will also have the courage, the persistence, the wisdom and the patience to transform those expectations into realities.

We at Edsel hope to become an important segment of this new sales and marketing expansion that promises a higher material standard of living to all of our people. We also hope that we learn to use this greater material wealth in a wholesome way.

International Marketing and Economic Development

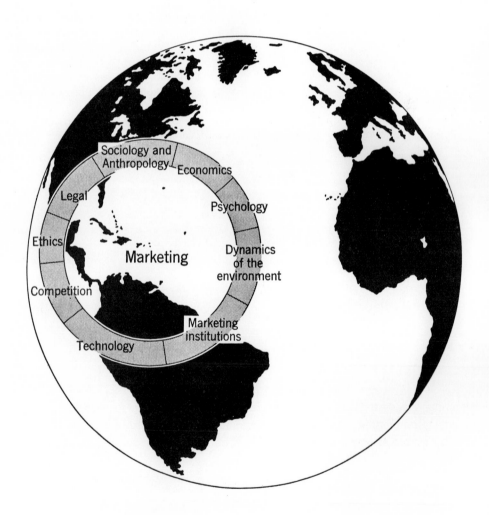

The role of marketing in expanding economies has not been adequately explored. Marketing in most countries has developed without any plan and too frequently without the realization that it has a positive role to play. Studies of international marketing have focused on the descriptive aspects of the national market. Certainly the individual differences among cultures and markets are important to an understanding of international marketing. For this reason, Part IV begins with the examination of these differences.

Important too is the role of marketing in a national market, which is examined in the second reading of Part IV. Finally, one of the most important marketing questions is discussed. What is the role of marketing in the economic development of a nation?

51. The World Customer

ERNEST DICHTER

Only one Frenchman out of three brushes his teeth.

Automobiles have become a must for the self-esteem of even the lowliest postal clerk in Naples or the Bantu street cleaner in Durban.

There is a supermarket in Apia, the capital of Western Samoa (which received its independence in January of this year). I found can openers and the cans to go with them in a remote village on the island of Upolu.

Four out of five Germans change their shirts but once a week.

Amazon Indians use outboard motors in deep green water alleyways.

What do these facts, and many others like them, portend for the future marketing manager? For top management in companies with foresight to capitalize on international opportunities? They mean that an understanding of cultural anthropology will be an important tool of competitive marketing. They mean that knowledge of the basic differences, as well as basic similarities, among consumers in different parts of the world will be essential. They mean that the successful marketer of the future will have to think not of a United States customer, nor even of a Western European or Atlantic community customer, but of a *world customer*.

For Western European countries, it is specific marketing facts and consumer purchasing behavior patterns which are of moment to today's businessman seeking new customers. At present, these countries comprise the biggest

✸✸ SOURCE: Reprinted by permission from *Harvard Business Review*, Vol. 40, No. 4, July-August 1962, pp. 113–122.

potential overseas market for most products. They are also the countries about whose consumers the most research information has been gathered. However, as some of the above examples illustrate, other parts of the world too are becoming potential markets, as human desires break the barricades of centuries in South America, Africa, and Asia.

Emergence of the European Common Market has forced businessmen and philosophers alike to take a look at the European as a distinct species. We now see the European as more than a Frenchman or an Austrian. The Atlantic community market and the world market may make us yet take a fresh look at what is alike and what is really different in humans, their desires, hopes, fears—in short, their motivations. Close observation of customers, and potential customers, all over the world reveals that there *are* some striking similarities, yet at the same time a considerable degree of permanent difference. From objective examination of these basic cultural similarities and differences, one may discern clues for serving the World Customer today.

In this article, I shall first point to a number of consumer behavior patterns relevant to international marketing, particularly within the Western European market but also in some of the less developed areas. Then I shall examine the differential role of national pride, which obviously affects and will affect the success of American-made products in Western European and other countries in the Atlantic market. Finally, in an effort to define and interpret the economic and psychological differences among world customers, I shall postulate six world market groups of nations, measured by the yardstick of middle class development.

THE DISTINCTIVE EUROPEAN

The United States company going into Europe has to study the culture and the psychology of the people of the country, not just its manufacturing facilities and markets in the technological sense. The advertising and sales managers have to learn that reaching customers in a given country involves a real understanding of the basic motivations which operate within that country.

In dealing with various European markets, the American businessman must open his eyes to certain paradoxes, stereotypes, and hidden competitors.

Apparent Paradoxes

There are paradoxes between the way in which American products are perceived and the way they are used. Thus, anti-Americanism is strongly coupled with a desire for many United States products, often out of pure snobbery, often because they are symbols of an affluent society. The Italian housewife considers her American sister a poor cook and a lady of leisure, but dreams day and night of owning a Hollywood kitchen.

A similar paradox is that of the West German businessman who scoffs at American know-how, pointing out the technical superiority of many of his national products, but proudly puts his elegantly uniformed chauffeur in a Ford, polished up to the last fold of its lacquered steel hull tuxedo.

Ingrained Stereotypes

The American businessman must cast off deeply ingrained stereotypes in analyzing the purchasing behavior of European consumers, in reference to product meaning, "purchasing morality," and quality consciousness.

We all "know" that French women are very fashion conscious. Yet a study recently showed that this was exactly one of those glib stereotypes that have little if any basis in reality. The purchase of a dress or coat is much more of an investment for the Frenchwoman than for the American woman. This results from differences both in income and in prices of fashion products. It is not enough, therefore, to tell a French shopper that a garment is fashionable. She also wants to know, in a way, the "trade-in value" of the dress or blouse. How long will the fabric last? How many years will she be able to wear it? These are promises and appeals which have to a very large extent lost their attraction to the American woman.

The European is very conscious of preservation. He collects and retains things. The only parallel that we have had in this country was during the period of World War II, when we developed a new kind of pride, a pride in doing without, a pride in not having bought a new car for several years, for example. This pride did not last very long. Just as soon as cars became available again, we reverted to our somewhat affluent American habit of replacing models quite rapidly. Yet this concept of "purchasing morality" still exerts influence in the United States for some products. For example, the average male still hesitates to buy two or three suits at one time because he feels that suits, together with many other articles of clothing, are highly overvalued, and therefore it is extravagant to buy more than one at the same time. On the other hand, most of us have learned that it no longer pays to resole shoes more than twice.

As for quality consciousness, as well as confidence in the trustworthiness of the manufacturer, this is quite different in different countries. In Australia or South Africa—and for that matter in England—you find on most toilet tissues the reassuring message that the manufacturer guarantees that the paper was not made out of secondhand rags, but only new rags and new raw materials.

Such a promise has become completely unnecessary in North America. Whatever advertising may be accused of, in many areas it provides the consumer, particularly in branded merchandise, with an assurance that he will not be cheated as long as he buys a well-known brand. It is true today that whether we buy a Westinghouse, a General Electric, or a Kelvinator refrigerator, we get more or less equal values as long as we pay about the same amount of money. What we have learned to buy is the freedom of individual choice. We buy images; we buy the sizzle because we have been reassured that the steak itself is of generally good quality. *In many European countries this confidence*, this almost blind reliance on the promise of the manufacturer, *has not yet been established*. Therefore, advertising approaches have to be based much more on definite proofs of quality.

Hidden Competitors

Another problem facing Atlantic marketers is that in many areas they are still dealing with hidden competitors, lurking in places unfamiliar in domestic marketing. Taking toilet tissue again, in some recent motivational research done in West Germany I found it was much too premature to promise the German consumer luxury softness or colors compatible with the bathroom fixtures. Instead, the hidden but real competitor with which the toilet tissue manufacturer has to contend is the newspaper and the old standby of the German equivalent of the Sears, Roebuck catalog. The West German family feels that toilet tissue, particularly the American luxury type, is wasteful and unnecessary. The advertising approach, then, has to deal much more with providing absolution and selling the concept that good quality toilet tissue is a part of modern life.

ETHOS OF NATIONALISM

Nationalism obviously plays a major role in determining consumer acceptance of nondomestically made products. Understanding its manifold aspects is a *sine qua non* for United States businessmen operating overseas.

National feeling manifests itself in many ways. Some of these have already been touched on briefly before. In this section, I shall show in greater detail how: (1) national pride can be a motivating sales factor employable by the astute overseas marketer as an asset; (2) longstanding cultural traditions in one nation can dictate the *discard* of advertising approaches proven successful in another nation; (3) stereotyped national *self*-illusions can alter the direction of marketing strategy.

National Pride

Admiration of foreign products often goes together with *hidden inferiority feelings* which are overcompensated by tearing the foreigner down. These products are the tangible symbols of foreign superiority. For example:

¶ In Venezuela, despite various forms of anti-Yankee sentiment, it is considered chic to smoke United States cigarettes. Even when the American brand name is used and the Venezuelan smoker can discover the little phrase "Hecho en Venezuela" on his package, the almost completely identical cigarette suffers at least a 50% prestige loss. A successful approach used in overcoming this problem was to convince Venezuelans that the people they secretly admired in a form of love-hatred—the Americans—indeed liked Venezuelan tobacco, used it for their own cigarettes, and had no negative feeling toward Venezuelan cigarettes.

A similar solution was found in connection with Venezuelan rum by serving this rum in hotels in Caracas frequented by United States businessmen and tourists. The Venezuelan could be convinced that if it was good enough for the supposed foreign connoisseur, then it certainly ought to be good enough for him.

¶ The French gasoline, *Total*, had a domestic marketing problem arising from a national inferiority complex. Gasoline, to the Frenchman, was for a long time represented by American and British companies. Gasoline and oil (to a lesser extent) are symbols of power. The Frenchman was not convinced that his own gasoline would have the same power as the foreign brands. The approach calculated to overcome this sentiment was to present *Total* as an international brand that happened to originate in France and the Sahara, but was accepted and well-liked in many other countries.

¶ In Morocco, sales of French pasteurized milk had dropped considerably with the advent of Morocco's independence. This stemmed partly from the exodus of the French army with its families, and also from Moroccan unfamiliarity with drinking pasteurized milk.

But the drop in milk sales was also due to other factors, psychological in nature. One was the lack of confidence in the quality of pasteurized milk—Moroccan women were accustomed to buying from street vendors who milked the cows in front of their own eyes and then ladled the milk out of the pail. The soulless, odorless, clean pasteurized milk in bottles was simply too far removed from the original natural source of milk for the women to realize that they were still receiving the same quality of product.

But even more interesting was a factor dealing again with the phenomenon of national pride. The company had changed the lettering on its milk bottles and milk cartons from French to Arabic. The purpose was to please the newly independent consumers. Research showed, however, that instead of being pleased, consumers reacted negatively to this attempt at flattery. They stated it in the following way: "What is good enough for the French people is good enough for us. We don't want Arab milk. We want good French milk that the Frenchmen drink themselves."

For *marketing purposes* it thus was necessary to re-establish confidence in the naturalness of pasteurized bottled milk by showing cows and having street vendors also peddle pasteurized milk. A second measure was to change the lettering on the milk bottles back to French. Both steps resulted in increased sales.

The little phrase "Made in . . . " can have a tremendous influence on the acceptance and success of products over and above the specific advertising techniques used by themselves.

In a recent study in West Germany, this query was posed as part of a projective test: "An important discovery has been made in the technical field which has a great influence on our daily life. Which country has made this discovery?" As many as 78% answered: "Germany." (The study is being repeated in other countries. It will be interesting to examine the answers.) We also asked the Germans to think of a new product which through an error in production caused the death of several hundred people. The task of the respondents was to indicate which country would be most likely to manufacture such a product. We found that Germans considered this most likely to happen in the East zone, Russia, or the satellite countries, and then up to 30% in Italy or France.

The strong positive attitude evidenced by Germans toward their own technical product influenced an advertising approach developed for Ford in Germany. Research showed that the name Ford had a strong American association. The reaction of Germans was: "Americans drive our cars, Volkswagen and Mercedes; therefore they must be convinced that German cars are better than their own; so why should we buy their cars?" When the German Ford was presented as an example of cooperation between American ingenuity and know-how and German thoroughness and efficiency, considerable sales success was achieved.

Inverted Morality

The influence of cultural traditions permeates a host of consumer behavior patterns.

The fact that 64% of Frenchmen don't brush their teeth is in part caused by the lack of running water in many communities. But a far more interesting aspect of this behavior could be explained on the basis of what I call "inverted morality." Here is an illustration of what can happen: In Puritanical cultures it is customary to think of cleanliness as being next to godliness. The body and its functions are covered up as much as possible.

But, in Catholic and Latin countries, to fool too much with one's body, to overindulge in bathing or toiletries, has the opposite meaning. It is *that* type of behavior which is considered immoral and improper. Accordingly, an advertising approach based on Puritanical principles, threatening Frenchmen that if they didn't brush their teeth regularly, they would develop cavities or would not find a lover, failed to impress.

To fit the accepted concept of morality, the French advertising agency changed this approach to a permissive one. The new approach presented the brushing of teeth as modern and chic but not as an absolute necessity which when neglected would result in dire consequences.

In line with the "inverted morality" notion is the fact that deodorant sales in France are lower than in most other countries. The majority, up to 80% of French housewives, use laundry soap instead of toilet soap. Only 20% of them have discovered perfumed, feminine soap which in the United States is frequently referred to as a "French type" of soap.

Self-Illusions

Often nationals of a particular country are completely mistaken themselves about their own main characteristics. Successful marketers must be as cognizant of these national self-illusions as they must be aware of the mistaken stereotypes noted earlier. For example:

¶ Germans still refer to themselves as a nation of poets and thinkers; yet the largest selling newspaper, *The Bildzeitung*, has a circulation of 2½ million based largely on sensationalism and tabloid treatment of news. Even German *advertisers* had to be shown that this circulation, although proven by audits, was indeed psychologically possible. The only way this could be done was to force the German advertiser to look at his own people, including himself, without hypocrisy and in the harsh light of reality.

¶ All references to economy, comfort, and warmth had only a minimal effect in getting Englishmen to install central heating. They all ran up against a barrier of traditional self-illusion that Englishmen are of a hardy race that does not need the softening and effeminate effect of central heating. Inroads could be made only when the health of babies was used as a rationalization and after reassurance was given to the English "he-man" that to feel comfortably warm would not be detrimental to his self-image of virility.

¶ Most Europeans are convinced that they are individualists and nonconformists. Studies have shown that this is to a very large extent an illusion. There is a widely expressed fear of losing individuality, but right now it is the European who is becoming the representative of the mass market while it is the American market which in turn relies more and more on psychological segmentations. United States manufacturers may produce individuality on a mass scale, but individuality has become the decisive appeal in many products and services.

National self-illusions are hardly restricted to other nations. In the United States, as in quite a few other countries, many of our ethical principles are still based on the concept that we have to work by the sweat of our brow. In Germany, this is even more so. *The more you work, the more moral you feel.* Yet at the same time our modern psychological development and automation have resulted in a situation where fewer and fewer people work with their hands. Service fields are increasing, and we have more and more leisure time. The recent victory of the electricians' union in New York introducing a five-hour day aroused the nation for many reasons. Particularly pertinent here is that it clashed with most of our cherished beliefs of the importance of achieving happiness through work.

We are now confronted with increasing leisure time. Our discomfort results to a large extent from a lack of hedonistic morality such as prevailed among the Greeks for whom life was here to be enjoyed by a few people who did not have to work and did not have to feel guilty about it.

Leisure pursuits are spreading rapidly. Labor-saving devices are multiplying, and they are being adopted all over the world. The major difference lies in the degree of manifest or latent guilt feelings which are aroused:

Instant coffee is used by the Dutch housewife accompanied by the verbal protest that she only uses it in an emergency. What happens, however, is that the number of emergencies has increased amazingly.

French farmwives are inclined to say that they need large kitchen stoves in order to do the cooking for their large farm families. Young farmwives, however, have begun to admire and gradually buy the smaller units used by their city sisters. They have discovered that they do not have to stay as long behind the stove, and so are finding interests in other roles than that of a kitchen slave.

BREAKING BOUNDARIES

Politically, in recent years we have watched a host of new nations emerge from erstwhile colonial status. It may be argued that many colonies would have been better off staying under the protection of enlightened colonial powers. Yet their desire for independence, no matter how premature we consider it to be, is so impulsive, explosive, and uncontrollable that no other solution remains than to satisfy this emotionally, humanly understandable hunger.

More important to the marketer is the fact that the same desire which spurred these political events has another dimension—viz., *in terms of consumption, whole centuries are being skipped in a world revolution of human expectations.*

Thus, from the viewpoint of the international psychologist's concern with the people still living in national units, we see the gradual development of the World Customer who breaks all boundaries:

¶ When a South African clothing manufacturer asks how to sell more long pants to previously half-naked Bantus, he is the first one to smash the barrier of apartheid, no matter how segregationistic his views may be. The moment one starts thinking of 10 million natives as consumers, one has to concern himself with their emotions and motivations.

Research revealed a greater psychological parallel between the emancipated Zulu and the emancipated white worker than between the nonemancipated Zulu and his emancipated tribal brother. The latter is ashamed when visited by his former ethnic peers. He has learned to speak English Afrikaans, has started to wear long pants, and often owns a car—a secondhand, dilapidated car, but nevertheless a car. He represents in many ways the same emotional conflict as that which existed between the first- and second-generation immigrants during the period of heavy immigration in the United States.

¶ In Australia until a few years ago 10% of the population was represented each year by newcomers, migrants, or—more euphemistically —"new Australians." These new Australians will change the basic Australian character in unrecognizable fashion within another ten years or so. As consumers, on the one hand, they want to eat, drink, and use the same products as the established Australians; on the other hand, they bring in their own customs and often superimpose Italian, German, or Spanish culture on the Australians.

Six Market Groups

How can we locate the World Customer at various stages of development? How can we measure nations?

The "consumer revolution" which we are witnessing is basically not a proletarian one, but is *a revolution of the middle class*. It is the degree of development of a large middle class which makes the difference between a backward and a modern country both economically and psychologically. That is the clue for appraising and interpreting different cultures, for measuring their achievement.

The most important symbol of middle class development in the world today is the automobile. It is the automobile which represents achievement and personal freedom for the middle class. And this restless middle class is the most important factor in the constructive discontent which motivates people's desires and truly moves them forward. In some countries, like the United States, West Germany, Switzerland, Sweden, and Norway, most people have enough to eat and are reasonably well housed. Having achieved this thousand-year-old dream of humanity, they now reach out for further satisfactions. They want to travel, discover, be at least physically independent. The automobile is the symbol of mobility; the automobile has become the self-mobile!

Using middle class development as a measure of achievement, if we were to visualize the social composition of each country in terms of a scale showing the size of its middle class, upper class, and lower class, we could probably define some six groups.

Group One: The Almost Classless Society, Contented Countries. In this group we would include primarily the Scandinavian countries. The middle class takes up almost all of the scale, with very few people left who could be considered really poor and few who are really rich. We are dealing with a socialistic security and equalization which sounds like paradise, but often leads to loss of incentives.

In these countries, products are viewed in a rather sober fashion. The car, for instance, is strictly utilitarian, and showing off with one's auto is not considered correct.

Studies have shown that reliability and economy are very important. Attitudes toward products are rational: they do not represent a special status value. There is generally a conservative attitude toward new gadgets and styles. Second cars are practically nonexistent.

Group Two: The Affluent Countries. This group includes the United States, West Germany, Switzerland, Holland, and Canada. Few people starve, and there is still some room at the top. The top of the middle class itself, however, often is high and desirable enough so that there is no need to break through and trespass into the unpopular and threatened class of financial aristocracy.

Among these countries the most advanced is the United States. What happens in many areas in the United States represents the latest and leading trends and permits us to predict what will happen in the next few years in the other affluent countries. People in affluent countries want greater individuality in their products. They dream of high-quality, repair-proof, almost custom-tailored articles.

While the German still uses his car for prestige purposes, in the United States the status value of cars has substantially diminished and has been shifted to other products and services such as swimming pools, travel, and education. The average American considers his car more like an appliance than a status symbol. Conspicuous cars like the Cadillac or the Lincoln try to emphasize their quiet elegance to avoid being considered cars for show-offs. There is increased attention to functional values and integration in car designs. Cars are not pampered; they are expected to do their job.

Group Three: Countries in Transition. In this group we may place England, France, Italy, Autralia, South Africa, and Japan. These countries still have a working class in the nineteenth century sense. But this class is trying to break out of its bondage and join the comfortable middle class. The upper classes still have privileges and can afford maids, Rolls-Royces, and castles; but their privileges are being rapidly whittled away. These countries have not had complete social revolutions. (The Labor government in England represented such an attempt but failed). Servants are still cheap but rapidly getting more expensive and less easily available. Many wage-earning groups suffer from low wages. Living standards are behind those of the United States and West Germany. The white-collar worker often makes less money than the factory worker, but he has not integrated yet with the developing labor-based middle class. Prestige still plays an important role.

Cars are pampered in these countries. They are an extension of one's personality. They are given pet names. They represent major investments. Cars are outward symbols of success.

There are still many first-car people, who have only now bought their first proof of "having arrived." Price plays an important role as an invitation to enter the automobile world—upgrading the buyer from bicycles and motorcycles. For top classes, some very expensive cars are available. Style plays a role with certain groups; there is much experimentation, curiosity, and desire for product adventure. Markets are still fluid, have not stabilized yet. There is resistance in all these countries against planned obsolescence. A lot of people hold onto their cars for six to ten years or more. American cars are considered to be too flashy and also too expensive.

Group Four: Revolutionary Countries. Venezuela, Mexico, Argentina, Brazil, Spain, India, China, and the Philippines are in this group. In these areas large groups of people are just emerging from near-starvation and are discovering industrialization. Relatively speaking, there are more extremely rich people, a small but expanding middle class, and a very large body of depressed economic groups that are beginning to discover the possibilities of enjoying life through the revolution in industry.

In these countries large sections of the population have not even reached the level of being consumers. These are the Indians living in many South American countries, the people living in villages in India and Indonesia, and so on.

Automobiles are available only to a relatively small group. They are expensive and considered a luxury. They are taxed so highly that they are beyond the reach of most people. American cars are considered the ideal. People want to show off. Small cars are bought as a way to get started. As the middle class develops, there should be an even further increase in the sale of small and compact cars, with the really rich people preferring big American cars.

Group Five: Primitive Countries. The newly liberated countries of Africa and the remaining colonies comprise the fifth group. In these countries there exists only a very small group of wealthy indigenous and foreign businessmen, new political leaders, and foreign advisers. The rest of the population is most often illiterate and ignorant and exists in a preconsumer stage, characterized either by barter or by almost complete primitive "self-sufficiency." The few cars that are sold are primarily for the government bureaucracy. There is no real car market as yet.

Group Six: The New Class Society. In Russia and its satellite countries, there is emerging a class of bureaucrats who represent a new form of aristocracy, while everybody else represents a slowly improving, low middle class. True, in these countries the extremely low income and the starving proletarians have disappeared.

The automobile, the modern home with its mechanized kitchen and mass-produced food items, and supermarket distribution represent the symbols of a new industrial society. By understanding the basic position of a country on this scale of development one can understand the role of products at present and one can also predict their future possibilities.

There is an interest in prestige cars. All the bourgeois symbols of capitalist countries are being copied—particularly those of the United States.

Our Greatest Opportunity

Many recent stories in the press—most of them picked up in foreign countries—make it appear that we ought to be ashamed of the good life we are leading. This recanting has its origin in a deep-seated guilt feeling which is unhealthy and dangerous. Some of the recanting is directed against a number of specific products, such as electrical gadgets, big cars, luxury and leisure time, and merchandise.

The real measuring rod of the success of one system over another should be based on the happiness of the citizens, their creativeness, and their constructive discontent. The desire to grow, to improve oneself, and to enjoy life to the fullest is at least equal, if not decidedly superior, to the goal of being ahead in a missile or a satellite program.

Our present life, therefore, should be presented as a challenge to the outside world—not in a boastful way, but as a life attainable by everyone through democratic and peaceful pursuits.

CONCLUSION

In most countries I have visited, I find that human desires are pretty much alike. The big difference lies in the level of achievement, in its many different forms.

In Iquitos, on the Amazon River, I recently visited an Indian tribe. They live in blissful fashion, hunting and planting bananas and yuccas. Who is smarter—we, the hard-working "civilized people"—or the contented Indians? Part of the answer was provided by the fact that our guide complained that there were fewer and fewer Indians for tourists to see. They were becoming "too civilized." In other words, these primitive people who were supposed to be happy are caught in the inevitable maelstrom of development. They smoke cigarettes and are beginning to wear jeans and shirts.

Growth and progress are the only possible goals of life. I believe that the clue to man's destiny lies in his relentless training toward independence, not only politically, but also in the psychological sense. We are beset by fears, by inhibitions, by narrow-minded routine thinking.

Step by step, year by year, we free ourselves more and more. Jets reduce physical distances; international trade and mass communications break down barriers. The world is opening up. The Common Market will broaden into an Atlantic Market and finally into a World Market. In order to participate effectively in this progressive development of mankind, it is essential to have a creative awareness of human desire and its strategy throughout the world—to understand and prepare to serve the new World Customer.

52. The Challenge of the Underdeveloped National Market

RICHARD D. ROBINSON

Marketing concepts most appropriate in the emerging states of Asia, Africa, and Latin America differ markedly from those to which we have grown accustomed in the United States. The difference begins with product design.

Rather than promoting products believed to generate the greatest financial return in the short run, Western firms selling in non-Western markets probably should place more emphasis on those products of greatest long-run benefit to the nations concerned and analyze most carefully the manner in which they are supplying those products to the market. Otherwise, Western managements may anticipate increasingly tight import restrictions for their products, blocked earnings, higher taxes, and eventual loss of foreign markets and assets.

The point is that one should expect heightened sensitivity to long-run national interests on the part of Asian, African, and Latin American governments as they become more sophisticated and skilled. Such sensitivity to national interest is what many unthinking Westerners have condemned with the epithet "nationalism."

A domestic marketing specialist in the United States may tend to look at the market from the point of view of the structure of present demand, so as to sell a new product or more of an existing product. The new might be new only in respect to style, brand, or packaging. Consumer wants are changed and expanded constantly in the process.

‡ SOURCE: Reprinted by permission from the *Journal of Marketing* (National Quarterly Publication of the American Marketing Association), Vol. 25, No. 6, October 1961, pp. 19–25.

But in India or Egypt, the marketing analyst —if sensitve to the national interest of the host country—must concern himself more with ascertaining what types of products would contribute most to increasing the national product, alleviating the nation's balance of payments situation, and sopping up inflationary pressures with a minimum commitment of scarce resources, including foreign exchange.

The stimulation of non-existing demands for new consumer goods or demands based on brand name, style obsolescence, or new packaging may well cause an unjustified waste of scarce materials and skills or an unnecessary commitment of them. Where resources are seriously limited in a per-capita sense, the Western businessman who remains insensitive to this national interest does so at his peril.

THREE LEVELS OF MANAGEMENT SENSITIVITY

There are three levels of management sensitivity.

The first has to do with management's awareness of the need to modify or redesign *products* so as to make them really appropriate to the markets into which they are moving. The second has to do with management's awareness of the need to measure its products against the long-run interests of non-Western markets—in other words, *impact* of products. The third level of sensitivity is management's awareness of the extent to which its product is politically *vulnerable*.

Sensitivity on all levels may well lead to product modification—even to invention—or, on the other hand, to self-imposed limitation in certain cases. Perhaps within these underdeveloped national markets some products should not be promoted at all, however modified or redesigned.

Product Design

Clearly, different United States products require different types of foreign markets. Some require large industrial markets; others, mass consumer markets. Still others need a professional or technical market, or a market in which public agencies buy, or a literate market, or a market in which the standard of living is high, and so on.

Since many of these characteristics are not found in markets outside of North America and Western Europe, the sales potential for certain products in many parts of the world is limited. Many American managements are well aware of the limitations placed on the degree to which they can expand foreign sales because of the special market characteristics demanded by the nature of their traditional products. Geographical and climatic conditions are also important variables; few American firms design products specifically for use in the jungle or the desert, or products for use by illiterates.

Generalizations that follow are based on the author's study of the attitudes and organization of 172 American companies in respect to overseas interests. This study was conducted over the 1956–58 period under the auspices of the Division of Research, Harvard Graduate School of Business Administration.

The necessity for substantially modifying or altering products to meet the specific demands of non-Western markets frequently discouraged American managements from taking serious interest in becoming active within these markets. It might be possible to service the European, Canadian, and Australian-New Zealand markets with surplus domestic production, but elsewhere such sales spillover was difficult to develop. The domestic product was simply not appropriate.

One executive pointed out that his company's principal product, asphalt roofing, was not appropriate in areas in which extreme heat was common, thereby ruling out much of the equatorial zone as a market.

Mining machinery produced by one firm could not be exported in large quantities because it was built specifically to fit conditions found in United States mines, conditions uncommon to other countries.

Management of a steel-castings company, the principal products of which were heavy castings for railway cars, cited many reasons why foreign customers did not wish to use cast steel, let alone the company's designs. Many foreign railways used buffers instead of couplers, rolled steel designs for the side frames instead of cast steel, and four-wheel freight cars instead of eight-wheel.

The president of one company stated that his firm's products were consumer goods and were to a very considerable extent culturally conditioned. "We block ourselves from many markets in South America, Africa, and other areas."

An American executive with a long experience in India commented that most United States companies were based on the North American customer. They had very little concern for customers elsewhere. Concrete evidence of such disregard was the little influence American firms had had in setting up world-wide standards. "United States industry has not even taken the trouble—or spent the money—to have its 1,700 national standards translated for use in foreign countries," the President of the American Standards Associations is reported to have said. "It is no coincidence that American industries doing the largest export business—the electrical and motion pictures industries, for example—are the ones that have developed international standards." [1]

In many cases where geographical and cultural influences on products were cited by management to explain their disinterest in foreign sales, the true reasons seemed to lie somewhat deeper. Too many managements had surmounted these difficulties. Asphalt roofing might not be good in extreme heats, but was it not impossible to develop a similar roofing which would be? Mining conditions might be quite different from those obtaining in United States mines, but surely appropriate machines could be built. Granted, the product of the steel castings company was not suited for sale in most foreign areas, but the development of an appropriate product was surely not as difficult as that encountered by such companies as the International Business Machines Company and the Westinghouse Electric Corporation.

One management was modifying the design

[1] *Time*, June 30, 1958, p. 74.

of its truck, which was to be produced and sold in Turkey. Changes were required by the rough roads, the high elevations, and extreme heat in some areas. Executives in a large automotive company observed that it was difficult for the larger, mass-production companies to alter products in this fashion to meet specific geographical and climatic conditions. But was great size necessarily related to inflexibility in this regard? The division manufacturing trucks in this case was probably little larger than the independent truck manufacturer who was modifying its product for the Turkish market.

Asked about the feasibility of manufacturing some sort of an intermediate type of machine in some foreign areas, a type no longer being used in the United States, a vice president of a farm machinery product replied that in a way his company was doing precisely that in Mexico; the tractor assembled in Mexico did not include all the latest hydraulic gadgets. Such a tractor would have required too much servicing and would have been too complicated for the ordinary Mexican farmer to operate.

Directly related to willingness to modify product design was the matter of quality. The experience of Corporation X in Africa is relevant.

The local African government had been buying from Corporation X, an American firm, hand-operated dusters for use in distributing pesticides in the cotton fields. The dusters were loaned to individual Negro farmers. The duster supplied by the corporation was a finely-machined device requiring regular oiling and good care.

But the fact that this duster turned more easily than any other duster on the market was relatively unimportant to the native farmers. Furthermore, the requirement for careful oiling and care simply meant that in a relatively short time the machines froze up and broke. The result? The local government went back to an older type French duster which was heavy, turned with difficulty, and gave a poorer distribution of dust, but which lasted longer in that it required less care and lubrication.

From the point of view of the small Negro cotton farmer, the quality of the French dusters was more appropriate than that of the American dusters. In this relative sense, the quality of the French machine was superior.

This view was reflected in a remark by the director of the international division of a large company to the effect that Europe could produce anything more cheaply and better than the United States. By "better" he meant better *relative to the demands of the foreign market.* He admitted that many American-made products were much better than their foreign counterparts in an absolute sense, but this superiority in quality was too expensive to be "within the circle of demand" of many foreign markets. For example, his company manufactured one item with an average life of thirty-five years. The trouble was that many people abroad could not afford to pay for a device lasting that long, and they were not impressed.

Another way of looking at quality was to consider that additional cost of a highly durable product represented an investment and, if the cost of capital were relatively high, as it was in many of the underdeveloped countries, it might not be economically feasible to purchase the more durable or higher-quality American product.

Some few firms had gone so far in product modification as to invent virtually new products. A pen company had designed a special, cheap, mass-produced pen for the Asiatic market. Landers-Frary and Clark was selling a newly-designed hand-operated corn mill in Latin America. Private Enterprise, Inc., had developed a wooden block with which to construct cheap housing in Central America. It was significant that those companies identified with substantial overseas interest demonstrated extraordinary ingenuity and flexibility in modifying their products so as to be appropriate to local geographical and cultural conditions. It was precisely those companies that had not been interested in foreign business which seemed to find their product most limited in respect to international sales.

Yet, in some cases, the problems faced by these latter firms did not seem nearly as great in this respect as those faced and overcome by the others. It seemed that *the fundamental interest and orientation of key members of management really determined the degree to which a product was limited geographically and culturally.*

An internationally minded management examined deliberately and systematically the products it intended to market within Country X from the point of view of the environment of Country X. It made no assumptions about the validity of an American-oriented product. Major environmental factors considered in relation to the design of a given product were:

Level of technical skills ⟶ Product simplification

Level of labor cost ⟶ Automation or manualization of product

Level of literacy ⟶ Remarking and simplification of product

Level of income ⟶ Quality and price change

Level of interest rates ⟶ Quality and price change
(Investment in high quality
might not be financially desirable.)

Level of maintenance ⟶ Change in tolerances

Climatic differences ⟶ Product adaptation

Isolation (heavy repair ⟶ Product simplification and reliability
difficult and expensive)   improvement

Differences in standards ⟶ Recalibration of product and
resizing

Availability of other products ⟶ Greater or lesser product
integration

Availability of materials ⟶ Change in product structure and
fuel

Power availability ⟶ Resizing of product

Special conditions ⟶ Product redesign or invention

The added effort in developing an appropriate product, given the anticipated reward, might be thus measured. But it appeared that relatively few managements had analyzed the pros and cons of developing non-Western markets in these or similar terms.

Product Impact

In designing, modifying, and promoting the sale of products in the underdeveloped markets, management should not assume that the economic and social benefits to be derived from these products are necessarily the same as when they are used within the American economy.

A representative of one firm explained that his company's export business was "absolutely nominal." Asphalt roofing, the firm's principal product, was expensive for a cheap labor market. It failed to compete with wood shake and slate. In most cases, there were few building code restrictions; and builders simply took the cheapest of the traditional products with little regard for comparative qualities or for the amount of labor required for installation. Although under some conditions asphalt roofing had absolute advantages over the traditional type of roofing, one of its principal advantages

was that it required less labor than most other roofing for both manufacture and installation.

Outside of the United States and Western Europe, this labor-conserving feature of a product would not provide any significant economic advantage. The relationship of labor to the cost of materials is quite different from that in the Western European and American environment.

The point is that logically preceding any substantial commitment of company time and money to foreign sales projects should be a careful, impartial study of the impact of the products involved on the economies and societies in which they are to be sold. Sooner or later, the government of the recipient nation will awaken to its own interests. Products might well be analyzed in terms of their impact on production and upon the productivity of local labor. The introduction of some products might reasonably be expected to induce directly an expansion of employment. Others might have the effect of improving the quality of local labor. Luxury products and those of a fundamentally labor-saving nature might not be appealing under all circumstances to the development-conscious foreign government.

Each society develops its own peculiar wants in terms of non-essential, consumer goods. The satisfaction of at least part of this demand may be important to the national economy in order to maintain incentives and to sop up inflationary pressures. At least partial satisfaction may likewise be politically compelling.

By reason of the chronic pressure on investment and balance of payments in many underdeveloped countries, responsible governments are loathe to divert a greater share than is necessary of their already inadequate resources to the satisfaction of these demands. In order to relate the promotion of a non-essential consumer product in Country X to the national interest, two guides are useful: (1) Can the product be made available with a relative minor commitment of scarce local resources? (2) Does there already exist an unsatisfied popular demand for the product?

A product produced locally by presently unemployed labor and which upvalues locally available materials is quite different from an imported good, the price of which includes expensive foreign labor and scarce foreign exchange. Similarly, a non-essential product that is presently known and is in demand is quite different from a product for which demand will have to be stimulated.

Coca-Cola in Egypt is quite different from Coca-Cola in Turkey. In Egypt it has been known for many years and is in great demand. The drink uses few resources and helps "soak up" inflationary pressure. In Turkey, the product would have to be promoted, thereby creating a *new* consumer demand. The economy is already straining to meet present consumer demands without cutting back investment in basic development. Clearly, the introduction of Coca-Cola is not necessary to induce incentive to produce. Of course, if it could be shown that Coca-Cola would constitute a consumption substitute for other goods, and involve fewer scarce resources than the others, then an argument might be made for the introduction of Coca-Cola.

Obviously the nature of a product may change substantially from one society to another. Both technical and social conditions may have a heavy impact. The type of mining involved may make it impossible to apply further units of labor, thereby giving an absolute advantage to mining machinery in terms of increasing production. Or the rural population in a particular area may not provide adequate labor to harvest and process the basic crops rapidly enough to prevent substantial damage in the case of adverse weather. This means that

machines, which otherwise might have no impact on over-all production, would have substantial impact. These machines then change in nature from mere labor-saving devices into labor-creating ones in that they effect an absolute increase in production.

This discussion is occasioned by two observations: (1) Very few managements seem to be concerned about the nature of their product in relationship to total economic development, and specifically to the development of the country in which their product is marketed. (2) There seems to be little management awareness that a product might not have the same characteristics in relation to the American market as in a specific underdeveloped economy.

Political Vulnerability of Product

Even though a product is appropriately designed for the market and its promotion is in the interest of the host society, a management may still run substantial risk if that product is politically vulnerable—that is, susceptible to public concern and governmental control.

The degree to which one is shielded from political interest is in part a function of the degree to which management has modified its product so as to be most appropriate to the market. It also depends on how well management has chosen it products from the point of view of their impact upon national economic interests.

But there are other criteria as well to be used in the determination of political vulnerability. Is the product of such a nature as to be politically important or to attract undue government attention? How irreplaceable is the foreign contribution contained in the product? Is local competition possible? Does the organization by which the product is made available recognize the interests of the host country?

Such public concern and control may on the one hand lead to protection within a market, or on the other hand to loss of market and assets. Some of the relevant criteria are suggested by the following questions:

1. Is the product ever the subject of important political debates in respect to adequacy of supply? (Sugar, salt, kerosene, gasoline, foodstuffs, transport facilities, public utilities, tires, medicines, etc.)

2. Is the production one on which other industries rest? (Cement, steel, power, machine tools, construction machinery, etc.)

3. Is the product one in which effective competition is difficult in small national markets?

4. Is the product one held to be essential either economically or socially? (Key drugs and medicines, laboratory equipment.)

5. Is the product important to agriculture? (Farm tools and machinery, pumps, fertilizers, seed, etc.)

6. Is the product of national defense significance? (Communications equipment, transport equipment, etc.)

7. Does the product include important components that would be available from local sources? (Labor, skills, materials.)

8. Is the product one for which competition from local manufacture may be reasonably expected in the foreseeable future?

9. Does the product relate to channels of mass communication media? (Newsprint, radio equipment, etc.)

10. Is the product primarily a service?

11. Does the use of the product, or its design, rest upon some legal requirement?

12. Is the product potentially dangerous to the user? (Explosives, drugs.)

13. Does the product induce a net drain on scarce foreign exchange?

If each of these questions were answered on a 1-to-10 scale, from a strong "yes" to a strong "no," the lowest scoring products would be among the most vulnerable to political pressures. It is often useful to ask how foreign ownership of a given industry or product source would be treated in the United States.

Political vulnerability may lead to labor agitation, public regulation (price fixing, allocation quotas, etc.); nationalization (in the sense of restricting ownership to local nationals); or socialization (public ownership) on the one hand—or on the other hand to favoritism and protection. Which way the pendulum swings depends largely upon the sensitivity and foresight of management in responding to political pressures before they become irresistible, also upon the effort management makes to relate its product to the specific needs of the market in respect to both design and impact.

Goods deemed to be essential (for example, high scores in questions 2, 4, 5, 6, and 9) often receive first claim to scarce foreign exchange in respect to importing. Likewise, these same products, if made within the country, often receive a high degree of encouragement and protection, up to and including government guarantee for the repatriation of profits and capital and an official prohibition against competing imports. Therefore, other than the possibility of national-

ization or socialization, the risk of investment abroad in the production of essential products is substantially less than that incurred in the case of less essential products.

CONCLUSION

Relevant variables from management to management are really two: (1) degree of management sensitivity to the long-run interests and desires of the emerging countries of Asia, Africa, and Latin America, and (2) the degree of flexibility shown by management in product design and modification, as well as choice in the manner of supplying a market. Inasmuch as this article deals with product criteria only, there is no discussion of developing the most appropriate sources of supply (American, local, third country) or of organization (wholly-owned subsidiary, joint venture, mixed venture, contract manufacturing, license).[2]

The present study revealed that very few American managements are what one might call internationally minded. The foreign business of most is conducted simply as a spillover of the domestic.

This finding begs the question of why some few managements have shown such remarkable interest, flexibility, and sensitivity as to the needs of foreign markets while most remain callously indifferent. The answer is possibly to be found in a number of variables—the history of the firm, the way in which it is organized, the characteristics of its product, the nature of the productive processes, the sources of raw materials, and so on. But in the final analysis, the interest, flexibility, and sensitivity of management rests with individuals. It is they who make the relevant decisions.

The United States has been "caught short" in business personnel trained adequately in the proposition that the market place is the world. American business desperately needs more men who are thoroughly knowledgeable of Asia, Africa, and Latin America. Without them, it will be exceedingly difficult to build lasting markets in these areas for United States business.

---

[2] For further treatment of this subject, see the author's articles "Conflicting Interests in International Business Investment," *Boston University Business Review*, Vol. 7, Spring 1960, pp. 3–13, and "Organizing International Business from a New Point of View," *Oregon Business Review*, Vol. 19, August 1960, pp. 1–6.

53. *Marketing and Economic Development*

PETER F. DRUCKER

MARKETING AS A BUSINESS DISCIPLINE

The distinguished pioneer of marketing, whose memory we honor today, was largely instrumental in developing marketing as a systematic business discipline—in teaching us how to go about, in an orderly, purposeful and planned way to find and create customers; to identify and define markets; to create new ones and promote them; to integrate customers' needs, wants, and preferences, and the intellectual and creative capacity and skills of an industrial society, toward the design of new and better products and of new distributive concepts and processes.

On this contribution and similar ones of other Founding Fathers of marketing during the last half century rests the rapid emergence of marketing as perhaps the most advanced, certainly the most "scientific" of all functional business disciplines.

But Charles Coolidge Parlin also contributed as a Founding Father toward the development of marketing as a *social discipline*. He helped give us the awareness, the concepts, and the tools that make us understand marketing as a dynamic process of society through which business enterprise is integrated productively with society's purposes and human values. It is in marketing, as we now understand it, that we satisfy individual and social values, needs, and wants—be it through producing goods, supplying services, fostering innovation, or creating

‡‡ SOURCE: Reprinted by permission from the *Journal of Marketing* (National Quarterly Publication of the American Marketing Association), Vol. 22, No. 3, January 1958, pp. 252–259.

satisfaction. Marketing, as we have come to understand it, has its focus on the customer, that is, on the individual making decisions within a social structure and within a personal and social value system. Marketing is thus the process through which economy is integrated into society to serve human needs.

I am not competent to speak about marketing in the first sense, marketing as a functional discipline of business. I am indeed greatly concerned with marketing in this meaning. One could not be concerned, as I am, with the basic institutions of industrial society in general and with the management of business enterprise in particular, without a deep and direct concern with marketing. But in this field I am a consumer of marketing alone—albeit a heavy one. I am not capable of making a contribution. I would indeed be able to talk about the wants and needs I have which I, as a consumer of marketing, hope that you, the men of marketing, will soon supply:—a theory of pricing, for instance, that can serve, as true theories should, as the foundation for actual pricing decisions and for an understanding of price behavior; or a consumer-focused concept and theory of competition. But I could not produce any of these "new products" of marketing which we want. I cannot contribute myself. To use marketing language, I am not even "effective demand," in these fields as yet.

THE ROLE OF MARKETING

I shall today in my remarks confine myself to the second meaning in which marketing has become a discipline: The role of marketing in economy and society. And I shall single out as my focus the role of marketing in the economic development, especially of under-developed "growth" countries.

My thesis is very briefly as follows. Marketing occupies a critical role in respect to the development of such "growth" areas. Indeed marketing is the most important "multiplier" of such development. It is in itself in every one of these areas the least developed, the most backward part of the economic system. Its development, above all others, makes possible economic integration and the fullest utilization of whatever assets and productive capacity an economy already possesses. It mobilizes latent economic energy. It contributes to the greatest needs: that for the rapid development of entrepreneurs and managers, and at the same time it may be the easiest area of managerial work to get going. The reason is that, thanks to men like Charles Coolidge Parlin, it is the most systematized and, therefore, the most learnable and the most teachable of all areas of business management and entrepreneurship.

INTERNATIONAL AND INTERRACIAL INEQUALITY

Looking at this world of ours, we see some essentially new facts.

For the first time in man's history the whole world is united and unified. This may seem a strange statement in view of the conflicts and threats of suicidal wars that scream at us from every headline. But conflict has always been with us. What is new is that today all of mankind shares the same vision, the same objective, the same goal, the same hope, and believes in the same tools. This vision might, in gross oversimplification, be called "industrialization."

It is the belief that it is possible for man to improve his economic lot through systematic, purposeful, and directed effort—individually as well as for an entire society. It is the belief that we have the tools at our disposal—the technological, the conceptual, and the social tools— to enable man to raise himself, through his own efforts, at least to a level that we in this country would consider poverty, but which for most of our world would be almost unbelievable luxury.

And this is an irreversible new fact. It has been made so by these true agents of revolution in our times: the new tools of communication—the dirt road, the truck, and the radio, which have penetrated even the furthest, most isolated and most primitive community.

This is new, and cannot be emphasized too much and too often. It is both a tremendous vision and a tremendous danger in that catastrophe must result if it cannot be satisfied, at least to a modest degree.

But at the same time we have a new, unprecedented danger, that of international and interracial inequality. We on the North American continent are a mere tenth of the world population, including our Canadian friends and neighbors. But we have at least 75 per cent of the world income. And the 75 per cent of the world population whose income is below $100 per capita a year receive together perhaps no more than 10 per cent of the world's income. This is inequality of income, as great as anything the world has ever seen. It is accompanied by very high equality of income in the developed countries, especially in ours where we are in the process of proving that an industrial society does not have to live in extreme tension between the few very rich and the many very poor as lived all earlier societies of man. But what used to be national inequality and economic tension is now rapidly becoming international (and unfortunately also interracial) inequality and tension.

This is also brand new. In the past there were tremendous differences between societies and cultures: in their beliefs, their concepts, their ways of life, and their knowledge. The Frankish knight who went on Crusade was an ignorant and illiterate boor, according to the standards of the polished courtiers of Constantinople or of his Moslem enemies. But economically his society and theirs were exactly alike. They had the same sources of income, the same productivity of labor, the same forms and channels of investment, the same economic institutions, and the same distribution of income and wealth. Economically the Frankish knight, however much a barbarian he appeared, was at home in the societies of the East; and so was his serf. Both fitted in immediately and without any difficulty.

And this has been the case of all societies that went above the level of purely primitive tribe.

The inequality in our world today, however, between nations and races, is therefore a new —and a tremendously dangerous—phenomenon.

What we are engaged in today is essentially a race between the promise of economic development and the threat of international world-wide class war. The economic development is the opportunity of this age. The class war is the danger. Both are new. Both are indeed so new that most of us do not even see them as yet. But they are the essential economic realities of this industrial age of ours. And whether we shall realize the opportunity or succumb to danger will largely decide not only the economic future of this world—it may largely decide its spiritual, its intellectual, its political, and its social future.

SIGNIFICANCE OF MARKETING

Marketing is central in this new situation. For marketing is one of our most potent levers to convert the danger into the opportunity.

To understand this we must ask: What do we mean by "under-developed"?

The first answer is, of course, that we mean areas of very low income. But income is, after all, a result. It is a result first of extreme agricultural over-population in which the great bulk of the people have to find a living on the land which, as a result, cannot even produce enough food to feed them, let alone produce a surplus. It is certainly a result of low productivity. And both, in a vicious circle, mean that there is not enough capital for investment, and very low productivity of what is being invested—owing largely to misdirection of investment into unessential and unproductive channels.

All this we know today and understand. Indeed we have learned during the last few years a very great deal both about the structure of an under-developed economy and about the theory and dynamics of economic development.

What we tend to forget, however, is that the essential aspect of an "underdeveloped" economy and the factor the absence of which keeps it "under-developed," is the inability to organize economic efforts and energies, to bring together resources, wants, and capacities, and so to convert a self-limiting static system into creative, self-generating organic growth.

And this is where marketing comes in.

Lack of Development in "Under-developed" Countries

First, in every "under-developed" country I know of, marketing is the most under-developed—or the least developed—part of the economy, if only because of the strong, pervasive prejudice against the "middleman."

As a result, these countries are stunted by inability to make effective use of the little they have. Marketing might by itself go far toward changing the entire economic tone of the existing system—without any change in methods of production, distribution of population, or of income.

It would make the producers capable of producing marketable products by providing them with standards, with quality demands, and with specifications for their product. It would make the product capable of being brought to markets instead of perishing on the way. And it would make the consumer capable of discrimination, that is, of obtaining the greatest value for his very limited purchasing power.

In every one of these countries, marketing profits are characteristically low. Indeed the people engaged in marketing barely eke out a subsistence living. And "mark-ups" are minute by our standards. But marketing costs are outrageously high. The waste in distribution and marketing, if only from spoilage or from the accumulation of unsalable inventories that clog the shelves for years, has to be seen to be believed. And marketing service is by and large all but non-existent.

What is needed in any "growth" country to make economic development realistic, and at the same time produce a vivid demonstration of what economic development can produce, is a marketing system:—a system of physical distribution, a financial system to make possible the distribution of goods, and finally actual marketing, that is, an actual system of integrating wants, needs, and purchasing power of the consumer with capacity and resources of production.

This need is largely masked today because marketing is so often confused with the traditional "trader and merchant" of which every one of these countries has more than enough. It would be one of our most important contributions to the development of "under-developed" countries to get across the fact that marketing is something quite different.

It would be basic to get across the triple function of marketing the function of crystallizing and directing demand for maximum productive effectiveness and efficiency; the function of guiding production purposefully toward maximum consumer satisfaction and consumer value; the function of creating discrimination that then gives rewards to those who really contribute excellence, and that then also penalize the monopolist, the slothful, or those who only want to take but do not want to contribute or to risk.

Utilization by the Entrepreneur

Marketing is also the most easily accessible "multiplier" of managers and entrepreneurs in an "under-developed" growth area. And managers and entrepreneurs are the foremost need of these countries. In the first place, "economic development" is not a force of nature. It is the result of the action, the purposeful, responsible, risk-taking action, of men as entrepreneurs and managers.

Certainly it is the entrepreneur and manager who alone can convey to the people of these countries an understanding of what economic development means and how it can be achieved.

Marketing can convert latent demand into effective demand. It cannot, by itself, create purchasing power. But it can uncover and channel all purchasing power that exists. It can, therefore, create rapidly the conditions for a much higher level of economic activity than existed before, can create the opportunities for the entrepreneur.

It then can create the stimulus for the development of modern, responsible, professional management by creating opportunity for the producer who knows how to plan, how to organize, how to lead people, how to innovate.

In most of these countries markets are of necessity very small. They are too small to make it possible to organize distribution for a single-product line in any effective manner. As a result, without a marketing organization, many products for which there is an adequate demand at a reasonable price cannot be distributed; or worse, they can be produced and distributed only under monopoly conditions. A marketing system is needed which serves as the joint and common channel for many producers if any of them is to be able to come into existence and to stay in existence.

This means in effect that a marketing system in the "under-developed" countries is the *creator of small business*, is the only way in which a man of vision and daring can become a businessman and an entrepreneur himself. This is thereby also the only way in which a true middle class can develop in the countries in which the habit of investment in productive enterprise has still to be created.

Developer of Standards

Marketing in an "under-developed" country is the developer of standards—of standards for product and service as well as of standards of conduct, of integrity, of reliability, of foresight, and of concern for the basic long-range impact of decisions on the customer, the supplier, the economy, and the society.

Rather than go on making theoretical statements let me point to one illustration: The impact Sears Roebuck has had on several countries of Latin America. To be sure, the countries of Latin America in which Sears operates—Mexico, Brazil, Cuba, Venezuela, Colombia, and Peru—are not "under-developed" in the same sense in which Indonesia or the Congo are "under-developed." Their average income, although very low by our standards, is at least two times, perhaps as much as four or five times, that of the truly "under-developed" countries in which the bulk of mankind still live. Still in every respect except income level these Latin American countries are at best "developing." And they have all the problems of economic development—perhaps even in more acute form than the countries of Asia and Africa, precisely because their development has been so fast during the last ten years.

It is also true that Sears in these countries is not a "low-price" merchandiser. It caters to the middle class in the richer of these countries, and to the upper middle class in the poorest of these countries. Incidentally, the income level of these groups is still lower than that of the worker in the industrial sector of our economy.

Still Sears is a mass-marketer even in Colombia or Peru. What is perhaps even more important, it is applying in these "under-developed" countries exactly the same policies and principles it applies in this country, carries substantially the same merchandise (although most of it produced in the countries themselves), and applies the same concepts of marketing it uses in Indianapolis or Philadelphia. Its impact and experience are, therefore, a fair test of what marketing principles, marketing knowledge, and marketing techniques can achieve.

The impact of this one American business which does not have more than a mere handful of stores in these countries and handles no more than a small fraction of the total retail business of these countries is truly amazing. In the first place, Sears' latent purchasing power has fast become actual purchasing power. Or, to put it less theoretically, people have begun to organize their buying and to go out for value in what they do buy.

Secondly, by the very fact that it builds one store in one city, Sears forces a revolution in retailing throughout the whole surrounding area. It forces store modernization. It forces consumer credit. It forces a different attitude toward the customer, toward the store clerk, toward the supplier, and toward the merchandise itself. It forces other retailers to adopt modern methods of pricing, of inventory control, of training, of window display, and what have you.

The greatest impact Sears has had, however, is in the multiplication of new industrial business for which Sears creates a marketing channel. Because it has had to sell goods manufactured in these countries rather than import them (if only because of foreign exchange restrictions), Sears has been instrumental in getting established literally hundreds of new manufacturers making goods which, a few years ago, could not be made in the country, let alone be sold in adequate quantity. Simply to satisfy its own marketing needs, Sears has had to insist on standards of workmanship, quality, and delivery—that is, on standards of production management, of technical management, and above all of the management of people—which, in a few short years, have advanced the art and science of management in these countries by at least a generation.

I hardly need to add that Sears is not in Latin America for reasons of philanthropy, but because it is good and profitable business with extraordinary growth potential. In other words, Sears is in Latin America because marketing is the major opportunity in a "growth economy" —precisely because its absence is a major economic gap and the greatest need.

The Discipline of Marketing

Finally, marketing is critical in economic development because marketing has become so largely systematized, so largely both learnable and teachable. It is the discipline among all our business disciplines that has advanced the furthest.

I do not forget for a moment how much we still have to learn in marketing. But we should also not forget that most of what we have learned so far we have learned in a form in which we can express it in general concepts, in valid principles and, to a substantial degree, in quantifiable measurements. This, above all others, was the achievement of that generation to whom Charles Coolidge Parlin was leader and inspiration.

A critical factor in this world of ours is the learnability and teachability of what it means to be an entrepreneur and manager. For it is the entrepreneur and the manager who alone can cause economic development to happen. The world needs them, therefore, in very large numbers; and it needs them fast.

Obviously this need cannot be supplied by our supplying entrepreneurs and managers, quite apart from the fact that we hardly have the surplus. Money we can supply. Technical assistance we can supply, and should supply more. But the supply of men we can offer to the people in the "under-developed" countries is of necessity a very small one.

The demand is also much too urgent for it to be supplied by slow evolution through experience, or through dependence on the emergence of "naturals." The danger that lies in the inequality today between the few countries that have and the great many countries that have not is much too great to permit a wait of centuries. Yet it takes centuries if we depend on experience and slow evolution for the supply of entrepreneurs and managers adequate to the needs of a modern society.

There is only one way in which man has ever been able to short-cut experience, to telescope development, in other words, to *learn something*. That way is to have available the distillate of experience and skill in the form of knowledge, of concepts, of generalization, of measurement—in the form of *discipline*, in other words.

THE DISCIPLINE OF ENTREPRENEURSHIP

Many of us today are working on the fashioning of such a discipline of entrepreneurship and management. Maybe we are further along than most of us realize.

Certainly in what has come to be called "Operation Research and Synthesis" we have the first beginnings of a systematic approach to the entrepreneurial task of purposeful risk-taking and innovation—so far only an approach, but a most promising one, unless indeed we become so enamored with the gadgets and techniques as to forget purpose and aim.

We are at the beginning perhaps also of an understanding of the basic problems of organizing people of diversified and highly advanced skill and judgment together in one effective organization, although again no one so far would, I am convinced, claim more for us than that we have begun at last to ask intelligent questions.

But marketing, although it only covers one functional area in the field, has something that can be called a discipline. It has developed general concepts, that is, theories that explain a multitude of phenomena in simple statements. It even has measurements that record "facts" rather than opinions. In marketing, therefore, we already possess a learnable and teachable approach to this basic and central problem not only of the "under-developed" countries but of all countries. All of us have today the same survival stake in economic development. The risk and danger of international and interracial inequality are simply too great.

Marketing is obviously not a cure-all, not a paradox. It is only one thing we need. But it answers a critical need. At the same time marketing is most highly developed.

Indeed without marketing as the hinge on which to turn, economic development will almost have to take the totalitarian form. A totalitarian system can be defined economically as one in which economic development is being attempted without marketing, indeed as one in which marketing is suppressed. Precisely because it first looks at the values and wants of the individual, and because it then develops people to act purposefully and responsibly—that is, because of its effectiveness in developing a free economy—marketing is suppressed in a totalitarian system. If we want economic development in freedom and responsibility, we have to build it on the development of marketing.

In the new and unprecedented world we live in, a world which knows both a new unity of vision and growth and a new and most dangerous cleavage, marketing has a special and central role to play. This role goes beyond "getting the stuff out the back door," beyond "getting the most sales with the least cost," beyond "the optimal integration of our values and wants as customers, citizens, and persons, with our productive resources and intellectual achievements"—the role marketing plays in a developed society.

In a developing economy, marketing is, of course, all of this. But in addition, in an economy that is striving to break the age-old bondage of man to misery, want, and destitution, marketing is also the catalyst for the transmutation of latent resources into actual resources, of desires into accomplishments, and the development of responsible economic leaders and informed economic citizens.

Marketing in Perspective

T he sober task of evaluating the marketing function is suggested by the three readings in Part V. The authors of these articles are marketing scholars who are appraising the role of marketing today. Actually, to some degree consumers the world over appraise the marketing effort as they express satisfaction or dissatisfaction with the various aspects of the marketing effort.

The marketing effort, as influenced by environmental forces, is immense and ever-changing; complete satisfaction with the effort is probably beyond the realm of possibility. Nevertheless, by constantly appraising contributions and costs of marketing, ways will doubtless be found to improve the total effort. Certainly it is to this end that much of marketing education is devoted.

Marketing in Perspective

54. *Efficiency Within the Marketing Structure*

ROLAND S. VAILE

THE NATURE OF MARKETING

Any consideration of efficiency of marketing must start with a clear recognition of the fact that there are two strikingly different aspects of marketing. In the first place the provision of time and place utilities requires certain physical functions in the movement and storage of commodities, while in the second place the use of these commodities by specific people requires change in ownership and market facilities for making such change. Efficiency may be considered with respect to either of these two general aspects of marketing.

Measurement of efficiency in the physical aspects of marketing involve such things as time and motion studies, the prevalence of cross-hauling, choice of channels of distribution so as to minimize effort and time, the extent to which advantage is taken of the economy of large-scale production in the handling processes, and the trends in the costs, both monetary and real, of performing the physical functions.

Measurement of efficiency of markets in respect of the necessary changes of ownership involves such things as:

1. The ease of making contact among prospective buyers and sellers.

2. The completeness of information concerning conditions of supply and demand and the promptness with which changes in these conditions are reported.

‼ SOURCE: Reprinted by permission from the *Journal of Marketing* (National Quarterly Publication of the American Marketing Association), Vol. 5, No. 4, April 1941, p. 350.

3. The adequacy of opportunity for "shopping" among different offerings in the formation of market judgments.

4. The existence and useableness of credit and similar facilitating instruments, one purpose of which is to provide a reasonable degree of equality in purchasing power as between buyers and sellers.

5. The accuracy with which prices reflect supply and demand conditions and thereby direct the use of resources not only in the physical aspects of marketing, but in other lines of production as well.

6. The extent to which the market organization permits manufacturing and similar production activities to be so carried out as to take advantage of the economies of large-scale production, but at the same time serves to prevent the effects of monopoly such as, for example, the restriction of output that results in a monopoly profit to the sellers.

7. The extent to which the market organization encourages the development of vertical integration and thereby avoids unnecessary changes in ownership.

8. The economic effects of attempts to shift the demand schedules for specific commodities —the effects, that is, upon individual sellers and individual buyers and business in general.

9. The extent or degree to which the market distributes income payments proportionally to the marginal product.

Neither of these two lists of consideration in the measurement of efficiency in marketing is complete. It is believed, however, that they illustrate the most important points of measurement in the test of efficiency.

55. Measuring the Cost and Value of Marketing

STANLEY C. HOLLANDER

When did marketing begin? When were the first criticisms of marketing voiced? We do not know the answer to either question, but we can be certain of two things. One is that the function of marketing, that is, trade and exchange, has been part of the human economic system for many thousands of years. The other is that criticisms and defenses of trading activities are almost as old as trade itself. In 1776, these criticisms provoked a thundering answer from Adam Smith:

The statute of Edward VI, therefore, by prohibiting as much as possible any middleman from coming in between the grower and the consumer, endeavoured to annihilate a trade, of which the free exercise is not only the best palliative of the inconveniences of a dearth, but the best preventative of that calamity: after the trade of the farmer, *no trade contributing so much to the growing of corn as that of the corn merchant.*[1]

Smith declared: "The popular fear of engrossing and forestalling [buying for resale] may be compared to the popular terrors and suspicions of witchcraft."[2] Today the fear of witchcraft seems to have abated; it has been many years since books attacking witches made the best-seller lists. But the persistent popularity of books attacking marketing suggests that the fear of engrossers and forestallers has not vanished. The attacks have, of course, aroused

a ready response, and the marketing journals have been filled with criticisms of the critics, interspersed with a modicum of self-criticism.

As is true of most such debates, the discussions have tended to generate considerably more heat than light. Only in fairly recent years have we had any really serious attempts to measure both the costs and the benefits of marketing in our society. The dearth of such studies is not the fault of the many serious and well-intentioned people who have debated the value of marketing. It is simply an indication of the complexity and magnitude of the problem.

A PRODUCTIVITY ANALOGY

The difficulty of measuring marketing productivity may be illustrated by attacking a comparable problem: attempting to measure the productivity of a magazine article. An examination of the silent post-mortem in which you will indulge after finishing this or any other article will suggest some of the difficulties we face when we try to evaluate the marketing system.

In either case, we are trying to determine a ratio. On the one hand, we have the inputs into the system—the social and individual contributions to the product or process, and on the other hand, we have the outputs—the social and individual benefits. If the benefits are high in proportion to the inputs, we describe the article, the product, or the system in question as *highly productive*. But if the ratio is low, then the system is not very productive. The concept is simple to state; the real problems arise when we attempt to apply it.

---

[1] *The Wealth of Nations* (New York: Random House, 1937), p. 499. Emphasis supplied.
[2] *Ibid.*, p. 500.

‡‡ SOURCE: Reprinted by permission from *Business Topics*, Vol. 9, No. 3, Summer 1961, pp. 17–27.

Types of Input

The reading experiences that provide the final tests of a magazine article's value result from two major categories of inputs. One group consists of those supplied by the publisher and the people and firms associated with him. These include the work of paper and ink manufacturers, printers and production craftsmen, the postal service and the newsdealers, editorial employees, illustrators, and even authors. Supposedly the value of their services is measured by the prices and wages these contributors receive during the process of assembling and distributing the magazine. But this supposition involves a number of assumptions to which we will want to return shortly. Magazines, like every other product and service, present a number of unique problems in social cost measurement. For example, publications that derive much of their revenue from advertising may incur heavy production and promotional expenses so as to attract the readership that will attract advertising, which in turn, may, in various ways, affect the prices and sales of the commodities advertised. Under such circumstances it is often difficult to determine the exact inputs provided by each participant. A similar quandary arises out of the eternal debate between the publishers and the postmasters-general over the relationship of postal charges to the costs of furnishing postal services.

Another group of inputs is extremely important and many of these are often overlooked. These are provided by the readers, and include their time and effort as well as whatever they may pay, directly or indirectly, for the publication. These inputs are analogous to the time, effort and money expended by consumers in both the shopping and the consumption process. And, from the standpoint of the individual consumer, these are the personal costs that must be balanced against the personal benefits.

Simple Evaluation

Let us start with the simplest version of this problem; the individual judgment each one of you will make after finishing this article or this issue of Business Topics. Undoubtedly, you will ask yourself whether it has been worth reading or not. Not *how* worthwhile, or *how* it compares with other things you might have read instead, but simply: am I pleased or not that I decided to take the time to read this article? This is the sort of judgment that we all make frequently.

Yet notice how often our reactions are ambivalent. We say of some experience or book or lecture, "I guess it was worthwhile," or "I don't know—it wasn't too bad," or "I'm rather glad I read it, and yet maybe I could have used the time more profitably."

Now it is no wonder that our judgments are sometimes vague. To decide that reading a particular article, or engaging in any other activity, is worthwhile involves a very complex accounting process. Very few of us have enough time to do all the things we would like to do, or to read all the things that we would like to read. The segments of time that we invest in reading a particular article may be especially precious segments, on a busy day or when there are many alternative activities clamoring for our attention. Then again, the time may consist of minutes spent in the dentist's anteroom, when there is little else that we can do and when we really only want a little intellectual anaesthesia before climbing into the chair. The article may demand considerable attention and intellectual effort, which we may consider as output, as a source of enjoyment (witness the pleasure many people derive from solving puzzles) or, under other circumstances and at other times, we may consider as input, as an unwarranted drain on our energies. The benefits of our reading are elusive and subtle. We may obtain intellectual exercise, new insight, stimulation and entertainment. Or our reading may prove stultifying, boring, or misleading. All of this we have to balance in some rough and ready fashion before we can say whether the magazine was, or was not, worthwhile.

Complexities of Evaluation

However, this is still at the kindergarten level in productivity evaluation. Let us look at two more problems of greater complexity. One arises out of the fact that such rough balance sheets are really inadequate for comparative purposes or for social appraisals. Suppose, in the course of a year, that each of us reads two hundred magazine issues. Each issue consumes its own combination of time, money and energy; each yields its own patterns of information, insight and entertainment. How can we compare these two hundred: can we rank them in an ordinal line, and will our judgments be consistent each time that we express them? How can we add these two hundred patterns into a composite figure if we want to compare this year's reading with last year's, or with the magazines we read ten years ago? How can we make comparisons between, say, the magazines published in the U. S. and those published in other countries, or between publications issued under various auspices? What measures can we use to quantify either the inputs or the outputs, and how do we relate them to each other? It is perfectly apparent that these considerations are frivolous and frustrating, yet this is exactly the sort of problem we face when we try to make comparative judgments about the productivity of marketing.

But the problem is still more complex. Magazine articles are written in the hope of reaching large audiences. Each member of that audience is an individual. Each has his own standards, each has his own alternative ways of spending his time, each seeks his own particular satisfactions and ends. None is a replica of the others. In evaluating the effectiveness of an article, how can we add all of their tastes, inclinations and judgments into a single composite whole? Shall we regard one person's intense pleasure as the equivalent of several people's mild displeasure? Shall we allow extra, or reduced, weight in our calculus to the connoisseurs, to those who are the most sensitive to small differences, or to those whose swings on the manic-depressive axis are the widest?

WEIGHING THE COSTS

Conceptualizing and evaluating are equally difficult in any attempt to aggregate all of the inputs and outputs of a complex economic systm. Given certain assumptions and conditions, it is relatively easy to measure the physical results of highly specific, small operations. For example, it is not too hard to determine which of two machines is more effiicient at punching out sardine cans. This may involve some judgments about the relative cost of labor, capital and raw materials in the future. For example, one machine may be more efficient at low levels of output and the other at high levels, so some judgments have to be made about the nature of future demand for sardine cans. But practical, workable estimates can be made, and some of these judgments work out fairly well. Similarly, we can compare two different methods of putting those sardine cans on the supermarket shelves, subject to some assumptions as to the total number of cans to be stacked, the cost of labor, and the alternative uses for the stockmen's time in the store. But the only available measure, aside from miscellaneous hunches, guesses and opinions, of whether the whole operation is worthwhile is whether enough people buy those sardines to warrant allocating the social energies necessary to produce canned sardines instead of something else.

There seem to be only two measures by which we can evaluate the total inputs into the total marketing system. One is hours of labor, the other is monetary costs. Both have their limitations.

Labor as a Measure

Labor hours are not all homogenous, and hence we have a problem if we try to use number of hours worked in marketing as the measure of marketing cost. How can we properly equate an hour of time worked by an unskilled laborer with an hour of time spent by a highly trained engineer or architect? They are both human beings. Moreover, the job that is assigned to the laborer may be far more burdensome than the work performed by the professional. But each hour of the skilled man's time represents an expenditure of the human capital invested in training, and so, in a sense, constitutes a higher cost than does an hour of common labor. The problem can be resolved through evaluating each hour of labor at its actual wage or salary rate, but this approach leads into the monetary problems we will face in a moment. Another difficulty, of somewhat less significance, bothers the statisticians who try to compute labor productivity figures. They argue whether it is more accurate to use actual hours worked as the labor investment, or whether paid vacations, holidays and sick leaves should be added. The issue is often described as the question of hours worked versus hours paid for. (Although it would drive the statisticians crazy, conceptually one might be justified in including some portion of the future hours to be spent in paid retirement as part of this year's "labor paid for.")

Another problem is more difficult. The number of hours invested in marketing measures, at any one moment, only a portion of the total cost of the system. Our economy also draws upon natural resources and upon the capital that the past has produced. We can only equate units of capital and units of labor by converting them to a common factor—their monetary value. This again leads us to the problems inherent in applying monetary measures to marketing input.

Money as a Measure

Some of these problems are technical in nature. For example, should we evaluate the capital equipment used in any one year on the basis of its original cost, original cost minus depreciation (and if so, at what rate), cost to reproduce, or cost to replace with modern equipment? How shall we measure the labor of unpaid family workers? What shall we do about deferred compensation? More basic problems center around two major assumptions that underlie the use of monetary costs as a measure of input. When we use monetary costs expended in the private sector as our measure, we are, in effect, assuming that the government's contribution to marketing, which is considerable, is roughly equal to the net tax burden (also considerable), that is levied upon marketing. If the contribution and the taxes are unequal, then one party is, in a sense, contributing more to the bargain than it derives from the other. Our other assumption is that the costs represent free market values, that each dollar earned represents equal sacrifices, that each dollar spent obtains equal pleasure, and that there has been no exploitation of any of the participants in the system.

But there is an even more fundamental problem. The United States Census uses a monetary concept, "the value added by manufacturing," to measure the output of the manufacturing industry. The value-added figure is obtained by subtracting the total cost of the materials (and some services) that manufacturing industry purchases from the total amount of its sales. Many writers now advocate using a similar concept in marketing. A moment's reflection, however, shows that this concept of output is roughly equivalent to a monetary cost measure of input. Profits are usually a relatively small portion of the total figure and certainly are, at least in part, the price of certain managerial and entrepreneurial services. So, under this accounting, input and output will always be roughly equal.

Consumer Satisfaction

The most difficult part of the whole business is to measure the real output of marketing. In spite of all talk about motivation research, hidden persuaders and the like, we really seem to know very little about what people want from the marketing system. An example from retail distribution may help to illustrate this point.

One school of thought holds that most people look upon stores very largely as places in which they can obtain merchandise. According to this point of view, people consider shopping as a nuisance, and are most satisfied when they can obtain their purchases with minimum expenditures of time, money, and effort. Some interesting experiments with shopping games and with records of consumer behavior tend to substantiate this view, although the results are by no means conclusive.[3] On the other hand, there is the view advanced by many motivational researchers and by some very successful merchants, that people like to shop. The advocates of this position maintain that shopping is an end in itself, apart from the goods that are purchased, and that the retail system should be designed to maximize the pleasures of shopping.[4] Now, of course, no hard and fast election can be made between these two approaches. Much depends upon the customer, the products being purchased, the place and the time. Some people seem to react to shopping differently than others.[5] Most people will display one attitude when buying antiques, and another when purchasing a tube of toothpaste. Some people, who normally try to rush in and out of the supermarket, will be willing, when traveling, to spend hours in the quaint native market place, probably much to the annoyance of the natives. If we have only ten minutes in which to catch a plane, we want the airport newsstand to have our favorite magazine readily accessible; if we have two hours to kill between planes we like the airport bookstore that permits uninterrupted browsing. But even after allowing for all of these differences, we find that a fundamental question for both managerial strategy and social evaluation in retailing has been answered only indifferently and on an *ad hoc* basis. The devices for identifying and measuring consumer satisfaction in any general sense are limited to votes in the market place, which is probably the most significant single argument for a free market place.

[3] Wroe Alderson, *Marketing Behavior and Executive Action* (Homewood, Illinois: Richard D. Irwin, 1957), p. 183

[4] See, for example, Pierre Martineau, "*A Store is More Than a Store*," Motivation in Advertising, Ch. 20, (New York: McGraw-Hill, 1957), pp. 173–85.

[5] An interesting classification of shoppers appears in Gregory P. Stone, "City Shoppers and Urban Identification," *American Journal of Sociology*, July 1954, pp. 36–45.

COST RESEARCH

A few unusually dedicated analysts have attempted to measure the costs of marketing in our society, in the face of all the difficulties we have noted and in spite of a number of technical obstacles we have not considered. In general, these people have been well aware of the problems and limitations inherent in their work. But they have felt that even a rough approximation of the actual figures would be ample reward for the herculean labors involved in such a task.

Stewart and Dewhurst

By far the best known single study of this sort is *Does Distribution Cost Too Much?* (New York: Twentieth Century Fund, 1938), a study conducted by Professors Paul W. Stewart and J. Frederic Dewhurst under the sponsorship of the Fund. Stewart and Dewhurst worked with census figures on purchases and sales, and other data, to trace the 1929 flow of commodities in this country from original sources (agriculture, importation, and extractive industries) to final buyers (consumers, institutions, public utilities, and export) via such intermediate levels as manufacturing and trade. Increases in value resulting from transportation and from wholesale and retail trade were assigned as costs of marketing, increases at the manufacturing level were apportioned between marketing and processing. Stewart and Dewhurst estimated that, in 1929, final buyers absorbed $65.6 billion worth of finished tangible goods, of which three-fourths, or $49 billion, went to individual ultimate family consumers. These figures do not include the consumption of services, such as haircuts, medical attention or personal transportation. Total marketing costs for this $65 billion worth of goods were estimated at $38.5 billion.

In other words, according to this analysis, retailing, wholesaling, transportation, advertising, selling and other marketing activities took 59¢ out of every consumption dollar spent on goods or tangible commodities. This figure, which as we shall see has been subjected to some very serious criticism, included marketing and transportation expenses at all levels. Thus, it embraced practically all of the selling and distribution expenses involved in transferring cotton to the yarn spinner, in transferring cotton yarn to the fabric weaver, and in transferring

fabric to the shirt manufacturer, as well as the marketing costs involved in moving finished shirts to the consumer. Stewart and Dewhurst were careful to point out that their figure, 59¢, was meaningless unless it was compared with what distribution did in return for its compensation. They also were careful to point out that a more efficient manufacturing system, turning out large quantities and obtaining economies of scale, would necessitate a more complex marketing system. Nevertheless, in reading their report one can sense a sort of physiocratic bias, a feeling that changes in form utility ought to be relatively more costly than changes in time, place and possession utility.

Barger Study

In 1955, Harold Barger, relying on the vast data collections assembled by the National Bureau of Economic Research, published his *Distribution's Place in the American Economy since 1869* (Princeton: Princeton University Press, 1955). This is generally regarded as the most authoritative work yet published on the subject. Barger limited his analysis to wholesale and retail trade, and did not include manufacturers' marketing costs, as did Stewart and Dewhurst.

Barger was not overly impressed with distribution's performance in some respects. He concluded, for example, that labor productivity per man hour increased in commodity production at an annual rate of 2.6 percent per year from 1869 to 1949. Contrasted with this, he found that productivity in distribution went up only about 1 percent per year. The analysis is somewhat limited, since the measure used, total volume handled, does not allow for changes in functions performed. However, probably most of the difference is due to the greater relative application of machinery and other forms of capital in manufacturing than in trade.

However, he did find that wholesaling and retailing accounted for only about 35- 36¢ out of the consumer's dollar in 1929. Since he was working with only a portion of the total distributive activity for that year, rather than with the whole, we should expect his figure to be smaller than the Stewart and Dewhurst 59¢. However most analysts, including Barger, believe that part of the discrepancy is really a correction of the old figure, that would reduce it by an indeterminate amount, perhaps 8 or 9¢.

Cox Study

For the last several years Reavis Cox and some of his associates at the University of Pennsylvania have been conducting an investigation of marketing costs to serve as a companion to, or as a revision of, the Stewart and Dewhurst study. Their work has not yet been published, although it should be released in the near future. Cox gave an advance presentation of some of their findings at the 1960 meeting of the American Statistical Association. There he disclosed that an analysis of the Bureau of Labor Statistics' massive input-output table for the U. S. economy in 1947 revealed that ultimate consumers that year took $96 billion worth of goods, of which $41 billion, or about 43 percent, went for distribution *activities*. This figure included the marketing expenses incurred by manufacturing firms, as well as the marketing activities of the distributive industries, i.e. wholesalers, retailers, transportation agencies and advertising agencies. The distributive industries themselves accounted for about 31.1 percent of the final value of all consumption goods, and a considerably smaller portion of the total final value of consumer services.[6]

Department of Agriculture

In addition to these three studies and many smaller scale attempts there has been the massive work of the United States Department of Agriculture in measuring what it calls "marketing margins" for agricultural products. Unfortunately for our purposes, the Department uses the word "marketing" to embrace almost everything that can happen to agricultural products once they leave the farm. It determines its so-called marketing margin for consumer food products by subtracting the farm value of raw foodstuffs and by-products from the final retail value of agricultural foods. This margin thus includes, for example, both the cost of grinding wheat into flour and the cost of baking bread. The procedure is somewhat analogous to saying that the cost of manufacturing Ford cars is part of the cost of marketing iron ore.[7]

The economists who prepare the USDA marketing margin reports are always extremely careful in explicitly stating just what is included in their figures, although the same cannot always be said for the people who use those figures in political debate. But the agricultural definition yields results which simply are not comparable to the marketing cost studies we have examined, however useful the Department's work may be for other purposes. In 1939, for example, the Department said that 63 percent of the consumer's farm food dollar was absorbed by marketing costs, a slightly higher figure than has been reported for the last several years. Professors Beckman and Buzzell of Ohio State University reanalyzed the 1939 figures and found that just about one-third of the total 63 percent was the cost of processing prepared and semi-manufactured goods. The true marketing cost was about 41 percent, a figure much closer to those reported in the Barger and Cox studies for consumer goods in general.[8]

THE ACTUAL OUTPUT

But even the most accurate marketing cost figure is relatively meaningless until it is compared with the work performed by marketing. Much of that work, as we have noted, consists of intangibles that resist quantification, and so we do not have an output figure to set against the cost percentage. But it is an inescapable fact that a dynamic, high level economy involves a very considerable amount of marketing work. Even the Soviets, who have not been outspoken admirers of our marketing system, are beginning

---

[6] 1960 Proceedings of the Business and Economics Section, ASA. Washington: American Statistical Association, 1961, pp. 319–22.

[7] The Department does usually make one reasonable but inconsistent adjustment in these figures. Consumer expenditures for restaurant meals are adjusted down to the retail store value of equivalent foodstuffs. The work of a restaurant chef is not treated as marketing, but the work of a cook in a frozen food plant is. In this connection though, it is only fair to say that increases in the sales of prepared food, the so-called "built-in maid services," fall short of explaining all of the recent changes in farm marketing and processing margins. Finally, we may note that in a recent unofficial study, two leading USDA economists added farmers' costs for machinery and purchased supplies into the total marketing margin reported for farm food products. Frederick V. Waugh and Kenneth E. Ogren, "An Interpretation of Changes in Agricultural Marketing Costs," *American Economic Review*, May 1961, pp. 213–27.
[8] T. N. Beckman and R. D. Buzzell "What Is the Marketing Margin for Agricultural Products?" *Journal of Marketing*, October 1955, pp. 166–68.

to pay us the compliment of imitation as their own economies emerge from the subsistence level. The western world is just beginning to notice such communist developments as a conference on advertising methods held in Prague in 1958, and attended by delegates from the Soviet Union, East Germany, Albania, Bulgaria, Poland, Czechoslovakia, Hungary, Rumania, Yugoslavia, China, Mongolia, North Korea and Vietnam.[9]

Dr. E. D. McGarry, of the University of Buffalo, has provided the best statement of what constitutes the actual output of marketing.[10] He lists six major functions of marketing which may be summarized as follows.

Six Functions of Marketing

1. *The contactual function:* the searching out of buyers and sellers. This is a not inconsiderable task. A typical supermarket may carry five to six thousand items produced by hundreds of different processors.[11] One study of twelve representative drug stores found that each carried an average of 1,300 proprietary items (minerals, vitamins, patent medicines, etc.) alone, out of a selection of perhaps 20,000 or 30,000 such items produced for distribution through drug stores.[12] The American consumer draws upon a

selection of literally tens, perhaps hundreds, of thousands of items. An elaborate and often unnoticed mechanism is needed to maintain contact between all of the people who use and produce both these items and their components, supplies and equipment.

2. *The pricing function:* in our society, the principal device for allocating our supply of scarce resources.

3. *The merchandising function:* the work of gathering information about consumer desires and translating it into practicable product designs.

4. *The propaganda function:* "the conditioning of the buyers or of the sellers to a favorable attitude toward the product or its sponsor." This is the most criticized of all the marketing functions. But probably few will dispute the need for some activity of this sort to support an economy in which consumption rises above subsistence and in which the advantages of scale are obtained through mass production in advance of sale.

5. *Physical distribution:* the brute job of transporting and storing goods to create time and place utility.

6. *The termination function:* something of a catch-all category, that includes both the process of reaching agreement in the case of fully negotiated transactions, and all of the contingent liabilities that remain with the seller after delivery takes place.

Since many of these functions are concerned with intangibles, facile evaluation of marketing performance seems unlikely, and perhaps impossible, even for the future. Probably room will always exist for debate concerning both the objectives of marketing and the means used to achieve these objectives. We may be certain that our present methods are not perfect. We may well anticipate the development of new and better techniques for the performance of many marketing tasks. Nevertheless, even though their work resists quantification, marketers need not apologize for their share of the consumer's dollar.

[9] Lazlo Sonkodi, "Advertising in a Socialist Economy," *Cartel*, July 1959, pp. 78–79. Sonkodi's source is, interestingly enough, a publication called *Magyar Reklam* (i.e. *Hungarian Advertising*). For a discussion of other Russian marketing developments, see Marshall Goldman, "Marketing—A Lesson for Marx," *Harvard Business Review*, January-February 1960, pp. 79–86.

[10] Reavis Cox and Wroe Alderson (eds.), "Some Functions of Marketing Reconsidered," *Theory in Marketing.* (Chicago: Richard D. Irwin, 1950), pp. 263–79.

[11] "The Dillon Study," *Progressive Grocer*, May 1960, p. D18.

[12] Burley, Fisher and Cox, *Drug Store Operating Costs and Profits* (New York: McGraw-Hill, 1956), p. 263.

56. Soliloquy in Marketing

PAUL MAZUR

Among the shrinking dimensions of our own free will there still survives the ability to create our own definition for many of the terms we use. Acting upon that premise, I would define marketing, narrowly, as the means of distributing the products created by manufacturing—and, more broadly, as the means of delivering to the people of a nation the materials and services which make up their standard of living. Obviously, I would *not* include either within the circumference or prerogative of marketing, any social dictum or moral arbiter of what people should or should not purchase.

Marketing and manufacturing will fail to fulfill adequately their job unless they are related to what the market will absorb. If manufacturing creates products of kinds which have inadequate acceptance, marketing efforts will fail to deliver to production the necessary sales quota.

Or if marketing lacks selling skill, again it will fail.

Or if products are manufactured in quantities that exceed the rate of acceptance at any particular time, then marketing will also fail to fulfill its necessary quotas; inventories will accumulate; and under the pressure of their liquidation, prices and profit margins will decrease, production will diminish in order to allow an excess of consumption over production to reduce the accumulation in the warehouses and on the shelves. This process will continue until supply and demand are again in balance and profits again are reestablished.

‡ SOURCE: Reprinted by permission from *Marketing: A Maturing Discipline*, Proceedings of the Winter Conference of the American Marketing Association, December 1960, pp. 10–17.

There have been in the past dramatic illustrations of the adverse influences of excessive production and inventory accumulation. The economy is, indeed, very sensitive to the failure to coordinate production to marketing. The dimensions of the latter, dealing as it does with masses of people, possess more inertia and are less flexible than is the volume of production.

The most recent illustration of the consequences of excessive supply has been drawn by the facts of the current year of 1960. This is the year that was labelled the start of the roaring sixties. But like an over-active political candidate, the rehearsal of the "roaring" strained the throat; and only a hoarse whisper has been the result to date.

On the other hand, one should not be misled by the facts of 1960. The promise was not fulfilled. But in large part this has been the result of an over-expanded promise rather than any over-all fact of economic recession. The Gross National Product for the current year has exceeded that of 1959 by nearly five per cent—a figure substantially larger than the norm of our secular trend. The individual quarters of 1960 have presented a stable Gross National Product of an annual rate of about 500 billions of dollars. But the first quarter included an inventory accumulation at an annual rate of 11.3 billions of dollars; the second, five billions; the third quarter had a decumulation of inventories at an annual rate of 1 billion; and the fourth probably about the same. The dollars representing the actual demand for goods and services have increased each quarter. In our slackening production, in pressure of competition, and in the squeezing of profit margins, we have been paying for our failure to correlate production to the probable or actual needs of marketing. And the punishment for this economic sin is speedy and positive.

In some segments of our economy like building, capital expenditures, and consumer durable goods, our national picture has been subject to some decline in consumption demand—resulting in softness in the market places. It is difficult to separate cause and effect, to determine how much of an adverse factor on demand, diminution of production can and will create. Also, it is increasingly true that services and consumption of non-durable goods are playing a greater and greater role; and their resistance to economic erosion can give to the total picture of the economy a relative bright hue, while the manufacturing segments are experiencing stagnation or even contraction.

Nineteen-Sixty, on the whole, has therefore been a year in which the growth has been modest; but in which marketing has not been adequate to distribute to the consumers all that production could and did create.

Marketing is charged with a truly great responsibility in an economy in which surpluses rather than deficits of supply are the general rule; and the United States is a nation of surpluses, not of scarcities. It is dramatically clear that we possess a surplus of foodstuffs, and the figures of the first quarter of 1960 prove that we have a surplus capacity for producing steel and automobiles. Nations like Russia and China and India are concerned with creating sufficient production to satisfy subsistence or even subsubsistence standards of living. In these countries of economic scarcity, the problems are overwhelmingly those of production and unimportantly concerned with distribution and marketing, except in the matter of physical transportation. In the nations of abundance, on the other hand, the problem is one of promoting demands adequate to absorb the production of the manufacturing mechanism.

Moreover, it seems abundantly clear that our capacity for production in the United States continues to increase, but with the use of relatively fewer people engaged in the actual process of production. In the period of the last ten years the *quantity* of production has increased 45 per cent, and the number of workers on the production lines has remained the same. The consequence of this phenomenon might be markedly increased unemployment—if this was politically acceptable. But in a nation dedicated to full employment, this choice is not acceptable. Increased production must mean that more and more people will be engaged in services and distribution and marketing, or the tempo of the private production requirements must be substantially quickened, or Government will create employment opportunities through its own enlarged activities.

It should be clear indeed that growth of the economy of the United States and *sufficient* growth are necessities not only for the fulfillment of a proper increase in the standards of private and public living, but also to give adequate employment opportunity to a labor force that expands through the fertility and productivity of man.

The trend which has indicated a marked increase of the number of men and women engaged in consumption, distribution, marketing, and services will most probably continue. More and more people will be involved in the packaging, selling, and moving of goods; more and more will be concerned with the supply of services relating to the goods sold. And if our production levels are to increase rapidly enough to employ both present employables, and also the increased number of workers who will become available, then the indices of production must continue to rise and at an increasing rate. This means a greater and greater task for the forces and workers in the fields of marketing and services.

It, therefore, does not seem too much of an assumption to conclude that with increasing productivity that must come if we are to maintain our position in the world's markets and also our very much higher level of wages, we must increase sales abroad and our standard of living at home continuously and uninterruptedly. And, to repeat, it is the task of marketing to deliver that improved standard of living for its advantage to our economy, but more particularly for the benefit to our families of men, women, and children.

The alternative to the successful assumption of the task by marketing is retrogression in the material status of the people and consequent economic recession on the one hand, or on the other, the increasing activity and power of an expanding Welfare State. The consequences might well be not only loss of economic status in this world of ideological struggle, but could also include the loss of freedom and the replacement of democratic government with one of many forms of statism—either benign or malignant, but in either case probably ruthless and dangerous in its potential.

Marketing, then, in our free society of competitive enterprise is charged with supplying the fuel that keeps the wheels of industry turning that they may pour out an avalanche of our material well-being.

Recently our economy has been hauled before rump courts to answer the charges made by self-appointed and self-anointed public prosecutors. We are charged with using up our natural resources too rapidly because we encourage men and women to adopt standards of waste in order to stimulate demands not found essential by these prosecutors' idea of necessity. And from another segment of the social-political compass we are accused of being too affluent. We are said to be too rich in our inventories of material things, too indolent and retrogressive in our social, political, and idealistic outlook, too poor in those sections of our activities more closely related to our social requirements like education, roads, etc. In these latter aspects of our living we are told that we are poverty stricken while we wallow in the pig trough of material, private affluence. Moreover, it is pointed out that the greater expenditures for these social requirements would, of course, be controlled by public officials—elected or appointed. The funds appropriated for these social segments would come from higher taxes imposed upon the disposable income of the mass of the citizens of the United States.

Now it is true, of course, that in part the critics of the "Waste-Makers" are correct. If we consume more in the way of finished goods, we must also use more raw materials. That, unfortunately, is an inescapable sequitur. The only way to assure the consumption of lesser amounts of raw materials is to produce and consume fewer pieces of finished goods. Under this philosophy, Africa, now beginning to stir itself upon its bed of an inexhaustible wealth of raw material, should be an ideal witness in the trial against us brought by the public prosecutors of the "Waste-Makers." Africa, China, South America, Russia are, it would seem, sounder economies than we because they use up less and less of their material wealth because of their very low level of material well-being.

Some of the charges and implications of the denouncers of our form of economies approach the ridiculous. They describe our clothing, houses, appliances, and automobiles as though they were built of paper, cardboard, and scotch tape. Except for the time span of existence, modern equipment, like the "one horse shay" of Oliver Wendell Holmes' poem, seems to stand up in apparent perfect shape and then suddenly disintegrate into a pile of junk and debris. One gains the opinion that our modern automobile of chrome and fins is built of material that will stand up only for the two years that presumably separate its birth in the factory and its burial on the junk pile. The resulting arithmetic is destroyed by the facts. Our population of cars is over 60 million. If their life span was as short as the two or three years the economic puritans claim, we would require a production of 15 to 25 million cars a year to maintain our automotive population. Our actual production both for replacement and new buyers due to the increasing number of family formations is around six and a half million. As a matter of actual fact, the junk pile seems to have to wait from between 10 or 11 years to claim the average car.

But, nevertheless, it is still true that 6,000,000 cars and 1,200,000 homes, millions of TV sets and refrigerators use a great deal of steel, glass, and rubber. If we elect to convert our economy from the kind it is, using so much raw material, to one that husbands its resources by non-use, by replacing carefully developed desires with stark necessities and basic needs, then we will, certainly, possess and keep more iron ore but also have fewer machines, fewer homes, autos, appliances, and fewer good six-lane concrete roads.

In short, we would have a much more puritan economy and a far less prosperous one. Under these aspects marketing would find it relatively easy to distribute to a hungry, even starved population, the products of such an inhibited production mechanism.

However, marketing and distribution would deliver to the citizens of the nation a lower and lower standard of living. This would continue until inevitably the Super-State of a tomorrow would take over the complete responsibility.

The second group of self-appointed public prosecutors of our National Economy charge that we are wasteful in private expenditures in this, our too affluent society. They claim that we should divert more of our funds from private purses to public purposes, and expend them for what these critics say are more desirable social needs.

Now most of us are of the opinion that our social requirements should be better satisfied. Our defense should be superlatively strong and, as far as is possible, independent of other nations. Our aid to underdeveloped countries should be part of a generous allotment made, by *many* nations, to raise the material levels of backward economies. We should be willing to admit that the growth factor of the United States should quicken its tempo to employ our people, to maintain our standards, to create a proper defense, and improve our social contributions to our people. However, we challenge the validity of the statement that the waste that is claimed to exist in the private channels of trade would be absent if the funds flowed through public canals of expenditure. We challenge the conclusion that the diversion of funds from the private to the public segments of the economy would protect freedom rather than develop a welfare state and even might actually reduce our Gross National Product and the disposable income of the average American family.

The income of the average American family is large as measured against other places and other times. Nevertheless, we produced more in the current year of 1960 than we absorbed. The forces of demand were powerful in 1960. But they were not potent enough to match production. The demands upon marketing to keep the wheels of our productive mechanism rolling in order to avoid recession or depression are indeed enormous. The burden on marketing is even greater if we are to employ the workers in an economy that continuously increases their productivity and ability to produce more and more goods with fewer and fewer workers on the production line. And the task becomes unbelievably large if we add to the desirable increase in our material standards of living, the urgent requirements for higher social contribution to education, roads, health, and defense.

There are many of us who fear these new or refurbished economic doctrines of growth through socialization. We hold that the needs for defense for society, for working opportunities, and for the people's well-being are most likely to be furnished and safeguarded by maintaining the economic mechanism and methods that exist. These have already contributed over the decades the highest level of material well-being the world and history have ever witnessed. To tear down the mechanism and replace it with a Rube Goldberg contraption is a dangerous pastime to impose upon our people and families.

In fact, many of us believe that we should bend our efforts rather to improving the tested mechanism we have built so that it can carry the heavy and increased weight that will come to it. We believe that growth can come more surely and safely from the expansion and intensification of better production methods, the

design and creation of new and better products, and above all by improving the techniques and methodology and application of more effective means of marketing that are researched and tested and used as skillfully as is true of our production methods.

Marketing and distribution have used increasingly better tools. But the gap is still wide between these segments of business and production. We have reached the stage where we know how to produce well; to distribute the products effectively the day must come when we must know how to market better. Moreover, the day will also come when in order to survive in world competition and to reinstitute and maintain a proper balance of international payments, we must learn how to produce much, much better than we do today. And to furnish the highly increased volume of sales upon which improved production and the general adoption of automation will depend, we must learn to market and distribute goods *much, much, much* better than we do presently.

It is an interesting footnote that history has written on the page allotted to 1959. That was the year when the idea of the European common market came into being. In this idea there may prove to be one of the more significant changes economic history will record. And it should be noted that it is not a machine or a manufacturing method that was created. Rather, it is a plan for merging six European nations into one common market, of converting six nations, each with an average population of 28 millions, into one market with a population of 170 millions. Out of that marketing device can come new products, new methods, new costs, new wage levels, and new standards of living.

Marketing certainly appears to have come of age. It has grown up. Now it must grow stronger and abler. Its weaknesses must be corrected; its strength augmented. But it is indeed unlikely that it must be either reinvented or redesigned.

The critics are many; and they seem to borrow their text from the Rubaiyat whose author Omar Khayyam said:

. . . could thou and I with Fate conspire
To grasp this sorry Scheme of Things entire,
    Would we not shatter it to bits—and then
Re-mould it nearer to the Heart's Desire!

We must indeed be on guard, lest by unwise efforts we remold our economic principles and actions and our marketing approach and methods into a disastrous device.

c